The International Lesson Annual
1993–94
September—August

THE INTERNATIONAL LESSON ANNUAL 1993–94

September–August

A Commentary and Teacher's Guide on
the International Sunday School Lessons
Uniform Series

Edited by
William H. Willimon and Patricia P. Willimon

Lesson Analysis by
WILLIAM H. WILLIMON
LINDSEY P. PHERIGO
GAYLE CARLTON FELTON
PAT McGEACHY
and
Enrichment Articles by
William H. Willimon and Patricia P. Willimon

ABINGDON PRESS
Nashville

THE INTERNATIONAL LESSON ANNUAL—1993–94

Copyright © 1993 by Abingdon Press

This book is printed on acid-free recycled paper.

ISBN 0-687-19157-2

Library of Congress ISSN 0074-6770

Unless otherwise noted, scripture quotations are from the New Revised Standard Version Bible, Copyright © 1989 by the Division of Christian Education of the National Council of the Churches of Christ in the USA. Used by Permission.

Scripture quotations marked RSV are from the Revised Standard Version of the Bible, copyright © 1946, 1952, 1971 by the Division of Christian Education of the National Council of Churches of Christ in the USA. Used by permission.

Scripture quotations marked NEB are from *The New English Bible.* © The Delegates of the Oxford University Press and The Syndics of the Cambridge University Press 1961, 1970. Reprinted by permission.

Scripture quotations marked KJV are from the King James Version of the Bible.

"Enrichment Article" on pp. 134-35 adapted from William H. Willimon, *On a Wild and Windy Mountain* (Nashville: Abingdon Press, 1984), pp. 36-40.

"Enrichment Article" on pp. 158-60 adapted from William H. Willimon, *Shaped by the Bible* (Nashville: Abingdon Press, 1990), pp. 15-22.

93   94   95   96   97   98   99   00   01   02 — 10   9   8   7   6   5   4   3   2   1

MANUFACTURED IN THE UNITED STATES OF AMERICA

Editors' Preface

We welcome you to another year of learning and discovery with the *International Lesson Annual*. Last year, we changed the format of the *International Lesson Annual* in order to give it more unity and coherence. Now, one writer leads you through an entire quarter of lessons. What may be lost in variety, we hope is gained in unity and coherence.

Increasing numbers of today's Christians are realizing the importance of equipment in the faith. As our society becomes more secular, the demands upon us as Christians are greater. We need to be well informed, well schooled in the faith, better able to witness to our faith, in word and deed, in our daily lives. This means that the work you do, in your adult class, in teaching the *International Lesson,* is more important than ever. Through detailed study of Scripture, applying the Bible to the challenges of everyday living, the *International Lesson* enables a new generation of Christians to grow in their faith. As an adult teacher in your church, growth in the faith could not occur without your dedication, preparation, and prayerful commitment to the study of the Bible. Because your ministry of teaching is so important, we try to do everything possible to make the *International Lesson Annual* the best teaching aid available for adult Bible study.

To lead you through the lessons for 1993–1994, we have assembled a lively group of biblical scholars and interpreters. This year's study begins with Genesis, the first book of the Bible. Will Willimon, Dean of the Chapel and Professor of Christian Ministry at Duke University, will lead you through some of the Bible's oldest and most engaging material. We will meet real people with real problems, being met by a living and loving God.

For our second quarter of lessons—December, January, and February— we will be led by Lindsey Pherigo, long-time Distinguished Professor of New Testament at St. Paul's Theological Seminary in Kansas City, Missouri. Dr. Pherigo is unusually well qualified to lead us through a study of the Gospel of Luke. He is the author of several books on this Gospel and has a lifetime of interpreting Scripture for future pastors.

In this year's *Annual,* Gayle Carlton Felton makes her first appearance as one of our expositors. A United Methodist minister who has taught both undergraduates and seminary students, Dr. Felton is Assistant Professor at the Duke Divinity School, Durham, North Carolina. Because Dr. Felton teaches courses in Christian Education, she understands well the challenges of teaching today's adults about Scripture. You will enjoy the way in which Dr. Felton leads us through the concepts and ideas of Paul's letter to the Romans.

Readers of the *International Lesson Annual* have long enjoyed the engaging writing of the Reverend Pat McGeachy, Associate Pastor, Downtown Presbyterian Church in Nashville, Tennessee. Adult teachers have come to love the way Pat McGeachy makes Scripture relevant and engaging. In the fourth quarter, we will move through the Exodus, and the early portions of

Deuteronomy. Because some of your adult class members may not be too familiar with this material, who better able to lead us in our study than Pat McGeachy?

As always, we enjoy your questions, criticisms, and comments regarding the *International Lesson Annual.* May God be with you during this new year of study and Christian growth.

William H. Willimon and Patricia P. Willimon,
Editors

Contents

SECOND QUARTER

The Story of Jesus: The Gospel of Luke

UNIT I: A SAVIOR IS BORN
(December 5–26)

UNIT II: JESUS' MINISTRY IN GALILEE
(January 2–30)

UNIT III: THE CROSS AND THE RESURRECTION
(February 6–27)

THIRD QUARTER

Good News for God's People: Romans and Galatians

UNIT I: RIGHTEOUS THROUGH FAITH
(March 6–27)

UNIT II: EMPOWERED BY THE SPIRIT
(April 3–24)

UNIT III: SET FREE BY GOD'S GRACE
(May 1–29)

FOURTH QUARTER

God Redeems a People

UNIT I: DELIVERANCE FROM OPPRESSION
(June 5–26)

UNIT II: PROVISIONS FOR PRESENT AND FUTURE
(July 3–31)

UNIT III: INSTRUCTIONS FOR LIFE
(August 7–28)

THE STORY OF BEGINNINGS: GENESIS

UNIT I: GOD'S CREATION OF AND RELATIONSHIP WITH HUMANKIND

William H. Willimon and Patricia P. Willimon

FOUR LESSONS   **SEPTEMBER 5–26**

Where did we come from? How did we get here? Those questions are basic, primal. They are questions about origins. If we can figure out where we came from, how we got here, then perhaps we can figure out *why* we are here. Our inquiry into our origins is really a question about our purpose.

Harvard biologist Stephen Jay Gould, speaking on our campus recently, spoke of this universe as, "An amazing, utterly unpredictable series of wonderful cosmic accidents." That is certainly one way to read our origins. We are here because of an amazing series of cosmic coincidences. According to this view there is no way to explain the existence of plants, animals, stars, and planets except as accident. We may be a marvelous accident, to be sure, but still an accident.

There is another way to speak of our beginnings. That view is found behind the first chapters of Genesis. The name *Genesis* means "beginning." Behind these primal stories is the conviction that our beginning was with God, that we are here, not through a series of cosmic accidents, but through the creativity of God. This affirmation gives significance to our daily living. Knowing were we came from, how we got here, gives meaning to how we live here.

The testimony about origins that is found in the first chapters of Genesis is more than biology or geology, fine as those scientific disciplines may be. Genesis is theology, a story about God. Genesis says that God is a creative, life-producing, order-evoking God. Beyond anything we can say about ourselves from a biological point of view, Genesis makes the stunning claim that we are created by God and placed on this earth for divine responsibility.

How did we get here? More to the point, *why* are we here? Those are the questions that we shall ask as we begin at the beginning in our study of Genesis.

God as Creator

Background Scripture: Genesis 1:1-25

The Main Question

The great southern writer Flannery O'Connor is reputed to have said, of people from parts of the United States other than the American South, "The trouble with most modern people is that they are not from anywhere."

In my part of the world, one still hears asked, when someone meets a new person, "Where is she from?" It is a question about origins, beginnings.

One hears that question asked less frequently today than in the past. We live today in a mobile society where people move frequently. Ask someone, "Where is your hometown?" and you may receive in answer the list of a dozen places.

To my mind, such mobility, such lack of origin contributes to the superficiality of modern life. We are not *from* anywhere. Therefore we lack some of the distinctiveness, some of the colorfulness of our parents' generation. We all tend to talk the same, to look the same, to think the same. If we do not know *where we are from,* how can we know, in the deepest sense of the phrase, *where we are?*

Recently, we asked a favorite professor on our campus to participate in a series of faculty discussions on the theme, "What I Believe and Why." Each person was to speak, in a personal way, about what he or she believed.

This professor began his presentation by saying, "You cannot know much about me unless you first know that I was born in Germany, just before the beginning of World War II and that I was born a Lutheran. In a way, everything else about me stems from those two facts about my birth." He then went on to explain how those two facts about his origins determined nearly everything about the course his later life.

Where did we come from? That is the basic, very revealing question behind today's lesson on the very first chapter of the very first book of the Bible.

Selected Scripture

King James Version

Genesis 1:1-15

1 In the beginning God created the heaven and the earth.

2 And the earth was without form, and void; and darkness was upon the face of the deep. And the Spirit of God moved upon the face of the waters.

3 And God said, Let there be light: and there was light.

4 And God saw the light, that it

New Revised Standard Version

Genesis 1:1-15

1 In the beginning when God created the heavens and the earth, 2 the earth was a formless void and darkness covered the face of the deep, while a wind from God swept over the face of the waters. 3 Then God said, "Let there be light"; and there was light. 4 And God saw that the light was good; and God separated the light from the darkness.

was good: and God divided the light from the darkness.

5 And God called the light Day, and the darkness he called Night. And the evening and the morning were the first day.

6 And God said, Let there be a firmament in the midst of the waters, and let it divide the waters from the waters.

7 And God made the firmament, and divided the waters which were under the firmament from the waters which were above the firmament: and it was so.

8 And God called the firmament Heaven. And the evening and the morning were the second day.

9 And God said, Let the waters under the heaven be gathered together unto one place, and let the dry land appear: and it was so.

10 And God called the dry land Earth; and the gathering together of the waters called he Seas: and God saw that it was good.

11 And God said, Let the earth bring forth grass, the herb yielding seed, and the fruit tree yielding fruit after his kind, whose seed is in itself, upon the earth: and it was so.

12 And the earth brought forth grass, and herb yielding seed after his kind, and the tree yielding fruit, whose seed was in itself, after his kind: and God saw that it was good.

13 And the evening and the morning were the third day.

14 And God said, Let there be lights in the firmament of the heaven to divide the day from the night; and let them be for signs, and for seasons, and for days, and years:

15 And let them be for lights in the firmament of the heaven to give light upon the earth: and it was so.

Key Verse: **In the beginning God created the heaven and the earth. Genesis 1:1**

5 God called the light Day, and the darkness he called Night. And there was evening and there was morning, the first day.

6 And God said, "Let there be a dome in the midst of the waters, and let it separate the waters from the waters." 7 So God made the dome and separated the waters that were under the dome from the waters that were above the dome. And it was so. 8 God called the dome Sky. And there was evening and there was morning, the second day.

9 And God said, "Let the waters under the sky be gathered together into one place, and let the dry land appear." And it was so. 10 God called the dry land Earth, and the waters that were gathered together he called Seas. And God saw that it was good. 11 Then God said, "Let the earth put forth vegetation: plants yielding seed, and fruit trees of every kind on earth that bear fruit with the seed in it." And it was so, 12 The earth brought forth vegetation: plants yielding seed of every kind, and trees of every kind bearing fruit with the seed in it. And God saw that it was good. 13 And there was evening and there was morning, the third day.

14 And God said, "Let there be lights in the dome of the sky to separate the day from the night; and let them be for signs and for seasons and for days and years, 15 and let them be lights in the dome of the sky to give light upon the earth." And it was so.

Key Verse: **In the beginning . . . God created the heavens and the earth. Genesis 1:1**

As You Read the Scripture

Genesis 1:1. The verb here is more dynamic than the passive, "Why God began to create. . . ." It is more "When God created. . . ." Creation is a dynamic, ongoing process.

Verse 2. The Spirit (literally, "wind") blew over the formless wastes.

Verses 3-5. Throughout Scripture, darkness is symbolic of chaos, terror. Thus the first act of creation establishes day.

Verses 6-8. This "firmament" was thought of as a kind of inverted bowl that rested upon the waters ("the deep"). The firmament was punctured with small holes (stars) and greater holes (moon and sun) in order that the light might shine through. Thus Hebrew cosmology (conception of the universe) involved water (symbol of chaos and nothingness) on which floated an upturned bowl ("firmament"). Under the bowl was dry land, lakes, and oceans that were flat masses floating upon the water. The land received light that shined through the holes in the firmament.

Verses 9-13. At the voice of God, living things appear. Throughout Scripture, "the word of God" is depicted as powerful and lifegiving. Here, the words of God have the power to cause living things to spring into being.

After each act of creation, God pronounces that the creation is "good." The notion that matter, the physical world, is somehow evil whereas the world of the spirit is good, is not a Hebrew idea. The created world, matter, the inhabitants of the earth, are good because they result from the creativity of a good God.

Verses 14-15. See the notes on the lights in the firmament in discussion of verses 6-8.

The Scripture and the Main Question

In the Beginning, God

In studying the familiar and beloved first chapter of Genesis, I think it important to get straight about what sort of literature we are reading here. Although there are people who would disagree with me here, I believe it important to note that we are reading *theology* when we read Genesis 1. Our text is making a claim about God.

Now, nearly all of Scripture makes some claim about God. The Bible is a book about God and God's dealings with humanity. We don't listen to Jesus' parable about the prodigal son and think that we are reading a text on family law. We are reading a story that Jesus told to help us better to understand the nature of God.

However, when we come to reading Genesis 1, some of us forget that the Bible is a book about God. We try to make the Bible into a book about science or history. Thus we debate whether the seven "days" that are described in Genesis 1 are actual twenty-four-hour days. We argue over the scientific accuracy of whether it took seven days or seven billion years to create animals on the face of the earth.

Recently, our local school system has been put through quite an ordeal when the school board was caught in the crossfire between those who want the theory of evolution taught in our schools (the theory that plants and animals evolved very slowly, over billions of years, through a process of natural selection) or "creationism" taught in our classroom. "Creationists" are said to be people who believe in the "scientific accuracy of the Genesis account of the creation of the world."

While I am all in favor of taking Genesis 1 with great seriousness, I think it also important to read this passage *on its own terms*. I find it inconceivable that the writer of Genesis was writing science. Science itself was not invented until about three thousand years after the story of Genesis had been told. What we are reading here is something infinitely more important to us than even science. We are reading a story about God, a narrative account that depicts something deeply significant in the divine nature.

I expect that the original writer of Genesis would be rather amused at our trying to defend Genesis based on its scientific validity. To defend Genesis in that fashion is, in a way, to concede too much to science, as if scientific truth were the only truth worth knowing.

The first chapter of Genesis is theological truth, divine truth, ultimate truth. Like most of the Bible, Genesis 1 is relatively disinterested in modern questions of *how* the earth was created, or *when* it was formed. Rather, Genesis, like most of the rest of the Bible is intensely interested in *who* created the world and *why* we were created. If you want a question to keep in your class' mind as we study the first verses of Genesis, let this be the question: *Who created us and why?*

Does Genesis say precisely how the world and its inhabitants came into being, precisely when all this took place, who knows? Yet be assured of this, however and whenever we came into being, it was God who gave us being.

In the beginning, God.

The Earth Was Without Form and Void

Our story beings with chaos, with bubbling, formless, terrifying void. Over this dark, chaotic nothingness, the Spirit of God hovered, like a wind blowing across dark waters.

When the ancient Hebrews thought of chaos, they thought first of the ocean, the deep, unapproachable waters of the sea. The waters that existed prior to God's creation are called "the deep." Other ancient peoples like the Phoenicians built ships and went forth to sea. The ancient Hebrews, on the other hand, preferred the good, solid, dry promised *land*. Israel was never too interested in tackling the sea. The sea was that dark force with which God struggled when God began creating something out of nothing, when God began pushing back dark waters in order to "let the dry land appear" (verse 9).

"The deep" continues as a biblical image of chaos and terror. In the days of Noah, when God decided to destroy the earth and its people, God simply stopped holding the dark waters back, let the water gush up from the depths, pour down from the firmament, and a great flood occured (Gen. 6–9). When the psalmist wants to describe life at its worst, those times when troubles overtake us and almost overwhelm us, the psalmist speaks of times when "your waves and your billows have gone over me." "The deep" is the image of chaos and trouble in life.

And the great act of divine creation is God's pushing back those dark, chaotic waters and bringing forth dry, solid land. On the first day, God creates light (vv. 1-5). Imagine the universe without light. On the following day, God "separated the light from the darkness" (verse 4). Presumably, before this act of separation, everything was confused, light was dark and dark was light. Now there is order, regularity, definition where once there had only been chaos. By the third day, God speaks, "let the dry land appear" (verse 9). On the fourth day God creates seasons, days, years, the sun and the moon. "And God saw that it was good" (v. 18).

What was good here is order, form, pattern. We wonder who first told this story. Perhaps it was told among the ancient Hebrews during their first, dim, dark days as a nomadic people. Imagine what it was like to be an ancient person. The darkness held great terror as you and your tribe huddled around the campfire in the evenings. The world was a place where demons caused illness, where the rain did not come for days and caused drought and famine. When your child became sick, there was absolutely nothing for you to do but wait and pray. You had little protection from natural calamity and disaster.

So this story was told as an affirmation that God is on the side of creativity, not chaos. God made the world. The world, despite the bad things that sometimes happen to us, is a good place created by a good and loving God. Our God is one who brought order out of chaos, life out of nothingness.

Some scholars believe that the final form of this story comes much later in Israel's history. They believe that it may date from the time of Israel's monarchy, when great stress was being placed upon the need for order and stability in the national life. If so, then this story stressed the need for us to discern and to affirm the divine order in life. Although we human beings, through our sinful choices and bad acts, may at times cause great chaos and confusion, God is on the side of order. God has ordained a certain pattern, a certain form to life. We are to honor and to respect that orderliness in the world.

Today's text begins in dark, chaotic, terror. It ends in light, order, beauty, and goodness. Behind the text is an assertion about the nature of God and God's created world: Whenever we encounter order, beauty, and goodness in life, these are signs of God's goodness and creativity. Whenever we encounter chaos, ugliness, and evil in life, God is busy battling these dark forces to bring something out of nothing, life out of death, light out of darkness.

And God Saw That It Was Good

As we have said, the people who first heard this story had a firsthand knowledge of how chaotic, mystifying, and terrifying life in this world can sometimes be. Even more so, they had a great appreciation for whatever order, beauty, and goodness God has created in this world.

We also have a firsthand knowledge of chaos, of the void.

Recently, an oncologist, a doctor who has given his life to the treatment of cancer, said to me, "Basically, cancer occurs when normal, expected processes of cell division go crazy." In cancer, a normal process of cell reproduction goes haywire. Cells reproduce themselves at a chaotic rate. A tumor grows. The results are terrifying.

The writer of Genesis might describe cancer as an experience of life "without form and void" (v. 2). Can you think of other chaotic experiences in life? For instance, mental illness is sometimes described as a time when we have "lost touch," when "we are losing a grip on reality." Where once we perceived life as predictable, understandable, and orderly, now life has become chaotic and terrifying. The void has bubbled up in our lives, the dark waters have overcome the dry land, and creation is in danger of being overwhelmed by chaos.

In such dark days we do well to remember the affirmation of Genesis One. "In the beginning God created. . . ." Our God does not stop creating. Our God does not stop being on the side of order and creativity. God keeps bringing order out of chaos, something out of nothing.

Remembrance of that affirmation, even in our darkest of days, can enable us to say, even in times of relative darkness and confusion, that life is "good, very good."

Helping Adults to Become Involved

Preparing to Teach

The aim of this lesson is to help class members to affirm the creativity and goodness of God even in their own times of darkness and confusion. Just as Genesis 1 claims that God brought order out of chaos in creating the earth, so God continues to bring order out of our chaos in our daily lives.

Prepare yourself by reading "The Main Question," "The Scripture and the Main Question," and "As You Read the Scripture." Underline material that strikes you as interesting and helpful. As you read, you might jot down ideas or illustrations from your own experience as these would be helpful in your presentation of the lesson.

You are fortunate in that the material that you will be presenting to your class from Genesis 1 is familiar to most of them. On the other hand, because these verses are so familiar, your class may need to be challenged to hear this material afresh. Also, as is mentioned in the beginning of the discussion in "The Scripture and the Main Question," some members of your class may have developed opinions about this material based on recent controversy between "evolutionists" and "creationists."

While it may not be a good idea to engage in that debate in your class today, it would be good for you to stress that this material from Genesis makes a *theological* claim. Rather than get into a debate over the scientific accuracy of Genesis 1, stress that these verses are making a statement about the nature of God that has relevance for our lives today.

Introducing the Main Question

Begin by paraphrasing, in your words, the material in "The Main Question." This will get your adults thinking about the questions behind Genesis 1.

Now walk your class through today's text, Genesis 1:1-19. Using the information in "As You Read the Scripture," explain to them the meaning of Genesis words like *the deep* and *the firmament*. It might help to draw on a chalkboard or on newsprint, a diagram of the cosmology of Genesis so that your class can picture the ancient view of the universe.

While this discussion will undoubtedly impress some of your adults with the difference between our modern ways of conceptualizing cosmology (with a round earth surrounded by space) and the Genesis depiction of a "firmament" floating on "the deep," you will want to assure them that this ancient text has meaning for us today, meaning we shall now explore.

17

Developing the Lesson

I. Introduction

Using the material at the beginning of "The Scripture and the Main Question," suggest to your class that the first chapter of Genesis is mainly of value to us, not as a scientific or historical description of how the world came to be, but as a theological assertion of *why* the world came to be.

II. In the beginning God

Before God, there was nothing but chaos. Take a moment, after reading aloud Genesis 1:1-8, and ask your class about its images of chaos. Recall the nature of life among ancient people before the days of modern medicine, science, weather prediction, machines, communication, and so forth. Ask them, what comes to their minds when they think of a world without light and without form? List their images of chaos and confusion on a chalkboard or newsprint. You may want to be a catalyst for their thinking by using the illustrations of cancer or mental illness that are mentioned toward the end of the discussions in "The Scripture and Main Question."

III. The earth was without form and void

Now that you have started your class thinking about our daily experiences of chaos, having listed several examples on a chalkboard or newsprint, note the way in which Genesis 1 depicts God as the master over chaos, the one who speaks and brings a world into being. Ask your class to think of biblical examples in which God, and later, Jesus, are depicted as ruling over life's occasional chaos and confusion. Examples that might come to mind are stories in which God delivers Israel from slavery or where Jesus cures suffering people or feeds hungry people.

You might simply go down the list of chaotic, confusing experiences, which you listed in the previous learning activity, and list beside them some biblical story or verse that speaks to God's creativity in the midst of life's chaos.

IV. And God saw that it was good

Is life good or bad? That is a question that may lie behind today's passage from Genesis 1. After having identified those circumstances in life that may cause us to doubt life's goodness and orderliness from time to time—sickness, hunger, emotional illness, personal distress, family crises, war—ask your class in what way the story of Genesis 1 might speak to someone in those circumstances.

How, in our daily lives, do we experience God bringing something out of nothing, form out of the void, light out of darkness? You might prepare for this activity by thinking ahead of some experience of your own in which you were reassured of God's creativity in the middle of the world's chaos. Share this experience with your class members to serve as a catalyst to their thinking.

Helping Class Members Act

The affirmation of Genesis 1 is a very ancient declaration about the goodness and love of God. Yet it has contemporary significance. Ask your class members in what ways you as individuals, and your church as a group, can display some of the divine goodness and creativity that Genesis 1 declares.

Every time we feed the hungry, we are demonstrating that God is not on the side of hunger, but on the side of fulfillment and health. Every time we wage war against illness, we are saying something about our God as a God of wholeness and life. Each time we speak up for peace and justice, we are asserting that God is on the side of goodness and order. We are thereby enacting, in our lives today, the truth of Genesis 1.

Planning for Next Sunday

We continue our exploration of the first book of the Bible next Sunday as we study Genesis 2, the creation of humanity. Ask your class to read Genesis 2 before they come to class next week.

Created in God's Image

Background Scripture: Genesis 1:26-31; 2:4-9, 15-25

The Main Question

We live in an age of great paradox. On the one hand, we have witnessed great advances in health care, the standard of living, and human well-being. On the other hand, ours is also an age in which human life is shockingly cheap. Advances in human well-being appear to be paralleled by declines in the value of the individual.

A few years ago, the United Nations proclaimed "The Year of the Child." The value of children in our world was emphasized. In that same year, about a million and a half abortions were performed in the United States and the incidence of child abuse was greater than ever before.

A few weeks before I began writing this lesson, the civil war began in Liberia. The other day rebel troops entered a Lutheran refugee camp and opened fire on a group of defenseless civilian refugees. Six hundred men, women, and children were slaughtered. A week later, it was noted in South Africa that more black South Africans have been killed this year by other black South Africans than the number of blacks who have been killed by whites in South Africa in the past ten years. Last year, two thousand New Yorkers were murdered by their fellow citizens.

Across our planet, it does seem as if the individual human life has become cheap, an expendable commodity. How can we restore the dignity and value of each human being?

That question is answered in today's lesson, a familiar passage from Genesis One. Having made all of the other animals, the Creator turns his attention to the supreme act of creation, humanity. Knowing that sublime account of our beginnings gives new value and dignity to our future.

FIRST QUARTER

"Then God said, 'Let us make humankind in our image, according to our likeness . . .'" (Gen. 1:26).

Selected Scripture

King James Version

Genesis 1:26-28

26 And God said, Let us make man in our image, after our likeness: and let them have dominion over the fish of the sea, and over the fowl of the air, and over the cattle, and over all the earth, and over every creeping thing that creepeth upon the earth.

27 So God created man in his own image, in the image of God created he him; male and female created he them.

28 And God blessed them, and God said unto them, Be fruitful, and multiply, and replenish the earth, and subdue it: and have dominion over the fish of the sea, and over the fowl of the air, and over every living thing that moveth upon the earth.

Genesis 2:18-25

18 And the LORD God said, It is not good that the man should be alone; I will make him an help meet for him.

19 And out of the ground the LORD God formed every beast of the field, and every fowl of the air; and brought them unto Adam to see what he would call them: and whatsoever Adam called every living creature, that was the name thereof.

20 And Adam gave names to all cattle, and to the fowl of the air, and to every beast of the field; but for Adam there was not found an help meet for him.

21 And the LORD God caused a deep sleep to fall upon Adam, and he slept: and he took one of his ribs, and closed up the flesh instead thereof;

22 And the rib, which the LORD

New Revised Standard Version

Genesis 1:26-28

26 Then God said, "Let us make humankind in our image, according to our likeness; and let them have dominion over the fish of the sea, and over the birds of the air, and over the cattle, and over all the wild animals of the earth, and over every creeping thing that creeps upon the earth."

27 So God created humankind in his image,
in the image of God he created them;
male and female he created them.

28 God blessed them, and God said to them, "Be fruitful and multiply, and fill the earth and subdue it; and have dominion over the fish of the sea and over the birds of the air and over every living thing that moves upon the earth."

Genesis 2:18-25

18 Then the LORD God said, "It is not good that the man should be alone; I will make him a helper as his partner." 19 So out of the ground the LORD God formed every animal of the field and every bird of the air, and brought them to the man to see what he would call them; and whatever the man called every living creature, that was its name. 20 The man gave names to all cattle, and to the birds of the air, and to every animal of the field; but for the man there was not found a helper as his partner. 21 So the LORD God caused a deep sleep to fall upon the man, and he slept; then he took one of his ribs and closed up its place with flesh. 22 And the rib that the LORD God had taken from the man he made into a woman and brought her to the man. 23 Then the man said,

God had taken from man, made he a woman, and brought her unto the man.

23 And Adam said, This is now bone of my bones, and flesh of my flesh: she shall be called Woman, because he was taken out of Man.

24 Therefore shall a man leave his father and his mother, and shall cleave unto his wife: and they shall be one flesh.

25 And they were both naked, the man and his wife, and were not ashamed.

"This at last is bone of my bones
    and flesh of my flesh;
this one shall be called
    Woman,
    for out of Man this one was
    taken."

24 Therefore a man leaves his father and his mother and clings to his wife, and they become one flesh. 25 And the man and his wife were both naked, and were not ashamed.

Key Verse: **So God created man in his own image, in the image of God created he him; male and female created he them. Genesis 1:27**

Key Verse: **God created humankind in his image, in the image of God he created them; male and female he created them. Genesis 1:27**

As You Read the Scripture

Genesis 1:26-28. Of God's eight creative acts, this is the only one in which the Creator speaks directly to the creature, denoting a special intimacy with this particular creature.

Verses 26-27. Scholars believe this account of the creation of humanity was recorded during Israel's time of exile, a time of tragedy and dislocation in Israel. One characteristic of the biblical literature of this period was its resistance to any attempt to image God (see Exodus 20:4; Deuteronomy 5:8). Imaging God might lead to idolatry, which makes all the more surprising and striking the Genesis assertion that there is only one image of God—humanity!

Verse 28. This creature is given dominion. Scholars generally agree that the "image of God" here relates to the practice whereby ancient kings often placed images of themselves in territories where they ruled so that the king's authority might be exercised even where the king was not physically present. Humankind is the image of this Creator and therefore is able to rule in behalf of the Creator.

Verses 29-31. The creature is to rule over the wonders of creation. These verses have come under criticism in recent years by advocates of ecological theology. Too often in our history, dominion over creation has meant abuse of creation. That is not implied here. To rule with dominion over creation is to rule as God might rule—with loving care for all creatures, which are created and called "very good."

Genesis 2:18-25. The "man" here is not a male, for male and female were not yet differentiated. "Man" here is better translated as "human creature," or "earthling." These verses tell not so much of the creation of woman as of the creation of males and females out of the primal human creature.

Verses 18-20. A wonderful array of creatures are created for the "man." But none are a fit companion.

Verses 21-23. Whereas the other creatures, like the "man," have been formed from the dust of the earth (Genesis 3:7), this new creature is literally built up from a rib. Woman is the result of a very special act of creation. This in no way implies subordination to the man; in fact, woman is seen as the crowning act of creation, the only creature who is qualified to be a truly equal partner with the man.

Verses 24-25. The writer uses the creation of male and female as a story explaining the origin of marriage and procreation of children. Male and female have dominion because they are given the ability to create new human beings even as God created them. The man and woman are inno-cent, unashamed, like little children. Sinlessness is not really implied here. All the text says is that they were naive and childlike in these very first days.

The Scripture and the Main Question

So God Created

Summer is now over. Here in September, we can look back on the joys of this past summer. Usually, one of the most enjoyable aspects of summer-time is the opportunity to be in nature, to revel in the glories of God's cre-ation. When a hot July sun arises in the sky, and the temperatures soar, how pleasant to be lying on a Carolina beach, doing absolutely nothing of any redeeming value other than doing absolutely nothing, glass of iced tea not too far away, the gentle rhythm of waves, the occasional cry of the sea-gulls.

In North Carolina we also have the mountains, with their cool evenings, the throbbing songs of crickets lulling you to sleep at night—summer, and nature seen from a rocking chair on a porch or from the side of a lake. Sit-ting there, rocking and enjoying, one is taught a simple truth—this is our Father's world. On some balmy North Carolina nights you can almost hear, above the crickets and the chirping frogs, a divine voice pronounce, "Good!" over it all, just as it spoke on the first evening of creation. The Lord saw all that he had made and said, "Good!" and so say we on a July evening in a cor-ner of God's garden called North Carolina. Very good.

And yet, one thing we modern, air-conditioned people sometimes over-look in our vacation-time assessments of nature is this: Out there, just beyond the front yard, in the woods, the little creatures are busily devouring one another! The big fishes beneath the placid surface of the lake are eating smaller fishes, which are eating still smaller fishes, which are eating proto-zoa, which are eating whatever they eat. Nature is not only a realm of chirp-ing crickets and soaring gulls but is also a tooth-claw-and-nail fight to the death for life. We humans are but the uppermost rung of a great ladder of survival, omnivores at the top of a food chain in which one organism lives only through the death of another. Something, plant or animal, suffered to bring you breakfast this morning, to say nothing of what you are planning on having for lunch.

This world, which at first appears only benign and lovely, this creation of God which we revel in on July vacations, is also a realm of life and death where everything is eating and being eaten. So Paul spoke, not of how lovely creation is when seen from a screened-in porch of his mountain cottage, but how creation—groans. "The whole creation has been groaning in travail. . . . not only the creation, but we ourselves," Paul wrote in Romans 8. "The cre-ation was subjected to futility." Groaning. Futility.

In the Great Chain of Being, which biologists know only as a chain of food, some creature is always giving up its life for another. Those chickens, on the way to their destiny, die so that I can live. In an older day, when grandmother went out into the back yard, grabbed a hen, rung her neck, and prepared her for the family's evening meal, there was probably a greater sense of the interconnectedness of all animal life, a greater sense of the dependency of humans upon other animals for the life we enjoy, perhaps even sometimes a sense of regret that so many animals and plants must die so that we can live.

Let Us Make Man in Our Image

All this we know. But as Professor Sibley Towner of Union Seminary has noted, here is a biblical assertion that we may not know: God set all this teeming creation in motion for one reason above all others—to make human life possible. Did you hear that in the scripture today? Over time, over what we now know to have been billions of years, little by little, God coaxed from this buzzing mass of creatures a creature so like God's own self that it was said to be in the very image of God. This creature, this Adam, male and female, is the crowning glory of God's creativity.

I'm talking about you. You, little Sarah Ferree-Clark who was born this month, and Joan of Arc, and Napoleon, George and Martha Washington, Atilla the Hun, all are in the image of God. And Scripture claims that the whole creation, the crickets, gulls, frogs live for our sakes. We alone enjoy such a direct relationship with God.

I suppose that sounds incredibly presumptuous or arrogant. Not so, says the ancient Hebrew who, on one starlit night in July, stood on a Near Eastern hillside, gazed into the heavens and exclaimed:

> O LORD, our Lord,
>   how magestic is thy name in all the earth!
>
> Thou whose glory above the heavens is chanted
>   by the mouths of babes and infants,
> thou hast founded a bulwark because of thy foes,
>   to still the enemy and the avenger.
>
> When I look at thy heavens, the work of thy fingers,
>   the moon and the stars which thou hast established;
> what is man that thou art mindful of him,
>   and the son of man that thou dost care for him?
> Yet thou hast made him little less than God,
>   and dost crown him with glory and honor.
> Thou hast given him dominion over the works of thy hands;
>   thou hast put all things under his feet,
> all sheep and oxen,
>   and also the beasts of the field,
> the birds of the air, and the fish of the sea,
>   whatever passes along the paths of the sea.
>
> O LORD, our Lord,
>   how majestic is thy name in all the earth!   (Psalm 8 RSV)

Little less than God. Sure, compared to the vastness of the starry heavens, we are but small specks of matter in a great universe. But the Bible says we have no equal in all creation. Of all the creatures, we are the only ones invited to talk to and to work with God. God has given us dominion, given us the earth and told us to subdue it. Listen to Genesis: "So God created man in his own image; . . . male and female he created them. And God blessed them, and God said to them, 'Be fruitful and multiply, and fill the earth and subdue it; and have dominion over the fish of the sea and over the birds of the air and over every living thing that moves upon the earth' " (RSV).

No other creature is so like God. While we don't really know precisely what "in the image of God" means, we can infer that it has something to do with dominion, with being partners with God in caring for the garden that God has planted. Genesis says that God chose not to rule the world directly. God chose not to oversee every tiny detail, like some insecure boss who can never let go but insists on having his hands on everything that happens in the office. God puts us in charge. Us.

And we need to be faithful stewards, not wasting any of God's creation, caring for all of God's creatures, since God spent so much time and effort creating every one. Far from destroying the garden with waste and pollution, the good steward is always looking for ways to increase and enhance life in God's garden. Realizing that God has made it all for us, with loving care, believing that God has entrusted to us the maintenance of a beautiful, varied, and wonderfully rich creation, it makes a difference to us what happens to the whooping crane, the snail darter, another human being. Some day we shall have to account to God for how we have tended the garden. Our stewardship shall be judged by the one who once bragged to Job, "Oh Job, would you look at that hippopotamus over there! How about the giraffe I built! What do you think of my donkey?" (Job 40). Life should only be taken by human beings, no matter how simple or primitive an organism it may be, with great gratitude to God for giving us such life and with reverence for the preciousness of each creature, no matter how small, to a loving Creator.

Thank you, chirping crickets, croaking frogs, soaring gulls and all the rest of you, for making human life possible not only through the evolution of the species but also through your contributions to the sustenance and the diversity of human life. Scripture reminds us that we wouldn't be here without you and none of us would be here were not each of us—frogs, crickets, mosquitos (?), gnats (?), hippopotamuses, wildebeests, bald eagles, every single human being—important to God.

And God Gave Them Dominion

All of which may make you want to get out of church today and get on with the business of doing absolutely nothing but sitting on some veranda and enjoying God's creation—sailing some mountain lake, following a little white ball down a carpet of green, bobbing atop an innertube down some cold stream, just sitting in your front yard this afternoon. Fine. But before you go, one more word that you might not have heard if you had not come to your adult class this September morning: You, as the human animal, male and female, are at the very pinnacle of God's marvelous creation. Of all creatures, you are, in the words of the psalmist, "little less than God." God has put you in charge. And you might not have heard that, just sitting on your veranda. Rejoice, thank God: You are human.

Isn't it interesting, whenever someone is caught in some act of violence, some moral failure, some sexual indiscretion, people inevitably say, "Well, he is only human."

"Well, it goes to show, preachers are only human." It's meant to describe us at our immoral, bumbling worst. Only human!

And it's just that attitude that today's scripture is meant to combat. We are human! God has put us, *us* in charge! We are co-creators, co-workers with God. God's garden is all ours. The whole, wonderful creation exists for our livelihood, cultivation, protection, and delight. We are human! Here is a great antidote to the widespread despair, self-doubt, and self-hatred that many humans feel today—the biblical proclamation that God has created us, little less than God, the very pinnacle of all creation, and given us dominion.

We are human!

Helping Adults Become Involved

Preparing to Teach

Today's lesson is concerned with the dignity and worth of humanity as created in God's image. You might begin preparation by listing instances in the modern world in which human life appears to be undervalued. Read the introduction found in "The Main Question." This material will set the tone for your preparation for today's lesson.

Here is a suggested outline for the lesson:

    I. Human Life Undervalued Today.
        A. Ways in which individual human life is undervalued.
        B. Discussion of possible reasons for the problem.

    II. Read Today's Key Scripture from Genesis (1:26-28; 2:18-25).
        A. Using material in "As You Read the Scripture," interpret the highlights of these passages for the class.
        B. Stress the concepts of "dominion" and "in the image of God."

    III. Discuss the Genesis Image of Humanity as the Pinnacle of God's Creation.
        A. Using the material in "The Scripture and the Main Question," lead the class in a discussion of the ways in which humanity rules over nature.
        B. Discuss ways in which "dominion" can lead to abuse of nature.

    IV. Discuss the Dignity of Humanity as Depicted in Genesis 1 and 2.
        A. What do we mean when we say that we are "only human"?
        B. What is the basis of the value of human life in Genesis?
        C. How might the image of humanity in Genesis 1 and 2 counter some of the tendencies in modern life to devalue humanity?

Introducing the Main Question

It is suggested, in "As You Read the Scripture," that the material which we study today from Genesis came from the period of Israel's terrible time of exile. One can imagine the feelings of hopelessness and helplessness that beset the people at this tragic time in history. Here, in the middle of tragedy, is a bold affirmation of the value of human life, the sacredness of humanity.

Following the suggested outline, begin by sharing with your class instances from modern life, from the newspaper this past week or from other sources, of ways in which human life appears to be little valued today. You are doing this in order to set up the problem—the worthlessness of human life—to which the joyful proclamation of Genesis 1 and 2 is the answer.

Developing the Lesson

Continuing to follow the suggested outline, lead your class in a verse-by-verse study of today's scripture from Genesis 1 and 2. You will find the material in "As You Read the Scripture," to be quite helpful as you lift out key concepts in the passages. Note that our suggested lesson plan does not enter into debates about the meaning of Genesis 2:18-25 for contemporary discussion about the relationship between men and women. That is an important discussion, but one in which, in the interest of time, we do not really engage in great detail in this proposed lesson. For now, suffice it to say that *both* male and female share in the dominion and honor that God has given to humanity.

In step III of the proposed outline, you should use the material found in "The Scripture and the Main Question." This material might be summarized by you, adding illustrations from your own experience. The illustrations in "The Scripture and the Main Question" attempt to make the point of today's scripture: humanity is at the pinnacle of creation, God's supreme act of creativity.

Ask your class about the ways in which this human "dominion" can be abused.

For step IV of your class outline, you might lead your class in a discussion of the often-heard phrase, "only human." Let the material found toward the end of "The Scripture and the Main Question," serve as a catalyst for your discussion. Ask your class: After hearing the message of Genesis 1 and 2, how is it possible for us ever to say that our actions are "*only* human?" Being "human," when seen through the eyes of today's scripture, may be a description of us at our best, rather than our worst.

Helping Class Members Act

Go back to the list that you and your class made at the beginning of this session, the list of the ways in which human life appears to be undervalued in today's world. Ask the class to think of specific ways in which the affirmation of humanity as God's creation, found in Genesis 1 and 2, is a response to the dehumanizing aspects of modern life.

You might close the session by reading aloud to the class the verses from Psalm 8 that are quoted in "The Scripture and the Main Question."

Planning for Next Sunday

Our study of important texts from Genesis continues with an exploration of one of the most perplexing of human problems—sin. How can it be that creatures who are created in the image of God should also be creatures who succumb to temptation?

Ask that question of your class as they leave today. It can serve as a springboard for next week's class discussion.

The Ultimate Temptation

Background Scripture: Genesis 3:1-13

The Main Question

Someone once asked the great Southern prophet, Carlyle Marney, "Where was the Garden of Eden?"

Marney immediately replied, "428 Elm Street, Knoxville, Tennessee."

"You're crazy," someone in the college audience replied, "it's somewhere in Mesopotamia or someplace like that."

"No," persisted Marney. "The Garden of Eden was in the home where I grew up on Elm Street in Knoxville. For it was there that one summer afternoon I asked my mother for some money to buy some candy. She refused. So I crept into her bedroom, got her pocketbook, took out a quarter, slithered out of the house and went to the store and bought the forbidden fruit. And after I had eaten it all, I went back to the house and I was so ashamed that I hid in the closet. It was there that she found me, crouching in shame, hiding there in the darkness. And it was there that she said to me, 'Where are you?' 'Who told you to do this?' 'What have you done?' "

The Garden of Eden story, though ancient in origin, is one known to us all. It is not a story about some ancient forebears in some misty corner of the ancient world. It is a story which cuts a path through each of our hearts. The address of the Garden of Eden is our address. We have lived there, have known the truth of this ancient tale of original blessedness, followed by disobedience and betrayal, shame, and fear. We have met Adam and Eve and they are us.

Where is the Garden of Eden?

Today's text suggests that each of us, in our own history, in our own life story, recapitulates this ancient account of testing, failure, and divine rebuke.

Where is the Garden of Eden?

Selected Scripture

King James Version	New Revised Standard Version
Genesis 3:1-13	*Genesis 3:1-13*
1 Now the serpent was more subtil than any beast of the field which the LORD God had made. And he said unto the woman, Yea, hath God said, Ye shall not eat of every tree of the garden?	1 Now the serpent was more crafty than any other wild animal that the LORD God had made. He said to the woman, "Did God say, 'You shall not eat from any tree in the garden'?" 2
2 And the woman said unto the serpent, We may eat of the fruit of the trees of the garden:	The woman said to the serpent, "We may eat of the fruit of the trees in the garden; 3 but God said, 'You
3 But of the fruit of the tree which is in the midst of the garden, God	shall not eat of the fruit of the tree that is in the middle of the garden, nor shall you touch it, or you shall

hath said, Ye shall not eat of it, neither shall ye touch it, lest ye die.

4 And the serpent said unto the woman, Ye shall not surely die:

5 For God doth know that in the day ye eat thereof, then your eyes shall be opened, and ye shall be as gods, knowing good and evil.

6 And when the woman saw that the tree was good for food, and that it was pleasant to the eyes, and a tree to be desired to make one wise, she took of the fruit thereof, and did eat, and gave also unto her husband with her; and he did eat.

7 And the eyes of them both were opened, and they knew that they were naked; and they sewed fig leaves together, and made themselves aprons.

8 And they heard the voice of the Lord God walking in the garden in the cool of the day: and Adam and his wife hid themselves from the presence of the Lord God amongst the trees of the garden.

9 And the Lord God called unto Adam, and said unto him, Where art thou?

10 And he said, I heard thy voice in the garden, and I was afraid, because I was naked; and I hid myself.

11 And he said, Who told thee that thou wast naked? Hast thou eaten of the tree, whereof I commanded thee that thou shouldest not eat?

12 And the man said, The woman whom thou gavest to be with me, she gave me of the tree, and I did eat.

13 And the Lord God said unto the woman, What is this that thou hast done? And the woman said, The serpent beguiled me, and I did eat.

die.' " 4 But the serpent said to the woman, "You will not die; 5 for God knows that when you eat of it your eyes will be opened, and you will be like God, knowing good and evil." 6 So when the woman saw that the tree was good for food, and that it was a delight to the eyes, and that the tree was to be desired to make one wise, she took of its fruit and ate; and she also gave some to her husband, who was with her, and he ate. 7 Then the eyes of both were opened, and they knew that they were naked; and they sewed fig leaves together and made loincloths for themselves.

8 They heard the sound of the Lord God walking in the garden at the time of the evening breeze, and the man and his wife hid themselves from the presence of the Lord God among the trees of the garden. 9 But the Lord God called to the man, and said to him, "Where are you?" 10 He said, "I heard the sound of you in the garden, and I was afraid, because I was naked; and I hid myself." 11 He said, "Who told you that you were naked? Have you eaten from the tree of which I commanded you not to eat?" 12 The man said, "The woman whom you gave to be with me, she gave me fruit from the tree, and I ate." 13 Then the Lord God said to the woman, "What is this that you have done?" The woman said, "The serpent tricked me, and I ate."

Key Verses: **And the serpent said unto the woman, Ye shall not surely die: For God doth know that in the day ye eat thereof, then your eyes shall be opened, and ye shall be as gods, knowing good and evil. Genesis 3:4-5**

Key Verses: **The serpent said . . . "God knows that when you eat of it your eyes will be opened, and you will be like God, knowing good and evil." Genesis 3:4-5**

As You Read the Scripture

Genesis 3:1-13. "No text in Genesis (or likely in the entire Bible) has been more used, interpreted, and misunderstood than this text," says Old Testament scholar, Walter Brueggemann (*Genesis,* John Knox Press, 1980, p. 41). With that caveat in mind, we begin our study. Scholars are generally agreed that this text is not a story about a "fall," a theoretical explanation of how sin came into the world. It is not concerned so much with origins as with the ways in which humanity copes with an undeniable fact of life—we are fallible and sinful. From the first it has been so; how then shall we live as fallible and sinful creatures?

Verse 1. The serpent is said to be "more subtil" than the rest of God's creatures. The serpent is savvy and astute, whereas the man and woman are not. The serpent begins with a question that deliberately distorts what God said. God did not say not to eat *any* fruit, only the fruit of a specific tree. Yet the seeds of doubt have been planted by the serpent.

Verses 2-4. Despite the woman's reply, the serpent counters with outright defiance of God.

Verse 5. Although we cannot say precisely what was this fruit of this forbidden tree, the serpent suggests that it is fruit that opens the eyes, so to speak, fruit that will make the man and woman as wise as God.

Verses 6-7. The man and the woman quickly succumb to the temptation. Woman here is not the evil temptress who has been sometimes depicted in church history. Both man and woman are equal here in their rebellion. They eat of the fruit and their eyes are opened. But how little they see! They wanted to be as wise as God. Now all they see is their nakedness.

Verses 8-11. The creatures who once conversed with God in the garden now cower in the bushes, afraid of God. Their much-desired "wisdom" has revealed to them only their nakedness and vulnerability.

Verses 12-13. When confronted by God with their rebellion and disobedience, the pitiful process of blaming begins. The serpent is blamed, the woman is blamed, and ultimately, God is blamed.

"What kind of God are you," the man implies, "that you should create such creatures like serpents and the woman to beguile me?"

The story is therefore not so much a story of temptation, or of sin, but of blaming.

The Scripture and the Main Question

"Did God Say?"

"And He said, 'I heard the sound of thee in the garden, and I was afraid, because I was naked; and I hid myself.' "

It's a story, primitive story, primordial, which means basic, deep; a true story. It's from Genesis, the beginning book of the Bible, beginning of humanity. Genesis means "in the beginning." In the beginning, God made man and woman and put them in the garden. God will keep the good garden. All man and woman must do is to enjoy, to "be fruitful and multiply"—which sounds enjoyable.

It's a story like the ones told to and by children—naive, fairytale-like, deep, true, like the fairytales told to you when you were young, which,

Bruno Bettelheim says, "speak the unspeakable and plumb the depths of our being."

Once upon a time, we had it all—with no business more pressing than "to be fruitful and multiply." Once upon a time we were like children, naked but unashamed, trusting and unafraid. We were a two-year-old after his bath, romping gleefully naked through the living room, free of the unnatural restraint called clothing. So we were. Undiapered and unashamed. The unselfconscious, trusting simplicity of children is the way God created us, so the story says, once upon a time. Let us assert what the story says and what it does not say.

Like any good story, this one doesn't explain, it narrates. *Contra* Augustine, this is not an explanation of how sin came into the world. The story does not say the man and the woman were at one time sinless. It just says they were naked and unashamed like children—they were only a few days old, remember. It is a story, not about sin, but about *self-consciousness*. And because it's a story about human life, it's a story about *limits*. You are free to enjoy the garden—only stay off that tree over there. The story does not ask, "Why that tree?" We're only told it's the "tree of the knowledge of good and evil." Therefore it's a tree of limits, for what makes us different from God is that we don't always know what is good, whereas God does. Because we're not God, we live with limits. Life has its limits. The story doesn't say why or how. It just states what everybody eventually learns—life, as good as it often is, has limits. (A) We don't know everything. (B) We shall die. It depicts rather than explains our first human testing, pushing at the limits. It's not a story about Satan (this creature is a "snake" who, in the first days of development, was smarter than man or woman). After all, we were only a few days old. Like most smart beings, the snake was good at raising questions.

"Are you sure that God said. . . ?"

"Why would God create such a fine tree and not allow you to eat. . . ?" Socrates said that the purpose of a good teacher is to raise the right questions (just like the snake!). The snake is but a device to move the story along to ask the questions, deep and threatening. Are there really limits to life? Maybe those limits apply to everyone else but me? Could a good God really say that we shall die?

Herein is our human dilemma. God has created us, male and female, the highest of animals. We have a wonderfully contoured cerebral cortex. Since Genesis, we have bypassed snakes. We can reason, ask why, all on our own now, with no need of help from snakes. We can create, achieve, discover, and invest. Can it be that creatures so marvelously endowed should also die? With all that we know, can it be that there is something left that we cannot or should not know? Did God really say that we should not eat of the fruit of the tree of good-evil, life-death?

"Did God say. . . ?"

"Did God say there are *limits* to life in the Garden?" Surely not. Limits. Ah, that's the talk of primitive people, before science, in time B.C.—before computers.

The man and the woman, these wonders of creation, have been given the garden. But they are also given boundaries. They are human, but also creatures. Being creatures, there are things they won't know, and they shall die. But having freedom, blessed with natural curiosity, they began to push against the limits. "Did God say you shall not eat the fruit of *any* of the trees?" asks the snake, grossly misrepresenting what God said. (The snake, by the way, appears to be the world's first theologian—asking questions, answering for God.)

The woman corrects the snake. "No, God said we are free to use all the trees, except for two." But the thought has been planted. The snake has suggested the possibility of an alternative way to God's way.

"Can it be that God, who has gone to such trouble to create us (and so wonderfully created, too), who has given us so many gifts, should also limit us?" The natural God-given boundary is now perceived as threat, a downright injustice. Death, the natural, expected boundary of life, has become the primary human agenda. What can we do about the preservation of our life? We must get organized and do something, take matters in hand, get moving!

"You will not die," says the serpent, moving from suggestion to outright rebellion. And why should we? It's not fair! So we take matters in hand. We were told that we were creatures destined to enjoy the Creator; that, as creatures, all we must do is trust. But *we wanted knowledge more than trust*. We were to entrust to God the meaning and significance of our lives, to let the Creator determine our destiny and worth as creatures. But that wasn't good enough. What good is a garden if we shall die? Not content to be creatures, we become creators. Look at what we can do and know if we just put our heads together! Go ahead, "a *little* knowledge is a dangerous thing." Eat up! Get wise.

Where Are You?

Now, it's the Creator's turn to question. "Where are you?" And the creature gives a pitiful answer. "I was afraid. I was naked. I hid." We wanted knowledge rather than trust, and look what we got—a forlorn creature, shivering in the bushes, cringing in terror. We wanted to step over the boundaries, stand up and be free, and for all of this, we now know only one thing—namely, *we are naked.*

The American philosopher Ernest Becker claims that all culture, science, art, industry, philosophy arises as response to this primordial fact. We are naked. That is, we are (despite our marvelous brains) fragile, exposed, vulnerable creatures who die. And now that we have outgrown God, who is there to give meaning, purpose to our short lives? We must do it ourselves, says Becker.

So, lacking immortality, security, and meaning beyond ourselves, we write books, do research, build houses, make clothes, endow chairs at universities, have children, make war, paint pictures—all as elaborate defenses against the primordial awareness that we are naked and therefore afraid.

What Have You Done?

Our nakedness is no more apparent than in our pitiful attempts at self-justification through blaming. When asked "What have you done?" the woman says, "The serpent beguiled me. . . ." The man says, "The woman gave me. . . ." We can't admit our actions. It takes secure, strong beings to be honest. The lying and blaming reveal the real truth about us: I was naked and afraid.

Dostoevski's *Crime and Punishment* tells of a bright student, Raskolnikov, who decides that he is smart enough to commit the perfect murder without being caught. He is intelligent, calculating, not like other weaker, less intelligent men. The novel is a story of his own self-destruction. Raskolnikov is punished, not by gods, but by the weight of his own offense.

So, in the birth of human self-consciousness and rebellion, man and woman are punished—not by God, but by the results of their attempt to secure their lives by themselves rather than through trust in God.

The story stands as an early critique of inadequate human attempts to overcome anxiety. It begins with man and woman losing their innocence, their childlike willingness to live as trusting creatures within God's creation. In the place of trust, we wanted knowledge. And look what we got.

Our attempt to know more is our effort to deal with our anxiety by circumventing the reality called God. If we can just know enough, get enough government research grants, build bigger and better systems of knowledge accumulation and dissemination, we can secure ourselves, carve out some enduring significance for ourselves.

"What you don't *know* about AIDS can kill you," says the poster on a bulletin board. Knowledge is power to escape anxiety.

The story, this old story, teaches otherwise. It is only God who creates, calls, permits, and prohibits and only God who can deal with our deepest anxiety.

It's a hard lesson for us to learn. We who have been told that our greatest need is for autonomy, liberation, and freedom, are not likely to heed the call to *trust*. Most of the sermons you've heard are calls to action, to use *your* potential, to achieve, live up to your great talent. This story suggests that this way is the *problem,* not the *solution.* The story says that any freedom which doesn't discern the boundaries of human life leaves us anxious. Any exercise of our potential that is not at the same time an admission of our boundaries is demonic because it is based on a lie.

Our culture's attempts to resolve its anxiety are largely psychological, economic, or some form of narcotic. Our public life is largely an exploitation of our common anxiety. Our best politicians, theologians, and advertisements seduce us, like the serpent, into believing that security is to be had apart from the reality of God.

Therefore, I must call you to listen to an old, deep, mysterious story of once-upon-a-time in our past. It is a story, not about Adam and Eve, but about us because each of *us,* in our own lives, recapitulates this primordial act of rebellion and self-deceit. The story therefore has the power to shock us into recognition that our lives are constituted and have enduring significance, not because we have learned so much, but because we learn to trust the "one in whom we live, and move, and have our being."

Helping Adults Become Involved

Preparing to Teach

As I write this lesson, a local politician, who has just been indicted for taking bribes, has been on the television claiming, "I was framed." He blames his indictment on the FBI's "sting" operation in which he was filmed taking money from a constituent.

The story told in today's lesson is a very old story and also a very new story. That will be an asset to you as a teacher as you prepare this lesson.

Begin your preparation by reading "The Main Question." Then, after having this material set in your mind the central concerns of today's lesson, read the assigned scripture, Genesis 3:1-13, using the material in "As You Read the Scripture" to help you understand these verses in depth.

While you are reading the scripture, keep asking yourself, "How do we, in our daily, contemporary lives, illustrate the truth of this text?"

Introducing the Main Question

Most of your group may already be familiar with the passage from Genesis 3 that we will study today. Begin by using the material in "The Main Question," perhaps retelling it in your own words.

Ask members of your group to share, from their own experience, their understanding of Marney's assertion that the Garden of Eden is located in each of our lives.

The story told in Genesis 3:1-13 claims that each of us, in our own moral development, recapitulates the account of "the fall" and its aftermath as reported there.

Developing the Lesson

Now read aloud Genesis 3:1-13 to your group. Using the material in "As You Read the Scripture," point out interesting details in the story to your group. It is such a good story, so well told, that it is able to stand on its own, so to speak. However, your class will be interested in some of the details provided by "As You Read the Scripture."

Because today's scripture is a story, with a beginning, middle, and end, you might let the form of the story itself in Genesis 3:1-13 determine the form of your class. That is, simply walk your adults through the various movements of the story from temptation, to the doubts placed in the woman's mind, to the man and woman's decision to disobey God, and the aftermath of accusation and blaming.

The material in "The Scripture and the Main Question" should be of great value in presenting the passage. As you discuss each of the major movements in the story, pause and ask your class if they can think of contemporary parallels from their own experiences.

"The Scripture and the Main Question" suggests that the man and the woman of Genesis 3:1-13 had a desire for knowledge, limitless knowledge and power more appropriate to the Creator than to creatures.

Can your group cite examples of how our continued human quest for knowledge and power often bring us to grief? Has your local community experienced any examples of human technology backfiring on its creators recently? Does your group see any parallels between the story in Genesis and our contemporary struggles with nuclear waste, ecological problems, military power, medical experimentation?

Rather than live in trusting dependence upon our God, we wish to become as gods unto ourselves, grasping for ourselves a sense of security that should be had only in relationship to God. Thus the story told in Genesis 3:1-13 continues.

The blaming that occurs in Genesis 3:12-13 is one of the most humorous (or the saddest!) aspects of this story. Ask your class to reflect upon that blaming. How does this attempt to "pass the buck" continue today as we attempt to shift the blame for our moral failures onto someone else's shoulders?

Helping Class Members Act

In a sense, today's scripture does not urge some course of action upon us. Rather, today's scripture is a vivid depiction of the way we are, the way life is. However, there are implications for action within the story.

Ask class members to take a moment, in silence, and focus upon one situation in their own lives in which they need to take responsibility for their behavior in the situation, to stop blaming others, and to move toward betterment of the situation. After a few moments of thoughtful silence, close today's session with a short prayer of your own.

Planning for Next Sunday

This Sunday we have focused upon the origin of our sin. What does God do with the sinfulness of his creatures? What is the divine response to human frailty and deceit? That will be the subject of next Sunday's lesson from Genesis. Ask class members to read the rest of Genesis 3 in preparation for that lesson.

LESSON 4   SEPTEMBER 26

God's Response to Sin

Background Scripture: Genesis 3:14-24; 6:5-8, 11-27; 9:8-13

The Main Question

The great modern theologian, Reinhold Niebuhr, who taught for many years at New York's Union Theological Seminary, once said that "the doctrine of original sin is the only empirically verifiable doctrine in Christianity." That is, even though many people may not believe in Christ, may neither understand nor affirm most of the creeds and doctrines of the Christian faith, everyone knows about sin.

Each of us knows firsthand of our capacity to make wrong choices, to strive for the wrong goals, and to pervert even the best of life's blessings into a curse for others and ourselves. Has anyone ever stated the human propensity for sin any better than St. Paul in his Letter to the Romans?

> I do not understand my own actions. For I do not do what I want, but I do the very thing I hate. . . . But in fact it is no longer I that do it, but sin that dwells within me. For I know that nothing good dwells within me. . . . I can will what is right, but I cannot do it. For I do not do the good I want, but the evil I do not want is what I do. Now if I do what I do not want, it is no longer I that do it, but sin that dwells within me (Romans 7:15-20).

Where did this strange human inclination to wrong come from? How did we get in this mess where each of us can say that, in countless ways, I "do not do what I want, but I do the very thing I hate"?

Many modern people do not like to admit their sinfulness. We like to think that we are basically nice people who are making progress. How could anyone who has lived through any portion of the twentieth century with its wars, concentration camps, and periodic brutality make such a claim?

Perhaps the chief evidence that "sin dwells within me" is my constant assertion that I am really a nice person after all—despite all of the empirical evidence to the contrary!

Today's lesson, in which we explore a number of separate but related passages from Genesis, speaks to the issue of human sin and its consequences.

Selected Scripture

King James Version

Genesis 3:22-24

22 And the LORD God said, Behold, the man is become as one of us, to know good and evil: and now, lest he put forth his hand, and take also of the tree of life, and eat, and live for ever:

23 Therefore the LORD God sent him forth from the garden of Eden, to till the ground from whence he was taken.

24 So he drove out the man; and he placed at the east of the garden of Eden Cherubims, and a flaming sword which turned every way, to keep the way of the tree of life.

Genesis 6:5-8

5 And GOD saw that the wickedness of man was great in the earth, and that every imagination of the thoughts of his heart was only evil continually.

6 And it repented the LORD that he had made man on the earth, and it grieved him at his heart.

7 And the LORD said, I will destroy man whom I have created from the face of the earth; both man, and beast, and the creeping thing, and the fowls of the air; for it repenteth me that I have made them.

8 But Noah found grace in the eyes of the LORD.

New Revised Standard Version

Genesis 3:22-24

22 Then the LORD God said, "See, the man has become like one of us, knowing good and evil; and now, he might reach out his hand and take also from the tree of life, and eat, and live forever"—23 therefore the LORD God sent him forth from the garden of Eden, to till the ground from which he was taken. 24 He drove out the man; and at the east of the garden of Eden he placed the cherubim, and a sword flaming and turning to guard the way to the tree of life.

Genesis 6:5-8

5 The LORD saw that the wickedness of humankind was great in the earth, and that every inclination of the thoughts of their hearts was only evil continually. 6 And the LORD was sorry that he had made humankind on the earth, and it grieved him to his heart. 7 So the LORD said, "I will blot out from the earth the human beings I have created—people together with animals and creeping things and birds of the air, for I am sorry that I have made them." 8 But Noah found favor in the sight of the LORD.

Genesis 9:8-13

8 And God spake unto Noah, and to his sons with him, saying,

9 And I, behold, I establish my covenant with you, and with your seed after you;

10 And with every living creature that is with you, of the fowl, of the cattle, and of every beast of the earth with you; from all that go out of the ark, to every beast of the earth.

11 And I will establish my covenant with you; neither shall all flesh be cut off any more by the waters of a flood; neither shall there any more be a flood to destroy the earth.

12 And God said, This is the token of the covenant which I make between me and you and every living creature that is with you, for perpetual generations:

13 I do set my bow in the cloud, and it shall be for a token of a covenant between me and the earth.

Key Verse: **And I will establish my covenant with you; neither shall all flesh be cut off any more by the waters of a flood; neither shall there any more be a flood to destroy the earth. Genesis 9:11**

Genesis 9:8-13

8 Then God said to Noah and to his sons with him, 9 "As for me, I am establishing my covenant with you and your descendants after you, 10 and with every living creature that is with you, the birds, the domestic animals, and every animal of the earth with you, as many as came out of the ark. 11 I establish my covenant with you, that never again shall all flesh be cut off by the waters of a flood, and never again shall there be a flood to destroy the earth." 12 God said, "This is the sign of the covenant that I make between me and you and every living creature that is with you, for all future generations: 13 I have set my bow in the clouds, and it shall be a sign of the covenant between me and the earth.

Key Verse: **I establish my covenant with you, that never again shall all flesh be cut off by the waters of a flood, and never again shall there be a flood to destroy the earth. Genesis 9:11**

As You Read the Scripture

Genesis 3:22-24. These verses come at the end of Adam and Eve's testing and failure. They have eaten the forbidden fruit and now they must suffer the consequences. They now know "good and evil," in other words, they now possess some of the divine ability to know good from evil. Knowing this, they are more like the Creator than like the creatures they were created to be. The text says that the Creator punishes them because, rather than trust the way God has created the world, they have sought to be gods unto themselves. They have eaten of the tree that brings knowledge, but they are now barred from the "tree of life," which is protected by a heavenly being with a flaming sword.

Genesis 6:5-8. After the expulsion from the Garden, human wickedness continues, even intensifies, so much so that God is greatly grieved at having created humanity. In anguish, the Creator decides to end his human experiment, blotting out all life, except for Noah. In both Genesis 3:22-24 and in 6:5-8, the Creator is depicted anthropomorphically, with very human feelings of regret, anger, and sorrow. Here is a very early depiction of God, a God who becomes angry and vengeful.

Genesis 9:8-13. And yet, here is also a God who, having punished humanity for its impudence and rebellion, once again reaches out to humanity. In these verses, just after the terrible flood and the preservation of Noah's family, God makes a promise or covenant with them (and every other living creature) that "never again shall there be a flood to destroy the earth."

As a sign of the promise, "I set my bow in the cloud." The story not only "explains" the origin of the rainbow but it also depicts the steadfastness of God's love. Even today, whenever humanity sees a rainbow arched in the sky after rain, it is reminded of God's great promise "never again" to give up on created life.

All three of today's key passages depict a God who is intimately involved with his creatures, so much so that he becomes angry and even destructive toward them in his divine anger. And yet, all three end with God's loving response to his wayward creation. God promises not to give up on creation, to keep looking at the rainbow and thereby remembering his promise not to destroy us for our continuing sinfulness.

The Scripture and the Main Question

Sent Forth from the Garden

"Therefore the LORD God sent him forth from the garden of Eden, to till the ground from which he was taken" (Genesis 3:23). With these somber words the account of our primal ancestors in the Garden ends. Whereas before we had happiness, constant communion with God, compatible companionship between the man and the woman, now we have hard work, thorns, enmity between the man and the woman, and distance from God.

The story of the expulsion from the Garden is a depiction of alienation, separation from our origins. Thus it is an honest story about our human situation.

I remember someone asking in a college religion class, "Is this story historically true?"

The professor responded, "I don't know that this story is historically true, in fact, I doubt that it is. I only know that it is *eternally true.*"

We can say the same about this story of Adam and Eve and their expulsion from the Garden. The contrast between their once idyllic existence in God's good Garden and their hard life in the rocky soil of the Near East is great. Their once happy time together as companions fit for each other is unlike their present existence where the male rules over the female (Genesis 3:16).

Pick up today's newspaper and you will see depicted there life outside the Garden. Just this morning, looking over our local newspaper, I find that last night, in our medium-sized American city, there were two assaults upon women, a husband was arrested after beating his young wife to death in a marital argument, and a little child was hospitalized after being whipped by her parents. In addition I find that two persons died of heart attacks while they were at work. So there is terrible tension between the sexes, violence against even the ones we love, and many of us are working ourselves to death. So it goes with life outside the Garden.

In the second major portion of today's scripture, we move beyond Eden to some years later, "when men began to multiply on the face of the ground . . ." (Genesis 6:1). If you thought that Adam and Eve were perhaps a couple of bad apples in our human barrel, think again. If you thought that our rebellion and sin were one-time events, then you are wrong. Generations later, "the LORD saw that the wickedness of man was great in the earth, and that every imagination of the thoughts of his heart was only evil continually" (Genesis 6:5).

God's great human experiment appears to have failed. Imagine the joy with which the Creator once greeted his supreme creation. See the delight the Creator took in creating man and woman, telling them to "have dominion" (Genesis 2). Now look at the tragic results of humankind's appearance on the earth. After Adam and Eve, we meet Cain and Abel, the firstborn of the human race (Genesis 4). Cain and Abel, the first children produced by Adam and Eve, become the first instance of fratricide. Having despoiled and been driven out of the Garden, now brother turns against brother in horrible violence.

Little wonder that the God who once looked upon his creation and exclaimed, "Good, very good," now says, "I will blot out man whom I have created from the face of the ground" (Genesis 6:7 RSV).

We may be shocked at such thoughts coming from the Creator. Genesis does not avoid depicting God as one who feels not only love, delight, joy, and happiness, but also anger and disgust. The Creator has given everything to the man and woman, but look how they have responded! Man and woman were to be the supreme acts of God's creativity. No wonder the Creator is disgusted and depressed by what he sees in human history.

"I am sorry that I have made them," says the Creator (Genesis 6:7).

As I thumb through this morning's newspaper, reading of the violence, the inhumanity, the sadness that we human beings inflict upon one another, I can easily imagine God looking down upon human life and saying, "I am sorry that I have made them."

Behold, I Establish My Covenant

And well might this have been the end of the story. Let's be honest—if you or I had been the Creator, we might have ended the abortive human experiment right here, after Cain's murder of his brother Abel.

Have you ever known parents who became so disillusioned by their own children that they rejected their children? I have. It is possible for a parent to try, try, and try again to love a child, only to have that child reject the parent's love, hurt the parent time and again, so that the parent eventually loses hope for the child, gives up, disinherits the child, and blots the child's name from their lives.

Such parental rejection is horrible to behold. And yet I have seen parents who have done so much for their children and yet whose children, as adults, have so terribly disappointed them that parental rejection was understandable.

If a human parent could ever feel driven, by an adult child's behavior, to totally reject that child, how much more might the Creator be driven to total rejection of the human race!

Such would have been the end of the drama of humanity. We would have all perished in a watery grave, blotted forever off the face of the earth, our brief time on this planet marked only by a sign, written in God's own hand, reading, "FAILURE."

But our rebellion and sin were not the last acts of the divine-human drama. Even while God was busy rearranging the human race through the waters of a terrible flood, God was also preserving the family of Noah on the great ark (Genesis 6-8).

Listening to the account of the great flood, we watch the dark storm clouds gather, see the first drops of rain, rain that eventually became a deluge. The waters rise, the rivers overflow, and there is gradual destruction of everything. The story of Noah and the flood is a horrifying, incomparable tale of death and destruction.

And yet, on those dark waters floated a boat that preserved life, both animal and human. The story of Noah and the ark is therefore not only a story of God's anger and regret at having created humanity; it is also a story of God's preservation of humanity.

Later, when the church thought about Christian baptism, it recalled the story of Noah on the ark and interpreted baptism in the light of the story of Noah. Even as sinful humanity was destroyed in the flood, so our sins were said to be washed in baptism. Even as a new humanity was formed from Noah's faithful family after the flood, so we rise to a new existence after our baptism. Thus some of the early church fathers spoke of baptism both as a "womb," the source of new life, and a "tomb," the death of our old, sinful selves.

The same God whose righteousness and goodness could not stand the sight of humanity's evil, is the God who reaches out to preserve humanity and make covenant with the descendants of Noah.

"Behold, I establish my covenant with you and your descendants after you. . . . never again shall all flesh be cut off by the waters of a flood . . ." (Genesis 9:9, 11).

Never Again

So what does the Creator do with the sinfulness of his creatures? That is the subject of today's scripture. There is punishment for sin, consequences. And yet there is also a God who keeps coming back to humanity, never completely gives up hope for the human race, takes up the experiment one more time where it left off. Herein is our hope.

There is punishment for sin. And yet, even with God's stern words to Adam and Eve (Genesis 3:14-24), the results of Adam and Eve's rebellion against God are not so much God's punishment as the horrible consequences of their behavior. It is not so much that God is busy handing out stiff sentences to them for their sin, but rather that their rebellion and disobedience have thrown the whole world off center.

Fortunately, the story does not end with the horrible consequences of our sin. Genesis 9:8-13 is the fitting ending to today's lesson. God comes back to the wayward earthlings and makes a covenant with them, a promise never to desert them or to abandon them to their own devices. The bow in the clouds is a reminder to God and to humanity of God's promise of faithfulness.

So that is the ultimate lesson to be learned from today's scripture from Genesis. It is not news that we are sinful, confused, self-destructive creatures. Everything we know about ourselves confirms the Genesis testimony that "the wickedness of man was [is!] great in the earth" (Genesis 6:5). What was news then and is still news today is God's amazing willingness to stick with us, to promise "never again" to give up on the human experiment.

The testimony of the Genesis 9 covenant is a great comfort to us in our times of despair over ourselves and our fellow human beings. It is great comfort to know that God will never again give up on us and desert us. Never again. Therein is our hope.

Helping Adults Become Involved

Preparing to Teach

One way to understand Scripture better is to be sure that we understand the questions for which Scripture is the answer. The material in "As You Read the Scriptures" and "The Bible and the Main Question" suggests that today's passages from Genesis were recorded as ancient Israel's response to the issue of human sin. What does God do with our sin? Is our future as the human race a future of terrible punishment for our continual rebellion against God or is our future one of communion with our Creator?

You might begin your preparation today, not by turning first to the scripture, but by turning first to your local newspaper. In "The Scripture and the Main Question," the newspaper is cited as evidence or proof of the Genesis assertion (6:5) that the imaginations of human hearts are "evil continually."

Look at your local newspaper for evidence or sin and disobedience. Clip some of those instances for use in beginning your class. This material, from contemporary news reports, can serve as a catalyst for your study of Genesis.

Now read over today's assigned scripture, using the material in "As You Read the Scripture" to augment your understanding of the passages.

You might use the following outline for your class:

I. From the first, humanity rebels against God.
   A. Adam and Eve, and their descendants, sinned against God.
   B. Today, the rebellion and moral chaos seen in Adam and Eve continues.
II. Despite our rebellion and its terrible consequences, God reaches out to us in love.
   A. God reached out and made an eternal covenant (signified by the bow in the clouds) with Noah and his descendants.
   B. God continues to take initiative with us, never deserting us.
III. God's covenant with us is the basis for our hope for the human race.

Introducing the Main Question

"The Main Question" suggests that the doctrine of original sin, the notion that humanity is always engaged in rebellion against God, is one of the most believable of Christian doctrines. Everyone knows about human sinfulness because there is so much evidence for it.

Begin your class by sharing with the class the clippings you have collected from your local newspaper that depict contemporary evidence of our sin. Many in your class may have read these same stories, so your presentation of them need not be detailed. You only want to get them thinking about the human condition in our sin.

Developing the Lesson

I. From the first, humanity rebels against God.

Begin with step one in your lesson outline. Read aloud to your class, or have them read, the selected scripture from Genesis for today's lesson. Using the material found in "As You Read the Scripture," fill in the background and context for these two passages. Suggest to your class that these ancient accounts of human sin have a contemporary sound to them. After all, we have just seen the same story described, in a different way, by our local newspaper.

Can your group identify any human tendencies, seen in the story of Adam and Eve or Cain and Abel, which bring us to grief today? For instance, Adam and Eve were not content to accept the limits that were placed upon them by the Creator. They overstepped the bounds imposed upon them by eating the fruit of the forbidden tree.

Can your group think of any parallels today? (For example, certain sorts of medical experimentation or genetic engineering may be seen as human beings attempting to take upon themselves those prerogatives that should be only God's.)

II. Despite our rebellion and its terrible consequences, God reaches out to us in love.

Today's texts from Genesis speak not only of our sin. The title of today's lesson is "God's Response to Sin." In a sense, today's lesson is not about us or our sin; it is about God and God's actions in the face of our sin. Read Genesis 9:8-13 for your class. Tell them that this story of the covenant is a story about what God does with our sin. Using the material in "As You Read the Scripture," as well as "The Scripture and the Main Question," set this passage in context. This passage occurs at the end of the devastating flood.

The story of our relationship with God does not end with God's wrath and punishment, and it does not end with our human failure. The story ends with God's gracious promise "never again" to destroy humanity, "never again" to quit working with humanity.

Ask your class if they can recall other biblical stories in which God reached out to us despite our sin and disobedience (God's forgiveness of King David after his affair with Bathsheba, Jesus' prayer "Father forgive them" as he hung on the cross, and others).

III. God's covenant with us is the basis for our hope for the human race.

Using the material toward the end of "The Scripture and the Main Question," highlight the way in which the story of the covenant in Genesis 9:8-13 is a basis for human hope. Even though we continue in our sin, even though we continue to be disobedient, God promises never to desert us.

Ask the group what specific ways this affirmation offers contemporary humanity hope even in our failures.

Helping Class Members Act

Knowing that God has promised to love us and to forgive us, never to give up on us, is not only a powerful comfort to struggling humanity, but also a means of encouragement. Ask the class to spend a moment in self-examination, thinking of one specific way in which they have not lived as they ought, and one specific means of responding more faithfully to God's faithfulness to us.

Planning for Next Sunday

Next week we begin a new unit, exploring the Genesis story of Abram and Sarai. Ask the class to read Genesis 15:1-18 in preparation for next week's class.

Unit II. THE BEGINNING OF A NEW RELATIONSHIP

FOUR LESSONS   **OCTOBER 3—OCTOBER 24**

The theme for this four-lesson unit on Genesis is, "The Beginning of a New Relationship." In the previous four lessons, we have followed the story of the origins of humanity, created in the image of God. But we have also followed a much more somber tale, the story of how humanity, once given half a chance to do so, besmirched that divine image with our sin.

We saw how, after the great flood, God made a promise to Noah and his family never again to give up on humanity, never again to send a great flood to destroy the human race. God set a great bow in the clouds to remind him of his covenant (Genesis 9:8-13).

Now for the rest of the story. Having promised to preserve the human race, even in its waywardness, how will God pull this off? How will God ensure that humanity keeps in communion with its Creator? What are God's plans for human destiny?

The story continues, depicting God as coming to a desert nomad named Abram on a starry night and promising to make of him a great, new family. This new family of a new covenant shall be a blessing to all families of the earth. This unit of lessons tells the story of that covenant, that blessing, and the beginnings of the people of Israel. In these lessons we shall observe the resourcefulness of a loving God, a God who has promised never to leave us, to make something out of us, some means of blessing to the whole world.

LESSON 5   **OCTOBER 3**

Trusting in God's Promise

Background Scripture: Genesis 12:1-3; 15:1-18

The Main Question

Jane was describing her religious pilgrimage to the group who had gathered in John and Sue's living room.

"I know that many of you grew up in the church, were raised in a Christian home, and were brought to church from as early as you can remember," said Jane.

"That was not my experience. My parents had very little church background and virtually no Christian commitment. Therefore I had no Christian training or formation. So, why am I here?" she asked.

"From as early as I can remember, I felt a tug at my heart. When I was young, even though I had never been told much about God, nothing about Jesus, I still felt drawn to God. I was fascinated by the Bible. Began reading it on my own when I was a teenager. Although I understood little of what I was reading, something within me made me want to know more. It was as if there were a voice within me encouraging me on, urging me to explore a land I knew nothing about, the land of faith."

Then Jane described how she eventually came to the church, shortly after her marriage, bringing her children with her. "From the first Sunday at St. John's, I knew that I was home. I knew that this was the place for me. I sought baptism and instruction."

"You certainly had a long search, didn't you?" said John.

"Yes, it was a long search. But it was not so much a matter of *my* search," replied Jane.

"What do you mean?" asked John.

"I mean that it was *God* who was searching for me, God taking the initiative with me, reaching out to me. If I'm here, home at last, I owe it all to God."

Sometimes we forget that our relationship to God is a matter of God's initiative, not ours. God has reached out to us, more often than we have reached out to God.

In today's lesson from Genesis, we study the primal story of divine initiative, the story of God's covenant with Abram. God reached out to this ancient nomad and made a promise to him.

God still reaches out to us.

Selected Scripture

King James Version

Genesis 15:1-16

1 After these things the word of the Lord came unto Abram in a vision, saying, Fear not, Abram: I am thy shield, and thy exceeding great reward.

2 And Abram said, Lord GOD, what wilt thou give me, seeing I go childless, and the steward of my house is this Eliezer of Damascus?

3 And Abram said, Behold, to me thou hast given no seed: and, lo, one born in my house is mine heir.

4 And, behold, the word of the LORD came unto him, saying, This shall not be thine heir; but he that shall come forth out of thine own bowels shall be thine heir.

5 And he brought him forth abroad, and said, Look now toward heaven, and tell the stars, if thou be able to number them: and he said unto him, So shall thy seed be.

6 And he believed in the LORD; and he counted it to him for righteousness.

7 And he said unto him, I am the

New Revised Standard Version

Genesis 15:1-16

1 After these things the word of the LORD came to Abram in a vision. "Do not be afraid, Abram, I am your shield; your reward shall be very great." 2 But Abram said, "O Lord GOD, what will you give me, for I continue childless, and the heir of my house is Eliezer of Damascus?" 3 And Abram said, "You have given me no offspring, and so a slave born in my house is to be my heir." 4 But the word of the LORD came to him, "This man shall not be your heir; no one but your very own issue shall be your heir." 5 He brought him outside and said, "Look toward heaven and count the stars, if you are able to count them." Then he said to him, "So shall your descendants be." 6 And he believed the LORD; and the LORD reckoned it to him as righteousness.

7 Then he said to him, "I am the

LORD that brought thee out of Ur of the Chaldees, to give thee this land to inherit it.

8 And he said, Lord GOD, whereby shall I know that I shall inherit it?

9 And he said unto him, Take me an heifer of three years old, and a she goat of three years old, and a ram of three years old, and a turtledove, and a young pigeon.

10 And he took unto him all these, and divided them in the midst, and laid each piece one against another: but the birds divided he not.

11 And when the fowls came down upon the carcasses, Abram drove them away.

12 And when the sun was going down, a deep sleep fell upon Abram; and, lo, an horror of great darkness fell upon him.

13 And he said unto Abram, Know of a surety that thy seed shall be a stranger in a land that is not theirs, and shall serve them; and they shall afflict them four hundred years;

14 And also that nation, whom they shall serve, will I judge: and afterward shall they come out with great substance.

15 And thou shalt go to thy fathers in peace; thou shalt be buried in a good old age.

16 But in the fourth generation they shall come hither again: for the iniquity of the Amorites is not yet full.

LORD who brought you from Ur of the Chaldeans, to give you this land to possess." 8 But he said, "O Lord GOD, how am I to know that I shall possess it?" 9 He said to him, "Bring me a heifer three years old, a female goat three years old, a ram three years old, a turtledove, and a young pigeon." 10 He brought him all these and cut them in two, laying each half over against the other; but he did not cut the birds in two. 11 And when birds of prey came down on the carcasses, Abram drove them away.

12 As the sun was going down, a deep sleep fell upon Abram, and a deep and terrifying darkness descended upon him. 13 Then the LORD said to Abram, "Know this for certain, that your offspring shall be aliens in a land that is not theirs, and shall be slaves there, and they shall be oppressed for four hundred years; 14 but I will bring judgment on the nation that they serve, and afterward they shall come out with great possessions. 15 As for yourself, you shall go to your ancestors in peace; you shall be buried in a good old age. 16 And they shall come back here in the fourth generation; for the iniquity of the Amorites is not yet complete."

Key Verse: **And I will make of thee a great nation, and I will bless thee, and make thy name great; and thou shalt be a blessing. Genesis 12:2**

Key Verse: **I will make of you a great nation, and I will bless you, and make your name great, so that you will be a blessing. Genesis 12:2**

As You Read the Scripture

Genesis 15:1-16. The Abram story begins earlier, back in Genesis 11. We are told a great deal about Abram and his nomadic family, but we are told nothing which, at this point, distinguishes them from any other ancient family. In chapter fifteen, we hear the story that designates this family as the recipients of a special divine promise. Now we shall learn why Abram is so important in God's scheme of things.

Verse 1. The story tells us that Abram was a very old man when met by God in this vision. In other words, Abram was already advanced in years, without children, which in that day, in that part of the world meant without a future. At this point in the narrative, his name is not yet changed to Abraham (see Genesis 17:5).

Verses 2-4. The voice says that Abram shall have a son of his own. This child shall be Abram's "reward." The notion of reward here is no this-for-that transaction. Rather, the reward shall be a sign to everyone that God has chosen Abram for special recognition and special responsibility.

Verses 5-6. In a memorable scene, the Lord shows Abram the stars in the sky and promises that Abram's descendants shall be as numerous as those stars.

Verses 7-11. In accordance with ancient custom, Abram makes a sacrifice to God both as sign of thanksgiving and as an offering to God to ratify the covenant. Abram is looking for some sign from God to reassure him of the truthfulness of the divine promise.

Verses 12-16. In the Lord's further explication of the promise, the Lord gives a preview of the history of this newly created covenant family. For four hundred years they shall be oppressed (Egyptian slavery) but, eventually, "they shall come out with great possessions."

The narrative does not ponder *why* the Lord chose this man and not some other to bear the promise. There is no indication that Abram was particularly virtuous or noteworthy. You will note that Genesis is full of inexplicable divine choices such as Abel over Cain (Genesis 4), Isaac over Ishmael (Genesis 21), Jacob over Esau (Genesis 25). God chooses whom God chooses.

The Scripture and the Main Question

Your Reward Will Be Great

If you take a moment to scan Genesis 12–14, you will see that these chapters concern a family of nomads whose leader is Abram. We learn that they have most of the problems of any human family—envy, jealousy, bickering. We learn that Abram is a person who feels close to God, who continually converses with God throughout the ups and downs of his family life. But why should we concern ourselves for so long with this family and not some other?

We are about to learn why.

Matters come to a head at the beginning of Genesis 15 when God says to Abram, "Do not be afraid, Abram, I am your shield; your reward shall be very great" (15:1). Abram responds that God's love for him is all well and good, but what sort of reward does God have in mind, since "I continue childless"?

The Hebrew word that our Bibles translate as "reward" does not mean reward in the sense of a wage for services rendered. Rather it means reward in the sense of special recognition given by a master to a faithful servant who has performed some special service to the master.

Through thick and thin, Abram and Sarai have served God. They have placed their hope in God, all evidence to the contrary. Take a moment and read the New Testament interpretation of Abram's faithfulness in Hebrews 11:10.

Abram knows that there can be little sense of "reward" for him and Sarai as long as he has no rightful heir. He will not be able to hold on to his land. He will not be able to continue his family name. No heir means no future, therefore no real hope. So Abram protests to God that all he has for a future is this adopted slave-boy. After Abram's double protestation, God repeats the promise one more time: " 'Look toward heaven and count the stars, if you are able to count them. . . . So shall your descendants be' " (Genesis 15:5).

What did Abram see when he looked toward the heavens? How did he make the move from a vision of natural wonder to a new vision of his own life? In looking up at those innumerable stars, was he overwhelmed by the glory and majesty of God? Gazing upon natural wonder, was Abram convinced of God's power and ability to keep his promise? Was his experience similar to that described in Psalm 8?

"When I look at the heavens. . . . the moon and the stars. . . ."

He Believed the Lord

Many Christian writers, from St. Paul to Martin Luther, have marveled at the acclamation of Genesis 15:6. Abram believed!

All evidence to the contrary (he and Sarai were childless and very old, remember, with nothing more to reassure him than the starlit heavens), Abram believed. He has no "proof." Nothing has as yet changed in his situation. Everything he knows about life, about conception and birth, about aging and death, tell him that the promise cannot be believed. And yet, Abram believes.

In a few verses, our story has moved Abram from disbelieving protest to belief. How does one make such a movement? What are the psychological or spiritual processes that occur in a person's mind which move that person from disbelieving scepticism toward believing faithfulness?

We don't know. The story does not tell us. Perhaps Abram had already experienced enough of God's faithfulness and goodness to be able to trust God's promise of an heir. Perhaps Abram felt that, in his circumstances, he had absolutely no reason to trust himself or his resources. Therefore if he was going to hope, he could only hope in God.

Perhaps. Or is it that such belief is not based upon experience or upon despair, but rather upon the gift of God? Belief, in the face of all the reasons for doubt, is nothing short of miraculous. If we believe, our belief is a gift of God, even before God gives us any other gifts.

Does this episode with Abram remind you of another confrontation between disbelief and belief that is found in the Gospels? In Matthew 16:15-17, Jesus asks his disciples who they believe him to be. Peter abruptly and quite without explanation blurts out, "You are the Christ, the Son of the living God."

Where does such a declaration of faith come from?

Jesus indicates that such faith is nothing short of miraculous, a miraculous gift: " 'Blessed are you, Simon Bar-Jonah! For flesh and blood has not revealed this to you, but my Father who is in heaven.' "

I know that there are people who have analytical minds, who base their belief upon careful weighing of the evidence, sorting out of the facts. I am not one of those people. For me, belief is not the result of logical deduction.

Rather, belief is a kind of leap, a stride into the unknown based upon nothing any more substantial than trust.

How is it for you?

Abram's belief, all evidence to the contrary, is a gift. He believed that God was capable, somehow, someway, of being true to his promises. Before he received the promised gift of an heir, Abram received the gift of faith. His was not a reasoned, deliberate, intellectual effort. Rather, Abram heard God's promise and believed. In his believing, in his leap of faith, I think Abram was a precursor of many of us who are his heirs in faith.

I Am the Lord

Even though Abram has come to believe in the promises of God, that does not mean that all doubts have been banished from his mind. At the promise of land and an heir, Abram responds,

"O Lord GOD, how am I to know that I shall possess it?" Abram asks God (Genesis 15:8 RSV).

How indeed? There is a sacrifice and God appears to confirm the sacrificial gift, speaking to Abram in a dream of the future of his family (15:12-16).

So Abram's journey with God continues. As yet, he has no proof, no definite evidence that God will be faithful to his promises. Abram ventures forth, trusting in those promises, believing that God is able to do what God promises to do.

Why do we read this ancient story today? Because Abram was one of the first of our race to walk with God. More than that, he was the very first to receive the promise of God. God told Abram he would make something out of him, bless him, use him to bless others. Abram trusted that promise, all evidence to the contrary.

Thus we remember him in your class today. He becomes a model of faith for those of us who come after him. And when we remember Abram, God's promise to him is fulfilled. God really did make a great nation out of this desert nomad. God really did give Abram a family.

When your class gathers this Sunday, we are Abram's family, a visible sign that God keeps God's promises.

Helping Adults Become Involved

Preparing to Teach

This week's lesson explores the mystery of trust in God's promise. Belief is always a mystery. Why is it that some people are confronted by the claims of the church and respond in faith and others do not? Why is it that belief comes easily for one but not for another? These are among the questions that you will be exploring in today's lesson.

Begin your preparation for teaching today's lesson by reading the key scripture for today, Genesis 15:1-16. Use the material in "As You Read the Scripture" to help you understand this passage in depth. As you read, think of this episode as an instance of God approaching someone, making a claim upon that person's life, and evoking a faithful response from that person. Has a similar experience happened to you or to someone you know?

Today's lesson can be organized according to the following outline:

I. God takes the initiative with us, reaching out to us before we reach out to God.
   A. Our relationship with God is first something God does to us.
   B. We are dependent upon God's initiative with us.

II. God reached out to Abram.
   A. God promised to make a great nation of Abram's family.
   B. Abram believed God, despite the evidence to the contrary.

III. Faith is a response to the initiative of God in our lives.
   A. Faith does not always have strong evidence to back it up.
   B. Faith is trusting response.

Introducing the Main Question

Open the class by retelling, in your own words, the opening illustration in "The Main Question." Ask the class, "Can you identify with Jane's testimony of the ways in which God has reached out to her?"

This illustration will stimulate your group to thinking about faith as the result of God's reaching out to us. Lead a discussion within your group about the specific ways in which they have found, in their own lives, God reaching out to them. Before coming to class, you might think of such examples from your own life. Share your examples from your own life with the group in order to free them to share their examples of faith as God's initiative.

Developing the Lesson

I. God takes the initiative with us, reaching out to us before we reach out to God.

Now introduce today's scripture by simply reading, or retelling in your own words, today's key scripture from Genesis 15:1-16. Using the material that is found in "As You Read the Scripture," set this passage in context. This event occurred very late in Abram's life. He had been walking with God throughout his life. But on this starlit night, Abram received a promise from God that suggested that Abram's future was still open and full of possibility.

Can any in your group identify with Abram? That is, have any of them been in a situation in which the future seemed closed and barren to them until they felt God reassuring them that he was with them?

Many older adults can identify with Abram. In our mature years, there is the natural feeling that our life's journey is over. We have either accomplished our goals in life or else adjusted to the reality that we will not meet all of our goals. Abram was old, he and Sarai had lived most of their lives with no children of their own. And yet, on this starlit night, Abram was promised a new and open future, an heir and a family.

II. God reached out to Abram.

Using the illustrative material found in "The Scripture and the Main Question," continue to lead your group in their reflection upon the story of God's covenant with Abram.

Discuss the notion of "reward" as it is found in this story. Can anyone in your group think of a time in his or her life when they received a "reward" from God, some recognition of faithfulness, which was unexpected and perhaps unsought?

Note, in your discussion, that the story does not claim that God *always* responds to our fidelity with rewards. Rather it says that, in Abram's case, God made a promise to recognize Abram's faithfulness with the gift of an unexpected child. How does your group feel about the story's assertion of a "reward" for faithfulness? When might this story lead to false or unrealistic expectations on the part of some believers?

The discussion in "The Scripture and the Main Question" suggests that, as Abram looked up into the starry night, he perhaps sensed some of the power and glory of God that made it easier for him to trust God's promise. Have any in your group had a similar experience of moving from recognition of God's majesty in nature (Psalm 8) to trust in God's faithfulness in their own lives?

III. Faith is a response to the initiative of God in our lives.

This discussion leads us to consideration of the final point in our lesson plan outline. The illustration about Jane in "The Main Question" suggested that we sometimes think of our faith as something that we do, something that we attain after personal struggle, our own achievement of belief. Today's scripture from Genesis 15 portrays faith as a mysterious response to the action of God in our lives.

Why is it that some people feel God's presence and respond in faith and others do not? Today's lesson suggests that faith is and remains a mystery. When there is faith, this is no cause for boasting or smug complacency. If we have faith, if we are able to trust the promises of God and to base our lives on them, it is as a gift of God, not our own achievement. God came to Abram, not Abram to God. Because God came first to Abram, then Abram was free to give himself to God.

After discussing this idea of faith as a gift of God, can your group think of experiences within their own lives, or within their life in the church, in which it appears that we sometimes confuse faith with human achievement?

Have they ever heard us speak of faith as if it were a cause for personal boasting rather than a cause for humble thanksgiving?

In my own work at a university, I frequently have young adults come to me and ask me what they can *do* to believe. Is there a book they can read, some technique to assuage their doubts and give them firm assurance of the reality of God?

I wish there were such techniques available! Certainly, we can place ourselves in situations where it is likely that we shall be encountered with God's love. One reason why we come to church is to strengthen our faith.

But when all is said and done, faith is not something we do but something God does. If we believe, it is because God first reached out to us.

Helping Class Members to Act

Today we have explored faith as a matter of God's initiative with us. But we are people who like to have our way rather than God's way. Ask the group, in preparation for next week's lesson, to think of one instance in their own life in which they felt God was leading them in a certain direction, but they wanted to go in another direction.

Planning for Next Sunday

Next Sunday we continue our study of the story of Abram by focusing upon Abram's wife, Sarai, one of the most interesting of Old Testament characters. Your group's thoughts about the conflict in their own lives between God's way and our way will be excellent preparation for our study of Genesis 16.

LESSON 6   OCTOBER 10

Our Way or God's Way?

Background Scripture: Genesis 16

The Main Question

The early Christian leader, Tertullian, once noted, "Christians are made, not born."

By that he meant that no one becomes a Christian by natural inclination, by innate disposition, or by birthright. In a sense, there are no second-generation Christians. You cannot inherit this faith; you must receive it for yourself.

This idea is not original with Christians. Israel before us saw itself as the creation of a loving God who took the initiative and reached out to Israel. When asked, "Who are we?" the Hebrew was taught to respond, "We were Pharaoh's slaves in Egypt; and the LORD brought us out of Egypt with a mighty hand; and the LORD showed signs and wonders, great and grievous, against Egypt . . . , that he might bring us in and give us the land which he swore to give to our fathers" (Deuteronomy 6:21-23)

Just as God reached out and made a covenant with Abram (Genesis 15:1-16), so God kept his promise and reached out to the Hebrew slaves in Egypt and brought them out "with a mighty hand."

In other words, Israel was made, not born, a creation by a loving God of a people out of a group of nomads who were once no people. Just as the Creator made a world out of nothing (Genesis 1), so God continues to create something out of nothing, a people out of a group of nobodies.

This is a key affirmation for both Jews and Christians. In reminding ourselves that we are a creation of God, out of nothing, we are reminded that our salvation, our relationship to God, is essentially up to God rather than up to us. Only because God has reached out to us are we thereby free to reach out to God.

One day, when Abram was very old, God came to him, as God may have come to you, saying, "I will make my covenant between me and you." That was the beginning of the story.

But God's reaching out to us is only the beginning. Response is required. When God extends the hand to us, we must reach out and grasp it. When

God's way is revealed to us, will we follow our way or God's way? The temptation to take matters into our own hands is always strong. Shall we wait patiently or shall we act on our own terms? That dilemma is at the heart of today's lesson.

God's way or our way?

Selected Scripture

King James Version

Genesis 16:1-4, 11-16

1 Now Sarai Abram's wife bare him no children: and she had an handmaid, an Egyptian, whose name was Hagar.

2 And Sarai said unto Abram, Behold now, the LORD hath restrained me from bearing: I pray thee, go in unto my maid; it may be that I may obtain children by her. And Abram hearkened to the voice of Sarai.

3 And Sarai Abram's wife took Hagar her maid the Egyptian, after Abram had dwelt ten years in the land of Canaan, and gave her to her husband Abram to be his wife.

4 And he went in unto Hagar, and she conceived: and when she saw that she had conceived, her mistress was despised in her eyes.

....

11 And the angel of the LORD said unto her, Behold, thou art with child, and shalt bear a son, and shalt call his name Ishmael; because the LORD hath heard thy affliction.

12 And he will be a wild man; his hand will be against every man, and every man's hand against him; and he shall dwell in the presence of all his brethren.

13 And she called the name of the LORD that spake unto her, Thou God seest me: for she said, Have I also here looked after him that seeth me?

14 Wherefore the well was called Beerlahairoi; behold, it is between Kadesh and Bered.

New Revised Standard Version

Genesis 16:1-4, 11-16

1 Now Sarai, Abram's wife, bore him no children. She had an Egyptian slave-girl whose name was Hagar, 2 and Sarai said to Abram, "You see that the LORD has prevented me from bearing children; go in to my slave-girl; it may be that I shall obtain children by her." And Abram listened to the voice of Sarai. 3 So, after Abram had lived ten years in the land of Canaan, Sarai, Abram's wife, took Hagar the Egyptian, her slave-girl, and gave her to her husband Abram as a wife. 4 He went into Hagar, and she conceived; and when she saw that she had conceived, she looked with contempt on her mistress.

....

11 And the angel of the LORD said to her,

"Now you have conceived and
    shall bear a son;
  you shall call him Ishmael,
    for the LORD has given heed to
    your affliction.
12 He shall be a wild ass of a man,
with his hand against everyone,
    and everyone's hand against him;
and he shall live at odds with all his
    kin."

13 So she named the LORD who spoke to her, "You are Elroi"; for she said, "Have I really seen God and remained alive after seeing him?" 14 Therefore the well was called Beerlahairoi; it lies between Kadesh and Bered.

15 And Hagar bore Abram a son: and Abram called his son's name, which Hagar bore, Ishmael.

16 And Abram was fourscore and six years old, when Hagar bare Ishmael to Abram.

15 Hagar bore Abram a son; and Abram named his son, whom Hagar bore, Ishmael. 16 Abram was eighty-six years old when Hagar bore him Ishmael.

Key Verse: **And Sarai said unto Abram, Behold now, the LORD hath restrained me from bearing; I pray thee, go in unto my maid; it may be that I may obtain children by her. And Abram hearkened to the voice of Sarai. Genesis 16:2**

Key Verse: **Sarai said to Abram, "You see that the LORD has prevented me from bearing children; go in to my slave-girl; it may be that I shall obtain children by her." Genesis 16:2**

As You Read the Scripture

Genesis 16:1-4, 11-16. Last week we met Abram. Today we deal with his wife, Sarai. In chapter fifteen, Abram was led by God to envision a new future. Even though Abram and his wife were old, very old, God says he will give them a child. Abram trusts God's promise, even though little that Abram knows of life confirms the promise. Abram's response is contrasted with that of Sarai. When confronted by life's barrenness, no heir, no child, Sarai takes matters into her own hands.

Verses 1-3. Sarai tires of waiting upon God to make good on his promises. She devises a plan whereby her husband, Abram, will conceive a child with Hagar, an Egyptian maid in Sarai's service.

Verse 4. When Hagar's child is born, Sarai immediately had contempt for her. More than simple jealousy is probably involved in Sarai's reaction to Hagar's pregnancy. Hagar is an alien and the prospect of her child becoming an heir to the family fortune is considered to be a great insult to the family name.

Verses 11-16. Verse 11 begins a curious insertion into the story of Abram and Sarai. The story of Hagar and her son, Ishmael, suggests that there is an alternative story taking place at the same time as the story of Abram and Sarai. God is not exclusively committed to Abram and Sarai to the exclusion of all other human families. God also cares about those on the outside. While Hagar and Ishmael represent, for Abram and Sarai, a threat to their need to trust the promise of God to make of them a great people, they are for us a reminder that God is infinitely resourceful, not limited even to his own chosen people, and deeply involved in human life. God is bringing about a variety of futures for a variety of peoples.

The Scripture and the Main Question

Now Sarai Bore Abram No Children

In last week's lesson we focused upon God's gracious promise to Abram and Sarai. God will make a great nation out of this old, childless couple. Despite all evidence to the contrary, God will work among them to create a future they dared not dream.

But that was last week, back in Genesis 15. Here we are in Genesis 16 and nothing has happened. Can God's promise be trusted? Will God keep God's promise? Will there be an heir? Is there a future?

Those were the questions that insinuated themselves into Sarai's mind. There has been a promise of a child, but still there is no child. Like a woman in labor, awaiting birth, Sarai is awaiting the birth of the future. Her situation is reminiscent of the way in which St. Paul describes our general human condition as the whole creation "groaning in labor . . . grown inwardly as we wait for adoption as children, the redemption of our bodies. For in this hope we are saved" (Romans 8:22-24, author's translation).

Trusting in God would be a relatively simply matter if God worked on our schedule. If God responds quickly, as we measure time, then trust is much easier. But as the early Christian writer once said, "With God, a thousand years is as one day." We can empathize with Sarai. She was already a very old woman. Her "biological clock" was ticking each day. The promise of a child was fine, but where is the child?

This is the situation that led Sarai to take matters into her own hands, to attempt to manipulate events to move things along. She urges her husband to have sexual relations with her Egyptian maid, Hagar. This is Sarai's plan to realize the promise of an heir, even though it is not God's plan.

And before we are too quick to criticize Sarai's plan, remember that Sarai and Abram have dwelt now for ten years in Canaan (Genesis 16:3). Ten years is a long time to wait for a promise to be realized. Ten years is an especially long time when one is the age of Sarai and Abram, toward the end of life.

Patience may be a central Christian virtue, but it is a virtue that we modern human beings seem to have in short supply. We are now accustomed to instant oatmeal, instant banking, instant everything. We want what we want and we want it now, with push-button speed.

"I have more money than time," I heard someone say the other day. We modern people are unaccustomed to waiting. In the gaps, in the long gaps between promise and fulfillment of promise, we are apt to lose heart, to give up, to become discouraged and take matters into our own hands.

That is what happened to Sarai and Abram. Exhausted by waiting, tired of hoping without seeing fulfillment of their hope, they decided to take matters into their own hands, to manipulate events to suit their vision of the future.

A person I know grew up in poverty. Even though he grew up poor, he had a great deal of ambition, the gift of ambition, one might say. He wanted to achieve much, to do well in business. He worked hard in school, always had a variety of after-school jobs while he was growing up. He wanted to do whatever was necessary to realize his dreams of success into business.

Unfortunately, he became impatient. He tired of waiting for his hoped-for success. He took shortcuts. He became involved in some shady business deals, hoping to make more money in less time.

Eventually, his shortcuts caught up with him. He was charged with fraud in a contract that he had made with the government. Convicted and sentenced to jail, he represents, in my mind, a parallel to the story of Abram and Sarai's impatience. Surely, God wanted him to succeed, to lift himself above his humble origins. But rather than take matters the slow, appropriate way, he did it his way. The results were tragic.

Sarai's idea to have her husband impregnate her maid Hagar has tragic consequences. "And when she saw that she had conceived, she looked with contempt on her mistress" (Genesis 16:4). Hagar has had a child, Ishmael, and now has contempt for the childlessness of Sarai. There is now deep division in the house of Abram, big trouble. Sarai's great project has ended in disaster. "Then Sarai dealt harshly with her, and she fled from her" (16:6).

The story suggests that, although God's ways often take time and require patience on our part, God's ways are superior to ours. We must pray, then, for patience.

The Lord Has Given Heed to Your Affliction

Hagar, the maid who cooperated with Sarai and Abram in their plan, now finds herself in a terrible situation. Sarai now despises her because Hagar is about to present Abram with his long-awaited child whereas Sarai is still childless. Sarai's "solution" to the problem of an heir has been no solution at all. Sarai now resents her maid and Hagar must flee for her life and for the life of her child. Hagar is now a fugitive, fleeing the wrath of her mistress (Genesis 16:7-9). Alone, fearful, Hagar is visited by an angel of the Lord who tells her that God has plans for her and her descendants, even as God had plans for Abram and Sarai and their descendants.

Although the main plot of this story is the history of Abram's family and their descendants, the story of Hagar and Ishmael is an important subplot. Hagar's story, and the promise of God to protect her and her child, suggests that God is not exclusively committed to Abram and Sarai. Even for Hagar the Egyptian, the outsider, the alien among Abram's people, there is divine concern. She shall be protected and blessed.

By inserting Hagar's story here, I think the ancient compiler of Genesis means to make a statement about the difference between the way we do things and the way that God does things. When we do things, we usually do them with an eye only to our own good. Sarai was busy manipulating events, using Hagar in a vain attempt to give Abram an heir, treating Hagar no better than if Hagar were a piece of livestock that Sarai and Abram owned.

Perhaps Sarai thought that, because of the divine promise of an heir, which had been made by God to her and Abram, God had concern only for their well-being and no one else's.

What Sarai needed to know was the great affirmation of Jewish faith—the Lord our God is one. There are not multiple deities, as if Hagar and the Egyptians have their gods and Abram and Sarai have theirs. It is not as if God works only among Abram's family and no others. The Lord our God is also their God. There is only one God, therefore Abram and Sarai's lives are caught up in the purposes of the same God who is busy with Hagar and her unborn child's lives.

This is a monotheistic (one God) lesson that we must learn and relearn. The same God who is busy with us is busy with our brothers and sisters. We may label our brothers and sisters as "Egyptian" or "servant" or some other designation by which we separate ourselves from them. But in God's eyes we are all one because there is one God.

The delightful subplot of the story of Hagar and the promises of God is a reminder that God is busy making promises to more people than those who are within the bounds of our family.

Hagar Bore Ishmael to Abram

"Abram was eighty-six years old when Hagar bore Ishmael to Abram" (Genesis 16:16). How strange and wonderful are the workings of God! How strange and surprising are the twists and turns of human history!

We are reading the story of an ancient family. However, all of the tension, jealousy, deceit, and difficulty remind us of contemporary family life. Part of the point of our story must be that God chooses to work within *this* family, despite its difficulties.

The loving God intervenes, works even within the confused events that are the result of Sarai's manipulation. Luther once said that "God can shoot with a crooked bow or ride a lame horse." Time and again in our history, when our great plans go astray and we become stuck with the mess of our own making, God is able to work within our mess to bring some blessing out of our curse. Such is the case with Hagar and her son, Ishmael. Such is the case with Abram and Sarai. Sarai tried to manipulate events and to make things come out right on her terms. A loving God intervened and enabled things to come out on his terms.

Helping Adults Become Involved

Preparing to Teach

It is important that you prepare yourself by having a good grasp of the scripture that you are trying to teach. Today's lesson from Genesis 16:1-16 comes in the middle of the story of Abram and Sarai. In your preparation to teach this material, it might be good for you to go back at least to Genesis 12 and scan the chapters leading up to Genesis 16 in order to set today's text in context.

A key idea in this lesson is the notion of God's surprising intervention within often confused human affairs. Read Genesis 16:1-4, 11-16, using the material in "As You Read the Scripture" to help you understand this material in depth.

For your class, use the following outline:

I. We often lose patience with God's plan and take matters into our own hands.
   A. God's plans often take time to accomplish.
   B. We are people who often trust our own efforts more than God's actions.
II. Human family life, though often confused and difficult, can be the arena for God's loving intervention.
   A. Sarai tried to take matters into her own hands and made a mess of the situation.
   B. God reached out to Hagar even though she was not part of God's original plan to bless Abram's family.
III. We ought to wait patiently for God's actions within our difficult situations.

Introducing the Main Question

Open the class by noting that we live in a society that values human initiative in righting wrong and contributing to progress. We are a society that values the person who is able to say, "I did it myself," and "I did it my way."

In such a society, the testimony of today's scripture may be difficult to hear. Now share, in your own words, the material found in "The Main Question." This will be a catalyst for your class to begin thinking about the ways we prefer to take matters into our own hands rather than to trust God.

Then read aloud the key scripture for today, Genesis 16:1-4, 11-16. Use any of the material which you found helpful in "As You Read the Scripture" to expand your class's understanding of these verses.

Developing the Lesson

I. We often lose patience with God's plan and take matters into our own hands.

Have your class note the way in which Sarai tried to manipulate matters to her own ends by using her servant, Hagar.

Using the material in "The Scripture and the Main Question," discuss this human tendency with your class. Can they cite examples from their own experience in which they lost patience in a situation, decided to take matters into their own hands, and ended up making matters worse?

You might retell the story of the man who wanted success, but who took illegal shortcuts to success, as told in "The Scripture and the Main Question."

In last week's lesson, we studied the promise that God made to Abram, the promise to give him an heir and to make a great nation out of him. Abram trusted God. But things took longer than Abram might have imagined. Now Sarai tires of trust and takes matters into her hands.

Is lack of patience a corollary of lack of faith? Can your group cite examples from their own lives in which this seemed to be true?

II. Human family life, though often confused and difficult, can be the arena for God's loving intervention.

Using the discussion in "The Scripture and the Main Question," note the surprising turn that our story takes when God reaches out to Hagar the fugitive and assures her of his protection. Note how this subplot runs beneath the main story of Abram and Sarai.

Thinking of modern family life, can members of your class cite parallels from contemporary experience of family that relate to the problems within Abram and Sarai's family?

For instance, a major problem in many congregations today is the problem of "step families," that is, families that are joined by a second marriage. How do stepparents manage to relate to children of a former marriage?

Can your group cite other examples of contemporary family stress?

You might want to list their examples on a chalkboard or newsprint.

After noting the ways in which God intervened in the mess in Abram and Sarai's family, ask your group if they have had experiences in which they came to feel that God intervened in their family difficulties.

I recall the man who told me, after years of struggle with his son, that his son quite unexpectedly, even miraculously, went through a dramatic religious conversion and was restored to his father after years of alienation. I am sure that father would claim that restoration as the result of God's intervention into the affairs of a troubled family.

III. We ought to wait patiently for God's actions within our difficult situations.

Sarai did not want to wait for fulfillment of the promise to provide her with a child. She devised a plan that brought great grief to her family and to her servant, Hagar. Our society has such great faith in the efforts of human beings, such great confidence in our own works. This story suggests that we must temper our confidence in ourselves and our own devices with faith in the ability of God to work for the future God desires.

Can your group think of ways in which we might gain more patience in trusting the promises of God? In what ways might this story be a source of patience for us in our family relationships?

Helping Class Members to Act

All of us, in our families, have issues that perplex us and bring us sadness. At the end of your session, ask the class to sit quietly and, in silence, think of one exasperating or seemingly impossible dilemma within their own family that needs God's loving intervention. Ask them silently to focus on that dilemma and then to pray for God's loving work in that situation. Close the session with a short prayer of your own.

Planning for Next Sunday

Our journey with Abram and Sarai continues. The promise, made earlier to Abram, is reiterated by God.

You and I live our lives on the basis of promises that we have made and kept, promises that we are still trying to keep, and even promises that we have not been able to keep, along with the promises that others make to us. Ask the group to think about promises that they have made which have made a difference in the way they have lived their lives.

God's Everlasting Covenant

Background Scripture: Genesis 17

The Main Question

I spend a great deal of time counseling young adults before their marriage. Being the pastor of a university chapel, naturally weddings are a big part of life around here. You may know that people appear to be waiting later in life to get married. The average age for marriage has been increasing in this country. Most of the young adults whom I prepare for marriage are past their mid-twenties.

Of course, maturity is a good thing. People are wise to wait to get married until they are ready. But sometimes I hear a note of hesitation among the words of these young adults which troubles me. Many of them, about half of them to be exact, have been raised in homes with divorced parents. Some of them have seen older brothers or sisters marry and then separate within a few years. They are therefore frightened, unsure of their own prospects for marital success. So they enter into marriage with great caution.

One of their frequent questions is, "With the world in the shape it's in, with the future so uncertain, and human beings so unpredictable, is it possible for me to commit my life to another person forever?"

How is it possible for one human being to promise to love another forever, without qualification?

My usual response is, "That's the very reason why the church has always insisted in the promises of marriage. Because life is so uncertain and unpredictable, you dare not go into the future without someone who has promised to be with you no matter what."

It is a great source of comfort, amid the vicissitudes of life, to know that someone has committed to be with us, through thick and thin, in ups and downs, no matter what happens to us.

Today's scripture from Genesis asserts that God has made such an everlasting promise to us.

Selected Scripture

King James Version

New Revised Standard Version

Genesis 17:1-14

1 And when Abram was ninety years old and nine, the LORD appeared to Abram, and said unto him, I am the Almighty God; walk before me, and be thou perfect.

2 And I will make my covenant between me and thee, and will multiply thee exceedingly.

3 And Abram fell on his face: and God talked with him, saying,

4 As for me, behold, my covenant is with thee, and thou shalt be a father of many nations.

5 Neither shall thy name any more be called Abram, but thy name shall be Abraham; for a father of many nations have I made thee.

6 And I will make thee exceeding fruitful, and I will make nations of thee, and kings shall come out of thee.

7 And I will establish my covenant between me and thee and thy seed after thee in their generations for an everlasting covenant, to be a God unto thee, and to thy seed after thee.

8 And I will give unto thee, and to thy seed after thee, the land wherein thou art a stranger, all the land of

Genesis 17:1-14

1 When Abram was ninety-nine years old, the LORD appeared to Abram, and said to him, "I am God Almighty; walk before me, and be blameless. 2 And I will make my covenant between me and you, and will make you exceedingly numerous." 3 Then Abram fell on his face; and God said to him, 4 "As for me, this is my covenant with you: You shall be the ancestor of a multitude of nations. 5 No longer shall your name be Abram, but your name shall be Abraham; for I have made you the ancestor of a multitude of nations. 6 I will make you exceedingly fruitful; and I will make nations of you, and kings shall come from you. 7 I will establish my covenant between me and you, and your offspring after you throughout their generations, for an everlasting covenant, to be God to you and to your offspring after you. 8 And I will give to you, and to your offspring after you, the land where you are now an alien, all the land of Canaan, for a perpetual holding; and I will be their God."

Canaan, for an everlasting possession; and I will be their God.

9 And God said unto Abraham,
Thou shalt keep my covenant therefore, thou, and thy seed after thee in
their generations.

10 This is my covenant, which ye
shall keep, between me and you and
thy seed after thee; Every man child
among you shall be circumcised.

11 And ye shall circumcise the
flesh of your foreskin; and it shall be
a token of the covenant betwixt me
and you.

12 And he that is eight days old
shall be circumcised among you,
every man child in your generations,
he that is born in the house, or
bought with money of any stranger,
which is not of thy seed.

13 He that is born in thy house,
and he that is bought with thy
money, must needs be circumcised:
and my covenant shall be in your
flesh for an everlasting covenant.

14 And the uncircumcised man
child whose flesh of his foreskin is
not circumcised, that soul shall be
cut off from his people; he hath broken my covenant.

9 God said to Abraham, "As for
you, you shall keep my covenant,
you and your offspring after you
throughout their generations. 10
This is my covenant, which you shall
keep, between me and you and your
offspring after you: Every male
among you shall be circumcised. 11
You shall circumcise the flesh of
your foreskins, and it shall be a sign
of the covenant between me and
you. 12 Throughout your generations every male among you shall be
circumcised when he is eight days
old, including the slave born in your
house and the one bought with your
money from any foreigner who is
not of your offspring. 13 Both the
slave born in your house and the
one bought with your money must
be circumcised. So shall my
covenant be in your flesh an everlasting covenant. 14 Any uncircumcised male who is not circumcised in
the flesh of his foreskin shall be cut
off from his people; he has broken
my covenant."

Key Verse: **And I will establish my
covenant between me and thee and
thy seed after thee in their generations for an everlasting covenant, to
be a God unto thee, and to thy seed
after thee. Genesis 17:7**

Key Verse: **I will establish my
covenant between me and you and
your offspring after you throughout
their generations, for an everlasting
covenant, to be God to you and to
your offspring after you. Genesis
17:7**

As You Read the Scripture

Genesis 17:1-14. These verses are another version (by the so-called priestly
source) of the covenant with Abraham (compare with the earlier tradition
in Genesis 15:7-21 which we studied in lesson 5, October 3). It is a more formally styled account of the story of Abram.

Verse 1. "God Almighty" is an English rendering of the Hebrew *El Shaddai*
which means literally, "God of the Mountains." This suggests a very early origin of this story that was later recorded by the priestly writer.

Verses 2-4. A covenant is a promise, usually made between a superior and
an inferior party.

Verse 5. Abram's name is changed to Abraham, a name that is somewhat related to the Hebrew for "father of a multitude." At a dramatic turning point in an ancient person's life, sometimes a name was changed to signify the change in life direction. Recall how Saul's name is changed to Paul in Acts 9.

Verses 6-8. The promise is for heirs, a family, and land. This nomadic tribe shall become a great people and have a land of their own.

Verses 9-14. Circumcision, an ancient practice that may have been borrowed from Israel's pagan neighbors, is variously explained in Exodus 4:24-26 and Joshua 5:2-9. It is here depicted as an outward sign of the promise made between Abraham and God. Technically speaking, one is not born into the people of Israel. One is adopted or initiated into Israel by the act of circumcision. Earlier, God made a covenant with Noah (Gen. 9:9-17, which we studied in lesson 4, September 26), but that covenant was with all of humanity. The covenant with Abraham, which is symbolized by circumcision, is only for Israel and its descendants. Thus the Old Testament has two significant covenants, the Noachian and the Abrahamic, one universal (a promise not to destroy the earth and its inhabitants after the flood) and the other more specific (a promise to form a new nation and to give this nation land).

The Scripture and the Main Question

I Will Make My Covenant Between Me and You

A covenant is a promise. In the Old Testament, the word *covenant* is usually used to indicate a promise between a superior party with an inferior one. Today's scripture, from Genesis 17, speaks of a promise between the Almighty God and Abram. And yet, a covenant first means anything that any promise means. What does a promise mean to us?

First, to make a promise to someone is *to commit* yourself to that person. You and I live in an age that appears to be fearful of long-term commitments. A few years ago, Susan Litwin wrote a book entitled, *The Postponed Generation.* The book was the fruit of her interviews with hundreds of young adults in the United States. Litwin found that there was a definite tendency, on the part of these young people, to postpone life, to wait longer and longer to get married, and to wander rather aimlessly between college and career. Why were they postponing their lives? Although there were a number of possible factors, Litwin concluded that a major factor in their tendency to postpone life was their fear of commitment.

This generation is so impressed with life's unpredictability, they have so little faith in their own ability to sustain commitment over time, that they are fearful of commitment. They keep waiting until all the factors are right, until they are absolutely sure that they are doing the right thing, that they keep putting off commitment indefinitely.

In fairness to these young adults it should be said that many of them have been raised by parents who failed to keep their own marital commitments. Perhaps because so many of them grew up during a time of spiraling divorce rates, they became doubtful of their own ability to make and to keep commitments to other people.

A second aspect of a promise is that a promise puts one at the mercy of the future. *All promises have an inherently future quality* about them. There is no way to do a "dry run" on a promise. We can carefully consider the pros and cons of our decisions. We can examine our own motives for making promises, but there is no way to be absolutely certain what a promise will require of us in the future. Every promise places me at the mercy of the future.

If I say, "I will meet you for coffee tomorrow at ten o'clock," I have put myself at the disposal of the future. To say to you, "I will meet you for coffee tomorrow at ten o'clock—unless something better turns up," that is hardly a promise at all. It is not fair for me to say, when I don't show up for coffee at ten o'clock the next day, "Well, I really did intend to meet you for coffee, but I did not know all the other interesting possibilities I would have today when I agreed to meet you." I must be willing, in making a promise, to encounter the future, come what may.

Every promise requires that I structure my future on the basis of that promise. After my promise, my world takes on different meaning. I stride into the future as one who has made commitment to another. Thus a promise is not simply at the mercy of the future; a promise changes my future. In my promising, I project myself into the future, I determine what sort of person I will be in the future, what course my life will take.

Therefore, promising is *an exercise of human creativity*. I am not simply an insubstantial cipher, blown to and fro by the wind. I can give my life direction, meaning, significance through my promising. My life need not be limited solely to myself and my own needs. I can take on responsibility for others through my promises. My life becomes infinitely richer and more meaningful through my promising. I become attached to the needs and cares of others. Because I have committed myself to others through my promises, my life becomes more complex and interesting.

A promise is therefore the creation of something new in the world. When I make a promise, I create a new reality that must be confronted and accounted for in the future. We speak of "making a promise," recognizing that, when we speak these words, we are creating something new that had not been there before our promise. We speak, in everyday parlance, of "breaking a promise," realizing that a promise not kept is an act of destruction, violence, in which something that once existed has been broken and destroyed.

A promise is not just some verbal report of an emotional state that we feel deep within our souls. A promise is a fact, a product of human creativity, an act whereby we add something to the world that makes a difference in what happens in the world.

Today, when we speak of the promise that God made to Abram and to his descendants, we gather up all of these beautiful human meanings of promise making and give them new significance because here is a promise, in Genesis 17:1-14, made by God.

The Father of the Multitude of Nations

We often think of our world as an insecure, unpredictable sort of place. How much more so was the world of Abram!

Imagine the world of this ancient nomadic man, wandering from place to place with his tribe. He was now very old, and you and I know that an increase in age carries with it an increase in our insecurity. Older persons often feel more dependent upon others for protection, transportation, finances. As our physical health begins to deteriorate, our sense of our own vulnerability increases. Today's passage begins by telling us that "Abram was ninety-nine years old" (17:1) when God appeared to him.

Added to Abram's age was the reality that he had no heir. There would be no one to pass on the family name, no one to ensure that the values and dreams of his family would be continued. Probably, at his death, Abram's family would be scattered, dispersed. His wife would be at the mercy of others. His servants would probably be scattered among other families. He and his family were in a very vulnerable situation.

How do we achieve security in life?

The way we ask the question may be part of the problem. How do *we achieve* security, we ask. Is security something that *we* work out for ourselves? Well, we purchase health and life insurance in order to provide us some security in the face of sickness and bereavement. We save money and care for ourselves. Perhaps, in our modern world where we have so much control over so many factors in life, we delude ourselves into thinking that we have control over everything in life. We deceive ourselves into thinking that— whereas Abram and his generation were primitive, vulnerable, and insecure—we are secure.

But in our better moments we must admit that we also are at the mercy of factors over which we have no control. We live in a world were there are terrible weapons present, weapons of mass destruction that can wipe away most of humanity in a few seconds. Our machines and technology have made our lives better in many ways but they have also extracted a price from us.

Much of our technology and most of our economy can be seen as our attempts to provide security for ourselves in an insecure world. However, the quest for security and stability in our lives can never be won by ourselves alone. There is no material, technological cure for death, for the perils of human existence. If we are to be secure, safe, serene in our thoughts about tomorrow, then we must be so as a gift. Our security must be based not exclusively upon ourselves or our efforts but rather upon our confidence that God is with us.

One great affirmation behind today's text is that insecure Abram, now toward the end of his life's journey, was encountered by God and reassured by God that his life counted for something. God had plans that went beyond Abram's efforts. God was busy working out a future for Abram's family that was more significant than what Abram had been able to do on his own.

Abram had made promises, promises to himself, to his wife, Sarai, to his family and servants. Abram, like any of us, had been faithful to many of the promises which he had made, and unfaithful to others.

Beyond Abram's promises, God was also making and keeping promises. God was busy being faithful, painting a picture on a larger canvas than that which Abram could see by himself.

"Behold, my covenant is with you, and you shall be the father of a multitude of nations," says God to Abram (Genesis 17:4).

In that covenant, new reality was created, new possibility appeared. Abram saw that his security, the significance of his life was, finally, not of his own devising.

I Will Give to You

As I counsel persons preparing to make the promises of marriage, I often tell them that one of the greatest gifts one person can give another is the gift of the promise to be with that person, throughout life, no matter what. In our lives we give many things to people whom we love, but we can give no greater gift than the gift of our promise.

To make a promise to someone, whether it be the promise of marriage or more mundane, less spectacular promises, is to give that person a gift. We link our lives with that person, yoke our future to their future.

Genesis 17 reiterates the promise made to Abram by God. Late in life, when his future seemed fixed, determined, and closed, old Abraham received a great gift from God—a promise. God promised to link himself to Abraham, to preserve him and his family into the future, to make something out of his family which they could not make for themselves.

Behind the text is the implicit claim that God also makes promises to us, promising to stand beside us, to be with us as we stride into our uncertain futures.

Any future, no matter how uncertain, is a much more liveable future when we are certain that God has promised to be with us.

Helping Adults Become Involved

Preparing to Teach

In today's lesson we will be linking an ordinary, everyday human experience, promise making, with the ancient Genesis account of the covenant made to Abraham. Therefore, as you prepare to teach this lesson, you might conceptualize your teaching task by thinking of the dual foci of this lesson—(1) we make promises to one another and these acts of promise making help us (2) to understand the abiding promise which God makes to us.

Begin your own preparation as a teacher for today's class by reading the material in "The Main Question." Then take a few moments to jot down on paper your own experiences of making promises. "The Main Question" focuses mainly on the promises made in marriage. But you will also want to think about promises which are made by parents to children, employers to employees, teachers to students, and so forth.

You will be able to use these experiences of promise making as you teach today's lesson.

Now read the assigned scripture from Genesis 17 and the helpful background material in "As You Read the Scripture," and "The Scripture and the Main Question."

Introducing the Main Question

Open your class by retelling, in your own words, the introduction to today's lesson in "The Main Question."

This material will initiate your class's reflection on the role of promises in our lives.

Now read to them the account of the promise made by God to Abram which is found in Genesis 17:1-14. Use the material in "As You Read the Scripture" to provide essential background information for this passage. You might want to remind your class of their study of the earlier account of the promise to Abram from Genesis 15:7-21.

Developing the Lesson

Share your list of important promises in your life with the class. Ask the class to add to the list, perhaps writing their responses on a chalkboard or newsprint. Which promises do they find the most difficult to keep? Which promises are rather "one-sided"? That is, which promises are analogous to a biblical covenant in which a superior party makes a promise with an inferior one? (See the discussion of the nature of biblical covenants in "As You Read the Scripture.")

Using the material which is found in the extended discussion of promises in "The Scripture and the Main Question," lead your class in an exploration of the nature of human promises. You will probably want to retell this material in your own words. As you do, try to think of examples from your own experience which illustrate some of the aspects of human promise making. Your own experiences will enable members of your class to relate this material to their own lives.

After exploring the various aspects of human promises—commitment, an exercise of human creativity, an exposure to the future, a gift of one person to another—relate these thoughts on human promises to the promise which God made to Abraham. This material will be used to expand your group's understanding of the nature of promises and their contribution to human life.

Read again today's scripture. Remind your group of Abraham's situation in life and the bleak prospects for the future of his family with no heir. Ask them to imagine that they were Abraham. What might be their thoughts on hearing God make such a promise to them?

Can any members of your class relate personal experiences from their relationship to God to the experience which Abraham had with God? Have they ever felt that God had made a promise to them, a promise which required great faith and trust on their part?

Thinking over what they know of scripture, can any members of your group cite any other biblical stories or passages which speak of important promises made by God? The story of Noah after the flood. Jesus' baptism. Jesus' promises to his disciples not to leave them alone but to always be with them and to comfort them in their struggles. Others? This exercise will remind your group of the central role of promise making and covenant throughout scripture.

Looking back now, perhaps four thousand years from the time when God made this promise to Abraham, does your class see concrete ways in which God's promise has been fulfilled? The nation of Israel? The existence of the church, God's extended family? The perseverance of the Jewish faith, despite all obstacles? The meeting of your adult class today!

Helping Class Members to Act

Ask the class to consider some of the promises which they have made to other people. Ask them to sit in silence and to focus on one of their most difficult promises to which they are attempting to be faithful. Close with a prayer of your own which asks for God's grace to be faithful to the promises which we have made to others and to God.

Planning for Next Sunday

We have focused on Abraham, the father of a new family of the covenant. Next Sunday we will focus on Sarah, the mother of the family. Just as Abraham had to confront God's covenant and consider its consequences for his life, so Sarah had to consider what the covenant meant to her. Ask the class to read Genesis 21:1-21 before coming to class next Sunday. Then ask them to come to class prepared to share one way in which they identify with Sarah and her experience of God as stated in Genesis 21:1-21.

God's Promise Fulfilled

Background Scripture: Genesis 21:1-21

The Main Question

Not long ago, Bishop Peter Storey, of the Methodist Church in South Africa, spoke in our university chapel. Bishop Storey had spoken there on two other occasions.

When he had visited before, Bishop Storey's pain over his homeland was self-evident. He had courageously spoken of the evils of apartheid, the tragedy of racial separation, the threat of violence. On those past occasions, the entire congregation had been moved by his plea for our prayers for the people of South Africa, black and white, as they struggled with their mammoth problems.

On his most recent visit, Bishop Storey brought a strikingly different message. Only a few weeks earlier, there had been a dramatic breakthrough in the situation. The South African Prime Minister had ordered Nelson Mandela to be released from jail. The Prime Minister had also promised that the structures of apartheid would be gradually dismantled.

Bishop Storey's sermon overflowed with joy and vitality. The changed situation in his homeland had filled him with great hope.

"On other occasions when I have been with you," he said, "my sermons were full of sadness and prophetic rebuke of a terribly unjust system. Today, my sermon will be different."

His sermon was different because the situation had taken a dramatic turn for the better. He did not say that the struggle was over, and he did not claim that everything was immediately changed. Yet something had changed. There would be a long road ahead for the people of South Africa, but now there were solid signs of hope and encouragement.

Leaving church that day, I was almost embarrassed by a statement made by one of the members of the congregation. "You know," she said, "it is rare that we hear such unqualified good news in a sermon."

65

I was embarrassed because she was right. Most of our sermons, much of our church life is mainly reiteration of everything that has gone wrong with us and our world. It is rare that we hear unqualified good news.

When things change dramatically for the better, when God begins to make good on divine promises, it is time to shout for joy. Such times are truly good news, truly gospel.

Today's scripture tells of the fulfillment of a promise to Abraham and Sarah, therefore it tells the good news of promises made, promises kept, promises fulfilled.

Selected Scripture

King James Version

Genesis 21:1-14

1 And the LORD visited Sarah as he had said, and the LORD did unto Sarah as he had spoken.

2 For Sarah conceived, and bare Abraham a son in his old age, at the set time of which God had spoken to him.

3 And Abraham called the name of his son that was born unto him, whom Sarah bare to him, Isaac.

4 And Abraham circumcised his son Isaac being eight days old, as God had commanded him.

5 And Abraham was an hundred years old, when his son Isaac was born unto him.

6 And Sarah said, God hath made me to laugh, so that all that hear will laugh with me.

7 And she said, Who would have said unto Abraham, that Sarah should have given children suck? for I have born him a son in his old age.

8 And the child grew, and was weaned: and Abraham made a great feast the same day that Isaac was weaned.

9 And Sarah saw the son of Hagar the Egyptian, which she had born unto Abraham, mocking.

10 Wherefore she said unto Abraham, Cast out this bondwoman and her son: for the son of this bondwoman shall not be heir with my son, even with Isaac.

11 And the thing was very grievous in Abraham's sight because of his son.

New Revised Standard Version

Genesis 21:1-14

1 The LORD dealt with Sarah as he had said, and the LORD did for Sarah as he had promised. 2 Sarah conceived and bore Abraham a son in his old age, at the time of which God had spoken to him. 3 Abraham gave the name Isaac to his son whom Sarah bore him. 4 And Abraham circumcised his son Isaac when he was eight days old, as God had commanded him. 5 Abraham was a hundred years old when his son Isaac was born to him. 6 Now Sarah said, "God has brought laughter for me; everyone who hears will laugh with me." 7 And she said, "Who would ever have said to Abraham that Sarah would nurse children? Yet I have borne him a son in his old age."

8 The child grew, and was weaned; and Abraham made a great feast on the day that Isaac was weaned. 9 But Sarah saw the son of Hagar the Egyptian, whom she had borne to Abraham, playing with her son Isaac. 10 So she said to Abraham, "Cast out this slave woman with her son; for the son of this slave woman shall not inherit along with my son Isaac." 11 The matter was very distressing to Abraham on account of his son. 12 But God said to Abraham, "Do not be distressed

12 And God said unto Abraham, Let it not be grievous in thy sight because of the lad, and because of thy bondwoman; in all that Sarah hath said unto thee, hearken unto her voice; for in Isaac shall thy seed be called.

13 And also of the son of the bondwoman will I make a nation, because he is thy seed.

14 And Abraham rose up early in the morning, and took bread, and a bottle of water, and gave it unto Hagar, putting it on her shoulder, and the child, and sent her away: and she departed, and wandered in the wilderness of Beersheba.

because of the boy and because of your slave woman; whatever Sarah says to you, do as she tells you, for it is through Isaac that offspring shall be named for you. 13 As for the son of the slave woman, I will make a nation of him also, because he is your offspring." 14 So Abraham rose early in the morning, and took bread and a skin of water, and gave it to Hagar, putting it on her shoulder, along with the child, and sent her away. And she departed, and wandered about in the wilderness of Beersheba.

Key Verse: **For Sarah conceived, and bare Abraham a son in his old age, at the set time of which God had spoken to him. Genesis 21:2**

Key Verse: **Sarah conceived and bore Abraham a son in his old age, at the time of which God had spoken to him. Genesis 21:2**

As You Read the Scripture

Genesis 21:1-14. Today's scripture brings us to the birth of Abraham and Sarah's long-awaited child. We have been studying this story for a month now, learning of the first promise to Abram on a starlit night (Genesis 15:1-16, October 3), of Sarah's attempts to take matters into her own hands with tragic results (Genesis 16:1-16, October 10), and of the reiteration of the covenant to Abraham with the command to circumcise as reminder of the covenant (Genesis 17:1-14).

Verses 1-3. The promise of an heir is at last fulfilled. The son is named Isaac, which means "laughter," perhaps in recognition of Sarah and Abraham's scornful laughter at the thought of having a child in their old age (Genesis 17:17).

Verses 4-7. Abraham circumcises the child, just as he was commanded to do in Genesis 17, in recognition of the covenant. For her part, Sarah is worried about what other people will say about so old a woman having a baby.

Verses 9-10. Recall that Sarah's slave, Hagar, had conceived a child through Abraham, the result of Sarah's scheme to provide Abraham with an heir. We studied these events in our lesson on October 10, Genesis 16:1-16. Sarah is jealous of Hagar and her child Ishmael.

Verses 11-14. You may recall, in our study of Genesis 16:1-16, that even though Hagar and her son Ishmael played no part in God's covenant with Abraham, God reached out to Hagar in her plight and promised to protect her. Just as God kept his promise to Abraham and Sarah, so will God keep the promise to Hagar. The story of Hagar and Ishmael becomes a subplot within the main story of Abraham and Sarah.

The Scripture and the Main Question

The Lord Visited Sarah

Today's scripture, Genesis 21:1-14, is the climax of the saga of the covenant that God made with Abraham. After the many chapters in which we have been following Abraham and Sarah, the final fulfillment comes rather quietly. Abraham and Sarah have had to wait many years for fulfillment. Now Abraham is a hundred years old. Great patience has been required of Abraham and Sarah. God made a promise to them and perhaps they thought God would make good on the promise a bit sooner. After all, they were very old and thought they had little time to waste.

But God kept the promise in God's own good time. It took time, a rather long time, particularly at their age, for the promise to be fulfilled.

In our study of Genesis 16:1-16 on October 10 we noted that Sarah became impatient and took matters in her own hands, encouraging her husband Abraham to impregnate her maid Hagar. This was not what God had in mind when God promised Abraham and Sarah an heir. The pregnancy of Hagar led to feelings of jealousy and hatred by Sarah.

One might think that the birth of a child to Sarah might end all that. After all, Sarah has at last had a child of her own so she need not feel jealousy or envy of Hagar.

Think again. Sarah continues to be troubled by her circumstances. Now that she has at last had a baby, the thing that troubles Sarah is that "every one who hears will laugh over me" (Genesis 21:6). She feels humiliated in being a woman her age with a baby.

Isn't this typical of us? Like Sarah, we pray and pray for God to give us something. Then, when our prayers are answered and we receive the gift that we so desperately desired, we complain! What does it take to please us?

To be fair to Sarah, she was in a rather embarrassing situation. Picture a woman, advanced in years, preparing to spend the rest of her life in a nursing home or geriatric center, finding instead that she is preparing a room for a nursery for her baby! Think of what the neighbors would say about that!

My own father and mother were forty when I was born. My father confessed to me, many years later, that when I was about four years old, he took me to run some errands with him. In one store, someone asked him, "Bob, is that your grandson with you?"

He was furious. Mainly, he was embarrassed.

Sometimes the gifts that God gives us are difficult for us to receive, even embarrassing to receive.

I know two married people who have been very good church members over the years. They dutifully brought their three children to church and did everything possible to instill good Christian values in their children. Now their children are grown. One of them is a missionary in Africa. Another is a lawyer who defends unpopular legal causes for poor people. The third child is in prison for refusing to pay taxes in order to protest the government's expenditures for the military.

Knowing them, and knowing their children, I think it could be argued that their children are the products of their Christian home. In bringing their children to Sunday school and church, these parents instilled Christian values in them, made them to see how important it was for them to stand up for their convictions, to do the right thing as they saw it.

That may be true. But I can tell you that these two parents are rather perplexed and perhaps even embarrassed by their adult children. While they were bringing them to church, teaching them the gospel, little did they know that God was blessing them with three children who would grow up to be people of unpopular causes and unconventional convictions.

Sometimes God blesses us in ways that surprise and embarrass us. Like Sarah, we come to have second thoughts about the blessedness of God's blessings!

God Has Made Laughter for Me

I remember an old preacher saying, "Better be careful what you pray for. God may answer your prayer."

Abraham and Sarah, more than anything in the world, wanted a child. Now God has at last given them a child. With that child comes embarrassment, the laughter of their shocked neighbors, and tension within their marriage. Sarah's jealousy over her servant Hagar and her child Ishmael continues (Genesis 21:8-14). She pleads with Abraham to send the child and his mother out into the wilderness. Abraham refuses. After all, Ishmael is his child.

Some promise fulfilled this is!

"There's a man calling who is really upset," my secretary said. "The man's mad over something you have done to his daughter."

"What?" I said.

"I hold you personally responsible," he began in a most exasperated and agitated tone.

"For what?" I asked.

"My daughter. We sent her there to get a good education. She is supposed to go to medical school. She is to be a third-generation neurologist. Now she has got some fool idea in her head about Haiti and I hold you personally responsible," he said.

"Please," I said. "Could we try to be rational?"

He told me who he was, who his daughter was. I knew her, but not that well. She ushered nearly every Sunday in the chapel. She had also been active in various campus causes and had been one of the organizers of last Spring's Mission Workteam. How could anybody be upset about a daughter like her?

"Like I said," he said, "she was supposed to go to medical school. Her grades are good enough. Now this."

"Now what?" I asked.

"Don't act dumb, even if you are a preacher," he shouted into the telephone. "You know very well. Now she has this fool idea about going to Haiti for three years with that church mission program and teaching kids there. She's supposed to be a neurologist, not a missionary for heaven's sake!"

"No pun intended," I said.

"None of this would have happened if it had not been for you. She has become attached to you, liked your sermons. You have taken advantage of her when she was at an impressionable age. That's how she got so worked up over this fool idea about going to be a missionary."

"Now just a minute. Didn't you take her to be baptized?" I asked.

"Well, yes, but we are Presbyterians," he said.

"And didn't you take her to Sunday school when she was little? You can't deny that. She told me herself that you used to take her to Sunday school," I said triumphantly.

"Sure we did. But we never intended for it to do any damage," he said.

"Well, there you have it," I said. "She was messed up before we ever got her. Baptized, Sunday schooled, Called. Don't blame this thing on me. *You* were the one who started it. You should have thought about what you were doing when you had her baptized."

"But we are only Presbyterians," he said, his once belligerent voice changing to a whimper.

"Doesn't make any difference. The damage was done before she ever set foot in our chapel. Congratulations, Mr. Jones, you just helped God make a missionary."

"We just wanted for her to be a good person. We never wanted anything like this."

"Sorry. You're really talking to the wrong person," I said, trying to be as patient as possible. "We only work with what we get. If you want to complain, you'll have to find her third-grade Sunday school teacher. The thing is quite out of our hands. Have a nice day."

I expect that poor man at one time, perhaps when his daughter was very young, prayed that God might be close to her, that God might guide her life in a way which was pleasing to God. Perhaps that man felt that he heard God promising to do just that.

Well, God kept his promise.

Be careful when you believe in the promises of God. God might just keep his promises, and then where would we be?

Helping Adults Become Involved

Preparing to Teach

Because today's lesson is the culmination of the saga of Abraham and Sarah and their problem of being childless, begin your preparation by scanning the preceding chapters of Genesis, beginning with chapter 12. You might want to scan the preceding lessons in this book, beginning with lesson 5, October 3. Read today's assigned scripture, Genesis 21:1-12. The material found in "As You Read the Scripture" will help you to understand this passage in depth by providing essential background information.

Your goal will be to help adults in your class to reflect upon the story of the fulfillment of the promise to Abraham and Sarah by the birth of Isaac and its implications for the promises that God makes to us. Here is a suggested outline for today's class:

I. God fulfills his promises.
   A. God fulfilled his promise to Sarah and Abraham with a son.
   B. Even though the promise took a long time to be fulfilled, it was fulfilled.

II. Sometimes the fulfillment of promises causes problems.
   A. Sarah was embarrassed at the thought that a woman so old would have a baby.
   B. After the birth of her child, Sarah hated Hagar and Ishmael.

III. God often gives us what we ask for, even when it causes us problems.
   A. We must be open and receptive to God's blessings.
   B. God's purposes are often larger than our opinions of our personal needs.

Introducing the Main Question

Today's lesson deals with God's promises and the circumstances that sometimes occur in our lives when God's promises are fulfilled. Begin the class by retelling in your own words the story of Bishop Storey's sermon found in "The Main Question." Ask your group whether they agree with the concluding statement that sometimes the church is as surprised as anyone when God's promises are fulfilled.

This will start your class thinking about God's promises and our response to the fulfillment of God's promises.

Developing the Lesson

I. God fulfills his promises.

Have someone read aloud to the class today's assigned scripture from Genesis 21:1-14. Lead your group in a more detailed look at this scripture, utilizing the material found in "As You Read the Scripture." Note the two responses of Sarah to the birth of Isaac, (1) embarrassment (Genesis 21:6-7) and (2) resentment of Hagar and Ishmael (Genesis 21:8-14).

Ask the members of the group to think back on their own life experiences in which they felt as if God were answering their prayers or making good on promises to them. Have any of them ever had the experience of asking God to give them something when their petition was granted? Of course, such experiences do not explain those times when we pray for something to happen and it does not happen. Today's scripture is focused upon the fulfillment of promises by God, not their lack of fulfillment.

II. Sometimes the fulfillment of promises causes problems.

Using the material in the opening section of "The Scripture and the Main Question," lead your group in a discussion of Sarah's response to the birth of Isaac and the fulfillment of her desire to present Abraham with an heir. Can your group have some sympathy with Sarah in her embarrassing situation? Can they understand Sarah's resentment of Hagar?

Have any members of your group had personal experiences that enable them to relate to Sarah's feelings?

A few moments ago, your group discussed their joy at having their prayers answered, their petitions to God granted. Have any of them had a situation to occur in their lives, or the lives of persons they have known, when an answered prayer became a great burden to them?

Here you might want to use the extended illustration found in the last part of "The Scripture and the Main Question," the story of the man who was angry because his daughter was drawn into mission work. Can any of your class identify with this man's ambivalent and even negative feelings about the path that his daughter was taking?

What does your group think about the preacher's statement that, "you had better be careful what you pray for because sometimes God may give you what you want"? How does that statement apply to the story of Abraham and Sarah?

Ask your group, "What is the most difficult gift God has ever given you?" Allow members to share these experiences with the class.

III. God often gives us what we ask for, even when it causes us problems.

Sarah and Abraham were receptive to God's gift of a child, even when the advent of that child caused personal and family problems for them. Today, many in our church are debating the morality of abortion. While this is a very controversial subject, and one which we cannot fully explore within the context of today's class, is there anything within today's story that helps your adults to think about this difficult issue?

How can we be more receptive to God's gifts, even when they are gifts that cause us difficulty? For instance, sometimes we pray to God for what *we* want. Is this prayer? Jesus prayed, "Nevertheless, not my will but thine be done." Perhaps we conceive of prayer in the wrong way. We think of prayer as a means of getting what we want rather than a means whereby God gets what God wants for us.

Sometimes God's gifts to us are confusing and difficult because we are not God and we have difficulty seeing beyond the confines of our own projects and desires. For instance, in our story, Sarah and Abraham wanted an heir so that they could ensure the survival of their family into the next generation. But God was busy working on a long-term plan whereby not only this family would be preserved but a great nation would come forth as well. In addition to this, Sarah and Abraham were worried only about their own family whereas God also cared for the family of Ishmael and Hagar. Because God's purposes and plans are considerably larger than our own, sometimes the fulfillment of God's promises confuses us.

Can it be possible that God is working out greater purposes through us than we are able to see with our own limited vision?

Helping Class Members to Act

We often think that our problem with God is one of how to get God to fulfill our requests and desires. Today's lesson suggests that our problem may be how to live with God's answered promises. Ask your group to take a moment and think quietly about prayers, desires, or needs that they have brought to God in the last few months. Ask them then to think about how their lives might change if God granted their desires.

How might we fashion our lives in such a way that we are open to all of God's blessings and fulfilled promises, even if they disrupt our lives and cause us to venture forth unto unexpected areas of living?

Planning for Next Sunday

For next week, ask your class to read Genesis 25:19-34. Also ask them to come to class prepared to answer this question: What is the greatest issue or problem facing contemporary Christian families?

Their responses will form the basis for our study of the family of Rebekah and Isaac.

In Unit III, "The Promise is Transmitted," we will continue the saga of the primal family of Israel that we began in Unit II. Abraham and Sarah have at last had a son, Isaac. That son, the heir to the family name, has now grown up to be a man and has a wife of his own. In other words, we are now in the second generation of the family begun that starry night when God asked Abraham to look up into the heavens and promised to make of him a great people as numerous as the very stars of the heavens.

As we shall learn in the lessons of this unit, the history of this family will not be easy. There are still great hurdles to be overcome, great obstacles. As in any family, the family of Isaac and Rebekah had their difficulties.

The adults who gather in your class for this unit of study also come from families who have difficulties, ups and downs, new challenges to meet and obstacles to overcome. Therefore our study will be of relevance to their lives as they attempt to live out their faith in God in the very ordinary, mundane struggles of their own families.

The stories we will be studying are all stories of ordinary people, very ordinary people, who were loved by God and who struggled to be responsive to God's love.

Of course, we also are ordinary people, so this series of lessons should have particular relevance for us.

LESSON 9   OCTOBER 31

Trouble in the Family

Background Scripture: Genesis 25:19-34

The Main Question

A few years into parish ministry I discovered that a major problem within my congregation was the contemporary problem of childless couples. Increasing numbers of young married couples want children but are unable to have children. Experts have speculated on the possible reasons for this phenomenon of infertility. Couples are waiting longer to have children, thus leading to decreased fertility. There may be certain chemical or biological factors in the environment that contribute to the problem. Whatever the reasons, infertility appears to be a growing problem that affects many couples. With fewer adoptive children available, the problem is compounded by having fewer options for childless couples who desire to adopt a child.

Infertility is only one problem faced by contemporary couples. Today's families are beset by many problems, many challenges. Today's scripture—which tells of trouble within an ancient family, the family of Isaac and Rebekah—sounds as recent as today's newspaper headlines.

One reason why we love the Bible is its utter honesty. The Bible, as honest a book as anyone could hope to read, depicts the family life of our ancestors in faith as no easy matter. This is not the family as seen on "The Brady Bunch" or "Father Knows Best." Here are real families engaged in real struggles. Because the Bible is so honest, so real, so true, it can be a trustworthy guide for us in our struggles with our families. The Bible asserts that God is with us in our families, supporting us, guiding us, making new possibility present. Knowing that God is with us, through thick and thin, in our families, can make all the difference for us.

How can we respond to troubles within our families? That is the important question that lies behind today's scripture from Genesis 25.

Selected Scripture

King James Version

Genesis 25:19-34

19 And these are the generations of Isaac, Abraham's son: Abraham begat Isaac:

20 And Isaac was forty years old when he took Rebekah to wife, the daughter of Bethuel the Syrian of Padan-aram, the sister to Laban the Syrian.

21 And Isaac intreated the LORD for his wife, because she was barren: and the LORD was intreated of him, and Rebekah his wife conceived.

22 And the children struggled together within her; and she said, If it be so, why am I thus? And she went to inquire of the LORD.

23 And the LORD said unto her, Two nations are in thy womb, and two manner of people shall be separated from thy bowels; and the one people shall be stronger than the other people; and the elder shall serve the younger.

24 And when her days to be delivered were fulfilled, behold, there were twins in her womb.

25 And the first came out red, all over like an hairy garment: and they called his name Esau.

26 And after that came his brother out, and his hand took hold on Esau's heel; and his name was

New Revised Standard Version

Genesis 25:19-34

19 These are the descendants of Isaac, Abraham's son: Abraham was the father of Isaac, 20 and Isaac was forty years old when he married Rebekah, daughter of Bethuel the Aramean of Paddanaram, sister of Laban the Aramean. 21 Isaac prayed to the LORD for his wife, because she was barren; and the LORD granted his prayer, and his wife Rebekah conceived. 22 The children struggled together within her; and she said, "If it is to be this way, why do I live?" So she went to inquire of the LORD. 23 And the LORD said to her,

"Two nations are in your womb,
 and two peoples born of you
  shall be divided;
the one shall be stronger than
  the other,
the elder shall serve the
  younger."

24 When her time to give birth was at hand, there were twins in her womb. 25 The first came out red, all his body like a hairy mantle; so they named him Esau. 26 Afterward his brother came out, with his hand gripping Esau's heel; so he was named Jacob. Isaac was sixty years old when she bore them.

called Jacob: and Isaac was three-score years old when she bare them.

27 And the boys grew: and Esau was a cunning hunter, a man of the field; and Jacob was a plain man, dwelling in tents.

28 And Isaac loved Esau, because he did eat of his venison: but Rebekah loved Jacob.

29 And Jacob sod pottage: and Esau came from the field, and he was faint:

30 And Esau said to Jacob, Feed me, I pray thee, with that same red pottage; for I am faint: therefore was his name called Edom.

31 And Jacob said, Sell me this day thy birthright.

32 And Esau said, Behold, I am at the point to die: and what profit shall this birthright do to me?

33 And Jacob said, Swear to me this day; and he sware unto him: and he sold his birthright unto Jacob.

34 Then Jacob gave Esau bread and pottage of lentiles; and he did eat and drink, and rose up, and went his way: thus Esau despised his birthright.

27 When the boys grew up, Esau was a skillful hunter, a man of the field, while Jacob was a quiet man, living in tents. 28 Isaac loved Esau, because he was fond of game; but Rebekah loved Jacob.

29 Once when Jacob was cooking a stew, Esau came in from the field, and he was famished. 30 Esau said to Jacob, "Let me eat some of that red stuff, for I am famished!" (Therefore he was called Edom.) 31 Jacob said, "First sell me your birthright." 32 Esau said, "I am about to die; of what use is a birthright to me?" 33 Jacob said, "Swear to me first." So he swore to him, and sold his birthright to Jacob. 34 Then Jacob gave Esau bread and lentil stew, and he ate and drank, and rose and went his way. Thus Esau despised his birthright.

Key Verse: **And the Lord said unto her, Two nations are in thy womb, and two manner of people shall be separated from thy bowels; and the one people shall be stronger than the other people; and the elder shall serve the younger. Genesis 25:23**

Key Verse: **The Lord said to her, "Two nations are in your womb, and two peoples, born of you, shall be divided; the one shall be stronger than the other, the elder shall serve the younger." Genesis 25:23**

As You Read the Scripture

Genesis 25:19-43. Our text begins immediately after the death of Abraham (Genesis 25:1-18). This text is the first phase of a long saga that narrates the tension between Jacob (Israel) and Esau (Edom). From the very first, from their birth, there is tension between these two brothers. The text on which we focus today speaks of Jacob's birth as a matter of careful divine planning and divine intervention. Behind Jacob and his life there is the moving hand of God, directing events, engaging in dialogue, moving the story on to its conclusion. Behind these rather mundane, not always edifying family affairs, God is working out his purposes.

Verses 19-20. A long, twisted story lies behind these verses. Great pains have been taken to secure a wife for Isaac (Genesis 24:1-62), child of the promise to Abraham and Sarah. One would think that, after all the care taken to find a suitable wife for Isaac, the family would experience smooth sailing from now on.

Verse 21. Yet the old problem of infertility, lack of an heir, reappears. Isaac prays to God for a child with Rebekah.

Verse 22. One would think, after Isaac's prayer is answered and Rebekah is pregnant, all would be well. But all is not well. Even in Rebekah's womb, there is trouble between her twins. This makes Rebekah depressed and she wonders why she lives in such turmoil.

Verse 23. The text interprets the prenatal struggle as a portent of things to come. The struggle between the twins in the womb shall have international consequences.

Verses 24-26. The oracle predicts strange events for these two boys. Even though Esau is the first born, and by all rights of primogeniture ("firstborn") he should inherit his family fortune. However, the tension in the womb is a foreshadowing of continuing struggle that will result in an overturning of the accustomed order of things, including the rights of primogeniture.

Verses 27-28. The tensions continue. The parents show favoritism to different sons.

Verses 29-34. Esau is depicted as dumb, easily tricked by his conniving brother, Jacob. In a fit of hunger, Esau sells his rights of primogeniture to his younger brother, preferring immediate relief for his hunger to long-term rights within the family. The story is meant to explain why, in later years, the nation of Israel achieved primacy over the nation of Edom.

The Scripture and the Main Question

Isaac Prayed to the Lord for His Wife

In the opening discussion in "The Main Question," we focused upon infertility as a growing problem among many contemporary couples.

Interestingly, infertility is an issue behind today's scripture from Genesis. If you have been following our study of the patriarchs, the progenitors of Israel, you have seen this problem before. Back in last month's study of Genesis 15, you will recall that infertility was the issue facing Abraham and Sarah. How could their family survive without an heir?

Now the problem of infertility arises again with Abraham and Sarah's son, Isaac. Today's scripture opens as Isaac intercedes to God for his wife and her situation. Rebekah is infertile. What shall become of the promise made to Abraham to make of him and his heirs a great nation? Has the promise been made and kept for only one generation, the generation of Abraham and Sarah? Must the promise perish in the time of Isaac and Rebekah? We are to understand infertility as these ancient people saw it. Infertility was not considered a biological or physiological problem. It was a spiritual issue. Without children, without heirs, then a couple was without a future. Children were the ancient Near Eastern equivalent of our Social Security system. If a person died without children, then that person died in abject poverty because there was no able-bodied person to care for the aging person.

In addition to these hard economic facts of life, infertility was also interpreted by many as a sign of divine disfavor, a "curse" upon the woman who was labeled as "barren." Undoubtedly, childlessness caused great tension, blaming, and hostility between married couples.

It is this problem of infertility, lack of children, and therefore *lack of a future* that is the concern of today's scripture from Genesis 25:19-34. Isaac and Rebekah have no children. Isaac prays to God for aid and "Rebekah his wife conceived" (Gen. 25:21).

Now this resolution of the story should have ended Isaac and Rebekah's problems as a married couple. Unfortunately, the birth of sons was the beginning of new problems rather than the end of all problems.

Isaac prays to God for a child. And with that prayer (people, be careful when you pray!) the trouble begins.

The Children Struggled Together

"Rebekah conceived," and even in her womb, there was trouble. There, in the mysterious uterine darkness, there is conflict for there is not one but two fetuses in the womb and they are already in dark struggle (Gen. 25:22).

Rebekah feels the conflict even before the children are born. Feeling the rumblings within she exclaims, "If motherhood is this, why do I live?" (v. 22).

"I thought you said this was going to be painless!"

Rebekah inquires of the Lord. The Lord explains, "At first I thought I'd just bless you with a child. Then I decided, while I was at it, to give you twins, just to make it interesting. Not just two boys, two whole nations in your womb, struggling. You thought this birth was a little something sweet to comfort you and the old man in your autumn years? No, I'm doing something cosmic here, big. That kick you just felt was me, kicking at the door of the future of the world!"

And Rebekah says, "This is your idea of a blessing?"

There is no such thing as "painless birth," particularly if that birth be a gift of God. *The promises of God paradoxically involve pain.*

I know a woman who, nearly Rebekah's age, after prayer gave birth to her first and only child. The child she called "Grace," the world labeled as having "Down's syndrome." How is there such pain in blessing? She has given now most of the rest of her life in working for the care and education of children like her Grace.

How is there such blessing in pain?

There is a mystery taking place here, still dark, while yet *in utero,* and there is conflict, serving as prelude to the rest of the story of Jacob.

Rebekah, in time, gives birth. The first twin is delivered, "red, all his body covered in hair." So they named the first, "Red," or Edom. And, pulling little Red out of the womb, they were startled to find that the second twin, the younger, had his brother's heel tightly clasped in his clutching little hand.

"Look at that! Wanted so bad to be first born that he's trying to hold his brother back!" said the attending obstetrician.

So they named him Jacob, which might mean, "Heel," the right name if ever there were one, as we shall learn later.

So we've got Red and his little brother, Heel.

Esau and Jacob. And though they were twins, they had nothing in common.

This isn't the "Bill Cosby Show." We're talking "Simpsons" here.

Esau was the macho type. Love to hunt, played football (with other hairy types), love to mix it up with the boys in rugby.

Jacob is described as "a quiet man, living in tents." In other words, Jacob stayed home, indoors, played the piano, cooked gourmet meals, felt that football encouraged violence.

No surprise: "Isaac loved having Esau . . . but Rebekah loved Jacob" (v. 28).

What kind of family is this? Dad loves one twin, Mom loves the other? What sort of parents are these where partiality and favoritism are shown to one and not the other?

They are real parents, your parents. Not that your parents love your little sister more than they love you—although they might.

"Dear, it's not that I don't *love* you, it's just that I find it difficult to be enthusiastic about your athletic exploits. I would be pleased if you read a book every once in a while."

The story told before the days of psychological rationalization, only says, "Isaac loved Esau. Rebekah had her money on Jacob."

One day Jacob was cooking, creating in the kitchen; he smelled a strange odor. It was Esau, coming in from hunting.

Esau says, "Let me have some of that red stuff you got, I'm starved."

"It's not 'red stuff'," says Jacob, "it's Boeuf bourguignonne."

"Whatever," says Esau, "let me have it!"

Little brother Jacob sees his chance. "How hungry are you?"

"I'm dying!" said Esau.

"Dying? Good. Let me have your birthright and I'll let you eat."

In other words, drop dead, big brother. Make me the older brother, the heir, the firstborn, head of the family. Subvert the entire pattern of Near Eastern social arrangement, the foundation upon which a whole culture is based, to hell with primogeniture, give me your birthright.

Esau was incapable of taking the long view. "What good's a birthright when I'm starving? Let me eat, you'll have the birthright."

"And Esau ate and drank, and rose and went his way" (Gen. 25:34), a way considerably downhill after that fateful exchange with little brother.

End of the Jacob and Esau saga, first part.

These Are the Descendants of Isaac

There is no moral to this Jacob/Esau story. For this is not so much a story about people like our parents, Isaac and Rebekah, or people like us, Jacob and Esau. You and I live and love in families, real families, where there are conflicts, unresolved tensions, competition between brothers and sisters, and unexplained, misunderstood feelings. This story of the birth of the sons of Isaac and Rebekah is a story about us in our families.

But this is also a story about the promises of God, about the way that God comes to real people in real families, working with them, blessing them, using them for divine purposes.

The story suggests that, in real human families like yours and mine, God is working out his purposes. That is the promise behind today's scripture.

Helping Adults Become Involved

Preparing to Teach

As you prepare this lesson, think for a moment about your own experiences in your family. We love our families and cherish them. Yet in any intimate human relationship, there are tensions, including our family relationships, especially our family relationships. Jot down on paper some of the tensions that are experienced by contemporary families. Recall that we asked your class to prepare for today's class by identifying at least one area of conflict in today's families. You will be able to use this in interpreting today's scripture from Genesis.

Now read today's assigned scripture, Genesis 25:19-34. Use the material in "As You Read the Scripture" to give you more detailed information on these verses. Note that this passage begins in the middle of the long narrative of the life of Isaac and Rebekah.

Organize your session as follows:

    I.   In the family of Isaac and Rebekah, there was conflict.
        A. The problem of Rebekah's infertility.
        B. The rivalry between the two sons.
   II.   In our families we often experience conflict.
        A. Conflict of unfulfilled dreams.
        B. Conflict of rivalry between family members.
 III.   Even within our family conflict, God is working to bless us.
        A. Sometimes God's blessings cause us difficulty.
        B. Despite the difficulty, God is with us in our families.

Introducing the Main Question

Begin today's class by sharing with your group your list of noteworthy tensions within today's families. Ask your group to share their lists of family difficulties. You might list these on a chalkboard or newsprint.

Using the material in "The Main Question" on infertility among contemporary couples, or material of your own devising on some current family problem, lead your group in a more in-depth look at some specific problem that causes frustration and difficulty among our families.

I. In the family of Isaac and Rebekah, there was conflict.

Read aloud, or retell in your own words, the story of the birth of twin boys to Isaac and Rebekah. You might use the free rendition of the story which is found in "The Scripture and the Main Question." After telling the story, ask your group if they detect parallels to some of the problems of Isaac's family in our families today. For instance, have they ever known families in which there was severe rivalry between the children?

II. In our families we often experience conflict.

Isaac and Rebekah struggled with the problem of infertility. They were both advanced in years but had no children. How do modern couples deal with the disappointments and frustrations which often come to people in marriage?

How does your group react to the story's claim that "Isaac loved Esau, . . . but Rebekah loved Jacob." Note that the Bible is not lifting this up as a positive parental characteristic. The Bible is simply noting the real, though not very admirable, characteristics of these two parents. Ask your class if they agree with the discussion, at the end of "The Scripture and the Main Question," in which it is asserted that there is no real "moral" to this story, rather this story is a true depiction of life within a real, very fallible, very believable family?

III. Even within our family conflict, God is working to bless us.

Today's lesson carries with it the notion that, when God blesses us, sometimes God's blessings are difficult for us. Sometimes blessings carry with them responsibility, or struggle, or pain. What does your group think of that assertion? How does the story of Rebekah illustrate the idea that blessings involve difficulty?

Whatever your group may think about the family life of Isaac and Rebekah, their conflicts with their children, their parental favoritism, behind the story is the Genesis claim that God was busy working with this family in order to use them for his purposes, in order that this family might bless many other families in the future.

Have any members of your class thought of God's working within their families in order to accomplish some larger purpose? How can it be said that God uses our families today for divine goals? Some of the material in "The Scripture and the Main Question" may be helpful here in illustrating the idea that God works within our families.

Helping Class Members Act

Today we have explored a matter close to many of our hearts, our families. Using the story of Isaac and Rebekah, we have tried to be honest about our families and the struggle that we sometimes encounter with life in our families.

Yet through all the struggle, Christians have confidence that God is using our family lives for his own good purposes. Lead your group in an experience of prayer in which you complete the petition, "God, help us in our families to. . . ." Invite members of the class to take turns completing that sentence prayer.

After all have had an opportunity to offer sentence prayers of petition, ask them to complete the prayer, "God, thank you for . . . in our families." Invite members of the class to take turns thanking God for some aspect of our family life.

Planning for Next Sunday

Have you ever been deceived by someone? Unfortunately, deception occurs in some business transactions. But what happens when deception occurs in our very own families? At the hands of those who are closest to us? Read Genesis 27:6-8, 15-27 before coming to next week's class. It is a story of deception close to home.

Deception in the Family

Background Scripture: Genesis 27

The Main Question

Most critics would agree that one of the greatest contemporary American plays is Arthur Miller's *Death of a Salesman*. Since this play first appeared in the 1940s, it has become a modern classic. No one would say that the play provides a pleasant evening's entertainment. However, most people would agree that it is a truthful, realistic, and often painful depiction of life in a modern American family.

The chief character in the play is Willie Loman, a traveling salesman, who must confront his own failure in business as well as the disintegration of his own family. That confrontation is not easy for Loman because he has an exalted opinion of himself and a bloated image of his work as a salesman.

Willie Loman is idolized by his son, Biff. The father craves the respect and admiration of his son. Unfortunately, the father is living a lie. He is failing at business, even though he is constantly giving his son advice on how to be successful. In addition to his failure in business, Loman is also failing at his marriage. He is having an extramarital affair.

Biff eventually learns the awful truth about his father. His father is a fake, a man who, though he preaches bravery and heroism, has been a coward. He is unable to admit to his wife and son that he has been unceremoniously fired by his boss.

The play ends in a flurry of accusation and invective, as father and son accuse each other of deceit. Biff has been fired for stealing from his employer. The father is also fired because of his deceitful ways with his boss.

Deception is never a pretty picture. It is particularly ugly when it occurs within the family, among people who are supposed to love and support one another. In today's scripture, we read an ancient story of deception, in which one brother is duped both by his twin brother and even by his own mother.

The text that we study today does not offer a pleasant picture of humanity. However, it is a picture that we must confront if we are to know the truth about ourselves and our families.

Selected Scripture

King James Version	New Revised Standard Version
Genesis 27:6-8, 15-27	*Genesis 27:6-8, 15-27*
6 And Rebekah spake unto Jacob her son, saying, Behold, I heard thy father speak unto Esau thy brother, saying,	6 Rebekah said to her son Jacob, "I heard your father say to your brother Esau, 7 'Bring me game, and prepare for me savory food to eat, that I may bless you before the LORD before I die.' 8 Now therefore, my
7 Bring me venison, and make me savoury meat, that I may eat, and	

bless thee before the LORD before my death.

8 Now therefore, my son, obey my voice according to that which I command thee.

....

15 And Rebekah took goodly raiment of her eldest son Esau, which were with her in the house, and put them upon Jacob her younger son:

16 And she put the skins of the kids of the goats upon his hands, and upon the smooth of his neck:

17 And she gave the savoury meat and the bread, which she had prepared, into the hand of her son Jacob.

18 And he came unto his father, and said, My father: and he said, Here am I; who art thou, my son?

19 And Jacob said unto his father, I am Esau thy firstborn; I have done according as thou badest me: arise, I pray thee, sit and eat of my venison, that thy soul may bless me.

20 And Isaac said unto his son, How is it that thou hast found it so quickly, my son? And he said, Because the LORD thy God brought it to me.

21 And Isaac said unto Jacob, Come near, I pray thee, that I may feel thee, my son, whether thou be my very son Esau or not.

22 And Jacob went near unto Isaac his father; and he felt him, and said, The voice is Jacob's voice, but the hands are the hands of Esau.

23 And he discerned him not, because his hands were hairy, as his brother Esau's hands: so he blessed him.

24 And he said, Art thou my very son Esau? And he said, I am.

25 And he said, Bring it near to me, and I will eat of my son's venison, that my soul may bless thee. And he brought it near to him, and he did eat: and he brought him wine, and he drank.

26 And his father Isaac said unto him, Come near now, and kiss me, my son.

son, obey my word as I command you."

....

15 Then Rebekah took the best garments of her elder son Esau, which were with her in the house, and put them on her younger son Jacob; 16 and she put the skins of the kids on his hands and on the smooth part of his neck. 17 Then she handed the savory food, and the bread that she had prepared, to her son Jacob.

18 So he went in to his father, and said, "My father"; and he said, "Here I am; who are you, my son?" 19 Jacob said to his father, "I am Esau your firstborn. I have done as you told me; now sit up and eat of my game, so that you may bless me." 20 But Isaac said to his son, "How is it that you have found it so quickly, my son?" He answered, "Because the LORD your God granted me success." 21 Then Isaac said to Jacob, "Come near, that I may feel you, my son, to know whether you are really my son Esau or not." 22 So Jacob went up to his father Isaac, who felt him and said, "The voice is Jacob's voice, but the hands are the hands of Esau." 23 He did not recognize him, because his hands were hairy like his brother Esau's hands; so he blessed him. 24 He said, "Are you really my son Esau?" He answered, "I am." 25 Then he said, "Bring it to me, that I may eat of my son's game and bless you." So he brought it to him, and he ate; and he brought him wine, and he drank. 26 Then his father Isaac said to him, "Come near and kiss me, my son." 27 So he came near and kissed him; and he smelled the smell of his garments, and blessed him and said,

"Ah, the smell of my son
is like the smell of a field that
the LORD has blessed."

27 And he came near, and kissed
him: and he smelled the smell of his
raiment, and blessed him, and said,
See, the smell of my son is as the
smell of a field which the LORD hath
blessed.

Key Verse: **And he said, Thy
brother came with subtilty, and hath
taken away thy blessing. Genesis
27:35**

Key Verse: **But he said, "Your
brother came deceitfully, and he has
taken away your blessing." Genesis
27:35**

As You Read the Scripture

Genesis 27:6-8, 15-27. This passage forms a counterpart to Genesis 25:19-
34. Read together, Genesis 25:19-34 and 27:1-45 deal with related themes.
The first theme is the transmission of God's promise and the inheritance of
a future from one generation to the next. God's promise is not a one-time
event. The family continues to be utterly dependent upon the faithfulness of
God if the promise is to continue throughout the generation. The second
theme that concerns these two major passages of Genesis is the tension and
the enmity between the two brothers, Jacob and Esau. As we noted in lesson
9 for October 31, God's promise is not without conflict. The family has been
blessed by God, promised the future. And yet within the family, there is this
intense competition between the brothers over who shall be the chief recipient of the promise.

Verses 6-8. We recall that Rebekah favored the younger son, Jacob (Gen.
25:27-28). She has now devised a plan whereby Jacob will deceive his father,
Isaac, whose "eyes were dim" (27:1). Isaac is preparing to die and desires
one last favorite meal before he dies.

Verses 16-17. Rebekah deepens her deceit by dressing Jacob in Esau's
clothes. It is obvious that this was no momentary moral lapse on her part.
Rather, Jacob and Rebekah are depicted as careful, calculating deceivers.
From our vantage point their behavior seems extreme. However, we must
understand that the blessing of the father is crucial for the future. The
blessed son will inherit most of the father's possessions and will be responsible for carrying on the family name in the future. Their deception is great,
but much is at stake in the blessing.

Verses 18-20. From deception, Jacob moves to outright lying. When
asked, who he is, Jacob answers, "I am Esau your firstborn" (27:19). Isaac is
skeptical, particularly because Jacob has killed and prepared the food so
quickly.

Verses 21-24. Isaac is still skeptical, and Jacob continues to lie. The scene
is a pathetic one, with the old man groping and confused and the cunning
younger brother deceiving his infirm father.

Verses 25-27. The old man asks Jacob to "come near and kiss me, my son"
(27:26). Does this kiss of deception remind you of another kiss long afterwards? Compare this with Luke 22:47-48. How ironic that a gesture of ten-
derness and trust should be the gesture of deceit! The scene ends with
Jacob, the usurper, the younger brother, overturning the traditional rites of
primogeniture (the rights of the firstborn) and receiving his father's blessing, the blessing which normally would have gone to Esau.

The Scripture and the Main Question

A Family Who Is Blessed

In last week's lesson, we began our exploration of life in a troubled family. We studied the births of Jacob and Esau (Gen. 25:19-34). At the birth of her sons, Rebekah had been told by God, "Two nations are in your womb, and two peoples, born of you, shall be divided; the one shall be stronger than the other, the elder shall serve the younger" (Gen. 25:23 RSV).

In the story, it does not take long for God's dark promise to be fulfilled. Already in the womb the twins struggle with each other. Jacob and Esau come out of the womb with Jacob clutching his brother's heel. No wonder they called Jacob, "The Grabber." In today's scripture, controversy between the brothers continues.

Jacob is the younger brother. That means that he has no claims on his father's property. However, this is a story about conventional, traditional social arrangements being overturned. Through a strange turn of events, the younger son will come to inherit the father's property and the older son, Esau, will be disinherited. How did this happen?

Today's scripture from Genesis 27 is a story about *blessing* and *deceit*.

First, let us consider this matter of *blessing in the Old Testament*. The story of the primal family, the family of Abraham, is a story that is preoccupied with blessing. The Lord appeared to Abraham and promised to bless him (Gen. 15:1-16). In previous lessons, we have explored the ways in which that promise to Abraham became a reality. Now, in studying the story of Isaac and his sons, Jacob and Esau, we are continuing to follow the narrative thread of blessing. We find that the blessing of God was not a matter for one generation, just for patriarchs and matriarchs like Sarah and Abraham. The blessing of God continues through the generations. The blessing of God is seen as an intrusion of divine power into human life. The blessing is not a once-and-for-all event but continues through time, through the generations, leading a blessed human family into the future.

It was because of God's blessing that Abraham and Sarah kept focused on the future, standing on tiptoes straining forward to God's promised future. It was by blessing that Isaac and Rebekah believed that God would bless them with children, even though they were very old. No wonder that the writer of the letter to the Hebrews thought of this story of blessing when he attempted to speak of the way God's love had persevered throughout the generations. Speaking of the saints of old, the writer to the Hebrews says, "And all these, though well-attested by their faith, did not receive what was promised, since God had foreseen something better for us, that apart from us they should not be made perfect" (Heb. 11:39-40 RSV). In writing to the Hebrews, this early Christian writer claimed Jesus as the fulfillment of God's blessing to the family of Israel so long ago.

What does it do to a family to believe that it is shaped by divine destiny? Today, most families seem to have no destiny. They struggle from day to day to make ends meet, just trying to get by. How many families see themselves as part of the larger purposes of God? How many families have any sense that the decisions that they make, the way they order their family life, the way they raise their children, spend their money, are matters of any lasting consequence?

The story of Jacob and Esau is a story about a family that felt that God's hand was upon them. In their daily lives, they saw themselves as somehow set apart, marked by God for special blessing and special responsibility.

That You May Bless Me

Just as Sarah attempted to manipulate events to her advantage (Gen. 16, lesson 6, October 10), so Rebekah seeks to manipulate events to the advantage of her favored son. Many verses earlier, we learned the shocking truth that "Isaac loved Esau, because he ate of his game; but Rebekah loved Jacob" (Gen. 25:28). Our story opens as Isaac prepares to bless his eldest son (his favorite son), Esau. But Rebekah and Jacob scheme in an attempt to deceive Isaac and win the father's blessing for Jacob, even though Jacob is the younger son and would not normally receive the father's blessing.

Thus we come to the second focus of our story. This story is not only a story of blessing, but also *a story of deception*. Are you shocked at the intrigue and deception that occur in Isaac and Rebekah's family? In last Sunday's lesson (Gen. 25:19-34) we noted that, according to Near Eastern laws of primogeniture, Esau should inherit his father's wealth. That was the conventional way of passing on goods to one's children. But in this story, the conventional practice of primogeniture is broken. The tragedy is that the break in the laws of primogeniture, the rising of the younger brother out of his inherited condition, comes by deception.

The story does not excuse or defend Rebekah and Jacob. They are busy, in the story about the pottage (Gen. 25:29-34), obtaining Isaac's blessing by deception. We may be shocked that our ancestors in the faith behaved this way. We know that Jacob will become the father of the nation of Israel. Is this any way for a founding father to behave? It is interesting that the story asks none of these moral questions. The story contents itself to depict the actions of this family. Perhaps this is the story's way of depicting life as it really is, rather than preaching at us about life as we wish it would be.

Have you ever had an experience of realizing that someone you looked up to, perhaps a revered ancestor, a grandparent or forebear, was a person of questionable character? We usually like to depict our ancestors as good and noble people. However, the truth is, they were probably a lot like us.

For instance, I have recently been reading a history of the Civil War. In this particular account, there is a long discussion of the Southern general, General Robert E. Lee. The historian notes that Lee was a man of great character and principle, deeply revered by his men. Unfortunately, Lee was also a person who experienced great military success in his leadership of the Army of Northern Virginia, in the Civil War. This success deluded him into thinking that he and his men were invincible. That delusion led to a great tragedy at Gettysburg. Despite the advice of his generals, and the feelings of his own men, Lee ordered his army into a disastrous battle. The historian commented, "The carnage at Gettysburg is the price that the South paid for Robert E. Lee."

One of the reasons that we read history is to learn about our ancestors. However, when history is told in a truthful way, we often learn things about our ancestors that we would rather not have known. Probably the chief lesson that we learn about our ancestors is that they are much like us!

There were tensions in Isaac and Rebekah's family from the very beginning, even when their children were still in the womb. In today's story, those tensions become vividly evident as Rebekah and her favorite son, Jacob, schemed against Isaac and his favorite son, Esau.

The deception ends in great anguish.

"Are you really my son Esau?" Isaac asks (27:24).

Jacob lies. "I am."

When the deception is discovered at last, "Isaac trembled violently," and Esau cried out, "with an exceedingly great and bitter cry" (27:33, 34 RSV).

The story begins in deception and deceit, and ends in horrible anguish. Esau realizes that he has lost his father's blessing, and Isaac sees that he has been part of a grave injustice against his elder son.

Is this not usually the way it is with deceit? When we participate in deception, we often reassure ourselves that no one will be hurt by our deception. We speak of "little white lies" as if lies are not really hurting anyone. Sometimes we say that we tell people a lie "for their own good." More often than not, we are not only deceiving someone else, we are deceiving ourselves. Our deception does cause other people pain. When we say that we are protecting other people, we are usually busy protecting ourselves. We deceive ourselves about our motives, telling ourselves that we are doing our deception for another person's good, when we are doing it for our own good. Anguish results.

After the deceit, the enmity and antagonism between the two brothers erupt violently. "Now Esau hated Jacob because of the blessing with which his father had blessed him, and Esau said to himself, 'The days of mourning for my father are approaching; then I will kill my brother Jacob'" (Genesis 27:41 RSV).

The family, which once had two sons who were twins in the same mother's womb, is now split apart in murderous hatred, murderous hatred that will not be healed for many years to come.

You can say many things about the Bible. You can say that it is ancient, that it is difficult to understand, that it is sometimes confusing. But you can never say that the Bible flinches from looking at us as we really are or telling the story of our lives as we really live them.

Helping Adults Become Involved

Preparing to Teach

Today's lesson will require you to lead your class in thinking about some potentially difficult subjects. All of us want to love our families and provide a warm, loving, and caring atmosphere for our children. However, family life is often a place where there are many tensions and difficulties. Your challenge will be to provide atmosphere so that members of your class may come this Sunday with a willing spirit to discuss these matters and to open their hearts to the guidance of Scripture.

Read Genesis 27 for yourself at one sitting. It is a marvelous story, told with great dramatic flair. It is not a pretty story, but it is a story that breathes with great vitality and realism. As you read today's assigned scripture, try to note your own feelings. Put yourself in the place of the participants of the story. How would you feel if you were moving through this narrative within your own family? The material that is found in "As You Read the Scripture" will be helpful to you in understanding this passage from Genesis in depth.

Your overall aim in this lesson is to point out the ways in which God's blessing touches us in our families. However, your class will at the same time explore the ways in which our deception causes pain for us as we live in the light of God's blessing upon us. You might therefore think of today's lesson as having a twofold focus. Use this outline as you teach today's lesson:

   I. What does it mean to be blessed by God in our families?
      A. The significance of blessing in the Old Testament.
      B. Our sense of God's blessing in our families today.
  II. Deception within our families.
      A. Rather than trust God's blessing, we take matters into our own hands.
      B. Deception is one of the means by which we bring pain to ourselves and to our families.
 III. God's blessing upon us remains steadfast, even in our deception
      A. God remained faithful to Isaac's family, despite their troubles.
      B. Despite our failings in our own families, God does not fail us.

Introducing the Main Question

In his book about evil in everyday life, *People of the Lie,* Scott Peck says that evil tends to be most viciously present when people are trying to do the most good—in families, in churches, in schools. As Christians, we know that Jesus was put on the cross by people—religious leaders, government officials—many of whom thought they were doing good.

Therefore we need not be overly surprised to encounter the evil of deception in the midst of family life. While we are busy living out the blessings of family life, we are also prone to inflict pain on one another. Begin today's class by retelling the story of Willie Loman and his son Biff in *Death of a Salesman* which is found in "The Main Question." Ask class members first to identify the positive aspects of their relationship and then the negative. Note how we sometimes deceive our parents and children because we love them. This will begin your class's thinking about the ambiguity of family life.

Developing the Lesson

I. What does it mean to be blessed by God in our families?

Isaac and Rebekah were blessed by God with children, even though they were advanced in years. Jews and Christians believe that our families are gifts of God. Ask your class to list (while you write on chalkboard or newsprint) the various "blessings" of family life. Which of these blessings imply responsibilities on our part? For instance, the blessing of children entails parental responsibility for the wise upbringing of our children.

Using the material on blessing that is found in "As You Read the Scripture" and "The Scripture and the Main Question," instruct your class on the meaning of blessing in the Old Testament.

II. Deception within our families.

Blessing implies giftedness. When we see our children as blessings, we mean that we see our children as gifts of a loving and generous God. In what ways do we forget that our blessings are gifts and look upon them as possessions or achievements? Do parents sometimes put pressures on their children, treating their children as their parental projects rather than as gifts of God? Discuss with your class the ways in which we sometimes forget that our families are blessings of God.

Rebekah found it difficult to be patient and wait upon God's blessing to be fulfilled. She took sides in the dispute of her children and tried to manipulate events. Retell the story from today's scripture, Genesis 27:6-8, 15-27. Ask your class to listen carefully to the story and then to suggest parallels to Sarah's actions in contemporary family life.

III. God's blessing upon us remains steadfast, even in our deception.

While in no way excusing Sarah and Jacob's deception of Isaac and their stealing of the birthright, behind the story of deception is another affirmation: God continues to love this fallible family and continues to use them for his purposes.

Have members of your class had experience with families which, while not the model of morality or goodness, still appeared to be used for good purposes?

Helping Class Members Act

Ask each member of the class to look at the list of family blessings and responsibilities that you composed early in today's class. Ask them to focus on one blessing and its attendant responsibility for personal action during the coming week. How will each of us respond in gratitude for God's gift of our family?

Planning for Next Sunday

Although Jacob now has the blessing that was intended for his brother, his problems are far from over; in fact, they may be just beginning. Having God's blessing does not mean that we are immune from disappointment. After these few sentences of introduction, ask class members to read Genesis 29:1-30 in preparation for next week's lesson.

LESSON 11   NOVEMBER 14

Dealing with Disappointment

Background Scripture: Genesis 29:1-30

The Main Question

He had "come up the hard way," as they say, born into a family with much poverty. However, from an early age he had much ambition. Even as a child, he wanted to learn, to achieve. Yet achievement was not easy in his neighborhood. The schools were inferior. Life on the streets around his home was difficult.

Even though he had dreams of attending college one day, he was forced to drop out of school when his mother became ill and had to quit her job. With no one else to support the family, he had to take a job as an errand runner for a large corporation downtown. From the age of sixteen on, he supported his family.

He still had a dream of succeeding. He studied as much as he could about the world, dreaming of a day when he might be able to go back to school. In his mid-thirties, after he had a small family of his own, he went back to high school in the evenings, after he finished work. In a couple of years, he had his high-school diploma and was very proud of himself. At last he would be able to advance, to achieve, to be given a job that was more suited to his abilities.

Unfortunately, it was not to be. "Once a janitor, always a janitor," seemed to be the attitude of his company. He applied for every opening in the company, but he was never advanced. Remaining at his post as an errand runner for thirty years, he became embittered and sad.

When he died in his late fifties, some said that he died of alcoholism, some said that it was a liver ailment brought on by his heavy drinking. But his wife knew better.

"I think that he died of a broken heart," she said. "He so wanted to make something of himself, to get ahead, to achieve. He just could not live with the great disappointment of what had happened to him in life."

In life, we all have disappointments. For some of us, the unfairness and injustice of life sometimes crush us. How is it possible, in the face of life's disappointments, to live with courage and hope? That is the question behind this week's study of the relationship between Jacob and Laban in Genesis 29.

Selected Scripture

King James Version	New Revised Standard Version
Genesis 29:15-30	*Genesis 29:15-30*

15 And Laban said unto Jacob, Because thou art my brother, shouldest thou therefore serve me for nought? tell me, what shall thy wages be?

16 And Laban had two daughters: the name of the elder was Leah, and the name of the younger was Rachel.

17 Leah was tender eyed; but Rachel was beautiful and well favoured.

18 And Jacob loved Rachel; and said, I will serve thee seven years for Rachel thy younger daughter.

19 And Laban said, It is better that I give her to thee, than that I should give her to another man: abide with me.

20 And Jacob served seven years

15 Then Laban said to Jacob, "Because you are my kinsman, should you therefore serve me for nothing? Tell me, what shall your wages be?" 16 Now Laban had two daughters; the name of the elder was Leah, and the name of the younger was Rachel. 17 Leah's eyes were lovely, and Rachel was graceful and beautiful. 18 Jacob loved Rachel; so he said, "I will serve you seven years for your younger daughter Rachel." 19 Laban said, "It is better that I give her to you than that I should give her to any other man; stay with me." 20 So Jacob served seven years for Rachel, and they seemed to him but a few days because of the love he had for her.

for Rachel; and they seemed unto him but a few days, for the love he had to her.

21 And Jacob said unto Laban, Give me my wife, for my days are fulfilled, that I may go in unto her.

22 And Laban gathered together all the men of the place, and made a feast.

23 And it came to pass in the evening, that he took Leah his daughter, and brought her to him; and he went in unto her.

24 And Laban gave unto his daughter Leah Zilpah his maid for an handmaid.

25 And it came to pass, that in the morning, behold, it was Leah: and he said to Laban, What is this thou hast done unto me? did not I serve with thee for Rachel? wherefore then hast thou beguiled me?

26 And Laban said, It must not be so done in our country, to give the younger before the firstborn.

27 Fulfil her week, and we will give thee this also for the service which thou shalt serve with me yet seven other years.

28 And Jacob did so, and fulfilled her week: and he gave him Rachel his daughter to wife also.

29 And Laban gave to Rachel his daughter Bilhah his handmaid to be her maid.

30 And he went in also unto Rachel, and he loved also Rachel more than Leah, and served with him yet seven other years.

21 Then Jacob said to Laban, "Give me my wife that I may go in to her, for my time is completed." 22 So Laban gathered together all the people of the place, and made a feast. 23 But in the evening he took his daughter Leah and brought her to Jacob; and he went in to her. 24 (Laban gave his maid Zilpah to his daughter Leah to be her maid.) 25 When morning came, it was Leah! And Jacob said to Laban, "What is this you have done to me? Did I not serve with you for Rachel? Why then have you deceived me?" 26 Laban said, "This is not done in our country—giving the younger before the firstborn. 27 Complete the week of this one, and we will give you the other also in return for serving me another seven years." 28 Jacob did so, and completed her week; then Laban gave him his daughter Rachel as a wife. 29 (Laban gave his maid Bilhah to his daughter Rachel to be her maid.) 30 So Jacob went in to Rachel also, and he loved Rachel more than Leah. He served Laban for another seven years.

Key Verse: **And it came to pass, that in the morning, behold, it was Leah: and he said to Laban, What is this thou hast done unto me? did not I serve with thee for Rachel? wherefore then hast thou beguiled me? Genesis 29:25**

Key Verse: **When morning came, it was Leah! And Jacob said to Laban, "What is this you have done to me? Did I not serve with you for Rachel? Why then have you deceived me?" Genesis 29:25**

As You Read the Scripture

Genesis 29:15-30. The story of Jacob, Laban, and Laban's daughters Leah and Rachel is one of the great narratives of the Old Testament. Told with dramatic flare, with humor and pathos, the story is distinguished for its honest depiction of real people caught in real-life situations. Beginning in chapter 29 of Genesis, Jacob meets Laban's lovely daughter, Rachel. It was love at first sight (29:10-14). Today's assigned text begins the story of Jacob's dealings with the devious Laban.

Verse 15. Jacob signs on to work for Laban.

Verses 16-20. When asked what he will work for, Jacob surprises Laban by saying that he wants to work for his daughter, Rachel. We are dealing with a story from a patriarchal society in which women had few rights and were treated as if they were the property of their fathers, a commodity to be bargained for and bought and sold. In a few verses, the narrator tells us that Laban's older daughter, Leah, was not nearly so attractive as her younger sister ("Leah's eyes were weak," v. 17). The narrator thus introduces a source of conflict into the story. Jacob loves Rachel, but Laban has on his hands two unmarried daughters. Jacob agrees to the rather severe job of working for Laban for seven years in exchange for the hand of Rachel. Due to his great love for Rachel, the seven years "seemed to him but a few days" (v. 20).

Verses 21-26. Laban tricks Jacob by giving him Leah instead of Rachel, explaining that, in his country, the younger daughter is always married after the older daughter has been wed. Because women were veiled in the Near East, Laban is able to make the switch without Jacob realizing that he has been tricked until he and Leah are alone. In order to marry Rachel, Jacob agrees to work another seven years! The listener may feel some satisfaction in knowing that Jacob, who has so willingly deceived others (Gen. 27:6-8, 15-27) is himself deceived.

Verses 27-30. Jacob, despite Laban's deception, completes his additional seven years in order to obtain the hand of his beloved Rachel. We are told that Jacob "loved Rachel more than Leah" (v. 30), a source of possible tension for the future.

The Scripture and the Main Question

What Have You Done to Me?

A number of sociologists have been measuring the level of well-being among the citizens of various nations. In an issue of *Public Opinion* (April/May, 1985), Ronald Inglehart and Jacques-Rene Rabier report on the results of happiness research. Interesting data have been accumulating since the early 1970s on the relative happiness of European nationalities. You may find the results to be surprising. When asked to rate their happiness level, the Irish turn out to be just about the happiest people in the Western world. The Republic of Ireland tops the happiness list with the people of Northern Ireland (surprise) a close second. These happy Irish are followed by Britain; the Netherlands; Denmark; and at number six, the U.S.A. The most unhappy Westerners are the Spanish, West Germans, the Japanese, and at the bottom, the reportedly miserable Italians.

Although researchers are reluctant to specify which factors contribute to happiness, one factor seems to be whether or not the nation has recently lost a war—thus we find the Japanese, West Germans, and Italians at the bottom feeling bad. Affluence seems to contribute to overall life-satisfaction. When asked to rate their satisfaction with life as a whole, the Danes, Swedes, Swiss, and Norwegians topped the list. But money alone doesn't produce happiness. Although the Irish earn only about a third of the per capita income of the U.S., they manage to be a good deal happier. They are positively delirious when compared to the Germans, even though individual Germans are almost three times wealthier. Affluence hasn't brought the Japanese much happiness. They are tied for last place with the Greeks, even though they earn over twice as much per capita.

Some have theorized that the more religious a people, the happier they are—the staunchly Catholic Irish and the equally staunch Afrikaner Protestants, for instance. Perhaps that is true. Religion, our faith in God, does seem to have an effect upon our attitude toward life. In this life you and I have much cause for unhappiness. We all face certain disappointments and defeats. Knowing that God is with us in our disappointments may help us to endure them. Believing that God is active in our world, bringing about the completion of his purposes, may help us to handle our defeats.

In today's scripture, Genesis 29:15-30, Jacob cannot believe that Laban has so deceived him. He is horribly disappointed and begins many years of service to Laban with the goal of obtaining Laban's daughter, Rachel, for his wife. The ancient story becomes for us an example of great disappointment, great unhappiness, and its consequences.

Why Have You Deceived Me?

Harvard's Eric Erickson says that a person's ability to trust is developed in the first six weeks of life. If, for some reason, the world appears to be untrustworthy to the infant of six weeks, Erickson believes that child's level of trust may be damaged for life.

Most children probably grow up thinking that the world is basically a good place. But then, as they grow, they experience the deception of others. Life does not always deliver what we want. People betray and deceive us. What to do then?

You can shake your fist at heaven and rage, say the world is out of joint. You can crawl off under a rock somewhere and howl at the injustice, the unfairness of it all, distort the face into a frown and offer unsolicited cynical comments about life, turn the voice into a whine.

Oh, I wanted to but you see my father never let me. . . .

I could have, if my wife had let me, but she just forbid me to. . . .

The professor was down on me from the first, never gave me a. . . .

Or you can say, *Que sera, sera.* The way things are is the way they are ordained to be. My little life is part of a larger pattern over which I have no control. Best to accept it, adjust, there is nothing to be done. Take up your little collections for relief somewhere, like pointing you toward the Atlantic Ocean with a teaspoon and saying, "Start dipping." Some are born well, some not so well. What can anybody do?

Or we can persevere like Jacob, convinced that someday, someway, a gracious God will help to make our dreams reality. Jacob labored for many years in that hope. Eventually, his dreams were realized. He married Rachel and they lived together as husband and wife. They did not live "happily ever after." This is a Bible story, not a fairy tale. But they did have a good marriage and achieved much together.

Perhaps when we are able to persevere, to continue, to keep on keeping on in the face of disappointment and defeat, this is the surest sign of our faith in the ultimate goodness of God.

Jacob Served Seven Years for Rachel

A coach remains a coach only when the won-loss record is in his favor. The corporate president stands up before a drooping sales graph and says to the shareholders, "Well, we lost six million this year but we're calling it a moral victory, a year of character building for our company." A week later, there's a new name on the front door.

I sit on my university's commencement committee. To my knowledge, we have never knowingly nominated anyone to speak to our graduates who has been a failure. We look for people who are tops in their field, the achievers and doers, shapers and movers. The graduates don't want to hear an address on, "Reasons Why My Last Three Marriages Ended in Divorce," or "The Day They Came In to Tell Me to Clean Out My Desk and Turn In the Key to the Executive Washroom."

And yet, the graduates know, just like that seventeen-year-old quarterback, that *disappointment is built into life.*

Failure. It's that sinking emptiness in the stomach when you look down the list of grades on the exam. There are your initials. At the bottom. That breathless expectation as the figures are being added only to be met with stunned realization that they will not tally in your behalf. It is the physician, returning from the operating room, surgical mask taken off to reveal a countenance that speaks without having to speak. Was the operation a success? No, I don't need to ask, do I?

It's packing up and moving from the house to separate apartments, packing last the book of wedding pictures that won't be viewed again because they are too painful.

It is the morning after the election. The unused boxes of buttons and bumper stickers. The balloons and confetti not needed, the desperate attempt to smile as if it doesn't hurt. "I want to thank all of you for all that you have done. We didn't win, but we made our point, I think. I'm sure that, if we had a few more weeks, we might have turned things around and . . . I want to thank everyone for everything. Some day, we'll look back on this as a good experience."

Failure. Defeat.

What to do with defeat? One response is cheap rationalization: It was a moral victory. I remember, as a young pastor, entering a woman's home where her husband had just died and she met me at the door with a fierce look on her face saying, "Preacher, don't tell me nothing about how 'he's better off now,' or 'he's in a better place' or any of that other stuff. He's gone!" She knew. She wasn't up for any of this preacher-talk. He was gone.

Today, in the face of failure, we have more skillful rationalizations. A typically modern response is to blame failure on some other person, or even to claim no knowledge or responsibility for the failure. "The woman whom you gave to be with me, she gave me fruit of the tree, and I ate." And she said, "The serpent whom thou created, he gave me the fruit to eat." Rationalization, blaming is not new, you see.

What to do with the defeat? One way to handle failure, we learn, is not to attempt anything too great, stretch ourselves too far, lest we fail. Life can be a series of successes, provided we don't ask too much of life. Insignificant successes are better than a big failure.

Today's story of Jacob's long struggle to obtain the hand of Rachel suggests another way: perseverance, persistence, hard-headed determination born of a commitment to one's dreams and faith in the ultimate goodness of God.

Helping Adults Become Involved

Preparing to Teach

While the subject of today's lesson is not a pleasant one to discuss, at least it is a subject we all know something about—disappointment. Building upon your class's personal experiences of disappointment in life, you will lead them in an exploration from an episode, a rather long episode, in the life of Jacob. Begin by reading Genesis 29:15-30, using the material in "As You Read the Scripture" to assist you in your study of this text. This text fits in with our study of the life of Jacob, a study that we began back in lesson 9, October 31. You may want to scan the past two lessons to remind yourself about Jacob and his life journey.

You will note, in your study of Genesis 29:15-30, that these fourteen years of Jacob's life were rather uneventful. Can you imagine giving that many years of your life to this one dream, the dream of having Rachel as his wife?

Undoubtedly, one of the meanings that Israel derived from this account of Jacob's long years of service to deceitful Laban was the need for persistence and perseverance in life. Jacob was persistent in getting what he wanted. When other more frail spirits might be utterly disillusioned by Laban's deceit, Jacob remained committed, serving Laban an additional seven years in order to win Rachel. We are to derive the same encouragement to persistence in our study of this text.

You can organize today's lesson on the following outline:

    I. Disappointment and defeat are facts of life.
       A. Many of us have dreams for ourselves which are not easily realized.
       B. The longer we live, the more disappointment we are liable to meet in life.
    II. Jacob experienced great disappointment in his desire to marry Rachel.
       A. Although he worked seven years for her, Laban tricked him.
       B. A week after his marriage to Leah, Jacob and Rachel were married.
       C. Even though he had been deceived, Jacob worked another seven years.
    III. Perseverance and persistence are virtues that are derived from our faith in the goodness of God.

Introducing the Main Question

Ask your class to begin today's session by listing, on chalkboard or newsprint, instances of disappointment that adults often face in life. In order to get your adults to begin thinking about the issue of disappointment, you might read to them, or retell in your own words, the story told in

"The Main Question." This exercise will prepare the way for your study of
Genesis 29:15-30.

Ask someone to read aloud Genesis 29:15-30.

Developing the Lesson

I. Disappointment and defeat are facts of life.

Who among us has not experienced some disappointment and defeat in
life? The list of typical adult disappointments demonstrates that disappointment is a reality with which we must learn to deal. Sometimes we set unrealistic goals for ourselves. Sometimes other people do not cooperate, as Laban
frustrated the goals of Jacob.

"The Scripture and the Main Question" has an extended discussion of disappointment and failure in our lives. Retell, in your own words, some of the
illustrations that are used there. This will enable your class to think in more
depth about this issue of disappointment.

Share with your group the recent research on national levels of happiness.
How does your group react to this material? In what way does religion help
us to deal with our defeats?

II. Jacob experienced great disappointment in his desire to marry Rachel.

The previous question provides a good lead-in to your assigned scripture
for today. Read aloud Genesis 29:15-30, the account of Jacob's deception by
Laban. Ask class members to put themselves in Jacob's place. How would
they feel? What interests them most, or what do they find most unusual
about this story? Here, the material in "As You Read the Scripture" may be
of help to you in discussing the passage.

Your class has met Jacob earlier. We have seen that Jacob himself is capable of deception (as he deceived Esau, his brother, in Gen. 27). What would
they describe as Jacob's chief characteristic of personality as revealed in Genesis 29:15-30?

*III. Perseverance and persistence are virtues that are derived from our faith in the
goodness of God.*

In "The Scripture and the Main Question," it is suggested that our faith in
God may be a great resource in dealing with disappointment and defeat in
life. In what way does the story of Jacob illustrate that assertion?

Ask your class to think back on times of disappointment or defeat in their
own lives. In what way was their faith in God a help for them in enduring
and persevering in these times of disappointment? Discuss together the ways
in which our faith, and our growth in faith such as occurs in this adult class,
provides us help in dealing with disappointment.

Helping Class Members Act

Ask everyone to think silently about their own life situation at this time.
Ask them, "If you were asked to rate your level of happiness, at this very
moment in your life, from one to ten, with ten being the highest amount of
happiness, what would your rating be?"

Allow them a few moments to think about the question and to respond in
their own hearts.

Then ask them, "Think back over our lesson today, over what you already know about the Christian faith and its beliefs. In what way does your relationship to God encourage you in this moment of your life?"

After a few moments of silence, close today's session with a prayer of your own that asks God to strengthen us during our times of disappointment.

Planning for Next Sunday

You and I face many divisions in our lives, gaps between the rich and the poor, the young and the old, men and women. Next Sunday's lesson will deal with how some of these divisions might be healed. To prepare, make a list in your own mind of some of the painful divisions in our families and in our society as a whole. Come to class prepared to discuss those divisions and how they might be healed. Read Genesis 33:1-14 in preparation for the lesson.

LESSON 12   NOVEMBER 21

Being Forgiven

Background Scripture: Genesis 33

The Main Question

There has been "The Donna Reed Show," "Ozzie and Harriet," "Father Knows Best," "Leave It to Beaver," "The Brady Bunch," "The Cosby Show," and for the nineties, the wildly popular "The Simpsons."

School principals in Ohio and California condemn Bart Simpson as "a poor role model"—bristle-headed little charmer that he is. Then there's prissy Lisa; blob of a baby, Maggie; and poor Homer and Marge. Here is the American family, warts and all.

In one episode Marge drags everyone to Sunday school, hoping to "get a little goodness into them." The teacher is trying to teach the children about heaven.

"Will my dog, Fluffy, go to heaven?" one child asks.

"No, heaven's for people," she tells the disappointed children.

Bart persists, "What if my leg gets gangrene and has to be amputated? Will it be waiting for me in heaven?"

The teacher answers authoritatively, "Yes."

"What about a robot with a human brain?" Bart presses.

The teacher has had it. "Is a little blind faith too much to ask of you people?"

School principals need not worry. "The Simpsons" is satire. They are us, who we *are* rather than who we wish we were on "The Cosby Show" or "Donna Reed Show."

And let's face it, humankind is a mess, and this is reflected in our families. Most of the real damage we do to one another is done in families. Perhaps we have developed into a society of strangers because we lack the resources to endure one another at close range.

Statistically, about half of us grew up amidst a marriage that failed.

Spouse abuse, child abuse, elder abuse, it's all in the family. Any law-enforcement officer will tell you that he or she would rather break up a bank robbery than to walk into a marital argument. More people are shot in bedrooms than in bars.

The median age for marriage, first marriage, has been rising every year over the past decades. People appear to marry tentatively, with utmost caution, tiptoeing with care, having seen so many chewed up in the machinery called matrimony.

There are so many painful divisions, in our families and in the human family. Is there any way for our divisions to be overcome and for us to be reconciled?

That is the pressing question behind today's scripture from Genesis and the continuing story of Jacob and Esau.

Selected Scripture

King James Version

New Revised Standard Version

Genesis 33:1-14

1 And Jacob lifted up his eyes, and looked, and, behold, Esau came, and with him four hundred men. And he divided the children unto Leah, and unto Rachel, and unto the two handmaids.

2 And he put the handmaids and their children foremost, and Leah and her children after, and Rachel and Joseph hindermost.

3 And he passed over before them, and bowed himself to the ground seven times, until he came near to his brother.

4 And Esau ran to meet him, and embraced him, and fell on his neck, and kissed him: and they wept.

5 And he lifted up his eyes, and saw the women and the children; and said, Who are those with thee? And he said, The children which God hath graciously given thy servant.

6 Then the handmaidens came near, they and their children, and they bowed themselves.

7 And Leah also with her children came near, and bowed themselves: and after came Joseph near and Rachel, and they bowed themselves.

Genesis 33:1-14

1 Now Jacob looked up and saw Esau coming, and four hundred men with him. So he divided the children among Leah and Rachel and the two maids. 2 He put the maids with their children in front, then Leah with her children, and Rachel and Joseph last of all. 3 He himself went on ahead of them, bowing himself to the ground seven times, until he came near his brother.

4 But Esau ran to meet him, and embraced him, and fell on his neck and kissed him, and they wept. 5 When Esau looked up and saw the women and children, he said, "Who are these with you?" Jacob said, "The children whom God has graciously given your servant." 6 Then the maids drew near, they and their children, and bowed down; 7 Leah likewise and her children drew near and bowed down; and finally Joseph and Rachel drew near, and they bowed down. 8 Esau said, "What do you mean by all this company that I met?" Jacob answered, "To find

8 And he said, What meanest thou by all this drove which I met? And he said, These are to find grace in the sight of my lord.

9 And Esau said, I have enough, my brother; keep that thou hast unto thyself.

10 And Jacob said, Nay, I pray thee, if now I have found grace in thy sight, then receive my present at my hand: for therefore I have seen thy face, as though I had seen the face of God, and thou wast pleased with me.

11 Take, I pray thee, my blessing that is brought to thee; because God hath dealt graciously with me, and because I have enough. And he urged him, and he took it.

12 And he said, Let us take our journey, and let us go, and I will go before thee.

13 And he said unto him, My lord knoweth that the children are tender, and the flocks and herds with young are with me: and if men should overdrive them one day, all the flock will die.

14 Let my lord, I pray thee, pass over before his servant: and I will lead on softly, according as the cattle that goeth before me and the children be able to endure, until I come unto my lord unto Seir.

favor with my lord." 9 But Esau said, "I have enough, my brother; keep what you have for yourself." 10 Jacob said, "No, please; if I find favor with you, then accept my present from my hand; for truly to see your face is like seeing the face of God—since you have received me with such favor. 11 Please accept my gift that is brought to you, because God has dealt graciously with me, and because I have everything I want." So he urged him, and he took it.

12 Then Esau said, "Let us journey on our way, and I will go alongside you." 13 But Jacob said to him, "My lord knows that the children are frail and that the flocks and herds, which are nursing, are a care to me; and if they are overdriven for one day, all the flocks will die. 14 Let my lord pass on ahead of his servant, and I will lead on slowly, according to the pace of the cattle that are before me and according to the pace of the children, until I come to my lord in Seir."

Key Verse: **And Jacob said, Nay, I pray thee, if now I have found grace in thy sight, then receive my present at my hand; for therefore I have seen thy face, as though I had seen the face of God, and thou wast pleased with me. Genesis 33:10**

Key Verse: **Jacob said, "No, please; if I find favor with you, then accept my present from my hand; for truly to see your face is like seeing the face of God—since you have with such favor received me. Genesis 33:10**

As You Read the Scripture

Genesis 33:1-14. This story begins after a twenty-year estrangement between Jacob and Esau. Jacob hopes that, despite what he has done to Esau—namely, duping him out of his birthright—perhaps he can win over Esau through elaborate gifts (Genesis 32:13-21). When he looks up and sees Esau coming toward him with a huge contingent of men (33:1), he is terrified.

Verse 1-2. Seeing his brother approaching him with so many men, Jacob naturally assumes that there is going to be a fight, so he divides up his family, perhaps hoping to save the lives of some, perhaps hoping that the women and children will bear the first onslaught of Esau's attack.

Verse 3. Bowing and scraping before another person is not Jacob's typical style. Always the resourceful one, Jacob, having given up hope of defeating his brother in battle, now attempts to ingratiate himself with his wronged brother through humility and the offering of gifts.

Verses 4-11. This is the tender, and surprising, scene of reunion. Jacob offers Esau a gift. Esau, surprisingly gracious, refuses, but eventually consents to accept the gift. In gazing at last upon the face of his estranged brother, Jacob says that he feels as if he is "seeing the face of God."

Verses 12-14. Now reunited, the brothers and their families journey together. Can Jacob at last be trusted to follow behind without tricking his brother? Is Jacob's concern for the frail ones in his contingent real or not? Esau must trust his now-reconciled brother and move on.

The Scripture and the Main Question

And Jacob Lifted Up His Eyes and Behold, Esau Was Coming

If you have been here on either of the last two Sundays, you know that we have been studying the story of a troubled family, our family. This isn't "The Brady Bunch." It's the Bible, so it's a true story, even if a not altogether inspiring one. This isn't Ozzie and Harriet. It's Isaac and Rebekah; big, dumb older brother Esau and scheming, slick, little upstart brother Jacob. While still in the womb, the two caused such a commotion, Rebekah went into bad pre-partum depression (Genesis 25:22). When she was delivered, the twins came out with Jacob clutching his brother's heel (Genesis 25:24-27). They called the second Jacob, which sometimes meant "Grabber" and other times meant "Heel." Either designation fit Jacob.

Mom loved Jacob, Dad loved Esau, says the story. (They were not model parents.) Jacob took advantage of Esau at a weak moment (most of Esau's moments were weak moments) and duped him out of his birthright. Then, with Mom's help, when old man Isaac was on his deathbed, Jacob dressed up in Esau's outfit and duped his father into blessing him rather than Esau, thus giving him all the family fortune.

Esau hated Jacob for what he had done (Is this television's "Dallas"?), determining to kill him right after Isaac's funeral. Mom (who, remember, unashamedly loved Jacob more than Esau, Genesis 25:28) caught wind of Esau's plan, called in Jacob, and sent him high-tailing it out of town, lying to poor, dying Isaac, telling him that she wanted Jacob to go visit Uncle Laban and find a nice girl to marry of their own race and religion.

But at least you can't accuse the Bible of being naive, romantic, or papering over human reality with sweet cliché—the way we do. We are listening in on the life of a family—in a way, the first family, a real family all mixed up with the fear, distrust, envy, and deceit, popcorn, trips to Disneyworld, and sitting on the front row at church.

It's a mess when such a family gets together, risky.

"Can't we just get through one Christmas vacation without a big fight?" they ask.

Well, there haven't been too many family reunions since Isaac died, and

Rebekah passed away since Jacob slipped out of town with his brother threatening to cut his throat for ruining his life.

"What about your younger brother?" friends of Esau ask. "You never mention him."

"My brother is a conniving little scoundrel," says Esau "I hate his guts."

And friends promptly change the subject.

In just about every family I know of, there is always someone who is not discussed, at least one person missing from the annual Christmas card photo.

"You never go home to see your family," they said to Jacob. He never replied.

But Esau Ran to Meet Him

It's now been ten chapters of Genesis and many years and Jacob has been told by God to go back home (31:13).

It is a perilous, risky journey Jacob is making, as are all reunions after division, homecomings after alienation. With so many cruel words, and so many years, will there be a meeting?

Have you ever walked the path back home that Jacob walks?

I don't think it's a path we like to walk, so much risk. Most couples I know who separate, divorce.

Most brothers and sisters who split up in squabbles over inheritances, stay that way.

Twenty years ago her parents said, "If you marry him with the color of his skin, don't ever set foot in this house again."

When she heard her father was dying of cancer, she called and asked, "Dad, do you want me to come back?"

He said, "No."

It is such a risky, perilous path to such a meeting. Jacob would not have taken it, I think, had he not been ordered by God. He could not have walked it were there not a cadre of angels escorting him back to the place of meeting or rejection, face to face with Esau.

Angels or no angels, he's scared. He sends messengers on ahead of him to say to his "Lord Esau" that, if he'll receive him home without blowing his head off, there will be oxen, donkeys, male and female slaves for him in the bargain (32:5). This stance is quite different from the haughty, arrogant way Jacob connived against Esau before.

"If I find favor in your eyes," Jacob says in deference, receive me. And, in utter fear and desperation, Jacob prays, prays the longest prayer in all of the Book of Genesis.

"Reconciliation was your idea, God. Save me from the hand of my brother. He may come kill us all."

Strange, isn't it, to see Mr. Jacob, Grabber that he is, on his knees. Shaking? Begging God like a baby.

"Besides, it was you, O God, who promised me, 'I will do you good and make a great people out of you' when you let down that ladder to me that night" (32:12). That's more like the old Jacob—bargaining, pleading, holding God to account.

Let us all pause and watch granddaddy Jacob. Because meeting is never without pain, dryness of the mouth, sweating palms. So we stare at one another across chasms of race, gender, nation, economic class. Though clearly commanded by God to make peace, to be reconciled, we don't risk such perilous meeting.

I've got my culture, you've got yours. To hell with 'em. Stay out of my life, I'll stay out of yours. Good fences make good neighbors.

A senior here at the university told me. "Watch. First semester, freshman year, nobody closes the door into the hall. We're all just one big happy family. But by second semester, after rush, after the newness wears off, the doors begin to close until it's just me and my friends in our room."

It takes great courage to come to meeting.

God Has Dealt Graciously with Me

Jacob's heavenly escort of angels (Genesis 32:1-2), I think, signifies that this isn't just a family matter, this conflict between Jacob and Esau. God has an interest in this reunion. Homecoming was God's idea, not Jacob's. Reconciliation is at God's initiative, not ours. Meeting is the primary biblical goal of life. Meeting.

And the angels suggest that God does not command what God does not enable us to do.

Next day, Jacob sends on ahead of him two hundred female goats, twenty male goats, two hundred ewes and twenty rams, forty cows, ten bulls, twenty female donkeys and ten male donkeys (32:13-15). Prayers to God are fine, but old Jacob knows that a few hundred goats and ewes help make reconciliation a bit easier for Esau to swallow.

Jacob even sends his wives and children on ahead of him (in a stunningly courageous move to ensure that, if Esau is in a murderous mood, his wives will find out first!).

"But Esau ran to meet him, and embraced him, and fell on his neck and kissed him, and they wept" (33:4) and there was meeting.

Remind you of a later story, told by Jesus in Luke 15? The boy, younger brother like Jacob, who got hold of his inheritance and like Jacob, went out and wasted it in a "far country"?

And that boy, like Jacob, "came to himself" when he remembered his family, remembered home. And he made a speech, a penitent speech in hopes of making reconciliation easier for his old man to swallow.

And while he was still at a great distance, his father ran and embraced him, and kissed him, and said, "My son which was lost is found, who was dead is alive."

We're in a mess, our family. We've done a better job of cutting our brother's throat than kissing the neck. Separated, alienated, staring at one another across great chasms.

The old story promises that God both commands and enables meeting.

Then in a curious turn, trusting Esau departs and invites Jacob to come with him to journey together. But Jacob begs off with a not very convincing excuse about nursing flocks. Is this the same old Jacob? Same old lies and tricks? Esau goes his way not knowing if his brother has really been changed or if he has been duped.

That's the way it often is in families, among brothers, sisters, races, nations. It's a mess, risky, uncertain, full of peril, our meetings. Nothing is easy, sure about our relationships in the Bible or in life.

But this old story promises that, even amid the mess, God both commands and enables meeting.

Helping Adults Become Involved

Preparing to Teach

Today's lesson, as the two previous ones, deals with the problem of conflict within the family. Using the story of Jacob's reconciliation to Esau, we will explore the problem of our being alienated from one another, particularly in our families, and how that alienation is overcome.

In preparation for your class this Sunday, read the assigned text from Genesis 33. Use the material in "As You Read the Scripture" to help you study the text in detail. As you read, try to put yourself in the place of Jacob. Then try to put yourself in Esau's place. What would be your feelings if you were he during this fateful encounter?

After you read the assigned scripture, take a moment and make a list of all the examples you can think of that illustrate divisions within our human families—divisions between the generations, divisions between rebellious family members and others, and so forth. Now list all the divisions you can name within society as a whole. You can use these thoughts to engage the adults in your class as you lead them through today's scripture. Now read "The Main Question" and "The Scripture and the Main Question" to stimulate further your thoughts about the challenge of reconciliation of our divisions.

Today's lesson could be organized on the basis of this outline:

    I. We face many painful divisions in our lives.
       A. There are divisions within our families.
       B. There are divisions within our society as a whole.
    II. Division between persons is a problem as old as the story of Jacob and Esau.
       A. While they were young, Jacob had deceived Esau.
       B. Jacob finally came back to Esau, asking forgiveness.
       C. Esau received Jacob graciously and the family was united again.
   III. Today we are challenged, in our families and in our society as a whole, to seek and to accept the forgiveness of others.

Pray for God's guidance as you lead the adults in your class in study of Genesis 33.

Introducing the Main Question

You will begin today's lesson the same way in which you began your own study of Genesis 33:1-14. Begin by having your class think of all the examples of division in their lives. First, have them think of divisions and causes of alienation within contemporary families. What are the aspects of our family life which cause barriers to be erected between persons in the same family?

Developing the Lesson

I. We face many painful divisions in our lives.
In "The Main Question," two different types of family television shows are

cited. One type of show depicts our families as free from strife, placid, and always happy. The other type of show is a bit more true to real life. Can you cite examples from contemporary television depictions of family life? You might describe some recent episode from a television show that illustrates the problem of divisions within families. Which type of show—the idealistic, romantic vision of family life, or the more honest, sometimes offensive type—is the most popular with American viewers?

II. Division between persons is a problem as old as the story of Jacob and Esau.

After you have started your class thinking about divisions within our families, turn now to your assigned scripture, Genesis 33:1-14, the story of the reconciliation of Jacob and Esau. Read this story to your class, stopping after each verse and describing the situation in more detail for your class. The material found in "As You Read the Scripture" should be of help to you in explaining this text in detail to your class.

Set the text in context. Remind your class of the deception of Esau by Jacob, which is the background for this episode of reconciliation.

Ask the class to imagine Jacob's inner thoughts as he approached the encounter with Esau. Then ask the class to imagine Esau's thoughts. What issues are at stake in this reconciliation? That is, what must each person give the other person if this reconciliation is to be real and lasting?

After looking at the scripture and thinking about problems of reconciliation in their own lives, ask your class which they think is more difficult: To forgive someone or to accept someone else's forgiveness? That is, who had the tougher task in our story: Jacob or Esau, the forgiver or the forgiven?

III. Today we are challenged, in our families and in our society as a whole, to seek and to accept the forgiveness of others.

How will our divisions ever be overcome unless we are willing to give and to receive forgiveness? Go back to the list of situations that exemplify division within our families and in our society as a whole, the list which your class devised at the beginning of this session. In what ways are each of these instances of separation also instances of the need for forgiveness? For instance, in the divisions that we sometimes experience between age groups or generations, the young often feel that the older generation has not given them the resources they need to cope with the challenges of life. Do children sometimes resent that they were "overprotected" by their parents and therefore ill equipped to handle the problems of adult life? Sometimes children, looking back on their relationship with their parents, feel that their parents were too severe in their discipline of them. Your group can cite other instances of the need for forgiveness if there is to be reconciliation.

What are the necessary requisites for forgiveness to be real and lasting? Refer back to the story of Jacob and Esau's reconciliation. What factors made their reconciliation possible? What makes reconciliation possible for us today?

Helping Class Members Act

Ask class members to look over the lists of instances of division within our families and in our society. Then ask each member of the class to choose one specific instance of division that in some way intersects with their own lives. Ask class members to state one concrete, specific action they could take that might help to heal, even if in a small way, that instance of division. Ask members to share, if they are willing, their examples of division and actions they might take to bring reconciliation to that division.

Planning for Next Sunday

Have you ever been blessed by anyone? Could you ever say of someone, "She was really a blessing to me?" Next Sunday we will be exploring the ways in which other people bless us and the ways in which we can be a blessing to others. Read a story about blessing, Genesis 48:9-19, before coming to class next Sunday.

LESSON 13   NOVEMBER 28

The Ability to Bless

Background Scripture: Genesis 48

The Main Question

"Then raising the cup to his lips, readily and cheerfully he drank the poison. Hitherto most of us had been able to control our sorrow; but now, when we saw him drinking, and saw that he had finished the draught, we could no longer forbear, and in spite of myself my own tears were flowing fast, so that I covered my face and wept, not for him, but at the thought of my own calamity in having to part with such a friend."

This is an account in *Phaedo* of the departure of Socrates as seen by one of his disciples.

Today's scripture is an account of the departure of Jacob (Israel) as narrated in Genesis 48.

You can tell much about a person by the way that person's life ends, by their last words and actions, by how they say Good-bye.

You and I live our lives amid so many comings and goings, some door is forever closing behind us. The other day I thought of all the people who have meant so much to me: former teachers, grandparents, aunts, uncles, scoutmasters, coaches. Where are they now? Everyone who is present for us will one day be absent from us. All of life is caught between the rhythm of presence/absence. Hello. Good-bye.

As I pastor, I have long known the value of pastoral presence. When people are going through significant joys or sorrows in their lives, it is important for their pastor to be present with them. However, in recent years I have become more attuned to the significance of pastoral absence. At the end of the counseling session, in the last moments before we leave someone's hospital room, in the last acts of worship at the end of the service, we pastors need to be aware of how our pastoral absence creates space for God's spirit.

Through our becoming absent, God might become present in a new way. The last words we speak before we leave are therefore deeply significant.

There are pastors who are too present to their people, always breathlessly running to and fro, always on call, always available, always having the right answer on the tip of their tongue for every faith dilemma. The pastor fills up all the empty spaces, stands between all the embarrassing gaps, so there is nothing left to explain, no sense of absence or void, nothing still empty so there is nowhere for God to come.

For the past weeks' lessons, we have been following the twistings and turnings of Jacob's story. Today, we come to the end of that story, the end of Jacob's life. We witness Jacob blessing his sons.

What role does blessing play in our lives today? How can we give new significance to our times of departure and absence? Those are some of the questions behind this Sunday's lesson.

Selected Scripture

King James Version

Genesis 48:9-19

9 And Joseph said unto his father, They are my sons, whom God hath given me in this place. And he said, Bring them, I pray thee, unto me, and I will bless them.

10 Now the eyes of Israel were dim for age, so that he could not see. And he brought them near unto him; and he kissed them, and embraced them.

11 And Israel said unto Joseph, I had not thought to see thy face: and, lo, God hath shewed me also thy seed.

12 And Joseph brought them out from between his knees, and he bowed himself with his face to the earth.

13 And Joseph took them both, Ephraim in his right hand toward Israel's left hand, and Manasseh in his left hand toward Israel's right hand, and brought them near unto him.

14 And Israel stretched out his right hand, and laid it upon Ephraim's head, who was the younger, and his left hand upon Manasseh's head, guiding his hands wittingly; for Manasseh was the first-born.

15 And he blessed Joseph, and

New Revised Standard Version

Genesis 48:9-19

9 Joseph said to his father, "They are my sons, whom God has given me here." And he said, "Bring them to me, please, that I may bless them." 10 Now the eyes of Israel were dim with age, and he could not see well. So Joseph brought them near him; and he kissed them and embraced them. 11 Israel said to Joseph, "I did not expect to see your face; and here God has let me see your children also." 12 Then Joseph removed them from his father's knees, and he bowed himself with his face to the earth. 13 Joseph took them both, Ephraim in his right hand toward Israel's left, and Manasseh in his left hand toward Israel's right, and brought them near him. 14 But Israel stretched out his right hand and laid it on the head of Ephraim, who was the younger, and his left hand on the head of Manasseh, crossing his hands, for Manasseh was the firstborn. 15 He blessed Joseph, and said,

"The God before whom my
     ancestors Abraham and
     Isaac walked,
the God who has been my
     shepherd all my life to this
     day,

said, God, before whom my fathers Abraham and Isaac did walk, the God which fed me all my life long unto this day,

16 The Angel which redeemed me from all evil, bless the lads; and let my name be named on them, and the name of my fathers Abraham and Isaac; and let them grow into a multitude in the midst of the earth.

17 And when Joseph saw that his father laid his right hand upon the head of Ephraim, it displeased him: and he held up his father's hand, to remove it from Ephraim's head unto Manasseh's head.

18 And Joseph said unto his father, Not so, my father: for this is the firstborn; put thy right hand upon his head.

19 And his father refused, and said, I know it, my son, I know it: he also shall become a people, and he also shall be great: but truly his younger brother shall be greater than he, and his seed shall become a multitude of nations.

Key Verse: **And his father refused, and said, I know it, my son, I know it: he also shall become a people, and he also shall be great: but truly his younger brother shall be greater than he, and his seed shall become a multitude of nations. Genesis 48:19**

16 the angel who has redeemed me from all harm, bless the boys;
and in them let my name be perpetuated, and the name of my ancestors Abraham and Isaac;
and let them grow into a multitude on the earth."

17 When Joseph saw that his father laid his right hand on the head of Ephraim, it displeased him; so he took his father's hand, to remove it from Ephraim's head to Manasseh's head. 18 Joseph said to his father, "Not so, my father! Since this one is the firstborn, put your right hand on his head." 19 But his father refused, and said, "I know, my son, I know; he also shall become a people, and he also shall be great. Nevertheless his younger brother shall be greater than he, and his offspring shall become a multitude of nations."

Key Verse: **His younger brother shall be greater than he, and his offspring shall become a multitude of nations. Genesis 48:19**

As You Read the Scripture

Genesis 48:9-19. Our scripture is part of the account of Jacob's (Israel's) adoption and blessing of Ephraim and Manasseh. The blessing is based upon the divine promise given earlier at Luz, or Bethel (Gen. 35:9-13). In adopting and blessing his grandsons, Jacob thereby gave them equal status to his eldest sons, Reuben and Simeon. The narrative is probably an attempt to explain how Joseph's heirs became divided into two tribes, Manasseh and Ephraim, each claiming full rank with the other tribes of Israel (Gen. 49:22-26).

Verses 9-10. The scene is a tender one. Jacob, once so resourceful and cunning, is now a very old, very frail man. Joseph's sons are brought to him for blessing. Here is a story about continuity of the family and its memories across the generations. You will recall that this family began in blessing (Gen. 12:1-3). Through numerous twists and turns in the story, the blessing has been kept alive.

Verses 11-14. The very presence of his grandsons, standing before Jacob, is to him a sign of the reality of his own blessedness. The physical gesture of laying on hands is a sign of the conveying of power from one person to another. We are not sure why Jacob blessed by "crossing his hands."

Verses 15-16. Here is a summary of the ancestral faith that has sustained Jacob through his life. Scholars believe this may be a very old bit of poetry, perhaps a recitation of the faith of Israel that may be much older than the written composition in Genesis. Note that these verses are completely focused upon the action of God. "The God before whom . . . the God who has led. . . ." The "angel" here is the one who came to Abram and Sarai and promised them an heir (Genesis 18:1-15).

Verses 17-19. During the act of blessing it is revealed that the younger son shall be as great as the older one. Thus the mysterious reversals, first experienced in the triumph of Jacob over his younger brother Esau, continue. This is a repetition of the earlier version of the blessing in verses 15-16.

The Scripture and the Main Question

That I May Bless Them

Today's scripture opens with Jacob, now a very old man near the end of his life, asking his son Joseph to bring his sons before him that he may give them his final blessing (Gen. 48:9).

It is important that we understand some of the significance of the act of blessing in the Bible so that we might better understand what is going on in this story of Jacob's blessing of his grandchildren.

The Lord told Moses that the function of Aaron's sons was to be priests. What do priests do? They bless:

> "Speak to Aaron and his sons, saying, Thus you shall bless the Israelites, you shall say to them:
> The LORD bless you and keep you,
> the LORD make his face to shine upon you, and be gracious to you;
> the LORD lift up his countenance upon you and give you peace."
> (Numbers 6:22-26)

One reason why we usually have a blessing or a benediction (literally: "good words") at the very end of our services of worship on Sunday is so that some of the power of the gathering might be transferred to others as we leave. When we are gathered, we receive strength and refreshment from the presence of others around us. We join our voices together in the hymns of the church. We pray together, listen together, praise together. When we depart, some of that power that we have felt when we were together inevitably dissipates. What shall become of us now that we are scattering?

In the act of the priest's blessing, the people of Israel were reassured that God's love and power went with them. "The Lord bless you and keep you . . . and give you peace."

The blessing, bestowed at the end of worship, was thus a powerful, visible, physical sign of the providence of God, of God's continuing presence with us even while we were absent from the congregation.

Jesus takes this ancient sign of transferral of power and transforms it. Jesus blesses children. He blesses meals, disciples. He commands his disciples not only to preach and heal but also to bless—to bless even those who curse them (Luke 6:28). Thus blessing becomes a shocking sign of the radical nature of his Kingdom. You can tell his disciples by how they bless. Even as God sends the blessings of rain and sun on the just and the unjust, God's people are to bless friend and enemy alike.

We have long since secularized our times of leave-taking, but the words we use, even today as we shake hands or embrace point back to the divine significance of the act of blessing. The French *adieu,* the Spanish *adios,* the English *good-bye* are all derived from "God be with you." They are all human well-wishings that commit another to the care of God.

Blessing becomes a bridge between what happens here and what happens there, a reassurance that we journey not alone. God is with us, as present to us as sun and rain, the hand of a friend.

I once heard the late Dr. Paul Pruyser of the Minninger Foundation say that he thought the supreme test for whether or not someone was ready to be turned loose as the pastor of a church was whether or not that person could bless someone. All the skills needed by a pastor, all the faith needed to sustain and evoke faith in the providence of God, are visible in that gesture, he said.

"The Lord bless you and keep you; The Lord make his face to shine upon you and be gracious to you. The Lord lift up his countenance upon you and give you peace."

And He Blessed Joseph

Today's text, Genesis 48:9-19, concerns the death of Jacob and the blessing of Joseph's sons. We are to read this story as a continuing story of blessing. The blessing that holds all of these stories in Genesis together is that primal blessing made to Abram that starlit night in Genesis 15:1-16 and Genesis 17:1-14. Abram is told that, even though he is quite old, God will bless him and Sarai with a child. Through that child, a great nation will come forth that shall bless the whole earth.

God kept his word. A child was born, Isaac. And to that child were born two more children, Jacob and Esau. The birth of children, the succeeding generations, became visible signs of God's faithfulness to his promise. So Jacob's blessing becomes the latest installment in the story of the transferral of the blessing of God across many generations.

In a way, the story is making the claim that if Jacob is able to bless his children, it is because God has blessed him. Perhaps that holds true for all of us. If we are able to be a blessing to others, to pass on wisdom, or material goods, or love to them, it is only because God has blessed us.

We are able to convey no blessing to others that we ourselves have not received from God.

In a tender scene, we see the old man Jacob calling his family together and passing on to them the same blessing, the same promise that has guided them through his life. The scene is one of a death-bed visitation by the family. In days gone by, people died in their homes, surrounded by a loving family. Today, most of us will die surrounded by strangers, people who are paid to care for us during our last hours.

One of the goals of the Hospice Movement is to enable terminally ill people to die, not in an impersonal institutional environment, but in a situation where there are people who love and care for them.

The God Who Has Led Me All My Life

You may have had an experience in which you were called to the deathbed of someone whom you love. Many generations ago, people hoped that they would not be cursed by a quick death. In fact, historians claim that cancer was the desired mode of death in the Middle Ages. Cancer, unlike a sword through the skull or a dagger through the heart, gave one time to die. If one died suddenly, it was thought, one was denied the opportunity to get one's affairs in order, to say the things that need to be said before death.

Today, most of us pray for the blessing of a quick death. Most people dread the thought of lingering in a terminal illness. We want to die in some way whereby we will not know that we are dying. Of course, no one would want to suffer for a long period of time if that can be avoided. However, our desire for a quick death may be testimony that for most modern people, dying has lost any meaning. We have nothing to do with our dying, nothing to say, no wise words to pass on to the young, no one to bless in our last hours.

Jacob, having lived such a rich and eventful life, has much to do in his last hours. Even when Jacob was in the womb with Esau (Gen. 25:19-34), there was struggle. When he was a young man, he had contended with his older brother for their family birthright (Gen. 27). He had conflict with his father-in-law to be, Laban (Gen. 29). Finally, late in life, he became reconciled to Esau, his estranged brother (Gen. 33). What a life!

In Jacob's mind, his life was not merely one of adventure, struggle, achievement, and disappointment. His life was a walk with God.

"The God before whom my fathers Abraham and Isaac walked, the God who has led me all my life long to this day . . ." (Gen. 48:15).

The promise made to father Abraham so long ago was a promise to walk with this family, a blessing upon them, the blessing of divine presence. That blessing was conveyed from Abraham to Isaac, then from Isaac to Jacob, and now from Jacob to Joseph and his sons. From one generation to the next, the promise is conveyed, the blessing is continued.

Helping Adults Become Involved

Preparing to Teach

Today's lesson offers your adults the opportunity to reflect upon the continuity of God's grace from one generation to the next. A few years ago, we did a survey of those who used *The International Lesson Annual* and found that the median age for the average adult who used the *Annual* was over fifty years. If that is true for your class, then your adults will already have thought of the need for the older generation to pass on to the young its wisdom and experience. On the other hand, if your group of adults are young adults, they will be able to affirm the need for the younger generation to learn from the life experiences of the old. Allow today's scripture to meet your adults where they are in their life cycle so that they will be enabled to identify with the scripture.

Prepare yourself by reading over the assigned biblical text, Genesis 48:9-19, using the material in "As You Read the Scripture" to help you understand the text in context.

In "The Main Question" and "The Scripture and the Main Question," you will find life-experience illustrations that will help you to link the concerns of the biblical text with the life concerns of your adult class.

You may organize today's class on the basis of the following outline:

    I. The act of blessing in the Bible and in worship.
        A. Blessing in the Old and New Testaments.
        B. Blessing in our Sunday worship.
    II. The transferral of power from one generation to the next.
        A. The need for the transferral of wisdom from the old to the young.
        B. The ways in which the old bless the young.
   III. Blessing one another in life and in the church.

Introducing the Main Question

Introduce today's class by sharing the material found in "The Main Question." Ask if anyone in the class has had the experience of wishing that a deceased grandparent or parent was still living so that this person could give needed guidance in some current situation. For instance, just the other day my wife said, "I wish that your mother were still alive so that we could call her and ask her what she would do in this circumstance."

That statement is an everyday affirmation of the pain of absence of a loved one and the need for the old to pass on to the young their wisdom and experience. Today's scripture deals with the passing of one generation, the blessing of the young by the old. Jacob is preparing for the most challenging absence of all, the absence of death. He calls his family in to bless them. This episode serves as the basis of our reflection on the dynamic of presence/absence and of blessing.

Developing the Lesson

I. The act of blessing in the Bible and in worship.

Have someone in your group to read aloud today's assigned scripture, Genesis 48:9-19. Using the material found in the first half of "The Scripture and the Main Question" and "As You Read the Scripture," guide your adults on a study of the act of blessing in Scripture and in our experience of Sunday worship. Note the antecedents of the act of blessing that are found in places throughout the Old Testament. Ask your group if they have ever noticed the benediction or blessing at the end of the Sunday service. Does this pastoral gesture have particular meaning for them? Comment on the ways in which our everyday language, in those moments when we say to another person, "Good-bye," relate back to the ancient experience of committing another person to the care and providence of God.

II. The transferral of power from one generation to the next.

While the act of blessing has significance in our worship, it also has its counterpart in everyday life. When a son or daughter leaves home to go to summer camp. When someone leaves home to go to college. When someone we love is going into the hospital for major surgery. When a loved one is near death. All of these may be opportunities for blessing. We are standing, in these moments, on the edge of absence. The absence may be only for a few days and a short, "Good-bye," will suffice. Or the absence may be until eternity, when someone we love is about to die.

Recall for your group the tender scene that occurs when Jacob calls in Joseph and his sons to bless them as we have read it in Genesis 48:9-19. Ask members of your class if they have had similar experiences of blessing of the old by the young. Encourage them to share these with the group. You might recall some experience of blessing from your own life and be prepared to share this with the class in order to initiate the discussion.

III. Blessing one another in life and in the church.

Toward the end of the discussion in "The Scripture and the Main Question," it is suggested that we lack the means sufficiently to pass on wisdom and experience from the older generation to the younger today. Does your class agree with that assertion? In what ways might the older generation do a better job of instructing the young, of blessing them before they depart? Does your class feel that the younger generation today wants to be instructed!

Have you ever told your pastor how much his or her blessing at the end of the service of worship on Sunday means to you? What are some other occasions in the life of the church when we are preparing for absence and therefore blessing would be appropriate?

For instance, when a family is preparing to move from one home to another and is therefore preparing to leave the congregation. When students are preparing to go away to college. When someone in the congregation is preparing to enter the hospital for serious surgery. Might these be moments when we could bless people in a public gesture of blessing and therefore commit these persons to the love and providence of God?

Helping Class Members to Act

During your discussion, your class may have suggested ways in which we can improve our blessing of one another in our daily lives and in the life of the church. Designate someone in your class to share these ideas with your pastor or worship committee.

Planning for Next Sunday

Next Sunday we leave Genesis and begin a new quarter of study on the Gospel of Luke. In preparation for that new unit of study, ask your class to read the first chapter of the Gospel of Luke. As they read, ask them to keep in their minds this question, "What is the Good News?"

THE STORY OF JESUS: THE GOSPEL OF LUKE

UNIT I: A SAVIOR IS BORN
Lindsey P. Pherigo

FOUR LESSONS   **DECEMBER 5–26**

The Gospel of Luke is one of the most beloved portions of Scripture. Most of our vivid impressions of Jesus come from Luke's testimony. If one counts Luke's second volume, the Acts of the Apostles, Luke is the author of nearly a third of the entire New Testament.

In this unit we will be dealing with material that will be familiar to many in your class. Even if someone has a very meager knowledge of Scripture, chances are that person will know the work of Luke. Each class will be challenged to confront this material in new and engaging ways.

Moving from the birth of Jesus in Bethlehem, the important ministry of John the Baptist, and the response of Mary, we venture into the early days of Jesus' ministry in Galilee. This unit concludes with a study of the crucifixion of Jesus and his resurrection. In the next three months we will therefore walk through the life of Jesus with Luke as our guide, step by step engaging the events of his life.

Members of your class are preparing to move into the Christmas season. As will be noted in the unit titled "A Savior is Born," most of our Christmas images come from the hand of Luke. This is a most appropriate time of the year to sit at the feet of Luke again, listening to his marvelous stories, being engaged by his unique presentation of the gospel and its implications for our lives.

LESSON 1   **DECEMBER 5**

Good News for Us

Background Scripture: Luke 1:5-25; 3:1-18

The Main Question

No one avoids making some mistakes. Some persons seem especially vulnerable to poor judgments. Most persons add to their mistakes by deliberately choosing to do harmful things, which are harmful to themselves, harmful to other persons, and harmful to society. These mistakes and harmful actions cause us to feel badly about ourselves. Our conscience bothers us. We are not happy with our moral and ethical failures.

All persons have a share in goodness also. We make some decisions that are not mistakes. We deliberately do some good things. That positive side of each person needs empowerment, so that the mistaken judgments and harmful actions can be reduced and good judgments and helpful actions increased. How can we get this empowerment?

No matter how we talk about the ideal of a "classless society," it seems to be inevitable in every society that people separate into different classes. The "upper" classes are "upper" because they have and control "the lion's share" of material things, especially money. Money is power, so the "upper" classes are the ones with power. Considering human nature, this situation usually leads to the exploitation of the "lower" classes by the "upper" classes. We need constantly to find some ways of correcting this social injustice.

We also tend to develop certain feelings of superiority that are rooted in other factors besides money and the power it brings. We may feel that our skin color or our education or our talent makes us superior persons. These feelings of superiority need correction also. These are the questions addressed in this lesson.

Selected Scripture

King James Version

Luke 3:2b-4, 7-17

2 The word of God came unto John the son of Zacharias in the wilderness.

3 And he came into all the country about Jordan, preaching the baptism of repentance for the remission of sins;

4 As it is written in the book of the words of Esaias the prophet, saying, The voice of one crying in the wilderness, Prepare ye the way of the Lord, make his paths straight.

....

7 Then said he to the multitude that came forth to be baptized of him, O generation of vipers, who hath warned you to flee from the wrath to come?

8 Bring forth therefore fruits worthy of repentance, and begin not to say within yourselves, We have Abraham to our father: for I say unto you, That God is able of these stones to raise up children unto Abraham.

9 And now also the axe is laid unto the root of the trees: every tree therefore which bringeth not forth

New Revised Standard Version

Luke 3:2b-4, 7-17

2 The word of God came to John son of Zechariah in the wilderness. 3 He went into all the region around the Jordan, proclaiming a baptism of repentance for the forgiveness of sins, 4 as it is written in the book of the words of the prophet Isaiah,

"The voice of one crying out in the wilderness
'Prepare the way of the Lord, make his paths straight.'"

....

7 John said to the crowds that came out to be baptized by him, "You brood of vipers! Who warned you to flee from the wrath to come? 8 Bear fruits worthy of repentance. Do not begin to say to yourselves, 'We have Abraham as our ancestor'; for I tell you, God is able from these stones to raise up children to Abraham. 9 Even now the ax is lying at the root of the trees; every tree therefore that does not bear good fruit is cut down and thrown into the fire."

good fruit is hewn down, and cast into the fire.

10 And the people asked him, saying, What shall we do then?

11 He answereth and saith unto them, He that hath two coats, let him impart to him that hath none; and he that hath meat, let him do likewise.

12 Then came also publicans to be baptized, and said unto him, Master, what shall we do?

13 And he said unto them, Exact no more than that which is appointed you.

14 And the soldiers likewise demanded of him, saying, And what shall we do? And he said unto them, Do violence to no man, neither accuse any falsely; and be content with your wages.

15 And as the people were in expectation, and all men mused in their hearts of John, whether he were the Christ, or not;

16 John answered, saying unto them all, I indeed baptize you with water; but one mightier than I cometh, the latchet of whose shoes I am not worthy to unloose: he shall baptize you with the Holy Ghost and with fire:

17 Whose fan is in his hand, and he will thoroughly purge his floor, and will gather the wheat into his garner; but the chaff he will burn with fire unquenchable.

Key Verse: **The voice of one crying in the wilderness, Prepare ye the way of the Lord, make his paths straight. Luke 3:4**

10 And the crowds asked him, "What then should we do?" 11 In reply he said to them, "Whoever has two coats must share with anyone who has none; and whoever has food must do likewise." 12 Even tax collectors came to be baptized, and they asked him, "Teacher, what should we do?" 13 He said to them, "Collect no more than the amount prescribed for you." 14 Soldiers also asked him, "And we, what should we do?" He said to them, "Do not extort money from anyone by threats or false accusation, and be satisfied with your wages."

15 As the people were filled with expectation, and all were questioning in their hearts concerning John, whether he might be the Messiah, 16 John answered all of them by saying, "I baptize you with water; but one who is more powerful than I is coming; I am not worthy to untie the thong of his sandals. He will baptize you with the Holy Spirit and fire. 17 His winnowing fork is in his hand, to clear his threshing floor and to gather the wheat into his granary; but the chaff he will burn with unquenchable fire."

Key Verse: **The voice of one crying in the wilderness; Prepare the way of the Lord, make his paths straight. Luke 3:4**

As You Read the Scripture

Luke 3. This description of John "the Baptizer" is one of the most detailed accounts that we have of John, brief as it is. It is a good reflection of the Christian understanding of the role of John.

Verse 2*b.* "The word" that came to John is a different word in the Greek text than "the Word" that "became flesh and lived among us" in John 1:14. Our text literally says "a word," like the words we speak. This puts John in the prophetic tradition. See Isaiah 1:10.

Verse 3. "The region around the Jordan" is a deliberately vague geographical indication. John's activity could have been anywhere between the Sea of Galilee and the Dead Sea. Tradition has favored the lower part of the Jordan, near Jericho. His proclamation of "a baptism of repentance" was both unique and traditional. The call of repentance was traditional, but associating it with baptism was unique.

Verse 4. The application of the citation from Isaiah 40 to John is an early Christian tradition found in all four Gospels. It clearly identifies John as the forerunner who came to prepare the way for Jesus.

Verse 7. John was calling sinners to repentance. They are a "brood of vipers," probably because their repentance was superficial. "The wrath to come" may refer to the tribulations expected before the end of this evil age and the coming of the kingdom of God, or it may refer to the Last Judgment.

Verses 8-9. John's exhortation to bear fruit (to be righteous and do good things) probably reflects the superficiality of the repentance of many who came to him. The same exhortation appears in Matthew 3:7-10. This probably indicates a common literary source that both Matthew and Luke used. This hypothetical source is usually called "Q" (after the German word for "source," *Quelle*).

Verses 10-11. Here John detailed what "fruits worthy of repentance" means. It includes sharing food and clothing with the poor. Compare Matthew 25:35-36.

Verses 12-13. "Fruits" also includes financial honesty.

Verse 15. Many scholars believe that John was a messianic figure in his own right. He and his followers maintained an independent existence in some rivalry to Jesus and his group (see John 3:22-26 and 4:1). All the Gospels, however, represent John as the one who prepared the way for Jesus. Luke goes farther than this and reports that John did not consider himself as the Messiah (Christ). See the Gospel of John also, at 1:8 and 1:20.

Verses 16-17. John witnessed to Jesus as one who would baptize with the Holy Spirit. This is fulfilled in Acts' account of Pentecost (Acts 1:5; 2:1-4). This led to the traditional understanding that Pentecost marked the beginnings of the church.

The Scripture and the Main Question

John the Baptizer's Call to Repentance

The first three Gospels agree in emphasizing the work of John as a call to repent. To repent means to realize that one is going in the wrong direction, and then to turn and go in the right direction. The old direction involves disobedience to God's will. The new direction is the path of obedience. Judaism defines righteousness as obedience to God's will. That will was revealed through Moses in the first five books of our Bible (the Torah).

Repentance is Judaism's solution to the problem of sin. Judaism taught that each of us has the power to obey or disobey God's will. Sin is our willful decision to disobey. We can use that same freedom to turn from the way of disobedience (to repent) and follow the paths of righteousness. It is finally our decision. John was calling on people to repent.

John's call is not out of date. We humans are still freely choosing to disobey, so we can still heed John's call.

The quotation from Isaiah 40:3 reads as follows:

> A voice cries out:
> "In the wilderness prepare the way of the LORD,
>   make straight in the desert a highway for our God."

Early Christian tradition, however, altered this pattern so the prophetic utterance would fit better the feeling of the first Christians that John was the fulfillment of this prophetic oracle. Therefore Luke's Gospel followed Mark (1:3) in presenting this prophecy this way:

> The voice of one crying out in the wilderness:
> "Prepare the way of the Lord,
>   make his paths straight."

Note the exact poetic parallelism in the original oracle in Isaiah. "In the wilderness" parallels "in the desert." "Prepare" parallels "make straight." "The way" parallels "a highway." "Of the LORD" Jesus, not God, and the phrase "in the wilderness" is attached to the one crying, rather than paralleling the (omitted) phrase "in the desert." John, of course, was the "one crying out in the wilderness."

Repentance Needs Empowering

Christianity rejected the Jewish belief that the problem of human sin can be solved by repentance. Sin is a larger problem than simply the wrong use of our human free will. God must deal with it. Some evil force in the universe is the root cause of human sin. Paul announced that "all, both Jews and Greeks, are under the power of sin" (Romans 3:9). We need to be rescued from this power. Christ Jesus was God's rescue agent. He is our Savior and Redeemer.

Although accepted and reconciled to God while we are still sinners (Romans 5:6-10), God's plan is to transform us into righteous persons. God does this by planting within us his own transforming Holy Spirit. See 2 Corinthians 3:18 and Romans 8:9-11.

Both Luke and Acts bring out what John did and what Jesus does by contrasting John's water-baptism with Jesus' spirit-baptism. This appears first in the testimony of John in Luke 3:16. It is repeated in Acts 1:5; 11:16; and 19:4-7. The story of the coming of the Holy Spirit at Pentecost in Acts 2:1-21 is the high point of this contrast.

Repentance requires more than an effort of the human will. Christians believe that repentance is very important, but we repent by the grace of God. Our experiences with God (Father, Son, or Holy Spirit) enable us to repent.

Personal Repentance

John called the people to personal repentance. They came to him repenting. Repentance is sometimes superficial. John's test for true repentance was to look for results. Some of those who came to him must have felt accepted by God simply because they were "sons of Abraham." John said, in effect, "Forget your roots; show me your fruits" (Luke 3:9).

The fruits that John expected from genuine repentance were practical deeds of concern for the naked, the hungry, and the oppressed. We today can test genuineness of our repentance the same way.

Jesus also taught this lesson. See especially the parable in Luke 13:6-9.

Social Reform

Thanks to the discoveries and insights of sociology, we now know that personal repentance, empowered by grace, is not enough. We are all participants in social groups that are more than the sum of the individuals that make them up. Individual reform must be accompanied by social reform.

The reformation of our social systems is very difficult because we know so little about how to do it. We know that even when individual repentance is genuine, society may remain unchanged. This is a major concern of the church of our time.

We can see a rudimentary concern for this in the life of the church as reported in Acts. There are two references to an early attempt to establish a Christian social structure. Acts 4:32-37 reports a sharing of goods that moves in the direction of this ideal. The model person in this society was Barnabas.

In another story, Ananias and Sapphira exemplify the human reluctance to enter fully into such a society (Acts 5:1-11). They both died when they withheld private possessions from communal ownership.

This notice of early Christian "consumer communism" is not attested in any other early Christian writing. Some historians therefore believe that it may have been a short-lived experiment, already abandoned before Paul wrote his letters. Others conclude that it is unlikely to have happened at all, but is an idealistic account of what the author of Acts believed must have happened in the community's infancy.

The story of Zacchaeus in Luke 19:2-8 also reflects the early church's awareness of social injustices that should be corrected. It offered no solutions, probably because of its expectation that the present evil age would soon be replaced by the coming of the kingdom of God. Trying to evangelize society was not on the church's agenda until modern times.

Helping Adults Become Involved

Preparing to Teach

The overall theme of this unit is Luke's story of the Advent of Christ: "A Savior Is Born." This first lesson focuses on "Preparing the Way." John the Baptizer prepared the way for Jesus by his call to repentance. This lesson studies Luke's report of John's preparatory work. Today's text may be outlined as follows:

     I. The beginnings of John's mission
    II. John's estimate of the sincerity of the people
   III. John's insistence on "fruits"
   IV. "Fruits" explained

     V. Repentance empowered
    VI. Persistence in sin punished

The first step in preparing to teach is to study "The Scripture and the Main Question." Then read carefully the selected scripture, using the commentary "As You Read the Scripture." Do not feel obligated to teach everything noted in this commentary. It is general background material for the teacher.

Introducing the Main Question

It will be helpful to explain to the class that the heart of the lesson is our need for personal and social reform. Perhaps "The Main Question" could be read aloud by one or more class members. A general discussion on what needs to be reformed could bring out the special concerns of your class. Or small groups could first explore this question, and then share their ideas with the others. There may be a tendency for the group to avoid individual traits that need reforming, since that's more personal. And yet, you may have some in the group who would welcome a chance to make a public confession. The group can then give real support to the confessor.

Social reform is usually controversial. It may be more helpful to limit the discussion to identifying societal elements that the group feels need to be reformed. Providing solutions is much more difficult and requires special skills.

Developing the Lesson

I. The beginning of John's mission
Remind the class of the key verse for this lesson. Point out its double meaning. We should "prepare the way of the Lord" even as John did.

To make John's work more familiar, it would help to have a large map of Israel. Note how the Jordan river snakes around. In Jesus' time its flow was much fuller than it is now because of the water pumped out for agricultural use. Note on the map the traditional place where John baptized, near Jericho. Locate also "Aenon near Salim" where John baptized according to John 3:23.

As the teacher, you should refresh your knowledge of the story of John's birth in the background scripture Luke 1:5-23. You may choose to summarize this story in the introduction stage of this lesson, or you may decide to use it only if needed for some class discussion.

II. John's estimate of the sincerity of the people
John's popularity must have attracted some insincere people. Perhaps going out to John for baptism got to be "in" thing to do. John sensed this insincerity, and denounced them strongly as a "brood of vipers." His anger reminds one of Jesus' anger at the hypocrisy of the scribes and Pharisees in Matthew 23:13-36 (much modified in Luke 20:45-47).

III. John's insistence on "fruits"
Jesus himself said "the tree is known by its fruit" (Matt. 12:33). On another occasion he used this same criterion for testing prophets: "You will know them by their fruits" (Matt. 7:16). He and John agreed on this. Real repentance shows results.

After this, have the class turn to James 2:14-26. How does this discussion of "faith without works" apply to John's principle?

Ask the class members to respond to this question: Do some persons today think they have something that makes them superior to others? Read the warning in Luke 3:8. What today parallels the "sons of Abraham" in this verse?

IV. "Fruits" explained

After reviewing John's explanation of proper fruits of repentance, have the class members propose fruits especially needed in today's world. Make a list of their responses on a chalkboard, flip chart, or newsprint on the wall.

V. Repentance empowered

Get a discussion going on our ability to repent. Have the class come up with examples of persons who don't (or can't) repent. Are some actions unforgivable? Can we really love our enemies, as Jesus taught? How can we repent of hateful attitudes? Is it even *possible* without help?

Christians believe that only by the grace of God can we repent and be righteous, that grace comes from God's Holy Spirit. The gift of that Spirit is what Jesus Christ brings to us. John's witness is that the Coming One (Jesus) "will baptize you with the Holy Spirit and with fire." The Holy Spirit empowers our repentance and our righteousness.

VI. Persistence in sin is punished

The "fire" that the Coming One will bring is God's judgment on those who refuse empowerment. It is the "ax" that will cut down unfruitful trees (v. 9). The wind blows the chaff away from the wheat. The chaff is then burned "with unquenchable fire." Have a class member read Psalm 1, and call special attention to verses 4 and 5.

Helping Class Members Act

Challenge the class members to think about the one thing in their lives that they would like most to change. Can they make the change? Why, or why not? How does grace fit into this? What role does our will play in making this change?

Planning for Next Sunday

Announce the topic for the next Sunday, "Yielding to God's Will." Note how well that ties into this week's lesson. Ask the class to be thinking ahead about two basic questions: (1) How do we know God's will? and (2) Why do we resist it?

Saying Yes to God

Background Scripture: Luke 1:26-56

The Main Question

This lesson focuses on the tension between what we are and what we think we should be. It extends further into the relationship between our own standards and those of God. Restated, the central issue is the tension between what we are and what God intends us to be.

Let us first suppose that our standards are rooted in our understanding of what God's will for us actually is. In this case there is no conscious recognition of any tension between our standards and God's will. Most of us probably believe that what we think is right is also what God thinks is right.

Let us next suppose that our standards are in some disagreement with what we understand to be God's will. Both of these suppositions force on us the question of how we get our notions of God's will.

To deal with this in a Christian setting, most of us would feel comfortable with an answer that says we get our knowledge of God's will from the Bible. Since the Bible is a complex religious deposit from both Judaism (the Old Testament) and apostolic Christianity (the New Testament) there is room for a wide range of opinions about how to learn God's will from the Bible. The most common approach would take seriously the commandments given through Moses and the teachings of Jesus. Restated, it is Moses plus Jesus that informs most Christians. Where tension occurs, Christians tend to follow Jesus.

No matter how we arrive at our understanding of God's will, there is still the gap between where we are and where we should be. To recognize this is the first step in bringing our life into harmony with God's will.

Selected Scripture

King James Version	New Revised Standard Version
Luke 1:26-38	*Luke 1:26-38*
26 And in the sixth month the angel Gabriel was sent from God unto a city of Galilee, named Nazareth,	26 In the sixth month the angel Gabriel was sent by God to a town in Galilee called Nazareth, 27 to a virgin engaged to man whose name was Joseph, of the house of David. The virgin's name was Mary. 28 And he came to her and said, "Greetings, favored one! The Lord is with you." 29 But she was much perplexed by his words and pondered what sort of greeting this might be. 30 The angel said to her, "Do not be afraid, Mary, for you have found favor with God. 31 And now, you will conceive in
27 To a virgin espoused to a man whose name was Joseph, of the house of David; and the virgin's name was Mary.	
28 And the angel came in unto her, and said, Hail, thou that art highly favored, the Lord is with thee: blessed art thou among women.	
29 And when she saw him, she was troubled at his saying, and cast in	

her mind what manner of salutation this should be.

30 And the angel said unto her, Fear not, Mary: for thou hast found favour with God.

31 And, behold, thou shalt conceive in thy womb, and bring forth a son, and shalt call his name JESUS.

32 He shall be great, and shall be called the Son of the Highest: and the Lord God shall give unto him the throne of his father David:

33 And he shall reign over the house of Jacob for ever; and of his kingdom there shall be no end.

34 Then said Mary unto the angel, How shall this be, seeing I know not a man?

35 And the angel answered and said unto her, The Holy Ghost shall come upon thee, and the power of the Highest shall overshadow thee: therefore also that holy thing which shall be born of thee shall be called the Son of God.

36 And, behold, thy cousin Elisabeth, she hath also conceived a son in her old age: and this is the sixth month with her, who was called barren.

37 For with God nothing shall be impossible.

38 And Mary said, Behold the handmaid of the Lord; be it unto me according to thy word. And the angel departed from her.

your womb and bear a son, and you will name him Jesus. 32 He will be great, and will be called the Son of the Most High, and the Lord God will give to him the throne of his ancestor David. 33 He will reign over the house of Jacob forever, and of his kingdom there will be no end." 34 Mary said to the angel, "How can this be, since I am a virgin?" 35 The angel said to her, "The Holy Spirit will come upon you, and the power of the Most High will overshadow you; therefore the child to be born will be holy; he will be called Son of God. 36 And now, your relative Elizabeth in her old age has also conceived a son; and this is the sixth month for her who was said to be barren. 37 For nothing will be impossible with God." 38 Then Mary said, "Here am I, the servant of the Lord; let it be with me according to your word." Then the angel departed from her.

Key Verse: **And Mary said, Behold the handmaid of the Lord; be it unto me according to thy word. And the angel departed from her. Luke 1:38**

Key Verse: **Then Mary said, "Here am I, the servant of the Lord; let it be with me according to your word." Then the angel departed from her. Luke 1:38**

As You Read the Scripture

Verse 26. "In the sixth month" means in the six month of Elizabeth's pregnancy. This leads to the traditional view that John was six months older than Jesus. "The angel Gabriel" was not an ordinary angel (messenger) but a *chief* among angels. He already had announced the coming of John (1:19). "Nazareth" is not mentioned in any writing source that still exists, prior to Christian writings. Nothing is known of it. It was apparently an unimportant village that Jesus made famous. Luke's version of Jesus' birth has become the popular one: Joseph and Mary traveled to Bethlehem for the birth of Jesus, then returned to their home in Nazareth. In Matthew's version they did not live there until after Jesus was born; then they migrated from Bethlehem and took up a new home in Nazareth. Both accounts agree in a Bethlehem birthplace, and a Nazareth home for Jesus.

Verse 27. "A virgin engaged": this indicates that Mary was in her late teens, already pledged to Joseph in an arranged marriage, as was customary. Joseph is identified as "of the house of David," the royal line. This establishes the necessary connection between Jesus and the Messianic hopes of the people. As Elizabeth's relative (1:36), Mary seems not to have been of David's lineage, but of the Levitical line of Aaron (1:5).

Verse 28. Gabriel's greeting was not in a dream as in Matthew's version (Matt. 1:20-14), but in a direct appearance. The purpose of the announcement's greeting was to point out that Mary had been specially chosen for this high honor.

Verse 29. Mary was understandably perplexed by this strange greeting. There is no indication that she knew he was an angel; compare the annunciation of Samson in Judges 13:2-11. Unlike Zechariah (Luke 1:13), it was not the appearance of the angel that "much perplexed" Mary but his words. Perhaps this reveals one aspect of her character, as Luke understood it; she had a reflective, reasoning mind.

Verse 30. The angel informed Mary of her special status.

Verse 31. The angel now cleared up Mary's puzzlement by announcing her forthcoming pregnancy. Following the pattern of the annunciation to Zechariah (Luke 1:13), the Annunciation was a complete surprise and included the name to be given to the one to be born. "Jesus" is the Greek form of "Joshua," meaning "Savior."

Verses 32-33. In two earlier annunciations (that of Samson and of John the Baptizer) the angel announced what the one to be born will accomplish. The same pattern appears here. Jesus "will be great," and "will be called the Son of the Most High." The political promise of the throne of David, with a reign that will last forever, was not verified historically. Most Christians have chosen, therefore, to give this a spiritual meaning, and refer it to the eternal kingdom that will follow the end of this evil age.

Verse 34. Mary now had a new problem; she was still a virgin.

Verse 35. The angel explained that God's Holy Spirit "will overshadow you," leaving her pregnant. This divine paternity made the child "holy" and the "son of God."

Verse 36. The angel informed Mary of Elizabeth's pregnancy (as the reader learned earlier in chapter 1). Elizabeth was Mary's "relative."

Verse 37. With God nothing is impossible (see Mark 10:27).

Verse 38. Mary now gave permission; she said yes to God.

The Scripture and the Main Question

The scripture for this lesson tells the story of Mary's reaction to the startling announcement of the angel Gabriel. It begins with her puzzlement. What was announced cannot be, in her understanding. Mary's puzzlement is a model of what often happens when our lives are confronted by the will of God.

God's will sometimes appears to demand the impossible. To experience hurt from another person may be so traumatic that the announcement that

God demands forgiveness is both puzzling and difficult to accept. Doesn't the sense of justice count for anything?

In such a circumstance one may naturally feel that God should hate the hurtful one as much as we do. As the psalmist says, "Do I not hate those who hate you, O LORD? . . . I hate them with a perfect hatred" (139:21-22). But the larger tradition of Israel already provided the corrective. "You shall not hate in your heart anyone of your kin . . . or bear a grudge against any of your people, but you shall love your neighbor as yourself" (Lev. 19:17-18). Jesus not only quoted this central tradition but also reinforced it with his well-known admonition to turn the other cheek, to love those who persecute you, to love your enemies (Matt. 5:39-48). To obey this radical representation of the will of God is very difficult for most of us. We tend to want to modify it enough to make it "obeyable."

There are many times in life when what we have been taught to think of as right (because it represents the will of God) may be hard to follow because it doesn't seem right in a particular circumstance. In such a situation it is hard to give up our feelings of "rightness" in order to obey the claims of a higher righteousness. Sometimes we should obey this higher righteousness even if it is hard, but other times we may feel it necessary not to obey what is presented to us as the will of God. "Yielding to God's will" is one side of the "coin"; the other side may well be the necessity of reconsidering and possibly revising our understanding of what God's will is for us.

How can we know which way to go? Sometimes we can learn from the experiences of others. This is especially helpful if the circumstances are very similar. For instance, most people need to "fit in" with—to feel comfortable in—the culture around us. Others feel the need to be critical of their culture. Many people before us have wrestled with this problem. Some recommend, as the best choice, accepting the status quo as it is. After all, the way things are is the way God intends them to be or else they would be different. Isn't this God's world, created as God willed it? It is better to adjust to the way things are, since the way things are is the way God willed it. Others see the status quo as needing serious revision and improvement. Without doubting the role of God as creator and sustainer of the world as it is, many people feel that something has gone wrong. The world is far from perfect. There are social and natural disasters that are hard to relate to an all-powerful creator God who is also perfectly good. Theologians call this the problem of "theodicy." In this awareness of an imperfect world, what does it mean to obey God's will? What now does "yielding to God's will" mean? It should be apparent by now that there is no easy solution. God has given us minds to use in reaching decisions for our own lives. As Jesus is reported in Luke 12:57, "Why do you not judge for yourselves what is right?"

Such an answer, of course, is not a complete denial of those guidance systems we usually depend on. It is more a warning that external data on the will of God must always be balanced with "internal" data—that is, what we believe to be the will of God is based on our experience, our interaction with tradition and Scripture, and our own ability to reason.

Just as help can come from the experiences and beliefs of others, these "others" can be contemporary with us, or they can belong to any past age. These latter, of course, must have left a known legacy—either in their work (writing, sculpture, architecture, music, visual arts, and so on) or in the traditions of their life-style and social interaction. We are not left alone to pull together all our data; we have much help from those who went before us.

Furthermore, our perception of God's will is influenced strongly by our own faith-stage. Everyone goes through several stages of faith. The earlier stages find the answer to God's will in external "authorities"—parents; teachers; one's peer group; one's nationality; one's religion, with its scriptural and denominational aspects. The more mature (and later) stages tend to rely more on one's own personal judgments.

Still, the main problem is *whether or not we are willing to follow the path of obedience,* no matter how we decide what the will of God is. We know the better but choose the lower. That's the human condition to which Christianity ministers. As "fallen" creatures, we are restored by Christ and empowered by him to begin preparation for life with God. Like Mary we are often puzzled and hesitate. But then Mary shows us what to do about it. We should raise critical questions, decide, and then act. Mary's yes to Gabriel becomes for us a model yes for every situation that is at first puzzling, but eventually turns out well as we obey God's will to the best of our understanding of that will.

One major problem for everyone is the ease with which we identify the will of God with the standards our culture group takes for granted as right ones. Most religions function to sanction the customs of their culture group. Christianity is no exception. Christianity is as deeply shaped by its culture group as it, in turn, shapes culture. We like to think that our religion always shapes our culture, but the reverse is functioning at the same time.

To distinguish between God's universal will and the various cultural standards that compete with it is a problem with which we all have to struggle. Sometimes we have to take an unpopular stand and say with Peter that we must obey God rather than man (Acts 4:18-20), and accept the consequences. That's what Mary did in our lesson today.

Helping Adults Become Involved

Preparing to Teach

This lesson raises some hard questions. It is a fine opportunity for serious and thoughtful class discussion. During your class, it will be easy to get sidetracked to questions about the details of the annunciation to Mary. These should be addressed, but since there is no way to settle them, the focus of the class lesson should be on the practical question of *knowing and doing the will of God in our lives today.* Here is an outline of today's lesson:

I.   The annunciation to Mary
II.   Mary's questions and acceptance
III.   How do we know God's will?
IV.   How do we do God's will?

First, read carefully the scripture lesson and try to anticipate the questions that class members might ask. Watch the clock on this first part so that it doesn't take more than a fourth of the class time. Be honest in admitting that we do not know the answers to questions about the reality of angels and God's use of them as messengers. Be aware of the way Matthew describes an annunciation to Joseph (in a dream), but there is no need to introduce this version unless a class member calls attention to it. If this happens, be prepared to report it correctly, and resist the temptation to supply easy answers.

Introducing the Main Question

Early in the class period move away from the discussion of the annunciation to Mary and describe the way the story leads to a very practical question. Obeying God's will depends first on knowing what that will is. That's a thorny enough question, and should be given the most time in the lesson period. Allow some time at the end to discuss the problem of doing God's will, once we accept some understanding of it.

Developing the Lesson

I. The annunciation to Mary

Read aloud the Annunciation verses without Mary's responses. Using the material in the section "As You Read the Scripture," share with the class any information that clarifies the text. Perhaps you can comment on individual parts as you read the text. Then let the class raise questions or make comments.

II. Mary's questions and acceptance

Note first the frank statements about Mary's puzzlement. Her questions are easily understood as a quite normal reaction. What is the significance of God's messenger (angel) approaching Mary directly? Ask the class if they think Mary could have refused to cooperate. What does her submission imply about our relation to God's will? Remember, and be prepared to acknowledge, the way Matthew's infancy story focuses on Joseph's acceptance of the situation, not Mary's. It is Mary's submission that gives us the main question of this lesson.

III. How do we know God's will?

Review first the section "The Main Question." It raises the question of how we know God's will and suggests that our Bible plays a major role in the answer for most people. Open a discussion on how the Bible helps (determines?) our understanding of God's will. What parts of the Bible are most influential? Who decides what parts are most authoritative? How do they respond to the message of a bumper sticker—God Said It, I Believe It, That Settles It?

Next bring into the discussion the ideas and questions expressed in the section "The Scripture and the Main Question." Ask the class to give an example (not necessarily from real life) where the common understanding of the will of God doesn't seem like the right thing to do. If the class doesn't respond with such an instance, read aloud Luke 6:29-30 and ask the class first if they regard that as a correct representation of the will of God. Focus especially on the second half of verse 30.

Be sure to raise the question of how the status quo relates to God's will, and how we should respond to that.

IV. How do we do God's will?

It isn't enough to know God's will. To know is not to do. Ask the class to list obstacles that hinder our full obedience to God's will. Central among these should be the problem of human nature. We naturally are self-centered and that hinders our surrender to God's will. Is the class in agreement that "human nature" is the basic obstacle?

How does the class understand the "good news" of Christianity? What has God done to rescue us from ourselves? Use the opportunity to restate the gospel. God is about the job of transforming us into new persons, of freeing us from that bondage that hinders our obeying God's will. A reading of 2 Corinthians 3:18 and Romans 6:17-18 will help the understanding of the class. Invite responses.

Helping Class Members Act

It is almost certain that your class will not endorse the status quo of any culture as a true expression of God's will. Have the class propose a list of specific things that exist in our culture that are not in accord with God's will. Be sure to include obvious items—such as hunger, poverty, inadequate medical services for the poor—but encourage the class to go beyond these to other items that are actually present in the class's community.

Then open a discussion on how individual persons can be responsive to God's will by doing something specific to make society what it should be, according to the class's understanding of God's will. Make a list on a chalkboard or newsprint of the actions an individual can do to be obedient to God's will. Be sure to keep the list focused on actions that improve conditions and on realistic actions that one can actually do.

Finally, open a discussion on how groups can be obedient to God's will by working to change the community conditions that violate it. Certain class members may already be active in group projects of a service club in the community. Then focus on what the church is doing. Is it doing anything? If not, why not? Challenge the class to be aggressive in moving the church into projects such as recycling. Ask the class members to propose several activities they believe to be efforts to obey God's will. Giving money to worthy projects is important, of course, either as an individual or as a group, but it does not take the place of actual, hands-on involvement.

Preparing for Next Sunday

In Christianity it is Jesus who gives us our clearest insight into God's will and who was God's agent for enabling us to do that will. His birth, therefore, is the beginning of what developed into our religion. Next week's lesson studies that momentous beginning.

God's Gift of a Savior

Background Scripture: Luke 2:1-20

The Main Question

The birth of Jesus was an event that passed almost unnoticed at the time. Later, it was seen to be of great significance. The infancy stories in Luke and Matthew were written long after Jesus' fame was recognized. They were written in the light of his later fame as the church's Lord and Savior. The stories witness to a faith not yet realized at the time of his birth. We might say that the significance of the birth stories reflects the esteem that Jesus later acquired. They reflect the true importance of the event rather than what actually happened.

Writing about another subject, the great German New Testament scholar, Martin Dibelius, noted that what was actually spoken at an event seldom expressed the real historical importance of that event. That is one of the difficult problems of the historian. Shall he or she report only what was actually said at an event (if, indeed, that was known), or should the historian write what *should* have been said to capture the true importance of the event?

Ancient Greek historians, including the Jewish historian Josephus, and the writer of Luke and Acts, preferred to try to describe a significant event in a way appropriate to its real importance.

Luke's story of the birth of Jesus follows this practice. It was an event of great importance for the future of humanity. The person to become the Savior of the world was heralded by a heavenly angel and serenaded by a heavenly chorus. The later Lord was born Lord. Jesus was already "Lord at his birth." This lesson is focused on this Lordship in order that he may be Lord of our lives today.

Selected Scripture

King James Version

Luke 2:4-20

4 And Joseph also went up from Galilee, out of the city of Nazareth, into Judaea, unto the city of David, which is called Bethlehem; (because he was of the house and lineage of David:)

5 To be taxed with Mary his espoused wife, being great with child.

6 And so it was, that, while they were there, the days were accomplished that she should be delivered.

7 And she brought forth her firstborn son, and wrapped him in swad-

New Revised Standard Version

Luke 2:4-20

4 Joseph also went from the town of Nazareth in Galilee to Judea, to the city of David called Bethlehem, because he was descended from the house and family of David. 5 He went to be registered with Mary, to whom he was engaged and who was expecting a child. 6 While they were there, the time came for her to deliver hr child. 7 And she gave birth to her firstborn son and wrapped him in bands of cloth, and laid him in a manger, because there was no place for them in the inn.

dling clothes, and laid him in a manger; because there was no room for them in the inn.

8 And there were in the same country shepherds abiding in the field, keeping watch over their flock by night.

9 And, lo, the angel of the Lord came upon them, and the glory of the Lord shone round about them: and they were sore afraid.

10 And the angel said unto them, Fear not: for, behold, I bring you good tidings of great joy, which shall be to all people.

11 For unto you is born this day in the city of David a Saviour, which is Christ the Lord.

12 And this shall be a sign unto you; Ye shall find the babe wrapped in swaddling clothes, lying in a manger.

13 And suddenly there was with the angel a multitude of the heavenly host praising God, and saying,

14 Glory to God in the highest, and on earth peace, good will toward men.

15 And it came to pass, as the angels were gone away from them into heaven, the shepherds said one to another, Let us now go even unto Bethlehem, and see this thing which is come to pass, which the Lord hath made known unto us.

16 And they came with haste, and found Mary, and Joseph, and the babe lying in a manger.

17 And when they had seen it, they made known abroad the saying which was told them concerning this child.

18 And all they that heard it wondered at those things which were told them by the shepherds.

19 But Mary kept all these things, and pondered them in her heart.

20 And the shepherds returned, glorifying and praising God for all the things that they had heard and seen, as it was told unto them.

8 In that region there were shepherds living in the field, keeping watch over their flock by night. 9 Then an angel of the Lord stood before them, and the glory of the Lord shone around them, and they were terrified. 10 But the angel said to them, "Do not be afraid; for see— I am bringing you good news of great joy for all the people: 11 to you is born this day in the city of David a Savior, who is the Messiah, the Lord. 12 This will be a sign for you: you will find a child wrapped in bands of cloth and lying in a manger." 13 And suddenly there was with the angel a multitude of the heavenly host, praising God and saying,

14 "Glory to God in the highest heaven,
and on earth peace among those whom he favors!"

15 When the angels had left them and gone into heaven, the shepherds said to one another, "Let us go now to Bethlehem and see this thing that has taken place, which the Lord has made known to us." 16 So they went with haste and found Mary and Joseph, and the child lying in the manger. 17 When they saw this, they made known what had been told them about this child; 18 and all who heard it were amazed at what the shepherds told them. 19 But Mary treasured all these words and pondered them in her heart. 20 The shepherds returned, glorifying and praising God for all they had heard and seen, as it had been told them.

Key Verses: **And the angel said unto them, Fear not: for, behold, I bring you good tidings of great joy, which shall be to all people. For unto you is born this day in the city of David a Saviour, which is Christ the Lord. Luke 2:10-11**

Key Verses: **Do not be afraid; for see—I am bringing you good news of great joy for all the people: to you is born this day in the city of David a Savior, who is the Messiah, the Lord. Luke 2:10-11**

As You Read the Scripture

Verse 4. David came from Bethlehem (1 Samuel 16:18-19), so the people expected a new Davidic king to come from Bethlehem also. Luke identifies Joseph as a descendant of "the house and family of David."

Verse 5. There is a textual problem here. Some texts describe Mary as engaged to Joseph; others as his wife. Scholar J. M. Creed noted that it would have been strange if Mary traveled with Joseph when she was only betrothed to him. That Mary was pregnant also makes it more likely that they were married. Luke's account (unlike Matthew's) gives no hint that her pregnancy was a problem for Joseph.

Verses 6-7. They arrived in Bethlehem in time for her delivery. Luke describes Jesus as Mary's "firstborn son," implying that others were to come after this first one. That Jesus was laid in a manger (a feed trough for animals) has become a fixture in popular Christmas traditions. (In Matthew he was apparently born at the home of Mary and Joseph.) Luke gives as a reason the capacity crowd at "the inn."

Verse 8. This verse has suggested to some that Jesus' birth took place at night.

Verse 9. An angel (messenger) appeared to the shepherds, along with a frightening appearance of "the glory of the Lord" (see Exod. 40:34-35).

Verses 10-11. The angelic messenger calmed their fears and announced the birth of the Messiah, also called "Lord" and "Savior." This is probably reading back into the birth the titles that actually were applied to Jesus only after his resurrection (see Acts 2:36 and Rom. 1:4). Luke calls Jesus "Savior" only this one time.

Verse 12. The angel gave the shepherds information that would help them locate the new baby.

Verses 13-14. "A multitude of the heavenly host" now joined the angel and the shepherds, praising God and proclaiming "on earth peace among those whom he favors," or "on earth peace, goodwill among people." That Jesus is associated with peace on earth is clear enough, but for whom is obscure.

Verses 15-16. The shepherds went into Bethlehem and found the baby in the manger.

Verses 17-18. The shepherds shared with Mary and Joseph what they had learned from the angel. This news caused amazement, but why should it, after the Annunciation account earlier? Had Mary forgotten that experience? It seems to have been the others ("all who heard it") who were amazed, because they were learning who this baby was for the first time. Since Joseph was not included in the Annunciation, perhaps he was amazed at the information the shepherds brought. The story of the shepherds does not seem to presuppose the Annunciation story.

Verse 19. The Greek word usually translated as "words" also means "things" or "events." Perhaps Mary was pondering these events. That Mary was really aware of the future greatness of her baby is made unlikely by her later refusal to support Jesus in his mission (see Mark 3:20-21 and 31-35). Luke, however, describes Mary as "pondering" on these experiences. She seems to have not understood Jesus' words in Luke 2:49, and again, Luke describes Mary as "treasuring all these things in heart" (2:51).

The Scripture and the Main Question

The Structure of the Birth Story

Luke's infancy story accomplishes several important things. First, it establishes the village Nazareth in Galilee as the home of Jesus' family. Then it confirms the Messianic expectation of the Messiah's birth in Bethlehem. Next it links Joseph with the line of David.

Luke's way of accomplishing two of these things is unique. He assumes (or knows) that Nazareth was the home of Joseph and Mary before Jesus' birth. A Roman tax law (difficult to verify) required a journey to Bethlehem, and Jesus was born there soon after their arrival. After tending to the requirements of the law of Moses, they returned home. This account in Luke has become the commonly adopted one.

Matthew's story is different. The Bethlehem birth is quite natural, because that's the home of Joseph and Mary. The problem Matthew faces is to account for Jesus' growing up in Nazareth. He accomplishes this by telling of Herod's "massacre of the innocents," the flight into Egypt, the return to an unsafe situation in Bethlehem and the migration to Nazareth. The popular solution to the contradictory patterns here is to add the individual events in Matthew's account (the star, the magi, the massacre, the flight into Egypt) to the story as Luke reports it. Matthew's basic pattern is unfamiliar to most Christians.

Both Luke and Matthew link Jesus to the Davidic royal line through Joseph's genealogy, even though both Gospels agree that Joseph was biologically unrelated to Jesus. There is no simple solution to this problem.

The Angel and the Angels

The appearance of the angel in Luke's story gives cosmic importance to the birth event. This is a very special birth. This is heightened further by "the glory of the Lord," which is a Jewish way of saying that God's very presence was with the angel. The significance of this birth is emphasized yet again by the "multitude of the heavenly host," with their famous "on earth peace" declaration.

It is important to note that his heavenly announcement heralds the coming of *a world savior,* not merely a Jewish Messiah. As the new religion discovered its identity and separated from its original Jewish setting it became a world religion, with Jesus proclaimed as "for all the people." This led to the eventual formation (in the sixth Christian century) of a Christian calendar based on the year of Jesus' birth. This calendar is now accepted worldwide. The years before the birth of Jesus were identified by B.C. (Before Christ) and those after his birth by A.D. (Anno Domine: the year of the Lord). Out of consideration for the non-Christians who use this calendar, it is becoming customary use B.C.E. and C.E., meaning Before the Common Era and the Common Era.

The angelic host announced "on earth peace" (the rest of that phrase is not clear). Christians today have a special interest in supporting peace movements. World peace is high on our agendas. Conflicts are inevitable, but war is a poor solution. We hope we can resolve conflicts by negotiation. That always involves compromises and some surrender of national autonomy to international controls. Jesus the Savior is also the Prince of Peace.

The Shepherds

In contrast to the impression left by Matthew's infancy story, with its introduction of the magi (the wise men) from the East, and the concern of King Herod, Luke's account pays attention only to shepherds. Shepherds were at the bottom of the social strata. God's angelic announcement of Jesus' birth came to the poor, the dregs of society. In this respect, the two infancy stories complement each other. The birth of Jesus was of significance to all, the rich and ruling class (Matthew) as well as the poor and outcast (Luke). This emphasis of Luke continues through the whole Gospel. Compare Luke's beatitudes (6:20-26) with Matthew's (5:3-10).

The shepherds bring no gifts to the baby Jesus, unlike the magi who bring treasures. It is sufficient for the shepherds to see with their own eyes what the angel made known to them. The story has a kind of intrinsic probability in that if a male child of the line of David were born in Bethlehem it could well have been an event that would have attracted much attention. Many would be asking, Is this one the long-awaited Messiah?

The Ponderings of Mary

The initial response of Mary to Gabriel's announcement—a "questioning before accepting" attitude—seems to continue with her reaction to the words of the shepherds. Although she "treasured all these words," she obviously had no awareness of their real meaning. She "pondered them in her heart." This same view of Mary is repeated yet again in the story of Simeon's statement about Jesus' future greatness (Luke 2:25-35). There the text simply reports that "the child's father and mother were amazed at what was being said about him" (2:33). That Joseph was amazed would not be surprising (in Luke's Gospel), but Mary's amazement is more difficult to understand. Finally, Mary's attitude is shown again in the story of Jesus staying in the Temple while his family started their return journey (2:41-51). This time it is the statement of Jesus that puzzles both parents; "they did not understand what he said to them" (2:50). At the end of Luke's infancy stories he reports that Mary "treasured all these things in her heart" (2:51). We should probably assume that she also kept pondering what they meant.

In the story of the adult Jesus it seems likely that Mary did not understand or sympathize with the ministry of Jesus. Luke reports a modified version of an incident where his mother and his brothers come to his house in Capernaum (according to Mark 3:19b) only to be rebuffed. Mark's account (on which Luke's is based) is more detailed and gives the reason for their coming; "they went out to restrain him, for people were saying 'He has gone out of his mind' " (Mark 3:21, note 3:31). Mark's terse statement was modified in Luke to eliminate the hostility of Jesus' family (compare Mark 6:4 with Luke 4:24).

Mary's failure to understand and support Jesus in his ministry makes it easier to understand the true nature of the infancy stories. They were written in the light of what Jesus became later on.

The ponderings of Mary do not interfere with the joy of the birth. New life is a joyous event, to be shared as well as enjoyed. The ultimate significance of the birth of one to become famous is not felt until the benefits of that famous one are made real in one's life. The birth that is most important is the birth of Christ in one's heart. At Christmastime we sing, "Be born in us today." That transforms an obscure event in history into a salvation event for us.

Helping Adults Become Involved

Preparing to Teach

This lesson follows the scripture closely. The natural outline is as follows:

I. The structure of the birth story
II. The angel and the angels
III. The shepherds
IV. The ponderings of Mary

First, read carefully the section "As You Read the Scripture." Then read "The Main Question." Finally study "The Scripture and the Main Question," making some notes of the parts you with to emphasize.

It will be helpful if you review Matthew's infancy narrative as recorded in 1:18–2:23. Do not plan to discuss it in great detail, but pay special attention to its overall structure, its way of emphasizing the cosmic significance of Jesus' birth, and its special focus on the upper levels of society.

Introducing the Main Question

It is important in this lesson to have a good grasp of the scripture itself and its relation to Matthew's version, but one must be careful not to spend too much time on the problems raised by the text itself. The final ten minutes need to be carefully reserved for a discussion applying the event of the Lord's birth to one's life today.

A major problem introduced by this study is, "What really happened?" Since that is very technical, the teacher should shift the emphasis to the *meaning* of the event. Discuss briefly the points made in "The Main Question." Let the class members see the problem and encourage them to propose ways of handling it. This will give them a better chance of understanding the intent of the Gospel writers.

Developing the Lesson

I. The structure of the birth story
See how many class members are familiar with the structure of Matthew's story. Ask why they have (presumably) taken Luke's structure for granted.

Help them see that each Gospel writer has the same basic aims; how each one accomplishes these aims can be very different. See if the class can express these common aims in the infancy stories. Put them on a chalkboard or newsprint. They should include:

1. Accounting for Jesus' birth in Bethlehem
2. Show how Jesus was of the royal (Davidic) line
3. Acknowledging that Jesus grew up in Galilee, in an obscure village named Nazareth
4. Recognizing the cosmic significance of Jesus' birth

Next, get the class to explain how each Gospel writer met these aims. Even though this lesson is from Luke's Gospel, comparing it at these points with Matthew's Gospel will help greatly to get a perspective that does not get bogged down in purely historical questions that cannot be answered.

II. The angel and the angels

This is Luke's way of telling the reader how important this birth really was. It is Luke's parallel to Matthew's miraculous star.

Explain to the class that *angel* is a Greek word that means "messenger." It can be translated either way. This angel is not identified as the angel Gabriel of Luke's Annunciation story (1:26). It is simply identified as an "angel of the Lord" (as in Num. 22:22-35).

Many people in biblical times believed in an order of created supernatural beings called "angels." Many people today still believe in their existence. Their reality is not the main issue in this lesson. We accept the ancient belief and go beyond the question of actuality to seek the *meaning* of the story. That meaning is plain. Luke is telling the reader that heaven is aware of this birth—indeed has planned it and will use this special person for the salvation of the world.

III. The shepherds

Twentieth-century Americans are mostly out of touch with shepherd life. Explain that in ancient Israel the sheep grazed openly and therefore had to be always accompanied by a shepherd. They often wandered too far to be brought back "home" every night, so shepherds often spent the night with their sheep.

Point out the lowly status of the shepherds. They were the least educated, least influential members of society. This class of persons was of special concern to the author of Luke's Gospel. It was entirely appropriate for Luke to include shepherds in the birth story of Jesus. As Luke has already stated, in the "Magnificat" of Mary (Luke 1:46-55), the aims of God to be carried out by the unborn child she is carrying include

> He has brought down the powerful from their thrones,
>   and lifted up the lowly;
> he has filled the hungry with good things,
>   and sent the rich away empty.

Ask the class to suggest how this emphasis on the lowly, in the Magnificat as well as in the version of the Beatitudes in Luke, relates to the shepherd theme in Luke's infancy story.

IV. The ponderings of Mary

It may be of concern to the class to learn that Mary was not a staunch supporter of the ministry of Jesus. Ask the class how that affects their understanding of the infancy story. Then tell them that Mary and Jesus' brother did become disciples after the Resurrection.

Helping Class Members Act

Divide the class into small groups of three or four for a brief (five-minute) discussion on the question, when did Jesus become *your* Lord? Explain that the purpose is not to embarrass anyone, but to reflect on how long it sometimes takes to recognize Jesus as Lord. Do not ask for any reports to the larger class. Close the class period by looking ahead to the next lesson.

Preparing for Next Sunday

What does acceptance of Jesus as Lord mean for one's daily life? The final lesson in this unit reflects on the temptations that come with Jesus' call, and how that can instruct us.

The First Christmas Pageant

William H. Willimon and Patricia P. Willimon

And he came to her and said, "Greetings, favored one! The Lord is with you! (Luke 1:28)

There is a little book that has become the major part of our family's Christmas reading-aloud repertoire—Barbara Robinson's delightful *Best Christmas Pageant Ever*. It is the uproarious, irreverent, deeply moving account of an unforgettable Christmas pageant at Second Presbyterian Church in which the chief culprits were "the Horrible Herdmans," who were absolutely the worst kids in the history of the world. They lied and stole and smoked cigars (even the girls) and talked dirty and hit little kids and cursed their teachers and took the name of the Lord in vain and set fire to Fred Shoemaker's old broken-down toolhouse.

What the Herdmans—Claude, Leroy, Ralph, Imogene, Ollie, and Gladys—do to the Nativity is a story that you must read for yourself.

My theory is this: you may never understand the Christmas story until you have seen it done (or undone) as only the kindergarten-church school classes can do it. You know how we usually conceive of the Nativity. In our hands, the people in the first Christmas come out looking as religious and inspired as the participants in the annual Perry Como Christmas Show.

But the disarming thing about children's Christmas pageants is that they never seem to work that way. No matter how fine the bathrobes or how professional the makeup, or how great the quantity of hay upon the stage, something invariably goes wrong. Mary, Joseph, and the rest of the cast never seem to look as dignified, as pious, or as sure of themselves as they do on Christmas greeting cards. The shepherds usually act as confused and dumbfounded as the sheep they are supposed to be watching over.

The wise men may look overdressed but rarely do they look overwise.

But last year, as I watched the children at my church giggle and stumble their way through the Incarnation, it occurred to me that this was exactly how Matthew and Luke were trying to tell us that it happened on that very first Christmas.

It was not as tied down and religious and neat as we like to tell it. Whatever that Advent was, it all must have been a little confusing, and unnerving, and even a little ridiculous. For it had to do with God—Lord of Lords, King of Kings, Suffering Servant, Prince of Peace—becoming flesh and dwelling among us. There has got to be something unnerving about that.

I venture that Mary did not look much like the queen of heaven that night in Bethlehem. I venture, with Luther, that she looked more like a rather confused, bewildered teen-ager from your church youth group who was about to giggle in her nervousness and had not the slightest notion of what to do with a baby or what her next line was supposed to be. And Joseph, if he had any feelings at all, must have felt embarrassed. After all, he was in an embarrassing situation. The shepherds, despite all that talk about "fear not," were as scared as you or I would be if a similar thing happened to us while we were at work.

This is how God is always with us. This is Emmanuel. We—like Mary, like Joseph, like the others—are busy at home minding our own business, falling in love, getting engaged, making plans, paying taxes, complaining about the government, entertaining strange relatives from the East bearing perfume, plodding through the everydayness of our lives in backwater towns; and then God chooses us to reveal something of himself to the world, to run some errand, perform some act of love through us. And we, whether we really like it or not, or have the experience or ability or understanding, get pushed onto the stage of history to act out our parts with stage fright, filling roles that are too big for us, wondering what the next line will be, doing our best to do what he wants us to do even when we are not sure why he wants us to play the part.

This is Emmanuel.

If by chance some winged, angelic messenger from God should appear to us this season, whether it be the angel Gabriel or an angel like most of the ones we see this time of year, with a median age of eight years, wearing an old bedsheet over tennis shoes and Levis, topped with tinseled halo and cardboard wings, I think that angel's word from the Lord would be the same as those first words that the angel spoke to Mary:

"Greetings, favored one!/the Lord is with you."

And with you, and you, and you. . . .

Choose to Serve

Background Scripture: Luke 3:21-22; 4:1-15

The Main Question

Life is full of alternative paths. Choices are always before us. Sometimes we have a clear image of a long-range goal and can see when some paths lead us off-track. Some of these by-ways are healthy, temporary diversions. Others are destructive of our long-range goals while appearing desirable and enjoyable. These destructive diversions would be classed as *temptations*. Some attractive and pleasurable paths are actually temptations that divert us from a chosen life path. How can we recognize and deal with these temptations?

Other persons have no clearly chosen long-range goal for their lives. For them, there are too many alternative paths from which to choose. With no objective to work toward, these choices take on a different importance. These persons must be evaluated according to their own value-systems. Temptation now is not what diverts us from our goal, but any choice that is lower in our scale of values than another higher choice. Why would one deliberately choose a lower option? Because it offers some kind of pleasure or reward that is preferred to the benefits of a higher option.

This lesson is about life's temptations. How do we recognize them? How do we handle them? Clues will come from a study of the temptations of Jesus as reported in Luke's Gospel. In this experience of Jesus we will be able to clarify the role of willpower and of evil impulses. We can choose some authoritative person to help us with temptations, and we can learn from our past experiences. We can also see a little (at least) of the future that lies ahead of each optional choice, and we can increase our awareness of the ever-present Holy Spirit to guide us into the greater goal and the higher choice.

Selected Scripture

King James Version

Luke 4:1-15

1 And Jesus being full of the Holy Ghost returned from Jordan, and was led by the Spirit into the wilderness,

2 Being forty days tempted of the devil. And in those days he did eat nothing: and when they were ended, he afterward hungered.

3 And the devil said unto him, If thou be the Son of God, command this stone that it be made bread.

4 And Jesus answered him, saying, It is written, That man shall not live

New Revised Standard Version

Luke 4:1-15

1 Jesus, full of the Holy Spirit, returned from the Jordan and was led by the Spirit in the wilderness, 2 where for forty days he was tempted by the devil. He ate nothing at all during those days, and when they were over, he was famished. 3 The devil said to him, "If you are the Son of God, command this stone to become a loaf of bread." 4 Jesus answered him, "It is written, 'One does not live by bread alone.' "

by bread alone, but by every word of God.

5 And the devil, taking him up into an high mountain, shewed unto him all the kingdoms of the world in a moment of time.

6 And the devil said unto him, All this power will I give thee, and the glory of them: for that is delivered unto me; and to whomsoever I will I give it.

7 If thou therefore wilt worship me, all shall be thine.

8 And Jesus answered and said unto him, Get thee behind me, Satan: for it is written, Thou shalt worship the Lord thy God, and him only shalt thou serve.

9 And he brought him to Jerusalem, and set him on a pinnacle of the temple, and said unto him, If thou be the Son of God, cast thyself down from hence:

10 For it is written, He shall give his angels charge over thee, to keep thee:

11 And in their hands they shall bear thee up, lest at any time thou dash thy foot against a stone.

12 And Jesus answering said unto him, It is said, Thou shalt not tempt the Lord thy God.

13 And when the devil had ended all the temptation, he departed from him for a season.

14 And Jesus returned in the power of the Spirit into Galilee: and there went out a fame of him through all the region round about.

15 And he taught in their synagogues, being glorified of all.

5 Then the devil led him up and showed him in an instant all the kingdoms of the world. 6 And the devil said to him, "To you I will give their glory and all this authority; for it has been given over to me, and I give it to anyone I please. 7 If you, then, will worship me, it will all be yours." 8 Jesus answered him, "It is written,
'Worship the Lord your God,
and serve only him.' "

9 Then the devil took him to Jerusalem, and placed him on the pinnacle of the temple, saying to him, "If you are the Son of God, throw yourself down from here, 10 for it is written,
'He will command his angels concerning you,
   to protect you,'
11 and
'On their hands they will bear you up,
   so that you will not dash your foot against a stone.' "
12 Jesus answered him, "It is said, 'Do not put the Lord your God to the test.' " 13 When the devil had finished every test, he departed from him until an opportune time.

14 Then Jesus, filled with the power of the Spirit, returned to Galilee, and a report about him spread through all the surrounding country. 15 He began to teach· in their synagogues and was praised by everyone.

Key Verse: **And Jesus answered and said unto him, Get thee behind me, Satan: for it is written, Thou shalt worship the Lord thy God, and him only shalt thou serve. Luke 4:8**

Key Verse: **Jesus answered him, "It is written, 'Worship the Lord your God, and serve only him.' " Luke 4:8**

SECOND QUARTER

As You Read the Scripture

Each of the first three Gospels reports that Jesus was tempted by the devil immediately following his baptism. In the earliest Gospel, Mark, Jesus' temptation is very briefly reported (Mark 1:12-13). Luke and Matthew have another account, much more detailed, which expands the account in Mark. Note that Luke fails to harmonize completely what he took from Mark and what he added to it. Did the temptations occur during the forty-day period (as Mark reports and Luke preserves) or did Jesus fast for forty days and then experience the temptations (as Luke's additional material reports)?

Luke 4:1. Luke apparently understands Jesus as led by the Holy Spirit within him, whereas Mark (and Matthew?) seems to think of the Spirit as an external force that "drove" him into the wilderness. "The wilderness" was the desert land adjacent to the Jordan valley. Scripture is not specific enough for us to know the location of the baptism.

Verse 2. The first part of the verse follows Mark and thinks of the temptations as occurring during the forty days. The second part has a forty-day fast preceding the first temptation.

Verse 3. The first temptation, to turn stones into bread, may have been a temptation for Jesus to relieve his own hunger. We could also understand it as a temptation to have a ministry that focused on feeding the hungry. The devil prefaced this temptation with "If you are the Son of God," making the temptation a test of his divine powers.

Verse 4. Jesus refused this test by quoting scripture (Deuteronomy 8:3). His ministry would go beyond meeting physical needs.

Verse 5. When the devil showed Jesus all the kingdoms of the world "in an instant," we should probably understand this as a visionary experience. Luke omitted the "very high mountain" of Matthew 4:8, which seems to assume a literal understanding.

Verses 6-7. Now the devil offered to give all these kingdoms to Jesus if Jesus would only worship the devil. This reflects the belief of early Christians that the devil had control of this world (see John 12:31; 14:30; 16:11 and 1 Corinthians 2:8; 2 Corinthians 4:4; and Colossians 2:15). These kingdoms, therefore, were his to give away. This rule of the devil, of course, was temporary. The early Christians believed that God would soon defeat the devil and be the supreme ruler once again.

Verse 8. Jesus refused this temptation also, again quoting from scripture (Deuteronomy 6:13).

Verses 9-11. Now the devil himself quoted scripture, tempting Jesus to test the promise of God to protect him in the kind of spectacular jumping stunt that the devil proposed. "The pinnacle of the temple" is probably the best translation of a Greek phrase which is not clear. The scripture the devil quoted is Psalm 91:11-12.

Verse 12. Jesus refused again, citing Deuteronomy 6:16.

Verse 13. The text leaves the door open for the devil to tempt Jesus again (see 22:31).

Verses 14-15. "Returned to Galilee" indicates a baptismal site somewhere in the part of the Jordan that was south of Galilee. Mark's author now introduces the reader to Jesus' Galilean ministry.

The Scripture and the Main Question

Being Human Means Being Tempted

A central Christian belief is that Jesus was both fully divine and fully human. The church took several centuries to define this doctrine clearly, and it has strongly affirmed it ever since. The real humanity of Jesus necessarily implies that he experienced temptation. The author of Hebrews had no problem with this and gave us our most emphatic statement about it (Heb. 2:17-18; 4:15). This in turn raises a question about the sinlessness of Jesus. This is a doctrine unknown to Luke (see Luke 18:19, which repeats a saying taken from Mark 10:18). That Jesus "although he was a Son [of God] learned obedience" (Heb. 5:8) clearly reflects a different view of Jesus from the doctrine of his sinlessness. (Is the declaration of sinlessness in Heb. 4:15 a later scribal addition?)

Since we are human, we too have temptations. Some of our temptations are exemplified by those of Jesus. Each temptation involves choices and each set of choices involves temptation. We will study the types of temptation Jesus experienced and relate them to our lives.

Materialistic Temptations

We all need enough food, shelter, and clothing so they do not demand attention or distract us from a life of service to others. When Jesus quoted Deuteronomy and affirmed "one does not live by bread alone," he was affirming that life was more than these basics. What, for example?

Learning is a lifelong adventure. Creating works of art in all its forms is important. Developing close personal relationships is important also. As one develops a sensitivity to the pain and hardships of others, one becomes active in helping them. We protect the welfare of future generations by being involved in earth-stewardship activities. All of these examples go beyond caring for one's own food, shelter, and clothing. "Life is more than food" (Luke 12:23).

But temptations abound, and we make "the basics" more and more luxurious. We are tempted to acquire the financial means for "gourmet" eating and for more clothes than we need, and luxury clothes at that. This extends to "shelter" as well. Some of the rich live in palaces or mansions far beyond their basic need for comfortable shelter.

To be able to have this luxury food, clothing, and living quarters requires devoting one's time to the acquisition of money. The temptation to be materialistic is constantly with us.

Setting Worship Priorities

The second temptation for Jesus was to worship wrongly. If he would only worship "the god of this world" (2 Cor. 4:4), he could have unlimited possessions. The same temptation faces many of us. We can believe that if we "sell out" to those who have money and power, we can have riches. It is a temptation closely related to the first one.

That to which we give our fullest attention is what we really "worship." Jesus, in his later ministry, taught us the right priority. When discussing our basic needs, Jesus urged his followers to "strive for his [God's] kingdom, and these things [the basics] will be given to you as well" (Luke 12:31). Putting first things first is an important principle. He went on to note that "where your treasure is, there your heart will be also" (12:34). Jesus urged his followers to put their treasure "in heaven, where no thief comes near and no moth destroys" (12:33).

It isn't that we actually "worship" the wrong things; we don't do that. But a case can be made for regarding those things to which we are most devoted as our real worship object. This may be the state; the work we're doing; any special "cause"; the pursuit of money, power, or fame; our family; the institutional church; or any of many other things. It isn't that these are, in themselves, bad. It's just that they really belong in second place to our devotion to God and God's kingdom. Jesus refused to worship anything except God.

Denying Responsibility

Jesus' third temptation was to depend on God to do it all. The devil wanted Jesus to test God's promise to protect his Messiah by jumping off the top (probably) of the Temple. Surely God would send angels to save him. Jesus refused to put God to such a test, and so should we.

God has given us humans the ability to think and to work. It was not part of the providence of God to give us all the answers. We see problems and work together to find solutions. We have made much progress over the course of human history.

Suppose, for example, we face the growing world population. This planet has a great variety of life forms. All of them are interrelated and interdependent. This includes plants, animals, insects, and all the sea creatures, besides humans. We now know that all life is one huge ecosystem. Human overpopulation threatens this system. What can we do? One temptation is to do nothing. "Nature will take care of itself." God will keep the population down by natural disasters and such. Or, to the contrary, we can be inspired by God to take steps to control human population and thus protect all of this planet's life forms.

The temptation to "leave it to God" is a common one. It is not disloyal to God to affirm our responsibilities. It is not that we should forget God and do it all ourselves. God is with us when we exercise our responsibility. God depends on us as much as we depend on God.

The New Life for Jesus

Our study passage for this lesson ends with an editorial summary of the next step in the story of Jesus. Having experienced the temptations and overcome them, Jesus chose his real life's work. "Filled with the power of the Spirit," he now turned to the work of teaching, preaching, and healing the people of Galilee. That story continues in the next lesson.

Helping Adults Become Involved

Preparing to Teach

This lesson completes the unit on the coming of our Lord. His call to ministry led to his final preparation, his temptation. This lesson focuses on *how the temptations of Jesus are related to some of our temptations today.*

The lesson falls naturally into five parts:

I.   Humanity means temptation
II.   Materialistic temptations
III.   Setting worship priorities
IV.   Denying responsibility
V.   The new life for Jesus

Study first the section "As You Read the Scripture." Then read "The Main Question" to begin to make the links between Jesus' temptations and ours today. Then study carefully "The Scripture and the Main Question," making special note of the ideas that your class may be most interested in discussing. It will be helpful background to refresh your familiarity with Matthew 6:19-34 and Luke 12:22-34, as well as Matthew 25:14-30 and Luke 19:11-27.

Introducing the Main Question

Challenge the class to express some of their temptations. Make no attempt yet to relate them to the temptations of Jesus. Make a list of what the class identifies as their current temptations either on newsprint or a chalkboard. Concentrate on setting a variety of temptations before the class. Do not encourage a discussion on how one might handle (overcome) any of these. That will be appropriate in later discussions today.

Next, read the whole scripture for this lesson to make the class familiar with the larger scene. Perhaps the reader should be a class member, reading from the New Revised Standard Version if this is available.

Then, tell the class that the study will make connections between Jesus' temptations and ours.

Developing the Lesson

I. Humanity means temptation

Introduce first the orthodox Christian doctrine of the full humanity of Jesus. He was not simply God in human form, but a real human being (and, of course, at the same time, fully divine, but this lesson deals with his humanity). Some persons in the class may be somewhat uncomfortable with this doctrine, but be careful not to get bogged down on this point. It will be sufficient just to remind everyone what orthodox Christians believe.

It may help to call the class's attention to the plain language about Jesus' humanity in Hebrews (2:17-18; 4:15; 5:8-9). Ask the class's opinion about whether one could be fully human and never experience guilt.

II. Materialistic temptations

Ask the class to give examples from their own observations of persons yielding to the temptation to build treasures on earth. The parable of the rich fool (Luke 12:16-21) will be appropriate for this.

How does one draw the line between what we need and having too much? Is *all* luxury forbidden to a disciple of Jesus? Are we willing to hear Luke 12:33 and obey it? Let the class attempt some answers.

When Jesus refused to turn stones into bread, his rebuke to the devil was "One does not live by bread alone." There are higher values to cultivate than material possessions. One should not understand Jesus here as meaning that a ministry to the world's hungry people is not appropriate. The whole pattern of his own ministry was to help people with their basic needs. He never, however, encouraged materialistic accumulations. Instead, he said, "It is easier for a camel to go through the eye of a needle than for someone who is rich to enter the kingdom of God" (Luke 18:25).

III. Setting worship priorities

Start a class discussion on what some people *really* worship. Is it agreeable to say we worship what we put first? See if anyone in the class can remember what Jesus told us to put first. If this does not come out of the class, then remind them that Jesus said to put the kingdom of God first. Luke records this in 12:31, but Matthew's way of reporting it is probably better known (Matt. 6:33), and in the King James Version. Share that with the class.

Ask the class how they would find out what they (individually) really worship. Is money a good indicator? If not, why not?

Get the class's reaction to some of these questions: Do some persons worship money? Power? The nation? Some special cause? The church? Ask for other specific examples.

Open a discussion on what it means to "strive first for the kingdom of God and his righteousness." Does it mean something specific enough to be helpful? Share ideas; there is no "right answer."

IV. Denying responsibility

Christianity is not fatalistic. Fatalism is a pre-Christian belief that all things are controlled by powers outside ourselves. Even though many Christians believe this, it is nevertheless not a part of orthodox Christianity. Fatalism removes all human responsibility. "What will be, will be" is fatalism.

It is ironic that trusting God to take care of things undermines human endeavor. Trusting God should not cause us to become inactive, accepting the status quo as "the will of God."

Jesus, in this third temptation, refused to put God to the test. He may well have believed that God would miraculously rescue him from the natural consequences of a normally fatal jump, but he felt it was wrong to make God prove that such trust was correct.

We, too, may be tempted to leave it to God. We should never feel like our efforts are in vain. Have the class list examples of yielding to this kind of temptation. Try the overpopulation problem or ecological concerns on the class members and get their responses.

Helping Class Members Act

Ask class members to what do they give money? To what do they give their time? What makes them feel strongly? What tempts them the most? This kind of discussion can help each of them to reassess their priorities and make some changes.

Preparing for Next Sunday

The lesson next Sunday sets out the way Jesus thought of his purpose in life. His mission was a service mission. Close the lesson with a short exposition of how temptation is always with us as we participate in the mission of Jesus.

UNIT II: JESUS' MINISTRY IN GALILEE

FIVE LESSONS   JANUARY 2–30

Often history's most important events happen in out-of-the-way places. St. Francis began an entire reformation of the church in a little Italian hill town called Assisi. Rosa Parks gave birth to the American Civil Rights Movement by refusing to move to another seat in a bus in Selma, Alabama.

Luke says that Jesus' ministry began, of all places, in his hometown synagogue in Galilee. Far from the centers of culture and commerce, isolated from many major events of the day, Galilee may appear to be an odd place to begin a revolution. And yet, Luke said that Jesus chose Galilee as a place to begin his revolution.

Out in Galilee, he preached, taught his disciples, and healed the sick. Perhaps Galilee represented a quiet place apart that was conducive for reflection and slow, careful instruction, which discipleship demanded. Perhaps Jesus did not want his disciples to be distracted by the hustle and bustle of a metropolitan area.

We do not know exactly why Jesus chose Galilee. However do we know this: Most of us live our lives in out-of-the-way places like Galilee. Most of the times in which we live are not important by the world's standard of greatness. And yet, all of this unit's scripture from Luke reminds us—*Jesus meets us where we are, even in out-of-the-way places; he comes to us and calls us to follow him.*

LESSON 5   JANUARY 2

Mission to People

Background Scripture: Luke 4:16-28

The Main Question

What does it mean to be a Christian? Is there a distinctively Christian life-style?

Our basic clue comes from the life-style of our Lord. The portrayal of Jesus in the Gospel of Luke is definitely the portrayal of one who said, "I am among you as one who serves" (22:27). As "one who serves," Jesus was involved in many kinds of service. He ministered to the whole person, not merely to the spiritual needs of the people. In addition to his teaching and preaching, he healed the sick and cast out the demons that were possessing some people. He vigorously opposed injustice and all forms of hypocrisy. He was perceived by the Jewish authorities as a threat to their practices, and was finally put to death by the Romans because he was regarded as a political threat to their rule.

Twice in Luke's Gospel Jesus sent his disciples out on mission. First he

143

sent the Twelve out, telling them "to proclaim the kingdom of God and to heal" (9:2). Later he "appointed seventy others and sent them . . . to every town and place where he himself intended to go" (10:1). They "returned with joy, saying, 'Lord, in your name even the demons submit to us!' " (10:17).

The scene where Jesus' mission is most clearly defined, however, is the one where Jesus returned to "Nazareth, where he had been brought up" (4:16). On that occasion he read a famous oracle from the prophet Isaiah and announced that he was the one it was talking about. God had "anointed me to bring good news to the poor, . . . to proclaim release to the captives and recovery of sight to the blind, to let the oppressed go free" (4:18). Today's lesson considers the ways in which Jesus' mission to people is our model.

Selected Scripture

King James Version

Luke 4:16-28

16 And he came to Nazareth, where he had been brought up: and, as his custom was, he went into the synagogue on the sabbath day, and stood up for to read.

17 And there was delivered unto him the book of the prophet Esaias. And when he had opened the book, he found the place where it was written,

18 The Spirit of the Lord is upon me, because he hath anointed me to preach the gospel to the poor; he hath sent me to heal the broken-hearted, to preach deliverance to the captives, and recovering of sight to the blind, to set at liberty them that are bruised.

19 To preach the acceptable year of the Lord.

20 And he closed the book, and he gave it again to the minister, and sat down. And the eyes of all them that were in the synagogue were fastened on him.

21 And he began to say unto them, This day is this scripture fulfilled in your ears.

22 And all bare him witness and wondered at the gracious words which proceeded out of his mouth. And they said, Is not this Joseph's son?

23 And he said unto them, Ye will

New Revised Standard Version

Luke 4:16-28

16 When he came to Nazareth, where he had been brought up, he went to the synagogue on the sabbath day, as was his custom. He stood up to read, 17 and the scroll of the prophet Isaiah was given to him. He unrolled the scroll and found the place where it was written:
18 "The Spirit of the Lord is upon me,
    because he has anointed me
        to bring good news to the poor.
He has sent me to proclaim release
        to the captives
    and recovery of sight to the blind,
        to let the oppressed go free,
19 to proclaim the year of the Lord's favor."

20 And he rolled up the scroll, gave it back to the attendant, and sat down. The eyes of all in the synagogue were fixed on him. 21 Then he began to say to them, "Today this scripture has been fulfilled in your hearing." 22 All spoke well of him and were amazed at the gracious words that came from his mouth. They said, "Is not this Joseph's son?" 23 He said to them, "Doubtless you will quote to me this proverb, 'Doctor, cure yourself!' And you will say, 'Do here also in your hometown the

surely say unto me this proverb,
Physician, heal thyself: whatsoever
we have heard done in Capernaum,
do also here in thy country.

24 And he said, Verily I say unto
you, No prophet is accepted in his
own country.

25 But I tell you of a truth, many
widows were in Israel in the days of
Elias, when the heaven was shut up
three years and six months, when
great famine was throughout all the
land;

26 But unto none of them was
Elias sent, save unto Sarepta, a city
of Sidon, unto a woman that was a
widow.

27 And many lepers were in Israel
in the time of Eliseus the prophet;
and none of them was cleansed, saving Naaman the Syrian.

28 And all they in the synagogue,
when they heard these things, were
filled with wrath.

things that we have heard you did at
Capernaum.' " 24 And he said,
"Truly I tell you, no prophet is
accepted in the prophet's hometown. 25 But the truth is, there were
many widows in Israel in the time of
Elijah, when the heaven was shut up
three years and six months, and
there was a severe famine over all
the land; 26 yet Elijah was sent to
none of them except to a widow at
Zarephath in Sidon. 27 There were
also many lepers in Israel in the time
of the prophet Elisha, and none of
them was cleansed except Naaman
the Syrian." 28 When they heard
this, all in the synagogue were filled
with rage.

Key Verses: **The Spirit of the Lord
is upon me, because he hath
anointed me to preach the gospel to
the poor; he hath sent me to heal
the brokenhearted, to preach deliverance to the captives, and recovering of sight to the blind, to set at liberty them that are bruised, to preach
the acceptable year of the Lord.
Luke 4:18-19**

Key Verses: **The Spirit of the Lord
is upon me, because he has anointed
me to bring good news to the poor.
He has sent me to proclaim release
to the captives and recovery of sight
to the blind, to let the oppressed go
free, to proclaim the year of the
Lord's favor. Luke 4:18-19**

As You Read the Scripture

Jesus' return to Nazareth is recorded in the first three Gospels. Matthew
follows Mark closely, but Luke's account seems to be an independent one.
Luke alone gives the Isaiah oracle that characterizes Jesus' mission to the
people.

Luke 4:16. "As was his custom" is an important part of Luke's emphasis on
the faithfulness of Jesus to his Jewish roots. This was not a special decision
on the part of Jesus to attend the synagogue on this particular sabbath; it was
his custom. The same emphasis, using the same phrase, is applied to Paul in
Acts 17:2.

Verse 17. Since Jesus had already become a well-publicized person (4:14-
15), it was probably not unusual that he would be invited to read from the
scripture. The sacred writings were in scroll form, so Jesus took the Isaiah
scroll and unrolled it until he came to the passage he wanted to read. He followed the accepted procedure, standing to read and sitting to preach (v. 20).

Verses 18-19. The oracle is in Isaiah 61:1-2*a*. It was quite an astounding claim for Jesus to make. The reference to being anointed by the Lord was at least a Messianic hint, and perhaps more than that. *Messiah* means "the anointed one." In Luke's view, however, the office of Messiah (Christ) was given to Jesus after his resurrection (Acts 2:36). We should probably understand this Nazareth event as reflecting the later status of Jesus, as also in the infancy narratives. The Isaiah text, however, functions well as an introduction to the main themes of Jesus' mission as portrayed in Luke. According to Luke his mission was mainly to the lower ranks of society.

Verse 22. The local response to Jesus' sermon (much abbreviated here) was favorable. Their surprise was that the one familiar to them only as "Joseph's son" had become such a praiseworthy person (4:14-15).

Verse 23. The response of Jesus to their approval is not what we would expect! Jesus anticipated their next move and accused them of wanting him to demonstrate "the things we have heard you did at Capernaum." Jesus chose Capernaum as his base of operations, and the townspeople in Nazareth had heard about his deeds there. Luke has not informed the reader about what these deeds were, but it is assumed that they are known. In Mark (6:1-6) and Matthew (13:53-58) Jesus' return to Nazareth is placed later in the story, making it easier for his fame to be known.

Verses 24-27. Having posed a question for the people of Nazareth, Jesus now answered it. He refused to do in his hometown what he did elsewhere. Luke's report of his refusal is a less specific statement than Mark's (Mark 6:4), omitting all reference to his family's rejection of him. Jesus then cites two stories from Israel's past to justify his refusal. In both Mark and Matthew Jesus does heal a few people there, but his work is hampered by their unbelief.

Verse 28. Now the townspeople reacted with "rage." We often react to a refusal just as they did.

The Scripture and the Main Question

Returning Home

Many persons have the experience of going away from home and then later returning. It is often a going away associated with going to college. Or it might be a military call, or a transfer in one's job. For whatever reason, the "going away, returning home" pattern is one familiar to many in our time.

Going away usually involves many new experiences, and experiences change a person. One seldom returns home unchanged. It is a somewhat different person that returns home.

Home is constantly changing also. In addition, the fresh perspective that one gets while away from home makes home seem different. One can't return to the home that was, because it is no more. "You can't go home again."

When Jesus returned to his hometown he was not the same person who left to be baptized. His baptismal experience and his temptation experience changed his life. In his new life he had already earned a considerable popularity. He left Nazareth known as a carpenter; he returned a popular preacher, teacher, and healer. His experience in returning is a lesson for us all.

The Service Mission

Upon his return he attended the synagogue on the Sabbath. He must have attended it many times before, but now he was a newly famous visitor. He used the occasion to inform the community of his new mission in life.

The oracle he read from Isaiah made his mission clear. Since he claimed to be its fulfillment, its contents described his mission. "The Spirit of the Lord" was upon him (remember his baptismal experience with the Spirit descending upon him). God had anointed him, meaning he was chosen to be (the future) Messiah. He was sent to proclaim good news to the poor. His ministry was a mission to all people, but especially to the ones neglected by the institutional religions of his time—the poor, the blind, the prisoners, and the oppressed.

This mission gets fuller expression in the life that followed this visit. As Luke unfolds the story, Jesus shows a noticeable concern for the "down and out." This is our clue for a Christian life-style. He encouraged his disciples to follow the path he blazed. He instructed them to preach, teach, and to heal the sick. His life-style was theirs too. It has become the model for Christians ever since.

Leaving home and then returning often gives us the opportunity to assess the home scene in a new way. With a new perspective we can observe its needs better. The needs of the poor people were not a principal concern of the religious institutions of Jesus' time. The same might well be said for our society today. It is time to be more sensitive to the needs of the poor and the oppressed, and to work at setting things right!

Initial Acceptance

To speak out boldly often gets approval, at first. Everyone admits the necessity of making changes. The needs of the poor are too obvious to deny, and who would like to be known as one who opposes helping the poor?

That initial acceptance is a common pattern. The "best people," in the "talk period," respond favorably to the changes needed. But when talk moves to action things are very different. Helping the poor means giving up some of what we have, and that's not so acceptable. Rescuing the oppressed means giving up some of our power and privileges, and that's not easy.

We can see this pattern in the story of Jesus returning to Nazareth. When Jesus made his startling announcement, "all spoke well of him" (4:22). But this initial approval did not last very long. When Jesus frustrated their hopes for special benefits, they turned on him and "were filled with rage" (4:28).

Rejection

The people of Nazareth not only rejected Jesus and his mission to serve people, but they tried to destroy him (see 4:29). How he was able to escape is not very clear (see 4:30). He resumed his ministry elsewhere.

The explanation offered in the Gospels is one that models the experience of many others who return home after establishing themselves elsewhere. Jesus quoted what may have been a proverbial saying when he said, "No prophet is accepted in the prophet's hometown" (4:24). The surprise of the townspeople was based on their familiarity with Jesus as a child and a young man. "Is not this Joseph's son?" (4:22), they asked.

It is the very familiarity of the hometown people with the earlier (non-famous) life of a native son or daughter that stands in the way of seeing him or her as famous. This pattern is a familiar one with all those who, like Jesus, have returned home. The famous one is known locally to be merely an ordinary person.

Many aspects of our society today reflect this same pattern. It is difficult for a parent, for example, to be recognized by his or her children as a real authority. A child may reject the idea of a wise parent only to accept it from a teacher or a book.

Many marriages exhibit the same pattern. One's spouse may have excellent solutions but these may not be authoritative until verified by some "authority." The spouse is too familiar to be an authority. What is an authority? Someone from out-of-town!

This rejection pattern based on over-familiarity is what we should expect in our mission. We will probably make more progress if we do not make our base in our hometown, or in our family, but in areas where we are the "out-of-towner," and thereby "authoritative." After all, as another half-true proverb puts it, "familiarity breeds contempt."

Let us not give up working for changes in our society because these changes are unpopular with those who are benefiting from the way things are now. The mission is "to bring good news to the poor," and "good news" goes beyond talking. The mission "to proclaim release to the captives" means to do whatever must be done to release them. The mission is to bring "recovery of sight to the blind." "The blind" represents the whole medical mission as well as the educational mission that sees blindness as ignorance and prejudice.

The mission "to let the oppressed go free" is a very difficult one. Money and power give the oppressors great strength. The oppressors and the oppressed are everywhere. Every community needs this mission. Oppression takes many forms—racism, sexism, classism, ageism, economic tyranny. The Church of Jesus Christ has a mighty job to do. Christianity is not a religion that limits itself to spiritual concerns. Its path was laid out by Jesus.

Helping Adults Become Involved

Preparing to Teach

Read "The Main Question" and plan to say it in your own words. Write out your own formulation to make sure it is precise and exact.

Next review the story in Luke about Jesus' return to Nazareth. It will strengthen your teaching base to read the other tradition of this event, found in Mark 6:1-6 and Matthew 13:53-58. The Markan tradition (copied in Matthew), has several interesting elements not in the Lukan tradition. It is not necessary to include these in the class discussion, but, as the teacher, you should be familiar with both versions in case someone in the class calls attention to the differences, or comments in such a way as to confuse the two accounts.

Make yourself familiar with the section "As You Read the Scripture." The comments there are primarily for the teacher's enrichment, rather than material to be formally taught.

The lesson material falls into four sections:

        I. Returning home
       II. The service mission
     III. Initial acceptance
     IV. Rejection

Introducing the Main Question

Be sure the story about Jesus' return to Nazareth doesn't become the main lesson. The lesson uses the story to get into life today. The focus of this lesson is on how *Jesus' mission gives us the model for our mission.* As preparation for the lesson proper, this study of Jesus' return should not occupy more than about one-third of the class time.

Developing the Lesson

I. Returning home

Ask class members to share any personal experiences that illustrate the "returning home" situation. Ask for "going away" experiences that made important changes in one's perspective on life in general. See what comments the class can make on how "hometown" changes in one's absence. Has anyone returned home to find greater acceptance than before?

II. The service mission

Ask the class members to name some specific needs in their own local community. Are there any who are poor? What responsibility does the church have to help them? Is that mostly a political problem? Have we in the church turned over the relief of the poor to our government? Stimulate a discussion on the poverty problem and its solution. Should we be resigned to the idea that there is no solution; "you always have the poor with you" (John 12:8)? This is not a saying which Luke preserves.

The solution to the poverty problem is not easy. Do not expect to solve it in your class discussion. It is important, nonetheless, to discuss it and to keep Christians sensitive to it.

Move from this discussion to the "release to the captive" aspects of the mission. Get the class to suggest meanings for our time. Who are the captives of our time and in our communities? Make a list of those things we are captured by and need freedom from. If no one suggests anything, you can "prime the pump." How about tobacco? How about TV? Then add their suggestions and soon it will be apparent that this is not out of date at all. As Paul put it so well in Galatians, "For freedom Christ has set us free" (5:1). What kind of captivity was in Paul's mind? Does it still exist? The gospel of grace promises freedom from all captivities?

Move next to "recovery of sight to the blind." What is the church's role in ministering to health needs? Have we turned all of that over to the medical world? Tell the class that next week's lesson will deal more fully with this part of the mission. In the carefully limited time you allot to this, however, be sure to broaden "the blind" beyond health matters, and note that the mission is concerned with other kinds of blindness.

Finally, turn to the phrase, "to let the oppressed go free." The word translated "oppressed" is a strong word that literally means "to break into pieces," as in Mark 14:3. It has a more figurative meaning in Isaiah's oracle, meaning "downtrodden" or "broken victims." The translation "oppressed" catches well its meaning. Ask the class to identify the oppressed of their own community. Is it Blacks? Hispanics? Native Americans? Women? The elderly? Once you have agreed on some examples, then raise the question of how our mission relates to these oppressed persons.

III. Initial acceptance

If the class has officially acknowledged the scope of the mission that the discussion has opened up, then they have illustrated the initial acceptance stage of the mission. These are included in what the church ought to be doing. This is not, of course, the total list of mission tasks, but only the ones pointed up in this lesson.

IV. Rejection

If the class illustrates the initial acceptance stage, does it also illustrate the rejection stage? This part of the lesson can be embarrassing. Simply ask how deeply involved your church, and your class in particular, has gone beyond the talk stage to the action stage. Or have they rejected this (or some of it) by their lack of any action?

Helping Class Members Act

See if anyone in your class can come up with any way to be actually (personally) involved in the larger mission of the church. What good news does your class have for the poor of the community? What can one do to be active in the freedom mission? What can one do for the "blind"—any kind of blindness? What can one do to root out oppression? Select some actual possible action and challenge the class to adopt it. It can be class action, individual action, or both.

Planning for Next Sunday

The next lesson expands on the healing mission of the church, as modeled by the ministry of Jesus. To prepare for this, ask two members of the class to discuss this with two physicians and bring a report to class. Ask two more members to discuss this with two "spiritual healers" of any kind, including Christian Science practitioners and/or "faith healers." Solicit volunteers to report on books on this subject as these might be available. Ask another class member to collect some experiences of unusual healings from anyone who has experienced this.

Called to Care

Background Scripture: Luke 4:31-43

The Main Question

How should the followers of Jesus be involved in the illnesses of persons? The answer is quite clear if we think only of spiritual illness. We are all aware that some persons have a religion that is "sick," even if we can't define "sick" precisely. They are spiritually ill. Christians are certainly involved in a mission to cure spiritual illnesses. But what about mental illness? Is the distinction between "spiritual" and "mental" always clear? Some forms of insanity are related to religious concepts.

There are also emotional illnesses. Are these a separate category, or do they belong with mental illness? Can we consider all non-physical illnesses as related forms of spiritual illness? Christians who follow the example of Jesus would certainly include all these ministries in their mission.

But isn't there a physical dimension to all of these? Is all illness related somehow to the body—its glands, nerves, and brain? Some would say that we cannot separate these so neatly. Bodily conditions affect our minds and emotions, at least, and our minds and emotions affect our bodies. Is the same true for our spiritual life? Does our body affect it? Does our spirituality affect our bodily health?

The account of Jesus in Luke (and in Mark and Matthew) would seem to be in full agreement with the "holistic" approach popular today. Jesus ministered to the whole person, not simply to their spiritual life. Shouldn't we, as followers of Jesus, minister to the whole person also?

Selected Scripture

King James Version

Luke 4:31-43

31 And [Jesus] came down to Capernaum, a city of Galilee, and taught them on the sabbath days.

32 And they were astonished at his doctrine: for his word was with power.

33 And in the synagogue there was a man, which had a spirit of an unclean devil, and cried out with a loud voice,

34 Saying, Let us alone; what have we to do with thee, thou Jesus of Nazareth? art thou come to destroy us? I know thee who thou art; the Holy One of God.

35 And Jesus rebuked him, saying, Hold thy peace, and come out of

New Revised Standard Version

Luke 4:31-43

31 He went down to Capernaum, a city in Galilee, and was teaching them on the sabbath. 32 They were astounded at his teaching, because he spoke with authority. 33 In the synagogue there was a man who had the spirit of an unclean demon, and he cried out with a loud voice, 34 "Let us alone! What have you to do with us, Jesus of Nazareth? Have you come to destroy us? I know who you are, the Holy One of God." 35 But Jesus rebuked him, saying, "Be silent, and come out of him!" When the demon had thrown him down before them, he came out of him

him. And when the devil had thrown him in the midst, he came out of him, and hurt him not.

36 And they were all amazed, and spake among themselves, saying, What a word is this! for with authority and power he commandeth the unclean spirits, and they come out.

37 And the fame of him went out into every place of the country round about.

38 And he arose out of the synagogue, and entered into Simon's house. And Simon's wife's mother was taken with a great fever; and they besought him for her.

39 And he stood over her, and rebuked the fever; and it left her: and immediately she arose and ministered unto them.

40 Now when the sun was setting, all they that had any sick with divers diseases brought them unto him; and he laid his hands on every one of them, and healed them.

41 And devils also came out of many, crying out, and saying, Thou art Christ the Son of God. And he rebuking them suffered them not to speak: for they knew that he was Christ.

42 And when it was day, he departed and went into a desert place: and the people sought him, and came unto him, and stayed him, that he should not depart from them.

43 And he said unto them, I must preach the kingdom of God to other cities also: for therefore am I sent.

without having done him any harm. 36 They were all amazed and kept saying to one another, "What kind of utterance is this? For with authority and power he commands the unclean spirits, and out they come!" 37 And a report about him began to reach every place in the region.

38 After leaving the synagogue he entered Simon's house. Now Simon's mother-in-law was suffering from a high fever, and they asked him about her. 39 Then he stood over her and rebuked the fever, and it left her. Immediately she got up and began to serve them.

40 As the sun was setting, all those who had any who were sick with various kinds of disease brought them to him; and he laid his hands on each of them and cured them. 41 Demons also came out of many, shouting, "You are the Son of God!" But he rebuked them and would not allow them to speak, because they knew that he was the Messiah.

42 At daybreak he departed and went into a deserted place. And the crowds were looking for him; and when they reached him, they wanted to prevent him from leaving them. 43 But he said to them, "I must proclaim the good news of the kingdom of God to the other cities also; for I was sent for this purpose."

Key Verse: **Now when the sun was setting, all they that had any sick with divers diseases brought them unto him; and he laid his hands on every one of them, and healed them. Luke 4:40**

Key Verse: **All those who had any who were sick with various kinds of diseases brought them to him; and he laid his hands on each of them and cured them. Luke 4:40**

As You Read the Scripture

Luke 4:31. Luke explains to his Gentile readers that Capernaum is "a city of Galilee." It was situated on the north end of the Sea of Galilee and was the home of Simon. Jesus made it his home also after he left Nazareth.

Verse 32. The astonishment of the people was caused by the manner in which Jesus taught. In contrast to the scribes (who continually quoted Moses as their authority), Jesus spoke "out of himself," a word in Greek usually translated as "with authority."

Verse 33. The belief in demon possession was common in Jesus' time. It was believed to be the cause of many illnesses, including what we would now call mental and emotional illnesses. Most modern persons have adopted other theories.

Verse 34. Since demons (evil spirits) were supernatural, they recognized Jesus as supernatural also. The phrase "Let us alone" is a cry of indignant surprise, used only here in the New Testament. They affirm a main point in the first three Gospels, that Jesus came to "destroy" the evil spirits that hurt persons. We should note carefully that Jesus in the Gospel of John does not cast out any demons. This Gospel has a different understanding of the mission of Jesus.

Verse 35. The command of Jesus is first to silence the demon with the imperative "Be silent" (more literally, "be muzzled"). It is one of many places where Jesus tries to keep his true identity a secret. The scholars call this "the Messianic Secret" theme. It originated in Mark, where it is important for the Gospel story. Luke retains it and explains it as part of the divine plan (for example, 9:45). Matthew formally retains it, but at the same time refutes it (for example, 14:33).

Verse 36. Jesus' power to heal those possessed by evil spirits excites wonder and amazement among the people.

Verse 37. Word about Jesus as a healer spread rapidly throughout Galilee.

Verse 38. Simon is abruptly introduced here. In Mark's earlier account (Luke's source) this story is preceded by an account of the call of the first four disciples, one of whom was Simon. Luke defers this call of Simon and the three others to a later point in his story, making Simon's appearance here a bit awkward. "Who is he?" the reader of Luke might well ask.

The mention of Simon's house indicates that this disciple made his residence in Capernaum. An old tradition has identified Simon's house, currently shown to visitors of Capernaum. The mention of Simon's "mother-in-law" tells us clearly that he was married. Luke emphasizes her illness, adding to Mark's "fever" (Mark 1:30) the adjective "high."

Verse 39. The high fever is treated as subject to Jesus' commands, much as an evil spirit, but it is not personified.

Verses 40-41. This is an editorial summary of Jesus' activity as a healer. Note that the illnesses in verse 40 are called "diseases" and are clearly different from the demons of verse 41. Note also the recurrence of the "Messianic Secret" theme.

The Scripture and the Main Question

Jesus and Evil Spirits

It is important to know the larger background of the stories about Jesus casting out evil spirits, or demons. These stories are part of a worldview that was popular among the people of Jesus' time. This worldview assumed that we humans are living on the battlefield of a great cosmic war between God and his adversary, Satan (see Rev. 12:7-12 for a progress report on how the war is going). God is winning the war, and has already driven Satan and his angelic army out of heaven. Satan and his "unclean spirits" have been thrown down to the earth where they are making their final stand (see Luke 10:18). The war will soon be over, and then the present evil age, which is ruled over by Satan (see 2 Cor. 4:4; Col. 2:15; John 12:31; 14:30, 16:11), will be replaced by the "Kingdom of God." Jesus proclaimed that "the Kingdom of God is at hand" and showed in his person the victory of God over Satan and his demons. The first three Gospels, following this worldview, tell how Jesus overpowered the demons and cast them out.

This worldview is still popular in some Christian circles. It is important to note, however, that this conception of the world is not the only one in the Bible. Some Christians of the Apostolic Age understood Jesus in a different cosmic setting. This is the case with the Gospel of John, where there is no cosmic war, and Jesus does no exorcisms. Furthermore, most of the Old Testament has a worldview that is different from either of these. In the Old Testament there is no cosmic war, no Satan as a power trying to take over the cosmos (universe), and very little attention to evil spirits. While today's lesson is not the proper place to explain these other cosmologies (worldviews), it *is* important to know that the cosmic war worldview is only *one* of the biblical understandings.

What do we of the twentieth century do with these stories of Jesus exorcising demons? It depends on what *our* worldview is. If it's the same as that of Jesus in the first three Gospels, then there's no problem. We just accept them literally. But suppose that worldview is not acceptable for us. Suppose we have a worldview that sees the cause of illness and disease as germs, bacteria, viruses, and genetic defects. Then the demon-possession theory of some first-century Jews is no longer helpful. We are then tempted to deal with these stories symbolically in order to affirm their value.

Early church theologians treated many of the biblical stories "allegorically." Allegory is a mode of interpretation that claims a "hidden" meaning of the text as the true meaning, rather than the literal meaning. The text says one thing, but it means another. With permission to interpret the text symbolically, what are the "evil spirits" in our world today?

Protestants, following Luther and Calvin, criticize the allegorical method because it makes the meaning of Scripture too dependent on the interpreter. And yet, there is a real need to see in "problem passages" some meaning beyond the literal when the literal is a problem. That may be part of the challenge of today's lesson.

Jesus' Concern for the Ill

When Jesus was at Simon's house, and found Simon's wife's mother "suffering from a high fever," he (Jesus) was concerned for her. He healed her with a word in Luke's version. In both Matthew (8:14-15) and Mark (1:29-31) Jesus touched her to heal her.

Speaking can be a very effective healing method. What we say to a person may contribute to their wellness. A Christian does not have to be a divine being to heal by speaking a healing word. Each of us should weigh our words carefully so as to minister to the problems of persons around us. We can also, of course, hurt people with our words and contribute to the problem rather than the solution.

This story is not only interesting for its disclosure of Simon (Peter) as a married man, but even more because *it shows the initiative of Jesus in the presence of illness.* We who claim to be his disciples can also take the initiative in caring for the ill of our time.

Jesus' Reputation as a Healer

The popularity of Jesus in Galilee seems to have been based, to some degree, on his healings. People brought their sick to him, persons with "various kinds of diseases." "He laid his hands on each of them and cured them." The emphasis here is on the healing properties of touching. It is well known in medical circles that touching plays an important role in healing. Babies that are held and touched are healthier than ones not touched very much. Touching often conveys a care and concern that goes beyond our spoken words.

Just why touching is healing is not fully known. Is there a "power-flow" from the one touching to the one touched? This would seem to be the view that lies behind the story of the woman with "the flow of blood" who was healed by touching "the fringe of his garment" (Luke 8:43-48). Jesus felt her touch and said, "I perceive that power has gone from me." Is the person of the toucher important? Do some persons have more healing power than others? Is the faith of the one touched an important factor also, or is it *the* important factor?

The Priority of the Kingdom Message

Beset by too many people seeking Jesus in order to hold him in one place, Jesus escaped and tried to have some solitary quality time. The people tried to keep him with them. Jesus protested that he had a special job to do—namely, to proclaim the kingdom of God in several cities. He said, "I was sent for this purpose."

This puts a proper check on his healing ministry. As important as this was, he did not want to make it his chief work. Proclaiming the gospel came first.

The problem here is that many ministers today see *only* the ministry of proclaiming the gospel as the mission-task. They do not yet have much concern for the health problems in their community, beyond occasional counseling (ministering to spiritual, mental, or emotional problems). The priority of preaching did not cause Jesus to abandon his healing ministry. As his disciples, what should we do?

Helping Adults Become Involved

Preparing to Teach

Make it a point to read about the church and its healing mission. My book *The Great Physician* (Abingdon, 1991) would be useful. Healing is a subject that people have strong opinions about, so the discussion moderator needs to be well-prepared.

You may organize this lesson as follows:

I. Jesus and evil spirits

155

II. Jesus' concern for the ill
III. Jesus' reputation as a healer
IV. The priority of the kingdom message

The central activity of Jesus' ministry was twofold: he healed the sick and proclaimed the kingdom of God. This lesson emphasizes the role of healing in the church today. To prepare further, read carefully "The Main Question," "As You Read the Scripture," and "The Scripture and the Main Question."

Introducing the Main Question

Ask the class what they think about the church's responsibility for a healing ministry. Once the discussion starts, ask for reports from those assigned last week. Let the reports be part of the larger discussion. Allow about one-third of the class time for this discussion, but be prepared to let it take longer if the discussion is going well.

Developing the Lesson

I. Jesus and evil spirits

Explain to the class the larger context of the stories about Jesus casting out demons. Be ready to answer questions about this cosmic-war cosmology. If the class has some members who do not find this worldview helpful, ask them to explain why it isn't helpful. If others find it helpful, ask them to explain why it helps them.

Ask if anyone has experienced an exorcism. Probably none have, but several may have seen a movie that includes it. If so, ask them to share the impression it made on them.

Then experiment with finding symbolic meanings for the "evil spirits" of the Gospel stories. Give the class free rein to speculate about helpful symbolic meanings.

II. Jesus' concern for the ill

Have a class member read verses 38 and 39. Then ask for implications anyone sees in the story. If they pick up on Simon's wife and home, you might want to read 1 Corinthians 9:3-5 to the class, but be aware of the difficult phrase behind "a believing wife"; its meaning is uncertain, and yet it is clear that the apostles traveled with women.

Healing Simon's mother-in-law's fever is a representative story to show Jesus' concern for the ill. Note that the initiative was his. Have the class consider the impact of "healing words" in human relationships. Does one have to be a special healer to speak healing words? Try to raise the consciousness level of your class members on this point.

III. Jesus' reputation as a healer

All four Gospels make it very clear that Jesus was a popular healer. What does that imply for his followers? Is healing a ministry that we should retain? Have we turned healing entirely over to the medical world?

Read verses 40 and 41 to the class. Point out the way Jesus healed a variety of "diseases." Ask the class if they think the Jews of Jesus' time could diagnose "diseases" accurately. Point out that in this general summary Jesus healed by laying on hands. Have a short discussion on the effect touching has on people. See if the class members have any experiences to share about the healing effect of touching.

You might want to contrast the reason for Jesus' fame in his own lifetime with the reason for his fame today. Such a contrast will help sensitize the class to our current neglect of a healing dimension in the mission of today's churches.

IV. The priority of the kingdom message

Read verses 42 and 43 to the class. As a fully human being Jesus, like all human beings, needed some time for himself. His popularity made that difficult. That's a common problem for celebrities. It is a bit curious that whereas Luke usually emphasizes Jesus as one who went apart to pray (see 5:16, for example), here prayer is not mentioned. His reaction to the people who wanted him to stay with them was a pointed statement that made it plain that his healing ministry, as important as it was, was not the real reason for his call. He could have healed many more people than he actually did, but even if he had healed everyone who was ill at the time, he would have done nothing to change the world.

See if the class can think of instances where doing good things keeps one from doing a more important thing. What was the more important thing for Jesus? Why was he sent?

"The good news of the kingdom of God" was the announcement that the war with Satan was about over and the new age—the kingdom of God—was almost here. Ask the class to explain how Jesus' two main emphases, the casting out of demons and the good news of the kingdom of God, are related.

Helping Class Members Act

At the very least, begin (or improve) a class project to call on the ill people of the community. Regular visitation can take the form of "taking turns," or weekly scheduling. Instruct the class members to use healing words and to touch the ill person. Keep a class register of visits made. Share the concern for healing in church work with your pastor and work toward including a healing dimension in the regular worship service, and/or supporting an existing one.

Planning for Next Sunday

Must we wait for the kingdom to come? Can't we live in it, at least partially, before it comes in its fullness? What would it be like to take seriously Jesus' statement that the kingdom is "among you" (Luke 17:21)? What it would require from us is next week's lesson. Have the class think about that as preparation. Tell them next week's scripture (Luke 6:20b-36), and ask them to reflect on it as preparation.

The Bible as the Church's Book

William H. Willimon and Patricia P. Willimon

Jesus returns to his hometown synagogue in Nazareth (Luke 4:16-30). What does Israel do on its holiest of days? Luke gives us a picture of the people of God gathered.

When he came to Nazareth, where he had been brought up, he went to the synagogue on the sabbath day, as was his custom. He stood up to read, and the scroll of the prophet Isaiah was given to him. He unrolled the scroll and found the place where it was written:

"The Spirit of the Lord is upon me,
because he has anointed me
  to bring good news to the poor.
He has sent me to proclaim release to the captives
  and recovery of sight to the blind,
  to let the oppressed go free,
to proclaim the year of the Lord's favor."

And he rolled up the scroll, gave it back to the attendant, and sat down. The eyes of all in the synagogue were fixed on him. Then he began to say to them, "Today this scripture has been fulfilled in your hearing." All spoke well of him and were amazed at the gracious words that came from his mouth. They said, "Is not this Joseph's son?" He said to them, "Doubtless you will quote to me this proverb, 'Doctor, cure yourself!' And you will say, 'Do here also in your hometown the things that we have heard you did at Capernaum.'" And he said, "Truly, I tell you, no prophet is accepted in the prophet's hometown. But the truth is, there were many widows in Israel in the time of Elijah, when the heaven was shut up three years and six months, and there was a severe famine over all the land; yet Elijah was sent to none of them except to a widow at Zarephath in Sidon. There were also many lepers in Israel in the time of the prophet Elisha, and none of them was cleansed except Naaman the Syrian." When they heard this, all in the synagogue were filled with rage. They got up, drove him out of the town, and led him to the brow of the hill on which their town was built, so that they might hurl him off the cliff. But he passed through the midst of them and went on his way. (Luke 4:16-30)

Jesus returns to his hometown synagogue. And what do they do? They hand him the scroll, the scriptures of Israel. They do not ask Jesus, "Tell us how it is for you." They do not ask him to report on his days at college, to share his feelings with them. They hand him the scroll. They ask him to read. Then he interprets, then he preaches. Watch closely as they hand him the scroll, for right there, in that action of handing Jesus the scroll, we see a movement that is at the very heart of the faith of Israel.

There may be religions that begin with long walks in the woods, communing with nature, getting close to trees. There may be religions that begin by delving into the recesses of a person's ego, rummaging around in the psyche. Christianity is not one of those religions.

Here is a people who begin in that action of taking up the scroll, being confronted with stories of God, stories that insert themselves into our accustomed ways of doing business and challenge us to change or else be out of step with the way things are now that God has entered human history.

They hand Jesus the scroll. He reads from the prophet Isaiah, speaking of that day when God would again act to set things right, come for Israel, lift up the downtrodden, and push down the mighty. The Spirit of the Lord is upon him to announce God's advent.

After reading, Jesus begins to interpret. Note that he interprets by setting other biblical stories next to Isaiah's announcement of God's advent. "God is coming among us. And the last time God came among us, during the days of the great prophet Elijah, many of our own people were hungry. But God's prophet fed none of them. Only a widow from Sidon, a foreigner, was nourished."

The congregation grows silent. The young preacher continues. "And were not there many sick people in Israel during the time of the prophet Elisha? Yes. But Elisha healed none of them. Only Naaman, a Syrian, a Syrian army officer."

And the once adoring congregation became an angry mob. As they led the young preacher out, he said to them, "I said nothing new. It's all in the book! It's all in *your* book!"

A distinctive community is being formed here by this reading and listening. A peculiar community is being criticized here as well. What sort of people are being called into being by such stories?

The Politics of the Bible

The church was called into being, as if out of nothing, as a people in dialogue with Scripture. Unlike conventional means of human organization, the church had no ethnic, gender, or national basis for unity. All it had were these stories called Scripture. These Scriptures rendered a person, a personality, Jesus. For this new and distinctive community called the church, Jesus of Nazareth, as the Messiah, became the interpretive framework for all reality, the organizing principle for all of life. Thus the function of Scripture was political, constitutive. By *political* I do not mean politics as it has degenerated in our own time—the aggressive securing of individual rights, the maximum number of personal desires elevated to the level of needs that are then pursued at all cost. The Bible is "political" in the classic sense of the word *politics*—the formation of a *polis*, the constitution of a people through a discussion of what needs are worth having, what goals are good.

Thus the Bible must be read "politically," that is, it must be read from the awareness of its desire to form a new people. We would not read Shakespeare's *King Lear* as history or as science. It is a drama. So we should not read the Bible as merely science, history, philology, or personal help. The Bible seeks to engender a people, a *polis*.

In defiance of sociological laws, without conventional cultural, or ethnic support, this new community conquered the Roman Empire in one of the most amazing cultural shifts ever seen in Western history. For instance, there was no value more dear to classical Romans than the family. All of Roman society was organized around the family headed by the *Pater Familias*, the father of the family. Marriage, political power, economic advancement, and civil rights were all based upon the family. Family name and status determined one's situation throughout life. Indeed, the military was virtually the only means of social advancement for someone born into a poor Roman family.

From the beginning, the church was—in complete contrast to Roman society—ambivalent or even hostile to the family. Early Christian leaders like Paul advised against marriage and familial attachments. Christian baptism had as its goal nothing less than the disruption of one's family, since one was "reborn" in baptism. The prior natural birth into a human family was overcome through the new birth of baptism so that one's family name was changed and one was given a new Christian name, a new identity based not on the old standards of family status but on the new standards of adoption into a new family—the church. In baptism the old distinctions by which the world lives were washed away.

"As many of you as were baptized into Christ have clothed yourselves with Christ. There is no longer Jew or Greek, there is no longer slave or free, there is no longer male nor female; for you are all one in Christ Jesus" (Galatians 3:27-28).

In other words, *the Bible had reality-defining power over the church.* Through Scripture we were taught to view and review the world through new categories. Among us there could be no deference to family name, gender, race, or economic position. All of those old, dated distinctions had become washed in the waters of baptism.

Scripture gave us a new story, a new narrative account of the way the world was put together, new direction for history, new purpose for being on earth. The world of Rome had many other stories that gave meaning to peoples' lives—eroticism, pantheism, polytheism, cynicism. To be a Christian was to be someone who had been initiated, by baptism, into this alternative story of the world.

It was not the case that ancient Romans felt some inner need in their lives, some vague feeling of emptiness and then went shopping about for a faith that would fill it, found Christianity, and then embraced it. Rather, it was that the church incorporated ancient Romans into their story of reality called Scripture. The church gave them a different story through which to make sense out of their lives.

When you read Scripture, you will note that narrative, story, is the Bible's primary means of dealing with truth. Occasionally, but only rarely, will the Bible attempt to define the essence of something. Socrates was interested in discovering a good working definition of big words like *truth* and *beauty,* but that is not the Bible's way of working. In the Bible a Jewish carpenter's son comes forward and says, "I am the way, the truth, the life." We must follow his story if we are to know truth.

Occasionally, but only rarely, will the Bible describe some inner, personal experience. Our time is an age in which people are greatly infatuated with themselves, their own feelings, their personal stories. The longest journey most of us venture is the rather short trip deeper into the recesses of our own egos. This is not the Bible's path to truth.

Rather, the Bible seeks to catch up our little lives into a grand adventure, a great saga of God's dealings with humanity, a saga begun in God's journey with Israel, continued in the surprising call of God even unto the Gentiles. The church is the product of that story.

Living in God's Kingdom

Selected Scripture: Luke 6:17-36

The Main Question

This lesson focuses on what it would be like to live now as though we were already in the kingdom of God. When Jesus taught the pattern of such a lifestyle it is plain that the poor, the hungry, the sad, and the persecuted will be the favored citizens in the kingdom of God. The rich, well-filled, "happy," and popular ones in this era will be the underdogs in the kingdom. It looks like a reversal of our ordinary values, a turning upside-down of the present order.

Not only that, but Jesus taught non-resistance to those who harm us, and non-recovery of items stolen from us. We are to do good to all, friend and foe alike.

The question is: *How practical are these instructions?* Do we really believe that we should live this way? If not, why not? If so, why do we fail to let them guide us?

There are many Old Testament "laws" (teachings) that we reject for one reason or another. For example, we regard the rules of warfare in Deuteronomy 20, or the treatment of a disobedient son in Deuteronomy 21:18-21, as ethically wrong and disobey them deliberately. Does this freedom extend to the teachings of Jesus? How could we modify Jesus' teachings to make them useful in our age? Or, *should* we? If not, why not? These are some of the tough, practical questions which lie behind today's lesson.

Selected Scripture

King James Version

Luke 6:20-36

20 And he lifted up his eyes on his disciples, and said, Blessed be ye poor: for yours is the kingdom of God.

21 Blessed are ye that hunger now: for ye shall be filled. Blessed are ye that weep now: for ye shall laugh.

22 Blessed are ye, when men shall hate you, and when they shall separate you from their company, and shall reproach you, and cast out your name as evil, for the Son of man's sake.

23 Rejoice ye in that day, and leap for joy: for, behold, your reward is

New Revised Standard Version

Luke 6:20-36

20 Then he looked up at his disciples and said:

"Blessed are you who are poor,
for yours is the kingdom of
God.

21 "Blessed are you who are
hungry now,
for you will be filled.
"Blessed are you who weep now,
for you will laugh.

22 "Blessed are you when people hate you, and when they exclude you, revile you, and defame you on account of the Son of Man. 23 Rejoice in that day and leap for joy, for surely your reward is great in heaven; for that is what their ancestors did to the prophets.

great in heaven: for in the like manner did their fathers unto the prophets.

24 But woe unto you that are rich! for ye have received your consolation.

25 Woe unto you that are full! for ye shall hunger. Woe unto you that laugh now! for ye shall mourn and weep.

26 Woe unto you, when all men shall speak well of you! for so did their fathers to the false prophets.

27 But I say unto you which hear, Love your enemies, do good to them which hate you,

28 Bless them that curse you, and pray for them which despitefully use you.

29 And unto him that smiteth thee on the one cheek offer also the other; and him that taketh away thy cloke forbid not to take thy coat also.

30 Give to every man that asketh of thee; and of him that taketh away thy goods ask them not again.

31 And as ye would that men should do to you, do ye also to them likewise.

32 For if ye love them which love you, what thank have ye? for sinners also love those that love them.

33 And if ye do good to them which do good to you, what thank have ye? for sinners also do even the same.

34 And if ye lend to them of whom ye hope to receive, what thank have ye? for sinners also lend to sinners, to receive as much again.

35 But love ye your enemies, and do good, and lend, hoping for nothing again; and your reward shall be great, and ye shall be the children of the Highest: for he is kind unto the unthankful and to the evil.

36 Be ye therefore merciful, as your Father also is merciful.

Key Verse: **Be ye therefore merciful, as your Father also is merciful. Luke 6:36**

24 "But woe to you who are rich,
    for you have received your
        consolation.

25 "Woe to you who are full now,
    for you will be hungry.
"Woe to you who are laughing now,
    for you will mourn and weep.

26 "Woe to you when all speak well of you, for that is what their ancestors did to the false prophets.

27 "But I say to you that listen, Love your enemies, do good to those who hate you, 28 bless those who curse you, pray for those who abuse you. 29 If anyone strikes you on the cheek, offer the other also; and from anyone who takes away your coat do not withhold even your shirt. 30 Give to everyone who begs from you; and if anyone takes away your goods, do not ask for them again. 31 Do to others as you would have them do to you.

32 "If you love those who love you, what credit is that to you? For even sinners love those who love them. 33 If you do good to those who do good to you, what credit is that to you? For even sinners do the same. 34 If you lend to those from whom you hope to receive, what credit is that to you? Even sinners lend to sinners, to receive as much again. 35 But love your enemies, do good, and lend, expecting nothing in return. Your reward will be great, and you will be children of the Most High; for he is kind to the ungrateful and the wicked. 36 Be merciful, just as your Father is merciful."

Key Verse: **Be merciful, just as your Father is merciful. Luke 6:36**

As You Read the Scripture

This passage in Luke has another form in Matthew's parallel. Luke's beatitudes (verses 20-26) are paralleled in Matthew 5:3-11. Luke's verses 27-36 are parallel in Matthew 5:33-48. In many cases there are considerable differences between the two versions. The teachings in Luke are more severe than in Matthew, and may therefore be closer to what Jesus actually said. The tendency of the church would be to soften radical teachings. Luke's setting is "on a level place" (6:17), whereas Matthew's setting is on a mountain (Matthew 5:1).

Verses 20-23. The promised blessings are for four classes of persons, the poor, the hungry, the sorrowful, and the hated. In Matthew the poor become the "poor in spirit," the hungry become "those who hunger . . . for righteousness," and the hated become "those who are persecuted for righteousness' sake." If, as appears likely, the early church found the more "radical" version of Jesus' teaching difficult to accept and modified it, does this sanction our need to modify it for our time?

Verses 24-26. Luke has four corresponding "woes" not found in Matthew's parallel. These woes emphasize the stark radicalness of the blessings; they are "the other side of the coin."

Verses 27-29a. To love one's enemies, to "do good to those who hate you, bless those who curse you, pray for those who abuse you," and to "offer the other" cheek to one who strikes you—all these teachings have passed into the church's tradition of valuable ideals. It is rare to find a Christian who is able to live like this, but they have seldom been questioned as worthy ideals for all.

Verses 29b-30. Now we have a greater problem. Capitalistic doctrines and the right of private property make it difficult for Christians living in such a society to obey these teachings, or even to accept them as valid ideals. They may be appropriate for the kingdom of God, which has no thieves or beggars, but in this present evil age are they useful guides?

Verse 31. This, of course, is the famous "Golden Rule." For many people it stands as the only rule we need. Taken together with the preceeding and succeeding verses, the "Golden Rule" becomes more difficult.

Verses 32-35a. There are three situations that are parallel to each other, and together make a powerful point. The love Jesus is teaching is not selfish, based on the benefits it accrues. It goes well beyond the exchange pattern of the kind of loving that is easy for anyone. We tend to balk again when we get to the teaching about lending. The right to own things and to keep them is dear to most of us. Jesus' instruction was to loan, "expecting nothing in return." Doesn't this put us at the mercy of any dishonest person? Is this good stewardship?

Verse 35b. The rationale for these teachings is a new kind of reward, a reward from God. That tends to undermine the apparent "altruism" of Jesus' radical teachings. Rewards on earth (in this age) are improper, but rewards from God (in the coming kingdom?) are all right. Should the motivation for the life-style Jesus teaches be God-given rewards?

Verse 35c. Our life-style should be patterned after God's. This is similar to the motivation in the Holiness Code in Leviticus 17–26, where Israel is to be holy because God is holy (for example, Leviticus 22:31-33).

Verse 36. Luke's version of this saying is less radical, rather than more radical, than Matthew's. To be perfect (Matthew) is one thing; to be merciful (Luke) is another. Both, however, assume that imitation of God is a legitimate ideal for humans.

The Scripture and the Main Question

The Blessings and Woes

Jesus blessed the poor and pronounced woes on the rich. Is there anything intrinsically good about being poor? Are the poor "better" people than the rich? Insofar as the rich are powerful, and take advantage of the poor to build up their riches, one could affirm this. The selfish refusal of the rich to take any responsibility for meeting the needs of the poor could be a partial explanation of Jesus' attitude. But *should* the rich give away all their possessions? Is there no justification for the accumulation of wealth in our society? Can we make an exception for the rich person who is a generous philanthropist (lover of mankind)? What is the right place of the wealthy in our society?

Are the world's hungry people better people than those who are well-filled? Of course, the presence of gluttony and gourmet eating in the face of starving persons is easy to condemn, but should the whole human population be leveled down to the average? Why? Is equality of possessions and food really a good ideal? Why, or why not?

What is intrinsically good about being sorrowful, or bad about being happy? Or why should popularity be bad in itself? Of course, to be hated on account of one's loyalty to Jesus is quite deserving of a blessing, but to pronounce a woe on the merely popular is harder to understand. Jesus himself seems to have been popular and well spoken of by many Galileans. These blessing and woes deserve much thought and discussion.

What to Do about Evil Persons

Jesus taught (in this lesson's verses) a policy of non-resistance to evil persons. Love your enemies, do good to those who hate you, and so forth. His teachings are quite the opposite of those in Psalm 109. But Psalm 109 is not representative of the noblest Hebrew sentiments.

We have a popular saying about not letting people "walk all over you." We praise "assertiveness." But permitting evil persons to oppress us is what Jesus seems to teach. We shouldn't resist a bully, or a tyrant, or a thief, and we should always give to beggars. How can a follower of the Jesus who also taught us to be good stewards, live by these teachings?

In our society we feel (usually) that society needs to be protected from evil persons. We tend to imprison evil persons as a protective measure for the rest of society. Is this wrong?

It will not do to say these teachings may have been appropriate in Jesus' society, but not in ours. His society had tyrants, bullies, thieves, and beggars also.

One plausible solution to these problems is to remember that Jesus seems to have shared the popular expectation that the great cosmic war between God and Satan was almost over. (Review, if necessary, the explanation in "The Scripture and the Main Question" in the January 9 lesson.) Jesus expected the coming kingdom of God in his own generation. See Luke 9:27, Mark 13:30, and Matthew 10:23. This expectation was still alive in Paul's time.

Jesus may have taught these radical instructions because he saw the End of this age as an event of his own generation. Then his ethical teachings would be, at least in part, "interim ethics," or ethics for the brief interim between his own time and the End. We can see Paul teaching "interim ethics" in 1 Corinthians 7:25-31.

The Golden Rule

This famous rule, in its positive form, seems original with Jesus. It has several negative parallels in both the East and the West. Confucius, for instance, when asked to give one word that would serve as a rule for all of life, gave the word "reciprocity," adding, "What you do not want done to yourself, do not do to others."

The problem with this popular rule is that it becomes quite relative. What I might want others to do to me might well be what others would not want me to do to them. Suppose, for example, I am an introvert married to an extrovert. I want to be left alone, therefore should I leave my extrovert spouse alone?

Our Motivations for Right Living

Jesus notes carefully that the good deeds of ordinary people are self-centered. Ordinary people like those who like them. They give to those who give to them. They lend to those who repay and lend to them. Jesus declares that this way of living is not unusual; all people tend to be this way. Jesus then urges us to be beyond this, to like those who don't like us, to give to those who don't give to us, to lend to those who won't lend to us and who might not repay.

Why should we live like this? The initial reason is the promise that "your reward will be great," but to make rewards the basic motivation is quite incompatible with the teachings just before the mention of reward.

In the law codes of the Torah (the first five books in the Old Testament) we can see three types of motivation for obedience. In the "Covenant Code" (Exodus 21:1–23:9), probably the oldest set of laws, there is no motivation offered. Yahweh commands obedience, and we obey because Yahweh commands it. This corresponds with the parental response to the child who questions the parental command, "Because I said so."

In the "Deuteronomic Code" (Deuteronomy 12–26) the motivation is clear and emphatic. Obedience will be rewarded and disobedience punished. This is the theological thread that runs through the histories of Israel, from Joshua to 2 Chronicles.

In the "Holiness Code" in Leviticus the motivation is imitation of Yahweh ("the LORD"). The people shall be holy because Yahweh is holy. This is the highest form of motivation in scripture.

This imitation-of-God motivation is the basic one presented by Jesus. Why should his disciples live as he taught them to live? Because God is kind to the wicked, the disciples of Jesus should be kind also.

The final statement reinforces this lofty motivation. Jesus tells his disciples to "be merciful, just as your Father is merciful."

Helping Adults Become Involved

Preparing to Teach

This lesson opens up rich possibilities for class discussion. As leader, you should be familiar with Matthew's version of these teachings, in chapter 5.

There is no easy way to decide which of the versions is closer to what Jesus actually said, except for the plausible guess that Luke's Beatitudes are somewhat closer to Jesus than Matthew's. The other sayings should be treated as independent forms of an earlier collection of sayings now lost. Of course, the original context in which Jesus said these things is now lost also. Their present context was created by the Gospel writer.

The lesson has four closely related parts:

I.   The blessings and woes (verses 20-26)
II. What to do about evil persons (verses 27-30)
III. The golden rule (verse 31)
IV. Our motivations for right living (verses 32-36)

Read "The Main Question" and the study the section "As You Read the Scripture." Note all the controversial items that could be good for class discussion as these appear in "The Scripture and the Main Question."

The intent of the many questions is not to cast doubts on the authority of Jesus. The questions are serious inquiries into the proper use of scripture in our Christian mission today.

Introducing the Main Question

Begin by asking for volunteer reactions to the scripture lesson. If these are not promptly expressed, then have a class member to read Luke 6:20-26, and get responses from that. Then have another class member read verses 27-36, and ask for responses to that. These initial reactions from the class members should express the idea in "The Main Question." Do not discuss these reactions yet; the right time will come as the lesson unfolds.

Developing the Lesson

I. The blessings and woes

Now the class can have an opportunity to discuss the four blessings and their corresponding woes. Bring in Matthew's variations on these four, and explain that the changes may reflect the way the early church struggled to make the blessings fit the actual circumstances of daily life. The presence of wealthy church members at an early date can be seen in James 2:1-7 and, somewhat later, in 1 Timothy 6:17-19. This last passage reflects the attitude toward the rich that has prevailed in the church ever since. Share these other scriptures with the class if appropriate to the discussion.

II. What to do about evil persons

Begin with ideas from the class, without reference to the verses that deal with this topic. It is quite unlikely that the class will produce sentiments as radical as Jesus' ideas. When the class has made some suggestions, including some personal experiences with evil persons, then remind them of Jesus' teachings. Now get reactions again.

See if someone in the class can understand in these teachings some general principle that we can more easily affirm. Or, just be very blunt and encourage the class to follow through on its ideas. If anyone affirms these teachings in their literal meaning, does he or she really practice them? If so, ask for specific instances.

If anyone is willing to question these teachings, is he or she willing to be forthright about that? If so, what does it do to our view of the authority of Jesus' teachings? That's another big topic, so do not let the discussion get bogged down there. Explain that questions like the authority of Jesus, or any other person in scripture, is a study in itself and requires different background information than this course supplies.

Present to the class the proposal that Jesus' radical ethical teachings are "interim ethics." Get responses from class members. Do not be dogmatic about this suggestion, either in affirmation or denial. Let each one adopt what is personally helpful. Luke 12:57 might be a good reminder verse.

III. The golden rule

Get the class to evaluate this rule as a sufficient guide for Christian living. Point out its general usefulness, and tell the class about the negative versions from other teachers. Quote the Confucian version for "The Scripture and the Main Question."

Point out that the value of the golden rule is limited because it tends to be relative. See if the class can come up with a better illustration than the one given in "The Golden Rule." Share that one as a starter.

IV. Our motivations for right living

Begin by reading verses 32-34. Point out the self-interest in the good behavior of most people. Jesus is calling for a higher righteousness than that.

Now read verse 35. It reflects two types of motivation, rewards and imitation of God. Explain why rewards cannot be the motivation Jesus was providing (verses 32-34 forbid that conclusion; one can be rewarded without reward being the motivation, as in Luke's beatitudes). The imitation-of-God motivation is certainly supported by verse 36. If you have time, present the motivations in the law codes of the Torah and ask for opinions from the class on the most effective motivation for them. Is the most effective one also the best one? Challenge each one to reflect on what motivates him or her to live an ethical life.

Helping Class Members Act

Ask the class to make a special effort to go beyond their usual life-pattern and do at least one thing that Jesus is calling for in the verses of this lesson. They are not to do this so they can report it to anyone, but simply because it's a higher righteousness. Next Sunday they will be asked to share the effect this extra something had on their self-understanding.

Planning for Next Sunday

Announce the topic of the next lesson, "The Cost of Discipleship." It follows naturally from this week's lesson. Have the class members think about whether the demands of the gospel make it more attractive or less.

The Cost of Discipleship

Background Scripture: Luke 9:51–10:12

The Main Question

Being an active member of a Christian church today does not make many demands on us. There is the need to support the institution by generous financial contributions, and some demands on our time, if only our attendance at worship. Furthermore, we are seldom actively involved in the mission of the church. At most, we make another financial contribution.

Jesus was not the creator of such a system. Granting that he was a Jew and did not intend to create a new religion (the majority scholarly opinion), he nevertheless made strong demands on his followers. It was very costly to be a true disciple of Jesus. He told the ruler "sell all that you own and distribute the money to the poor" (Luke 18:22) in order to become a disciple. Peter declared, "Look, we have left our homes and followed you" (Luke 18:28).

Riches were a special impediment to discipleship. "How hard it is for those who have wealth to enter the kingdom of God!" (Luke 18:24). Discipleship seems to demand poverty.

Is this costly discipleship required for our salvation? How does discipleship relate to salvation? And what is our role in the mission of the church today? Do we (should we) still proclaim the nearness of the kingdom of God? Is preparation for the coming of the kingdom still the highest priority? This lesson deals with these tough, costly questions.

Selected Scripture

King James Version

Luke 9:57–10:12

57 And it came to pass, that, as they went in the way, a certain man said unto him, Lord, I will follow thee whithersoever thou goest.

58 And Jesus said unto him, Foxes have holes, and birds of the air have nests; but the Son of man hath not where to lay his head.

59 And he said unto another, Follow me. But he said, Lord, suffer me first to go and bury my father.

60 Jesus said unto him, Let the dead bury their dead: but go thou and preach the kingdom of God.

61 And another also said, Lord, I will follow thee; but let me first go bid them farewell, which are at home at my house.

New Revised Standard Version

Luke 9:57–10:12

57 As they were going along the road, someone said to him, "I will follow you wherever you go." 58 And Jesus said to him, "Foxes have holes, and birds of the air have nests; but the Son of Man has nowhere to lay his head." 59 To another he said, "Follow me." But he said, "Lord, first let me go and bury my father." 60 But Jesus said to him, "Let the dead bury their own dead; but as for you, go and proclaim the kingdom of God." 61 Another said, "I will follow you, Lord; but let me first say farewell to those at my home." 62 Jesus said to him, "No one who puts a hand to the plow and looks back is fit for the kingdom of God."

62 And Jesus said unto him, No man, having put his hand to the plough, and looking back, is fit for the kingdom of God.

1 After these things the Lord appointed other seventy also, and sent them two and two before his face into every city and place, whither he himself would come.

2 Therefore said he unto them, The harvest truly is great, but the labourers are few: pray ye therefore the Lord of the harvest, that he would send forth labourers into his harvest.

3 Go your ways: behold, I send you forth as lambs among wolves.

4 Carry neither purse, nor scrip, nor shoes: and salute no man by the way.

5 And into whatsoever house ye enter, first say, Peace be to this house.

6 And if the son of peace be there, your peace shall rest upon it: if not, it shall turn to you again.

7 And in the same house remain, eating and drinking such things as they give: for the labourer is worthy of his hire. Go not from house to house.

8 And into whatsoever city ye enter, and they receive you, eat such things as are set before you:

9 And heal the sick that are therein, and say unto them, The kingdom of God is come nigh unto you.

10 But into whatsoever city ye enter, and they receive you not, go your ways out into the streets of the same, and say,

11 Even the very dust of your city, which cleaveth on us, we do wipe off against you: notwithstanding be ye sure of this, that the kingdom of God is come nigh unto you.

12 But I say unto you, that it shall be more tolerable in that day for Sodom, than for that city.

1 After this the Lord appointed seventy others and sent them on ahead of him in pairs to every town and place where he himself intended to go. 2 He said to them, "The harvest is fruitful, but the laborers are few; therefore ask the Lord of the harvest to send out laborers into his harvest. 3 Go on your way. See, I am sending you out like lambs into the midst of wolves. 4 Carry no purse, no bag, no sandals; and greet no one on the road. 5 Whatever house you enter, first say, 'Peace to this house!' 6 And if anyone is there who shares in peace, your peace will rest on that person; but if not, it will return to you. 7 Remain in the same house, eating and drinking whatever they provide, for the laborer deserves to be paid. Do not move about from house to house. 8 Whenever you enter a town and its people welcome you, eat what is set before you; 9 cure the sick who are there, and say to them, 'The kingdom of God has come near to you.' 10 But whenever you enter a town and they do not welcome you, go out into its streets and say, 11 'Even the dust of your town that clings to our feet, we wipe off in protest against you. Yet know this: the kingdom of God has come near.' 12 I tell you, on that day it will be more tolerable for Sodom than for that town."

SECOND QUARTER

As You Read the Scripture

The scripture for this lesson teaches two themes. The first is *the cost of discipleship*, the second is *the mission of the disciples.* Both sections have parallels in Matthew's Gospel, but the mission instructions in Matthew are addressed to the Twelve. Matthew has no Mission of the Seventy.

Luke 9:57-58. The "someone" of Luke is a scribe in Matthew 8:19. Jesus' reply to the enthusiastic would-be disciple was apparently intended to point out the cost of becoming a follower. The Son of Man (Jesus) had no home most of the time. He was an itinerant beggar, according to the conditions of the mission later described. It is probable that Jesus *did* have a home in Capernaum (see Mark 3:19*b*), but he was traveling most of the time. In effect Jesus was contrasting his insecure life-style with the security of foxes and birds.

Verses 59-60. The Jewish scholar C. Montefiore once commented that honoring parents was so deeply rooted in the Jewish consciousness that these sayings of Jesus in verses 59-62 have not a wholly Jewish ring. They should not be universalized into a principle for all times and seasons. They stress the urgency of the kingdom mission. Over the centuries of Christian history that initial urgency has largely disappeared.

Verses 61-62. A third would-be disciple requested a final home-visit first, but Jesus refused to accept him. This encounter is found only in Luke, whereas the other two are also in Matthew. The two common to both Gospels are apparently from a common source that no longer exists. This third example ends with a fine proverbial saying about persistence that Luke may have adapted to this setting. The point Luke makes is that the kingdom mission has no room for workers who are not fully dedicated.

Luke 10:1. The "seventy" are otherwise unknown in early Christian writings. The number is seventy-two in some ancient manuscripts. The same confusion between seventy and seventy-two appears in the account of the nations in Genesis 10 (depending on whether one reads the Hebrew text or the Greek translation). Luke's mission of the Seventy (two) is probably based on the traditional number of the nations according to Genesis 10.

This account has interesting parallels in the mission of the Twelve. Some of the instructions to the Seventy are found addressed to the Twelve in Matthew's Gospel. This suggests that Luke has created a mission to the whole world as a supplement to the mission to Israel.

Verse 4. The instructions here are different from the ones to the Twelve in Mark 6:8-9, but all accounts have the same frugality. The "missionaries" are to take nothing with them, except the clothes on their backs. They are forbidden to take any money, no bag (of personal things), not even sandals. They are to live on the generosity (hospitality) of the people they meet.

Verses 5-6. "Peace" (*shalom*) is the usual Jewish greeting. It is a complex word that means bestowing health and all good things, much richer than our "hello." Upon arrival at a house if the tenants respond in a friendly way, the "shalom" greeting will benefit them. If they are unfriendly, the shalom blessing will return to the "missionary." This assumes an objectivity to the blessing similar to the type illustrated by the story of Isaac's blessing of Jacob (Gen. 27).

Verse 7. "The laborer deserves to be paid" is a succinct phrasing of Paul's argument in 1 Corinthians 9:3-18, and is actually quoted as scripture in 1 Timothy 5:18.

Verses 8-12. If a town is friendly, the "missionaries" are to heal the sick and announce the nearness of the kingdom. Towns that reject them will be severely punished "on that day" (the Judgment Day).

The Scripture and the Main Question

The Would-Be Disciples

"Someone" was enthusiastic about what Jesus was doing and declared his desire to follow Jesus wherever he went. However, he had not counted the cost, and apparently deserted Jesus when he discovered the life the disciples led.

The second person (also unnamed) was called by Jesus to be a disciple, but he requested a deferment so he could bury his father. If the father was already dead, it would only mean a short delay. But suppose he meant to delay discipleship until his father died. In either case, Jesus seems to have considered that the urgency of the kingdom of God announcement took precedence over everything else.

This second encounter (and the next one also) is reminiscent of the call of Elisha in 1 Kings 19:19-21. Reread that episode.

The third disciple-applicant only wanted to bid farewell to his family, but Jesus refused to permit even that postponement.

How familiar these would-be disciples seem! Which of us has not postponed work for the kingdom? "I'll surely tithe when I make a bigger salary." "Next year I should have more time to teach Sunday school." "When I retire I'll be very active in the church." Discipleship demands immediate action.

In last Sunday's lesson we saw how Jesus demanded his disciples to give up their possessions and be poor. That is probably the most difficult requirement for discipleship. Jesus taught bluntly (in Luke 14:33) "none of you can become my disciple if you do not give up all your possessions."

We probably cannot absolutize this requirement, making it a general, absolute rule, without running into trouble with other passages in Luke, including other teachings of Jesus. For instance, Luke's account in 8:1-3 presupposes that the women-disciples mentioned there did *not* give up their possessions, for if they had done so, how could they have provided for Jesus (and the Twelve?) "out of their resources"? And how do we relate the poverty passages to the stewardship passages (Luke 16:1-13; 19:1-27)?

Discipleship and Salvation

Many Christians confuse discipleship with salvation. This is mostly because in one of the principal sources of Christianity (Judaism) there is a close relationship that often makes discipleship equivalent to salvation. In Judaism *salvation is based on our meeting some conditions.* In the usual Jewish way of understanding this, our salvation depends on our acceptance of the Torah as God's will, and then obeying it. Since no one can be perfectly obedient, perfect obedience is not required. God forgives our failures, however, if we repent (another condition). Thus our salvation depends on the right blend of obedience (righteousness) and repentance.

This general understanding of conditioned obedience was also that of the earliest (Jewish) disciples. The Torah was still valid, but fulfilled by Jesus, the new Moses and the Messiah. This was essentially the understanding of the author of the Gospels of Matthew and Luke (and Acts, of course). Therefore, Jesus' teachings in these two Gospels practically equate discipleship and salvation. The Torah is eternally valid (Matt. 5:17-20; Luke 16:17), only the righteous will enter the kingdom (Matt. 5:20; 7:21), and sinners must repent (Luke 13:1-5).

Orthodox Christianity, however, following especially the Apostle Paul, believes that our *salvation is an unearned gift*. "By grace you have been saved through faith, and this is not your own doing; it is the gift of God" (Eph. 2:8; see also 2 Cor. 5:19; Rom. 5:6-11). For Christians, salvation is free but discipleship is costly. It is our God-given salvation that enables and empowers our discipleship. Or, put differently, righteousness is not a requirement for salvation, but salvation is necessary for us to be righteous. God, in Christ, has given us salvation so that we can be righteous. True righteousness is the result of salvation rather than its cause.

The Mission of the Seventy

Luke and Acts (volumes one and two of an originally connected work, now separated by the Gospel of John) were written partly to inform a certain otherwise unknown person (Theophilos) about the rise of Christianity. This work tells how a small Jewish sect spread over the Roman Empire. The idea that Jesus was for the whole world, not just for Jews, lies behind the story of the sending out of the Seventy (a story found only in Luke). The Seventy (or seventy-two) seem to stand for all the different peoples of the (then known) world. Jews relied on Genesis 10 as the explanation of the different "nations" that existed after the great flood. All the people in the world came from their common ancestor, Noah. Noah's sons produced the seventy (two) peoples. Luke seems to be preparing the way for the world mission of the church with the Mission of the Seventy (two). The story serves Luke's purposes too closely for it to be undoubtedly historical. The unlikely occasion of thirty-five (or -six) pairs of "missionaries" all returning at the same time helps us to focus on the *meaning* of the story rather than its historicity. What does this story of those who were first "sent out" by Jesus mean for those of us who are sent out today?

The Mission Today

The two accounts of Jesus sending out the Twelve (Luke 9:1-6) and the Seventy (10:1-12) may be of limited help in creating the church's mission today. The Latter Day Saints of Utah do take the sending out in pairs literally, and have achieved a measure of success for their plan. The Jehovah's Witnesses have a similar mission strategy. Perhaps the "mainline" churches should reexamine the feasibility of using this technique. Neither the Latter Day Saints nor the Jehovah's Witnesses take literally the instructions to live off the hospitality of the people sought out. Neither do they heal the sick nor cast out demons. Instead they exhort their hearers with their denominational tenets.

The mission of "mainstream" Christianity may be much more complex than in previous centuries. We educate, tend the sick medically, and feed the hungry, while witnessing to the salvation that motivates and enables these good and helpful deeds. The good news for the world is no longer an announcement of the nearness of the kingdom of God; it is a proclamation of God's graceful acceptance of us as sinners and God's purposeful enablement of our obedient discipleship.

Helping Adults Become Involved

Preparing to Teach

Enrich your knowledge of the discipleship theme by studying several important discipleship passages in Luke, especially 13:22-30; 14:12-14, 25-33; 18:9-14, 18-30; 19:1-10. Feel free to use these passages if the discussion warrants it. Study carefully the scripture for this lesson, and the section "As You Read the Scripture." Then read "The Main Question" and "The Scripture and the Main Question," making careful notes of points you think would help your class discussion to be meaningful.

This lesson has four sections:

I. The would-be disciples
II. Discipleship and salvation
III. The mission of the seventy
IV. The mission today

Introducing the Main Question

The discipleship theme makes most of us Christians uncomfortable. Ask the class to report on any feelings they may have experienced if they actually tried to practice the "higher righteousness" of Jesus' teachings. Then ask them how they feel about being an example of a disciple. What "grade" would they give themselves?

Then ask what it is that interferes with their becoming the ideal disciple. Move to the scripture text now and read about the three "would-be" disciples, without discussing them. Recall the exaltation of the poor in last week's lesson, and add the blunt statement in 14:33. Ask the class to react to that verse.

This lesson takes a hard look at the poverty requirement and tries to clarify the meaning of discipleship by some tough questions. The lesson also includes the mission of the church and how it has changed since the time of Jesus.

Developing the Lesson

I. The would-be disciples

Have a class member put himself or herself in the place of the rejected "someone" of 9:57. Let them tell the class how they feel about Jesus' rejection of them. Do the same with the other two incidents. Then have the class give examples of how modern disciples tend to put off doing some discipleship actions. Use the questions in the section "The Would-Be Disciples" in "The Scripture and the Main Question," if nothing is volunteered by the class. Or add them to what the class members suggest.

Raise the poverty question and relate it to the contrary teachings about stewardship and the stories of women supporting Jesus (and the Twelve?) out of their resources, and Luke's story of Zaccheus.

II. Discipleship and salvation

It is very important for the class to understand this topic. Teach first the Jewish understanding, and point out that Jesus was a Jew and had no quarrel with this understanding (for example, Matthew 23:2). Jesus, after all, was a Jew, not a Christian. Make sure the class understands the Jewish view before going further.

Then present the orthodox Christian view, as explained in "The Scripture and the Main Question." When this is clear to everyone, then point out that both Matthew and Luke present discipleship as a requirement for salvation. Help the class to see that this was a legitimate viewpoint in the earliest development of Christianity, but needs now to be understood from the whole Christian perspective as represented by exponents like Paul.

It will be very helpful to illustrate the main points in this discussion with relevant passages from the New Testament. This is not "proof-texting" because it does not make an individual verse support a viewpoint different from the meaning of that verse in its context. It is simply illustration.

It is important in this discussion to guard against making discipleship demands conditions for salvation. To do that would be to teach a "works-righteousness" view of salvation, which is not the orthodox Christian view of salvation as a gracious gift of God.

III. The mission of the seventy

There are several related passages that should be well known by the leader of the class even if they don't enter into the discussion. They report the Mission of the Twelve (see Mark 6:7-13; Matt. 10:5-23; Luke 9:1-6). Several of the sayings in the mission of the Seventy appear elsewhere as instructions to the Twelve.

Read the following paragraph to the class: "Seventy" was a popular number in Jewish tradition. Seventy scholars translated the Hebrew Bible into Greek, according to tradition. Moses appointed seventy judges (in Num. 11:16). Seventy elders accompanied Moses on Mount Sinai (Exod. 24:9). The Sanhedrin (the governing body in Jerusalem) had seventy members. Josephus, in the Jewish War against the Romans in 66 C.E., appointed seventy "rulers" of Galilee. Based on Genesis 10, there were seventy "nations" in the world.

IV. The mission today

This is a much larger topic and deserves more time and space than this lesson allows. Ask the class to comment on the appropriateness of the mission instructions for our mission today. Let the class members make the points they feel are important. It is likely that they will bring out the most important observations. Let this discussion be related to the discipleship theme, for certainly all disciples are part of the church's mission.

Helping Class Members Act

Draw from the class several resolutions to be better disciples in the future. See if the class itself can be a better disciple-group by some specific action that is new and different from past actions. Put these on the board and stimulate the class members to review their discipleship level and improve it with specific items.

Planning for Next Sunday

Announce that next Sunday's lesson is on alienation and reconciliation, both on the human-human level and the human-God level. Ask the class to reflect on the role a disciple should play in the whole reconciliation process.

Lost and Found

Background Scripture: Luke 15

The Main Question

Every family experiences some tensions among some of its members. Estrangement is a common family characteristic. Sometimes this results in a disruption of the family, as in divorce, or in separation. A daughter may be at loggerheads with a parent. Sibling rivalry may become severe. A parent may not be able to "turn loose." A son may develop values that clash with those of the rest of the family. Division of inherited property may occasion bitter feelings among the children.

And yet, "blood is thicker than water," as the saying goes. To belong to a family can give much-needed security. To not belong can make one feel isolated and alone.

Alienation within families is often caused by hurtful actions or selfish desires. Sometimes the cause is simply thoughtlessness. Actions can be misunderstood. Sometimes there is real wrongdoing that causes the trouble. Whatever the cause, reconciliation is always possible and usually desired.

One important and common solution to these estrangements is a willingness to repent (apologize) and a willingness to forgive. This week's lesson deals with these problems through a study of the parable of the lost son (the "prodigal" son).

How easy is repenting and forgiving? Can we just do it, at will? Does the Christian gospel go beyond this and offer a better way? If so, what is that better way?

Selected Scripture

King James Version	New Revised Standard Version
Luke 15:11-24	*Luke 15:11-24*
11 And he said, A certain man had two sons:	11 Then Jesus said, "There was a man who had two sons. 12 The

12 And the younger of them said to his father, Father, give me the portion of goods that falleth to me. And he divided unto them his living.

13 And not many days after the younger son gathered all together, and took his journey into a far country, and there wasted his substance with riotous living.

14 And when he had spent all, there arose a mighty famine in that land; and he began to be in want.

15 And he went and joined himself to a citizen of that country; and he sent him into his fields to feed swine.

16 And he would fain have filled his belly with the husks that the swine did eat: and no man gave unto him.

17 And when he came to himself, he said, How many hired servants of my father's have bread enough and to spare, and I perish with hunger!

18 I will arise and go to my father, and will say unto him, Father, I have sinned against heaven, and before thee,

19 And am no more worthy to be called thy son: make me as one of thy hired servants.

20 And he arose, and came to his father. But when he was yet a great way off, his father saw him, and had compassion, and ran, and fell on his neck, and kissed him.

21 And the son said unto him, Father, I have sinned against heaven, and in thy sight, and am no more worthy to be called thy son.

22 But the father said to his servants, Bring forth the best robe, and put it on him; and put a ring on his hand, and shoes on his feet:

23 And bring hither the fatted calf, and kill it; and let us eat, and be merry:

24 For this my son was dead, and is alive again; he was lost, and is found. And they began to be merry.

younger of them said to his father, 'Father, give me the share of the property that will belong to me.' So he divided his property between them. 13 A few days later the younger son gathered all he had and traveled to a distant country, and there he squandered his property in dissolute living. 14 When he had spent everything, a severe famine took place throughout that country, and he began to be in need. 15 So he went and hired himself out to one of the citizens of that country, who sent him to his fields to feed the pigs. 16 He would gladly have filled himself with the pods that the pigs were eating; and no one gave him anything. 17 But when he came to himself he said, 'How many of my father's hired hands have bread enough and to spare, but here I am dying of hunger! 18 I will get up and go to my father, and I will say to him, "Father, I have sinned against heaven and before you; 19 I am no longer worthy to be called your son; treat me like one of your hired hands." ' 20 So he set off and went to his father. But while he was still far off, his father saw him and was filled with compassion; he ran and put his arms around him and kissed him. 21 Then the son said to him, 'Father, I have sinned against heaven and before you; I am no longer worthy to be called your son.' But the father said to his slaves, 'Quickly, bring out a robe—the best one—and put it on him; put a ring on his finger and sandals on his feet. 23 And get the fatted calf and kill it, and let us eat and celebrate; 24 for this son of mine was dead and is alive again; he was lost and is found!' And they began to celebrate."

Key Verse: **For this my son was dead, and is alive again; he was lost, and is found. And they began to be merry. Luke 15:24**

Key Verse: **"For this son of mine was dead and is alive again; he was lost and is found!" And they began to celebrate. Luke 15:24**

As You Read the Scripture

The larger scripture lesson is all of Luke 15. This chapter consists of three successive parables on the same theme. The glad tiding of God's love for the penitent sinner proclaimed by Jesus is one of Luke's favorite themes. Note Luke 15:7, 10, and 24. See Luke 13:1-5 also. Reconciliation is a central theme in the Jewish understanding of salvation.

Luke 15:12. This division of property before the death of the father was not common, but does have some parallels in Jewish history. According to Deuteronomy 21:17 the oldest son received "a double portion of all that he has."

Verse 13. "A distant country" is probably intentionally vague, but it does stress a deep separation.

Verse 15. A Jewish saying was, "Cursed is the man who tends swine." Pig-tending was degrading work for a Jew.

Verse 16. These "pods" came from the carob-tree, common in the Mediterranean area.

Verse 17. The phrase "came to himself" was a common Greek idiom, equivalent to the Jewish idiom "return to God."

Verse 18. Note that the initiative lies with the penitent sinner, who intends to go to his father and confess his sin.

Verse 19. The penitent son did not expect full restoration to his former place in the family. He hoped only to join the hired hands.

Verse 20. The father's acceptance was immediate and preceded the son's confession. This, however, should not be taken to indicate acceptance without repentance, for this would contradict the main theme of the three stories about lostness—namely, joy over a repentant sinner. It is not necessary to make this parable into an allegory. It makes its point by being an illustrative incident from ordinary life.

Verse 21. The penitent son made a formal confession and disclaimed any right to his former status in the family.

Verses 22-23. The robe, ring, and sandals signify the full restoration of the lost son back into the family circle. The response of the father exemplified the special joy when something lost is found. The loss of a possession increases our estimation of its value, and regaining it gives us a greater happiness than enjoying the things we have never lost.

Verse 24. A person in "a distant country" could be completely out of touch with family in Roman Empire days. From the family's perspective that person might as well be dead. That's the sense in which the happy father proclaimed that his "dead" son was alive again. That called for a big celebration.

The Scripture and the Main Question

Estrangement Within the Family

It is obvious that there were tensions in the family of the prodigal son. The younger son wanted to leave home. He requested his inheritance and decided to go to a distant country. The story doesn't tell us why he wanted to leave. Perhaps it was the open jealousy of the older brother. Perhaps he just felt too provincial and wanted to see the world.

Many families would understand this from their own experiences. Sibling rivalry often makes life miserable for the underdog. The rivalry can be academic, as when a younger child follows an older brother or sister in school, but can't measure up to the superior work of the older one. Or, it can be in athletics or in music or in debate or any other activity.

Estrangement can be the result of a normal growing up. Parental control may be rejected (or modified) because one's peer group is the major influence behind one's decision. A certain amount of this is normal, to be expected and tolerated until it's passed. In the tension period, however, it can cause serious estrangement.

Personality clashes may be a main problem. These can be parent-parent, parent-child, or child-child, and usually remain fairly constant in the family history.

And then there are some persons who just seem to be "mean." They deliberately hurt another family member. This may cause retaliation from the hurt one, "to get even." Or it can be outwardly ignored even though most psychologists would say that it isn't really ignored but just pushed out of sight into the subconscious.

Misunderstandings are frequently the cause of estrangement. An action or some words may be seen or heard in a sense not at all intended.

Possessions are frequent sources of estrangement also, especially when an estate is being divided up or when things are "passed on" to the next generation. It is often difficult to be fair from anyone's perspective.

Babies and school-age children are always financial burdens, but they are (usually) accepted without special hostilities. Young people sometimes expect so much financial help from their parents that they actually undermine the parents' financial security. Those expectations can be sinful and the source of estrangement.

Spouses can be unfaithful, neglectful, irritating, unreasonably jealous, or possessive. These tensions (and others) can lead to separation and/or divorce, with many attendant child problems.

The parable of the lost son raises all these kinds of questions in our lives today. It can not only model the problems, but can also model one important solution.

Admitting Mistakes

The younger son learned the hard way. Most of us learn the hard way. That is, our parents' wisdom could prevent many mistakes if only the children would let it. "But Mom, I want to do it myself!" We learn from experience, but we get experience by making mistakes. We have to be permitted to make mistakes.

The son in "the distant country" made so many mistakes that he became destitute. We are like that. We keep on making mistakes until we "hit bottom." Then we're ready to "wise up" and get help. Hopefully there will come a time when the one who insisted on making his or her own mistakes will wake up. The younger son "came to himself" and realized the mess he had gotten himself into. When we reach this point it is time for a change. We "take stock" of ourselves and make plans for changes.

Regrets are part of this experience, but regrets alone don't restore a relationship that mistakes have broken. The younger son realized he was lost, and that he alone was to blame. He was ready to make a new start. Like that son, anyone can make a new start. The lure of family security can bring a prodigal home again, once he or she has "come to himself [or herself]."

The son couldn't undo what had been done. We can't either. What was done will remain done no matter how strongly we regret having done it. Neither can we really expect a person whom we have hurt to "forgive and forget." He or she may forgive, but how does one forget? It is like learning something. Once learned, it can't be unlearned. The son's father could forgive and accept the son's repentance, but could he forget? The other son could neither forgive nor forget. Reconciliation offered is sometimes rejected. To accomplish reconciliation is a more complicated procedure.

Reconciliation

How to be reconciled after a period of alienation is something most people think is quite simple. Here's the customary formula. What caused the alienation? If it was caused by an unalterable element, such as a serious personality clash, the alienation remains fairly constant, and one must simply put up with it. But most alienations are caused by changeable elements. To oversimplify an example, let us set up an estrangement that was caused by something an "offender" did to an "offended." The formula for reconciliation is one that begins with the offender taking the initiative, confessing responsibility for the alienation and asking forgiveness from the one offended. If the offended one accepts this confession and apology, he or she can forgive the offender and reconciliation is accomplished.

Theologically, this is the Jewish doctrine of salvation. Sin, freely chosen, alienates the sinner from a holy God. Repentance, also freely chosen, restores the relationship because God is merciful and always accepts sincere repentance. Note that in this understanding God does not cause the alienation and does not initiate the reconciliation.

Even though most Christian church members would probably identify with this view of reconciliation, it nevertheless is not the orthodox Christian understanding of our relationship to God. It could be argued that the orthodox pattern of our reconciliation to God should also be the pattern for reconciliation between human persons who are estranged.

What is the *Christian* pattern? It, too, is simple but harder to accept and still harder to apply to our human alienations. It says that sin does not separate us from God. God accepts us while we are still sinners (Rom. 5:6-11). God initiates the reconciliation and accomplishes it apart from and before our repentance. Reconciliation is God's unconditional gift to a still sinful humanity. The earliest Christians did not agree on how God does this! For Paul, the cross was God's rescue act, presented as a "mystery." For the Gospel of John, on the other hand, it was God as the Word becoming flesh and dwelling among us.

Of course acceptance does not mean that God approves of sinners. God also is working within the sinner to transform the sinner into a righteous person—a "new creation."

Transferred to human relationships, the orthodox view of reconciliation suggests that the initiative of reconciliation comes from the offended one, not the offender. Following Paul, the offended one voluntarily suffers the offense, and the mystery of suffering accomplishes the reconciliation. On the other hand, following John, the offended one puts himself (herself) into the "shoes" of the offender (becomes incarnate in their life) and somehow this creates a new oneness that is reconciliation.

Jesus' parable is clearly the Jewish view, not that of Paul or John. The one who offends takes the initiative and seeks reconciliation.

Helping Adults Become Involved

Preparing to Teach

If available from a school, church, or library near you, obtain a copy of Clarence Jordan's expanded Cotton Patch Version of the parable of the lost (prodigal) son. It is one of his recordings, read by Jordan himself.

This lesson explores personal relationships in families, using the parable of the lost son as the starting point for discussion. The lesson has three parts:

I. Estrangement within the family
II. Admitting mistakes
III. Reconciliation

Begin by getting in mind the topics of family alienations and reconciliations in "The Main Question." Then study "As You Read the Scripture" and "The Scripture and the Main Question." Make special note of questions to raise and points to emphasize in class discussion. Realize that everyone in the class will have personal experiences on this topic. Plan to utilize these experiences in class discussion.

Introducing the Main Question

This is one topic that involves everyone. Encourage the class members to think about their own family relationships and invite them to share these if they wish to. Explain that the aim of this lesson is to give class members a chance to reflect on their own family relationships and to improve their quality.

Developing the Lesson

I. Estrangement within the family

On a chalkboard (or on newsprint) write down the different kinds of hostilities (alienations) that the class members identify. Try to establish the variety of these tensions to include parents, children, grandchildren, and grandparents. If there are some in "The Scripture and the Main Question" that the class doesn't suggest, add them to the list.

If you were able to get the recording of Clarence Jordan's expanded reading of the parable of the lost son, let the class hear it at this point. Follow this with comments about the modernization of this version. Even though the second part of the parable (the role of the older son) is not part of this lesson, let the class hear the way Clarence Jordan retold the whole parable.

If there are those in your class who have done professional counseling, identify them and value their opinions.

II. *Admitting mistakes*

Start a class discussion about how easy or hard it is to admit past mistakes and to be truly repentant. Do the class members think anyone can always repent? Why do some people find it hard to repent?

What different forms can repentance take? Does true repentance always involve change? How does "guilt" fit in here? Conscience?

Remind the class of the story of Job who refused to admit to any wrong-doing only to "encounter God" and then repented of his self-righteousness and arrogance.

Let the class see (hear) the relationship of the three stories about the lost being found. Call special attention to the way the first two are interpreted as sinners repenting, even though the sheep and the coin did not repent. Their lostness and "foundness" are clearly interpreted as alienation from God and reconciliation through repentance. The repentance theme then moves beyond the interpretation and right into the third story, which is left uninterpreted.

III. *Reconciliation*

This section may be difficult to explain. The common pattern will already be familiar to the class. It may be more effective not to present the common pattern but to let it come out of class discussion. Write its stages on the chalkboard or newsprint. The results should look like this:

Stage One: Person A offends person B = Alienation
Two: Person A repents
Three: Person A makes restitution
Four: Person B may forgive person A
Five: Reconciliation: the relationship is restored

Then ask the class to evaluate this common pattern. Do they have any reservations about its effectiveness? If no criticisms are offered, ask the class if repentance is required for reconciliation. (The usual answer is yes.) Then ask the class if we are free to repent. (The usual answer again, yes.) Now ask what Christ came to do? What was the saving work of Christ?

In other words, if we can heal alienation by our own sincere repentance, then why do we need Christ? This question will open the door to explain the specifically Christian understanding of reconciliation. Do this in your own words, and then quote the explanation in part III of "Helping Adults Become Involved."

Get the class reaction to these ideas. Leave them to think about this and assure them that the topic of salvation will be continued into the next unit.

Helping Class Members Act

Challenge the class members to reflect on situations in their own family and take some specific action to enrich their family life. This is not for reporting next Sunday, but only for their personal advantage.

Preparing for Next Sunday

This lesson ends unit II, "Jesus' Ministry in Galilee." Next Sunday begins unit III, "The Cross and the Resurrection." Next Sunday's lesson looks at the salvation theme again from a different perspective. Read Luke 18:15-30 in preparation.

UNIT III: THE CROSS AND THE RESURRECTION

FOUR LESSONS   **FEBRUARY 6–27**

You can tell a lot about an organization on the basis of what symbol it uses to represent itself. A university may use the symbol of book, or a lighted flame, symbols of knowledge and wisdom. A stock-trading firm uses the image of a bull, telling us that they are "bullish" on the stock market.

You and I gather within a human organization that takes as its symbol the cross. The cross, a symbol of the worst of human cruelty, is the church's symbol of victory. For us Christians, the cross symbolizes the very heart of our faith. The cross is a sign both of the world's rejection and murder of Jesus. At the same time, paradoxically, it is also a symbol of the power of God. In the cross, God turned the worst that humanity could do into the most powerful presentation of what God could do.

In this unit, we will follow Luke's presentation of the last events of Jesus' early ministry. We will see how, even though Jesus preached love, he received hate from the world. He obediently suffered death on a cross. And yet, in God's amazing act, Jesus was raised from death to life.

These are among the core Christian themes that we will be studying during this unit.

LESSON 10   **FEBRUARY 6**

Exercising Childlike Faith

Background Scripture: Luke 18:15-30

The Main Question

This lesson continues the salvation theme and adds a new element. It is based on two passages in Luke, both of which have versions in Matthew and Mark that have interesting and significant variations.

It will be helpful to focus on three questions. *First,* what does the teaching about being like a child mean? *Second,* what can we learn about the first three Gospels from the variant passages, and what can we learn about Jesus' teachings as well? *Third,* what new insights do these two passages give us in our continuing study of the doctrine of salvation and its relation to riches?

The problem with the first question is the lack of precision in the biblical texts, a problem characteristic of the other two Gospel versions as well.

The second question helps us understand the way the different convictions of the Gospel writers have influenced what they report about Jesus' teachings.

The third question returns to the theme of the lesson for January 23 and continues discussing the thorny problem of wealth as an obstacle to salvation. It also forces us to deal with the reward motive for our discipleship. Are we exchanging temporary rewards now for better and eternal rewards later? That seems like a shrewd business deal instead of a "childlike faith."

These are among the questions that today's lesson attempts to answer.

Selected Scripture

King James Version

Luke 18:15-30

15 And they brought unto him also infants, that he would touch them: but when his disciples saw it, they rebuked them.

16 But Jesus called them unto him, and said, Suffer little children to come unto me, and forbid them not: for of such is the kingdom of God.

17 Verily I say unto you, whosoever shall not receive the kingdom of God as a little child shall in no wise enter therein.

18 And a certain ruler asked him, saying, Good Master, what shall I do to inherit eternal life?

19 And Jesus said unto him, Why callest thou me good? none is good, save one, that is, God.

20 Thou knowest the commandments, Do not commit adultery, Do not kill, Do not steal, Do not bear false witness, Honour thy father and thy mother.

21 And he said, All these have I kept from my youth up.

22 Now when Jesus heard these things, he said unto him, Yet lackest thou one thing: sell all that thou hast, and distribute unto the poor, and thou shalt have treasure in heaven: and come, follow me.

23 And when he heard this, he was very sorrowful: for he was very rich.

24 And when Jesus saw that he was very sorrowful, he said, How hardly shall they that have riches enter into the kingdom of God!

25 For it is easier for a camel to go through a needles eye, than for a rich man to enter into the kingdom

New Revised Standard Version

Luke 18:15-30

15 People were bringing even infants to him that he might touch them; and when the disciples saw it, they sternly ordered them not to do it. 16 But Jesus called for them and said, "Let the little children come to me, and do not stop them; for it is to such as these that the kingdom of God belongs. 17 Truly I tell you, whoever does not receive the kingdom of God as a little child will never enter it."

18 A certain ruler asked him, "Good Teacher, what must I do to inherit eternal life?" 19 Jesus said to him, "Why do you call me good? No one is good but God alone. 20 You know the commandments: 'You shall not commit adultery; You shall not murder; You shall not steal; You shall not bear false witness; Honor your father and mother.' " 21 He replied, "I have kept all these since my youth." 22 When Jesus heard this, he said to him, "There is still one thing lacking. Sell all that you own and distribute the money to the poor, and you will have treasure in heaven; then come, follow me." 23 But when he heard this, he became sad; for he was very rich. 24 Jesus looked at him and said, "How hard it is for those who have wealth to enter the kingdom of God! 25 Indeed, it is easier for a camel to go through the eye of a needle then for someone who is rich to enter the kingdom of God."

of God.

26 And they that heard it said, Who then can be saved?

27 And he said, The things which are impossible with men are possible with God.

28 Then Peter said, Lo, we have left all, and followed thee.

29 And he said unto them, Verily I say unto you, There is no man that hath left house, or parents, or brethren, or wife, or children, for the kingdom of God's sake,

30 Who shall not receive manifold more in this present time, and in the world to come life everlasting.

Key Verse: **Verily I say unto you, Whosoever shall not receive the kingdom of God as a little child shall in no wise enter therein. Luke 18:17**

26 Those who heard it said, "Then who can be saved?" 27 He replied, "What is impossible for mortals is possible for God."

28 Then Peter said, "Look, we have left our homes and followed you." 29 And he said to them, "Truly I tell you, there is no one who has left house or wife or brothers or parents or children, for the sake of the kingdom of God, 30 who will not get back very much more in this age, and in the age to come eternal life."

Key Verse: **"Truly I tell you, whoever does not receive the kingdom of God as a little child will never enter it." Luke 18:17**

As You Read the Scripture

Luke 18:15. In Mark, Jesus is indignant at the disciples when they rebuke those bringing children. Both Matthew and Luke omitted this indignation. Luke also omitted the reference to Jesus embracing the children. Luke changed Mark's "children" to "babies," but reverted to "children" in verses 16 and 17.

Verse 16. All three report that the kingdom "belongs" to children, but capacity in the children seems needed to give point to the saying.

Verse 17. "To receive the kingdom of God as a little child" is a requirement for entrance into the kingdom. But what does it mean? Luke has recorded the saying unchanged (from Mark 10:15), but Matthew (18:3) changed it, as well as moved it to an earlier setting.

Verses 18-19. The "certain ruler" of Luke is "a man" in his Markan source (10:17), and "someone" in Matthew. The man addressed Jesus as "Good Teacher" in both Luke and Mark, but simply as "Teacher" in Matthew.

Verse 20. The commandments given probably represent all ten of the famous "Ten Commandments." Jesus was probably not selecting from the ten only these five as necessary.

Verse 22. Luke omitted Mark's note that Jesus "loved him." Luke strengthened the requirement by adding "all" to Mark's statement. Jesus in all three accounts promised "treasure in heaven" as compensation for poverty on earth.

Verses 24-25. Luke greatly weakened his Markan source; compare these verses with Mark 10:23-25. The saying about the camel was probably an oriental hyperbole (exaggeration for emphasis). Since in Aramaic (Jesus' language) the word for "camel" and the word for "rope" are easily confused, it is possible that we should read "rope" here. In any case the often-heard explanation that "the eye of a needle" was the name of a low gate in the

Jerusalem wall that required a camel to go through on its knees is a medieval sermonic fiction.

Verse 26. Luke rephrased Mark 10:27, reducing the emphasis on the impossibility of meeting the requirements for entering the kingdom of God. The amazement and astonishment of the disciples in Mark was omitted by Luke. The difference between the salvation doctrine of Mark and Luke is only hinted at here. Mark came from a Gentile-Christian community that shared with Paul a conviction that the Crucifixion was God's rescue act for humanity, whereas Luke came from a Jewish-Christian community that did not relate the cross to our salvation. Note that Mark 10:45 is changed by Luke (12:27) to a servant motif. Luke, in preserving the statement about the impossibility of "mortals" qualifying for entrance into the kingdom, seems to have been not fully aware that he was compromising his own convictions about repentance and righteousness as basic requirements for salvation.

Verses 28-30. Jesus reassured the disciples that the life of poverty that they have voluntarily embraced will be richly rewarded. Luke did not retain Mark's qualification that their "rewards" in this age will be "with persecutions" (Mark 10:40). The meaning of the promise that they will have more than they have given up, even in this time, may refer to the larger fellowship of discipleship as the replacement for the families they have left. See Mark 10:30.

The Scripture and the Main Question

What Is a Childlike Faith?

The reputation of Jesus as a healer who laid hands on those he healed may be the explanation for people bringing "even infants" to Jesus. They were probably seeking a blessing for their offspring. When the disciples tried to prevent this, Jesus pronounced, "It is to such as these that the kingdom of God belongs." He then followed that with the dictum, "Whoever does not receive the kingdom of God as a little child will never enter it."

These sayings are "framework sayings." They provide only a framework. The meaning has been left to the hearer (or reader). Children have many traits. They are helpless as infants, born self-centered, unaware of and unconcerned for the needs of those around them (especially the parents), lovable, ignorant, messy, expensive, and they unconsciously impose burdens on their caretakers. Unless betrayed, they trust their parents and have the capacity to obey or disobey. They sleep a lot, too, as infants. Which traits did Jesus have in mind?

Since Jesus was talking to adults about conditions they must meet, we have to look for some quality in children that is not only theirs but can be a quality in adults as well.

Some Christians seem to think the ignorance of children ought to be preserved into adulthood. They say things like: "If ignorance is bliss, 'tis folly to be wise." "You be careful not to let that school ruin your faith." The only thing Christian leaders need is the guidance of the Holy Spirit: "book-learning" is relying on human resources. Granting that education does change one's ideas, it nevertheless brings us closer to the truth, which is God's nature. Ignorance is not the answer.

Of course, Jesus must have meant some *good* quality in children. That rules out their self-centeredness, messiness, and all those qualities. A renowned biblical scholar believes that Jesus means a simple and absolute trust in the God's will. We must surrender, without misgiving and without reserve, to God's grace. This idea is characteristic of many others. It remains uncertain, and it is less than helpful that the Gospel writers have preserved for us a saying of Jesus that proclaims a condition for salvation not clearly defined.

Learning from the Differences

Let's first look at the theological presuppositions behind the three accounts of the "certain ruler" (Luke) who asked Jesus about the requirements for eternal life. In the earliest one (Mark, the source for both the others) when the man replied that he had kept the commandments, Jesus told him, in effect, that wasn't enough. Luke has preserved Mark's viewpoint. There is still one thing lacking. "Sell all that you own and distribute the money to the poor" (Luke 18:22). There's no commandment in the Torah (the Law of Moses) that says we must sell everything and give the money away. Why does Jesus make poverty a condition for eternal life?

In Matthew's account there are two important changes. Matthew didn't like Jesus' repudiation of his own goodness, so he altered the story to "correct" this impression. Then, at the point where Mark and Luke report that he still lacks "one thing," Matthew's account makes the poverty instruction a "counsel of perfection" rather than a requirement. A "counsel of perfection" is something not required but adding it makes one more perfect. In theology a "counsel of perfection" is called a "work of supererogation." Both terms mean something beyond what is required. It is like a project in school that isn't required, but gives extra credit.

This is quite agreeable with Matthew's usual position on salvation. It is a reward for obedience (righteousness). It is closely related to Jewish thinking on salvation.

In Christian theology eternal life is not a reward of obedience or for anything else. Eternal life is God's gift, through Jesus Christ. Mark's account, saying that even perfect obedience to the Torah does not ensure eternal life, is therefore closer to later Christian orthodoxy than Matthew's account. So much of Luke-Acts reflects the Jewish understanding that Luke's use of Mark without changing it as Matthew did, is puzzling. Perhaps Luke did not see the full implications of Mark's version.

The Anti-Wealth Theme

It is characteristic of the first three Gospels that wealth is an impediment to salvation. We studied that theme in the January 23 lesson. This week's lesson stresses "how hard it is for those who have wealth to enter the kingdom of God." Hard, but not impossible? Other sayings in Luke, such as the one in 14:33, make poverty a requirement for discipleship.

Perhaps the requirement Jesus gave to the "ruler" was not intended to apply to everyone. Perhaps it was a special requirement for this particular person. It seems reasonable that Jesus would often speak to particular situations, not intending that the particular become a universal.

Or perhaps the "ruler" was invited to be one of Jesus' special disciples, as Mark's account suggests. That Jesus "loved him" and invited him to "follow him" are details that Luke omits. Then we have to assume that the special disciples had a more stringent life-style than "ordinary" disciples who stayed in their family and workplace. The teaching of the rabbis agreed with Jesus that riches often hindered the life of obedience, but they did not sponsor "poverty-cults."

The Reward Motivation

In all three of the Gospels called "synoptic" (because of their striking agreements), heavenly rewards are frequently promised to the followers of Jesus. In this week's scripture, Jesus reassured the disciples that what they had to give up to become disciples will be restored, and more. This restoration is even promised for "this age," with "eternal life" the reward "in the age to come." The "this age" restoration of family may be explained by Jesus' saying in Luke 8:21.

For "the age to come" rewards, see Luke 6:35 and 16:25 in addition to the scripture for this lesson. How do we respond to these reward promises? Are we motivated by them? Does this tempt us to be content with poverty "in this age"? How does this affect our current attitude that poverty is a disgrace and should be eliminated entirely?

Helping Adults Become Involved

Preparing to Teach

Two themes dominate this lesson. Give the first third of your class time to the first theme, *"Being like a child."* Then take a shorter time slot to discuss a minor theme, *What can we learn from a study of the variations in the scripture as found in each of the first three Gospels?* Reserve the last half of the class time for a discussion of Jesus' sayings about riches and the life of a disciple. Work the reward motivation theme into the riches discussion.

The four divisions of this lesson:

     I. What is a childlike faith?
    II. Learning from the differences
   III. The anti-wealth theme
   IV. The reward motivation

List the three leading questions presented in "The Main Question." Then study the "As You Read the Scripture" section. Now you will be ready for "The Scripture and the Main Question." Formulate your discussion topics and "starter-questions."

Introducing the Main Question

Announce to the class the principal themes in the form of questions. They will probably already be familiar with the sayings of Jesus about children and the kingdom of God. Explain that one class aim is to ask what that means.

They will probably already know that the stories and sayings have variations from Gospel to Gospel. Announce that this lesson takes those variations seriously because they reveal the way the Gospel writer's convictions affect the wording. How do one's convictions affect what one says?

Warn the class that the lesson includes hard sayings about rich people being excluded from salvation. Can wealth itself exclude the rich one? That question gives us the chance to think again about motivation by expectations of rewards.

Developing the Lesson

I. What is a childlike faith?

Draw from the class their notions of the qualities of a young child, both good ones and bad ones. Add the traits from "What Is a Childlike Faith?" in the "Scripture and the Main Question" section, if they haven't been suggested by the class.

Have a class member read verses 15-17. Inform the class that Matthew, Mark, and Luke all have the first saying, and in identical wording (except Matthew has "kingdom of heaven" instead of "kingdom of God" in Mark and Luke). Then point out that whereas Mark and Luke have identical accounts of the second saying, Matthew changes both the wording and its place in the story. Read the saying in Matthew 18:3. Now the class can discuss what Jesus really said and what it means.

Ask the class members to name childlike qualities. Write them on the chalkboard or newsprint. At this stage include both good and bad traits. Add to the class list any that you think of, and refer to Matthew 18:4, raising a question about what it says. Does the class think a child is humble?

Explain "framework sayings," as described in "The Scripture and the Main Question." Use these sayings as good examples. Invite class members to share what they would put into this framework. Since there is no way to be sure here, quote the biblical scholar's opinion from "The Scripture and the Main Question," and leave the question open.

II. Learning from the differences

Make the transition to this topic by staying with the child sayings and comparing Matthew's version (18:3) with Luke's (18:17). How does "receiving . . . as a child" reflect a different viewpoint than "changing and becoming like children"?

The next example may be easier for the class and more instructive as well. Call attention to the beginning of the story of the ruler who asked about eternal life. Ask the class to respond to Jesus' reaction to being addressed as "good" (in Luke's more accurate presentation of Mark 10:17). Is anyone bothered by it? Why? Then make the conjecture that Matthew was bothered by it because he changed it. Read Matthew 19:16-17. Let the class guess why Matthew made this change. What does it tell us about the convictions of the authors of Luke and Matthew?

Move next to the answer to the ruler's question. In Luke, following Mark (10:21), perfect obedience to the Torah is not enough. In Matthew (19:21) it is enough, but he is urged to go beyond the requirements to "extra-credit." What does that tell us about the convictions of Luke and Matthew?

III. The anti-wealth theme

A previous discussion (in the lessons for January 16 and 23) on wealth as an obstacle to salvation probably did not settle the question. The class has another chance to discuss it in this lesson.

What impression does the class have about the ending of the story of the ruler seeking eternal life? Was Jesus saying that his salvation depended on his becoming poor?

Read to the class the story of Zacchaeus (Luke 19:1-10). Why didn't Zacchaeus have to sell all *his* possessions?

Remind the class of the parable of the pounds (Luke 19:11-27). Matthew has a parallel version (Matt. 25:14-30). Jesus here seems to have taught that we should have possessions and use them wisely. How does the class relate these teachings to the ones that require poverty? Perhaps the issue is whether we *have* money or we *love* money. One cannot *love* money and qualify for the kingdom.

IV. The reward motivation

This, too, has already been in the discussion. Have the class consider Luke 18:22 and any other saying familiar to the class that promises rewards. See if they can accept the idea that the giving of rewards is not necessarily the motivating factor, but just the consequent factor.

Helping Class Members Act

Ask the class members to select at least one person outside the class and talk with that person about variations in the text of the Bible. How does that person relate these variations to concepts of inspiration and scriptural authority? The class member should be prepared to present his or her answers to these questions.

Preparing for Next Sunday

Next week the lesson focuses on the consequences of our actions. Ask the class to think ahead on the questions, Are consequences always sure to happen? and Do they happen sometimes, but not always?

LESSON 11   FEBRUARY 13

Accountable for Our Actions

Background Scripture: Luke 20:1-19

The Main Question

Everyone knows that actions have consequences. What we do will affect something or someone. Of course, what we think may well affect what we do, but it's our actions that have visible consequences.

To what extent are we accountable for the consequences of our actions? Are we completely accountable? Partly accountable? Sometimes accountable and sometimes not accountable? Hardly ever accountable? Why is there this range of possible answers?

We can see the problem more clearly in its extreme forms. A deliberate, "cold-blooded" act of killing another human being, without provocation and without danger to the killer, is legally called "first-degree murder." That implies other degrees of murder. Then there's "involuntary manslaughter," for which the killer is less accountable than "first-degree murder." If the killing is purely in self-defense, accountability dwindles even more. If the killer is clearly insane, then accountability is gone altogether. Of course, this only illustrates degrees of accountability and opens up the complexities of the problem.

The scripture lesson is a parable that illustrates full accountability for our actions. The wicked tenants are fully accountable and will suffer destruction for their wickedness. But life is more complicated than this. Just how do we assess our own accountability and the accountability of those around us? And what about the various groups we are in; can they be held accountable? That includes, of course, our church and our country.

Selected Scripture

King James Version

Luke 20:9-19

9 Then began he to speak to the people this parable; A certain man planted a vineyard, and let it forth to husbandmen, and went into a far country for a long time.

10 And at the season he sent a servant to the husbandmen, that they should give him of the fruit of the vineyard: but the husbandmen beat him, and sent him away empty.

11 And again he sent another servant: and they beat him also, and entreated him shamefully, and sent him away empty.

12 And again he sent a third: and they wounded him also, and cast him out.

13 Then said the lord of the vineyard, What shall I do? I will send my beloved son: it may be they will reverence him when they see him.

14 But when the husbandmen saw him, they reasoned among themselves, saying, This is the heir: come, let us kill him, that the inheritance may be ours.

15 So they cast him out of the vineyard, and killed him. What therefore shall the lord of the vineyard do unto them?

16 He shall come and destroy these husbandmen, and shall give

New Revised Standard Version

Luke 20:9-19

9 He began to tell the people this parable: "A man planted a vineyard, and leased it to tenants, and went to another country for a long time. 10 When the season came, he sent a slave to the tenants in order that they might give him his share of the produce of the vineyard; but the tenants beat him and sent him away empty-handed. 11 Next he sent another slave; that one also they beat and insulted and sent away empty-handed. 12 And he sent still a third; this one also they wounded and threw out. 13 Then the owner of the vineyard said, 'What shall I do? I will send my beloved son; perhaps they will respect him.' 14 But when the tenants saw him, they discussed it among themselves and said, 'This is the heir; let us kill him so that the inheritance may be ours.' 15 So they threw him out of the vineyard and killed him. What then will the owner of the vineyard do to them? 16 He will come and destroy those tenants and give the vineyard to others." When they heard this, they said, "Heaven forbid!" 17 But he looked at them and said, "What then does this text mean: 'The stone that the builders rejected has

the vineyard to others. And when they heard it, they said, God forbid.

17 And he beheld them, and said, what is this then that is written, the stone which the builders rejected, the same is become the head of the corner?

18 Whosoever shall fall upon that stone shall be broken; but on whomsoever it shall fall, it will grind him to powder.

19 And the chief priests and the scribes the same hour sought to lay hands on him; and they feared the people: for they perceived that he had spoken this parable against them.

become the cornerstone'? 18 Everyone who falls on that stone will be broken to pieces; and it will crush anyone on whom it falls." 19 When the scribes and chief priests realized that he had told this parable against them, they wanted to lay hands on him at that very hour, but they feared the people.

Key Verses: **And he beheld them, and said, What is this then that is written, The stone which the builders rejected, the same is become the head of the corner? Luke 20:17**

Key Verses: **But he looked at them and said, "What then does this text mean: 'The stone that the builders rejected has become the cornerstone'?" Luke 20:17**

As You Read the Scripture

"The Parable of the Wicked Tenants" is, in its present form, an allegory rather than a true parable. In an allegory, each principal element in the story is a symbol for something else. Because this story reflects back on the crucifixion of Jesus, it is not likely to be a teaching of Jesus "in the days of his flesh." It could easily have been one of his parables, however, transformed in the preaching of the early church into the present allegory.

Luke 20:9. The "man" stands for God, the "vineyard" is Israel, his chosen people. The vineyard as a symbol for Israel was a common one, as shown by Psalm 80:8-16 and Isaiah 5:1-7. The "tenants" are the hierarchy now in charge of the people (the vineyard). The "man" going to another country for a long time is God, no longer directly governing his people.

Verses 10-12. The three "slaves" sent to collect the owner's share represent the prophets God sent to warn the hierarchy that their management of the "vineyard" wasn't good. The prophets all died a violent death at the hands of the hierarchy, according to a popular book of Jesus' times, *The Lives of the Prophets*. In the allegory the three are treated progressively worse.

Verses 13-15. The "beloved son" is Jesus, who was put to death by the "tenants." "Thrown out" and then "killed" stands for taking Jesus outside the walls and crucifying him. Now what will God do to the present hierarchy?

Verse 16. God will destroy those tenants, meaning the Jewish hierarchy, and turn the "vineyard" over to others. This is explained further in 22:28, where the disciples are depicted as "judging the twelve tribes of Israel." To "give the vineyard to others" stands for the Christian claim to be the true Israel. Christianity as the true Israel is a major theme of Luke-Acts. His hearers (identified as "the people" in v. 9) were shocked by this, as their response shows. The destruction of "those tenants" took place in the Jewish war with the Romans in 66-70 C.E.

Verse 17. In response to the "heaven forbid" reaction of the people, Jesus countered by asking them what a well-known text meant by the rejected stone becoming "the cornerstone"? In this usage, the text (Ps. 118:22) refers symbolically to Christ as the rejected stone that became the cornerstone of the true Israel (see also Acts 4:11 and 1 Pet. 2:4-7).

Verse 18. Early Christians understood the prophecy in Daniel 2:34-35 as a prophecy that was fulfilled by the coming of Christ.

Verse 19. The "hierarchy" understood that the story was critical of them and predicted their downfall, so naturally they wanted Jesus "put away." Jesus' original parable may well have been directed against the hierarchy. They, in turn, may well have wanted Jesus silenced because of his criticism.

The Scripture and the Main Question

We Reap What We Sow

Near the end of the letter of Paul to the Galatians, in its present canonical form, the reader is warned not to take Paul's gospel of radical grace too seriously. "After all," this scribal addition seems to say, "in the end you are going to get exactly what you deserve." Of course, this contradicted the main point of the letter. From the viewpoint of Judaism, this warning was quite appropriate. We often do get what we deserve. The parable of the wicked tenants illustrates well the belief that God's judgment—God's justice—will finally catch up with those who disobey God's will. When we read that parable we can see at once its affinity to the cardinal principle of Judaism.

> The Lord watches over the way of the righteous,
> but the way of the wicked will perish. (Psalm 1:6)

Actions do have consequences. Those who believe that those consequences follow a pattern of strict justice tend to explain good and bad experiences as the just consequences of previous actions. What did I do to deserve this? is a frequent question. We are fully accountable for our actions and fully deserve the consequences.

We sometimes try to avoid taking the responsibility for unfortunate consequences that we have caused. We may try to shift the blame, or "pass the buck." Of course, if the consequences are positive, we may encourage others to believe that our actions were the cause of the good results. We tend to deny the blame but claim the credit.

These are some limiting factors, however, that modify this stern individualism. To be reminded of these factors is not to encourage anyone to seek excuses for their own accountability. Instead, to be aware of them may give each of us a more sympathetic and understanding attitude toward those others around us.

What Can We Change?

Some of our actions are not willfully chosen actions. We may just do them without thinking. We call these actions "habits." Our "habits" become part of how we are known. We are "creatures of habit."

Habits are functionally important. We perform many required actions by habit, relieving us of the problem of making a decision on every little thing that comes up in life. Habits are what make us predictable to those around us.

As useful and necessary as habits are, they still may be "good" or "bad." Our bad habits may be harmful to ourselves, and/or annoying (at the least) to others. Are we accountable for our bad habits? The answer depends on how much control you believe we have in creating and changing our habits. Most of us, I think, would answer, "Yes, we are accountable for our bad habits."

The question gets harder to answer when we move from habits to "compulsions." My dictionary defines a compulsion as "an irresistible impulse to act in a certain way, regardless of the rationality of the motivation," and "an act or acts performed in response to such an impulse." If such an action is irresistible, is the actor accountable for his or her actions?

Our problem gets even more difficult yet when we proceed to the next stage. Some people have "addictions," and addictions are usually regarded as more severe than compulsions. My dictionary reports that the word *addict* comes from a Latin word (*addictus*) meaning "given over to another as a slave." We most commonly use the concept in reference to certain drugs, but lately the concept of addiction is being used much more widely. Is a "couch potato" a television addict?

We purposefully stop short of actions performed by persons who are insane. Should insane people be held accountable for their actions? But aren't habits, compulsions, and addictions part of "normal" lives? It is a vague line that separates sane from insane.

As Christians we are people who are saved by the grace of a loving God, who accepts us as we are and dwells within us to make us over into the image of Christ. How can we defend any other life-style than that of accepting the people around us as they are and acting as God's instruments of transforming grace in their lives?

Are We Products of Society?

We have become much more aware these days of how we are shaped by the society in which we live. We call this "socialization." The feminist movement has called our attention to the ways we socialize our boys to be boyish and our girls to be girlish. Are what we formerly believed to be "natural" qualities really socializations?

Our problem here can be most easily seen in the more extreme forms. In certain small groups within our larger society, the socialization process may be at least partly responsible for the emergence of criminal personalities. How accountable are these persons for their actions? Is it an aberrant society that is really accountable? Is accountability divided sometimes between an individual and society?

This aspect may be easier to grasp if put in terms of peer pressure (but that's socialization, too). If we are in a peer group that believes in doing things the larger society believes is wrong, and we follow our peer group, where is the accountability?

Those who study ethical behavior patterns and stages of faith believe, on the basis of their research, that most people never get free from peer-group controls. Shall we hold the peer group accountable for the actions of their members?

For example, consider a peer group in our society that believes formal education ("schooling") is harmful. Out of sheer ignorance, a person in that peer group may do something that is harmful or even criminal. Shall we hold that person accountable? "Ignorance of the law is no excuse" is the way we usually answer. But is that answer right?

What We Must Accept

The famous prayer of Reinhold Niebuhr reminds us to change what we can change and to accept what we cannot change. We cannot change others, so our choice is to accept them as they are or to refuse to accept them. Persons with bad habits can change those habits. Persons need help in reforming their habits, but in the last analysis they must themselves make the change.

People need more help when dealing with undesirable actions caused by compulsions or addictions. They need the grace of God, but that grace comes through the people around them, not directly from the sky. We all need to be agents of grace, but at the same time we all need to be objects of the grace of God so we can change also. The process of redemption is interactive. We are all in need of being changed; we are all agents of God in the changing of those around us.

Helping Adults Become Involved

Preparing to Teach

Since there is more than usual in this lesson for the teacher to present, rather than utilizing mainly class discussion, it is important to study carefully "The Scripture and the Main Question." The scripture, this week, is the basis for the first part of the lesson only. Be familiar with the parable, but do not make it the central emphasis. "As You Read the Scripture" raises hard questions about the authenticity of the parable being actually from Jesus, but since that is not the main point of this lesson, do not let that question replace "The Main Question."

    I.   We reap what we sow
   II.   What can we change?
  III.   Are we products of society?
  IV.   What we must accept

Introducing the Main Question

Do not begin with the parable. Begin by raising the question of our accountability. Point out that actions have consequences and ask how responsible we are for our actions. Get class members to respond without any further development of the problem. After a short time of collecting class opinions, but not yet discussing them, raise the questions found at the end of "The Main Question."

Developing the Lesson

I. We reap what we sow

Now is the time to have a class member read aloud the parable. Explain the symbolic (allegorical) meaning to the class, and then ask them to venture opinions about the time period the parable fits most appropriately. Does it fit the lifetime of Jesus? Why, or why not? Help the class to see why the scholars believe it is not in its original form, and why it is probably an early church modification of what Jesus taught. This matter aside, what does the parable say about the accountability of the tenants for their actions?

Make the points in support of the tenants' accountability in "We Reap What We Sow" in "The Scripture and the Main Question" section. Then announce that these are some problems with believing in full individual accountability.

II. What can we change?

Open a discussion on habits. Get the opinions and experiences of class members about the universality and power of habits. Ask them to what extent is a person responsible for his or her habits? Have them give examples of bad habits.

Then move on to "compulsive" acts. Read the dictionary definition in the lesson material. Does the class agree that some actions are irresistible? If so, where's the accountability?

It will not be easy, and it is not necessary, to make a definite distinction between compulsion and addiction. Addictions are often related to what are often called "habit-forming" drugs. That illustrates well the way our three words *habit, compulsion,* and *addiction* cannot be isolated from one another, but are often interchangeable. For a milder situation we tend to talk about habits; for severe ones, we prefer compulsion or addiction.

There's lots of room for discussion and disagreement when we begin to "excuse" people of accountability for actions done by compulsion or addiction. How far does the class feel we should move in that direction? Do not expect full agreement with the lesson material or between class members. The intent is to get people to think, and thus to improve their personal relationships as well as to make some personal changes.

Be sure to discuss only "normal" persons. See if the class agrees that all "normal" people have "habits" that are so strong as to be called compulsions or addictions. Have them supply examples of compulsive acts from their personal experiences.

III. Are we products of society?

Class members are probably most familiar with the socialization process that affects our gender classification. Does our society effectively create gender traits that are not rooted in "human nature"? Is it natural for baby girls to be dressed in pink and baby boys in blue? Is it natural for a young woman who wants to get married to "shut up and wear pink"? What other examples of socialization can your class suggest?

Raise now the more difficult aspect of how peer pressure affects our actions. Should one's individual background be a factor in deciding on his or her accountability? Should cult groups be held accountable for the actions of their members? Should the members be excused? Do they share accountability?

SECOND QUARTER

Ask the class to share the family socialization that has affected them. This can be too personal to share, so examples can come from observation of other families, if necessary or helpful. Are sexual attitudes the result of family/societal socialization? Racial attitudes? Let the class provide different types of examples.

Finally, ask how inheritance (genetic) factors are related to accountability. How about a violent temper? Is one accountable for actions caused by an inherited trait?

IV. What we must accept

Steer the class discussion away from one's own accountability and focus the discussion on understanding others. How does a topic like this affect the way we relate to others? Study carefully the material in this part of the lesson. Present the theological lesson slowly and deliberately, asking for responses that the theological material might cause.

Finally, challenge the class members to adopt a new level of understanding of others. Challenge them to be instruments of God's grace in the lives of those around them.

Helping Class Members Act

Ask class members to keep a private list of actions in their daily lives that they will take more responsibility for changing. Then, on another private list, have them note those actions of others that have become more acceptable to them because of increased understanding of why they act as they do.

Preparing for Next Sunday

The lesson next week focuses on the servant theme in a Christian lifestyle. This relates closely to the accountability and "agents of grace" themes of the lesson this week. Before next week, think about being a servant to all around you.

LESSON 12   FEBRUARY 20

Acting as a Servant

Background Scripture: Luke 22:1-30

The Main Question

Jesus taught that among his followers "the leader" must "be like one who serves" (v. 26). He identified himself as "one who serves" (v. 27).

Why is the figure of the servant a model of the life-style of Jesus' followers? Is there some inherent goodness in being a servant? Don't we need good bosses as well?

196

We give lip-service to this servanthood ideal, but we don't become servants, we hire servants. What does "being a servant" mean?

Everyone is already a servant to something. We can't avoid serving, and we're caught up in several servanthoods. The only question is *what* do we serve? Isn't it time to examine carefully what we serve and do some critical thinking about whether we wish to stay in our present servanthoods or change to others? Surely some are more worthy of our services than others. Shouldn't we serve only the best?

Perhaps truth is the highest service-object. God is truth. Jesus in John's Gospel claims to be the truth: "I am the way, the truth, and the life" (John 16:4). Here the problem is that truth-serving often gets us in trouble with the church. Should it?

Jesus probably had in mind service to others. That kind of service is important for our own salvation because it is action that is corrective of our basic, natural self-centeredness. Jesus' death for the salvation of humanity was his greatest act of service. That was foreshadowed in the Last Supper.

Selected Scripture

King James Version

New Revised Standard Version

Luke 22:14-30

14 And when the hour was come, he sat down, and the twelve apostles with him.

15 And he said unto them, With desire I have desired to eat this passover with you before I suffer:

16 For I say unto you, I will not any more eat thereof, until it be fulfilled in the kingdom of God.

17 And he took the cup, and gave thanks, and said, Take this, and divide it among yourselves:

18 For I say unto you, I will not drink of the fruit of the vine, until the kingdom of God shall come.

19 And he took bread, and gave thanks, and brake it, and gave unto them, saying, This is my body which is given for you: this do in remembrance of me.

20 Likewise also the cup after supper, saying, This cup is the new testament in my blood, which is shed for you.

21 But, behold, the hand of him that betrayeth me is with me on the table.

22 And truly the Son of man goeth, as it was determined: but woe

Luke 22:14-30

14 When the hour came, he took his place at the table, and the apostles with him. 15 He said to them, "I have eagerly desired to eat this Passover with you before I suffer; 16 for I tell you, I will not eat it until it is fulfilled in the kingdom of God." 17 Then he took a cup, and after giving thanks he said, "Take this and divide it among yourselves; 18 for I tell you that from now on I will not drink of the fruit of the vine until the kingdom of God comes." 19 Then he took a loaf of bread, and when he had given thanks, he broke it and gave it to them, saying, "This is my body, which is given for you. Do this in remembrance of me." 20 And he did the same with the cup after supper, saying, "This cup that is poured out for you is the new covenant in my blood. 21 But see, the one who betrays me is with me, and his hand is on the table. 22 For the Son of Man is going as it has been determined, but woe to that one by whom he is betrayed!" 23 Then they began to ask one another, which one of them it could

unto that man by whom he is betrayed!

23 And they began to inquire among themselves, which of them it was that should do this thing.

24 And there was also a strife among them, which of them should be accounted the greatest.

25 And he said unto them, The kings of the Gentiles exercise lordship over them; and they that exercise authority upon them are called benefactors.

26 But ye shall not be so: but he that is greatest among you, let him be as the younger; and he that is chief, as he that doth serve.

27 For whether is greater, he that sitteth at meat, or he that serveth? is not he that sitteth at meat? but I am among you as he that serveth.

28 Ye are they which have continued with me in my temptations.

29 And I appoint unto you a kingdom, as my Father hath appointed unto me;

30 That ye may eat and drink at my table in my kingdom, and sit on thrones judging the twelve tribes of Israel.

be who would do this.

24 A dispute also arose among them as to which one of them was to be regarded as the greatest. 25 But he said to them, "The kings of the Gentiles lord it over them; and those in authority over them are called benefactors. 26 But not so with you; rather the greatest among you must become like the youngest, and the leader like one who serves. 27 For who is greater, the one who is at the table or the one who serves? Is it not the one at the table? But I am among you as one who serves.

28 "You are those who have stood by me in my trials; 29 and I confer on you, just as my Father has conferred on me, a kingdom, 30 so that you may eat and drink at my table in my kingdom, and you will sit on thrones judging the twelve tribes of Israel."

Key Verse: **But ye shall not be so; but he that is greatest among you, let him be as the younger; and he that is chief, as he that doth serve. Luke 22:26**

Key Verse: **But not so with you; rather the greatest among you must become like the youngest, and the leader like one who serves. Luke 22:26**

As You Read the Scripture

This lesson is based on three units of scripture. The first is the story of the Last Supper (vv. 14-23). The second teaches the servant theme (vv. 24-27). In the third, Jesus makes some extraordinary promises to his disciples (vv. 28-29). The Last Supper is narrative material; in the second unit Luke uses a dispute among the disciples to teach servanthood and identifies Jesus as a servant; the third unit has no setting but preserves sayings known to Matthew also.

Luke 22:15. This Passover seems to have had a special significance for Jesus. Did he have something to tell his disciples that would be especially effective at the Passover meal?

Verse 16. The text of the New Revised Standard Version hardly makes sense. How could Jesus refuse to eat the Passover, and then eat it? A better text reads "never *again* shall I eat it until . . ." (the Revised English Bible, following other ancient manuscripts). Check other available translations. The saying reflects an awareness of the danger he was in and his expectation of execution.

Verses 17-20. This section is beset with difficult problems. In the longer form now in the New Revised Standard Version there is a cup-bread-cup order found no place else. In the shorter form (omitting 19*b*-20 as an interpolation, or something added to the text), there is a cup-bread order, which is also unusual, but not completely limited to Luke. The material that is probably added (19*b*-20) is copied almost verbatim from 1 Corinthians 11:24*b*-25. If omitted, Luke's narrative fits well with the general picture of Luke-Acts, which has no awareness that the Last Supper was the occasion for Jesus' inaugurating the Lord's Supper (Paul's view). Actually this connection seems to have been unknown to Matthew, Mark, and John as well, even though all four Gospels were written after Paul had come and gone. In later church tradition, Paul's account in 1 Corinthians became the orthodox view.

Verses 21-23. The notice of a betraying disciple at table with them was the cause of some consternation, but in Luke the betrayer was not identified at the supper. In Matthew he is (Matthew 26:25).

Verse 24. This setting is radically different from Mark 10:35-45. Luke transforms the selfish request of James and John into a general statement about a dispute among the disciples over who is the greatest.

Verses 25-27. Compare Mark 10:42-45. The servanthood theme is preserved without tarnishing the reputation of James and John the way Mark does. The saying at the end of verse 27 is Luke's substitute for the ending in Mark (10:45*b*). Luke's view of the "work of Christ" for our salvation was unrelated to Jesus' death. Luke did not regard Jesus' death as a "ransom," as in Mark 10:45. He therefore substituted the servant ideal, with Jesus as the model, for Mark's belief in the death of Jesus as a "ransom for many."

Verses 28-30. This unit, also in Matthew, is placed by that author in a different setting (Matthew 19:28). Both settings are editorial creations of the Gospel writers. These teachings are not in Mark or John. They represent Jesus as making special promises to the disciples. They will sit "at the captain's table" in the kingdom and rule over Israel, as well.

The Scripture and the Main Question

From the historian's viewpoint, the story of the Last Supper and its connection with the Lord's Supper (the Holy Eucharist) is made up of pieces that are very difficult to put together. Was it on the fourteenth day of the Jewish month Nisan (Mark, Matthew, and Luke) or the day before (John)? Was or was it not a Passover meal? Did Jesus instruct the Twelve to repeat the Supper (Paul), or was it a one-time event (the Gospels)? Did Jesus focus on the bread and wine as symbols of his body and blood (the synoptic Gospels), or did he wash the disciples' feet (John)? Did he identify Judas at the meal, or not? Is this shorter text of Luke authentic, or was there an early scribal interpolation taken from 1 Corinthians 11:24-25?

This lesson does not attempt to solve these problems, although some attention is paid to some of these questions in the "As You Read the Scripture" section. We shall simply study the story as reported in Luke's Gospel, with the longer form of the text (as printed in the New Revised Standard Version).

There is a real sense in which the greatest service Jesus did was to die for our redemption. The Last Supper was the prelude to that final act of service. Jesus in the Gospel of John (10:15*b*) said, "I lay down my life for the sheep." Again, he said, "No one has greater love than this, to lay down one's life for one's friends" (John 15:13).

The Last Supper prepared the disciples for what followed.

The Last Supper, as described in the Gospel of John (13:1-30), in some ways fits the servant theme more obviously than in the other Gospels. The foot-washing scene is symbolized in the United Methodist deacon logo—the towel and the bowl. *Deacon* is one of the words (in Greek) for servant. A diaconal minister is a servant-minister.

The Ideal of Servanthood

We often stereotype the social position of a servant. A domestic servant, for example, is near the bottom of the social scale. But servanthood, in the Christian sense, has nothing to do with our place on a social scale. It is just as much an ideal for persons at the top of the scale as for those on the bottom. The "boss" should serve his employees, for example, just as devotedly as the employees should serve the boss.

Servanthood is an attitude that is ever sensitive to the needs of others. Jesus' example cuts across political, business, and domestic lines, giving us an opportunity to apply the concept in any life situation. He contrasts the king who lords it over his people with the way the disciples should behave. "Not so with you," Jesus said to his disciples.

The contrast between "the greatest" and the "youngest" is a bit strange. The leader should serve. Then Jesus added to the discussion a table-servant (a "waiter," we would say). The rhetorical questions in verse 27 indicate that the one at the table is "greater" than the one who serves, yet Jesus declared himself to be among them "as one who serves."

The material in Luke is a thoroughly revised version of Mark 10:35-45. Mark's story was not well received by either Matthew or Luke. Each of them revised it, but quite independently. Mark's story was probably revised because it cast James and John in a bad light. Luke dropped both names and changed it into a general "dispute," and Matthew (20:20-28) introduced the mother of James and John as the one asking the special favor for her sons. The original story (Mark) is the most effective setting for the teachings about servanthood.

We sometimes equate serving others with waiting on them, as a server in a restaurant. That concept considers only the desires of others. Real serving is more concerned with their needs. There are many levels of needs, and serving others takes all levels of needs into consideration.

At the most basic level—food, shelter, and clothing—we serve when we are part of meeting those basic needs. Matthew (only) has a very effective statement of Jesus on that level of need (Matt. 25:31-46). The Epistle of James is also quite explicit here (James 2:14-17). Most Christians are aware of this kind of serving, and are more or less active in it.

But people need more than food, clothes, and shelter. They need to be healthy and that usually requires access to medical services. Most of the world's poor people are deprived of adequate medical services. Christians are sensitive to that need also, and many are serving this need to some degree (but not enough).

People need education, and Christians are active here also, to some degree. Everyone needs to feel useful, and to *be* useful, to feel important because one is making a meaningful contribution to society. Are the disciples of Jesus meeting that need?

Everyone needs to be loved. Jesus said we should love even our enemies. His one commandment in John's Gospel is that we "love one another" (John 13:34). The Epistle called I John tells the reader, "Beloved, let us love one another, because love is from God; everyone who loves is born of God and knows God. Whoever does not love does not know God, for God is love" (4:7-8).

This need of everyone to be loved is not as successfully met by Christians. We have no trouble loving the lovable, but the rest have a need that isn't fully met (remember the January 16 lesson?).

Serving others means ministering to their needs on all levels. It is a hard, challenging call that Jesus gives to his followers.

The Promises

The last unit in the scripture selected for this lesson is not directly related to the two earlier units. Jesus is quoted as speaking to his closest disciples. He talks here in the language of the preaching of the early church. We must always remember when reading the Gospels that they include teachings of the Risen Lord of the post-resurrection period as well as remembered sayings of Jesus from "the days of his flesh." To know how to sort these out to recover a more accurate portrait of the historical Jesus is a task that requires highly specialized training. Those not so trained have no option but to accept the considered judgment of the "experts."

It was only after the early church realized that Jesus (now the Risen Lord) was the divinely chosen Messiah (Christ) that it could talk about Jesus as the king in the kingdom he proclaimed. In these promises, that's taken for granted. The "trials" of the early Jesus are in the past, and the Risen Lord is declaring to the faithful that "stood by" him that hé will share his kingdom with them. The image of the kingdom of God as a banquet is one that was familiar to the early church. The disciples will share his reign, even reigning over the "twelve tribes of Israel." See Revelation 20:4 for a similar promise, only there it is made to the Christian martyrs only. Servants of Christ are also the beneficiaries of Christ's service to them.

Helping Adults Become Involved

Preparing to Teach

The aim of this lesson is to help class members put their lives up against the ideal of servanthood and see how well it fits. The three scripture units in this lesson are independent of one another, making this lesson seem to be somewhat fragmented. Try to use the servant theme to tie them together.

The lesson material follows the scripture units closely, and therefore falls into three sections.

SECOND QUARTER

      I.   The Last Supper
     II.   The servanthood theme
   III.   The promises

Read all three sections carefully, beginning with "The Main Question," then going to "As You Read the Scripture" and "The Scripture and the Main Question." Think about the difficulty of serving human needs. Make a preliminary list of needs your church is meeting well, and another list of needs your church is not meeting well.

Introducing the Main Question

Ask the class members how comfortable they are when told they should be servants. See if that way of saying it provokes a negative response. Ask the class members to suggest community needs that they are aware of and list them on a chalkboard or newsprint. Then ask them to help make a list of "things" in your community that Christians (or people) are actually serving well already. Put the question in terms of slavery: What kinds of "slavery" exist in your community? This should help them realize that servanthood is already in practice, *but what are people serving?*

Developing the Lesson

I. The Last Supper
Begin by asking class members to tell in their own words the story of the Last Supper. It is quite likely that they will know the traditional account—that is, that Jesus instituted the Lord's Supper at the Last Supper. Do not introduce all the problems associated with the Supper, but it would be helpful for the class members to realize that the traditional ritual of the Lord's Supper comes from Paul (1 Corinthians 11:23-25). Explain the textual problem in Luke's account and have a class member read the account omitting the end of verse 19 and all of verse 20. Then ask if, without this part, there is any creation of a ritual. Finally, compare the omitted part to 1 Corinthians 11:24-25. Do not force a conclusion on the class members, but encourage each one to adjust to this information as seems proper.

The Last Supper clearly anticipates the arrest and execution that follows shortly afterward. See if someone in the class can relate Jesus' willingness to die to the Main Question, the ideal of servanthood. If not, use the lack of response as an opportunity to move to the next part.

II. The servant theme
Begin by having a class member read the earlier form of the occasion for the teachings on servanthood (Mark 10:35-41). Then explain to the class that the unflattering picture of James and John led both Matthew and Luke to change this story. Read Matthew's change first (Matt. 20:20-24). Then read Luke's change, which was very different. Luke reduced the story to just one verse (v. 24)! The servant teachings that follow in Luke are similar to those in Matthew (20:25-28) and Mark (10:42-45), except that Luke changes the "ransom" theme to the servant theme.

Draw from the class members their ideas about serving others. What do they think Jesus meant? Make a list of the kinds of service a Christian can practice.

Read Matthew 25:31-46 aloud and ask if that's a complete list of what we should do. If not, what else?

It will stimulate thought and self-examination if you ask the class if anyone has done *any* of the service listed in Matthew 25.

Now go beyond the "basic" needs and let the class suggest needs not mentioned in Matthew 25. Add your ideas to the discussion.

Explain to the class the word *deacon* and how it's related to the *diaconal ministry.* Is serving the job of the ministers? Should all Christians live with the servanthood ideal?

Be sure the class discussion gets beyond the concept of servant as a person in the lower levels of society. The leaders are no less obligated to serve than the "hired servants."

Suggest to the class that focus on the needs of others may be a help in overcoming our natural self-centeredness. Do not, however, encourage the idea that we can get free from self-centeredness by our own service to others. Serving others will help, of course, but getting free from our self-centeredness is too big a job for us to accomplish. It requires the grace of God, working through others around us, including those whom we are serving.

III. The promises

Helping Class Members Act

For this topic, action by the class is very appropriate. What can the class do beyond what it may be doing already? Ask the class members to adopt a definite service project. It could be a prison visit, for instance. Let them be creative and make the decision.

Preparing for Next Sunday

The last lesson in this unit reflects on the crucifixion and resurrection of our Lord. Think ahead on how dying may be the start of a new life. Ask each class member to formulate his or her ideas about the meaning of death and what lies beyond death. This will be easier for most persons if they engage others in conversation about this topic. Invite the class members also to discuss the resurrection event with several people.

From Death to Life

Background Scripture: Luke 23:32-47; 24:13-35

The Main Question

Out of the familiar story of the crucifixion and resurrection of Jesus several important questions arise besides the historical ones. This lesson does not present a solution to historical problems that are insoluble, but it does ask questions that help us to think about important aspects of our lives.

Jesus died in circumstances that he could have avoided. What are you willing to die for? Would it be special persons? Would it be some principle?

Jesus died and the disciples experienced him as alive after his death. Is there a life after death? What kind? Does "eternity" begin then? How does what you believe about eternal life affect your life now? We ordinarily think of going from life to death; should we think of going from death to life? Is the traditional Christian belief that death is a "rite of passage" to another kind of life really just a "hope"? Is there any evidence?

The scripture says that Jesus' suffering was the pathway that led him to his own perfection (Heb. 5:8-9). It also did something to transform others. Those earliest disciples experienced his death and the new life that followed as personal transformation. Christians ever since have continued to experience this transformation. How does suffering have redemptive results? The questions are hard ones; the answers are important.

Selected Scripture

King James Version	New Revised Standard Version

Luke 23:32-46

32 And there were also two other, malefactors, led with him to be put to death.

33 And when they were come to the place, which is called Calvary, there they crucified him, and the malefactors, one on the right hand, and the other on the left.

34 Then said Jesus, Father, forgive them; for they know not what they do. And they parted his raiment, and cast lots.

35 And the people stood beholding. And the rulers also with them derided *him,* saying, He saved others; let him save himself, if he be Christ, the chosen of God.

36 And the soldiers also mocked

Luke 23:32-46

32 Two others also, who were criminals, were led away to be put to death with him. 33 When they came to the place that is called The Skull, they crucified Jesus there with the criminals, one on his right and one on his left. 34 Then Jesus said, "Father, forgive them; for they do not know what they are doing." And they cast lots to divide his clothing. 35 And the people stood by, watching; but the leaders scoffed at him, saying, "He saved others; let him save himself if he is the Messiah of God, his chosen one!" 36 The soldiers also mocked him, coming up and offering him sour wine, 37 and saying, "If you are the King of the

him, coming to him, and offering him vinegar,

37 And saying, If thou be the king of the Jews, save thyself.

38 And a superscription also was written over him in letters of Greek, and Latin, and Hebrew, THIS IS THE KING OF THE JEWS.

39 And one of the malefactors which were hanged railed on him, saying, If thou be Christ, save thyself and us.

40 But the other answering rebuked him, saying, Dost not thou fear God, seeing thou art in the same condemnation?

41 And we indeed justly; for we receive the due reward of our deeds: but this man hath done nothing amiss.

42 And he said unto Jesus, Lord, remember me when thou comest into thy kingdom.

43 And Jesus said unto him, Verily I say unto thee, To day shalt thou be with me in paradise.

44 And it was about the sixth hour, and there was a darkness over all the earth until the ninth hour.

45 And the sun was darkened, and the veil of the temple was rent in the midst.

46 And when Jesus had cried with a loud voice, he said, Father, into thy hands I commend my spirit: and having said this, he gave up the ghost.

Luke 24:33-34

33 And they rose up the same hour, and returned to Jerusalem, and found the eleven gathered together, and them that were with them,

34 Saying, The Lord is risen indeed, and hath appeared to Simon.

Key Verse: Saying, The Lord is risen indeed, and hath appeared to Simon. Luke 24:34

Jews, save yourself!" 38 There was also an inscription over him, "This is the King of the Jews."

39 One of the criminals who were hanged there kept deriding him and saying, "Are you not the Messiah? Save yourself and us!" 40 But the other rebuked him, saying, "Do you not fear God, since you are under the same sentence of condemnation? 41 And we indeed have been condemned justly, for we are getting what we deserve for our deeds, but this man has done nothing wrong." 42 Then he said, "Jesus, remember me when you come into your kingdom." 43 He replied, "Truly I tell you, today you will be with me in Paradise."

44 It was now about noon, and darkness came over the whole land until three in the afternoon, 45 while the sun's light failed; and the curtain of the temple was torn in two. 46 Then Jesus, crying with a loud voice, said, "Father, into your hands I commend my spirit." Having said this, he breathed his last.

Luke 24:33-34

33 That same hour they got up and returned to Jerusalem; and they found the eleven and their companions gathered together. 34 They were saying, "The Lord has risen indeed, and he has appeared to Simon!"

Key Verse: They were saying, "The Lord has risen indeed, and he has appeared to Simon!" Luke 24:34

As You Read the Scripture

The heart of Luke's Passion Story is the first unit in this week's lesson, and two verses from Luke 24 represent the more complex story of Jesus' resurrection appearances.

Luke 23:32-33. All the Gospels report that Jesus was executed with two "criminals" (Luke) or "robbers" (Mark).

Verse 34. To whom was Jesus' prayer of forgiveness referring? To the two criminals? the soldiers crucifying him? Pilate and the Roman leaders? the Jewish authorities? The casting of lots for his clothing was probably a detail earlier tradition had "learned" from Psalm 22:18.

Verse 35. On the mocking of Jesus, see Psalm 22:7-8.

Verses 36-37. The mocking of the soldiers is a story placed in a different setting in Mark (15:30) and Matthew (27:41-42). The "sour wine" offering (by "the bystanders" in Mark and Matthew) may be related to Psalm 69:21b.

Verse 38. The inscription over Jesus' cross is reported in all the Gospels, but the exact wording is different in each one.

Verses 39-42. That one of the crucifixion companions taunted Jesus and that the other rebuked him for it is a tradition found only in this Gospel. Luke has a special interest in repentance, as seen by the story of the penitent harlot (Luke 7:36-50), the penitent Zacchaeus (19:1-10), the theme of repentance in the three stories of chapter 15, the penitent publican (18:9-14), and the necessity of repentance for salvation (13:1-9), all found exclusively in Luke's Gospel.

Verse 43. Jesus promised that "this day" he and "the penitent thief" would be together in "Paradise." In Jesus' time Jewish authorities held the idea of immediate transaction at death alongside the more traditional idea of a waiting period before a Last Judgment. The rabbis felt no special need to be consistent on this. Both ideas have coexisted ever since.

Verses 44-45a. Luke repeats from Mark 15:33 the noon time note ("the sixth hour"), and the three hours of darkness. Luke (alone) adds an explanation for the darkness. (A solar eclipse at Passover is impossible. Passover is always at full moon when sun and moon are on opposite sides of the earth.)

Verse 45b. Luke reports the tearing of the Temple curtain before Jesus' death, instead of afterward, as in Mark. This probably refers to the curtain that shielded the Holy of Holies from everyone, except the High Priest who could enter (only) once a year. Mark intended a symbolic meaning, that access to God is now open to all, through the cross. Luke copies Mark without realizing that its symbolism is contrary to his theology of repentance as the key to salvation. For Luke, it was only a miracle.

Verse 46. Luke's source reports only that Jesus "gave a loud cry and breathed his last" (Mark 15:37). Luke added a Psalm verse (Ps. 31:5a) to supply content to the last cry. Compare Acts 7:59.

Luke 24:33-34. Jesus' post-resurrection appearances, as reported by Luke, were confined to the Jerusalem area. The disciples were forbidden to leave the city (24:49; Acts 1:4). The first appearances were either to two disciples walking to Emmaus (24:13) or to Peter (24:34). Matthew reports a first appearance to Mary Magdalene and "the other Mary" (Matt. 28:8), John reports that the appearance was to Mary Magdalene alone (John 20:14-18), Paul to "Cephas" (1 Cor. 15:5). The New Testament evidence is not in agreement on where and when these appearances took place, or to whom, or the manner of Jesus' resurrection body. The profound effect these appearances had on the disciples, however, convinces many historians that the faith of Christians in a living Christ is well grounded.

The Scripture and the Main Question

The Crucifixion

Crucifixion was a common form of Roman execution. It was used only for non-citizens; citizens were usually beheaded. Political revolts against Roman rule were usually punished by crucifixion executions. When Jesus was a "preschooler" in Nazareth, a regional revolt was put down by the Roman legions. The rebels that survived the insurrection were crucified on the road leading in and out of the capital city of Galilee, Sepphoris. Josephus, the first-century Jewish historian, wrote that the number of the crucified at Sepphoris was 2000. Nazareth was only four miles away.

It is not clear how crucifixion caused death. Those executed usually lived on the cross longer than the six hours that Mark's Gospel reports. Jesus may have been flogged so severely that it hastened his death. He may have willed to die. He may have experienced heart failure. We simply do not know.

We do know, from many sources, that the suffering was intense in a crucifixion. That experience has given us the now common word, "crucial," which means "of supreme importance in determining an outcome." It comes from the latin word, "crux," meaning "cross."

The Power of Jesus' Death

It is strange, in some ways, that the emblem of a cruel execution has become the characteristic symbol of the Christian church. The cross, especially as a decorative pendant worn by both men and women, far outnumbers any other Christian symbol. Almost every Christian worship center features a cross as its central object.

The explanation is that redemption comes from suffering. *Our* redemption is the result of *his* suffering. The theological explanations offered in the course of Christian history have varied to fit the times that produced them. These explanations are not the reason for the power of the event and its symbol, but only rationalizations after the fact. Its power comes from our experience. However explained, the experience of being "redeemed" (set free), of being "saved," of being "born again," is often the result of some contemplation of the suffering of Jesus on the cross. Paul called it "the power of God" (1 Cor. 2:5). Many people feel this power when participating in the Lord's Supper.

It is important to note that even though "the power of God" comes to many people through the medium of the cross, other persons find this power in other ways. This was true in the earliest Christian community, and has continued to be true ever since. For Paul and the authors of the Gospel of Mark, 1 Peter, and Hebrews, the death of Jesus was God's rescue act, our salvation event. Other persons of the New Testament reflected experiences of salvation in other ways.

We can only make guesses. The ultimate answer is that it pleased God to reach us in different ways. It appears likely that the very first disciples, those who knew Jesus in the flesh, experienced their redemption directly from the power of his presence. These disciples did not experience "the power of God" through the death of Jesus; they already had it. This would account for the parts of the New Testament that perpetuate a tradition that goes back to an original disciple group, and is *not* cross-centered (such as the Gospels of Matthew, Luke, and John).

Others, like Paul, joining the community after Jesus' resurrection, found "the power of God" in his crucifixion and resurrection.

The general principle that emerges from the experiences of Paul and others after him is that *vicarious suffering is redemptive.* At least, it *can* be redemptive. (There's nothing automatic about redemption coming from suffering.) This is not just a result of Jesus' suffering; it is a possible result from *any* vicarious suffering. *Vicarious* means that one person suffers and another one benefits from it. As we interact with one another, we act as instruments of God's grace as we suffer vicariously for others. This is a mystery worth much pondering. We aren't agents of redemption by being kind; we are such agents as we suffer for another.

The Resurrection

The death of Jesus, powerful in itself, is nevertheless incomplete without the resurrection. The cross often (and mysteriously) brings a sense of divine acceptance just as we are. The resurrection is the clue to the indwelling power that is at work to transform us into what we ought to be.

We have no account of the resurrection of our Lord. It is not described in the New Testament, nor anywhere else in early Christian literature. No one was there, so there are no witnesses. What we *do* have is appearances (sightings) of Jesus after his death and burial.

Scholars have pored over the New Testament accounts of these post-resurrection appearances. They have explored every detail and proposed many explanations. They have written a library of books on the subject, and still more appear every year. There is much that is unsettled, and will remain unsettled. The data is insufficient for a final conclusion to the study.

One thing is certain, and that's enough for our faith. That one thing is *the conviction of those who experienced appearances of the Risen Lord that they were real.* He who was "Jesus of Nazareth" was alive and present in the community of his disciples in a new spiritual way. That confidence is at the heart of the Christian religion.

Jesus' resurrection was not a return to life, like the resurrection of Lazarus. Jesus' resurrection was *a new life beyond death.* It was life after death; not a return to the life that was but a new beginning.

Our Life Beyond Death?

That prompts a question for us. Will we, too, experience a life beyond death? The church has traditionally taught that death is real only for the physical body. Our real self is an immortal spirit that is "housed" in our bodies but "set free" at death.

What then? What does our naturally immortal spirit (soul) do upon release from the body? In one tradition it goes directly to one of two eternal destinies, heaven or hell. The promise of Jesus to the penitent thief on the companion cross, ("Today you will be with me in Paradise") reflects this tradition. In another tradition the soul must wait until the kingdom of God comes, and then it will be reunited with its resurrected body and only then go into an eternal destiny, either heaven or hell.

Both of these traditions are pre-Christian beliefs that the church retained. Respectively, one is a Greek heritage, the other Persian (Iranian).

Helping Adults Become Involved

Preparing to Teach

The focus of this lesson is on the crucifixion and resurrection appearances of Jesus. This focus is not on the events themselves, but their meaning for us. The best preparation is to take time to clear up in your own mind (as teacher) what you think about the questions this lesson raises. This is not so that you can present your ideas as the truth. However, you *can* lead the discussion with a sense of direction that will assist the class members to come to their own conclusions. For your meditation, read first "The Main Question." Then go directly to "The Scripture and the Main Question." The "As You Read the Scripture" section should be studied for background enrichment and for ease in handling questions that might arise in the discussion.

Today's lesson has four sections:

     I. The crucifixion
    II. The power of Jesus' death
  III. The resurrection
  IV. Our life beyond death?

Introducing the Main Question

Everyone is interested in their own personal survival. Is death the end or is there something beyond? If so, what?

Thinking about the death and resurrection of Jesus may give us the opportunity to reflect on how his death and resurrection affect us.

Present to the class the way the author of the Epistle to the Hebrews understood the meaning of the sufferings of Jesus (Heb. 5:8-9). Ask the class members to report what they see this scripture saying about two things. First, what was the effect of suffering on Jesus himself? Second, what did it enable him to do for others?

The class reflections on these two questions will prepare the members for "The Main Question" of this lesson. Do not let the class dodge the plain meaning of these verses by saying they don't mean what they say. Don't allow a class member to say what they *really* mean, over against what they actually say. Simply comment that the allegorical method of reading scripture is not an accepted Protestant way of reading scripture.

Developing the Lesson

I. The crucifixion

Tell the class the background information about Roman crucifixions, as explained in the lesson. See if there are any comments or questions about this. Then move to the meaning of the event. Begin by explaining the word *crucial.* Ask for questions and answer them to the best of your ability.

As you prepare to move to the next part, explain the difference between experiencing the power of the cross and giving a theological explanation of it. Urge the class to focus on their own experiences that demonstrated the power of the cross. If any wish to tell about their experiences encourage them to do so.

II. The power of Jesus' death

Give the class a preliminary description of the way vicarious suffering redeems. It not only has an effect on the sufferer, but has even more effect on the object of the suffering. See if any class member can report a life-experience to illustrate this.

Open a class discussion on vicarious suffering. Is it ethical? The ethics question is a real one. If (when) a situation means one person is suffering for another's benefit, we think that may be morally all right. But if the sufferer is seen as being punished for the sins of another, then we object to that as *not* moral.

How willing is the class to suffer vicariously? Can they be honest and frank about this? What can they do that would test this?

What can an individual class member do that would be a case of voluntary vicarious suffering? Can anyone in the class give an example?

III. The resurrection

Ask the class members to share with the others how they understand the resurrection. Are there some in the class who aren't sure it was real? Why do they think this way?

What would those who have no doubts say about having no doubts? Ask for sharing on this.

Are the class members satisfied with the conviction of the earliest community that their experiences with the Risen Lord were real?

Explain that the early Christians' experience of the spiritual presence of the Risen Lord has been the witness of Christians ever since. Can the class report personal confirmations of this? Invite them to share such experiences. This inner presence is (or can be?) a transforming power in the life of a Christian. That's the Church's witness to the meaning of the risen Lord's presence.

IV. Our life beyond death?

This discussion is important enough for a significant time-block, so save time for it.

Ask how many believe in their own life after death. Does anyone in the class feel that death is the end? What are the implications of saying, "This is all there is," in regard to this life?

Present the ideas from the lesson material and solicit class response to these ideas. Use the resources of class discussion for most of your time.

Helping Class Members Act

This is not an action lesson. It is reflective. Suggest that each class member select several persons whom they respect as having both good judgment and good information and engage them in reflective dialogue on these subjects.

GOOD NEWS FOR GOD'S PEOPLE: ROMANS AND GALATIANS

UNIT I: RIGHTEOUS THROUGH FAITH
Gayle Carlton Felton

FOUR LESSONS   MARCH 6–27

· The first eight lessons in this quarter focus on Paul's letter to the Christian community in the Italian capital city of Rome. Because Paul's purpose was to explain his understanding of the Christian faith, this material is quite heavy with theological concepts. Hence, these lessons provide a valuable opportunity to deepen our own insights into the basic truths of the faith to which we have committed ourselves. Our study should be a joyous endeavor, for the heart of Christianity is gospel—the good news of what God has done for us in Jesus Christ.

The lessons from Romans are divided into two units, the first entitled "Righteous through Faith." Lesson 1, "The Power of God for Salvation," depicts the human need for salvation and our helplessness to do anything to achieve it for ourselves. In the second lesson, "God's Gift of Redemption," it is made clear that in all God's dealings with humankind—in both the Old and the New Covenants—salvation is a gift of God's grace to be received in faith. God's great love for sinful persons was revealed by the death of Christ, which makes our reconciliation with God possible. This is the message of Lesson 3, "The Gift of Life in Christ." The last lesson in the unit, "Deliverance from Sin," emphasizes that our participation through baptism in the dying and rising of Christ enables us to enter into a new spiritual realm of life.

LESSON 1   MARCH 6

Saved by Faith

Background Scripture: Romans 1:1-17

The Main Question

During the early weeks of 1991, many people in Kuwait City gathered anxiously to listen to shortwave radio broadcasts announcing that American and Coalition forces were on the way to rescue them from the horrors of Iraqi occupation. For Paul, all humanity, and, indeed, all of creation, is under enemy occupation—hopelessly lost in sin and completely helpless to rescue itself. Like the citizens of defeated and devastated Kuwait, we wait and pray for deliverance. And there is good news to broadcast throughout the land.

THIRD QUARTER

Through the power of Christ's resurrection from the dead, God has made freedom from sin available; the Rescuer has come! The Kuwaitis celebrated in the streets with exuberant relief and joy, greeting the Coalition troops with outpourings of affection and shouting praises of the American president. They recognized that their salvation had been won for them when they were unable to achieve it by their own unaided efforts. They received it in trust and gratitude. Paul introduced himself and his message to the Christians in Rome by telling them that he was a messenger, chosen by God to proclaim such a gospel to persons of all nations and religious backgrounds. Human beings are in desperate need of the salvation that they can do nothing to achieve for themselves; we must simply receive in faith the salvation that God freely offers.

What does an old-fashioned and suspiciously theological-sounding word like *salvation* mean to us as modern persons? Do we really need divine intervention to deliver us in our culture, with its passion for personal fulfillment and confidence in technological sophistication? What can we do to accomplish our own salvation?

Selected Scripture

King James Version

New Revised Standard Version

Romans 1:1, 3-17

1 Paul, a servant of Jesus Christ, called to be an apostle, separated unto the gospel of God, . . .

3 Concerning his Son Jesus Christ our Lord, which was made of the seed of David according to the flesh;

4 And declared to be the Son of God with power, according to the spirit of holiness, by the resurrection from the dead:

5 By whom we have received grace and apostleship, for obedience to the faith among all nations, for his name:

6 Among whom are ye also the called of Jesus Christ:

7 To all that be in Rome, beloved of God, called to be saints: Grace to you and peace from God our Father, and the Lord Jesus Christ.

8 First, I thank my God through Jesus Christ for you all, that your faith is spoken of throughout the whole world.

9 For God is my witness, whom I serve with my spirit in the gospel of his Son, that without ceasing I make mention of you always in my prayers;

10 Making request, if by any

Romans 1:1, 3-17

1 Paul, a servant of Jesus Christ, called to be an apostle, set apart for the gospel of God, . . .

3 the gospel concerning his Son, who was descended from David according to the flesh 4 and was declared to be Son of God with power according to the spirit of holiness by resurrection from the dead, Jesus Christ our Lord, 5 through whom we have received grace and apostleship to bring about the obedience of faith among all the Gentiles for the sake of his name, 6 including yourselves who are called to belong to Jesus Christ,

7 To all God's beloved in Rome, who are called to be saints:

8 First, I thank my God through Jesus Christ for all of you, because your faith is proclaimed throughout the world. 9 For God, whom I serve with my spirit by announcing the gospel of his Son, is my witness that without ceasing I remember you always in my prayers, 10 asking that by God's will I may somehow at last

means now at length I might have a prosperous journey by the will of God to come unto you.

11 For I long to see you, that I may impart unto you some spiritual gift, to the end ye may be established;

12 That is, that I may be comforted together with you by the mutual faith both of you and me.

13 Now I would not have you ignorant, brethren, that oftentimes I purposed to come unto you, (but was let hitherto,) that I might have some fruit among you also, even as among other Gentiles.

14 I am debtor both to the Greeks, and to the Barbarians; both to the wise, and to the unwise.

15 So, as much as in me is, I am ready to preach the gospel to you that are at Rome also.

16 For I am not ashamed of the gospel of Christ: for it is the power of God unto salvation to every one that believeth; to the Jew first, and also to the Greek.

17 For therein is the righteousness of God revealed from faith to faith: as it is written, The just shall live by faith.

Key Verse: **For I am not ashamed of the gospel of Christ: for it is the power of God unto salvation to every one that believeth; to the Jew first, and also to the Greek. Romans 1:16**

succeed in coming to you. 11 For I am longing to see you so that I may share with you some spiritual gift to strengthen you—12 or rather so that we may be mutually encouraged by each other's faith, both yours and mine. 13 I want you to know, brothers and sisters, that I have often intended to come to you (but thus far have been prevented), in order that I may reap some harvest among you as I have among the rest of the Gentiles. 14 I am a debtor both to Greeks and to barbarians, both to the wise and to the foolish 15—hence my eagerness to proclaim the gospel to you also who are in Rome.

16 For I am not ashamed of the gospel; it is the power of God for salvation to everyone who has faith, to the Jew first and also to the Greek. 17 For in it the righteousness of God is revealed through faith for faith; as it is written, "The one who is righteous will live by faith."

Key Verse: **For I am not ashamed of the gospel; it is the power of God for salvation to everyone who has faith, to the Jew first and also to the Greek. Romans 1:16**

As You Read the Scripture

Romans 1:1, 3-15. Unlike most of Paul's letters, Romans was written to a church he had never visited. These verses contain Paul's introduction to these Christians of himself and his understanding of the gospel. He uses the customary form of Greek letter writing of that time, but expands each of the elements in order to make his own points.

Verse 1. The sender of the letter identifies himself as Paul, who is a servant or slave of Christ. He understands himself to be "an appointed agent assigned to God's great story" (Clarence Jordan).

Verses 3-4. The gospel, or good news, is the story of Jesus. God had promised the people of the Old Testament that the One who would be sent to save them would be a descendant of the great King David. (See 2 Samuel 7 and Isaiah 9:6-7 for Old Testament examples of the basis for this expectation and Acts 2:29-30 for an instance of its use in early Christian preaching.) But Jesus was much more than human; he was also the Son of God as evidenced by his resurrection from the dead. The use of the words *Jesus Christ our Lord* is significant. *Jesus* was a personal name whose meaning might be rendered as "God saves." *Christ* was a title in Greek, parallel to the Hebrew term *Messiah* and meaning "anointed one." Because kings and priests were anointed with oil as a sign of their being set apart to service by God's Spirit, this term had evolved into a designation of the long-anticipated Savior to be sent by God. *Lord* was a Greek word that had developed special significance, since it was often used to refer to God in the Greek version of the Hebrew Scriptures.

Verses 5-6. Through Christ, Paul had received his commission to preach the gospel to all nationalities, including the people in Rome.

Verse 7. The recipient of the letter is identified as the Christian community in Rome. The term *saints* does not imply special piety or status, but includes all believers—all those who are consecrated to the service of God. In wishing them both grace and peace, Paul combines a variation of the conventional Greek greeting with the traditional Hebrew salutation.

Verses 8-15. Paul elaborates on the customary prayer of thanksgiving to make clear to the Romans his hope of fulfilling his long-felt desire to visit them. He is planning a mission trip to the westernmost portions of the Roman Empire (Spain) and hopes to receive their help in this venture. Note that Paul praises these Christians and speaks with considerable tact of his anticipation of their mutually benefiting each other when he comes.

Verses 16-17. Here is summarized the theme of the letter and of Paul's understanding of the Christian gospel. With its pride and pomp, as well as its vast array of religious groups, the imperial capital was an intimidating place in which to preach Christ. But Paul asserts that he is not afraid because he knows that it is the authentic story of the supernatural reality of divine power. God offers salvation to all persons, both to Jews and to Gentiles. This salvation is not dependent upon the keeping of legal regulations or even the adherence to an ethical code of behavior. To be brought into this right relationship with God, human beings can only receive it in faith—trust in the loving goodness of God.

The Scripture and the Main Question

The Human Situation: The Need for Salvation

All of the lessons in this unit explore the offer of salvation that God makes to human beings. This wonderful offer cannot, however, be appreciated without our recognition of our desperate need for salvation. Paul's understanding of human beings as sinful and lost (see Romans 3:23) is confirmed in our own personal and corporate experience. We search futilely for meaning and purpose, for a cause or a power great enough to commit our lives to. A poignant cartoon depicts a person holding a white flag, saying, "I'm ready to give up the struggle, but can't find anybody to surrender to." We, too, realize that our lives are empty, even in the presence of achievements and acquisitions; we seek direction; we need help. Our needs are not always dramatically apparent; nineteenth-century Transcendental writer Henry David Thoreau insisted that the majority of the people he knew led "lives of quiet desperation." In the very midst of our most sincere efforts to live well, we know brokenness and anxiety. We suffer from a restless craving, a busy searching for identity and purpose, a hunger we cannot satisfy. The Southern author Flannery O'Connor described us all when she spoke of one of her characters as a boy with "the bottom split out of his stomach so that nothing would heal or fill it but the bread of life." We are alienated from other people, as evidenced by the discord and violence that mark our society from the international to the domestic levels. We are estranged from our own best selves and seek healing through drug and psychoanalytic therapies. We are in a state of enmity with the natural world, which we threaten with depletion, pollution, and even annihilation. And most tragically, we are in rebellion against God and therefore nothing else in our lives can be whole or healthy. As Augustine expressed it, "O God, Thou hast created us for Thyself and our hearts are restless until they find their rest in Thee."

The Power of God for Salvation

Against this bleak backdrop of meaninglessness and estrangement, Paul proclaims the gospel—the good news that God has acted to save us. The use of the term *gospel* is characteristic of the writings of Paul; in this opening section of Romans he uses it five times. What we cannot do for ourselves, God does for us. The God of the biblical story does not wait to be discovered by humans in need, but takes the initiative, acts first, reaches out to erring children with the love of a parent who hurts with the pain that they inflict upon themselves by their stubborn refusal to accept God's graciousness. God acts to vindicate, to deliver, to save. A new relationship is thus made possible between ourselves and God. Our separation is overcome through the personal intervention of God on our behalf. One of the most characteristic teachings of John Wesley, the founder of Methodism, was that of prevenient grace—the gracious action of God that precedes anything human beings can do and enables us to respond to the divine offer of salvation as we, in our sinful condition, are unable to do alone. God, who in the Old Testament revealed the divine nature and will through the history of the Hebrew people, has acted in Jesus Christ to establish a new covenant relationship with humankind. By the power manifested in the resurrection of Christ from death, we are reconciled to God, restored to the loving relationship with the Divine that we were created to enjoy. In the new life that we experience as God's gift of salvation, we are empowered to reconciliation with other persons, our inner selves, and the rest of the created order.

"Through Faith for Faith"

The word *faith* is used in several different ways in the New Testament. Sometimes it means intellectual assent to the truth of certain facts or belief that is strong enough to motivate action. As applied to God, the term usually connotes faithfulness or reliability. In the later books of the New Testament, *faith* seems to mean "the faith," understood as the basic teaching of Christianity. But for Paul, *faith* is usually synonymous with "trust"—the recognition of our complete dependence upon God and our willingness to rely totally on divine love and strength. Verses 16-17 emphasize that God's act of salvation can be appropriated by us in no other way. So long as we attempt to earn, to merit, or to comprehend, we cannot receive. We must instead recognize that we are mired in sin so deeply as to be unable to extricate ourselves, surrender our futile efforts at do-it-yourself salvation, and simply and humbly accept the gift that God gives. Trust is both the necessary and the sufficient condition for our salvation; nothing else is required. Such recognition of our own inadequacy and acceptance of salvation as something that God gives rather than something we accomplish is particularly difficult for middle-income Americans, as it was for the strictly religious Jews of Paul's time. We want to view ourselves as strong and competent, as independent and self-reliant. We are uncomfortable, even embarrassed, by the gospel message, which insists that we are weak and helpless, utterly dependent upon God to rescue us.

In attempting to illustrate the meaning of this kind of faith, Paul quotes from Habakkuk 2:4. A further look at this inspiring prophet of the Old Testament may be helpful. Habakkuk lived in a time when his nation was enduring the horrors of invasion by cruel foreign conquerors, coupled with political corruption and social injustice at home. In addition, the entire agricultural economy of Judah had collapsed (see Habakkuk 3:17). Because of either drought or military conquest, all crops had failed. There were no figs, no grapes, no olives, no grain. The sheep, goats, and cattle were gone. The result would surely be suffering and starvation. Yet in this terrible situation, Habakkuk affirmed that he would rejoice in the Lord and joy in the God of his salvation (see 3:18).

Here is a beautiful and profound description of faith as trust that rests in the assurance that God's action for salvation can be relied upon utterly. God's part is to rescue us from the sinful condition of our lives; our part is to trust what God has done and is doing for us. To speak of God as righteous is to describe the divine character of lovingkindness, of graciousness and mercy. God's righteousness is also understood as the divine action in history on behalf of human beings. For us to be righteous, as the word is used in verse 17, is to have accepted God's forgiveness, to have been justified and restored to right relationship with God—to have been saved. This can become a living reality in our lives only when we accept it in faith.

Helping Adults Become Involved

Preparing to Teach

Today's lesson begins an eight-week study of the book of Romans with the general title of "Good News for God's People." This lesson introduces many of the themes that will be significant throughout these two units. It will be helpful for you to read a brief introduction to the book of Romans in a study Bible or commentary as well as carefully noting the material provided at the beginning of this unit. A quick reading through the entire book of Romans (less than twenty pages in most Bibles) will give you a sense of Paul's style of writing and some of his major concerns, as well as raising questions to be wrestled with throughout the series.

Read "The Scripture and the Main Question" for an overview of the issues. Read Romans 1:1-17 along with the information provided in "As You Read the Scripture."

The content of the lesson can be organized as follows:

    I. Introduction

II. Paul's introduction of himself and his message (verses 1-15)
III. The need for salvation
IV. Salvation through the action of God
V. Salvation received only through faith

Bring several clippings from newspapers and magazines that can be used to illustrate our need for salvation both as individuals and as a society.

Introducing the Main Question

The lesson should encourage and enable persons to reflect on the meaning of sin, salvation, and faith in the teachings of Paul and in the experience of their own lives as Christian disciples.

Read "The Main Question" and prepare to share the analogy of a conquered people to help your students understand. Lead a brief discussion based on the questions suggested.

Developing the Lesson

I. Introduction

The reality of sin and the need for salvation are not popular subjects with many modern Christians, who may associate these ideas with a kind of old-fashioned oppressive religion they feel they have outgrown. In an age with so much emphasis on self-esteem and self-affirmation, such ideas may appear detrimental, even dangerous. But the accuracy of the Bible's portrayal of the human condition is continually proven in our own individual and corporate experiences of failure, loneliness, depression, anxiety, greed, and violence. The fulfillment and freedom, the joy and peace we crave are, indeed, available to us, but only through the power of our loving God, who has chosen to intervene in human history to bring us salvation. When we accept in simple faith God's gift of salvation in Jesus Christ, we are empowered to live new lives of witness and service.

In our study of the book of Romans during these eight sessions, we will explore these ideas and seek to understand their significance to us.

II. Paul's introduction of himself and his message (vv. 1-15)

Since the people of the church in Rome were personally unacquainted with Paul, and may even have heard unflattering reports about his ministry, he writes to them with considerable care in order to establish his credibility and ensure his acceptance. Paul affirms his understanding of his calling to the apostolic role, which gave him not only authority to preach the gospel, but also a special commissioning to preach to both Jews and Gentiles. He expresses eager anticipation of his planned visit to Rome and expectation of reciprocal blessings to be shared.

III. The need for salvation

In these verses Paul alludes to a theme that he develops in much more detail in the latter part of chapter 1 and in chapters 2 and 3. It will be helpful to read these sections and incorporate some of their teachings into the lesson at this point. It is simply impossible to explain Paul's understanding of salvation without first clearly comprehending the human situation of needing to be saved. This is where you can use the newspaper and magazine clippings to stimulate thoughtful discussion of human sinfulness and need.

IV. Salvation through the action of God

Encourage your students to consider the variety of ways by which we try to achieve our own salvation. What do people commonly mean when they speak of being saved or of being a Christian? Usually most of the answers that a class will suggest emphasize human decision and behavior. Contrast that view to what Paul is stressing about the effort God has undertaken to make our salvation possible.

V. Salvation received only through faith

Using the material in the earlier parts of this lesson, guide the class in efforts to define what salvation is. Encourage them to consider some of the various meanings of faith and, particularly, what Paul signifies by faith as the only means through which salvation may be received. It may be helpful to divide into small groups to discuss these questions briefly and then share ideas with the class.

Helping Class Members Act

Lead a discussion of some of the following questions. (Remember that you should be prepared with thought-provoking ideas to share in case the discussion lags or digresses.) What are some of our personal and corporate experiences that show human separation from God and from the way God would have us live? What difference might it make in our understanding of God if we realized that God has and is taking the initiative to save us? What changes might it make in our lives if we practiced living by faith?

Challenge the members of the class to devote a portion of their personal prayer time during the upcoming week to honest self-examination before God about ways they are alienated from God, from other persons, from the natural environment, and from their own best selves. Encourage them to be open to God's assurance that such separations can be healed through reliance on divine strength and guidance.

Planning for Next Sunday

Ask the class members to read chapters 12, 13, and 17 of Genesis. Explain that next week's lesson focuses on the Old Testament character of Abraham (first called Abram), whom Paul uses as a model for the kind of faith Christians should have. If possible, have a volunteer prepare to report briefly on the major events in the life of Abraham. Ask all students to think of other biblical and historical figures whose lives exemplify what it means to rely on God in faith. Ask them to consider whether they know personally individuals who so live.

Receiving God's Gift

Background Scripture: Romans 3:21–4:25

The Main Question

Many contemporary Christians are uncomfortable and even confused when asked to deal with material from the Old Testament. The New Testament seems so much more familiar to us, so much easier to understand. Paul, however, makes clear throughout his writings, and especially in this portion of the letter to Rome, that the action of God in Jesus Christ must be seen as a continuation and fulfillment of the work of redeeming the world, which God began during the earliest period of human history. The Old Testament relates the story of God's efforts through the history of the Hebrew (Israelite or Jewish) people to bring human beings back into right relationship with God. To rescue humanity from the wreckage that sin had made of the good order God had created, God chose Abraham and Sarah to be the ancestors of a people through whose history God would work to reveal the divine nature and will. It is preeminently the person Abraham whom Paul sees as a compelling example of the kind of faith that all persons must have if they are to be able to accept God's gift of redemption.

In this lesson we will focus on God's action for salvation as recorded in the Old Testament, especially in the figures of Abraham and his descendants. How do you understand God as pictured in the stories of the Old Testament? Is this the same God whom we know through Jesus? How did God try to rescue humans from the brokenness caused by sin in the period before the coming of Christ? How does God seek to redeem us today? How can understanding the connections between the Old and New Testaments in our Bible enable us to grasp and respond to what God is doing for us?

Selected Scripture

King James Version	New Revised Standard Version
Romans 4:13-25	*Romans 4:13-25*
13 For the promise, that he should be the heir of the world, was not to Abraham, or to his seed, through the law, but through the righteousness of faith.	13 For the promise that he would inherit the world did not come to Abraham or to his descendants through the law but through the righteousness of faith. 14 If it is the adherents of the law who are to be the heirs, faith is null and the promise is void. 15 For the law brings wrath; but where there is no law, neither is there violation.
14 For if they which are of the law be heirs, faith is made void, and the promise made of none effect:	
15 Because the law worketh wrath: for where no law is, there is no transgression.	
16 Therefore it is of faith, that it might be by grace; to the end the promise might be sure to all the	16 For this reason it depends on faith, in order that the promise may rest on grace and be guaranteed to

seed; not to that only which is of the law, but to that also which is of the faith of Abraham; who is the father of us all,

17 (As it is written, I have made thee a father of many nations,) before him whom he believed, even God, who quickeneth the dead, and calleth those things which be not as though they were.

18 Who against hope believed in hope, that he might become the father of many nations; according to that which was spoken, So shall thy seed be.

19 And being not weak in faith, he considered not his own body now dead, when he was about an hundred years old, neither yet the deadness of Sara's womb:

20 He staggered not at the promise of God through unbelief; but was strong in faith, giving glory to God;

21 And being fully persuaded that, what he had promised, he was able also to perform.

22 And therefore it was imputed to him for righteousness.

23 Now it was not written for his sake alone, that it was imputed to him;

24 But for us also, to whom it shall be imputed, if we believe on him that raised up Jesus our Lord from the dead;

25 Who was delivered for our offences, and was raised again for our justification.

all his descendants, not only to the adherents of the law but also to those who share the faith of Abraham (for he is the father of all of us, 17 as it is written, "I have made you the father of many nations")— in the presence of the God in whom he believed, who gives life to the dead and calls into existence the things that do not exist. 18 Hoping against hope, he believed that he would become "the father of many nations," according to what was said, "So numerous shall your descendants be." 19 He did not weaken in faith when he considered his own body, which was already as good as dead (for he was about a hundred years old), or when he considered the barrenness of Sarah's womb. 20 No distrust made him waver concerning the promise of God, but he grew strong in his faith as he gave glory to God, 21 being fully convinced that God was able to do what he had promised. 22 Therefore his faith "was reckoned to him as righteousness." 23 Now the words, "it was reckoned to him," were written not for his sake alone, 24 but of ours also. It will be reckoned to us who believe in him who raised Jesus our Lord from the dead, 25 who was handed over to death for our trespasses and was raised for our justification.

Key Verse: **For the promise, that he should be the heir of the world, was not to Abraham, or to his seed, through the law, but through the righteousness of faith. Romans 4:13**

Key Verse: **For the promise that he would inherit the world did not come to Abraham or to his descendants through the law but through the righteousness of faith. Romans 4:13**

As You Read the Scripture

Romans 4:13-17. The contrast being developed here is that between obedience to the Law and trusting acceptance of the promise of God. God's gift to Abraham was not a reward for obeying the Law, but a free grant to Abraham, who had faith to receive it.

Verses 13 and 14. The promise to Abraham may be found in Genesis 17:2-5 and 22:17-18 and was repeated to his descendants Isaac and Jacob (see Gen. 26:2-4; 35:10-12). Abraham was not chosen by God to receive this promised blessing because he was obedient to the Law, but simply because of his faith through which he was righteous—acceptable to God. If persons were able to earn God's promised gift of salvation, then faith would be of no value.

Verse 15. The Law brings divine anger upon those who disobey it, but when there are no rules of Law there are no violations. Paul's understanding of the role of divine Law is more complicated than this one verse suggests, but here he wishes to emphasize that the Law is decidedly not the vehicle through which salvation for humans can be achieved.

Verse 16. Because the fulfilling of God's gracious promise of redemption depends solely on accepting it in faith, all who have such faith are true descendants of Abraham. He is presented as the ancestor of all those who share his faith response, not simply those who are of his physical lineage.

Verses 17-25. The faith of Abraham in the divine promise that he would be the progenitor of many nations is used by Paul here as a counterpart of the faith that those who would be Christians must have in the resurrection of Jesus Christ.

Verse 17. God is not limited to working within the possibilities that human beings perceive in order to fulfill the divine promises. Rather, God has power to make the dead live and bring into being those things that do not yet exist. The implied reference here is to the startling birth of Isaac and to the miraculous resurrection of Christ.

Verses 18 and 19. Believing, although he did not understand, Abraham trusted God's promise to make him the father of many nations, even though all common sense and physical evidence indicated that such a thing was impossible. Abraham was almost a hundred years old, and although he had fathered a son in earlier years, his chances for parenthood at this point in his life appeared exceedingly slight. Worse, his wife, Sarah, whom God had insisted would be the mother of the promised child, was not only ninety years of age herself, but had been unable to bear children throughout her life.

Verses 20 and 21. In the face of overwhelming evidence to the contrary, Abraham, after some initial doubt (see Gen. 17:17), was able to believe with ever-growing conviction that God both could and would fulfill the promise. His faith increased as he praised God until he had no doubt, but trusted fully in the divine grace.

Verses 22-25. Paul concludes this part of his argument by repeating what he had asserted in verse 3 of this chapter: that Abraham's faith "was reckoned to him as righteousness." The term *reckoned* was used in commercial transactions to mean "counted" or "credited." Paul uses it, as does Psalm 32:2, which he quotes in verses 7-8. All who believe in the promise fulfilled in Jesus will, like Abraham, be accepted by God.

The Scripture and the Main Question

God's Action for Salvation in the Old Covenant

In the second century a Christian named Marcion created such a stir in the church that he was excommunicated as a heretic. What was Marcion's crime for which the church judged him so dangerous that he must be removed? Marcion rejected the Old Testament, insisting that it was not relevant or appropriate for Christians, claiming that the God of the Old Testament was a different being from the God who was made known in Jesus Christ. While perhaps few Christians would be quite so bold in expressing themselves today, it remains true that many find the Old Testament perplexing and disturbing and view the God they believe is described there with suspicion and even distaste. Why then has the Christian church for two thousand years insisted that the books of the Old Testament are sacred Scripture containing the authentic word of God? Why would Paul choose an Old Testament character, Abraham, as the model of the faith Christians should have?

To be a Christian is to recognize Jesus Christ as the unique revelation of God's nature and will; indeed, as divinity in human form. But to believe this is not to deny that God has partially revealed the divine Self in other ways. As Christians, we believe that God was acting, was reaching out to human beings, throughout human history—long before God took human flesh in the person of Jesus. Here is the key to the importance of the Old Testament to us: God was working in the history of the Hebrew people for many, many centuries before the time of Jesus. The ultimate revelation of God in Jesus Christ—the fullest knowledge of God that human minds can comprehend in this life—can be understood and appreciated only against the backdrop of God's long activity in the life of the Hebrew people as that story is recorded in the Old Testament. To understand God as revealed in Christ, we must know God as revealed in the Old Testament. To comprehend the fulfillment of the divine promises in the New Covenant relationship made possible through Christ, we must understand the yearnings of God's people in the Old Covenant.

According to the Old Testament account, God created a world of beauty and harmony in which humans could live in loving relationships with the natural world, with one another, and with God. But humans quickly misused the gift of free will and chose to put their own desires ahead of the will of God. As a result of this rebellion and selfishness, the entire created order was blighted by sin and humans were alienated and lost. Having cut themselves off from their right relationship with God, their lives in all aspects were characterized by brokenness, estrangement, and violence (see Gen. 3–11). The call of Abraham (Gen. 12) represented God's new beginning in human history. God took the initiative to overcome the tragedy caused by human sin. Through Abraham and Sarah and their descendants, God would work to reestablish the relationship between God and human beings that sin had destroyed. The kind of relationship into which God called Abraham and the people who would descend from him was that of a covenant.

A covenant is two-sided—a mutual, reciprocal relationship—in which both parties make promises and accept responsibilities. This was clearly not a covenant between equals. The sovereign God of the universe chose, motivated by love, to bind the divine Self to human beings. God took the initiative to act in order to make salvation possible because humans were helpless in the sinful separation they had chosen for themselves. The covenant was not established solely for the benefit of the people of Israel—Abraham's descendants—but in order that through them all peoples might be brought back into right relationship with God (see Gen. 12:3: "In you all the families of the earth shall be blessed"). They were given the privilege and the burden

222

of being God's chosen instrument for the redemption of the world. The covenant was renewed with the people of Israel under the leadership of Moses when God brought them out of slavery in Egypt and made clear their responsibility by giving them the Law on Mount Sinai. Later God affirmed the covenant with the royal dynasty of King David.

Throughout the history of the Old Covenant/Testament, the people of Israel failed repeatedly to fulfill their obligations to God. They fell continually into the worship of false gods, into social injustice and oppression, into personal self-centeredness and greed. Although they frequently suffered punishment for their sins, God always offered forgiveness and the opportunity to begin anew. While the people were rebellious and violated the covenant, God remained ever faithful, continually showing forth the divine nature of lovingkindness and the desire to reconcile the descendants of Abraham to God and through them to reconcile the whole world.

Abraham as Our Exemplar of Faith

Paul makes it clear that this covenant relationship with God is now available to all persons, not just those who are biologically descended from Abraham. He is our ancestor in the faith because from him we can learn what faith really is. God chose Abraham for reasons that remain hidden in the heart of God, but certainly not because of anything that Abraham had achieved or deserved. The Jewish people have always realized that God's choice of them as the people of the covenant does not imply any special merit or superiority. God's giving to Abraham righteousness, forgiveness, and right relationship with God was an act of free grace. Only God can make us righteous and, thus, acceptable to God. This is a difficult concept, for we would much prefer to do it ourselves; we would rather be paid what we earn than receive charity we do not deserve. Worse than the laborers in Jesus' parable of the vineyard (Matt. 20), we resent not only divine generosity to others, but also that which is offered to us. But before God, all our claims of worthiness disintegrate into dust and we are forced to realize that apart from God we are of little value. The divine work of salvation must depend on grace, for if it were left to us, our sinfulness would destroy it. Through divine power, the promises are fulfilled and the work of salvation continues. Abraham is our exemplar of how to receive by faith the promise of salvation. When instructed to leave homeland and family, "Abram went, as the LORD had told him" (Gen. 12:4). When informed by God while he was childless that his descendants would be as numerous as the stars in the heavens, "he believed the LORD; and the LORD reckoned it to him as righteousness" (Gen. 15:6).

Helping Adults Become Involved

Preparing to Teach

Begin your preparation by reading the background scripture Romans 3:21–4:25. Use "As You Read the Scripture" to assist you in understanding the verses that are our emphasis in this session. Notice the prominence of Abraham in Paul's thought. As you read "The Main Question" and "The Scripture and the Main Question," you may be surprised to find so much material about the Old Testament. The reason for this is that Romans 4:13-25 is a passage that simply cannot be understood without some knowledge of the Old Testament background that Paul possessed and that he assumed most of his readers in Rome would be familiar with. He believes that the best way he can explain to them what it means to accept salvation by faith is to use the example of Abraham. Using the information presented above, you will be able to make this connection clear to your students if you have studied and taken notes on it yourself in advance.

A workable outline of the lesson is as follows:

I. Importance of the Old Testament for Christians
II. Understanding the idea of covenant
III. Faith rather than law
IV. Abraham as an example of faith

Be sure to have Bibles for every student. Try to have at least one copy each of the Good News Bible and the Revised English Bible; their translations of Romans 4:13-25 are particularly helpful.

Introducing the Main Question

Ask the class to share their understandings of what the Old Testament teaches and, especially, their opinions or feelings about it. Explore with them in a preliminary way the questions of the relationship between the Old and New Testaments and why the Old Testament is still significant for Christians. Have them name familiar Old Testament characters and relate briefly what they remember about these people.

The main point underlying this lesson is the contrast between two ways of seeking right relationship with God: through obedience to the Law and by receiving in faith God's act of grace. The Old Testament personality Abraham is presented as a model of the latter.

Developing the Lesson

I. Importance of the Old Testament for Christians

Build on the discussion with the class which you based on the suggestions in "Introducing the Main Question" by encouraging them to continue sharing their recollections and views concerning the Old Testament. Present the material offered in "The Main Question" and in "The Scripture and the Main Question" quite thoroughly, in order to enrich their understandings.

Some class members may express concern about portions of the Old Testament in which God is portrayed as being more judging and punishing than loving and forgiving or about occasions when the Hebrew people understood God to be directing them to do things that we would consider unjust, even cruel. There are real difficulties in some of the Old Testament material, and this should be honestly acknowledged. You will certainly not be able to solve all of these problems, but some helpful ideas can be offered. The Hebrews of the Old Testament were a very ancient people whose understanding of God was somewhat limited. While having brought them into covenant relationship, God had not revealed to them the fullness of the divine nature and will. God's revelation to humankind was progressive, gradually unfolding and increasing over time. Proof of this is God's eventual act of sending Jesus as the revelation of God in human flesh. To be a Christian is to understand that we know God best through Jesus and that anything that contradicts the nature of God as revealed in Jesus is most likely the result of the limited perceptions of the human authors.

It will be helpful to use a chalkboard or newsprint to outline major events of God's action for salvation during the Old Testament period. Use the information in "The Scripture and the Main Question."

II. Understanding the idea of covenant

Basic to God's plan of salvation is the establishment of covenant relationships with human beings. Explain the concept of covenant, using the material in "The Scripture and the Main Question." Use the example of marriage as a covenant, although it differs from the biblical pattern because it is between equals. Emphasize the love and graciousness of the Creator God of the universe, who chose to enter into covenant bonds with sinful humanity.

III. Faith rather than law

The development of this point needs to be based on the ideas presented in last week's lesson; you may wish to reemphasize them briefly. Have Romans 4:13-25 read aloud from the Good News Bible and the Revised English Bible as class members follow in other translations. Use the material in "As You Read the Scripture" to help you summarize the main points.

IV. Abraham as an example of faith

With the previous points in the lesson established, it should not be difficult to make clear how Paul uses the example of Abraham. Have a volunteer (or do it yourself) report on the major events of Abraham and Sarah's lives and, as time allows, encourage others to contribute, based on their reading of the assigned Genesis material.

Helping Class Members Act

Challenge class members to study Old Testament material; encourage especially the reading of the books of Genesis and Exodus. As a result of this lesson, they should be able to see that understanding much of the New Testament depends on familiarity with the Old Testament.

Ask the students to think seriously about the covenants in their own lives and how they as individuals live within them. What do we learn about the nature of God when we realize that God freely entered into covenant relationship with us? What are the differences between the divine and human sides of the covenant and how they are lived out? How can we emulate Abraham and Sarah in our own relationships with God?

In the Old Testament the covenant between God and the descendants of Abraham and Sarah involved responsibilities to care for the poor and oppressed. Are there covenants that middle-income American Christians, as an especially privileged people, are expected by God to honor with other persons in the society and in the world? How can we be a people through whom God will bless "all the families of the earth"?

Planning for Next Sunday

Ask the class to read Romans 5 and Jeremiah 31:31-34. Note especially what Jeremiah says about the new covenant. Why is a new covenant needed? How will it differ from the old?

Being Reconciled to God

Background Scripture: Romans 5

The Main Question

Almost two thousand years ago a man named Jesus, called by his followers "Christ," traveled the roads of Palestine, preaching, teaching, and healing. After a brief career, he was arrested, brutally executed, and buried in disgrace. On the third day after his death, he arose to life again through the power of God. So what? What difference can this story possibly make to persons living in a world so different and so far away from that one? To be Christian is not only to accept this story as true, but it is also to believe that this story gives meaning to our lives today. Our deepest questions about existence—who we are and who God is—are answered by the death and resurrection of Jesus Christ.

The verses in Romans 5 that we are studying today are a kind of theological commentary on the meaning of Christ's death and resurrection. Paul is focusing especially on the crucifixion of Christ, attempting to explain his understanding of what it accomplished for us. As we have seen in the last two lessons, Paul believed that human beings are hopelessly separated from God and depend on God's action for salvation. Reconciliation between God and humanity is made possible by the death of Christ; it is not possible any other way. Here Paul is exploring how this is so. How does the death of Jesus Christ function to heal the brokenness between humans and God? What does the crucifixion show us about God? What does it mean to be reconciled to God? What does it mean to be justified and how can this be accomplished? How does the resurrection of Christ make new life available to us? These are some of the questions the lesson examines.

Selected Scripture

King James Version	New Revised Standard Version
Romans 5:6-17	*Romans 5:6-17*
6 For when we were yet without strength, in due time Christ died for the ungodly.	6 For while we were still weak, at the right time Christ died for the ungodly. 7 Indeed, rarely will anyone die for a righteous person—
7 For scarcely for a righteous man will one die: yet peradventure for a good man some would even dare to die.	though perhaps for a good person someone might actually dare to die.
8 But God commendeth his love toward us, in that, while we were yet sinners, Christ died for us.	8 But God proves his love for us in that while we still were sinners Christ died for us. 9 Much more surely then, now that we have been
9 Much more then, being now justified by his blood, we shall be saved from wrath through him.	justified by his blood, will we be saved through him from the wrath of God. 10 For if while we were ene-
10 For if, when we were enemies,	mies, we were reconciled to God

we were reconciled to God by the death of his Son, much more, being reconciled, we shall be saved by his life.

11 And not only so, but we also joy in God through our Lord Jesus Christ, by whom we have now received the atonement.

12 Wherefore, as by one man sin entered into the world, and death by sin; and so death passed upon all men, for that all have sinned:

13 (For until the law sin was in the world: but sin is not imputed when there is no law.

14 Nevertheless death reigned from Adam to Moses, even over them that had not sinned after the similitude of Adam's transgression, who is the figure of him that was to come.

15 But not as the offence, so also is the free gift. For if through the offence of one many be dead, much more the grace of God, and the gift by grace, which is by one man, Jesus Christ, hath abounded unto many.

16 And not as it was by one that sinned, so is the gift: for the judgment was by one to condemnation, but the free gift is of many offences unto justification.

17 For if by one man's offence death reigned by one; much more they which receive abundance of grace and of the gift of righteousness shall reign in life by one, Jesus Christ.)

through the death of his Son, much more surely, having been reconciled, will we be saved by his life. 11 But more than that, we even boast in God through our Lord Jesus Christ, through whom we have now received reconciliation.

12 Therefore, just as sin came into the world through one man, and death came through sin, and so death spread to all because all have sinned—13 sin was indeed in the world before the law, but sin is not reckoned when there is no law. 14 Yet death exercised dominion from Adam to Moses, even over those whose sins were not like the transgression of Adam, who is a type of the one who was to come.

15 But the free gift is not like the trespass. For if the many died through the one man's trespass, much more surely have the grace of God and the free gift in the grace of the one man, Jesus Christ, abounded for the many. 16 And the free gift is not like the effect of the one man's sin. For the judgment following one trespass brought condemnation, but the free gift following many trespasses brings justification. 17 If, because of the one man's trespass, death exercised dominion through that one, much more surely will those who receive the abundance of grace and the free gift of righteousness exercise dominion in life through the one man, Jesus Christ.

Key Verse: **But God commendeth his love toward us, in that, while we were yet sinners, Christ died for us. Romans 5:8**

Key Verse: But **God proves his love for us in that while we still were sinners Christ died for us. Romans 5:8**

As You Read the Scripture

Romans 5:6-11. The theme of this section is that reconciliation between humans and God is made possible through the death of Jesus.

Verse 6. Christ died for us when were lost in our sins, separated from God, and totally unable to do anything to help ourselves. This occurred at the right time—the time of our need—according to the plan determined by God.

Verse 7. Human heroism to the point of giving our lives for others is rare and usually involves dying for those who are admirable persons. Divine love is here illustrated in contrast to human behavior.

Verse 8. The proof of God's amazing love is the death of Christ on behalf of sinners, undeserving and unlovely.

Verse 9. Christ's death makes our justification possible—we are forgiven and put in right relationship with God. Therefore, we need no longer be in fear of the judgment of God upon our sinfulness.

Verse 10. We are no longer God's enemies; the crucifixion of Christ has given us peace with God. Now that we are God's friends, we will surely be ultimately saved by the power of the resurrected Lord.

Verse 11. The basis of our confidence is not anything in ourselves, but simply the divine gift of new life in relationship with God. In this we can rejoice exuberantly.

Verses 12-17. The emphasis in these verses is on the role of Christ as the second Adam. Because the work of Christ overcomes the results of the sin of Adam, new life for humanity is made possible.

Verse 12. Here Paul introduces the difficult idea of original sin—that the violation of the divine will by the first human beings somehow caused sin to be passed on to all of their descendants. This has been a much-debated doctrine in the history of Christianity, and there are diverse explanations of just why and how this inheritance of sin operates. The main point is the actuality that all persons are infected by sin and, hence, are subject to death. Adam is used by Paul as an inclusive representative of the entire human race.

Verses 13-14. The reality of death for human beings is evidence that sin has been in the world since the beginning, even though it was not always recognized as such. Until the giving of the law through Moses, sin was not "reckoned"—that is, sin was not entered into the accounts ledger, as in bookkeeping records—even though sin and its consequences were universal.

Verse 14. A transgression is an act of breaking the covenant with God, of violating the divine will, as Adam did. Adam is not only the representative of sinful humanity, but he is also the prototype of Christ.

Verses 15-17. Paul takes care not to equate the sin of Adam with the grace of Christ. In this way he avoids setting up a dualistic understanding of good and evil as equal powers contending against each other for control of human destiny. Once the rule of sin had become established, it took a much greater act of power to overthrow it. The crucifixion of Christ is an incomparably more significant act than the trespass of Adam, for grace and new life are far superior to sin and death. Indeed, grace can destroy the power and effects of sin.

When Paul uses the word *many* in these verses, he means to imply "all"; in Adam all died, and in Christ all may have new life.

The Scripture and the Main Question

In a "Dennis the Menace" cartoon, Dennis and his friend Joey are leaving Mrs. Wilson's kitchen, happily munching on freshly baked cookies. Dennis observes perceptively to his buddy: "Mrs. Wilson doesn't make you cookies because you're good, but because she's so good!" Here is a parable of the grace of God. We are the recipients of divine love not because of anything we are or do, but purely because of who God is. The death of Jesus Christ on the cross most starkly and powerfully portrays the depth and wonder of that love. This is a major part of the revelation of the nature of God, who comes to us through Jesus—God loves sinful people enough to send Christ to suffer death for us.

The New Covenant

As we discussed last week, God had begun to reveal the divine nature and will in Old Testament times by working through the history of the descendants of Abraham and Sarah—the Hebrews, or nation of Israel. God had entered into a covenant relationship with Israel, promising to bless all persons through them. In the time of Moses, God gave the law to spell out the ways in which God's people were to live. But in spite of God's continual faithfulness and repeated forgiveness, the Hebrew people proved unable to obey God's will. Over and over again, they violated the covenant and alienated themselves from God; they did not have the power to be righteous. In Jeremiah 31:31-34, there is recorded a prophecy of the new covenant that God will make with the people, a covenant that would include the changing of their hearts so that they might become capable of living in relationship with God. In Paul's account of the institution of the Lord's Supper in 1 Corinthians 11:23-26, Jesus, taking the cup, declares, "This cup is the new covenant in my blood." Jesus asserts that in his death on the cross the prophesied new covenant is being established. A new relationship between God and humankind is being made available; the power of sin, which had made obedience to the old covenant impossible, is being destroyed.

Because sin had become so pervasive and so powerful, the death of Christ was essential to set us free. Paul understands sin to have had its origin in the violation by Adam of the rules God had prescribed to govern life in the Garden of Eden (see Gen. 3). Paul is not interested in the details of Adam's transgression, and it is not necessary for us to take this story literally in order to take it seriously. The point is that human beings from the beginning of history have placed their own wills ahead of the will of God; we have self-centeredly sought our own way, invented our own values rather than discovering those God has established for us. The spelling book used in schools in the early Puritan colonies of New England illustrated the letter A with the rhyme "In Adam's fall, we sinneth all." As a founding ancestor of the human race (a concept much more clearly understood in ancient times than in our day), Adam's action represented and involved each of his descendants. But truly, as the Hebrew people themselves understood, each of us is our own Adam. Each of us repeats in our own life the pattern of transgression of God's will, which separates us from loving relationships. The doctrine of original sin, though not popular in contemporary Christianity, accurately portrays the nature of human beings individually and corporately.

The Seriousness of Sin

Paul emphasizes the deep seriousness of sin, which has ensnared human beings with the consequences of physical and spiritual death. Christ is the second Adam because he rescues us from the situation that Adam's sin put us in. As Adam disobeyed God, Christ obeyed perfectly and so overcame the results and power of sin. Christ's death opens up for us new lives in reconciled relationship to God. A dramatic image of this is found in the crucifixion account in Matthew 27:51. When Jesus died on the cross, the curtain of the Temple was "torn in two, from top to bottom." Why? Because this curtain had so long separated the Holy of Holies—the place in the innermost part of the Temple where God was thought to dwell—from the areas where worshipers were permitted to go. The tearing away of this curtain represented the destruction of the barrier between God and humankind. In the death of Christ, reconciliation is accomplished and we are turned from enemies of God into friends.

Reconciliation, as we have stressed in previous lessons, is the act of God, not something that we could achieve for ourselves. God chose to deal with human rebellion and estrangement through the death of Christ. This manifests both the magnitude of sin and the depth of divine love. In Christ's death, "evil is buried in an avalanche of grace." Human beings can be justified—forgiven of sin—and admitted into a new quality of life characterized by restored relationship to God.

The Cross and Our Salvation

The death of Christ on the cross makes our salvation possible. There the depths of divine love are revealed as nowhere else, for on that cross the Almighty God suffered for us. But there also, as nowhere else in human history, we see the fullness of the evil of which human beings are capable. Remember the old spiritual that asks us hauntingly, "Were you there when they crucified my Lord? Sometimes it causes me to tremble." The cross should make us tremble as we are confronted with the ugliness and horror of human sin. But in the cross we see not only sin, but also the beauty of God's love, which overcomes it. We are confronted with the power of suffering love, which transforms us. It is popularly said that "God helps those who help themselves," but the cross says that, "God saves those who cannot help themselves." This is the meaning of the death of Christ. The most powerful force in all creation is revealed—the love of a suffering God who yearns so desperately for us wayward children that God is willing to go to any length to reconcile us and restore us into loving relationship. God's love revealed in the death of Christ overcomes the brokenness caused by sin and brings us into an intimate communion that will extend not only through this life but through all eternity. We receive, as Paul puts it, "the abundance of grace and the free gift of righteousness" (v. 17). It is almost overwhelming to realize that Jesus Christ died because of how much God loves us. Unwilling to abandon us to our futile efforts to save ourselves, God acts at great cost to rescue us. The cross of Christ reveals not only how much God loved humankind two thousand years ago, but also how much God continues to love each of us today and every day. Like the hymn writer, Isaac Watts, surely we must respond, "Love so amazing, so divine, demands my soul, my life, my all."

Helping Adults Become Involved

Preparing to Teach

As you prepare to teach, it is important to review the major points of the two previous lessons in this series. This entire unit can best be considered as a whole, with each of the individual lessons building on the others in order to present a progression of ideas. Be certain that you are clear as to how these lessons relate to one another.

Read carefully the material in "The Main Question" and "The Scripture and the Main Question," seeking to identify the major points. Read all of Romans 5; use "As You Read the Scripture" for help with verses 6-17.

The content of the lesson can be organized around these three foci:

    I. God saves sinful humanity through the death of Jesus Christ.
    II. Christ as the second Adam
   III. New life in reconciliation with God

It will be especially important today to have Bibles available for all students. A variety of translations is helpful, particularly a Revised English Bible. Try to bring into class several examples from advice columns (like Ann Landers and "Dear Abby") that talk about broken and/or reconciled relationships. You will also need a chalkboard or newsprint and paper and pencils.

Introducing the Main Question

Use the material in "The Main Question" to plan your own introduction to the lesson. Emphasize how the death of Christ served to make human salvation possible and what relevance that truth has for us today.

Developing the Lesson

I. God saves sinful humanity through the death of Jesus Christ.

An understanding of the concept of grace—God's free, unmerited favor—must underlie all of our attempts to comprehend how human salvation is possible. Use the "Dennis the Menace" story in "The Scripture and the Main Question" and encourage your class to discuss it as a clue to grasping the idea of divine grace. Move on to suggest that, as strange as it sounds, God's grace is made available to us through the death of Christ. How could a brutal execution be a revelation of God's love? Try to stimulate the class to discuss these and related questions without proposing final answers at this point.

Using the material in "The Scripture and the Main Question" as well as your notes from the past two sessions, briefly recount the workings of God in the history of the Hebrew people in the Old Testament period. Review the concept of covenant, especially as we discussed it last week in relation to Abraham and his descendants. Have the class look together at Jeremiah 31:31-34 and discuss the need for a new covenant. Using 1 Corinthians 11:23-26, discuss Jesus' understanding of himself as initiating the new covenant. Covenants were traditionally ratified in ceremonies involving the use of blood as the sign of the covenant relationship. These motifs can be identified in the account of the Lord's Supper and the crucifixion, which it commemorates.

II. Christ as the Second Adam

Paul's explanation of how salvation is made possible for us through the death of Christ relies heavily on his idea of Christ as the prototype for right-eousness and new life, as Adam was the prototype for sin and death. This concept was much easier to grasp in ancient societies than it is today. The people to whom Paul addressed himself thought much more in corporate and communal terms than in the individualistic and personal concepts with which we are today more familiar. Read verses 6-11, 12-14, and 15-17 aloud from the New Revised Standard Version and the Revised English Bible, as well as from other versions. Often different words expressing the same thoughts communicate effectively to different people. Encourage your class to discuss various understandings of the idea of original sin. Using "The Scripture and the Main Question," guide them to the realization that within each of us is an inherent tendency toward evil, but that we are responsible for our decisions and, hence, our own sins.

III. New life in reconciliation with God

Use the advice columns to stimulate discussion about brokenness and reconciliation in relationships. The purpose is to move persons not only to think about, but also to feel the pain of estrangement and the joy of restoration. Using ideas from "The Scripture and the Main Question," lead the class in examining what it means to be reconciled to God. From being at enmity with God, we have been made God's friends; from being in conflict, we have become at peace; from separation, we have been restored to relationship; from alienation, we have been brought to communion; from hostility to God, we have been blessed with intimacy. These wonderful gifts come to us as the result of the death of Christ, which overcame the power of sin and gave us new life.

Helping Class Members Act

Not all of the questions your class members might raise about the death of Jesus can be resolved in this class session—or, indeed, at all. Some of the answers we would like to have will remain hidden in the mystery of God. The main point of this lesson, however, should be clear by now: Through the benefits made available to us by the death of Christ, we are justified and our sins are forgiven; we are reconciled and brought back into loving relationship with God. Lead the class in exploring the implications of this fact for our daily lives. How should justified and reconciled persons live—not only in terms of relationship to God, but in relationship with other persons, with ourselves, with the natural environment? What are some of the actual differences that the results of the death of Christ should make in our beliefs and in our behavior?

Have the class look together at 2 Corinthians 5:17-21. These verses present an understanding of reconciliation that is virtually identical to that in Romans 5, but they go on to speak about the "ministry of reconciliation" that God has given us, making us "ambassadors for Christ." Talk about what this means. Have class members make a list, which you will record on a chalkboard or newsprint, of specific ways we can work to further the ministry of reconciliation in this broken world. Ask members to make private lists of ways they can be instruments of God's reconciling love in their personal lives and relationships. Do as much of this in class as time allows and then encourage your members to continue in their private devotions during the coming week.

Planning for Next Sunday

Encourage class members to think about experiences of baptism in their own lives and in those of their children. Ask each person to take a few moments during the week to write a brief paragraph about his or her understanding of the meaning of baptism.

Delivered from Sin

Background Scripture: Romans 6

The Main Question

In his great hymn "O For a Thousand Tongues to Sing," Charles Wesley says of Jesus:

> He breaks the power of canceled sin,
> He sets the prisoner free.

Paul would certainly have responded with an "Amen." We have already established that Paul portrays human beings as prisoners helpless in the grip of sin, and that the death of Jesus makes possible our deliverance. Now we begin to examine the new life into which we enter when we are delivered from sin. How is the new life different from the old existence under the power of sin? What characteristics of the Christian life manifest that it is a life of freedom from the bondage in which original sin and our own sinfulness had enslaved us?

Deliverance from sin, Paul says, comes through the experience of our dying and rising with Christ. But how is it possible for us to have such intimacy with Jesus that we can share both his death and his life? Paul asserts that it is in and through the sacrament of Christian baptism that we are so united with Christ. This idea is clearly a much different understanding of baptism than what many of us are familiar with. Too often the baptism of infants is viewed only as a pretty ceremony in which parents pledge to raise the child properly, and the baptism of adults is understood solely as a service in which the person joins the church and promises to try to live a good life. Paul has something much more powerful and more mysterious in mind. For him, baptism is a supernatural experience in which we share the death of Christ and, hence, escape the bondage of sin. It is an act of God through which we rise from death and are brought into a new community of those who share the life of Christ.

Selected Scripture

King James Version	New Revised Standard Version
Romans 6:3-14, 20-23	*Romans 6:3-14, 20-23*
3 Know ye not, that so many of us as were baptized into Jesus Christ were baptized into his death?	3 Do you not know that all of us who have been baptized into Christ Jesus were baptized into his death? 4
4 Therefore we are buried with him by baptism into death: that like as Christ was raised up from the dead by the glory of the Father, even so we also should walk in newness of life.	Therefore we have been buried with him by baptism into death, so that, just as Christ was raised from the dead by the glory of the Father, so we too might walk in newness of life.
5 For if we have been planted together in the likeness of his death,	5 For if we have been united with him in a death like his, we will cer-

233

we shall be also in the likeness of his resurrection:

6 Knowing this, that our old man is crucified with him, that the body of sin might be destroyed, that henceforth we should not serve sin.

7 For he that is dead is freed from sin.

8 Now if we be dead with Christ, we believe that we shall also live with him:

9 Knowing that Christ being raised from the dead dieth no more; death hath no more dominion over him.

10 For in that he died, he died unto sin once: but in that he liveth, he liveth unto God.

11 Likewise reckon ye also yourselves to be dead indeed unto sin, but alive unto God through Jesus Christ our Lord.

12 Let not sin therefore reign in your mortal body, that ye should obey it in the lusts thereof.

13 Neither yield ye your members as instruments of unrighteousness unto sin: but yield yourselves unto God, as those that are alive from the dead, and your members as instruments of righteousness unto God.

14 For sin shall not have dominion over you: for ye are not under the law, but under grace.

....

20 For when ye were the servants of sin, ye were free from righteousness.

21 What fruit had ye then in those things whereof ye are now ashamed? for the end of those things is death.

22 But now being made free from sin, and become servants to God, ye have your fruit unto holiness, and the end everlasting life.

23 For the wages of sin is death; but the gift of God is eternal life through Jesus Christ our Lord.

Key Verse: **For the wages of sin is death; but the gift of God is eternal life through Jesus Christ our Lord. Romans 6:23**

tainly be united with him in a resurrection like his. 6 We know that our old self was crucified with him so that the body of sin might be destroyed, and we might no longer be enslaved to sin. 7 For whoever has died is freed from sin. 8 But if we have died with Christ, we believe that we will also live with him. 9 We know that Christ, being raised from the dead, will never die again; death no longer has dominion over him. 10 The death he died, he died to sin, once for all; but the life he lives, he lives to God. 11 So you also must consider yourselves dead to sin and alive to God in Christ Jesus.

12 Therefore, do not let sin exercise dominion in your mortal bodies, to make you obey their passions. 13 No longer present your members to sin as instruments of wickedness, but present yourselves to God as those who have been brought from death to life, and present your members to God as instruments of righteousness. 14 For sin will have no dominion over you, since you are not under law but under grace.

....

20 When you were slaves of sin, you were free in regard to righteousness. 21 So what advantage did you then get from the things of which you now are ashamed? The end of those things is death. 22 But now that you have been freed from sin and enslaved to God, the advantage you get is sanctification. The end is eternal life. 23 For the wages of sin is death, but the free gift of God is eternal life in Christ Jesus our Lord.

Key Verse: **For the wages of sin is death, but the free gift of God is eternal life in Christ Jesus our Lord. Romans 6:23**

As You Read the Scripture

In the scripture selections we have read in the earlier lessons of this unit, Paul focused on the need for and the provision of justification for human beings and our reconciliation to God. In this chapter he shifts his attention to the nature of the new life made available to those who accept God's gift by faith.

Romans 6:3-14. After dying and rising with Christ in baptism, we enter into a new character of existence. Having been freed from the dominion of sin, we can live as God's people.

Verses 3-4. Paul presents Christian baptism as an analogy to the death and resurrection of Christ. We die, are buried, and rise to newness of life. The mode of baptism by immersion is probably what Paul is here picturing. But the relationship being developed is more than an analogy. Indeed, it is through baptism that we truly participate in both Christ's death and his resurrected life. The word *glory* in verse 4 probably means the power of God as manifested in the resurrection.

Verse 5. To be "united with him" literally means to be "planted together" in the sense of being grafted onto. The emphasis is on the intimacy of the union of the believer and Christ. It is instructive to note the tenses of the verbs in this verse and again in verse 8. Our justification/reconciliation has been accomplished; our ultimate salvation is to be a reality in the future.

Verses 6-7. The crucifixion of Christ, in which we participate through our baptism, has destroyed the power of evil. The "body of sin" refers to the whole self when it was enslaved by sin. This old self has been destroyed—annulled or canceled out—by our death to sin, and we enter a new order of existence where sin has no legitimate place.

Verse 8. Having already experienced our death to sin through Christ's death, we look forward confidently to the fullness of resurrected life.

Verses 9-10. The death and resurrection of Christ were unique events that can never be, nor need ever be, repeated. They were sufficient to break the dominion of evil with its attendant death.

Verse 11. As a result, not only is Christ free from the power of sin and death, but so are we. A new community of human beings has been created—a community that exists in the newness of life, which is a sharing in the life of God through Jesus Christ.

Verses 12-13. In this new order of existence, it is possible for persons to live righteously, so Paul proceeds to moral exhortations. "Passions" refers to all evil desires, not just those associated with sexuality or even physicality. Similarly, "members" is to be understood as including all human faculties. All that we are as persons can now be presented to God through the moral freedom won for us by Christ.

Verse 14. This verse again looks to the future when the freedom from sin, now begun, will be complete.

Verses 20-21. While in bondage to the power of sin, we were unable to serve the power of righteousness. That kind of life can end only in spiritual destruction, both temporal and eternal.

Verses 22-23. In slavery—perfect obedience—to God we find real freedom in a life of growing holiness. The eternal life that we receive is a free gift from God, not a reward achieved.

THIRD QUARTER

The Scripture and the Main Question

Newness of Life

The material in the sixth chapter of Romans marks a distinct movement in Paul's presentation of his basic theological understandings. He has been concerned up to this point largely with describing the human situation of helpless sinfulness; the action of God in Hebrew history and, preeminently, in Jesus Christ to justify and reconcile us; and the necessity of receiving God's free gift in faith. Now he is moving into a discussion of the nature of the new life available to us once we are delivered from the control of sin. Paul emphasizes the decisive break between the old order of existence and the new. The person who has received by faith the benefits of Christ's death and resurrection is a new creature (2 Cor. 5:17). Having experienced a death to sin, he or she is no longer a natural human being, but has been transformed into one who is spiritual. Spiritual persons manifest new values and interests; they are members of a new race of human beings. Indeed, such transformed persons can be best described not as individuals, but as members of a new community or order of relationships. To be "in Christ" is to be a member of the Body of Christ.

Significance of Baptism

Our entrance into this new community, the Body of Christ, comes through baptism (see 1 Cor. 12:13). Deliverance from sin can come only through death, and in baptism our death—which results from both Adam's sin and our own—has been accomplished. A graphic representation of the relationship between baptism and death is seen in the common practice in the early church, still found today especially in Greek Orthodox churches, of using baptisteries shaped like tombs. One who entered such a baptistery and was immersed in the water it contained experienced a dramatic sense of the reality of death and burial. The old self with its bondage to sin was understood to be drowned in the water of the sacrament. But this death is an essential prelude to birth into the new life. As the nineteenth-century baptismal service in American Methodism prayed, "O merciful God, grant that the old Adam in this child may be so buried, that the new man may be raised up in him." The new person who emerged from baptism was one whose life was in intimate union with the life of Christ—indeed, a life grounded in and empowered by that of Christ. Such a person is in love with God as known in Christ and committed to the service of Christ. He or she lives in close fellowship with the presence of Christ through the Holy Spirit and is directed by that indwelling presence in the living out of the Christian commitment.

A Change of Masters

Paul pictures sin as a malign power that holds humans helpless within its grip. This death grip is broken by the death and resurrection of Christ and our identification with him expressed in our baptism. We are, thus, saved *from* sin, but we must also be saved *to* something. Human beings cannot remain in a state of moral neutrality. We always have some master; we cannot escape both sin and God. This is at least partially what Jesus was describing in his parable of the unclean spirit, which, after going out of a person, returns later with seven spirits worse than itself to take up residence in the person (see Luke 11:24-26). Freed by the work of Christ, we are empowered to make moral decisions; we can choose our master, but we will have some master simply because we are creatures and not God. (See Josh. 24:14-28 for an Old Testament account of the call to decision for or against God.) Bondage to sin as master is a terrible enslavement because it separates us from God, makes us increasingly evil, and ultimately destroys us spiritually and physically. Acceptance of Christ as master is a wonderful liberation because it reconciles us to God, empowers us to grow in holiness of life, and ultimately brings us eternal life. As an old English prayer puts it: "In Thy service is perfect freedom."

"Free at Last . . . "

In one of his stirring speeches, Martin Luther King, Jr., exuberantly quoted the words of an old spiritual: "Free at last, free at last; thank God Almighty I'm free at last!" This is precisely the attitude Paul believes Christians should manifest. We must grasp the amazing truth that the death and resurrection of Jesus Christ have delivered us from the bondage of sin; we must apprehend our freedom. Paul J. Achtemeier tells the story of several fish he kept in a small bowl when he was in college. Later, when he placed those fish in a large aquarium, he was struck to see that they continued, in spite of their enlarged opportunity, to swim around in the same tight circles to which they had become accustomed in their earlier confinement. The fish did not recognize their freedom, and so they could not utilize it. So, too, with us. We must recognize that the moral consequence of our freedom is that we can choose not to sin. Note that Paul does not exhort his readers to moral endeavor until he explains their deliverance from bondage. Unless they realize the power they have received through union with Christ, they will be unable to live lives of righteousness. Indeed, our lives are grounded in and draw upon the power of the resurrected life of Christ. We have been made alive to God; our new lives in the new age have begun.

Our lives in Christ are both present reality and future hope. As the old preacher put it: "I ain't yet what I'm gonna be, but, thank God, I ain't now what I used to be." Our deliverance from enslavement to sin is an accomplished fact. It was achieved by the death and resurrection of Christ with which we came to participate in our baptism. But like a person newly released from prison, we must practice living in freedom. We must work in cooperation with God's grace to overcome the old habits, to destroy the impulses to evil, to allow the life of Christ to express itself more and more through us. Such work requires spiritual discipline and humble reliance on the strength we draw from our union with Christ and our comradeship with others seeking to so live. Our salvation is a process, not an event; a journey, not a destination. The sanctification of which Paul speaks is our growing increasingly holy, increasingly consecrated or set apart for God. We are "being saved" as we become more and more "conformed to the image of his Son" (Rom. 8:29). Salvation has, then, an eschatological nature. Our salvation will only be fully achieved, our baptism truly fulfilled, when God gives us eternal life.

Helping Adults Become Involved

Preparing to Teach

Read all of Romans 6, using "As You Read the Scripture" for assistance. Read "The Main Question" and "The Scripture and the Main Question"; make notes on what you consider the major ideas to be presented.

The major points of the lesson may be outlined as follows:

      I.   Baptism as dying and rising with Christ
     II.   Freedom from sin
    III.   New life in Christ
   IV.   Salvation as present and future

You will need a sufficient supply of Bibles and hymnals for use during the session. A chalkboard or newsprint will be helpful also.

Introducing the Main Question

All regular churchgoers have witnessed the sacrament of Christian baptism, and almost all of your class members likely have been baptized themselves and have had their children baptized. Because of this familiarity, a good starting point for the lesson is a brief discussion of personal baptismal experiences and understandings. Encourage the class to analyze the meaning of the sacrament. Why do we baptize persons? Why do we baptize infants? What does the service of baptism do? What does it express?

Make clear to the class that for Paul the sacrament of baptism is a dramatic and life-changing experience through which we participate in the dying and rising of Jesus Christ; we are set free from enslavement to sin and are empowered to live new lives in Christ. How does our understanding of baptism diverge from that of Paul? Why are our ideas so different?

Developing the Lesson

I. Baptism as dying and rising with Christ

Most Christians refer to baptism as a sacrament—a special ceremony, instituted by Christ, through which God's grace comes to human beings. We believe that because baptism is an act of God through God's church, something real and highly significant happens to persons who receive it. Paul says in verses 3-5 that baptism washes away sin, clothing persons in righteousness, and, especially, through baptism we are "dying and being raised with Christ" so as to "share in his final victory." Use the "Significance of Baptism" section of "The Scripture and the Main Question" to help you explain these concepts.

II. Freedom from sin

Use "A Change of Masters" in "The Scripture and the Main Question" and the commentary on verses 6-11 in "As You Read the Scripture" as your guides to the main points. Encourage the group to think and talk about contemporary situations of bondage to evil masters—various addictions, uncontrollable impulses, and oppressive circumstances will provide examples. Are there occasions in life when it is true that "the devil made me do it"? Christians know God in Christ as the One who sets us free. Read Luke 4:16-21; here Jesus, in his first opportunity to speak in his hometown, quotes from the prophet Isaiah about God's gift of freedom. Remind the class of incidents in the Old Testament where God acted to provide freedom for God's people, especially the Exodus from slavery in Egypt (see Exod. 10–14) and the return from Babylonian captivity (see Isa. 40). Are there occasions of rescue or deliverance in your life or in the lives of your class members that could be shared?

III. New life in Christ

Have the class look closely at verses 12-14 and 20-23 and use the commentary in "As You Read the Scripture" to enhance their understanding of the concepts. The "Newness of Life" portion of "The Scripture and the Main Question" will also be helpful. The emphasis in this section of the lesson is on the character of the new life under the Lordship of Christ.

IV. Salvation as present and future

A characteristic doctrine taught by the founder of Methodism, John Wesley, was the understanding of salvation as a process, a reality to be more and more fully actualized throughout life. Wesley thought in terms of an order of salvation, which included justification, forgiveness of sins and restoration of right relationship with God (reconciliation); regeneration, spiritual birth into a new order of existence; sanctification, growth in holiness of life toward "Christian perfection" in which one is motivated purely by the love of God; and glorification, the heavenly state of freedom from all sin and being like Christ. Notice how Paul emphasizes a similar sense of process and fulfillment. Use the section "Free at Last . . . " to present this concept.

Helping Class Members Act

Encourage class members to examine their own lives honestly and prayerfully to determine their progress in the process of growth toward fullness of salvation. Make it clear that while sanctification comes through the grace of God working within us, it is up to us to practice the spiritual disciplines that make us receptive to God's action in changing us. Ask your pastor to have a congregational service of baptismal reaffirmation.

Planning for Next Sunday

Next Sunday we will begin a new unit of lessons, also based on the book of Romans. In preparation for this transition, ask your students to think during the week about the unit we have now completed and make a brief list of the major points they have learned.

A preliminary reading of Romans 8 and of the resurrection account in Mark 16 would also be helpful.

UNIT II: EMPOWERED BY THE SPIRIT

FOUR LESSONS APRIL 3–24

This unit is a continuation of the study of the letter of Paul to the church at Rome, which was begun in the last unit, "Righteous through Faith." It builds on the theological understandings your class members have gained from that unit. After a consideration of the significance of the Easter experience, the focus shifts to more practical, rather than primarily theological, concerns. Such a transition from doctrinal issues fundamental to Christianity to application in matters of Christian living was a characteristic pattern in Paul's letters.

The opening lesson of the unit is entitled "A Glimpse of Glory." Here students are invited to enter into the experience of the women who went to the tomb on the morning of the first Easter and are asked to seek to grasp what it means to be Easter people. Lesson 2, "Life in the Spirit," examines the contrast between two ways of living—in the flesh and in the Spirit. Those who have the Spirit of Christ dwelling within them are called to minister to others and have a variety of gifts bestowed on them by God. The third lesson, "Using Our Gifts in Serving," focuses on how Christians are to conduct themselves in the daily routine of life so as to use these gifts in service. In the concluding lesson of the unit, "Living for Others," students are challenged to examine their own moral behavior and their attitudes toward the behavior of others.

LESSON 5 APRIL 3

Sharing Christ's Glory

Background Scripture: Mark 16:1-8; Romans 8:12-27

The Main Question

"Something is loosed to change the shaken world, and with it we must change." This quotation from Stephen Vincent Benét is an appropriate comment on our Scripture selections for today. The Easter story from Mark tells of "something loosed" with the power to change the world; the verses from Romans attempt to describe how our lives are to be changed by that event. The women who sorrowfully approached Jesus' tomb early that morning were concerned about the important, practical question of how they would remove the heavy stone from the entrance. The young man in a white robe whom they met there lifted their minds totally out of such mundane concerns when he informed them that Jesus had been raised from the dead. There was no corpse to anoint with spices, no dead Master to mourn—only a tomb, eloquent in its emptiness. Mary Magdalene, Mary, and Salome felt the power of a God who could snatch Christ from the grasp of death. They realized, although they could not have expressed it, that something was, indeed, "loosed to change the shaken world." Nothing in human existence would ever be the same again; they were rightly struck speechless with amazement.

By the time of Paul such speechlessness had been replaced with commentary and analysis as those who sought to follow the resurrected Christ tried to comprehend the meaning of these events. They, too, experienced the power; they knew that the resurrection of Christ had inaugurated a new order of life for persons who would be led by the Spirit of God. What did it mean for them to be "children of God," to be "joint heirs with Christ"? What does it mean for us? How are we to live out the privilege of such incredible intimacy with the God who raised Jesus from the tomb?

Selected Scripture

King James Version

Mark 16:1-8

1 And when the sabbath was past, Mary Magdalene, and Mary the mother of James, and Salome, had bought sweet spices, that they might come and anoint him.

2 And very early in the morning the first day of the week, they came unto the sepulchre at the rising of the sun.

3 And they said among themselves, Who shall roll us away the stone from the door of the sepulchre?

4 And when they looked, they saw that the stone was rolled away: for it was very great.

5 And entering into the sepulchre, they saw a young man sitting on the right side, clothed in a long white garment; and they were affrighted.

6 And he saith unto them, Be not affrighted: Ye seek Jesus of Nazareth, which was crucified: he is risen; he is not here: behold the place where they laid him.

7 But go your way, tell his disciples and Peter that he goeth before you into Galilee: there shall ye see him, as he said unto you.

8 And they went out quickly, and fled from the sepulchre; for they trembled and were amazed: neither said they any thing to any man; for they were afraid.

New Revised Standard Version

Mark 16:1-8

1 When the sabbath was over, Mary Magdalene, and Mary the mother of James, and Salome bought spices, so that they might go and anoint him. 2 And very early on the first day of the week, when the sun had risen, they went to the tomb. 3 They had been saying to one another, "Who will roll away the stone for us from the entrance to the tomb?" 4 When they looked up, they saw that the stone, which was very large, had already been rolled back. 5 As they entered the tomb, they saw a young man, dressed in a white robe, sitting on the right side; and they were alarmed. 6 But he said to them, "Do not be alarmed; you are looking for Jesus of Nazareth, who was crucified. He has been raised; he is not here. Look, there is the place they laid him. 7 But go, tell his disciples and Peter that he is going ahead of you to Galilee; there you will see him, just as he told you." 8 So they went out and fled from the tomb, for terror and amazement had seized them; and they said nothing to anyone, for they were afraid.

Romans 8:12-17

12 Therefore, brethren, we are debtors, not to the flesh, to live after the flesh.

13 For if ye live after the flesh, ye shall die: but if ye through the Spirit do mortify the deeds of the body, ye shall live.

14 For as many as are led by the Spirit of God, they are the sons of God.

15 For ye have not received the spirit of bondage again to fear; but ye have received the Spirit of adoption, whereby we cry, Abba, Father.

16 The Spirit itself beareth witness with our spirit, that we are the children of God:

17 And if children, then heirs; heirs of God, and joint-heirs with Christ; if so be that we suffer with him, that we may be also glorified together.

Key Verses: **The Spirit itself beareth witness with our spirit, that we are the children of God: And if children, then heirs; heirs of God, and joint-heirs with Christ; if so be that we suffer with him, that we may be also glorified together. Romans 8:16-17**

Romans 8:12-17

12 So then, brothers and sisters, we are debtors, not to the flesh, to live according to the flesh— 13 for if you live according to the flesh, you will die; but if by the Spirit you put to death the deeds of the body, you will live. 14 For all who are led by the Spirit of God are children of God. 15 For you did not receive a spirit of slavery to fall back into fear, but you have received a spirit of adoption. When we cry, "Abba! Father!" 16 it is that very Spirit bearing witness with our spirit that we are children of God, 17 and if children, then heirs, heirs of God and joint heirs with Christ—if, in fact, we suffer with him so that we may also be glorified with him.

Key Verses: **It is that very Spirit bearing witness with our spirit that we are . . . heirs of God and joint heirs with Christ—if, in fact, we suffer with him so that we may also be glorified with him. Romans 8:16-17**

As You Read the Scripture

Mark 16:1-8. Mark's account of the first Easter is the briefest and most enigmatic of any in the four Gospels, yet it pulsates with the emotion of witnesses to astounding events.

Verses 1-2. The Jewish Sabbath, or holy day, had begun at sundown on Friday, only a few hours after Jesus died on the cross. Because of the prohibition of work on the Sabbath, Jesus' followers had been forced to bury his body hastily. So as early as there was sufficient light to allow them to move about on Sunday, the first day of the work week, three of the women disciples went to the tomb. Their intended task was to finish anointing the body with spices, in accordance with the burial practices of their culture.

Verses 3-4. The burial place of Jesus was most likely a cave with niches or shelves cut into the sides to hold bodies. Whole families were often interred in the same cave, but the other three Gospels tell us that this tomb had not previously been used. The large stone would have been flattened and rounded so as to roll in a trench and, by its very weight, seal the opening of the cave.

Verses 5-6. The white attire of the young man may indicate that he was a messenger from God. As is so often the case in Scripture, the first words of the heavenly messenger are an attempt to calm the fear of his hearers. He informs the women very straightforwardly that the Jesus whom they seek is not there, because he has been raised from death. He offers them the supporting evidence of the empty tomb.

Verses 7-8. The young man instructs the women to tell the disciples that Jesus will meet all of them in Galilee "just as he told you." Clearly the horror of the crucifixion events had blotted from their minds any recollection of Jesus' promise to meet them after his death, or at least had shattered any credibility it might have seemed to have.

Romans 8:12-17. These verses constitute an element often found in Paul's letters: a section of moral exhortation and encouragement.

Verses 12-13. Paul contrasts two ways of life, that of the flesh and that of the Spirit. The "flesh" does not mean simply the physical body, but rather the enmeshment in sin and mortality, which are inherent aspects of being human. Both life and death have a dual meaning here; they refer to both the physical and the spiritual realms. At the end of verse 12 occurs one of Paul's typical breaks in the midst of a sentence, when his thoughts take him off in a related, but different, direction.

Verse 14. Those who live under the direction of God's Spirit are incorporated into God's family and enjoy the enormous privilege of being children of God.

Verses 15-16. The privilege of being God's children is highlighted by contrasting that status, with its spirit of adoption, to the status of slavery, with its spirit of fear. Before being enabled to participate in God's Spirit, we were slaves to sin; now we have been adopted by God as children with rights to inheritance. Both *Abba*—the Aramaic word for "Father"—and the Greek form of the word are used to convey a sense of our intimacy with God.

Verse 17. Rejection by the world is a sign that we no longer belong there, but are identified with Christ.

The Scripture and the Main Question

Appropriately on this Easter Sunday, we focus our attention on the Resurrection, looking first at the story as told in Mark and then at Paul's exhortation to Christians to understand ourselves as a people whose lives have been changed by that event.

The Women at the Tomb

The four Gospels record variations in their accounts of the Resurrection, but one fact upon which they all agree is that the first to receive the glorious news were women. In a time when our society is still troubled about the proper place of women in both secular and religious arenas, this fact has great relevance. Mary Magdalene was a close companion of Jesus during his earthly ministry; she is mentioned at least a dozen times in the Gospels. We know less about Mary, the mother of James, and Salome, but in Mark 15:40-41 we are told that all three had followed and provided for Jesus in Galilee and had come to Jerusalem with him along with many other women. (See also Luke 8:1-3.) We can only imagine the scandal that such unconventional behavior must have stirred up, especially in an age when women were relegated exclusively to the domestic sphere and to the roles of wives and mothers.

THIRD QUARTER

Without disparaging the role of the main disciples, it is important to recognize the deep significance of God's choosing to reveal the best news the world has ever heard—that Christ had risen from death—to women first. All customs and stereotypes that have long restricted women to second-class status were shattered at the empty tomb.

The Resurrection: God's Victory

In perhaps the most majestic of all Easter hymns, "Christ the Lord Is Risen Today," Charles Wesley exults:

> Love's redeeming work is done,
> Fought the fight, the battle won,
> Death in vain forbids him rise,
> Christ has opened paradise.
> Lives again our glorious King,
> Where, O death, is now thy sting?
> Once he died our souls to save,
> Where's thy victory, boasting grave?

While the earliest disciples, both men and women, reacted to the news of the Resurrection with a mixture of fear and amazement, of doubt and hope, their emotions were soon transformed into joy. And throughout Christian history since that time, this has been the characteristic mood of Easter—joyous celebration of triumph. God has intervened to rescue us from slavery to sin and to bring us back into right relationship with God. To accomplish this deliverance, God sent Jesus to live a human life, to die and to be raised from death. His resurrection shattered the bondage that sin and death have exercised, and human beings were freed to live as God's people. God's victory has been won once and for all! And because of God's love for us, we share in this divine victory!

Living as Easter People

The good news for us is that God's victory in the Resurrection makes it possible for us to live new lives both in this world and in the world to come. Wesley's great hymn expresses this as it continues:

> Soar we now where Christ has led,
> Following our exalted Head,
> Made like him, like him we rise,
> Ours the cross, the grave, the skies.

Through God's grace we participate in Christ's triumph over sin and death. For this reason, it is so appropriate that a contemporary hymn refers to Christians as "Easter people" and asserts that "Every day to us is Easter" ("Easter People, Raise Your Voices," *The United Methodist Hymnal,* 304). The seal of the Resurrection for us is our possession of the Spirit of God, which is a kind of advance installment, or down payment, guaranteeing the future glory we will share with Christ when our salvation is complete. Romans 6:17 calls us "heirs of God and joint heirs with Christ." It is mind-boggling to realize that we inherit, we receive possession of, the very life of God, just as Christ did. The power that raised Christ from death is at work in our lives as well.

Verses 14-17 of Romans 6 emphasize the close relationship that has been established between God and the people who live by God's Spirit. With our emancipation from the bondage of sin and our reconciliation to God, we have been incorporated into the divine family, adopted as God's own children. No longer are we to conceive of God as unreachably remote or as frighteningly wrathful. God is our loving Parent with whom we can enjoy the warm fellowship of an affectionate family. In Old Testament legal procedures, truth was established by the testimony of two witnesses. Just so, the authenticity of our status as beloved children is proven by the collaborating testimony of God's Spirit witnessing with ours.

The concepts in this passage were very significant to John Wesley as he developed his theology during the early days of the Methodist movement. In one of his sermons, Wesley offers this explanation: "The testimony of the Spirit is an inward impression of the soul, whereby the Spirit of God directly witnesses to my spirit, that I am a child of God; that Jesus Christ hath loved me, and given Himself for me; and that all my sins are blotted out, and I, even I, am reconciled to God" ("The Witness of the Spirit, I" in Albert C. Outler, editor, *The Works of John Wesley, Volume I: Sermons I* [Nashville: Abingdon Press, 1984], p. 274). This witness of the Spirit was the source of Wesley's important doctrine of assurance—that we can know ourselves to have been forgiven and accepted by God. His description of his Aldersgate experience echoes the themes we have been considering: "In the evening I went very unwillingly to a society in Aldersgate Street, where one was reading Luther's preface to the *Epistle to the Romans.* About a quarter before nine, while he was describing the change which God works in the heart through faith in Christ, I felt my heart strangely warmed. I felt I did trust in Christ, Christ alone for my salvation; and an assurance was given me that he had taken away *my* sins, even *mine,* and saved *me* from the law of sin and death."

Helping Adults Become Involved

Preparing to Teach

This lesson does not appear to fit quite neatly into the scheme being followed in this study of Romans. Doubtless this is true, and appropriately so, because today is Easter Sunday and our attention is inevitably drawn to the Resurection above all else. In a deeper sense, however, this Resurrection focus is pertinent, for the reality of the death and resurrection of Christ undergirds all of Paul's understanding of the Christian faith.

I urge you, as you prepare to teach, to read not only the material in Mark 16:1-8, but also the accounts of the Resurrection in the Gospels of Matthew, Luke, and John. Read also Romans 8:12-27. Spend some time planning and practicing the guided meditations that are suggested below.

The material of the lesson can be very simply outlined as it falls into two main emphases:

I.   Witnessing the glory of God in the Resurrection of Christ
II. Sharing Christ's glory in Christian living

You will need Bibles and hymnals for all students.

THIRD QUARTER

Introducing the Main Question

The focus of the lesson may be expressed in two questions: What does the Resurrection of Christ accomplish in God's plan for human salvation? What is the significance for our lives of the fact that Jesus was raised from death?

Developing the Lesson

I. *Witnessing the glory of God in the Resurrection of Christ*

Have the class read together a prayer for Easter Vigil or Easter Day from a hymnal (e.g., *The United Methodist Hymnal*). Point out and try to stimulate discussion of the link this prayer makes between the Resurrection of Christ and the lives of Christians.

Using the commentary on Mark 16:1-8 in "As You Read the Scripture," help your students understand the setting of the Resurrection events.

Try using a guided meditation to stimulate the class to experience something of the emotions of the first Easter. Ask the members to relax by getting comfortable and breathing deeply and slowly. Encourage them to close their eyes to avoid distractions. Tell them to try to imagine themselves as being present on the morning of the Resurrection, there at the tomb. Coax them to feel the cool morning air and the damp grass underfoot, to hear the birds beginning to sing and a distant rooster's crow. Remind them they are going to the grave of a dearly beloved friend and teacher who has just been brutally executed. Use your imagination to help your students identify with the scene and with the women. Read aloud, with as much expression as you can, the Resurrection account in Mark or in one of the other Gospels if you prefer. Read slowly and with frequent pauses. When you finish reading, allow a period of silence and then encourage your students to share their responses. You should expect some of your class members to react to this exercise much more positively than others; for many it can be a very powerful experience.

Use the material in "The Main Question" to communicate the awesomeness of the Resurrection and what it means for us. This is the time to use "The Women at the Tomb" and "The Resurrection: God's Victory" sections of "The Scripture and the Main Question."

II. *Sharing Christ's glory in Christian living*

Use the "Living as Easter People" material and lead a discussion on the significance of that name for Christians. Emphasize how the Resurrection has made living changed lives possible for us. A point of special importance here is Paul's affirmation of the intimate relationship now existing between God and God's people. Talk about and list some of the images we use to try to comprehend God—Creator, King, Judge, and others. Why is the image of God as loving Parent so powerful? Try the guided meditation approach again, asking the class to enter into attitudes of prayerful receptivity. Have them imagine themselves in a familiar, favorite room where God is sitting in a large comfortable chair. They approach, climb up, and settle into God's lap for cuddling. Remind them that God may be envisioned as either Father or Mother, depending on which role better stimulates their sense of loving intimacy. In many places in Scripture God is imaged as female (e.g., Deut. 32:18; Isa. 42:14; 46:3; 49:15; 66:7-9, 13; Matt. 23:37; and Luke 15:8-10). Encourage discussion of their responses to the meditation experience. Was it easy or difficult to imagine getting into God's lap to be hugged? Why? It is

of great significance that the Christian faith teaches us to trust in the relationship of loving intimacy that God has given to us.

Helping Class Members Act

Urge your class members to read the stories of Easter and of the post-Resurrection appearances of Christ in the four Gospels during their devotional
time in the coming week. Motivate them to try the approach of imaginatively
and emotionally placing themselves into these stories as participants. Ask
them to think and pray about what it means to be Easter people as we go
about the routine of our daily lives.

Challenge your class, and yourself, to practice imaging and praying to
God as a loving Mother, being assured that God transcends all distinction of
gender by which humans are limited. There are persons in our society for
whom the image of God as Father is not a positive one, because of their negative experiences with human fathers. All of our attempts to talk about God
in human language require the use of metaphors or other figurative language. We are really saying that God is *like* a father, or judge, or rock. Individuals differ as to which names for or descriptions of God they find most
meaningful. The point is to experience the caring and nurturing communion with God that we can enjoy because of the victory over sin won in the
Resurrection. The closest analogy in our human experience to the love God
has for us is the love of a good parent. The gender of the parent is not the
issue; the quality of the relationship is what is important.

Planning for Next Sunday

With next Sunday's lesson we return to the major themes of Paul as presented in the letter to Rome. Ask class members to read Romans 8:1-11, 26-
28, 35-39. The contrast to be developed in that lesson is between life in the
flesh and life in the Spirit. Building on their understanding of the meaning
of those terms as presented in this week's lesson, ask them to make brief
notes of aspects in both personal and corporate life that seem to exemplify
either flesh or Spirit. One interesting and revealing way to do this would be
to look analytically at television programming, movies, and popular music.
What values are being expressed in them?

Living in the Spirit

Background Scripture: Romans 8:1-11

The Main Question

I remember when I was a child hearing conversations between my father and his friends about their hunting dogs. Often one would ask another about an animal, "What kind of spirit does he have?" These men knew that the kind of spirit a dog possessed would determine how that dog would hunt. In the Scripture passage we are considering today, Paul asks that same question, knowing that the decisive factor in a person's life is the spirit by which he or she is controlled. To be "in Christ" is to be in possession of the Spirit of life—the Spirit of God. This is the Spirit that animates those who have committed themselves to Christ and have participated, through baptism, in his dying and rising to new life. The very Spirit of God indwells such a believer, empowering that person to live in righteousness, free from the dominion of sin. Paul repeatedly contrasts such a life with that which is "in the flesh." The fleshly or carnal life is one of self-idolatry and rebellion against God; its end is both physical and spiritual death. Even if one who is controlled by the spirit of flesh should seek to obey the will of God as expressed in divine law, that person will be unable to do so. But God has sent the divine Son to destroy the bondage of sin, and because of his victory, those who follow him receive in faith the gift of a new spirit—the Spirit of Christ.

In this lesson we will examine this contrast between life in the flesh and life in the Spirit. We will seek to understand what it means to be possessed by and in possession of God's Spirit. We will explore the kind of transformation the Spirit brings about in our lives as individuals and as the church—the Body of Christ.

Selected Scripture

King James Version

Romans 8:1-11

1 There is therefore now no condemnation to them which are in Christ Jesus, who walk not after the flesh, but after the Spirit.

2 For the law of the Spirit of life in Christ Jesus hath made me free from the law of sin and death.

3 For what the law could not do, in that it was weak through the flesh, God sending his own Son in the likeness of sinful flesh, and for sin, condemned sin in the flesh:

4 That the righteousness of the

New Revised Standard Version

Romans 8:1-11

1 There is therefore now no condemnation for those who are in Christ Jesus. 2 For the law of the Spirit of life in Christ Jesus has set you free from the law of sin and of death. 3 For God has done what the law, weakened by the flesh, could not do: by sending his own Son in the likeness of sinful flesh, and to deal with sin, he condemned sin in the flesh, 4 so that the just requirement of the law might be fulfilled in us, who walk not according to the

law might be fulfilled in us, who walk not after the flesh, but after the Spirit.

5 For they that are after the flesh do mind the things of the flesh; but they that are after the Spirit the things of the Spirit.

6 For to be carnally minded is death; but to be spiritually minded is life and peace.

7 Because the carnal mind is enmity against God: for it is not subject to the law of God, neither indeed can be.

8 So then they that are in the flesh cannot please God.

9 But ye are not in the flesh, but in the Spirit, if so be that the Spirit of God dwell in you. Now if any man have not the Spirit of Christ, he is none of his.

10 And if Christ be in you, the body is dead because of sin; but the Spirit is life because of righteousness.

11 But if the Spirit of him that raised up Jesus from the dead dwell in you, he that raised up Christ from the dead shall also quicken your mortal bodies by his Spirit that dwelleth in you.

flesh but according to the Spirit. 5 For those who live according to the flesh set their minds on the things of the flesh, but those who live according the Spirit set their minds on the things of the Spirit. 6 To set the mind on the flesh is death, but to set the mind on the Spirit is life and peace. 7 For this reason the mind that is set on the flesh is hostile to God; it does not submit to God's law—indeed it cannot, 8 and those who are in the flesh cannot please God.

9 But you are not in the flesh; you are in the Spirit, since the Spirit of God dwells in you. Anyone who does not have the Spirit of Christ does not belong to him. 10 But if Christ is in you, though the body is dead because of sin, the Spirit is life because of righteousness. 11 If the Spirit of him who raised Jesus from the dead dwells in you, he who raised Christ from the dead will give life to your mortal bodies also through his Spirit that dwells in you.

Key Verse: **For the law of the Spirit of life in Christ Jesus hath made me free from the law of sin and death. Romans 8:2**

Key Verse: **For the law of the Spirit of life in Christ Jesus has set you free from the law of sin and of death. Romans 8:2**

As You Read the Scripture

Romans 8:1-11. These verses are pivotal for our understanding of the major points in the letter to the Romans, for many of Paul's themes are summarized here. The salient emphasis is on the nature of the new life made available to us through Christ.

Verse 1. Those who are in Christ have escaped from the threat of judgment and its consequence, death.

Verse 2. Here begins the contrast that will permeate the whole passage. "Law" does not refer to the Old Testament legal code, but means "principle" or "rule." In the new order of life, God's presence in the Spirit replaces the old law.

Verse 3. This verse is phrased rather confusingly, but continues to develop the contrast. God has accomplished what we were unable to do. Sin, if not annihilated, is at least condemned and its power broken. God has done this by sending Christ to live and die in, as Goodspeed's translation puts it, "our sinful human form." Jewish readers would have seen here a reference to the sin offering that the priests were commanded by God to offer in order to make atonement (see Lev. 4:2-3; 6:25; 14:19).

Verse 4. The "just requirement of the law" might be epitomized by Galatians 5:14: "For the whole law is summed up in a single commandment, 'You shall love your neighbor as yourself.' " Only through the Spirit are we able to fulfill the law.

Verses 5-6. Those persons who are carnal and those who are spiritual have different interests, values, commitments, and live very different lives. The carnal life will result in death; indeed, to live in sin is to be already dead spiritually. The spiritual life is characterized by peace and a quality of existence that is eternal.

Verses 7-8. The person whose mind is controlled by the spirit of carnality and self-centeredness is under the dominion of sin. She or he is alienated from and in rebellion against God.

Verse 9. Christians are not such persons, but rather are indwelt by the Spirit of God; this is the test of whether or not one belongs to God. Paul uses the terms *Spirit, Spirit of life, Spirit of God,* and *Spirit of Christ* synonymously.

Verse 10. Similarly, "Christ . . . in you" apparently means the same as the Spirit's being in us and also the same as being "in Christ." The idea in all cases is that the presence and power of God are in control of the life of such a person, so that he or she is freed from the control of sin and enabled to live in obedient relationship with God. Even so, the aftereffects of sin yield their consequences in the fact that the physical body is mortal and will experience physical death. But because of the restored relationship with God, which we enjoy in Christ, we possess the Spirit that gives eternal life.

Verse 11. Even our physical bodies will not be left in the state of death. Because the Spirit of God, who raised Jesus from the dead, is the same Spirit that now lives in us, we will also be raised from death. Christians, then, enjoy both physical and spiritual life now and throughout eternity. The Creator of the body and of the spirit has acted in the death and resurrection of Jesus to liberate both from the bonds of sin and to reconcile us to God as whole persons.

The Scripture and the Main Question

"In the Likeness of Sinful Flesh and to Deal with Sin"

In verse 3 of this chapter, Paul states without elaboration two of the most fundamental doctrines of the Christian faith: Incarnation and Atonement. Familiarity with these concepts is essential to our comprehension of the other points Paul makes. Christianity is distinguished from other religions by its affirmation that in the person of Jesus Christ, God took human form and entered the realm of human existence. The word *incarnation* literally means "the act of becoming flesh." In Christ we find revealed all that the human mind can comprehend about the nature of God. In a way too profound for our understanding, Jesus was both fully human and fully divine. When we want to know what the ultimate reality at the heart of this universe is like, we look at Jesus. When we want to know what we are supposed to be like, we look at Jesus.

Atonement literally means "to make at one." Christianity proclaims that by the death of Jesus, the separation between human beings and God was overcome. The gulf was bridged; the rift was healed; the rebellion ended. Humankind was reconciled to God, and the relationship of love and trust that God had intended was restored. There are a variety of ways to attempt to explain just how the Atonement occurred, but the fact of our being put right with God is what is important.

"The Spirit Has Set You Free"

The concept of freedom from the bondage of sin made available to us through the death of Christ has been mentioned numerous times in this series of lessons, just as it was repeatedly stressed by Paul. Because it is such a significant idea, it merits fuller exploration. There are, of course, many varieties of freedom, and even when our thoughts are restricted to the sphere of spiritual life, freedom has a range of dimensions of which we will treat just a few. Perhaps the primary focus of Paul's thought is our freedom from the helpless state of enslavement to sin. Almost all orthodox Christian theologians have historically agreed about the basic condition of humans without Christ—they are lost in sin, spiritually dead and unable to change their plight. Different ideas have, however, been argued about just how the work of Christ changes this predicament. John Wesley, to whom United Methodism looks back for its doctrines, contended that by the atonement of Christ's death, all persons were rescued from this state of helpless slavery. Not all persons were then saved, but all then *could be* saved. Wesley emphasized what he called prevenient grace—the grace of God that precedes any action on the part of human beings and, indeed, that makes any right action on our part possible. All persons have been given sufficient grace to enable us to respond to God's offer of salvation if we so choose. We are no longer hopelessly trapped in sin, but have been empowered by Christ's atonement to turn to God. Our wills are freed to choose to obey God and, if we so choose, God continues to bestow additional grace so that we may grow in holiness of life.

Another aspect of the freedom made available to us in Christ is liberation from paralyzing guilt about the past. Often persons are unable to forgive and accept and love themselves, even though they profess to believe that God does. Isn't this a way of suggesting that we have higher standards than does God? Surely if the holy God against whom we have been in rebellion can blot out the guilt of our past, we should ourselves be able to release it. Paul Tillich, in a famous sermon entitled "You Are Accepted," describes the problem:

> It is that mixture of selfishness and self-hate that permanently pursues us, that prevents us from loving others, and that prohibits us from losing ourselves in the love with which we are loved eternally. . . . The depth of our separation lies in just the fact that we are not capable of a great and merciful divine love toward ourselves. (*The Shaking of the Foundations* [New York: Charles Scribner's Sons, 1948] p. 158.)

Tillich goes on to use as an example the experience of Paul when he met Christ on the Damascus road while Paul was on the way to execute his vigorous attacks on Christians: "And when he found that he was accepted, he was

able to accept himself and to be reconciled to others." The sermon concludes with Tillich's description of the moment of grace when we realize
that God is reaching out for us in love and forgiveness:

> Sometimes at that moment a wave of light breaks into our darkness,
> and it is as though a voice were saying: 'You are accepted. *You are
> accepted,* accepted by that which is greater than you. . . . Do not seek
> for anything; do not perform anything; do not intend anything. *Simply
> accept the fact that you are accepted!'* . . . Sometimes it happens that we
> receive the power to say 'yes' to ourselves, that peace enters into us
> and makes us whole, that self-hatred and self-contempt disappear, and
> that our self is reunited with itself. Then we can say that grace has
> come upon us.

Modern psychologists and theologians agree that a profound motivating
fear of human beings comes from our awareness of our mortality; unlike
other natural creatures, we know that we are going to die. Because of this
haunting knowledge from which we cannot escape, we are ridden with anxiety, which causes us to clutch frantically the things that seem important in
our present life. Paul teaches that physical death is a consequence of the sinful condition that characterizes all human existence—original sin. But,
although we will all die physically, we can live spiritually in a quality of life
that is eternal. Even more, those who receive through the Spirit the life of
God will experience, beyond the bounds of physical death, the transformation of their bodies so that as whole persons we will live in everlasting communion with God. Our faith in these truths provides us with a confidence
and peace that evidences our liberation from the gnawing fear of death.
Thus we are enabled to live our lives with different attitudes, values, and
commitments than do those who are still bound in sin. The American poet
William Cullen Bryant expresses this idea beautifully in his poem
"Thanatopsis":

> So live, that when thy summons comes to join
> The innumerable caravan that moves
> To the pale realms of shade, where each shall take
> His chamber in the silent halls of death,
> Thou go not, like the quarry-slave at night,
> Scourged to his dungeon, but, sustained and soothed
> By an unfaltering trust, approach thy grave
> Like one who wraps the drapery of his couch
> About him, and lies down to pleasant dreams.

Helping Adults Become Involved

Preparing to Teach

This lesson brings together and builds upon many of the major themes
that have been developed in the previous lessons on Romans. An excellent
preparation for the teacher would be to review these past five lessons, noting
the chief points presented in each. From such a review, one would enter well
prepared into the planning of this lesson.

Read Romans 8:1-11, using "As You Read the Scripture" for assistance.

Then peruse "The Main Question" and "The Scripture and the Main Question" sections and list the points you perceive will be most meaningful to your class. Because so many ideas are presented here, you may wish to select the ones to focus on in teaching the lesson.

A very simple way to outline the major points is as follows:

> I.   Introduction
> II. Living in the flesh
> III. Transformed lives through the indwelling Spirit

Consider making copies for students, to use in class and take home with them, of the quotations in "The Spirit Has Set You Free" section taken from Paul Tillich's "You Are Accepted." A chalkboard or newsprint should be available, as well as Bibles and hymnals for all.

Introducing the Main Question

The essential point of the lesson is the contrast between two ways of living. What does it mean to live "in the flesh"? What does it mean to live "in the Spirit"? Paul asserts that God has given us the ability to choose between these ways of living. Which one are you following?

Developing the Lesson

I. Introduction

Use the material in "The Main Question" to introduce the central ideas of the lesson. Ask your students to share the notes they made during the week about aspects of life, both personal and corporate, that exemplify life in either the flesh or the Spirit. Discuss these with the purpose of making clear the contrast.

II. Living in the flesh

Explain that Paul's condemnation of life in the flesh does not mean that everything material or physical is bad. Indeed, God is the Creator of the physical world, and God pronounced it good. Evil comes as a result of misusing the physical and misaligning our priorities. The relevant questions are not simply how we act, but what are our interests, values, and commitments. The life in the flesh of which Romans speaks is a life characterized by carnality, self-centeredness, and rebellion against God. It will culminate in both spiritual and physical death.

III. Transformed lives through the indwelling Spirit

The possession of the Spirit of God provides believers with the evidence that they are being saved and enables them to lead lives vastly different from those lived in the flesh. Work through Romans 8:1-11 with your students, using "As You Read the Scripture" to help communicate the chief points.

Since our hope of salvation is grounded in the incarnation and atonement of Christ, it is important that your class understand these basic doctrines. Use the material in the "In the Likeness of Sinful Flesh and to Deal with Sin" section. You may also wish to use a theological dictionary or wordbook for more help; your pastor should have this resource.

"The Spirit Has Set You Free" section contains material that you may present to help the class understand the concept of spiritual freedom. Explain John Wesley's concept of prevenient grace.

Distribute copies of the quotations from Paul Tillich's "You Are Accepted" and have the class read and discuss them together. Try to stimulate as much sharing as possible about the various experiences and feelings of the group. Be prepared to suggest some leading questions to generate discussion; some examples are the following:

> What does it mean to have in our lives "a mixture of selfishness and self-hate"?
> Does that description seem true to your experiences?
> What must we do to be accepted by God?
> Why does being accepted by God make us better able to accept ourselves and others?

The subject of death and our attitudes toward it should evoke considerable discussion. Share the selection from "Thanatopsis" by Bryant (which some of your students may have memorized during their school days) and elicit reactions. To many people, one of the most powerful aspects of the Christian faith is the assurance that death is not the termination of all that we treasure. This assurance becomes increasingly precious to persons as they become older or as they experience the death of loved ones. A salient truth about life in the Spirit is that it is a life that survives physical death. As Emily Dickinson puts it in one of her many poems about death: "This world is not conclusion; A sequel stands beyond."

Helping Class Members Act

Urge the class members to take the Tillich quotations home with them and use them in their prayer time during the week. Ask them to focus on coming to a deeper realization of being accepted by God through the work of Jesus Christ and an enhanced understanding of what changes that truth can make in their lives.

Challenge your students to make honest and searching assessments of their own lives. What characteristics of life in the flesh do they see manifested? How can they open themselves more completely to the transforming presence of the Spirit? What marks of the life of the Spirit are they manifesting? How can these be strengthened? What are their feelings about death, especially their own death? If these feelings need to be changed, how can the power of the indwelling Spirit be allowed to accomplish this?

Christians live not only as individuals, but also as citizens of the society. While the life of the Spirit will never be perfectly manifested in the secular world, are there ways in which Christians might be influential in curbing some expressions of "the flesh" or, at least, in protecting themselves and their children from them?

Planning for Next Sunday

Ask the class members to read Romans 12 and Philippians 2:1-4, 14-16; 4:8-9. Encourage them to think about and list the gifts God has given to them that they can use in service to others.

Using Gifts to Serve

Background Scripture: Romans 12

The Main Question

Tommy was returning home from an errand to the store when he tripped and spilled groceries all over the sidewalk. Apples bounced down the walkway; egg yolks oozed from their carton; milk ran over the curb. Many people were passing by, stepping around and sometimes on his scattered mess. The child sat crying. After a few moments a man leaned down, put his hand on the boy's shoulder, and said, "Don't cry. Come on, I'll help you." He gave the child his handkerchief to dry the boy's tears. Carefully and patiently the man helped the boy gather up his purchases, repack what could be used and dispose of the ruined ones. Finally he said, "Come on in this store, Tommy. I'll buy you a candy bar to make you feel better." Tommy looked up through eyes still blurred with tears and asked, "Mister, are you God?" The man smiled, "No, son," he said, "but I am one of God's servants."

The focusing question for today's lesson is this: How are Christians to conduct themselves in the daily routine of life? One of the important answers to that question is that Christians are to live lives of service. To serve means to care for, to minister to, to be of benefit to, to meet the needs of others. Christians are persons whose lives have been transformed by the presence and power of God's Spirit. We have received this gift of divine grace not just for ourselves, but so that we might "in the midst of a crooked and perverse generation . . . shine like stars in the world" (Phil. 2:15). It is both trite and sentimental, yet it is still true that "what the world needs now is love, sweet love." Disciples of Jesus Christ are to be the exemplars of that love by using our God-given gifts in service.

Selected Scripture

King James Version

Romans 12:1-18

1 I beseech you therefore, brethren, by the mercies of God, that ye present your bodies a living sacrifice, holy, acceptable unto God, which is your reasonable service.

2 And be not conformed to this world: but be ye transformed by the renewing of your mind, that ye may prove what is that good, and acceptable, and perfect, will of God.

3 For I say, through the grace given unto me, to every man that is among you, not to think of himself

New Revised Standard Version

Romans 12:1-18

1 I appeal to you therefore, brothers and sisters, by the mercies of God, to present your bodies as a living sacrifice, holy and acceptable to God, which is your spiritual worship. 2 Do not be conformed to this world, but be transformed by the renewing of your minds, so that you may discern what is the will of God—what is good and acceptable and perfect.

3 For by the grace given to me I say to everyone among you not to think of yourself more highly than

more highly than he ought to think; but to think soberly, according as God hath dealt to every man the measure of faith.

4 For as we have many members in one body, and all members have not the same office:

5 So we, being many, are one body in Christ, and every one members one of another.

6 Having then gifts differing according to the grace that is given to us, whether prophecy, let us prophesy according to the proportion of faith;

7 Or ministry, let us wait on our ministering: or he that teacheth, on teaching;

8 Or he that exhorteth, on exhortation: he that giveth, let him do it with simplicity; he that ruleth, with diligence; he that sheweth mercy, with cheerfulness.

9 Let love be without dissimulation. Abhor that which is evil; cleave to that which is good.

10 Be kindly affectioned one to another with brotherly love; in honour preferring one another;

11 Not slothful in business; fervent in spirit; serving the Lord;

12 Rejoicing in hope; patient in tribulation; continuing instant in prayer;

13 Distributing to the necessity of saints; given to hospitality.

14 Bless them which persecute you: bless, and curse not.

15 Rejoice with them that do rejoice, and weep with them that weep.

16 Be of the same mind one toward another. Mind not high things, but condescend to men of low estate. Be not wise in your own conceits.

17 Recompense to no man evil for evil. Provide things honest in the sight of all men.

18 If it be possible, as much as lieth in you, live peaceably with all men.

you ought to think, but to think with sober judgment, each according to the measure of faith that God has assigned. 4 For as in one body we have many members, and not all the members have the same function, 5 so we, who are many, are one body in Christ, and individually we are members one of another. 6 We have gifts that differ according to the grace given to us: prophecy, in proportion to faith; 7 ministry, in ministering; the teacher, in teaching; 8 the exhorter, in exhortation; the giver, in generosity; the leader, in diligence; the compassionate, in cheerfulness.

9 Let love be genuine; hate what is evil, hold fast to what is good; 10 love one another with mutual affection; outdo one another in showing honor. 11 Do not lag in zeal, be ardent in spirit, serve the Lord. 12 Rejoice in hope, be patient in suffering, persevere in prayer. 13 Contribute to the needs of the saints; extend hospitality to strangers.

14 Bless those who persecute you; bless and do not curse them. 15 Rejoice with those who rejoice, weep with those who weep. 16 Live in harmony with one another; do not be haughty, but associate with the lowly; do not claim to be wiser than you are. 17 Do not repay anyone evil for evil, but take thought for what is noble in the sight of all. 18 If it is possible, so far as it depends on you, live peaceably with all.

Key Verse: **Having then gifts differing according to the grace that is given to us, whether prophecy, let us prophesy according to the proportion of faith. Romans 12:6**

Key Verse: **We have gifts that differ according to the grace given to us: prophecy, in proportion to faith. Romans 12:6**

As You Read the Scripture

The letters of Paul in the New Testament are typically divided into two major parts: a theological section that expounds the doctrines of Christianity and an ethical section that deals with the practical application of those beliefs in daily life. With chapter 12 we enter the ethical teaching portion of the letter to the Romans.

Romans 12:1. Paul's appeal to commit themselves wholly to God is based on the mercies God has freely offered in Christ. "Bodies" does not mean the physical organism only, but the whole self; all that one is must be devoted to God. The "living sacrifice" is in contrast to the animal sacrifices the Jews and other religious groups used as a central part of their worship.

Verse 2. Believers must resist temptations and pressures to fall back into a pattern of living that is no different from that of the secular world. The continuing work of the Spirit will make the believer increasingly able to obey the will of God.

Verses 3-13. These verses are an appeal for unity within the Christian community. They describe how one is to live in love with one's brothers and sisters in Christ.

Verse 3. Inflated egos are a threat to the harmony of any community and are especially inappropriate for Christians, who should realize that their faith is a free gift from God, not an excuse for pride.

Verses 4-5. Paul uses here the analogy he develops more completely in 1 Corinthians 12. As the physical body is composed of many organs with varying functions, so the Christian community is composed of many diverse persons, all of whom are united in Christ.

Verses 6-8. There is a wide variety of roles and abilities within the community, and all are gifts from God. All persons are to fulfill their specific callings and exercise their particular talents. The list of gifts is not meant to be exhaustive, but to provide examples.

Verses 9-13. These verses may be best understood as a brief synopsis of 1 Corinthians 13.

Verses 9-10. Christians are to relate to one another in warm and sincere affection, being both courteous and respectful.

Verses 11-12. Service is to be rendered with unflagging enthusiasm and diligence. For Christians, hope is a perspective on life—a confidence in the outworkings of the divine purpose. Persistence in prayer is essential, for if one is to live as these verses describe, one must constantly draw upon the strength of God.

Verse 13. Hospitality was not a matter of etiquette, but a paramount virtue in the biblical world and a necessity for travelers.

Verses 14-18. These verses instruct the believer in how to live in love with the secular world, even with adversaries.

Verse 14. To "bless" is to wish for a person's good and to speak well of him or her.

Verse 15. Christians are to have compassion—which literally means to "feel with"—for other persons.

Verse 16. Arrogance and conceit are divisive, destructive of the harmony between people, and improper for Christians.

Verses 17-18. Peace is to be the hallmark of the relationship between Christians the secular world.

The Scripture and the Main Question

"As a Living Sacrifice"

It is only after he has explained repeatedly and in detail, throughout the first eleven chapters of the letter, how the act of God in Jesus Christ has reconciled us and made a new quality of life possible that Paul moves on to talk about the implications of these truths for our daily living. When persons are in bondage to the power of sin, there is no point in exhorting them to live better. They are simply powerless to act on their intentions, no matter how noble they may be. But when we are put into right relationship with God and receive the indwelling presence of the Holy Spirit, we are then free to live as God wills. To devote ourselves to God's service "as a living sacrifice" is our appropriate response to God's gracious action. All that we do, for God and for other people, is in response to the initiative of God, which both motivates and empowers us.

All Christians are to live like Christ, to continue the work of Christ in the world, and that means to live as ministers—as servants. God has not called us into such ministries of service without equipping us with gifts we can use. To hear, as we so often do in the church, persons belittling themselves and their capabilities is not to witness attractive modesty, but rather a lack of trust in God and appreciation for what God has bestowed. Our gifts are certainly diverse, and some are much more obvious and dramatic than others. But God values, and the ministry of the church needs, the full exercise of the gifts of all.

Our service will be of many kinds and includes not only what we do, but also who we are. I have a poster in my office with the simple statement, "Be kind, for everyone you meet carries a heavy burden." We can all participate in the priceless ministry of kindness. John Wesley, who started the Methodist movement, was an exemplar of the life of service. A little rhyme attributed to him provides an excellent motto:

> Do all the good you can,
> To all the people you can,
> As long as ever you can.

To devote our lives to such service is not really to surrender ourselves in any negative sense, but rather to fulfill ourselves, to be the kind of persons God has freed us to be.

"One Body in Christ"

Perhaps the first locale for our service is within the community of Christians—the church itself. As persons reconciled to God and to one another, we are a part of a new order of existence to be lived out in a community of grace. It is sobering, perhaps even frightening, to realize that the church is to function as a model of the harmony and love that God is working to establish in all of creation. Throughout his correspondence with various churches, Paul places heavy emphasis on the theme of how Christians are to live with one another within the church. He advocates courtesy, humility, and mutual esteem. It is especially essential that Christians respect the diverse gifts of persons within the community and allow and encourage their full use without grasping for superiority and demeaning others. John Wesley insisted that "the Bible knows nothing of solitary religion." Individual believers must learn what it means to live as Christians by participating in the community, by being socialized in the church. Within the family of Christians, we learn and practice the virtues of Christlike living, which we can then exercise in ministry to the secular world.

"Live Peaceably with All"

The best way to communicate the truth of the Christian gospel to those who do not know it is to live in such a way that in our lives the outreaching love of God is powerfully manifest. Mother Teresa, the great saint of Calcutta who has devoted her life to the neediest of God's children, says of her work: "God is writing a love letter to these people and I am his pencil." While we are not all able to give ourselves so dramatically in service, we are able to show forth Christ's love in our daily living.

In the latter verses of Romans 12, Paul pictures such lives characterized by compassion and forgiveness. A woman once observed two little girls who were daily playmates having an angry spat. Sally gathered up her toys and stalked away, shouting back to Mary that she would never play with her again. Mary declared loudly that she would never play again with Sally even if Sally wanted to. Just a few hours later, the woman was surprised to see Sally and Mary playing together quite happily. Curious, she approached the girls and said, "I don't understand. Just a little while ago, I heard both of you declare that you would never, never play with each other again. But now here you are, having a good time together. Tell me what happened." The two little girls looked at each other with shy smiles, and Mary answered, "Well, me and Sally are good forgetters!" Christians are to be good forgetters, willing to forgive and try again.

Helping Adults Become Involved

Preparing to Teach

This lesson and next week's concluding lesson of the unit deal with practical issues of living as Christians, rather than the theological questions that were the focus of previous lessons in the series on Romans. The two aspects are by no means unrelated, for ethical living is the fruit of doctrinal truth.

Read Philippians 2:1-4, 14-16 and 4:8-9 for a sense of Paul's understanding of the Christian life. Using the material in "As You Read the Scripture," work carefully through Romans 12. Take time to assess honestly your own gifts and service in the light of these verses.

Have Bibles, sheets of paper, and pencils available for all students, as well as a chalkboard or newsprint for your use in class.

The major points of the lesson may be outlined as follows:

    I. Introduction
   II. Lives of service
  III. Living in the Christian community—the church
  IV. Ministry to the secular world

Introducing the Main Question

How are Christians to conduct themselves in the daily routine of life? This is the salient question of the lesson. Specifically, the Scripture deals with the ministry of Christians using their God-given gifts, how Christians relate to one another within the church, and how they live in relationship to the secular world.

Developing the Lesson

I. Introduction

It will be helpful to your students for you to make clear that the material of this lesson represents a shift in subject matter from the past sessions. Use the material in the first paragraphs of "As You Read the Scripture" and "The Scripture and the Main Question" to explain this change from doctrinal to ethical concerns. Successful living of the kind of life Paul portrays in Romans 12 is possible only when one has experienced the redeeming grace of God and has received the Spirit. This chapter exhorts Christians to express their new lives of reconciliation and freedom from sin through practical application in their relationships with other people.

II. Lives of service

Share the story in "The Main Question" to stimulate reflection about what it means to be a servant of God and, hence, of other people. Have the class concentrate together on verses 6-8. List on the chalkboard or newsprint the kinds of gifts they understand to be mentioned here. Encourage your students to go beyond this list and add other gifts that they think can be employed in service to others. Ask each person to spend a few moments writing down a list of the gifts he or she possesses. (Those who worked on this during the week can use their lists as starters.) Have the students get together in groups of two or three, preferably with persons they know fairly well but who are not family members, and add to each other's list of gifts. Additions may be made to the master list on the board out of these conversations.

Use the material in "As a Living Sacrifice" to present the idea of the Christian responsibility for service.

III. Living in the Christian community—the church

Use the material in "One Body in Christ" to introduce the idea of the church as a model community of Christians living in love. Your two goals in this part of the lesson might be to have persons comprehend the role of the church as an example for the world and to motivate a searching assessment of your own church. Focus on verses 3-5 and 9-13. Have the class members make a list, which you record on the board, of the characteristics of a Christian community that Paul commends. Have them add to the list their own suggestions. Ask the group to evaluate your own local church by these criteria. How well are you fulfilling the church's function of manifesting Christian love to the world? What are the areas of weakness or difficulty that need to be addressed if your church is to exemplify the new order of spiritual existence?

IV. Ministry to the secular world

Use the "Live Peaceably with All" section to present the chief ideas. Concentrate on verses 14-18, using the same technique of listing attributes on the board as the class identifies them in the Scripture. How are Christians to relate to persons who are not believers and even to those who may be hostile to Christianity? How are Christians to be different from other persons? A central point you must endeavor to make is that Christians are to strive to live in peace with the secular world without conforming to its values and expectations. The translation of verse 2 in J. B. Phillips's *Modern English Bible* may provide insight: "Don't let the world around you squeeze you into its own mould, but let God re-make you so that your whole attitude of mind is changed."

Helping Class Members Act

Challenge the class members to keep a daily record next week, and perhaps for longer, of any ways they minister to other people. Ask them to be aware of how they are using or neglecting their gifts. Urge them to assume increased responsibility for their church as a model community of love. Remind them of the old ditty, "What kind of church would this church be, if every member were just like me?"

The parable of the talents and the depiction of the great judgment in Matthew 25:14-46 would provide valuable scriptural foundation for personal assessment and recommitment to service during the week's devotional times. One of the themes of both the Old and the New Testaments is God's special concern for the poor and oppressed. God's people must devote themselves in service to the needy and powerless.

Planning for Next Sunday

Ask the class to read Romans 14 and 15 and think about the responsibility of Christians to live for others. Since both of these lessons are expositions on the theme of Christian love, encourage the students to read 1 Corinthians 13, especially in contemporary English translations.

Living for Others

Background Scripture: Romans 14

The Main Question

The Christian community in Rome was composed of persons from a variety of religious backgrounds. Many of them were Jews; many were from Greek cultic groups. They brought a wide range of previous practices and beliefs into the church, and sometimes this made it difficult for them to agree on just what were acceptable behaviors for followers of Christ. Particular points of difference had to do with which foods and beverages were proper and how various festival days should be observed. Paul himself had been a very strict Pharisee prior to his conversion to Christianity and had rigorously adhered to all the Jewish dietary laws and Sabbath observances. In view of this, it is ironic that Paul now identifies himself with the "strong" who realize that such observances are of little significance. Such an attitude of freedom is a telling indication of how dramatic had been Paul's change in understanding of how God is to be obeyed. As a person in Christ, Paul knew that his salvation was an unmerited gift of God to be received by faith, and not a reward for any actions on his own part. Paul recognized, however, that the freedom he experienced was not perceived the same way by every Christian. He was deeply concerned about the threat to harmony in the church community caused by such differences of conviction. He warns the Roman Christians about the dangers of judgmental attitudes of self-righteousness, which seek to impose one's own views upon everyone else. But he was also profoundly troubled about the detrimental effects on "weaker" brothers and sisters of the irresponsible use of one's freedom in Christ. How are some of these same issues present in our own church community? How are Christians to live?

Selected Scripture

King James Version	New Revised Standard Version
Romans 14:7-19	*Romans 14:7-19*
7 For none of us liveth to himself, and no man dieth to himself.	7 We do not live to ourselves, and we do not die to ourselves. 8 If we
8 For whether we live, we live unto the Lord; and whether we die, we die unto the Lord: whether we live therefore, or die, we are the Lord's.	live, we live to the Lord, and if we die, we die to the Lord; so then, whether we live or whether we die, we are the Lord's. 9 For to this end Christ died
9 For to this end Christ both died, and rose, and revived, that he might be Lord both of the dead and living.	and lived again, so that he might be Lord of both the dead and the living.
10 But why dost thou judge thy brother? or why dost thou set at nought thy brother? for we shall all	10 Why do you pass judgment on your brother or sister? Or you, why do you despise your brother or sister? For we will all stand before the

stand before the judgment seat of Christ.

11 For it is written, As I live, saith the Lord, every knee shall bow to me, and every tongue shall confess to God.

12 So then every one of us shall give account of himself to God.

13 Let us not therefore judge one another any more: but judge this rather, that no man put a stumbling-block or an occasion to fall in his brother's way.

14 I know, and am persuaded by the Lord Jesus, that there is nothing unclean of itself: but to him that esteemeth any thing to be unclean, to him it is unclean.

15 But if thy brother be grieved with thy meat, now walkest thou not charitably. Destroy not him with thy meat, for whom Christ died.

16 Let not then your good be evil spoken of:

17 For the kingdom of God is not meat and drink; but righteousness, and peace, and joy in the Holy Ghost.

18 For he that in these things serveth Christ is acceptable to God, and approved of men.

19 Let us therefore follow after the things which make for peace, and things wherewith one may edify another.

judgment seat of God. 11 For it is written,

"As I live, says the Lord, every
    knee shall bow to me,
and every tongue shall give
    praise to God."

12 So then, each of us will be accountable to God.

13 Let us therefore no longer pass judgment on one another, but resolve instead never to put a stumbling block or hindrance in the way of another. 14 I know and am persuaded in the Lord Jesus that nothing is unclean in itself; but it is unclean for anyone who thinks it unclean. 15 If your brother or sister is being injured by what you eat, you are no longer walking in love. Do not let what you eat cause the ruin of one for whom Christ died. 16 So do not let your good be spoken of as evil. 17 For the kingdom of God is not food and drink but righteousness and peace and joy in the Holy Spirit. 18 The one who thus serves Christ is acceptable to God and has human approval. 19 Let us then pursue what makes for peace and for mutual upbuilding.

Key Verse: **Let us therefore follow after the things which make for peace, and things wherewith one may edify another. Roman 14:19**

Key Verse: **Let us then pursue what makes for peace and for mutual upbuilding. Romans 14:19**

As You Read the Scripture

Romans 14. In the opening verses of the chapter, Paul writes about the controversy in the church, which is described in "The Main Question." He makes reference to two groups within the community—the weak and the strong—whose disagreements focus on questions about the eating of meat and the observance of special days. (There is a similar discussion in 1 Cor. 8.) Throughout the remainder of the chapter he attempts to defuse this controversy by urging attitudes of tolerance and charity.

Verses 7-9. If we were answerable to no higher authority than our own selves, we could do whatever we choose. But this is not true of Christians, who belong to Christ. Divine authority governs every aspect of our existence, both in life and in death. Christians also are not free to think of themselves only as individuals. The death and resurrection of Christ have made possible a new kind of life in a new community. Christians belong to and are accountable to both Christ and Christ's people.

Verses 10-12. Those who are weak in the faith are tempted to pass judgment on their stronger sisters and brothers who behave in ways that the weaker cannot accept. Those who are strong are, likewise, tempted to have feelings of contempt for those whose behavior is much more restricted than the strong believe necessary. Paul insists that neither party is in any position to judge the other. Indeed, we all have enough to do tending to our own business. Judgment is the prerogative of God alone, whose servants we all are, and we are not to usurp divine authority. We will all ultimately experience divine judgment; that is sufficient. This judgment, however, will not be for the purpose of determining whether we are saved. Such a view would be in direct contradiction to Paul's emphasis on salvation by faith in God's grace alone. Rather, the judgment will be an occasion of accountability for the quality of life one has maintained. Verse 11 is a rather loose quotation of Isaiah 45:23, which Paul uses to illustrate the absolute sovereignty of God over all persons.

Verse 13. Beginning with this verse, Paul addresses the strong in faith, the group in which he places himself. They must take great care that their actions do not, either by accident or by intention, cause a weaker Christian to falter.

Verses 14-15. Paul is himself fully persuaded that the old dietary laws are no longer binding on God's people, but this is not the most significant question. It is crucial for every person to be able to obey the dictates of his or her own conscience. If the action of any Christian causes another to violate his or her own scruples, then that action is wrong. Exercising one's freedom in trivial matters, like food, is so much less important than the risk of causing another Christian to falter.

Verse 16. This is a difficult verse, but it probably refers to the danger of having those outside the church disparage Christians because of internal dissension in the community.

Verses 17-19. Echoing words of Jesus, Paul reiterates that goodness and harmony in the community of people indwelt by the Spirit are of infinitely greater importance than matters like food and drink.

The Scripture and the Main Question

Respecting Our Differences

The crux of the issue Paul addresses in this chapter is the differences in life-styles within the Christian community. What actions are appropriate for Christians? What is right by Christian standards? Above all, Paul stresses the necessity for tolerance—openmindedness—in answering these questions. This does not mean that he was unconcerned about matters of morality or believed that Christians should be able to do anything they pleased. It means, rather, that Paul recognized that some questions are simply matters of opinion or preference. These differences can often be the result of very human influences rather than of depth of spiritual insight or commitment. We are all products of the cultural environment in which we have been raised and have, in many ways, internalized the values that are most familiar to us. What was believed to be right in our home, among our friends, in our church is often what we continue to uphold. Too frequently we fail to examine these opinions to determine where they came from and upon what they are grounded. One of the memorable experiences of my life as a young adult made this truth very real to me. I had been raised in a home and church that taught that the use of alcoholic beverages was absolutely wrong, and it never occurred to me to question that principle. One afternoon I walked into the snack bar at a country club where I was playing golf and was confronted by the scene of an Episcopal priest, sitting at a table and wearing his clerical attire, nonchalantly drinking a can of beer. I was stunned! It took me a long time to process that experience and to realize that his definition of proper Christian behavior was very different from the one I had been taught, but was not necessarily for that reason wrong.

Paul warns us against the danger of self-righteousness, of generalizing our personal preferences and convictions into binding standards for everybody and condemning those who fail to conform to them. Like Jesus before him, Paul exhorts us to avoid playing judge of our sisters and brothers in the faith. Each of us is ultimately answerable only to God, who alone knows us and our situations fully. In truth, human judgment is always based on shaky ground because what is right for one person may not be for another in a different condition. Too often it is weakness of faith, not strength, that makes persons demand stricter standards of behavior for themselves and for others. Doubt may be the parent of rigidity and severity. The safer and certainly the more Christlike stance is one of loving acceptance of sincere differences between Christians.

Majoring in the Minors

Nothing said above is meant to imply an "anything goes" approach to Christian moral behavior. There are surely some absolute standards of right and wrong. The problem comes when we identify our personal views as those absolutes. It is helpful to recognize that many of the issues about which Christians debate are actually of quite minor consequence. Paul makes clear his opinion that many of the things about which the church of his day was quibbling were morally indifferent. Clarence Jordan expresses this well in his *Cotton Patch Version* of Romans 14:1 and 17: "Accept a brother whose faith is immature, but don't get into a hassle with him over petty points . . . for the God movement is not doughnuts and coffee, but justice and peace and joyfulness in the Holy Spirit." Too much insistence on conformity of standards and behavior can be evidence of a works-righteousness approach to salvation. Christians are not only freed from futile striving to achieve salvation, but are freed *to* lives of joy in fellowship with Christ.

Deciding What to Do as Christians

An inescapable aspect of living as a Christian in the midst of a sinful world is the necessity continually to make moral decisions. Upon what criteria should such decisions be made? Clearly Paul asserted that Christians are free from legalistic adherence to a strict moral code of "do's and don'ts." One of the distortions of Christianity throughout history has been the attempt to turn a vital faith based on a personal relationship with Jesus Christ into a sterile list of prescribed and prohibited behaviors. An equally dangerous tendency, however, has been the temptation to allow freedom to degenerate into license and to excuse morally corrupt actions by persons who cloak themselves in religiosity. One of the ways to assess an action is to look at the consequences that will result from it. Paul uses this criterion in his advice to the strong Christians at Rome. An act that is in itself quite acceptable may be wrong if it has detrimental effects on other persons. This does not mean that one should always be determined by what other people will think or say about what one does. There are plainly many times in life when we must act according to our own best understandings of God's will, even when other persons disagree with us. The question is one of the appropriate balance between rights and responsibilities. As Christians we have the right to do many things we may choose not to do because of the negative effects on other people.

This is especially true when the right in question involves something trivial, something that is not worth the risk of weakening the faith of a sister or brother. This is the point Paul makes about eating meat and observing special days. There may be grave wrong in an action, even if not wrong in itself, which carries with it the danger of undoing what Christ has done for another person. Christians are called not to flaunt our freedom, but to loving and responsible use of it. This will mean, at times, restricting our exercise of freedom for the sake of others. When I taught courses in American government in a high school, I found that the students were very concerned about their freedom and were quite touchy about the limitation of it by any governmental authority. I tried to illustrate the necessity for responsibility as well as rights by swinging my arm about freely and proclaiming that since it was my arm, I could do with it whatever I wished. The student in the front desk began to get the message as my rapidly moving hand approached nearer and nearer. The whole class understood when I said, "My right to swing my arm ends where your nose begins." As frivolous as the illustration is, it accords with Paul's point. As citizens or as Christians, we are not isolated individuals, but a part of a community. Christians are to act in ways that contribute to harmony in the Body of Christ and to growth in grace and holiness by its members. In so doing we meet the ultimate test of our behavior: that it be Christlike.

Helping Adults Become Involved

Preparing to Teach

This lesson concludes the eight-session series on the letter to the Romans. You should spend some of your preparation time reviewing the major points we have emphasized in these two units of study. Today's lesson continues to explore the question of how one lives as a Christian.

Read all of Romans 14 and 15, using the commentary in "As You Read the Scripture" for help with the verses being featured. Be certain that you clearly understand the controversy between the groups Paul calls the "strong" and the "weak" in the church. The material in "The Main Question" provides a summary of the issues.

You will want to spend some time thinking about the relevance to your class, your church, and your community of the questions raised in this lesson. If possible, select class members to be prepared to role play the controversy in the early church and/or similar controversies today.

The structure of the lesson may be developed as follows:

    I. Introduction
   II. Threats to harmony in the Christian community
  III. Loving tolerance rather than self-righteous judgment
  IV. Responsible use of freedom for the sake of others

A chalkboard or newsprint for use in listing main points will be helpful. Bibles should also be available.

Introducing the Main Question

Imagine that you are a longtime member of the church, highly respected by everyone as an upstanding Christian. You are going on a weekend camping trip with a group of new church members, most of whom are recent converts to Christianity. What are some things you would be sure to do, and even to be seen doing, on the trip? What are some actions you would try to avoid, or at least to avoid being observed doing? Examine and evaluate your motives for your behavior.

It has been said that the truest test of the sincerity of a person's religious commitment is what that person would do if she or he could be absolutely certain that no one else would ever know about it. Consider this statement and explain why you agree or disagree.

Developing the Lesson

I. Introduction
Use the material in "Introducing the Main Question" to stimulate discussion highlighting the questions with which the lesson deals. Present the "respected Christian on a camping trip" situation to the class first and encourage as much participation as possible in exploring it. Read the suggested test of a person's religious sincerity and allow time for thought and comments. Be sure that the class sees the limitations of such a test in the light of the issues in this lesson.

II. Threats to harmony in the Christian community
Remind the class of the emphasis in last week's lesson on Paul's concern for the unity of Christians. Explain the situation and issues in the church at Rome (and at Corinth; see 1 Cor. 8) that were threatening to divide the community. Use the information in "The Main Question" as the basis of your summary.

III. Loving tolerance rather than self-righteous judgment
Ask the students who have prepared a role play to present it at this time. It will be especially helpful if they can "get into the mood" and project something of the intensity of self-righteousness and contempt that characterized the debate in Paul's day. Perhaps they could move from an exchange about the issues in the early church to a similar one about contemporary issues. Allow an opportunity for responses and analysis by the class when the role play is concluded.

Use the ideas and illustrations in the "Respecting Our Differences" and "Majoring in the Minors" sections of "The Scripture and the Main Question." Encourage the class members to share their own experiences of encountering differences in opinions, preferences, and behavior that were the result of differing cultural backgrounds or life circumstances. Discuss the very human tendency to establish our expectations and standards by looking in the mirror. Explore our willingness to be judgmental about the attitudes and actions of other people. Perhaps the old Native American adage applies here: "Never judge a person until you have walked a mile in his [or her] moccasins." Lead the class in making a list, which you will write on the chalkboard or newsprint, of present-day questions of behavior about which sincere Christians differ sharply. These may be local issues, such as appropriate use of the church facilities, or national ones, such as military spending. They may involve personal behavior, such as the use of alcoholic beverages, alternate life-styles, or abortion. What are the appropriate stances for Christians to take on these matters? What are the criteria by which we can make such decisions?

IV. Responsible use of freedom for the sake of others

Use the material in "Deciding What to Do as Christians" to raise concerns about rights and responsibilities. Emphasize the biblical concept of the community of faith as opposed to the contemporary American ideal of individualism. How can we be true to ourselves and exercise our God-given freedom and, at the same time, fulfill our responsibilities to other members of the community?

You will need to be honest about the fact that the issues raised in this lesson are very complex and do not have simple solutions. There are no hard and fast rules to apply easily in every case. Help your class to recognize the necessity of balancing values and prayerful decision making based on the desire to be Christlike.

Helping Class Members Act

Encourage your students to be especially aware this week of the decisions they make about their behavior and to intentionally analyze their motives. Challenge them to self-examination of their inclinations to be self-righteous and judgmental of the behavioral choices of others. Motivate them to consider whether their attitudes and actions contribute to the loving tolerance Paul believed was necessary for harmony in the Christian community.

How can individual Christians work toward making the church as a whole more just and accepting of those who are different? Who are some of the groups of persons on whose behalf we are called to be active?

Planning for Next Sunday

Next week's lesson will be the first in a new unit of five lessons on the letter to the Galatians. Since this is such a brief book (not more than five pages in most Bibles), ask the class to read it through, preferably in one sitting, to begin to grasp the major themes and to note points of particular interest or confusion.

UNIT III: SET FREE BY GOD'S GRACE

FIVE LESSONS   MAY 1–29

The lessons in this unit focus on the brief, but very important, letter written by Paul to the churches in Galatia. Although the identities of these
churches are uncertain, they were almost surely located in central Turkey
and were composed largely of persons who were Gentiles rather than Jews.
The letter, one of Paul's earliest, was probably written between A.D. 50 and
55. Galatians is often called "the Magna Carta of Christianity" because of its
affirmation of the freedom Christians receive from God. The letter was occasioned by a movement to insist that Gentiles who were to be Christians must
first become Jews—obey the requirements of the law of Moses. Paul vehe-
mently asserts a radical understanding of grace and justification by faith
alone.

The first lesson, "Delivered from Bondage," introduces the major themes
of the letter. "Adopted as God's Children" teaches us the difference that it
makes in our self-concepts and in our relationships when we recognize that
we belong to God. The third lesson, "Given the Birthright of Freedom,"
examines some misunderstandings of Christian freedom, as well as how
Christians can deal with physical illness. In the fourth lesson, "Bear Fruit of
the Spirit," the emphasis shifts to a consideration of how Christians are to
live out their freedom in relationship to others. The last lesson, "Express
Christ's Love in All Relationships," talks about the distinction of Christian
love.

LESSON 9   MAY 1

Delivered from Bondage

Background Scripture: Galatians 1–2

The Main Question

This is a very angry letter! Paul is deeply upset by what has happened
in the Galatian churches, and he tells them so in no uncertain terms!
Paul had visited these churches at least once, perhaps twice; he had been
well received personally, and his message was warmly accepted. The people of Galatia, a province of the Roman Empire located in what is today
central Turkey, were largely Gentiles rather than Jews. Apparently rather
soon after Paul had left the area, the churches had been visited by other
itinerant Christian preachers whose interpretation of the Christian life
did not accord with what Paul had taught. These "agitators," as Paul
called them, were probably Jewish converts to Christianity. They urged
the Galatians to conform to the Jewish legal requirements in order to be
true Christians. Especially, they insisted, men must be circumcised to be

included in the community of God's people. Many of the Galatians heeded these arguments and, in effect, became Jews in order to become Christians. When news of these happenings reached Paul, he was furious and wrote this letter of reprimand and explanation. To him, a very basic theological issue was at stake here: How are human beings to be saved? To accept the requirements of the law was to seek to earn one's salvation, to add something else to what had been accomplished by the work of Christ. Paul insists that salvation comes *only* through faith in God's gracious gift; to require anything more is to make salvation dependent upon human striving rather than upon Christ's death and resurrection. "How could you," Paul asks, "reject the freedom you have been given in Christ and return to the slavery of legalism?"

Selected Scripture

King James Version

New Revised Standard Version

Galatians 1:6-7

6 I marvel that ye are so soon removed from him that called you into the grace of Christ unto another gospel:

7 Which is not another; but there be some that trouble you, and would pervert the gospel of Christ.

2:11-21

11 But when Peter was come to Antioch, I withstood him to the face, because he was to be blamed.

12 For before that certain came from James, he did eat with the Gentiles: but when they were come, he withdrew and separated himself, fearing them which were of the circumcision.

13 And the other Jews dissembled likewise with him; insomuch that Barnabas also was carried away with their dissimulation.

14 But when I saw that they walked not uprightly according to the truth of the gospel, I said unto Peter before them all, If thou, being a Jew, livest after the manner of Gentiles, and not as do the Jews, why compellest thou the Gentiles to live as do the Jews?

15 We who are Jews by nature, and not sinners of the Gentiles,

16 Knowing that a man is not justified by the works of the law, but by

Galatians 1:6-7

6 I am astonished that you are so quickly deserting the one who called you in the grace of Christ and are turning to a different gospel—7 not that there is another gospel, but there are some who are confusing you and want to pervert the gospel of Christ.

2:11-21

11 But when Cephas came to Antioch, I opposed him to his face, because he stood self-condemned; 12 for until certain people came from James, he used to eat with the Gentiles. But after they came, he drew back and kept himself separate for fear of the circumcision faction. 13 And the other Jews joined him in this hypocrisy, so that even Barnabas was led astray by their hypocrisy. 14 But when I saw that they were not acting consistently with the truth of the gospel, I said to Cephas before them all, "If you, though a Jew, live like a Gentile and not like a Jew, how can you compel the Gentiles to live like Jews?"

15 We ourselves are Jews by birth and not Gentile sinners; 16 yet we know that a person is justified not by the works of the law but through

the faith of Jesus Christ, even we have believed in Jesus Christ, that we might be justified by the faith of Christ, and not by the works of the law: for by the works of the law shall no flesh be justified.

17 But if, while we seek to be justified by Christ, we ourselves also are found sinners, is therefore Christ the minister of sin? God forbid.

18 For if I build again the things which I destroyed, I make myself a transgressor.

19 For I through the law am dead to the law, that I might live unto God.

20 I am crucified with Christ: nevertheless I live; yet not I, but Christ liveth in me: and the life which I now live in the flesh I live by the faith of the Son of God, who loved me, and gave himself for me.

21 I do not frustrate the grace of God: for if righteousness come by the law, then Christ is dead in vain.

faith in Jesus Christ. And we have come to believe in Christ Jesus, so that we might be justified by faith in Christ, and not by doing the works of the law, because no one will be justified by the works of the law. 17 But if, in our effort to be justified in Christ, we ourselves have been found to be sinners, is Christ then a servant of sin? Certainly not! 18 But if I build up again the very things that I once tore down, then I demonstrate that I am a transgressor. 19 For through the law I died to the law, so that I might live to God. I have been crucified with Christ; 20 and it is no longer I who live, but it is Christ who lives in me. And the life I now live in the flesh I live by faith in the Son of God, who loved me and gave himself for me. 21 I do not nullify the grace of God; for if justification comes through the law, then Christ died for nothing.

Key Verse: **I am crucified with Christ; nevertheless I live; yet not I, but Christ liveth in me; and the life which I now live in the flesh I live by the faith of the Son of God, who loved me, and gave himself for me. Galatians 2:20**

Key Verse: **I have been crucified with Christ; and it is no longer I who live, but it is Christ who lives in me. And the life I now live in the flesh I live by faith in the Son of God, who loved me and gave himself for me. Galatians 2:19*b*-20**

As You Read the Scripture

The letter opens in Paul's typical pattern—he identifies himself as sender, the churches of Galatia as the recipients, and he extends greetings. But immediately differences become obvious: There is no section of thanksgiving as is customary with Paul, no expression of gratitude or commendation. Indeed, the tone is more of a threat (see 1:8-9, where the language in the Greek is very strong).

Galatians 1:6-7. Paul expresses his indignant amazement that the Galatians are so quickly turning against God. The verb translated "deserting" has the connotation of "participating in a mutiny." They are accepting another version of Christianity, but there is no other gospel—good news—than what Paul has preached to them. The new message to which they are responding is a dangerous distortion of the truth.

Galatians 2:11-14. In attempting to explain his position, Paul tells the Galatians about a confrontation he had with Peter in Antioch involving the same issues.

Verse 11. "Cephas" is the Aramaic form of the name "Peter." Peter had been recognized, at least informally, as the leader of the original disciples of Jesus. After Pentecost he took an active leadership role in the early church and was widely respected and influential. Antioch was a rather cosmopolitan city in Syria in which the church was composed of both Jewish and Gentile converts.

Verse 12. While in Antioch, Peter had table-fellowship with Gentile Christians without scruples concerning the Jewish dietary laws. However, when representatives of the Jerusalem church, under the leadership of Jesus' brother James, arrived, they apparently reprimanded him for this practice, and Peter withdrew from such common meals.

Verse 13. Other Jewish Christians followed Peter's lead and withdrew as well. Even Barnabas, a highly respected leader in Antioch and a frequent traveling companion of Paul, had gone along.

Verse 14. Paul accuses Peter and the others of hypocrisy and asks how, recognizing their own freedom in Christ from the requirements of the law, they can expect the Gentiles to obey that same law.

Verses 15-21. These verses include Paul's synopsis of the entire gospel as it was relevant to the Galatian situation.

Verses 15-16. Note that Paul retains the idea of the Jews as chosen people, although his reference to the "Gentile sinners" is not a moral judgment, but a comment about their relationship to the law. He sees two options for the accomplishment of human salvation—it comes either through obedience to the law *or* by faith in Christ. To be "justified" is to be made "upright" or "righteous," to be "acquitted" and "accepted." Such a change in a person comes only through faith in Christ, and that faith is itself a divine gift.

Verses 17-18. This verse is difficult, but apparently means that those Christians who exert effort to obey the law in order to be saved are in danger of falling back into sin. Such an approach, Paul insists, has been superseded and must not be restored.

Verses 19-21. These verses are the climax of the argument. Paul rejects all appeals to legalistic requirements and affirms that Christ's death and our identification with him are alone what matters.

The Scripture and the Main Question

The Authority of the Law

The controversy that occasioned the letter to the Galatian churches cannot be understood without comprehending the authority of the law in Judaism. *Torah,* meaning "Law" or "Teaching," was to be found in the first five books of the Hebrew Bible. By the time of Jesus, it had been explained, elaborated, and applied at great length. Traditionally, Torah was said to include 613 laws. Devout Jews believe that God's will was expressed in Torah and that God was served in the conscientious observance of it. While there were laws governing every aspect of life, an important part of Torah was the dietary code found in Leviticus 11 and Deuteronomy 14. Because of the necessity of consuming only foods that were considered "clean"—acceptable to God—and had been prepared in the prescribed manner, eating with persons of other religions was largely prohibited. Further, the act of eating together was itself in Jewish culture a religious activity during which God was thanked for the bounty of the earth and persons were bonded in fellowship. Strict adherence to the food laws was considered imperative if the Jews were to maintain themselves as a distinct people in covenant relationship to God. It is against this background that the withdrawal of Peter and the other Jewish Christians from table-fellowship with Gentile Christians must be seen.

An inviolable requirement of Torah was the circumcision of Jewish male babies on the eighth day after their birth. Circumcision was considered the sign of the covenant established between God and Abraham and continued with Abraham and Sarah's descendants. To be uncircumcised was to be outside the community of God's people. Male converts to Judaism were required to be circumcised as a part of their initiation rituals.

No Other Gospel

Before his conversion to Christianity, Paul had been a member of the Pharisees, the party in Judaism who were most insistent on the strict keeping of Torah. When he refers in his letters to "the law," it is usually this code and its expansions he has in mind. It is a measure of the transforming nature of his conversion that Paul's mind changed so radically on this subject. Paul sees clearly that the point at issue was a theological one that pierced to the very heart of the gospel and threatened to destroy it. In the first two chapters of this letter, he uses the Greek word for "gospel" thirteen times as he struggles to persuade his readers that their actions deny the essence of Christianity. Their emphasis is in the wrong place, because they are concerned with what they can do rather than what God in Christ has already done. Their misguided approach to seeking right relationships with God will actually result in making them sinners once again.

The essentials of Paul's theology, and of Christian doctrine, are presented in Galatians 2:11-21. This passage has been of great significance in the history of Christianity through the centuries. The Protestant reformer Martin Luther devoted eighty pages to these eleven verses in his commentary on Galatians in the sixteenth century.

Justification by Faith

Sola fide ("faith alone") might be called the motto of the Protestant Reformation, which Martin Luther and others led against the Roman Catholic Church. "Justification by faith" is an abbreviated way of expressing the theological truth that might be better phrased "justification through faith in God's grace alone." One way of understanding justification is with a courtroom metaphor. To be justified is to be pronounced not guilty, acquitted and accepted. It is also to be upright or conformed to a standard, as the term has existed in Christianity between the Roman Catholic understanding of justification as involving an infusion of grace by which one receives righteousness and the Protestant Reformers' understanding that in justification God declares us righteous and treats us as if we were. John Wesley's view was that justification has to do not so much with the declaring of a status as with the establishing of a relationship. Divine power continues to work in justified persons to make them holy; the Spirit of Christ comes to dwell within.

God's act of justification is made available through the death and resurrection of Christ. It is a free and gracious gift offered out of divine love. The appropriate and essential human response is faith, but in truth, humans are so helpless without God that even our very capacity for faith comes from God. Hence, faith is a gift, not an accomplishment. It does not earn us credits or give us claims on God. Divine grace always precedes anything that we can do in response; it comes to us with no strings attached. Faith is our trust, our absolute confidence, in the goodness and faithfulness of God. Such faith reshapes our lives because it enables us to share in the death to sin and resurrection to new life first experienced by Jesus. We share in that new life and in the continuation of that ministry to the world. Charles B. Cousar, in his commentary on Galatians in the *Interpretation* series, offers a beautiful description of faith:

> Faith is not a reliance on one's accomplishments or *one's lack of accomplishments,* but a trust in the accomplishments of God.

Positively, faith in Christ is the offering of a glad word of thanksgiving for God's goodness focused in the gift of his Son. It is the standing ovation we give when we have caught only a fleeting glimpse of or have been thoroughly gripped by the drama of Good Friday and Easter. With people crowded row on row in front and behind we find ourselves a part of an audience on its feet with applause, whistles, and shouts of "Bravo!" Then in a strange way, almost as if in a dream, we are transformed from isolated spectators into a company of participants, no longer looking on but actually on stage. A moment comes, when moving about from scene to scene, we realize that we are not intruders into someone else's play. We belong here. This is our place, our part. The cross and resurrection are not only Jesus' but also ours. Faith becomes obedience—not the superficial, formalized adherence to the demands of the law, but conformity to the prime figure in the drama, following him about as he moves among the mass of humanity declaring good news to the poor and release to the captives, binding the brokenhearted, giving garlands instead of ashes, and above all announcing the year of the Lord's favor.

Helping Adults Become Involved

Preparing to Teach

Since this is the initial lesson in a five-session study of the letter to the Galatians, it would be valuable to spend some time familiarizing yourself with the setting, issues, and themes of the whole book. Some ways to do this include reading through all six chapters, preferably in one sitting, noting the material in the unit introduction and in "The Main Question," studying the introduction to the book in a study Bible (the Oxford Annotated NRSV, for example), and getting information about Galatians from a commentary. If you have taught or studied the last two units of lessons on Romans, you will find that many of the major themes are already familiar.

Read Galatians 1 and 2 with care, using "As You Read the Scripture" for help with the verses that are printed in the lesson. Be certain that you can explain the situation of controversy in Galatia and why Paul was so upset. "The Main Question" and the section entitled "The Authority of the Law" in "The Scripture and the Main Question" should make this clear. Reflect on this situation in the Galatian churches and see what similar problems or questions you can think of from our own day, perhaps from your own church.

Use the following lesson outline:

I. The crisis in the Galatian churches
II. The attractions and dangers of legalism
III. Trusting in God's grace through faith

Consider making copies of the quotation from Charles Cousar at the end of "The Scripture and the Main Question" for students to use in class and to take home. A chalkboard or newsprint should be available as well as enough Bibles and hymnals for all.

Introducing the Main Question

A main objective of your teaching this lesson is to convey an understanding of the controversy between Paul and the "agitators" who were troubling the Galatian churches. The question at issue is simply this: How are we to be saved from sin and death? What can we do to achieve this? What does God do?

Developing the Lesson

I. The crisis in the Galatian churches

Try to explain clearly the problem that had arisen in the Galatian churches and why Paul was so distressed about it. The information in "The Main Question" and "The Authority of the Law" should enable you to do this. Be sure to make it clear that the issue was not a trivial one nor a matter of Paul's jealousy of other teachers, but a question relating to the very essence of Christianity. Write on the board or newsprint simple statements of Paul's views and those of the "Judaizers" (as those who insisted on observing the law were called).

Lead the class in a discussion of similar disagreements in the church today. Examples might be the insistence in some churches that persons be immersed in water for their baptism to be valid, the tendency of some churches to require speaking in tongues, the prohibition in some churches of the wearing of makeup or jewelry, the assertion by some that the drinking of alcoholic beverages is a mortal sin. Doubtless your group will be able to think of other examples. Evaluate all of these against Paul's understanding of how persons are reconciled to God.

II. The attractions and dangers of legalism

Suggest this definition of legalism for the class to consider: "the obeying of certain rules and the performing of certain actions in order to get oneself into right relationship with God." Have the class make a list, which you will record on the board, of any such rules and actions in your church, your family, or your own views.

Statistics show that the more conservative, even legalistic, churches are currently growing in membership. Why do you think this might be true? What are some of the attractions of legalism that have made it such an enduring position among Christians through the centuries? You may suggest these possibilities if the class members do not: (1) the security gained by having certain visible signs of salvation, comparable to circumcision in the early church—specific actions or prohibitions that may be understood as evidence of being right with God; (2) the comforting sense of being obedient to God because one has kept certain rules, even though other parts of one's life may be less than Christlike; (3) the pride of piety, especially in an achievement-oriented society in which we like to take credit for things ourselves. Is it possible that like the Galatians we run the risk of adding falsely to the gospel?

III. Trusting in God's grace through faith

The material you need for presenting this climactic portion of the lesson is found in the "No Other Gospel" and "Justification by Faith" sections of "The Scripture and the Main Question." Lead the class in looking closely at Galatians 2:19-21, where Paul's emphasis is summarized. If possible, have these verses read from different translations in order to get insights into their meaning.

Almost all surveys of the preferences of American Christians indicate that the most popular hymn is "Amazing Grace." Using your hymnals, have the class read or sing this hymn together. Talk about the theological ideas it presents and compare them to Paul's understandings. Why do you think this hymn is consistently so popular?

Distribute sheets with Charles Cousar's quotation about faith (from "The Scripture and the Main Question"). Spend as much time as your schedule allows reading and discussing parts of it; compare Cousar's ideas to those of Paul.

Helping Class Members Act

Encourage the class to take the Cousar quotation home with them and use it in their personal devotions during the week as they meditate on the meaning of faith. Challenge them to examine their personal lives and that of their church to discover what is really believed—not simply what is said—about how persons come into saving relationship with God. Do they attempt throught beliefs and behaviors to achieve salvation for themselves?

What are some of the ways less conservative churches might meet the needs of their people for security in their relationship with God, without resorting to rigid legalism?

Planning for Next Sunday

Next week's lesson is entitled "Adopted as God's Children" and focuses on Galatians 3:1–4:7. Ask all students to read this passage carefully during the week.

If there are persons in your class who have adopted children and who would be comfortable talking about it, ask them to be ready to share their experience and feelings.

Adopted as God's Children

Background Scripture: Galatians 3:1–4:7

The Main Question

A little boy was growing up very unhappy. His mother had never been married, and she had always refused to reveal to anyone the name of his father. Because of this mystery, the boy was the object of much gossip and speculation. Other children, reflecting what they had heard at home, shunned him except to taunt with hurtful names. Adults stared at him, looking for telltale traces of physical resemblance to men in the village. When the boy was about twelve years old, he began to attend services at the little church. He was attracted there by the tall, bearded minister, who thundered forth powerful sermons about the love of God. However, the boy was always very careful to slip quickly out of the church immediately at the end of the service, before anyone would have a chance to speak to him. On one Sunday morning, however, he found his exit blocked by a very large woman stationed in the aisle in conversation. Delayed in his escape, he was stunned to feel suddenly the heavy hand of the preacher on his shoulder. Turning, he looked up into the man's face. The preacher stared directly into his eyes for a few moments and then announced in his booming voice, "Son, I know who you are; you're the child of. . . ." "Oh no," thought the boy, "he's going to guess who my daddy is, right here in church!" and he froze in horror. "Yes, son, I know who you are," the preacher continued. *"You're the child of God. Now go out and live like it!"* The man who told this story about his own life testified that he left that church with an entirely different sense of who he was. He overcame his disadvantages and eventually went on to serve two terms as governor of his state. What a difference it makes in our lives when we know that in Christ we are God's children!

Selected Scripture

King James Version	New Revised Standard Version
Galatians 3:1-5, 23	*Galatians 3:1-5, 23*
1 O foolish Galatians, who hath bewitched you, that ye should not obey the truth, before whose eyes Jesus Christ hath been evidently set forth, crucified among you?	1 You foolish Galatians! Who has bewitched you? It was before your eyes that Jesus Christ was publicly exhibited as crucified! 2 The only thing I want to learn from you is this: Did you receive the Spirit by doing the works of the law or by believing what you heard? 3 Are you so foolish? Having started with the Spirit, are you now ending with the flesh? 4 Did you experience so much for nothing?—if it really was for
2 This only would I learn of you, Received ye the Spirit by the works of the law, or by the hearing of faith?	
3 Are ye so foolish? having begun in the Spirit, are ye now made perfect by the flesh?	

4 Have ye suffered so many things in vain? if it be yet in vain.

5 He therefore that ministereth to you the Spirit, and worketh miracles among you, doeth he it by the works of the law, or by the hearing of faith?

....

23 But before faith came, we were kept under the law, shut up unto the faith which should afterwards be revealed.

4:7

7 Wherefore thou art no more a servant, but a son; and if a son, then an heir of God through Christ.

Key Verses: But when the fulness of the time was come, God sent forth his Son, made of a woman, made under the law, to redeem them that were under the law, that we might receive the adoption of sons. Galatians 4:4-5

nothing. 5 Well then, does God supply you with the Spirit and work miracles among you by your doing the works of the law, or by your believing what you heard?

....

23 Now before faith came, we were imprisoned and guarded under the law until faith would be revealed.

4:7

7 So you are no longer a slave but a child, and if a child then also an heir, through God.

Key Verses: But when the fullness of time had come, God sent his Son, ... to redeem those who were under the law, so that we might receive adoption as children. Galatians 4:4-5

As You Read the Scripture

Galatians 3:1-5. The intensity of Paul's feelings of anger, disappointment, and frustration are very apparent here. The word *foolish* in verses 1 and 3 means "unthinking" or "thoughtless" rather than "stupid." It seems to Paul as if the minds of the Galatians have been taken over by some alien force, as if they are under an enchanted spell that has made them forget the truth they once knew so well. The gospel of Christ crucified as atonement for their sins has been made as clear to them as if it had been displayed on a public placard for all to see. They have received the Holy Spirit, even evidenced by the working of miracles among them. Paul reminds them forcefully that the indwelling presence of the Spirit has been given to them by God purely because they believed the message they heard preached. Their obedience to regulations or any other "works" on their part was irrelevant. The Galatians should know this because they have experienced it in their own lives and community.

Verses 23-24. The legal requirements of the Old Testament code—the law—served a divine purpose prior to the coming of Christ into the world. The law served as a kind of preparation for the salvation that was to be made available in Christ by revealing to people that they were unable in their own ability to live obedient to God's will. The law functioned as a custodian or tutor during the time in which people were spiritual minors.

Verses 25-26. The word *faith* here, as in verse 23*a*, refers to the Christian faith. Christ perfectly fulfilled the law and, thus, made it obsolete. The emphatic "you are *all* children" introduces a theme that will be developed further. Children of God have the full privileges of their status and so no longer need the discipline of the law.

Verse 27. As he makes clear elsewhere (see Rom. 6:3-8), it is in baptism that one is identified with Christ and becomes a child of God. The closeness of the relationship with Christ into which one enters is expressed in the metaphor of a garment. Baptismal services in the early church often included dressing in new clothes as a symbol of newness of life. Here Paul speaks of Christ as that garment.

Verse 28. Paul here announces the revolutionary doctrine of equality of all persons in the new life given through and in Christ. Human distinctions and discriminations must disappear in the new age Christ has inaugurated.

Verse 29. Christians are true descendants of Abraham. As the people of faith, they inherit the promises of God in the new covenant.

Galatians 4:1-3. Children are minors who lack legal rights and so must wait until the freedom of adulthood to be able to inherit property. Without Christ, persons of all ages are enslaved to the demonic forces of the spiritual world (see Rom. 8:38) and are deprived of their rightful status as heirs of God.

Verses 4-5. At the appropriate time in history, God sent the divine Son into the world as a human person to redeem, or set free, enslaved humanity. Here the metaphor shifts from inheritance of property to adoption as children.

Verses 6-7. As adopted children, Christians are heirs to the promises of God and enjoy intimate relationship with God as a loving Parent.

The Scripture and the Main Question

"The Fullness of Time"

One of the characteristics that distinguishes Judaism and Christianity from other world religions is the understanding of history. In Eastern religions, history typically has little significance; it is seen as a repetitive round of events, a cycle from which we long to escape. The Judeo-Christian tradition, by contrast, has a linear understanding of history. History began with God's act of creation. It is the stage upon which the divine drama of salvation is played out, and it will be brought to consummation by the action of God to fulfill the divine purposes. The God of the Bible is revealed primarily in and through the events of human history, which truly becomes salvation history. Therefore, history takes on profound significance for persons of biblical faith.

Christians believe that God chose to reveal the divine nature and will to persons of the Old Testament era through the history of the Hebrew (or Israelite or Jewish) people. One element of God's covenant with the people chosen as the instrument of divine action in the world was the law, Torah. The law made clear how God wanted people to live, but, perhaps even more important, it also made clear that human beings were incapable of obeying God. They were too sinful, too weak to do what they knew God wanted them to do. The law did provide some direction and some restraint for people in a time before the coming of Christ. Paul compares its function to that of the slave whose duties included taking the Roman boy to his school, seeing that he did his lessons, and in general keeping him out of trouble by exercising discipline over him. This function of the law, and therefore the law itself, became obsolete when Christ inaugurated a new age and a new relationship between people and God.

Galatians 4:4-7 is often used in the church as a Christmas lectionary selection because it celebrates the birth of Christ. Not by accident or coincidence, but "in the fullness of time"—in the time of God's own choosing—the second Person of the Trinity, who existed from the beginning, was born of a human mother in the form of human flesh. He was Jesus, the long-promised Christ, who came into human history and set us free from the bondage of sin. There is no more need for law to regulate the relationship between God and humans, for in Christ we become God's true children and are set free to love and obey God through the continual working of the divine Spirit within us.

"Did You Experience So Much for Nothing?"

Paul's appeal to the Galatian Christians is not based solely on understandings of history, or of incarnation and redemption. He appeals also on the basis of what they have themselves experienced. He is astonished that they seem to have forgotten that the presence and power of God had been manifest among them. How could they doubt? Paul feels much as Jesus does when he walks with two disciples along the Emmaus road soon after the Resurrection. When they express disappointment about Jesus' execution and confusion about the rumors of an empty tomb, Jesus calls them "foolish" (Luke 24:25)—the same word Paul uses in Galatians 3:1, 3. The Galatian Christians and the disciples on the Emmaus road refused to believe the very evidence of their own experiences with Christ.

We can experience the presence of God in our lives. We can know the transforming power of a personal relationship with Jesus Christ. We can enjoy the assurance that comes from the fellowship of the Holy Spirit with our own spirit.

"Adoption as Children"

The wonderful relationship Christians have with God can best be understood as that between a loving Parent and beloved children. The purpose of God's action in history is to bring us back into that kind of relationship. Created to be God's children, we have forfeited that status by rebellion and selfishness and so have become slaves of sin. Through Christ we are redeemed. In Paul's day, the word *redeem* was used for the act of buying a person out of slavery. Sometimes the purchase price was first paid to the temple god and the freed person technically became the property of the god. Just so, Christ has paid the price for our redemption; we are freed from slavery to sin, and we obtain a new status: children of God. Just as human children often resemble their parents physically, as well as in temperament and behavior, so also we possess a moral likeness to God. Just as these resemblances often become more obvious as human children grow older, so also we are to grow more and more into likeness to God as known in Christ.

"All of You Are One in Christ Jesus"

The revolutionary character of Paul's declaration in Galatians 3:28 is not often appreciated. We may be certain that his first-century readers literally gasped in shock when they first read this statement. Even today, if we were fully to apprehend what is being said here, we would also be shocked and deeply shamed by how far short the Christian community falls from fulfilling this ideal. What is at stake is a redefinition of all human relationships according to the profoundly simple principle that all persons are of equal worth before God and should be so treated in the human community. Differences are real but irrelevant; there is no superiority. Any inequality in the valuing of persons is fatal to the spiritual unity of Christians; it is a lethal influence in the life of the church. To know oneself as a child of God is to recognize God's equal love and acceptance of persons who are very different.

The most common bases of discrimination in Paul's day were the same as in ours—race, religion, social and economic class, and gender. No struggles have been more difficult or more protracted within the church. The last half of this century has been marked by enormous changes in race relations in this country. But the statement of Martin Luther King, Jr., remains true: "The most segregated hour of the week is 11:00 on Sunday morning." Racism continues abroad in the land and it lurks—sometimes just below the surface, sometimes boldly above—within the church, an ugly, evil contradiction of the gospel message. Sexism, while at last being identified and attacked in our society, is pervasive and malignant in both the secular world and the church. There is much to be done if Paul's great insight is to become reality.

Helping Adults Become Involved

Preparing to Teach

All five of the lessons in this unit are closely related, since the brief letter to the Galatians concentrates on the major theme of Christian freedom. It will be helpful to your class for you to reiterate the major points covered in the first lesson. Review these as you prepare to teach.

Read Galatians 3:1–4:7. Use the information in "As You Read the Scripture" for help in organizing the main ideas.

The salient emphases in the lesson are as follows:

I. The function of the law
II. Becoming children of God
III. The equality of all persons in Christ

Bibles and hymnals should be available for everyone; a chalkboard or newsprint will allow you to emphasize points and record input in discussions.

Introducing the Main Question

A contemporary gospel song insists, "To be God's children, you got to be born again!" What does this mean? Aren't all people God's children? What then does Paul mean when he says that "in Christ Jesus you are all children of God through faith" (Gal. 3:26)? How are God's children supposed to live? How should Christians act toward persons who are different from us in race, religion, nationality, social class, wealth, or gender? All of these questions are dealt with in today's lesson.

Developing the Lesson

I. The function of the law

The entire letter to the Galatian churches deals with the theme of law and freedom for Christians. An excellent way to begin this session is to review the major points from last week's study. Be certain that everyone understands and recalls the points of controversy between Paul and the Galatian Christians.

Use the material in "The Fullness of Time" section of "The Scripture and the Main Question" to remind the class of the significance of the law, or Torah, for the Jewish people of the first century. This material will also enable you to explain the understanding of history that is characteristic of the biblical religions, both Judaism and Christianity. This concept is important for comprehending Paul's view of the law as having once had a valid function, but then being rendered useless by the coming of Christ into the world.

II. Becoming children of God

John Wesley insisted that Christians could receive through Christ not only the gift of salvation, but also the assurance that they were, indeed, in a saving relationship with God. Some groups of Christians continue to deny that it is possible to have such assurance; some even assert that it is dangerous spiritual arrogance to claim so. But Wesley was not saying that Christians could take their salvation for granted or be sure that they were for all time "right with God." Like Paul, he believed that God graciously bestows on us such an undeniable sense of the divine presence and power that we can know ourselves to be in loving relationship with God. This is what it means to be "children of God"—to enjoy a relationship with God like that of children with their ideal parents.

Use the material in "Did You Experience So Much for Nothing?" to make these points. Have the class look in your hymnal for hymns that are classified as hymns of assurance. Ask class members to select favorite stanzas or phrases and share them aloud. Many hymns contain references to the personal experience of believers through which the saving presence of Christ is known. A familiar example is the Easter hymn "He Lives" with its stirring refrain: "You ask me how I know he lives? He lives within my heart." This is the experience that Paul is trying to rekindle in the hearts of the Christians of Galatia.

Explain that Paul likened the experience of being brought into right relationship with God to that of being adopted as a beloved child. Ask those persons who have adopted children to share their experience with the class. Guide the discussion in such a way as to emphasize the anticipation, joy, and love of the parents as well as the wonderful change in situation for the children. The material in "Adoption as Children" will help you to develop the analogy to God's adoption of us.

III. The equality of all persons in Christ

Write the words of Galatians 3:28 on the board or newsprint. It is fine if this takes up both time and space; the point is to catch the attention of the class. Use "All of You Are One in Christ Jesus" to help your students understand the radical nature of this declaration in Paul's day. Encourage the class to make a list of ways we fall short, as individuals and as a church, of fulfilling this ideal.

Helping Class Members Act

As you look in the mirror, literally and figuratively, this week practice thinking of yourself as a child of God. Do the same as you look at other people.

Planning for Next Sunday

Ask the class to read Galatians 4:8-31.

Freed to Grow

Background Scripture: Galatians 4:8-31

The Main Question

We could not figure out how the bird had gotten in, but there it was—a large black and white woodpecker frantically seeking a route of escape. The glass walls of our sun porch formed a particularly frustrating prison, for every direction appeared to be a way out. Perhaps even more unsettling, every surface presented the picture of a frightened woodpecker as the bird saw its own image reflected in the glass. We propped open the door that was the only way to freedom, but the bird seemed to fear that opening more than the walls. Desperately, it flung itself against the glass, seeking to break free. I found a long-handled broom and tried gently to guide the woodpecker toward the door, but succeeded only in terrorizing it more. We tried going away and allowing the bird time to calm down in the hope that it would then find its way out alone. An hour later, it was clinging to the light fixture in the ceiling, looking stunned and battered. Eventually we realized that more drastic intervention was essential if the bird were to be protected from destroying itself in its wild lunges toward freedom. We donned heavy work gloves and between the two of us managed after a long struggle to grab the exhausted creature and take it outdoors, where we released it to fly away. Imagine our astonishment and chagrin when the confused woodpecker finally flew—straight through the open door back into its sun porch prison!

That experience makes me better able to comprehend the feelings of Paul as he dealt with the Galatians. What might he say if he were speaking to us today? What are some of the wrong ways in which we seek freedom? Why do we fail to recognize and claim it when we should?

Selected Scripture

King James Version	**New Revised Standard Version**

Galatians 4:8-20

8 Howbeit then, when ye knew not God, ye did service unto them which by nature are no gods.

9 But now, after that ye have known God, or rather are known of God, how turn ye again to the weak and beggarly elements, whereunto ye desire again to be in bondage?

10 Ye observe days, and months, and times, and years.

11 I am afraid of you, lest I have bestowed upon you labour in vain.

12 Brethren, I beseech you, be as I am; for I am as ye are: ye have not injured me at all.

13 Ye know how through infirmity of the flesh I preached the gospel unto you at the first.

14 And my temptation which was in my flesh ye despised not, nor rejected; but received me as an angel of God, even as Christ Jesus.

15 Where is then the blessedness ye spake of? for I bear you record, that, if it had been possible, ye would have plucked out your own eyes, and have given them to me.

16 Am I therefore become your enemy, because I tell you the truth?

17 They zealously affect you, but not well; yea, they would exclude you, that ye might affect them.

18 But it is good to be zealously affected always in a good thing, and not only when I am present with you.

19 My little children, of whom I travail in birth again until Christ be formed in you,

20 I desire to be present with you now, and to change my voice; for I stand in doubt of you.

Key Verse: **But now, after that ye have known God, or rather are known of God, how turn ye again to the weak and beggarly elements, whereunto ye desire again to be in bondage? Galatians 4:9**

Galatians 4:8-20

8 Formerly, when you did not know God, you were enslaved to beings that by nature are not gods. 9 Now, however, that you have come to know God, or rather to be known by God, how can you turn back again to the weak and beggarly elemental spirits? How can you want to be enslaved to them again? 10 You are observing special days, and months, and seasons, and years. 11 I am afraid that my work for you may have been wasted.

12 Friends, I beg you, become as I am, for I also have become as you are. You have done me no wrong. 13 You know that it was because of a physical infirmity that I first announced the gospel to you; 14 though my condition put you to the test, you did not scorn or despise me, but welcomed me as an angel of God, as Christ Jesus. 15 What has become of the good will you felt? For I testify that, had it been possible, you would have torn out your eyes and given them to me. 16 Have I now become your enemy by telling you the truth? 17 They make much of you, but for no good purpose; they want to exclude you, so that you may make much of them. 18 It is good to be made much of for a good purpose at all times, and not only when I am present with you. 19 My little children, for whom I am again in the pain of childbirth until Christ is formed in you, 20 I wish I were present with you now and could change my tone, for I am perplexed about you.

Key Verse: **Now, however, that you have come to know God, or rather to be known by God, how can you turn back again to the weak and beggarly elemental spirits? How can you want to be enslaved to them again? Galatians 4:9**

As You Read the Scripture

Galatians 4:8-11. In these verses Paul exhorts his readers to resist the temptation to regress into a state of spiritual slavery, and instead to claim the freedom that is theirs in Christ.

Verse 8. The reference here is to the demonic spirits that were believed to exercise great control over the lives of persons (see v. 3). Paul does not deny their reality, but insists Christians are free from their power.

Verse 9. The ignorance of their former state is contrasted with the knowledge of the spiritual relationship with God. Paul corrects himself to place the emphasis on God's knowledge of us. God's action is always prior to anything we can do. To be known by God is to be in right relationship or intimate fellowship. Paul expresses his astonishment that, after experiencing such a relationship, the Galatians would deliberately seek to return to spiritual slavery.

Verse 10. These special observances were probably both the festival seasons of the Jewish religious calendar and the customary practices of various Gentile cults.

Verse 11. Paul is deeply disappointed and discouraged, feeling that his efforts to teach them the gospel have been rendered futile.

Galatians 4:12-20. In this poignant portion of the letter, Paul appeals to the Galatian Christians on a different basis—that of the shared affection they had enjoyed with him in the past.

Verse 12. Paul has given up all his special privileges and his special obligations as a Jew. He urges the Galatians to imitate him in this freedom. Before this time, they had done him no wrong, but now they do by turning away from the gospel he proclaimed.

Verses 13-14. Paul had first visited these churches at a time when he was quite sick. He praises the Galatians because they did not let his illness keep them from accepting and hearing him. Sickness was often believed to be a sign of God's punishment for one's sins, but the Galatians did not so interpret Paul's condition. The verb rendered "despise" literally means "to spit out"; people would often spit in the presence of an afflicted person in order to ward off the evil spirit responsible for the illness.

Verse 15. These people had received the sick Paul with warm affection. The expression about tearing out the eyes and giving them to Paul is probably a metaphor for giving something very precious. Some commentators interpret this verse as an indication that Paul's illness involved his eyes, but this is conjecture.

Verse 16. Remembering the close friendship he enjoyed with them while he was in Galatia, Paul dreads being seen as their enemy. However, he must be faithful to the gospel message.

Verses 17-18. Those who are urging the Galatians back to the law are hypocrites who desire to turn them against Paul. He intimates that they do not care sincerely for the Galatians, as he does.

Verses 19-20. These verses express the depth of Paul's concern. This is the only place in all his letters where he uses the term of endearment "my little children." The metaphor of childbirth conveys the pain and labor he is enduring. He wishes he were with them; he is at his wit's end to know what else to say.

The Scripture and the Main Question

"How Can You Turn Back Again . . . to Be Enslaved?"

Paul is not only dismayed, but also perplexed at the willingness of the Galatian Christians to surrender the freedom they have experienced in Christ and submit themselves again to spiritual bondage. But freedom is not always an easy thing to enjoy and, especially, to trust. It brings with it a whole set of dangers and problems from which a state of slavery insulates us. Remember the response of the Israelites whom Moses had led out of slavery to Egypt. So often, when danger or deprivation threatened, they whined about wanting to return to Egypt and berated Moses for rescuing them. They would have accepted the oppression of bondage for the guarantee of food and protection, traded liberty in the wilderness for slavery in familiar surroundings.

Why do we sometimes choose to return to the burdens of slavery rather than to accept the gifts that freedom provides? In some cases, we may simply be confused, like the woodpecker in the story above. What appears to be freedom may be bondage disguised. We may seek freedom in the wrong places and ways. We may fail to recognize freedom, especially if it involves surrendering ourselves to a higher power, and continue futilely dashing ourselves against the glass walls of our prisons. In other situations, we fear freedom because it comes with risks to our security. A newspaper article related the pathetic story of a prison inmate whose greatest fear after thirty years of incarceration was that he might be released and forced to cope with the demands of life outside the walls. Anyone who has worked with battered women knows the frustration of trying to counsel freedom to persons who are so ridden with guilt and negative self-image that they have convinced themselves they deserve oppression. The attraction of freedom may be unable to overpower the chains of guilt. Another enemy of freedom is doubt—the suspicion that it simply cannot be this easy: "Surely there is something else that I must do." This was the situation of the Galatian Christians, and it is common among Christians today. It is frequently a disguised variety of the pridefulness that insists, "I can and will do it for myself."

"My Condition Put You to the Test"

Paul had been suffering from a serious illness when he first came to Galatia. While we cannot be certain that this illness was related to the "thorn . . . in the flesh" that he speaks of in 2 Corinthians 12:7-9, it seems clear that Paul was afflicted by chronically poor health. Scholars have speculated widely on the precise nature of his condition; some suggest that it was malaria; others, epilepsy; still others, migraine headaches. A recurrent theory postulates an eye condition that interfered with his vision. Those who argue for this possibility cite Galatians 6:11, where Paul speaks of writing in "large letters." The exact diagnosis is unimportant, but for Christians who suffer physically themselves it is relevant that Paul was similarly beset. In the ancient world, illness was associated with demon possession, and Paul himself refers to "a messenger of Satan to torment me" (2 Cor. 12:7).

Christians today often struggle with illness, not simply because of the physical effects, but also due to feelings of guilt and confusion. Every pastor has been asked, "Why is God doing this to me?" Such a query is particularly painful when the sick person prays faithfully for healing and does not receive it. Paul, too, had repeatedly "appealed to the Lord about this, that it would leave me." While many questions will remain unanswered in this life, we can learn some things about illness from the biblical witness. God, like a loving parent, does not want us to suffer and, indeed, loves us enough to suffer along with us.

Second, God can use our infirmities for good purposes, to make us into better persons through them and manifest the divine power in our afflicted lives (see 2 Cor. 12:9). When I was in my mid-twenties, I suffered a stroke that, while rather minor in overall consequences, left me with a severe impairment of balance for some years. Now, a quarter of a century later, I vividly recall the feeling of lying in bed knowing that I was unable to get up and move to another room without help. After some improvement, I still used a cane for many months and could not drive a car. As frightening and painful as that experience was, I now look back on it as one of the most significant times of my life. It was during those months that I learned patience, appreciation for the joy of life, and most of all compassion for those who suffer physically. I know that I am a better person—a wiser minister, a more empathetic teacher, a warmer human being, a more committed Christian—because of that struggle with illness. The Christ whose heart was broken by human sin and whose body was broken on the cross uses our brokenness, lifts our suffering out of meaninglessness and transforms it to become a vehicle through which we become more like God. Oddly, illness becomes one of the means through which we come to realize our freedom in Christ. We are freed because we have faced some of the worst life has to threaten; we are freed because we have been forced to surrender reliance on ourselves and simply trust in God. We are freed because we have learned that external circumstances cannot determine who we are; our ultimate reality is our relationship with Jesus Christ.

"Christ Is Formed in You"

In very feminine imagery, Paul describes both himself and the Galatian Christians as anticipating childbirth (see 4:19). As Barbel Wartenberg-Potter expresses it: "He is a mother bearing them all over again in the pains of their birth in the faith, as he did when he first preached to them. And what was his message? . . . That they themselves be the womb in which Christ could grow and become life in and for them . . . that Christ might fill them with his liberating presence". (Philip Potter and Barbel Wartenberg-Potter, *Freedom Is for Freeing: A Study Book on Paul's Letter to the Galatians.* [The Women's Division, General Board of Global Ministries, The United Methodist Church, 1990], p. 67). Just as a mother surrenders her body to be the nurturing vessel for the unborn child, so also Christians surrender themselves to the Spirit of Christ, which grows within them more and more. As a mother serves the needs of the developing baby in her womb, Christians devote their lives in service to those about them. This is what true freedom means; we are set free by Christ not simply for our own pleasure, but to serve. In Martin Luther's essay "The Freedom of the Christian," the paradox of the Christian life is presented: "A Christian is the most free lord of all, and subject to none. A Christian is the most willing servant of all, and subject to everyone" (John Dillenberger, ed., *Martin Luther: Selections from His Writings* [New York: Anchor Books, 1961], p. 53).

Helping Adults Become Involved

Preparing to Teach

Read Galatians 4:8-31, preferably from several different translations. Use the material in "As You Read the Scripture" to assist you in comprehending the chief ideas being presented. Reacquaint yourself with the Old Testament story of the Exodus; skim chapters 3 through 14 of Exodus or read the account in a children's Bible storybook. Read 2 Corinthians 12:5-10 to see what Paul says about his struggles with "a thorn . . . in the flesh"—probably a chronic illness. Read carefully "The Main Question" and "The Scripture and the Main Question"; make your own list of what you see as the major points. Think about happenings in your own life that illustrate these points.

The following outline may be used:

> I. Choosing bondage
>   A. Forces that enslave
>   B. The attractions of slavery
> II. Dealing with physical illness
> III. Being loving, hurting ministers

Have Bibles, pencils, and paper available for all, as well as a chalkboard or newsprint for your use.

Introducing the Main Question

Read aloud to the class the story of the woodpecker in "The Main Question." Ask the students whether they have ever felt the way that bird must have felt. Stimulate a discussion about freedom and how we go about seeking it, both rightly and wrongly. Make a column on the board headed "Slavery" and one headed "Freedom." Have the class make lists, which you record, of all the experiences, feelings, and characteristics they can think of that belong in either list. Encourage them to do this in a brainstorming, free-association style. Be sure that "sickness" and "health" appear in the lists.

Developing the Lesson

I. Choosing bondage
  A. Forces that enslave

Divide the class into groups of three or four. Ask them to read Galatians 4:8-11 and list what Paul says about the forces that were enslaving the Galatians. As they share their findings aloud, record them on the board. The combined list should include these items: beings that are not gods, weak spirits, special observances. Have the groups suggest some things that we tend to make into gods—all-powerful objects of our loyalty and service.

What are some of the fears that bind us? What are examples of empty rituals and old habits from which we have trouble getting free?

B. *The attractions of slavery*

Use the material in the "How Can You Turn Back Again . . . to Be Enslaved?" section of "The Scripture and the Main Question." Focus on the four reasons for resisting freedom that are suggested: (1) confusion about what or where freedom is, (2) security provided by familiar circumstances, (3) guilt and lack of self-esteem, (4) unwillingness to surrender and trust what we cannot comprehend.

In a wonderful book called *Jacob the Baker: Gentle Wisdom for a Complicated World,* Noah ben Shea has a chapter entitled "Freedom Is Not the Absence of Slavery: It Is the Memory." Write this title on the board and encourage the class to analyze it. Help them to see that real freedom is enjoyed by those who have once experienced bondage, but have been rescued from it. The lively recollection of slavery motivates us to retain our new freedom. Apply this truth to the situation of the Christians in Galatia and to our lives today.

II. *Dealing with physical illness*

Have the students read 2 Corinthians 12:7b-9. Use the material in "My Condition Put You to the Test" to help them grasp the important points here. Either in small groups, if your class is large, or all together, encourage them to share personal stories of illness and its effects on their lives. Make a list together of all of the negative and positive effects you can think of. Compare Paul's feelings and beliefs about his own "thorn in the flesh" to those of the class members. Discuss various ideas held by Christians about the causes of illness. Try to make it clear that while there is much we do not understand, we can know and trust the love of God as we see it expressed in Jesus Christ.

III. *Being loving, hurting ministers*

Working either individually or in small groups, have the class list the qualities they believe are essential in a good pastor. Encourage them to use Paul as an example, noticing especially his anguished care for the Galatians despite his anger with them. After discussing these qualities, point out that *all* Christians are called to be ministers of the gospel of Christ and, thus, these qualities of character should be exemplified in the lives of us all.

Henri Nouwen wrote a powerful book titled *The Wounded Healer.* Explore the meaning of this phrase with the class. What are some of the "wounds" we suffer? How can pain enable us to function as "healers" in the lives of others? Paul is, of course, an example of this, but more important, so is Christ, who was called the Suffering Servant (see Isa. 53).

Conclude by using the material in "Christ Is Formed in You" to relate this discussion to the theme of freedom.

Helping Class Members Act

Allow a few minutes for each person to think about the meaning of freedom in her or his own life. Especially encourage reflection on various expressions of spiritual freedom that individuals may need. Urge the recording of these thoughts on paper and the continuation of this process in private meditation.

Challenge your students to identify acquaintances who are ensnared in various types of bondage and seek ways to help them toward freedom. Doing this would be especially easy in the case of persons suffering from physical infirmities. Every class member could become a volunteer, a visitor, or a telephone friend for a person confined at home or in a hospital or nursing home. Urge them to think and pray seriously about how their own "wounds" might enable them to be ministers of freedom and healing in the lives of others.

Planning for Next Sunday

Encourage reading and reflection upon Galatians 5.

LESSON 12   MAY 22

Enabled to Bear Fruit

Background Scripture: Galatians 5

The Main Question

Following the pattern of most of his letters, Paul moves at this point in his message to the Galatians into a consideration of the ethical implications of the doctrinal positions he has been explaining. How are Christians who have been liberated from sin and law to live in that freedom? What are the practical ramifications of spiritual freedom for moral conduct? What character qualities are to be exemplified in Christians?

C. S. Lewis in *Beyond Personality* offers some relevant insights:

> If there are rats in a cellar you are most likely to see them if you go in very suddenly. But the suddenness does not create the rats; it only prevents them from hiding. In the same way the suddenness of provocation does not make me an ill-tempered man: it only shows me what an ill-tempered man I am. The rats are always there in the cellar, but if you go in shouting and noisily they will have taken cover before you switch on the light. Apparently the rats of resentment and vindictiveness are always there in the cellar of my soul. . . . I can to some extent control my acts. . . . But I cannot, by direct moral effort, give myself new motives. (In *Mere Christianity* [New York: Macmillan, 1960], pp. 164-65.)

Paul is concerned in Galatians 5 with the rats that hide in the cellars of Christian lives and show themselves in behaviors that are incompatible with our relationship to Christ. He is especially distressed about attitudes and actions that are destructive of community among Christians and of their witness of love to the world. Through the transforming power of the Spirit working in our lives, we can increasingly manifest in mutual loving service the virtues of Christlikeness.

Selected Scripture

King James Version	New Revised Standard Version

Galatians 5:1, 13-26

1 Stand fast therefore in the liberty wherewith Christ hath made us free, and be not entangled again with the yoke of bondage.

....

13 For, brethren, ye have been called unto liberty; only use not liberty for an occasion to the flesh, but by love serve one another.
14 For all the law is fulfilled in one word, even in this; Thou shalt love thy neighbour as thyself.
15 But if ye bite and devour one another, take heed that ye be not consumed one of another.

16 This I say then, Walk in the Spirit, and ye shall not fulfil the lust of the flesh.
17 For the flesh lusteth against the Spirit, and the Spirit against the flesh: and these are contrary the one to the other: so that ye cannot do the things that ye would.
18 But if ye be led of the Spirit, ye are not under the law.
19 Now the works of the flesh are manifest, which are these; Adultery, fornication, uncleanness, lasciviousness,
20 Idolatry, witchcraft, hatred, variance, emulations, wrath, strife, seditions, heresies,
21 Envyings, murders, drunkenness, revellings, and such like: of the which I tell you before, as I have also told you in time past, that they which do such things shall not inherit the kingdom of God.
22 But the fruit of the Spirit is love, joy, peace, longsuffering, gentleness, goodness, faith,

Galatians 5:1, 13-26

1 For freedom Christ has set us free. Stand firm, therefore, and do not submit again to a yoke of slavery.

....

13 For you were called to freedom, brothers and sisters; only do not use your freedom as an opportunity for self-indulgence, but through love become slaves to one another. 14 For the whole law is summed up in a single commandment, "You shall love your neighbor as yourself." 15 If, however, you bite and devour one another, take care that you are not consumed by one another.
16 Live by the Spirit, I say, and do not gratify the desires of the flesh. 17 For what the flesh desires is opposed to the Spirit, and what the Spirit desires is opposed to the flesh; for these are opposed to each other, to prevent you from doing what you want. 18 But if you are led by the Spirit, you are not subject to the law. 19 Now the works of the flesh are obvious: fornication, impurity, licentiousness, 20 idolatry, sorcery, enmities, strife, jealousy, anger, quarrels, dissensions, factions, 21 envy, drunkenness, carousing, and things like these. I am warning you, as I warned you before: those who do such things will not inherit the kingdom of God.

22 By contrast, the fruit of the Spirit is love, joy, peace, patience, kindness, generosity, faithfulness,

23 Meekness, temperance: against such there is no law.

24 And they that are Christ's have crucified the flesh with the affections and lusts.

25 If we live in the Spirit, let us also walk in the Spirit.

26 Let us not be desirous of vain glory, provoking one another, envying one another.

23 gentleness, and self-control. There is no law against such things.

24 And those who belong to Christ Jesus have crucified the flesh with its passions and desires. 25 If we live by the Spirit, let us also be guided by the Spirit. 26 Let us not become conceited, competing against one another, envying one another.

Key Verses: **But the fruit of the Spirit is love, joy, peace, longsuffering, gentleness, goodness, faith, meekness, temperance; against such there is no law. Galatians 5:22-23**

Key Verses: **By contrast, the fruit of the Spirit is love, joy, peace, patience, kindness, generosity, faithfulness, gentleness, and self-control. There is no law against such things. Galatians 5:22-23**

As You Read the Scripture

Galatians 5:1, 13-26. These verses contain ethical exhortations to the churches of Galatia as to how they should live in the new freedom that God in Christ has given them.

Verse 1. Here in a concise statement is Paul's manifesto of Christian liberty. Christians are urged to hold tenaciously to that freedom and refuse to be harnessed with human legalisms like a beast of burden.

Verse 13. The word *opportunity* meant in Greek "a base of operation; a point from which to launch an attack." Freedom carries the danger of misuse through self-indulgence and immorality. What Christians are truly called to is not servility or exploitation, but mutual loving service.

Verse 14. The quotation is from Leviticus 19:18, but the point is that Christians are to love others not in order to fulfill a commandment, but out of lives transformed by the Spirit of Christ.

Verse 15. This verse doubtless reflects the actual situation in Galatia, where factions were fighting like wild animals and some were tempted to moral looseness.

Verses 16-18. Sharp opposition is established here between the two ways of living—in the flesh and in the Spirit. Paul insists that there can be no compromise due to the irreconcilable conflict. The phrase "I say" intensifies his personal appeal to his readers. The "desires of the flesh" are not simply those associated with the physical body, but all of the sinful impulses of human nature. Escape from the dominance of these passions is possible only by having a new master. With the Spirit of Christ acting as our guide, we are able to live good lives in freedom.

Verses 19-21. Freedom from the requirements of the Law may be misinterpreted as a license to sin, misused as justification for immorality. In typical Greco-Roman style, Paul provides a catalog of "works of the flesh"—vices to which we are prone until we are transformed by the Spirit and to which we are tempted even in the midst of that transformation. The first three listed may be classified as sins of sensuality involving exploitative gratification of the desires of the physical body. "Idolatry" and "sorcery" refer not only to the reprehensible practices associated with pagan worship, but also to the attitudes upon which those practices were based. The remainder of the list deals with behaviors that are destructive to the harmony of the Christian community as well as to the individuals who are guilty of indulging in them. Those who continue to be guilty of such behaviors are not truly members of the community of God's people, neither in this present time nor in the age to come.

Verses 22-23. Paul is emphatic that he is portraying the stark differences between the two ways of life. Using the cataloging technique again, he lists the virtues exemplified by persons living under the control of Christ's Spirit. These qualities are not so much the results of human efforts as they are the outgrowth of divine love reproducing itself within Christians.

Verses 24-26. Such spiritual fruit can be produced only after our sinful, selfish nature has been put to death and we are living in accord with the mind of Christ.

The Scripture and the Main Question

"Called to Freedom"

One of major themes of the letter to the Galatians, and indeed of all of Paul's theology, is that Christians have been set free from slavery to sin and to the Law. The question being addressed in this chapter is how we are to live in this new condition of freedom. Some may be tempted to use their freedom from the restraints of law as an excuse for self-indulgence and immoral behavior. If no prohibitions bind Christians, then why should we not do whatever we choose? If our salvation comes through God's grace and not our merit, why bother to behave ethically? Paul answers that our new life of freedom is life in Christ, life indwelt by the Spirit of Christ. In such a relationship we are guided, molded, and eventually transformed. Paul's mention of a yoke (Gal. 5:1) reminds us of Jesus' use of this metaphor (Matt. 11:29-30); we are yoked with Christ so as to live like him. We are authentically free—not to be and do anything we wish, but to actualize the image of God in which we have been created. As C. S. Lewis puts it, "Finally, if all goes well, turning you permanently into a different sort of thing; into a new little Christ, a being which in its own small way, has the same kind of life as God; which shares in His power, joy, knowledge and eternity."

As persons transformed by our relationship to Christ, we are unconcerned about earning rewards; we find ourselves freely overflowing with the grace of the Spirit. We are not required to give ourselves to others, but we are set free to be able to do so. Ethical Christian living is possible in no other way than to be motivated and empowered by divine love to respond to the needs of other persons. One aspect of this ethical freedom is that our attitudes and actions do not depend on the responses of those with whom we interact. A woman was once asked why she continued to smile and speak pleasantly each morning to a co-worker who consistently responded with either sarcasm or a snarl. She replied, "I know how I should behave, and I will not allow someone else to determine that for me."

"Become Slaves to One Another"

In Exodus 9:1, God's word to the Egyptian pharaoh who holds the Israelites in slavery is, "Let my people go, so that they may worship me." The freedom into which Christ has called us is a freedom *for* something. We are to utilize it in meeting each other's needs through acts of loving service. Jesus repeatedly stressed this aspect of responsible Christian living. When James and John sought preeminence among the disciples, Jesus reminded them that "whoever wishes to become great among you must be your servant, and whoever wishes to be first among you must be slave of all" (Mark 10:43-44). When he has finished the humble ministry of washing the disciples' feet on the evening of the Last Supper, Jesus urges them to emulate him: "You also ought to wash one another's feet. For I have set you an example, that you also should do as I have done to you" (John 13:14-15). What is demanded of us is not a set of specific actions, but an all-encompassing attitude toward life in which we understand ourselves as servants to one another. Ethical decision making is often complex because we are not conforming to a code of behavior or an abstract principle of morality. Instead, we deal with particular situations as they arise and seek to do what love requires in each context. This kind of servanthood does not end in grim self-repression, but in joyous self-fulfillment.

"The Works of the Flesh"

It should be reemphasized that Paul's use of the term *flesh* in Galatians 5:16-21 does not mean simply the physical body, but is instead an expression by which he refers to the sinful nature of humanity and the actions resulting from the indulgence of those impulses. *Fornication* probably meant prostitution, especially as practiced as a part of pagan worship, and, more broadly, any kind of sexual immorality. *Impurity* is a rather general term connoting any evil attitudes or actions that interfere with right living. Selfish willfulness with implications of violence against others is described as *licentiousness*. For the Jews, *idolatry*—the act of creating our god in our own image—was the root of all sin. The term *sorcery* refers to the use of drugs for magical purposes in some of the pagan cults of the day. Magic was a leading competitor of Christianity in Paul's time (see Acts 8:14-24). It was a system of practices, devoid of ethics, that tried to manipulate God into performing to please human desires. The next eight behaviors Paul lists are evils that destroy the harmony of the community. They exemplify alienation and hostility between persons rather than the loving mutual service for which Christians have been freed. *Enmities* means multiple hatreds, while *strife* suggests discord and contention. An attitude of utter selfishness is the root of *jealousy*. The Greek word used here for "anger" connotes volatility or flashes of uncontrolled rage. "Quarrels, dissensions, factions" all suggest the kind of self-obsessed ambition that ruthlessly exploits other people and tears a community into warring parties. *Envy* is the same Greek word that is used to describe the attitude of Jesus' enemies, which caused them to conspire to bring about his execution (see Mark 15:10 and Matt. 27:18). Having surrendered oneself to evil spirits—the gods of wine—was thought to underlie "drunkenness and carousing." Plainly Paul seeks to evoke in the minds of his readers the full range of sinfulness of which we are capable.

"The Fruit of the Spirit"

Fruit is singular, probably to suggest the organic nature of these qualities all growing out of the Christian personality, healed and unified by Christ. They are all manifestations of the divine love that indwells the Christian in the person of the Spirit. *Joy* is not so much the opposite of sorrow as the mind-set of rejoicing in Christ no matter the external circumstances. *Peace* is much more than the absence of strife. It is an inner quality of serenity that "looks on tempests and is never shaken." By *patience* Paul probably means persistence or endurance, being "long-tempered" in the trying situations of life. Both *kindness* and *generosity* are essential Christian attitudes and behavior patterns. *Faithfulness* here likely means trustworthiness. *Gentleness* is the same Greek word that is translated as "meek" in the third beatitude (see Matt. 5:5). It connotes submission to the will of God. *Self-control* is essential if we are to master our sinful impulses and manifest this fruit of the Spirit.

Helping Adults Become Involved

Preparing to Teach

As you prepare this lesson, note that with the fifth chapter of the letter to the Galatians Paul has moved from explaining theological concepts to exhorting them about ethical life-styles. This is a typical transition for Paul, who customarily grounds his discussion of Christian living on a previous presentation of doctrinal truths. Having argued forcefully in the first four chapters for the Galatians to realize their freedom in Christ, he now describes how that freedom is to be lived out. It will be beneficial to review the major points of doctrine that have been emphasized.

Read Galatians 5 carefully, using the material in "As You Read the Scripture." Make a list of your objectives for this lesson by asking yourself what points in this chapter are most relevant to the lives of your students. In order to personalize this material, try listing "works of the flesh" and "fruit of the Spirit" that you see in your own life.

The chief points of the lesson can be organized in this simple outline:

      I. Introduction
     II. Crucifying the sinful self
   III. Free to live
   IV. Bearing the fruit of Christ's Spirit

Collect several newspaper and magazine clippings—headlines and pictures are especially good—that illustrate "works of the flesh" and "fruit of the Spirit" as they are evidenced in contemporary life.

Have Bibles, pencils, and paper available for all students. A chalkboard or newsprint for writing and displaying will help you present your points.

Introducing the Main Question

"There may be several good evidences that a tree is a fig tree; but the highest and most proper evidence of it, is that it actually bears figs." So wrote the great American theologian Jonathan Edwards in his *A Treatise concerning Religious Affections*. This is precisely the point Paul makes. The attitudes and actions of a person's life are the proof that she or he has been freed by Christ from slavery to sin and law. The contrast between the two ways of life is sharp and clear. Christians are so intimately related to the Spirit that the qualities of Christlikeness manifest themselves as outgrowths of that union.

THIRD QUARTER

Developing the Lesson

I. Introduction

Relate to the class the C.S. Lewis story about rats in the cellar as found in "The Main Question." Encourage discussion of this analogy and how true they believe it to be in their own lives.

Point out that with the material in this lesson Paul shifts his emphasis from theological ideas to ethical admonitions. Remind the students of the similar shift in Romans 12 to practical application of doctrine in Christian living.

II. Crucifying the sinful self

Use the material in "The Works of the Flesh" portion of "The Scripture and the Main Question" and the comments on Galatians 5:13-21 in "As You Read the Scripture" to lead the class to an understanding of what Paul means by the "works of the flesh." Be certain that they are clear that Paul does not condemn all that has to do with the physical body. Use a display of newspaper clippings to stimulate discussion about manifestations of this kind of living in contemporary society. Make a list on the board headed "Works of the Flesh" and encourage the group to suggest those they see in our personal and corporate lives.

Be sure that the class understands that "crucifying the sinful self" is a process that continues over time. Even though the contrast between the two ways of life Paul describes is sharp, it is not accomplished instantaneously. Even committed Christians whose lives are indwelt by the Spirit usually harbor at least a few "rats in their cellars."

III. Free to love

Share with the class these comments by Charles B. Cousar:

> Persons freed by Jesus Christ are given the vocation to love one another. Paul does not hesitate to state this calling in the form of a command, an all-encompassing command without loopholes, which claims the total attention of the ones commanded. There may be contexts in which it is difficult to determine exactly what love demands, but there are no occasions where the command can be set aside, no conditions under which Christians are obligated to do something less. . . . Freedom is the basis for love, and love is the proper exercise of freedom. (Charles B. Cousar, Galatians in series *Interpretation: A Bible Commentary for Teaching and Preaching* [Louisville: John Knox Press, 1982], p. 133.)

Encourage discussion of these ideas. Use the material in "Called to Freedom" and "Become Slaves to One Another" to present the major points of this section.

IV. Bearing the fruit of Christ's Spirit

Write on the board the quotation from Jonathan Edwards, which is found at the beginning of "Introducing the Main Question." Discuss this quotation to make clear what Paul is saying about the Christian life. Display clippings that illustrate examples of "fruit of the Spirit" in contemporary people and society. Use the material in "The Fruit of the Spirit" and the commentary on

Galatians 5:1, 22-26 in "As You Read the Scripture." Under the heading "Fruit of the Spirit," lead the class in making a list on the board of particular expressions of such qualities as they see them manifested today.

Helping Class Members Act

Distribute three sheets of paper to each student and have them divide each sheet into three columns. The resulting nine sections should each be labelled with one of the examples of "fruit of the Spirit"—love, joy, peace, patience, kindness, generosity, faithfulness, gentleness, self-control. Challenge the group to take these sheets home and use them to record specific instances in their own lives in which their behavior toward other persons expresses one of these attributes. Encourage them to strive intentionally to manifest these qualities as fully and as often as possible, while being aware that what they are really doing is allowing the Spirit of Christ to produce fruit in and through them. Urge the class to find opportunities for loving service not only to friends, but also in the arenas of the larger society. The crying needs for ministries of peace and justice in the world must be met by persons motivated by the gospel of Christ.

Planning for Next Sunday

Ask the class to read Galatians 6 in preparation for concluding this unit.

Challenged to Love

Background Scripture: Galatians 6

The Main Question

Although the word *love* does not appear in the sixth chapter of Galatians, what is being described is the life of love that is to be characteristic of Christians. In their introductory text to a study of Christian ethics, Louis W. Hodges and Harmon L. Smith offer helpful insights into the nature of Christian love:

While Christianity does not specify precisely what one is to do it does show unmistakably the way a Christian is to decide to do. You are obliged always to do love, the one absolute to which all concrete decisions are relative. . . . In contrast to love conceived as an inner feeling Christian love is active. It is not so much something you feel as something you do. . . . Christian love is none other than the very giving of the self in service to the neighbor. To love is to put oneself at the disposal of neighbor for the neighbor's good. Love of neighbor means to go actively about the business of seeing to it that the real needs of the neighbor are met. (Harmon L. Smith and Louis W. Hodges, *The Christian and His Decisions: An Introduction to Christian Ethics* [Nashville and New York: Abingdon Press, 1969], pp. 25-26.)

In this lesson we will recognize the source of such love in the cross of Christ and the transformed life through the Spirit, which is made available to us. We will examine the implications of such love in the ways Christians relate to God and to other persons. What are the responsibilities involved in the command to love? What are appropriate attitudes toward one's own virtues? How are we to treat persons who have slipped into sinful behavior? How are we to understand the justice and judgment of God? How are Christians to live in the inescapable tension between the demands of this present world and the requirements of God's will? What does it mean to understand ourselves as a new creation living in a new order of existence?

Selected Scripture

King James Version

Galatians 6:1-10, 14-18

1 Brethren, if a man be overtaken in a fault, ye which are spiritual, restore such an one in the spirit of meekness; considering thyself, lest thou also be tempted.

2 Bear ye one another's burdens, and so fulfil the law of Christ.

3 For if a man think himself to be something, when he is nothing, he deceiveth himself.

4 But let every man prove his own work, and then shall he have rejoicing in himself alone, and not in another.

5 For every man shall bear his own burden.

6 Let him that is taught in the word communicate unto him that teacheth in all good things.

7 Be not deceived; God is not mocked: for whatsoever a man soweth, that shall he also reap.

8 For he that soweth to his flesh shall of the flesh reap corruption; but he that soweth to the Spirit shall of the Spirit reap life everlasting.

9 And let us not be weary in well doing: for in due season we shall reap, if we faint not.

10 As we have therefore opportunity, let us do good unto all men,

New Revised Standard Version

Galatians 6:1-10, 14-18

1 My friends, if anyone is detected in a transgression, you who have received the Spirit should restore such a one in a spirit of gentleness. Take care that you yourselves are not tempted. 2 Bear one another's burdens, and in this way you will fulfill the law of Christ. 3 For if those who are nothing think they are something, they deceive themselves. 4 All must test their own work; then that work, rather than their neighbor's work, will become a cause for pride. 5 For all must carry their own loads.

6 Those who are taught the word must share in all good things with their teacher.

7 Do not be deceived; God is not mocked, for you reap whatever you sow. 8 If you sow to your own flesh, you will reap corruption from the flesh; but if you sow to the Spirit, you will reap eternal life from the Spirit. 9 So let us not grow weary in doing what is right, for we will reap at harvest-time, if we do not give up. 10 So then, whenever we have an opportunity, let us work for the good of all, and especially for those

especially unto them who are of the household of faith.

....

14 But God forbid that I should glory, save in the cross of our Lord Jesus Christ, by whom the world is crucified unto me, and I unto the world.

15 For in Christ Jesus neither circumcision availeth anything, nor uncircumcision, but a new creature.

16 And as many as walk according to this rule, peace be on them, and mercy, and upon the Israel of God.

17 From henceforth let no man trouble me: for I bear in my body the marks of the Lord Jesus.

18 Brethren, the grace of our Lord Jesus Christ be with your spirit. Amen.

Key Verse: **As we have therefore opportunity, let us do good unto all men, especially unto them who are of the household of faith. Galatians 6:10**

of the family of faith.

....

14 May I never boast of anything except the cross of our Lord Jesus Christ, by which the world has been crucified to me, and I to the world. 15 For neither circumcision nor uncircumcision is anything; but a new creation is everything! 16 As for those who will follow this rule—peace be upon them, and mercy, and upon the Israel of God.

17 From now on, let no one make trouble for me; for I carry the marks of Jesus branded on my body.

18 May the grace of our Lord Jesus Christ be with your spirit, brothers and sisters. Amen.

Key Verse: **So then, whenever we have an opportunity, let us work for the good of all, and especially for those of the family of faith. Galatians 6:10**

As You Read the Scripture

Galatians 6:1-10. Paul continues to instruct these churches as to how they are to conduct themselves in the daily living of their faith.

Verse 1. It is unfortunately quite easy to get out of step with the guiding Spirit and to slip into unintentional sin. The emphasis is on the restoration of such a transgressor to right relationship with God and with the community, rather than on punishment of the offense. In the latter portion of the verse, Paul switches to the use of the singular pronoun to emphasize that each individual must look carefully to his or her own potential for transgression.

Verse 2. The burdens we are mutually to bear are the shortcomings of us all. Reciprocal forgiveness and reconciliation are ways through which we satisfy "the law of Christ"—the principle of love.

Verse 3. The contrast between "nothing" and "something" is as sharp as the Greek words could express. The danger is that we may become conceited and fail to recognize that we owe everything to Christ.

Verse 4. Everyone is to evaluate and critique her or his own behaviors and attitudes, rather than focusing on those of others. The word *test* is used for the process of trying metals for purity.

Verse 5. This verse is not contradictory of verse 2, but complements it. It refers to the responsibility for self-examination, which all Christians have.

Verse 6. The people of the church are obligated to care for the needs of their teachers—probably both material and spiritual.

Verses 7-8. The Greek for "mocked" literally means "to turn up one's nose." God cannot be ignored or slighted, for the divine moral law controls the outcome of events. One's rewards will be determined by the allegiance to which one's efforts are devoted.

Verse 9. The agricultural metaphor is continued with the emphasis placed on the necessity of resisting fatigue or "burnout" if we are to receive rewards from God.

Verse 10. "So then" is a typical Pauline expression as he sums up the application of his argument. Christians are to strive actively to promote the welfare of all persons and to be especially diligent in serving others within the church community.

Verses 14-18. The letter closes with a powerful reaffirmation of the themes Paul has been presenting.

Verses 14-15. The crucifixion of Christ is central to Paul's understanding of the Christian faith. It is the pivot of history, having changed the orientation of his life and that of all persons. This is why such legalities as circumcision are irrelevant. A new world order has been established by divine action.

Verse 16. "This rule" is the new standard, or measuring stick—the new values of the new order. Paul here prays for both the Christian church and the Jewish community.

Verse 17. For Paul, there is now nothing further to be said or done. His own relationship with Christ is evinced in his scars from various persecutions, which he views as the master's brand upon a slave.

Verse 18. Just as the letter begins with grace (1:3, 6), so also does it end. The closing "brothers and sisters" appears in no other epistle and is surely an additional indication of his affection for the Galatians.

The Scripture and the Main Question

Restoration Rather than Punishment

One of the recurring problems in any community of persons is that of how to deal with those who violate the regulations and standards of the group. Unfortunately, the community of the Christian church must face such situations frequently; being in Christ does not mean that persons are immediately exempt from all moral weakness and offenses. During some periods in the earlier history of the church, offenders were dealt with quite severely—often ostracized from the community and required to perform various public as well as private acts of penance before they could be readmitted. Today, most Christian churches tend to err in the opposite direction and fail to uphold clear moral expectations for their people. When members fall into sin, other people in the church become quite uncomfortable, not knowing how to behave in relationship to the offender. Lacking any system of discipline, we often simply gossip. Lacking any program for restoration, we frequently allow, if we do not push, transgressors to leave the church community.

Paul was sufficiently realistic to realize that Christians, while freed from bondage to sin, were not yet immune from occasional yieldings to temptation. He thought it important that the churches of Galatia know how to treat those who fall in order to restore such persons to the life of the community. Interestingly, Paul expresses no concern for punishment of the offender by the church, perhaps recognizing that this function was best left to God. He urges instead attitudes of compassion and empathy. Christians are to be nonjudgmental in relation to their sisters and brothers who err. Indeed, Paul urges Christians to go beyond attitudes of gentle acceptance to actually share the pain felt by the offender and actively help that person to bear it.

"Those Who Are Nothing Think They Are Something"

One reason for the gentle treatment of those within the community who transgress is the reality that, at one time or another, in one way or another, every Christian will succumb to the temptation to sin. Paul vigorously warns his readers against the dangers of self-righteous presumption and harsh judgment. We are reminded of Jesus' parable of the Pharisee and the tax collector praying in the Temple (Luke 18:9-14). Jesus condemns the smug self-congratulatory attitude of the devout religious person and commends the humble honesty of the sinner. This is the person who is truly in right relationship with God. Paul too points out that an attitude of condescension and condemnation toward others is a great offense to God. It is dangerous to withhold generous forgiveness from others unless one can be very sure one will not be in need of it: no one can rightly have that certainty.

One of our less admirable human qualities is the tendency to take credit for our positive attributes and the good actions we perform. I object to the saying: "What you have is God's gift to you; what you are is your gift to God." In truth, all we have and are that is good is the gracious gift of a loving God who uses many influences and people to help us. The story is told of a little girl who was having quite a struggle in learning how to print her name. At kindergarten during the day, teachers worked diligently, holding her hand and helping her learn the shapes of the letters. At home in the evenings and weekends, parents and siblings practiced with her patiently, guiding her pencil slowly to form the name. Finally one day the child succeeded. She excitedly carried the paper to her visiting grandmother and exclaimed, "Look, Grandma, and I did it all by myself!" Even maturing Christians are not free from the tendency to claim all the credit for ourselves.

"Don't Turn Up Your Nose at God"

The stress in Christianity upon forgiveness and gentleness is not to imply that God ignores the misdeeds of human beings. Indeed, the God of the Bible in both the Old and New Testaments is a God of justice and judgment. It is not so much that God specifically sends punishments on us. Rather, this universe, because it was created by a just God, is governed by moral law. Therefore, actions have inherent consequences. In the Scripture, sowing and reaping are often employed as a metaphor for these consequences and for the time of judgment. The fruit of the Spirit that Christians are to bear cannot be harvested successfully unless the proper seeds have first been sown and germinated with deep roots in the life of the Spirit.

Crucified to the World

The verb in Galatians 6:14*b* should be understood in the present progressive tense: the crucifixion between ourselves and the world is ongoing rather than completely accomplished. God's dramatic intervention in history in the life, death, and resurrection of Jesus Christ was world-changing. Henceforth, a new, reconciled relationship between God and the created order is made possible. But this new relationship is only progressively actualized in the conditions of human existence. Christians live in a state of tension between this world—this present sinful age—and the world to come—the future in which God's purpose will be fulfilled. We live in loyalty to a different master and so are called to live lives the present world cannot accept.

Boasting in the Cross

The cross of Christ with its horrible suffering might seem an unlikely, even inappropriate, object of boasting. But Christians view Good Friday from the perspective of Easter. The victory over sin and death won by the Resurrection gives meaning not only to the suffering of Christ, but to human suffering as well. This does not mean that we have all the answers to the difficult questions about tragedy and pain in life. We do, however, have the assurance that life has purpose and direction, that evil is not final, and that God, who loves us like an ideal parent, is ultimately in control.

Some of the most powerfully affirmative words of the entire Bible are those in Galatians 6:15b: "A new creation is everything!" God's action in Jesus Christ has established a new world order in which we are called to participate. In 2 Corinthians 5:17 (NEB), Paul expresses it this way: "For anyone united to Christ, there is a new creation: the old order has gone; a new order has already begun." Christians are the people of the new creation, enabled by the Spirit of Christ to live a new and eternal quality of life. C. S. Lewis puts it plainly: "Every Christian is to become a little Christ. The whole purpose of becoming a Christian is simply nothing else" (*Mere Christianity*, p. 153).

Helping Adults Become Involved

Preparing to Teach

A valuable way to begin your preparation is with a review of the major themes that have been presented in the four previous lessons on Galatians.

Read carefully Galatians 6, using "As You Read the Scripture" for assistance. Also reread 1 Corinthians 13, in which Paul offers his most comprehensive treatment of the theme of this lesson—Christian love in action.

The following outline covers the chief points of the lesson:

    I. Introduction and review
   II. Responsibilities involved in the command to love
       A. The distinctiveness of Christian love
       B. Dealing with those who slip into sin
       C. The dangers of self-conceit
  III. Living in the new creation
       A. The centrality of the cross
       B. A new people in a new age

Make copies for all students of the quotations from Hodges and Smith in "The Main Question" and "Introducing the Main Question." Bibles, hymnals, pencils, and paper should be available for everyone. A chalkboard or newsprint will be very useful also.

Introducing the Main Question

How is Christian love to be manifested in our living? This question and its implications are the focus of this concluding lesson in the series on Galatians. Louis W. Hodges and Harmon L. Smith will aid our comprehension of the issues:

> The distinctive character of Christian love lies not so much in what it demands that one do as in the reasons for making those demands. . . . [Christian love] is love of someone for [that person's] own sake, i.e., a relationship based on the fact that the person needs to be loved. [Christian love] is to give oneself to the other unreservedly, not counting the gain, without regard to qualities of the other, but solely because the other person has need of you. It is love of someone not because of who [that person] is or because of what [that person] is, but simply that he [or she] is. The epitome of this kind of relationship is demonstrated in the life and death of Jesus. (*The Christian and His Decisions*, pp. 26-27.)

Developing the Lesson

I. Introduction and review

Allow each class member to spend a few minutes with pencil and paper to make notes on his or her recollections of the main points that have come out of the study of Galatians thus far. Make a list on the board by sharing notes; be sure to use your own list so as to be certain to include everything.

Use the material in "The Main Question" to introduce the lesson. Distribute the copies of the Hodges and Smith quotations to move into the second part of the outline.

II. Responsibilities involved in the command to love

A. The distinctiveness of Christian love

Divide the class into small groups and allow some time for discussion of the quotations. Reassemble and share ideas. Be certain that the group understands that Christian love is unconditional, that it involves loving persons simply because they are loved and valued by God, that it is made possible by the love of God known to us through Jesus.

B. Dealing with those who slip into sin

Use the "Restoration Rather than Punishment" section of "The Scripture and the Main Question" and the relevant portions of "As You Read the Scripture." Encourage the class to talk about examples (though not, of course, individuals) of the difficulties we have in the church in dealing with members who commit sin.

C. The dangers of self-conceit

The section entitled "Those Who Are Nothing Think They Are Something" offers help in presenting this point. Another C. S. Lewis quotation may provoke some valuable discussion: "Whenever we find that our religious life is making us feel that we are good—above all, that we are better than someone else—I think we may be sure that we are being acted on, not by God, but by the devil."

III. Living in the new creation

  A. The centrality of the Cross

A good way to introduce this concept might be to have the class read together some hymns that focus on the meaning of the Cross. Two examples, based on Galatians 6:14, might be "Ask Ye What Great Thing I Know" and "When I Survey the Wondrous Cross." Others with similar ideas are "In the Cross of Christ I Glory," "Beneath the Cross of Jesus," and "Jesus, Keep Me Near the Cross."

Have the class look carefully at Galatians 6:14 and use the material in the last three parts of "The Scripture and the Main Question" to develop its meaning.

  B. A new people in a new age

There are three orders of existence in the Christian understanding of history. First there is the created order as described in Genesis 1–2—a universe characterized by loving, harmonious relationships in accord with the will of God. Then sin intruded as humans put their own wills ahead of that of God and in their selfish rebellion started the fallen order. All of human history has been lived in this fallen order. With the life, death, and resurrection of Christ, God inaugurated the redeemed order of existence. Perhaps it might better be called the *redeeming* order, for it is a process through which God and God's people work through the years for renewal and reconciliation. Finally the redeemed order will become a full reality when the divine purposes are fulfilled and the creation is restored to harmony under the rule of God.

Use the last paragraph of "Boasting in the Cross" to close, emphasizing the new creation that began with Jesus and that we as God's transformed people are to work toward making complete.

Helping Class Members Act

Encourage discussion of how the responsibilities involved in the command to love are being, or are failing to be, fulfilled in your lives as individuals, as a church, and as a society. Be as specific and as honest as possible. What are attitudes and actions toward those who fall into sin? Are we judgmental and self-righteous rather than gentle and restorative? How Christian are our attitudes and actions toward ourselves? Can we love ourselves as God does and still humbly see our shortcomings? Do we accept and use all that is good about us as a gracious gift for which we deserve no credit?

Planning for Next Sunday

Prayerfully consider how the themes of this unit apply in your life.

FOURTH QUARTER

GOD REDEEMS A PEOPLE: EXODUS AND THE LAWS

UNIT I: DELIVERANCE FROM OPPRESSION
Pat McGeachy

FOUR LESSONS   JUNE 5–26

If you try to read the Bible straight through from beginning to end, you will get bogged down for a long time in the desert. So, this quarter, we are taking a rapid trip through the wilderness with the wandering children of Israel, dealing with key passages from four of the five "books of Moses."

This unit, based on the early chapters of Exodus, looks at the plight of the Israelites, who had been enslaved by the Egyptians, God's concern for the Israelites, the coming of Moses, and the mighty acts by which God rescued the Israelites and started them on the way to freedom in their own land. There is advice and counsel here for us in the twentieth century, for God is with us in our troubles and will guide us out of them, if we will trust and obey.

Questions raised in this unit deal with a number of deeply felt needs. Does God really care for us in the dilemma of human life in this century? Are we enslaved by false goals and misplaced allegiance? Do our cries for help go unheard? In what sense is each of us called by God for jobs that need to be done? How can we hear and identify such calls? How can we be moved to obedience? What addictions keep us from doing what we ought to do and what we want to do? Are we stuck with them? We are beset from behind by modern equivalents of the Egyptians, and the way ahead is blocked by deeper waters than the Red Sea. Is there any use in complaining to God? Can miracles occur in our era?

It is the thesis of these lessons that a New Exodus is under way in Jesus Christ, and that we can avail ourselves of that delivering power to find new hope and freedom.

LESSON 1   JUNE 5

God Cares

Background Scripture: Exodus 1–2

The Main Question

I haven't kept count, but I would guess that in the past forty years I have been in close touch with about two thousand people who have had some sort of misfortune in their lives, many so serious that they would speak of

305

them as calamities or disasters. From them I have learned to respect the remarkable capacity of ordinary people to deal victoriously with such troubles. However, even among those whose faith is strong, I often hear the disturbing question, How could God let this happen? So pervasive is this question that many books have been written in an attempt to deal with it. One of the most popular of such writings has been the best-seller by Harold Kirschner, *When Bad Things Happen to Good People.* His struggle with the problem can be summed up like this: I would rather believe in a God who is not all powerful than to believe in a God who does not care. It is important to all of us to believe that we make a difference to God.

This question arises not only when bad things happen to us, but also whenever we stop and think about the negatives of nature, both great and small. Why did God make mosquitoes? What is the possible good in an earthquake? In such a vast, seemingly infinite universe, how can life on our planet make a difference to anyone? Why should an earthquake make any more difference to the universe than disturbing an anthill does to us?

Does God care? Is there anybody out there? We have to deal in this lesson with an enslaved people, under intolerable oppression. It should not surprise us that they too cried out our question. And it should comfort us to hear the answer that came.

Selected Scripture

King James Version

Exodus 1:8-11

8 Now there arose up a new king over Egypt, which knew not Joseph.

9 And he said unto his people, Behold, the people of the children of Israel are more and mightier than we:

10 Come on, let us deal wisely with them; lest they multiply, and it come to pass, that, when there falleth out any war, they join also unto our enemies, and fight against us, and so get them up out of the land.

11 Therefore they did set over them taskmasters to afflict them with their burdens. And they built for Pharaoh treasure cities, Pithom and Raamses.

2:1-9, 23-25

1 And there went a man of the house of Levi, and took to wife a daughter of Levi.

2 And the woman conceived, and bare a son: and when she saw him that he was a goodly child, she hid him three months.

New Revised Standard Version

Exodus 1:8-11

8 Now a new king arose over Egypt, who did not know Joseph. 9 He said to his people, "Look, the Israelite people are more numerous and more powerful than we. 10 Come, let us deal shrewdly with them, or they will increase and, in the event of war, join our enemies and fight against us and escape from the land." 11 Therefore they set taskmasters over them to oppress them with forced labor. They built supply cities, Pithom and Rameses, for Pharaoh.

2:1-9, 23-25

1 Now a man from the house of Levi went and married a Levite woman. 2 The woman conceived and bore a son; and when she saw that he was a fine baby, she hid him three months. 3 When she could hide him no longer she got a

3 And when she could not longer hide him, she took for him an ark of bulrushes, and daubed it with slime and with pitch, and put the child therein; and she laid it in the flags by the river's brink.

4 And his sister stood afar off, to wit what would be done to him.

5 And the daughter of Pharaoh came down to wash herself at the river; and her maidens walked along by the river's side; and when she saw the ark among the flags, she sent her maid to fetch it.

6 And when she had opened it, she saw the child: and, behold, the babe wept. And she had compassion on him, and said, This is one of the Hebrews' children.

7 Then said his sister to Pharaoh's daughter, Shall I go and call to thee a nurse of the Hebrew women, that she may nurse the child for thee?

8 And Pharaoh's daughter said to her, Go. And the maid went and called the child's mother.

9 And Pharaoh's daughter said unto her, Take this child away, and nurse it for me, and I will give thee thy wages. And the woman took the child, and nursed it.

....

23 And it came to pass in process of time, that the king of Egypt died: and the children of Israel sighed by reason of the bondage, and they cried, and their cry came up unto God by reason of the bondage.

24 And God heard their groaning, and God remembered his covenant with Abraham, with Isaac, and with Jacob.

25 And God looked upon the children of Israel, and God had respect unto them.

Key Verse: **And God heard their groaning, and God remembered his covenant with Abraham, with Isaac, and with Jacob. Exodus 2:24**

papyrus basket for him, and plastered it with bitumen and pitch; she put the child in it and placed it among the reeds on the bank of the river. 4 His sister stood at a distance, to see what would happen to him.

5 The daughter of Pharaoh came down to bathe at the river, while her attendants walked beside the river. She saw the basket among the reeds and sent her maid to bring it. 6 When she opened it, she saw the child. He was crying, and she took pity on him, "This must be one of the Hebrews' children," she said. 7 Then his sister said to Pharaoh's daughter, "Shall I go and get you a nurse from the Hebrew women to nurse the child for you?" 8 Pharaoh's daughter said to her, "Yes." So the girl went and called the child's mother. 9 Pharaoh's daughter said to her, "Take this child and nurse it for me, and I will give you your wages." So the woman took the child and nursed it.

....

23 After a long time the king of Egypt died. The Israelites groaned under their slavery, and cried out. Out of the slavery their cry for help rose up to God. 24 God heard their groaning, and God remembered his covenant with Abraham, Isaac, and Jacob. 25 God looked upon the Israelites, and God took notice of them.

Key Verse: **God heard their groaning, and God remembered his covenant with Abraham, Isaac, and Jacob. Exodus 2:24**

As You Read the Scripture

Exodus 1. This chapter is designed to account for the nervousness of the Egyptians over the increasing presence of the Israelites in their country. Note how many words are used to describe their multiplication. See especially verses 7, 12, and 20.

Verse 5. For a detailed accounting of this number, see Genesis 46:8-27. There may have been a good many more, if you add wives, grandsons, daughters, granddaughters, and servants. By the time of the Exodus the number was a considerable multitude (see Exod. 12:37-38, which numbers only the adult males). Some say it was in the millions.

Verse 8. The pharaoh mentioned here may have been Rameses II (about 1340 B.C.), one of the great Egyptian kings, famous for his monuments and temples, but others date this time as much as a hundred years earlier. At any rate, the times have changed, and the old "cousin system" no longer works. The new king may not have known Joseph personally, but, whoever he was, he obviously had introduced a new policy with respect to the Israelites.

Verses 8-14. The new king tried to "deal shrewdly"—that is, to play a political game in which he kept the Israelites in subjection, but made use of them as laborers. He tried to "eat his cake and have it too." But there was something remarkable about this people; no matter what the king did, they remained a problem to him.

Verse 17. The midwives were more concerned about their human obligations than about the orders of their king. Their actions make us think of a few brave Christians during the Nazi persecutions, who gave safe haven to their Jewish friends.

Exodus 2. Even before their cries (v. 23), God was preparing for Israel's deliverance by raising up a leader. After the fact we can look back and see that God knows our needs even before we ask (see Matt. 6:32). This story of Moses' birth probably became a part of the tradition after he had become a famous leader, much like our stories about George Washington as a boy.

Verse 6. The natural compassion of the midwives is also found in Pharaoh's daughter. There are clearly times when our instincts are wiser than the rules imposed on us by society.

Verse 10. The story skips over the boyhood and young manhood of Moses (as does the story of the young Jesus in the Gospels). According to Acts 7:22, he was educated in things Egyptian. Could he have learned something of monotheism from his teachers, or did this come from his Hebrew traditions? Though some of the earlier pharaohs had tried to put all their gods together into one, most scholars believe that Egypt was still polytheistic at this time. Perhaps, trained in both Egyptian and Hebrew traditions, Moses came to a deeper understanding of God, as did Paul, who understood both Jewish and Greek traditions.

Verse 14. The Israelites do not yet trust Moses. He has not, so to speak, won his spurs. Before he can be accepted by them, he must undergo a time of preparation.

Verses 15-22. Moses' time in Midian can be compared to that of John the Baptist in the wilderness (Luke 1:80) and Paul in Arabia (Gal. 1:17).

The Scripture and the Main Question

"The Times, They Are A-changin' "

I remember when the cost of sending a letter by first-class mail was three cents. And we had what was called a "penny post-card," with the one-cent stamp printed on it in green ink, so that you could actually communicate across the country for a penny, including the cost of the paper. At the time that I am writing this, the cost of a first-class stamp costs twenty-nine cents, an increase of almost 1,000 percent! If that doesn't seem like a lot, consider what it costs to buy a house these days, in comparison to what it cost a generation ago. Times do change.

Population growth is even more dramatic. When the first census was taken in the United States in 1790, there were fewer than four million people in the entire country. I would tell you how many there are today, but the figure grows so rapidly that by the time this gets into print any estimate would be out of date. I can only say that in 1790 the center of population in the young country was somewhere east of Baltimore, Maryland; today it is across the Mississippi River, somewhere in the state of Missouri. Demographers tell us that more people are alive in the world today than all who ever lived in history!

You can say, "Well, all things are relative." And they are, but quantitative changes become qualitative. When an electric fan blade rotates very slowly you can almost count the turns, but when it reaches a certain speed it becomes invisible. When the population gets to a certain level, it becomes an environmental disaster. All this means that, like it or not, the whole tenor of our lives changes; we wake up one day and there has arisen a pharaoh who knew not Joseph. Things just don't work as they used to.

In ancient Egypt, both for the Hebrews and for the Egyptians, life had become unmanageable. The king of Egypt tried to keep things the same through oppression, but that was like sitting on the lid of a pot to keep it from boiling over. Sooner or later, a disaster happens. I have seen it happen in churches that have outgrown their building or whose neighborhood has undergone a radical population shift. Some of us try to keep things the same by sitting on the lid. We try to keep our church a suburban congregation when it has become an inner-city church. Or we get angry, split over whether to relocate. It doesn't have to be done that way. And it didn't have to be done that way in ancient Egypt. The two populations, Egyptians and Hebrews, could have learned to live together creatively in their new situation. Or they could have come to a peaceful decision about sending out colonies. Instead, because the pharaoh "hardened his heart," they set out on a collision course that, in the long run, turned out to be a disaster for the Egyptians.

A Life of Slavery

Most of us in free America have a hard time identifying with those who live, or have lived, in a totalitarian state or who have been literally enslaved by others. The television series "Roots," based on the book by Alex Haley, helped us to get a feeling for the life of slaves, but to understand it completely, as they say, "you had to be there." Even today in America there are slaves. There are those who are enslaved by addictions. There are people trapped in destructive marriages or living with parents who treat them as slaves. And there is not one of us who has not known, at some time in our lives, what it is like to be a slave to that universal human condition known as sin.

On the larger level, there are conditions that create slavery. Grinding poverty is one such condition and, related to that, there is ignorance. Think what it would be like to live in a world where all the jobs go to people who are skilled at language or computer programming when you can barely read and write. I can picture a young man, sitting in his parents' dilapidated house, looking out at what appears to be a wonderful world of expensive cars, important jobs, and all sorts of luxuries that are beyond his reach. I can hear him say to himself, "Nobody gives a rap about me." His options are few, and unless something happens to intervene, he is liable to give up, to turn to crime, or to waste his life on the seductive world of drugs, with their momentary pleasures that in the end destroy. I can see an elderly woman, rocking in a lonely room, out of touch with the world that speeds past her window, unable to communicate with her children and grandchildren, listening to the ticking of an out-dated clock and wondering, "Does anybody care?"

God Cares

The cries of those persons are not unlike the cry of the Israelites in Exodus 2:23-25:

After a long time the king of Egypt died. The Israelites groaned under their slavery, and cried out. Out of the slavery their cry for help rose up to God. God heard their groaning, and God remembered his covenant with Abraham, Isaac, and Jacob. God looked upon the Israelites, and God took notice of them.

It is the central message of the Christian gospel that God cares. In the language of John 3:16, we would say that God loved the world so much that Jesus, a latter-day Moses, came into the world, at enormous sacrifice, to rescue us from slavery, that the world through him might be saved. To the young man without money and education, to the elderly woman cut off from the world of her children, and to you and me, in whatever trap we find ourselves, God comes. The psalmist gave the promise long ago (Ps. 145:18-19; see also 34:17-18):

> The LORD is near to all who call on him,
>   to all who call on him in truth.
> He fulfills the desire of all who fear him;
>   he also hears their cry, and saves them.

But they will not hear this good news unless Moses comes to them. And who will be Moses in our time? Can it be that we are still in Egypt and that the church still has a job to do in this rapidly changing world? Does God have a task for us?

Helping Adults Become Involved

Preparing to Teach

Because this is the first lesson of a new quarter, and an introduction to the wilderness experience of the Israelites, prepare by giving yourself a fresh overview of the first five books of the Bible, sometimes called the Pentateuch, or the Five Books of Moses. One way to do this, if you have a Bible that has paragraph subheads or brief summary phrases at the top or bottom of the pages, is to scan quickly through your Bible from Genesis through Deuteronomy, reading only those subheads. Another way would be to find a commentary that contains outlines of each of the books, and scan those outlines. (The *Abingdon Bible Dictionary,* for example, has a summary of the contents of each book listed under its name.) If you promise not to tell, I'll let you in on a secret that some preachers use when we want to refresh ourselves with a considerable amount of biblical history and haven't time to read 187 chapters. Get a good children's Bible storybook and read the material covering these chapters!

At the very least, make sure you know where we are dipping into the Bible's history, at the time of the Exodus. Don't worry if you can't pin down the date exactly, because the Bible is not clear on this point, and scholars disagree. I have a *very* much oversimplified chronology that helps me put things into perspective; you can use it if you like, remembering that in some cases I am off by as much as a 100 years or so, but these dates are easy to remember:

2000	1500	1000	500	+	500	1000	1500	2000
Abraham	Exodus	David	Fall of Babylon		Jesus Christ	Fall of Rome	East-West Split	Reformation	Today

Note that our lesson begins at the period in history almost as many years before Christ as Columbus's voyage came after Christ.

When you have completed this exercise, read the background scripture for this week's lesson and try to imagine what it would be like to have been a slave in ancient Egypt. Here is my outline of the material:

    I. The multiplying Israelites (chap. 1)
       A. Their increasing numbers (vv. 1-7)
       B. The cruel oppression (vv. 8-14)
       C. The courageous midwives (vv. 16-22)
    II. The coming of a deliverer (chap. 2)
       A. The birth of Moses (vv. 1-4)
       B. Pharaoh's daughter (vv. 5-10)
       C. The killing of the Egyptian and Moses' flight (vv. 11-22)
       D. God and the people's groaning (vv. 23-25)

Introducing the Main Question

This shouldn't be a hard question to introduce because it is universal. Give each class member a three-by-five card and ask them to write on one side the answer to this question: Have you ever been a slave to anybody or anything? On the other side, they are to name something that really worries them. Ask the class to keep these cards for themselves and to think about what they have written as the lesson proceeds. And give them these questions to think about: Does God care about your captivity? Does what you worry about matter to God?

FOURTH QUARTER

Developing the Lesson

I. The multiplying Israelites (chap. 1)

Briefly set the stage by reminding the class that the descendants of Jacob have been in Egypt for over four hundred years. You may wish to discuss with them the sorts of changes, talked about in "The Scripture and the Main Question," that have happened to us in our own lifetimes.

A. Their increasing numbers (vv. 1-7)

To help in understanding the point of view of both the Egyptians and the Israelites, think about the differences made in the United States by the growth of ethnic populations. Perhaps in your community a particular group will be most obvious.

B. The cruel oppression (vv. 8-14)

Help the class to see what a mistake it is to oppress and subjugate such newcomers in our midst. We are only beginning to discover in America what a wonderful gift the diverse ethnic communities are. Both we and the Egyptians could have avoided much pain if we had only responded to their presence in a positive way.

C. The courageous midwives (vv. 16-22)

These courageous women may have been Egyptian citizens; the verse could be translated "the midwives of the Hebrew women." At any rate, their obligation as human beings outweighed their duty to the king. In the face of this terrible form of birth control they could only do what they thought God would have wanted them to do. They were practicing a form of civil disobedience.

II. The coming of a deliverer (chap. 2)

Even before the people cried out, God knew their needs and was preparing a deliverer.

A. The birth of Moses (vv. 1-4)

This familiar story and the next one are well known to Sunday school children.

B. Pharaoh's daughter (vv. 5-10)

C. The killing of the Egyptian and Moses' flight (vv. 11-22)

This unfortunate event turns out to have good consequences (see Rom. 8:28).

D. The people's groaning (vv. 23-25)

These three verses are an expression of our main question: Does God care? Though the scripture says God remembered, please note that God had known about it all along, and was already working on their deliverance.

Helping Class Members Act

Ask the class to reflect in the coming week on the presence of God in whatever difficulties they may have, and to see and feel what a difference it makes to know that God cares.

Planning for Next Sunday

Ask the class to read Exodus 3:1–4:27, to keep their eyes open for burning bushes, and their ears open for God's call.

God's Call and Our Response

Background Scripture: Exodus 3:1–4:17

The Main Question

God calls everybody. We are used to thinking about God calling persons to be pastors or missionaries or some specifically religious task, but we forget that God calls all of us. The word most commonly used in biographical sketches to mean what a person does for a living is *vocation*. If we want to talk about what we do on our own time, we call it our *avocation*. Now, of course, the word *vocation* means a "calling." (Note the root *vocal*, or "voice," hiding in the word.) Even though you may not think of what you do with your life as a "calling," it is, or it should be. There are those whose calling is to raise children or grow cabbages or serve as a career diplomat. There are many callings in the world. So many, in fact, that Christians often have difficulty distinguishing among them. (Because I have many interests, I applied to schools of medicine, architecture, and music before I ended up in theology school. I even once wrote to Walt Disney, wondering if he would like to hire me as an animator; fortunately, he thought better of it.)

Here are some key questions to ask yourself when you are considering a call: How do you know it is God calling? If you decide it is God, then how do you respond? Is it possible to refuse God? What if you don't feel good enough to do what you think God wants?

Let me sum these questions up in one: How can we hear, understand, and obey the call of God? The familiar story of Moses and the blazing bush is a good one to help us find an answer to that.

Selected Scripture

King James Version	New Revised Standard Version
Exodus 3:10-15a	*Exodus 3:10-15a*
10 Come now therefore, and I will send thee unto Pharaoh, that thou mayest bring forth my people the children of Israel out of Egypt.	10 "So come, I will send you to Pharaoh to bring my people, the Israelites, out of Egypt." 11 But Moses said to God, "Who am I that I should go to Pharaoh, and bring the Israelites out of Egypt?" 12 He said, "I will be with you; and this shall be the sign for you that it is I who sent you: when you have brought the people out of Egypt, you shall worship God on this mountain."
11 And Moses said unto God, Who am I, that I should go unto Pharaoh, and that I should bring forth the children of Israel out of Egypt?	
12 And he said, Certainly I will be with thee; and this shall be a token unto thee, that I have sent thee: When thou hast brought forth the people out of Egypt, ye shall serve God upon this mountain.	
13 And Moses said unto God,	13 But Moses said to God, "If I

313

Behold, when I come unto the children of Israel, and shall say unto them, The God of your fathers hath sent me unto you; and they shall say to me, What is his name? what shall I say unto them?

14 And God said unto Moses, I AM THAT I AM: and he said, Thus shalt thou say unto the children of Israel, I AM hath sent me unto you.

15 And God said moreover unto Moses, Thus shalt thou say unto the children of Israel, The LORD God of your fathers, the God of Abraham, the God of Isaac, and the God of Jacob, hath sent me unto you:

come to the Israelites and say to them, 'The God of your ancestors has sent me to you,' and they ask me, 'What is his name?' what shall I say to them?" 14 God said to Moses, "I AM WHO I AM." He said further, "Thus you shall say to the Israelites, 'I AM has sent me to you.'" 15 God also said to Moses, "Thus you shall say to the Israelites, 'The LORD, the God of your ancestors, the God of Abraham, the God of Isaac, and the God of Jacob, has sent me to you'."

4:1-5, 10-12

1 And Moses answered and said, But, behold, they will not believe me, nor hearken unto my voice: for they will say, The LORD hath not appeared unto thee.

2 And the LORD said unto him, What is that in thine hand? And he said, A rod.

3 And he said, Cast it on the ground. And he cast it on the ground, and it became a serpent; and Moses fled from before it.

4 And the LORD said unto Moses, Put forth thine hand, and take it by the tail. And he put forth his hand, and caught it, and it became a rod in his hand:

5 That they may believe that the LORD God of their fathers, the God of Abraham, the God of Isaac, and the God of Jacob, hath appeared unto thee.

4:1-5, 10-12

1 Then Moses answered, "But suppose they do not believe me or listen to me, but say, 'The LORD did not appear to you.'" 2 The LORD said to him, "What is that in your hand?" He said, "A staff." 3 And he said, "Throw it on the ground." So he threw the staff on the ground, and it became a snake; and Moses drew back from it. 4 Then the LORD said to Moses, "Reach out your hand, and seize it by the tail"—so he reached out his hand and grasped it, and it became a staff in his hand—5 "so that they may believe that the LORD, the God of their ancestors, the God of Abraham, the God of Isaac, and the God of Jacob, has appeared to you."

....

10 And Moses said unto the LORD, O my Lord, I am not eloquent, either heretofore, nor since thou hast spoken unto thy servant: but I am slow of speech, and of a slow tongue.

11 And the LORD said unto him, Who hath made man's mouth? or who maketh the dumb, or deaf, or the seeing, or the blind? have not I the LORD?

....

10 But Moses said to the LORD, "O my Lord, I have never been eloquent, neither in the past nor even now that you have spoken to your servant; but I am slow of speech and slow of tongue." 11 Then the LORD said to him, "Who gives speech to mortals? Who makes them mute or deaf, seeing or blind? Is it not I, the LORD? 12 Now go, and I will be with

12 Now therefore go, and I will be with thy mouth, and teach thee what thou shalt say.

your mouth and teach you what you are to speak."

Key Verse: **Come now therefore, and I will send thee unto Pharaoh, that thou mayest bring forth my people the children of Israel out of Egypt. Exodus 3:10**

Key Verse: **So come, I will send you to Pharaoh to bring my people, the Israelites, out of Egypt. Exodus 3:10**

As You Read the Scripture

Exodus 3. This is one of the key chapters in all of the Bible, and one of the great theophanies (appearance of God). Others you may want to look at are Isaiah 6:1-9 and 1 Kings 19:1-18. Elijah's experience is especially interesting because it happened at the same place as Moses' vision: Mt. Horeb (or Sinai). Christians sometimes think of the coming of Jesus as the great theophany, though we must remember that he was much more than a mere "appearance."

Verse 1. Midian, where Moses had been living, was a region in the Arabian desert near the Gulf of Akabah, the eastern of the two fingers reaching north from the Red Sea; the western gulf is Suez. If you visualize the Arabian Peninsula pointing down like a triangle between these two gulfs, Mt. Sinai (also called Mt. Horeb, meaning "desert") is midway between them.

Verse 6. In addition to taking off his shoes, Moses hid his face, another sign of respect. But it may also simply mean that God was too bright to look at (see Exod. 19:21 and 33:18-20). In spite of this, there were times when the people did see God (Exod. 24:11) and survive.

Verse 14. The name of God is here associated with the Hebrew verb *hayah,* "to be." The name is usually translated "I Am What I Am," though it can be the future, "I Will Be What I Will Be," or even causative, "I Cause to Happen What I Cause to Happen." In any case, it is a proper name, and one considered so holy by pious Jews that it is never pronounced. (This is connected, of course, to the third commandment, Exod. 20:7). Ancient Hebrew was written without vowels, but these were later added as small dots, or "pointings." When the four consonants YHWH were encountered, the vowels to another Hebrew word, *adonai,* meaning "the Lord" were written in it, instead of the vowels for *Yahweh.* To this day, a Jew who reads aloud the Hebrew Bible always says "adonai," instead of the divine name. But so do we! Note that in your Bible, either King James or New Revised Standard Versions, YHWH is always translated LORD, with four capital letters.

Before we leave this, note how, in John 8:58-59, Jesus comes close to blaspheming, in the eyes of the other Jews, by saying, "Before Abraham was, I am." Elsewhere in this Gospel are other "I am" statements on the part of Jesus (see John 6:35; 8:12; 10:7, 11; 11:25; 14:6; 15:1). Do you think they, too, might be related to the divine name?

Exodus 4:1-17. These verses tell the story of Moses' reluctance, for which we can be grateful. Like the rash mistakes of Simon Peter, these human failings on the part of the great Lawgiver are a comfort to us ordinary mortals.

Verses 1-5. God teaches Moses three magic tricks. The first is to turn his shepherd's staff into a snake. Serpent tricks were common among the Egyptians; see 7:11-12. Only this first trick is recorded as actually being done by Moses.

Verses 6-8. The second trick: the leprous hand.

Verse 9. The third trick: turning water into blood.

Verses 10-17. Moses' real reluctance is his lack of experience at public speaking; Aaron is selected as his mouthpiece.

The Scripture and the Main Question

Going about Your Business

When I was a very young man, I felt called to preach, but I wasn't sure that my call was genuine. So I asked my father, "How do you know if you are called?" "Try as hard as you can," he said, "to get into something else. Then, if you still end up as an ordained minister, you will know that you were called." Of course, he was being a little facetious, but in essence he was right. It's a little like fishing with a cork. Lots of time the float bobs and jiggles, and you think you have a bite, but when you really do get a bite, there is no question about it. What was Moses doing when the call came? He was carrying out his family responsibility, taking care of the sheep. The best way to prepare yourself for God's call is to go faithfully about the business of being a good person. Thus Samuel (1 Sam. 3) and Isaiah (Isa. 6:1-9) went about their business in the Temple, and thus Jesus' first disciples (Mark 1:16-20) went about the business of fishing, and there, in the midst of their faithful daily work, God's call came. Thus did the call reach John Wesley, faithfully at his prayers, and thus it will come to you and to me.

The Burning Bush

When God's call comes, it is often in the most unexpected manner. Who would have looked for a burning bush? What do you think it looked like? Do you suppose it gave off heat? Note that the bush was "blazing, yet it was not consumed." In this way it has become for many a symbol for the church. We are to be "on fire for the Lord," but not burned up or destroyed by our zeal. Instead, we are to increase in both warmth and light for others.

And the church, like a burning bush, continues to be a channel of God's call for many. But the call does not always come in a religious setting. In Moses' case, it was out in the desert, and for Peter, Andrew, James, and John, it was on the shore of a lake. For some people, God's call comes in the form of a pressing need, such as compassion for the homeless or the ill. On the strength of such concerns fine teachers or physicians have been born, and only later did they begin to theologize about their calling, to realize that it had been God searching for them all along. Some find the call coming largely from within, through the exercise of a talent or gift. A young actor spent many years sharpening his skills to entertain people, only to discover that all along God had been preparing him to use those skills to reach people with the gospel. The Apostle Paul's preparation was somewhat like this. He spent a lifetime learning theology and honing his rabbinical mind to razor sharpness, until God put him to work as the great explainer of the faith. If you want to be called of God, become the best person you know how to be, and God will use you for good and glory.

The Name of God

In our day, people's names are usually a device for identification; a number would do as well. But in earlier times people's names hinted at their occupations (Carter, Wright, Cooper, Smith) or their physical characteristics (Black, White, Short). In the Bible there are numerous accounts of people having their names changed to say something about their character or their calling—Jacob to Israel, Simon to Peter. Names in the Scriptures seem almost to have a spiritual power about them. Surely the name of God is no exception.

Note that in the Bible the vast majority of people have the name of God in their names, either in the form of *el* (Daniel, Elizabeth, Elisha, Samuel) or in the form of *YHWH* (Joshua, Isaiah, Jesus). But what does God's name mean, all by itself?

> God's name is holy and terrible (Ps. 111:9).
> God's name is to be called upon (Joel 2:32).
> God's name is to be given glory (Ps. 115:1).
> God's name is given to God's children (Rev. 14:1).
> God's name is to be hallowed (Matt. 6:9).
> God's name is the source of our help (Ps. 124:8).

(I haven't room to continue this exercise, but you can do it yourself; look up *name* in a concordance and browse through the references.)

Reality

Let us, for the moment, take God's name literally. If God says to us, "My name is I AM," then, in a sense, we are being told that whatever exists is God. To put it another way, a believer says, "All things are important." An atheist says, "Nothing matters."

Of course, no responsible atheist would say such a thing. And every believer knows that you can't be too careful not to say, "Everything is God"; that belief is called Pantheism. Augustine said that you can look at anything in the universe, say a tiny flower, and say of it, "This also is Thou." But, Augustine added, you also have to say, "Neither is this Thou."

If God really is I AM, then all the universe somehow partakes of God. God's name is everywhere, all around us, but we fail to notice. Just as, I suppose, a fish in the ocean doesn't know that he is wet, so also we do not sense God all around us. Unless, as sometimes happens, a bush catches on fire or we hear someone speak "with authority, and not as the scribes" (Matt. 7:28), and we are suddenly given a glimpse of the truth that lies all around us. To see this is to have your life changed forever. You may ever after wish to pray:

> God be in my head, and in my understanding;
> God be in my eyes, and in my looking;
> God be in my mouth, and in my speaking;
> God be in my heart, and in my thinking;
> God be at my end, and at my departing.

Helping Adults Become Involved

Preparing to Teach

Of course you will want to read the two chapters for this week. Decide in advance how you are going to deal with the divine name, YHWH. In some older versions of the Bible, YHWH was mistakenly translated Jehovah, combining the consonants of *YHWH* (*J* and *Y* are interchangeable in Hebrew) and the vowels of *adonai,* "Lord." *Jehovah* became a much-loved word in some of our hymns, and even became part of the name of one denomination, but it is a questionable form of the word.

In the spirit of Exodus 20:7, I like to avoid using the divine name altogether, but in teaching this lesson you will occasionally need to say it out loud. In its written form, the difficulty can be avoided, as the Bible does, by printing it LORD, but that isn't clear when it is spoken. I think you will need to use a chalkboard or a magic marker on newsprint to help make yourself clear this week.

In addition, as you prepare to help the class think about the meaning of God's call to them, reflect on your calling as a church school teacher. I am trying to think seriously about my calling as a writer of these lesson helps. We must all keep this in mind. You may want to pray Henry Davies' prayer, which I have printed above.

Here is this week's outline:

    I. Moses' experience of God (Exod. 3:1-22)
       A. The burning bush (vv. 1-6)
       B. The call to Moses (vv. 7-12)
       C. The Name of God (vv. 13-15)
       D. Further instructions (vv. 16-22)
    II. Moses' reluctance (Exod. 4:1-17)
       A. Moses is given the signs (vv. 1-9)
          1. The rod/serpent (vv. 1-5)
          2. The leprous hand (vv. 6-8)
          3. The water into blood (vv. 9)
       B. Aaron appointed as spokesperson (vv. 10-17)

Introducing the Main Question

If you know your class members well, and they are comfortable in talking about such things, ask them to talk about times they have felt or heard God calling them. If you think they would be shy about this, here are some ways to get them talking:

1. Divide them into pairs for the conversation.
2. Start them with an easier question, such as, How did you (or your spouse) decide on your chosen career? To get married? To live where you presently live?
3. Then go to the tougher question: How did God call you?
4. Then let them share with the larger group.

Developing the Lesson

I. Moses' experience of God (Exodus 3:1-22)
A. The burning bush (vv. 1-6)

It is true, as I suspect the conversation about our calling will reveal, that most of us have never experienced a burning bush or anything very much like it. But that should not be surprising. God's direct entries into human history are rare; only a few people actually knew Jesus of Nazareth. Most of us have less-direct encounters with God. But that does not make our encounters less real than that of Moses. Do your best to help your class get the feel of that hot, windy desert, and how something more than wind raised the hair on the back of Moses' neck. Picture·him standing, barefoot, with his face in his hands (v. 6).

B. The call to Moses (vv. 7-12)

Help your class to notice five things. (1) In these verses we have the answer to the questions raised in last week's lesson: Does God care? (2) The appearance of God is good news, not bad. (Keep in mind the phrase "a land flowing with milk and honey." We shall meet it again.) (3) There is a specific task for Moses (vv. 10.). (4) Moses is not at all sure he wants to do it (v. 11). (5) But God promises to be with him.

C. The Name of God (vv. 13-15)

I think this is the core of the lesson, and indeed, one of the watershed verses in the Bible. To know God's name, and more, to know that *this* is God's name, is to begin to have some idea of what holiness is all about. From the moment God names this name, polytheism is on the way out. From this moment, the end is in sight for all false gods.

D. Further instructions (vv. 16-22)

The writer repeats the instructions that God has given to Moses, and adds some details. The "spoilation of the Egyptians" in verses 21-22, was used as a metaphor by Augustine for the Christian faith's borrowing from other cultures.

II. Moses' reluctance (Exod. 4:1-17)

I don't blame Moses for his lack of ease with the task God appointed him to. Indeed, I am grateful. I have two statues of Moses on my desk, one by Michelangelo and the other by a modern sculptor; in both he is depicted as muscular and powerful. It's good to know that he sometimes felt inadequate (see Psalm 90). It is "the wounded healer" alone who can cure.

Helping Class Members Act

There are two things we would you should hope to see happen to your class members as a result of this lesson: (1) that they hear God's call and (2) that they act on that call. It is hard to say which of these tasks is the harder. But if you lead a lot of horses to the water a lot of times, at least some of them will eventually drink. Go for it!

Planning for Next Sunday

Have the class members read the story of the battle between God and the pharaoh in chapters 6–12, asking, "In what sense is this like *my* struggles?"

God Sets People Free

Background Scripture: Exodus 6:2-9; 11:1-3; 12:21-36

The Main Question

Have you ever been a slave?

I made that six-word sentence a whole paragraph (in spite of what I was taught in composition class) because I wanted to make myself think deeply about it. My first answer to the question was, "Of course not! I was born a free person in a free country, and nobody owns me. I have never been a slave."

But, on deeper reflection, I believe that I have been, and to some extent still am, a slave. I am a slave to my prejudices. (Even the ones I think I have gotten rid of sometimes rise up to haunt me.) I am a slave to my habits. (Did you know most people put the same shoe on first every morning? Try putting the other one on first and see how it feels.) I am a slave to my body. When it gets tired or sick, I have to obey it and lie down. I am a slave to my culture, the traditions in which I have been raised.

On deeper reflection, I find that there are other forms of slavery. Experts tell us that a main characteristic of one who is a slave to drugs or alcohol is denial. Addiction is a hard thing to admit, especially to yourself. There are hidden masters, prejudices that we are only dimly aware of or not at all. And these are the most dangerous, for they poison us subtly. For example, a woman, perhaps because of an unfortunate relationship with her father, has a secret hatred of men. Without knowing this, she may have real difficulty being a good wife and mother.

Is there any hope for us slaves? Are we stuck with our mental, physical, and spiritual deformities? "No," says Moses. Read on.

Selected Scripture

King James Version

Exodus 6:5-7

5 And I have also heard the groaning of the children of Israel, whom the Egyptians keep in bondage; and I have remembered my covenant.

6 Wherefore say unto the children of Israel, I am the LORD, and I will bring you out from under the burdens of the Egyptians, and I will rid you out of their bondage, and I will redeem you with a stretched out arm, and with great judgments:

7 And I will take you to me for a people, and I will be to you a God:

New Revised Standard Version

Exodus 6:5-7

5 "I have also heard the groaning of the Israelites whom the Egyptians are holding as slaves, and I have remembered my covenant. 6 Say therefore to the Israelites, 'I am the LORD, and I will free you from the burdens of the Egyptians and deliver you from slavery to them. I will redeem you with an outstretched arm and with mighty acts of judgment. 7 I will take you as my people, and I will be your God. You shall know that I am the LORD your God, who has freed you from the burdens

and ye shall know that I am the LORD your God, which bringeth you out from under the burdens of the Egyptians.

11:1

1 And the LORD said unto Moses, Yet will I bring one plague more upon Pharaoh, and upon Egypt; afterwards he will let you go hence: when he shall let you go, he shall surely thrust you out hence altogether.

12:29-33

29 And it came to pass, that at midnight the LORD smote all the firstborn in the land of Egypt, from the firstborn of Pharaoh that sat on his throne unto the firstborn of the captive that was in the dungeon; and all the firstborn of cattle.

30 And Pharaoh rose up in the night, he, and all his servants, and all the Egyptians; and there was a great cry in Egypt; for there was not a house where there was not one dead.

31 And he called for Moses and Aaron by night, and said, Rise up, and get you forth from among my people, both ye and the children of Israel; and go, serve the LORD, as ye have said.

32 Also take your flocks and your herds, as ye have said, and be gone; and bless me also.

33 And the Egyptians were urgent upon the people, that they might send them out of the land in haste; for they said, We be all dead men.

Key Verses:* Wherefore say unto the children of Israel, I am the LORD, and I will bring you out from under the burdens of the Egyptians, and I will rid you out of their bondage, and I will redeem you with a stretched out arm, and with great judgments. And I will take you to me for a people, and I will be to you a God. Exodus 6:6-7*a

of the Egyptians.

11:1

1 The LORD said to Moses, "I will bring one more plague upon Pharaoh and upon Egypt; afterwards he will let you go from here; indeed, when he lets you go, he will drive you away.

12:29-33

29 At midnight the LORD struck down all the firstborn in the land of Egypt, from the firstborn of Pharaoh who sat on his throne to the firstborn of the prisoner who was in the dungeon, and all the firstborn of the livestock. 30 Pharaoh arose in the night, he and all his officials and all the Egyptians; and there was a loud cry in Egypt, for there was not a house without someone dead. 31 Then he summoned Moses and Aaron in the night, and said, "Rise up, go away from my people, both you and the Israelites! Go, worship the LORD, as you said. 32 Take your flocks and your herds, as you said, and be gone. And bring a blessing on me too!"

33 The Egyptians urged the people to hasten their departure from the land, for they said, "We shall all be dead."

Key Verses:* Say therefore to the Israelites, 'I am the LORD, and I will free you from the burdens of the Egyptians and deliver you from slavery to them. I will redeem you with an outstretched arm and with mighty acts of judgment. I will take you as my people, and I will be your God. Exodus 6:6-7*a

FOURTH QUARTER

As You Read the Scripture

Exodus 6:2-9. God renews the call to Moses. Some scholars think that this section is an added account by a later editor. In any case, it is a repetition of what we had already been told in the last lesson.

Verse 3. We are told here that Abraham and the other patriarchs were not familiar with the name Yahweh, but it is certainly used in the Genesis story. (See, for instance, Gen. 15:1, 16:2, and 22:14.) This could be because the writer of those parts of Genesis used it by anticipation or that, though the name was used then, its deeper significance was not understood. The name God Almighty (see Gen. 17:1) is the usual translation of the Hebrew *El Shaddai*, the meaning of which is obscure, but clearly has something to do with power. (In Joel 1:15, the word is used to describe God's ability to destroy the enemy.)

Verse 6. The most important word in this passage is *redeem*, which hints at an even more significant name of God. *Redeemer* in Hebrew means an "advocate," actually, in a legal sense, "one who will take the case on my side." Its most familiar use is in Job 19:25, but it did not become popular to speak of God in this way until the time of Isaiah's prophecy concerning the deliverance from Babylon. (See Isa. 41:14; 43:14; 63:16; and other places.) It is never used as a name for Jesus in the New Testament, but since then it has become one of the most beloved ways in which Christians speak of our Lord.

Exodus 6:10–10:29. Our lesson skips over these chapters, but to put our story in its proper context, we should at least review their contents. They deal with Moses' sense of inadequacy, leading to the choice of Aaron as his mouthpiece, and the impressing of the Egyptian king with nine plagues:

> Blood (7:14-25)
> Frogs (8:1-15)
> Gnats (8:16-19)
> Flies (8:20-32)
> Cattle disease (9:1-17)
> Boils (9:8-12)
> Hail (9:13-35)
> Locusts (10:1-20)
> Darkness (10:21-29)

Each of the stories is interesting in its own way, but we do not have time to deal with them in this lesson.

Exodus 11:1-3. After the first nine plagues, we are here given a brief reminder of how the people of Israel are to take booty from the Egyptians. Could this be considered their "just" reward because of all the slave labor they had contributed to their captors? In any event, they were able to get away with it, partly because of the status of Moses in the sight of the Egyptian authorities.

Exodus 11:4–12:20. The succession of plagues is interrupted to tell the story of the institution of the first Passover.

Exodus 12:21-36. The tenth plague is the destruction of the firstborn sons of Egypt; the Israelites are delivered by the Passover. The stubborn Pharaoh finally gives in and recognizes Yahweh, whom he calls by name (v. 31) and asks for a blessing for himself. In the end the Egyptians are glad to see them go, booty and all.

The Scripture and the Main Question

Idols

It is hard to overestimate the subtle power of false gods. They always promise a great deal, and, seen in the right way, they do have their place, but they cannot save, though they possess the power to destroy us. Let me illustrate by speaking of two familiar ones.

Mammon, as Jesus called him, or "Cash," is the most common false god (see Matt. 6:24). You may not believe you worship Mammon, but if you are like me you feel a lot better about life when your bills are paid. A popular response to the question, "How are you?" goes like this: "There's nothing wrong with me that a few thousand dollars wouldn't cure." So it often seems, and, when used as a servant of God, money can be a blessing. It is the *love* of money (1 Tim. 6:10), not money itself, that is the root of all evil. But to come under the sway of Mammon, to make him God, is ultimately to destroy oneself.

Patria, or "Native Land," is another false god. When we are "one nation under God" we can be a blessing. But blind patriotism is, as Samuel Johnson said, "the last refuge of a scoundrel." All sorts of crimes can be covered up under the name of national security. We are blessed to live in a land where we are encouraged to criticize our politicians and be skeptical of their promises.

There are many other false gods—Pleasure, Popularity, Status—each with its own temple and priests and priestesses. And they all have in common three things: (1) they are tempting; (2) they can destroy us; and (3) they cannot save us.

When Jacob's children (with their way paved by Joseph) moved to Egypt, it seemed the right thing to do. There was a famine in the land, and Egypt offered hope. There they did achieve a measure of status and security. But in the long run they became slaves to the very security they had sought. Even after they escaped, part of them longed to return to that security (Exod. 16:3).

The Struggle

The struggle that takes place in Exodus 6–12 is not between Moses and Pharaoh. It is between the Lord, who made heaven and earth, and the gods of the Egyptians. Moses and Pharaoh are the representatives of those forces, but the real forces transcend both of the men. When Moses was in need of help, God provided the words for his mouth, Aaron to speak them, the trick staff that turned into a serpent, and the terrible plagues. And when Pharaoh sought to stave off the inevitable, his heart was hardened. Who did this hardening? Curiously, the text has it three ways. Sometimes (Exod. 10:20, 27ff.) we read that "the LORD hardened Pharaoh's heart." But at other times (Exod. 8:15; 1 Sam. 6:6) it says that he hardened his own heart. And at still other times (Exod. 7:13; 9:7) it simply says, "Pharaoh's heart was hardened." It is as though predestination and free will are opposite sides of the same coin. The battle going on in the heart of the Egyptian king is a cosmic battle; the gods are wrestling within him.

The same is true for us in our spiritual struggles. The spirit of this world entangles us (Matt. 13:19) and prevents us from hearing God. On the other hand, when we earnestly try to pray, the Holy Spirit "intercedes with sighs too deep for words" (Rom. 8:26). When Jesus struggled with his own temptation, we are told that "he was with the wild beasts; and the angels waited on him" (Mark 1:13). A holy war was going on in the heart of the son of a Nazarene carpenter. Indeed, there are those who think that the Crucifixion, in addition to being a terrible earthly calamity, with all its cruel blood and pain, was the terrestrial setting for a cosmic conflict. The forces of darkness were almost victorious; that was the death and the "descent into hell." But the forces of good (God) ultimately triumphed; that was the Resurrection. Perhaps there was something of this in the mind of the writer of Ephesians (6:12), when he said, "Our struggle is not against enemies of blood and flesh, but against the rulers, against the authorities, against the cosmic powers of this present darkness, against the spiritual forces of evil in the heavenly places." We are not alone in our struggle.

Slavery

I tried to indicate, in suggesting the main question of this lesson, that though we may not be Israelites in Egypt, we are all slaves. In that brief statement, the question of who is the slave and who is the free person had to be skipped over. But let's say a word about it now. In a master-slave culture, the masters are also victims of the system. Of course, anyone would rather be a master than a slave, but it is true that a society that permits slavery is destructive at both levels. Sociologists know that when slavery was a reality in the United States, the moral fiber of the ruling class was undermined. What hurts my brothers and sisters also hurts me.

Perhaps this will be easier to understand if you think of it this way: All the enslavements in our society today—drugs and alcohol, greed, ignorance, illness, prejudice, and so on—are costly to the whole of society. We all pay for these sins. And so both the Egyptians and the children of Israel suffered under Pharaoh's regime. It turned out to be fatal to the Egyptians' firstborn sons, to their army, and to their pride. And in the end, such evils could be fatal to us. We need to cry to God in our slavery to sin, and ask that the true Lord, the great I AM would deliver us from the lesser gods to whom we give an unhealthy allegiance. Such a new exodus would be painful to our society, as it was to Egypt of old, but in the long run it would be good for us. Perhaps someone you know, perhaps you, may be a latter-day Moses, about to be surprised by a burning bush.

Helping Adults Become Involved

Preparing to Teach

Although only three passages are listed as background scripture for this week, they are cream skimmed from a much longer section consisting of seven chapters. You will want to read them all. If you agree with me that this section, in addition to its historical lesson, is also about the struggle between good and evil forces in the world, about false gods and our slavery to them, and about our deliverance from such idolatry, then you will want, in addition to your study, to look at your own slavery. This isn't easy to do; I've tried it myself and have a hard time being honest with myself. Maybe this prayer will help.

Almighty and Eternal God, you alone are the ruler of this world and of my life. Forgive me for the ways in which I have put other gods before you, especially those I am not conscious of. Give me the courage to look them fully in the face, that I may reject them and serve only you. Forgive me for worshiping my own security and not putting my trust entirely in you. Forgive me for seeking selfish pleasures and not trusting you to enrich my life with joy. Forgive me for valuing my own reputation more than the truth and my own ease more than the fight for the right. Help me not to reject the worldly gifts that I am in danger of worshiping, but to tame them, to saddle them in your name and ride them into your battle, that both they and I may be your servants. This I ask in the name of Jesus Christ our Lord. Amen.

Here's my outline:

    I. The call to Moses renewed (6:2-9)
  III. The reluctance of Moses—the nine plagues (6:10–10:29)
  III. The plundering of the Egyptians (11:1-3)
  IV. The institution of the Passover (11:4–12:20)
   V. The tenth plague and the Passover (12:21-36)

Introducing the Main Question

This may be a very difficult main question to get across. Perhaps your class will not agree that the story of the plagues of Egypt is about our moral and spiritual struggle with the idols that hold us captive. But I strongly believe that this is true and that, if you can convince your folks of it, you will have done them a favor. Those slaves who do not know they are slaves are slaves indeed; the hidden master is more dangerous than the one who is visible. We moderns are inclined to laugh at primitive people with carved wooden idols, or at the pantheon of gods of ancient Greece and Rome, with their strange, often sub-human, moral confusion. But, in our amusement, let us not overlook the gods we worship today. I have found that letting a class engage in the following game is a useful and fairly painless way to get at it. Put a list on the board with the following three headings:

The God	The Temple	The Priest or Priestess

Then see if they can come up with some examples:

The God	The Temple	The Priest or Priestess
Eros	The Playboy Club	Hugh Hefner
Mammon	The S and L	Donald Trump
Mars	The Pentagon	Norman Schwarzkopf
Societia	The Country Club	Miss Manners

It can be fun, but also disturbing, and may get them to thinking.

Developing the Lesson

I. The call to Moses renewed (6:2-9)
Tell briefly the story in this passage, ending by emphasizing the words, "They would not listen to Moses, because of their broken spirit and their

cruel slavery." Help the class to see that it is difficult for those who are enslaved either to ask for help or to believe in it when it is offered. That is why it is so hard for us to see our own need to escape from the bonds of idolatry.

II. The reluctance of Moses—the nine plagues (6:10–10:29)

Although this section isn't included in our background scripture, briefly go over it, at least naming the nine plagues, and making sure that this passage is seen in its proper context.

III. The plundering of the Egyptians (11:1-3)

The business about spoiling the Egyptians is a problem for Christians. It almost seems as though God was being a kind of trickster. And, in truth, there is a good bit in early Hebrew history that makes us think this way. Jacob, for instance, is quite the clever fellow at cheating his brother, Esau, and conning his Uncle Laban. He reminds one of the clever coyote in comics, the trickster in Native American lore, or the Br'er Rabbit figure in Uncle Remus tales. Note what Augustine said about this in our comments on 3:21-22 in last week's lesson, and look ahead to 12:35-36. Maybe the Egyptians had this coming, but it still makes us feel that this behavior was somewhat questionable.

IV. The institution of the Passover (11:4–12:20)

V. The tenth plague and the Passover (12:21-36)

If the plundering bothers us, the killing of the firstborn bothers us even more. Jesus Christ has given us an understanding of God that completes the image raised in the Old Testament. But we can at least say about the image of God in the book of the Exodus that God is righteous, clearly on the side of the underdog, the slave, and is ready to set things right. Moreover, God delivers those who are willing to put their trust in the Lord. In this sense, the God of the Exodus is very much like Jesus Christ, our Passover Lamb (see 1 Cor. 5:7).

Helping Class Members Act

The best way to handle this lesson, instead of thinking gleefully about attacking the Egyptians with plagues, is to think about attacking the spiritual demons that plague us, using the whole armor of God (Eph. 6:10-17). You might conclude this lesson with that passage, and perhaps a prayer like the one I suggested for you to pray as you prepare to teach this lesson. However you do it, help them to be on the lookout for the idols that might snare us in today's world. Send them searching for their "Egypt."

Planning for Next Sunday

Next week's lesson is on the familiar story of the Red Sea crossing. Since it is so familiar, make sure that the class members read the two chapters carefully. Ask them whether they believe in happy endings.

God Gives Us Victory

Background Scripture: Exodus 13:17–14:31

The Main Question

I once attended a school whose basketball team lost thirty-seven straight games. The string of losses started in one year, lasted all the way through the next, and on into a third. Two coaches lost their jobs, and the discouragement of the students knew no bounds. It was depressing. We began to think that there was no such thing as a happy ending.

Is there? We have all known periods in our lives when things went from bad to worse and stayed there. Although we knew how to quote such old bromides as "even this will pass," that didn't help much. And it's not true anyway. It may pass, but it will come around again. Sooner or later we will die. As Psalm 90 has it:

> The days of our life are seventy years,
>   or perhaps eighty, if we are strong;
> even then their span is only toil and trouble;
>   they are soon gone, and we fly away. (Ps. 90:10)

An ancient tradition says that the ninetieth psalm is Moses talking. Was he really that much of a pessimist?

Well, Exodus 13 and 14 are about an incredible, astonishing happy ending. Just at the last minute, the Israelites escaped by the skin of their teeth. A little boy told his mother that the Seabees built Moses a pontoon bridge. When she questioned him, he said, "Well, if I told you what they told me in Sunday school, you wouldn't have believed me." Would we? Do we believe in miracles? Is there hope for our world?

Selected Scripture

King James Version	New Revised Standard Version
Exodus 14:21-31	*Exodus 14:21-31*
21 And Moses stretched out his hand over the sea; and the LORD caused the sea to go back by a strong east wind all that night, and made the sea dry land, and the waters were divided.	21 Then Moses stretched out his hand over the sea. The LORD drove the sea back by a strong east wind all night, and turned the sea into dry land; and the waters were divided. 22 The Israelites went into the sea on dry ground, the waters forming a wall for them on their right and on their left. 23 The Egyptians pursued, and went into the sea after them, all of Pharaoh's horses, chariots, and chariot drivers. 24 At the morning watch the LORD in the
22 And the children of Israel went into the midst of the sea upon the dry ground: and the waters were a wall unto them on their right hand, and on their left.	
23 And the Egyptians pursued, and went in after them to the midst	

of the sea, even all Pharaoh's horses, his chariots, and his horsemen.

24 And it came to pass, that in the morning watch the LORD looked unto the host of the Egyptians through the pillar of fire and of the cloud, and troubled the host of the Egyptians,

25 And took off their chariot wheels, that they drave them heavily: so that the Egyptians said, Let us flee from the face of Israel; for the LORD fighteth for them against the Egyptians.

26 And the LORD said unto Moses, Stretch out thine hand over the sea, that the waters may come again upon the Egyptians, upon their chariots, and upon their horsemen.

27 And Moses stretched forth his hand over the sea, and the sea returned to his strength when the morning appeared; and the Egyptians fled against it; and the LORD overthrew the Egyptians in the midst of the sea.

28 And the waters returned, and covered the chariots, and the horsemen, and all the host of Pharaoh that came into the sea after them; there remained not so much as one of them.

29 But the children of Israel walked upon dry land in the midst of the sea; and the waters were a wall unto them on their right hand, and on their left.

30 Thus the LORD saved Israel that day out of the hand of the Egyptians; and Israel saw the Egyptians dead upon the sea shore.

31 And Israel saw that great work which the LORD did upon the Egyptians: and the people feared the LORD, and believed the LORD, and his servant Moses.

Key Verses: **Thus the LORD saved Israel that day out of the hand of the Egyptians; and Israel saw the Egyptians dead upon the sea shore. And Israel saw that great work which the**

pillar of fire and cloud looked down upon the Egyptian army, and threw the Egyptian army into panic. 25 He clogged their chariot wheels so that they turned with difficulty. The Egyptians said, "Let us flee from the Israelites, for the LORD is fighting for them against Egypt."

26 Then the LORD said to Moses, "Stretch out your hand over the sea, so that the water may come back upon the Egyptians, upon their chariots and chariot drivers." 27 So Moses stretched out his hand over the sea, and at dawn the sea returned to its normal depth. As the Egyptians fled before it, the LORD tossed the Egyptians into the sea. 28 The waters returned and covered the chariots and the chariot drivers, the entire army of Pharaoh that had followed them into the sea; not one of them remained. 29 But the Israelites walked on dry ground through the sea, the waters forming a wall for them on their right and on their left.

30 Thus the LORD saved Israel that day from the Egyptians; and Israel saw the Egyptians dead on the seashore. 31 Israel saw the great work that the LORD did against the Egyptians. So the people feared the LORD and believed in the LORD and in his servant Moses.

Key Verses: **Thus the LORD saved Israel that day from the Egyptians; and Israel saw the Egyptians dead on the seashore. Israel saw the great work that the LORD did against the**

Lord did upon the Egyptians; and
the people feared the LORD, and
believed the LORD, and his servant
Moses. Exodus 14:30-31

Egyptians. So the people feared the
LORD and believed in the LORD and
in his servant Moses.
Exodus 14:30-31

As You Read the Scripture

Exodus 13:17-22. This passage tells of the march to Etham. Succoth was
the first camp the Israelites made after leaving Rameses, not far from Lake
Timsah. This is not to be confused with another camp of the same name
near the Jordan. Succoth means "booths" or "huts," and is a name of a
feast (Num. 23:39-43) still celebrated by Jews today, but, again, is unrelated to the Egyptian Succoth. Nobody knows for certain where Etham was.
The most direct route to what we today call the Holy Land would have
been northeastward, along the Mediterranean coast, a journey of only a
couple of hundred miles. But this would have taken them through what we
now call the Gaza Strip, the country of the Philistines, a warlike people.
God decided to take them by a roundabout way that, in the end, involved a
wilderness journey of many years. Could another of God's reasons have
been the necessity of trying, training, and toughening the people in the
wilderness?

Verse 18. What we translate as "the Red Sea" is in Hebrew called the
"Sea of Reeds," and probably refers to the northwestern finger of the Red
Sea, which is today called the Gulf of Suez. Geologists tell us that in prehis-
toric times the Gulf of Suez extended much farther to the north and
included Lake Timsah and the Bitter Lakes. In 1869, the Suez Canal was
built from the Gulf to the Mediterranean. The point at which most people
believe the Israelites went over is now the southern section of the canal,
just north of the modern city of Suez. Those who seek a natural explanation for the remarkable deliverance point out that, under certain conditions, a good strong wind could have swept the relatively shallow area
almost dry.

Verse 19. The Exodus had been predicted by Joseph (see Gen. 50:24-25),
and now, with that wonderful respect for ancestors that has characterized
Hebrew tradition through the years, the old patriarch's remains are ten-
derly carried home. According to Joshua 24:22, his remains were eventually
buried at Shechem, which is now called Nablus, in the very center of the
Holy Land.

Verses 21-22. The pillar of smoke and fire symbolizes the divine leading
and protection of God. Fire signals were often carried at the head of
armies on the march. (The pillar did in fact sometimes go behind them;
see 14:19-20.)

Exodus 14. The miraculous deliverance became for Israel the decisive
event in their history. Again and again, the psalms and the writings of the
prophets refer to it. (See Pss. 106:6-12; 136:13-15; and Isa. 15:10-11.) Faithful Jews look back to this saving act much as Christians look back with gratitude to the life, death, and resurrection of Jesus. *Exodus* is a Greek word
meaning "the road out." The return from captivity in Babylon is seen by
Jews as a new exodus (Isa. 40:3-5), and for Christians this same image is
applied to deliverance in Christ (Mark 1:2-3).

The Scripture and the Main Question

"The Road Less Traveled"

Journeys don't always turn out the way we expect, but there is something about the unexpected turn that opens the door to undreamed-of possibilities. Like the wise men, the Israelites are about to go home by another way. Having met God, whether at a burning bush or a manger, we are never again the same people. The hesitant Moses, who had fled from Egypt and was reluctant to return, is not the same person; he is turning into a leader of remarkable ability. The children of Israel, having experienced the Passover, are not the same people; once sedentary slaves, they have become wilderness wanderers. And you too will be different if you go by another way. My father once advised me, "Never propose marriage to anyone until you have been with her on a camping trip." He meant that people behave in one way on dates, going to movies, dining in restaurants, but you find out who they really are when the bacon falls in the campfire and the smoke gets in their eyes.

Of course the forty years of wilderness wandering were not a camping trip. But they had their effect on the traveling Israelites. They left Succoth a rag-tag crowd of ex-slaves; they arrived at the Jordan a well-organized nation, with a code of laws unsurpassed in ancient history. They had learned to appreciate what it means to live by grace, being led from oasis to oasis by God, depending for their survival, not on the labor of their own hands, but on manna from heaven. To this day, faithful Jews annually celebrate the Feast of Booths (called Succoth, but not after the campsite from which they left; the Hebrew word for "booths" is *succoth*). It is a festival designed to remind them that, even living in cities, we still ultimately depend on God for our survival (see Lev. 24:42-43).

"Cloud by Day and Fire by Night"

One of the reasons I like to go camping is that I like to get lost. I don't mean really lost (that is a terrifying experience) but sufficiently confused so that it takes some effort to orient myself—there are surprises around every corner. (My wife does not share this enthusiasm. One of the more interesting discussions we are likely to have when traveling in a strange country centers around my tendency to take short cuts in places I have never been before.) The "blue highways" are more interesting than interstates.

And life is like that. If you go daily in the same routine, never varying, it may help you develop good habits, but what it doesn't do is give you that wonderful sense of the unexpected that makes for a rich excitement in the way you live. Occasionally someone will use the phrase "the foreseeable future." But just how much of the future can you foresee? Ten minutes? The truth is that we have no notion what might happen in the next ten minutes. This would be utterly terrifying if we did not know that God is going before us, leading us into the unknown tomorrow, and serving as our rear guard when we lie down to sleep at night. What a wonderful thing it is to be snug in the wilderness, with a guide you can trust and adventures about to happen!

A Happy Ending

But will they be good adventures? Sometimes disasters loom about us; Egyptian chariots pursue, and unchartered waters lie ahead. But for the people of God, that should not matter. "In the world you face persecution," said Jesus. "But take courage; I have conquered the world!" (John 16:33). Jesus' own life is the supreme example. Seen from the outside, his life appears to be rather a failure. He was never successful in the eyes of the world. His days of ministry were too brief, and they ended in death—or so it seemed to the pagan eyes that watched it all. "He saved others; he cannot save himself" (Mark 15:31). But that was not the end of the story. Out of despair, out of dark, out of doom, utterly unexpectedly, came a resurrection. There is a Red Sea baptism through which we must all pass (1 Cor. 10:1), our Good Friday, but an Easter is promised.

This good news is almost impossible to believe. Cynics and skeptics say that real life is harsh and hard. So it is. The desert through which we wander is inhospitable. There *are* Egyptian armies behind us, and there *are* Red Seas before us. We were not promised a rose garden. And you can tell me many stories of good, innocent people whose lives are filled with sadness. But that is not the point. The point is that there is victory even in those lives, for something else is behind and before us: a pillar of fire and cloud. The cynical eyes cannot see them. But, and those who have traveled this road long enough know what I mean, after a while eyes of faith begin to see them there. When I was a little boy I was afraid of the dark. I saw lions and tigers and bears in the bushes, and at night I would cover my head with a sheet to ward off the monsters. I cannot tell you when it happened, but at some point along the way it dawned on me that the dark bore no ultimate danger. Now I know that the dark unknown tomorrow and the creepy embarrassing past, whatever they may bring, cannot harm me. My life is hidden with Christ in God (Col. 3:3), and nothing in death or in life can separate me from that love (Rom. 8:38-39).

A Celebration

It is not part of our lesson this week, but I can't help pointing out that as soon as the crossing of the sea had taken place, an impromptu celebration was held (Exod. 15). It is the first place in the Bible where the word *song* appears. At its climax, Miriam, Moses' sister, and all the women, dance with tambourines. It was a resurrection morning, and I wish I could have been there.

Helping Adults Become Involved

Preparing to Teach

The story of the Red Sea crossing is as well known as any story in the Bible. Even secular people know this story; it is part of our culture. In fact, it is so well known that there are probably things in it we have forgotten. I know that when I re-read this story for this lesson, my eye fell on chapter 14, verse 20, which I had seen before but never stopped on: "and it lit up the night; one did not come near the other all night." It conjured in my mind visions of a night in the desert, with the protecting hand of God there to ward off the enemy. I thought of my camping days as a youngster, and there came fresh to me the verse in Revelation 21:3 (my paraphrase):

> Behold, the tent of God is in the midst of the people.
> God will pitch a tent with them and be their God;
> they will be God's people.

And that colored my whole understanding of this event. I don't insist that you have the same images, but I do encourage you to read the scripture carefully, expecting it to speak to you afresh.

Here's my outline:

I. The journey from Succoth (13:17-22)
II. The Egyptians pursue (14:1-14)
III. The crossing of the sea (14:15-22)
IV. The destruction of the Egyptians (14:23-31)
V. The celebration (15:1-21)]

Introducing the Main Question

I suspect your class has some skeptics; at least there will be some in there. Not that they won't believe the old story, or say that they do, but that they don't believe that sort of thing happens nowadays. You just don't get many Red Sea partings in the twentieth century. So it may be difficult for them to identify with this story. Begin by asking the straightforward question: Do you believe in miracles? Perhaps they will be willing to discuss this for a while, and maybe one or more of them will have a story to tell that illustrates a Red Sea crossing in their own lives. If not, perhaps you can tell them one from your own experience. If all else fails, you can share this one from mine:

> I was in a hospital waiting-room full of friends. My wife was undergoing delicate brain surgery to correct an aneurism. It was nothing that anyone said to me, though their presence was certainly part of it, nor was it a conscious prayer that I prayed, although I was doing a lot of praying, but suddenly, it came over me that everything was going to be all right. Not that she would necessarily live or be perfectly normal again, but that everything was going to be all right. And from that point on, it was. She did get well, completely. I had crossed over a Red Sea of fear and doubt and was forever safe on the other side.

Developing the Lesson

I. The journey from Succoth (13:17-22)

Read these verses, or tell the story briefly, and then let the class talk for a while about life as an adventure, a camping trip, a wilderness journey, a quest, or however you prefer to put it.

II. The Egyptians pursue (14:1-14)

Tell this story and let the class talk about things that pursue us in our daily lives. What are our fears? Do they usually materialize? How do we deal with them? Do we need to hear the voice of Moses saying, "Do not be afraid, stand firm, and see the deliverance that the Lord will accomplish for you today"?

III. The crossing of the sea (14:15-22)

Tell or read this story, and again let the class speak of deliverances that may have occurred in their lives. Ask them if they think life is supposed to have a happy ending. Is life a comedy or a tragedy?

IV. The destruction of the Egyptians (14:23-31)

Tell this story, and ask the class what they think the Egyptian version of this story would be. What report do you suppose the survivors gave when they got back to Pharaoh? (It is not likely that he was drowned; you don't go charging into empty oceans if you are the pharaoh.) Do you think Jesus would have had compassion on the Egyptians? Does God?

V. The celebration (15:1-21)

End on a note of celebration. If your class would enjoy doing it, you might want to end this lesson with a song. Pick a good resurrection hymn. Or, if you like, try my version of Miriam's song (Exod. 15:21). I sing it to the tune of "My Darlin' Clementine":

Sing a song unto the Lo-rd, who has triumph'd gloriously;
For the horses and the riders have been thrown into the sea.
You might like to use a tambourine.

Helping Class Members Act

I think the response to this particular lesson needs to be not so much an action as an attitude. That is, you can't very well say, "Go out and divide an ocean." What you need to say to the class members is something like: "Go into the wilderness of life and live victoriously, knowing that God will protect you from the troubles that pursue you and the troubles that lie ahead." How can you best get this across? If you can't think of anything, at least give them a good send-off, such as this: "Go out into the world in peace. Have courage; hold on to what is good; return to no one evil for evil; strengthen the fainthearted; support the weak; help the suffering; honor everyone; love and serve the Lord, rejoicing in the power of the Holy Spirit."

Planning for Next Sunday

Next week's lesson is about manna (Exod. 16). Ask your class to read it and reflect on this question: Do we really expect God to give us each day our daily bread?

UNIT II: PROVISION FOR PRESENT AND FUTURE

FIVE LESSONS   JULY 3–31

This unit, which continues studying Exodus, looks at God's care for the people in the wilderness, the people's development into a strongly monotheistic nation with a sophisticated code of laws and a developing system of government. Moses' leadership skills are tested as he guides them through the difficulties of the desert. God provides manna, the law, and the rules for worship that will enable his people to be cared for, both physically and spiritually. In spite of the people's failure and mistrust, God remains faithful and forgiving. We are called upon, now as then, to remember God's care, to acknowledge God's power to act on our behalf, and to accept the responsibility of giving ourselves to God's service.

Questions asked by this unit are relevant today. They include such matters as, Where does your true security lie? Can we be faithful to God in the uncertainties of these times? How can the church best be organized to meet its appointed tasks? Should lay people be more involved in what we do? Do we need a revival of the Ten Commandments in our time? Can they be seen as positive, powerful moral principles, rather than as merely negative moralisms? Are we reverent enough? And, in our failure, can we expect God to forgive us? Can we be called upon to play leadership roles like that of Moses? Are we conscious of God's presence in our midst? And does this make a difference in the way that we live from week to week?

Such questions belong, not simply to ancient Egypt, but to our twentieth-century world. We will do well, this quarter, to study them, take them to heart, and learn to live by their answers.

LESSON 5   JULY 3

God Provides

Background Scripture: Exodus 16

The Main Question

As I write this, the world's economy is in recession, and it makes a lot of us somewhat nervous. I don't worry too much about it because I have been through a number of recessions; in fact, I was born during the Great Depression, which was a good deal worse. My family did pretty well. Preacher's kids rarely go hungry; in a depression people seem to be drawn closer to the church. I can remember going with my father to take baskets of food to some of the church officers who were out of work. But, like many Depression babies, I was raised to be very uneasy when the money is low. My parents, without meaning to or saying it out loud, managed to instill in us children the notion that if we weren't stingy with our pennies we would all end up in the poor house.

The result of all of this is that my mood swings with my bank account. When, at the end of the month, all my bills are paid and there are still a few dollars in the bank, my depression goes away, and I find myself whistling. But I don't approve of this in myself; it is a very dangerous way to be. It is a mistake to let one's moods depend on the state of one's pocketbook. "You cannot serve God and Mammon [the great god Cash]." The main question raised by today's lesson is, "Where does your security lie?" If your sense of well-being depends on the groceries in the pantry, however important that may be, you are as shaky as the Israelites in the wilderness who tried to squirrel away the manna for the morrow and found it spoiled. What makes you feel secure?

Selected Scripture

King James Version

New Revised Standard Version

Exodus 16:2-7, 13-18

2 And the whole congregation of the children of Israel murmured against Moses and Aaron in the wilderness:

3 And the children of Israel said unto them, Would to God we had died by the hand of the LORD in the land of Egypt, when we sat by the flesh pots, *and* when we did eat bread to the full; for ye have brought us forth into this wilderness, to kill this whole assembly with hunger.

4 Then said the LORD unto Moses, Behold, I will rain bread from heaven for you; and the people shall go out and gather a certain rate every day, that I may prove them, whether they will walk in my law, or no.

5 And it shall come to pass, that on the sixth day they shall prepare *that* which they bring in; and it shall be twice as much as they gather daily.

6 And Moses and Aaron said unto all the children of Israel, At even, then ye shall know that the LORD hath brought you out from the land of Egypt;

7 And in the morning, then ye shall see the glory of the LORD; for that he heareth your murmurings against the LORD; and what *are* we, that ye murmur against us?

Exodus 16:2-7, 13-18

2 The whole congregation of the Israelites complained against Moses and Aaron in the wilderness. 3 The Israelites said to them "If only we had died by the hand of the LORD in the land of Egypt, when we sat by the fleshpots and ate our fill of bread; for you have brought us out into this wilderness to kill this whole assembly with hunger."

4 Then the LORD said to Moses, "I am going to rain bread from heaven for you, and each day the people shall go out and gather enough for that day. In that way I will test them, whether they will follow my instruction or not. 5 On the sixth day, when they prepared what they bring in, it will be twice as much as they gather on other days." 6 So Moses and Aaron said to all the Israelites, "In the evening you shall know that it was the LORD who brought you out of the land of Egypt, 7 and in the morning you shall see the glory of the LORD because he has heard your complaining against the LORD. For what are we, that you complain against us?"

13 And it came to pass, that at even the quails came up, and covered the camp: and in the morning the dew lay round about the host.

14 And when the dew that lay was gone up, behold, upon the face of the wilderness *there lay* a small round thing, *as* small as the hoar frost on the ground.

15 And when the children of Israel saw *it,* they said one to another, It *is* manna: for they wist not what it *was.* And Moses said unto them, This *is* the bread which the LORD hath given you to eat.

16 This *is* the thing which the LORD hath commanded, Gather of it every man according to his eating, an omer for every man, *according to* the number of your persons; take ye every man for *them* which are in his tents.

17 And the children of Israel did so, and gathered, some more, some less.

18 And when they did mete *it* with an omer, he that gathered much had nothing over, and he that gathered little had no lack; they gathered every man according to his eating.

13 In the evening quails came up and covered the camp; and in the morning there was a layer of dew around the camp. 14 When the layer of dew lifted, there on the surface of the wilderness was a fine flaky substance, as fine as frost on the ground. 15 When the Israelites saw it, they said to one another, "What is it?" For they did not know what it was. Moses said to them, "It is the bread that the LORD has given you to eat. 16 This is what the LORD has commanded: 'Gather as much of it as each of you needs, an omer to a person according to the number of persons, all providing for those in their own tents.' " 17 the Israelites did so, some gathering more, some less. 18 But when they measured it with an omer, those who gathered much had nothing over, and those who gathered little had no shortage; they gathered as much as each of them needed.

Key Verse: Then said the LORD unto Moses, Behold, I will rain bread from heaven for you; and the people shall go out and gather a certain rate every day, that I may prove them, whether they will walk in my law or no. Exodus 16:4.

Key Verse: Then the LORD said to Moses, "I am going to rain bread from heaven for you, and each day the people shall go out and gather enough for that day. In that way I will test them, whether they will follow my instruction or not." Exodus 16:4

As You Read the Scripture

Verse 1. Nobody knows for certain where the wilderness of Sin is, but we do know that the Israelites had been wandering about a month and a half, so their supplies must have been running low.

Verse 2. This is not the only "murmuring" Moses had to listen to on the journey. (See also 14:10-12 and 15:24.) His great skills as a leader were constantly being put to the test.

Verse 3. (See also Num. 11:4-5.) The term *fleshpot* has become a synonym in our day for any place in which sensual gratification can be found. But in our text it simply meant the stewpot where the slaves got their daily rations. The cry of the people can be paraphrased, "We may have been slaves in

Egypt, but at least we weren't dying of hunger." The people are beginning to lose faith in the Lord's leadership, and hence, in Moses.

Verse 4. God's instructions come first to Moses and are then explained to the people by Moses and Aaron. Only a day's worth of manna is to be given at a time, which will test the people's faith.

Verse 5. (See also 22-30.) The custom of keeping the Sabbath had evidently already been begun among the Hebrews, though it is not formally pronounced until this chapter, and is given as one of the commandments in chapter 20. We know that the Babylonians had Sabbath rests prior to this time. This marks the beginning of its becoming a strict observance for the children of Israel.

Verse 7. "The glory of the Lord" can mean simply "proof of how wonderful God is" and can refer simply to the manna itself, but in the light of verse 10, what is meant is a supernatural appearance, not unlike what is called a halo in religious art or, more properly, an aureole or golden glow. The pillar of fire that went before them is another such manifestation.

Verse 13. The account in Numbers 11:4-31 says that the quail were easy to catch (tired from their migratory flight), but that instead of providing nourishment for the people they turned out to be the origin of a deadly plague. Here they seem to be associated with the coming of the manna in some way.

Verse 15. "It is manna" (KJV) or "what is it?" (NRSV)—both translations give some problems, but since the writer adds, "for they didn't know what it was," the latter reading makes more sense. Although what is today called manna is from the sap of the tamarisk tree, what is described here (and in v. 31) doesn't sound like that. The writer clearly means that it was something miraculous that they had never encountered before. (For New Testament references, see John 6:31-53 and 1 Cor. 10:1-5.)

Verse 18. An omer is about a gallon. Amazingly, everybody had enough. (See 2 Cor. 8:13-15.)

Verse 29. How far were you allowed to walk on the Sabbath? Later rabbinic rules set the limit at 2,000 cubits (about three-fifths of a mile), the radius of the camp around the tabernacle (Josh. 3:4).

Verse 34. The symbolic jar stood near the Ark of the Covenant.

The Scripture and the Main Question

Murmurings

This lesson is about security. In Lesson 3 we had a good bit of discussion about false gods, in which we seek security, and suggested that the slavery in Egypt was one example of such. If it was difficult to see then how anyone could worship the idea of being a slave, it should become clearer now, for the people are in the wilderness and long for the security, however painful, they once had.

This account is by no means the only one about murmuring in the story of the wilderness wandering. (See Exod. 15:22-25; 17:1-8; Num. 14:1-4; 16:41; Deut. 1:27; and Ps. 106:24-27.) Jesus had to put up with such murmurings (John 6:41-43), and so did the early church leaders (Acts 6:1). It seems to be a sort of built-in problem for faith communities. With the wrong sort of leadership, it could be that such murmuring is appropriate. People have a right to gripe and complain. But in this case, the complaint is against God and, therefore, is altogether inappropriate.

Are we ever guilty of complaining against God? My guess is that, if you have ever given your class a tough assignment, you have heard some mutterings and grumblings among your pupils. And you have probably done some murmuring yourself. The question we need to ask as we go through this lesson is this: Is my griping appropriate?

Fleshpots

For a graphic description of what it was like to eat as slaves back in Egypt, see Numbers 11:4-6. Not everybody is tempted by the same things. I can pass up most desserts without a problem, but I have to keep my distance from homemade biscuits and gravy; my wife, on the other hand, can make biscuits without sampling them, but needs to stay clear of the chocolate dessert bar. However, when you are in the wilderness, running low on food and water, you crave neither of those things; you crave sustenance itself. You don't need dessert in the desert; you need daily bread.

The people's desire was legitimate. It is not a sin to be hungry; what's sinful is failing to trust God. There are two ways to violate that trust: to long for the fleshpots of Egypt and to squirrel away the manna. They are both forms of false security, and we call those who put their trust in such false idols "greedy" or "misers." It is a form of idolatry to want things to last forever, to be the same. We are called in Christ to forget "what lies behind and [strain] forward to what lies ahead" (Phil. 3:13), to press on, trusting God to take care of us. To want things to last forever is to want immortality, to "be as God" (Gen. 3:5). In fact, I think you could make a case that even things like plastic flowers, artificial turf, photographs, and tape recordings are a little dangerous.

There is, of course, a healthy kind of conservatism, a responsible regard for the past. Those who do not remember their history are condemned to repeat it. You *are* supposed to "look to the rock from which you were hewn,/ and to the quarry from which you were dug" (Isa. 51:1). Where do you find your true security? The lesson in Exodus 16 is clear: The only true basis of security is God.

True Security

If you ever get to travel on the Rhine you will enjoy a wonderful glimpse into the medieval world of kings and their castles. Every few thousand yards you come upon another feudal stronghold, with its battlements and turrets. Most of them are tourist hotels and museums now, but they tell of a time when those who had the strength walled themselves in from their neighbors, surrounded by moats and drawbridges or perched on inaccessible crags. It seems a strange and far-away thing, but I have been in suburban American neighborhoods that made me feel much the same way. They may not have moats around them, but they do have guard dogs and security alarm systems. Some of them do not even have windows, but the owners exist in an artificial climate, controlled by thermostats. (Beware when the power goes off for more than a few hours!)

To shut yourself off from people is to shut yourself off from life. Our true security should come, not from walls around us, but from an internal trust in the One who has promised to care for us

> though the earth should change,
>   though the mountains shake in
>   the heart of the sea;
> though its waters roar and foam,
>   though the mountains tremble
>   with its tumult. (Psalm 46:2-3)

For years I read Jesus' encouraging words in Matthew 16:18 exactly backwards. "On this rock," he said to Peter, "I will build my church, and the gates of Hades will not prevail against it." I pictured the church, all surrounded with battlements and gates, which the powers of darkness were storming. But it is the other way around! We are supposed to be storming their gates. We are not to wall ourselves up in false security, but to be on the march. God will be with us in the wilderness, supplying our every need, and our task is to be faithful. So I am always stirred whenever we sing "How Firm a Foundation":

> Fear not, I am with thee, O be not dismayed,
> For I am thy God and will still give thee aid.
> I'll strengthen and help thee, and cause thee to stand
> Upheld by my righteous, omnipotent hand.

Let us, then, be on the march. God will not desert us in the desert. The very rocks will provide us with water, and there will be manna enough for all.

> The soul that on Jesus still leans for repose,
> I will not, I will not desert to its foes;
> That soul, though all hell should endeavor to shake,
> I'll never, no, never, no, never forsake.

Helping Adults Become Involved

Preparing to Teach

It goes without saying that you will need to read Exodus 16 several times as you prepare for this lesson, and check your commentaries. And, of course, you will want to pray for God's guidance in helping you properly interpret this chapter for and with your class. There is no substitute for adequate preparation. Having said that, I think there is something to be said, in regard to this lesson, for being unprepared. That is, your true security is not in your preparation, but in trusting God's guidance along the way. So, to be consistent with what the lesson seems to be saying, you needn't have all your *i*'s dotted and your *t*'s crossed. God will provide manna along the way, in the guidance of the Spirit and in the participation of your class members, who also have their gifts to bring. Go at it with confidence, not in yourself, but in the Master Teacher who goes with you.

Here's the outline for this lesson:

     I. Longing for the fleshpots (16:1-3)
    II. The promise of bread from heaven (16:3-12)
   III. The giving of the manna (16:13-21)
   IV. The institution of the sabbath (16:22-30)
    V. The ceremonial jar of manna (16:31-36)

FOURTH QUARTER

Introducing the Main Question

One way to get at the question of true security is to ask it in this form: When do you feel the safest? If that doesn't cut it, try reversing the question: What is most likely to make you uneasy? Then search for the security that removes that unease. Think of it this way: I'm afraid of flying. Therefore, I feel the safest when I'm on solid ground.

Ask your class to make a list of things that give us a sense of security. Their answers might include money in the bank, a strong military, a smaller national debt, plenty of food in the pantry, a good neighborhood watch program, having family gathered around us. Then get them to discuss what true security means to them. They will probably agree that most earthly forms of security are illusory. Even the "solid ground" under our feet is spinning through space as the earth rotates.

Another way to get at the question of security is to start with the prayer of our childhood, and ask what sorts of feelings it brings up:

> Now I lay me down to sleep;
> I pray thee, Lord, my soul to keep.
> If I should die before I wake;
> I pray thee, Lord, my soul to take.

In any event, after you have raised this issue, go through the outline of the lesson with them, asking them to keep the main question in mind.

Developing the Lesson

I. Longing for the fleshpots (16:1-3)

Bring in the passage from the book of Numbers here, with its vivid description of what the Egyptian soup kitchen was like. Then have the folks chat for a little while about hungers they may have in life. Not all of them will be for food. Help them to understand that while it is unhealthy to complain, God does want us to ask for daily bread (Matt. 6:11). It is not that God doesn't already know we need it (Matt. 6:32), but that we need to be ever conscious of how we live at all times by God's grace.

II. The promise of bread from heaven (16:3-12)

Twice in this section the phrase "the glory of the LORD" is used. Do you ever think of the sandwiches in your lunchbox as a manifestation of God's glory? There is a sense in which that glory rests on the whole creation, for those who have eyes to see it.

III. The giving of the manna (16:13-21)

The basic sense of this section is that the manna was altogether the gift of God, that there was exactly enough for everybody, and that they should not try to hoard any extra. The concept of false security is easy to see here.

This might be a good place in the lesson to introduce other places in the Bible where manna is mentioned (e.g., Num. 11:7-9; Deut. 8:3; Neh. 9:15; Ps. 78:21-25; Josh. 5:10-12; John 6:31-35, 58; Heb. 9:4; Rev. 2:17). You might get class members to look these up and reflect on how they relate to the main theme of the lesson.

IV. The institution of the sabbath (16:22-30)

There was one exception to the rule that they must gather only enough manna for one day—it was okay to save something for the sabbath. Everyone ought to have a rainy day account. However, we must not let that be our chief source of permanent happiness; then it will become an idol.

V. The ceremonial jar of manna (16:31-36)

The pot of manna in front of the Ark was nothing more, and nothing less, than a solemn reminder that God's grace had cared for the people. It is a little like the "first dollar" that you see framed in a business, so that they won't forget their humble beginnings. Or like things we keep in a scrapbook or a church historical society. There should be such things, but even they can become idols.

Helping Class Members Act

Conclude by sending your folks out with a sense of liberty. I remember once going on a trip and taking absolutely nothing with me but the clothes on my back, a toothbrush and some cash. Since I was taking a bus, I didn't need my driver's license. I felt sort of naked, and without an I.D. I would not be able to cash a check. At the same time, however, it was a sort of delicious feeling. It was at once both frightening and exhilarating. See if you can send your class out feeling both free and secure, knowing that God will take care of them.

Planning for Next Sunday

Have the class members read Exodus 18 and think about church government.

God Gives Confidence

Background Scripture: Exodus 18

The Main Question

I hate administration. I love the part of my work that involves words: preaching, teaching, writing Bible study helps. And I love the part that involves encounters with people: marrying, baptizing, visiting. But I hate administration. I'm a doer, not a facilitator. The worst job I have is calling people on the phone and saying, "Would you be willing to chair a committee?"

But administration is an essential part of the church's life, and when it is done well, it is a people thing, not a mere pushing of papers. Someone has said that the best thing you can do for another person is to ask that person to help you. People need to be needed; they want to be a part of things.

James Dittes wrote an excellent book a few years back, called *The Church in the Way*. Dittes's title has a double meaning. Sometimes, when we are busy with the busyness of the church, we think, "If it just wasn't for all these blasted meetings, the church could get on about its business." But the way is the Way, and there's an end to it. A good administrator sees to it that meetings *are* the church. They should be conducted in such a way that people love one another as they learn to work together. That is what the church is all about (Eph. 4:15-16).

As Moses learned, on the good advice of Jethro, to organize his people, he set in motion the beginnings of church government as we know it today. The main question for us to consider, as we study our assignment this week, is this: Can we learn to work with one another, "so that all may learn and all be encouraged" (1 Cor. 13:31)?

Selected Scripture

King James Version	New Revised Standard Version
Exodus 18:13-25	*Exodus 18:13-25*
13 And it came to pass on the morrow, that Moses sat to judge the people: and the people stood by Moses from the morning unto the evening.	13 The next day Moses sat as judge for the people, while the people stood around him from morning until evening. 14 When Moses' father-in-law saw all that he was doing for the people, he said, "What is this that you are doing for the people? Why do you sit alone, while all the people stand around you from morning until evening?" 15 Moses said to his father-in-law, "Because the people come to me to inquire of God. 16 When they have a dispute, they come to me and I decide between one person and
14 And when Moses' father in law saw all that he did to the people, he said, What is this thing that thou doest to the people? why sittest thou thyself alone, and all the people stand by thee from morning unto even?	
15 And Moses said unto his father in law, Because the people come unto me to inquire of God:	

16 When they have a matter they come to me; and I judge between one and another, and I do make them know the statutes of God, and his laws.

17 And Moses' father in law said unto him, The thing that thou doest is not good.

18 Thou wilt surely wear away, both thou, and this people that is with thee: for this thing is too heavy for thee; thou art not able to perform it thyself alone.

19 Hearken now unto my voice, I will give thee counsel, and God shall be with thee: Be thou for the people to Godward, that thou mayest bring the causes unto God:

20 And thou shalt teach them ordinances and laws, and shalt shew them the way wherein they must walk, and the work that they must do.

21 Moreover thou shalt provide out of all the people able men, such as fear God, men of truth, hating covetousness; and place such over them, to be rulers of thousands, and rulers of hundreds, rulers of fifties, and rulers of tens:

22 And let them judge the people at all seasons: and it shall be, that every great matter they shall bring unto thee, but every small matter they shall judge: so shall it be easier for thyself, and they shall bear the burden with thee.

23 If thou shalt do this thing, and God command thee so, then thou shalt be able to endure, and all this people shall also go to their place in peace.

24 So Moses hearkened to the voice of his father in law, and did all that he had said.

25 And Moses chose able men out of all Israel, and made them heads over the people, rulers of thousands, rulers of hundreds, rulers of fifties, and rulers of tens.

another, and I make known to them the statutes and instructions of God." 17 Moses' father-in-law said to him, "What you are doing is not good. 18 You will surely wear yourself out, both you and these people with you. For the task is too heavy for you; you cannot do it alone. 19 Now listen to me. I will give you counsel, and God be with you! You should represent the people before God, and you should bring their cases before God; 20 teach them the statutes and instructions and make known to them the way they are to go and the things they are to do. 21 You should also look for able men among all the people, men who fear God, are trustworthy, and hate dishonest gain; set such men over them as officers over thousands, hundreds, fifties, and tens. 22 Let them sit as judges for the people at all times; let them bring every important case to you, but decide every minor case themselves. So it will be easier for you, and they will bear the burden with you. 23 If you do this, and God so commands you, then you, then you will be able to endure, and all these people will go to their home in peace."

24 So Moses listened to his father-in-law and did all that he had said. 25 Moses chose able men from all Israel and appointed them as heads over the people, as officers over thousands, hundreds, fifties, and tens.

Key Verse: **Moreover thou shalt provide out of all the people able men, such as fear God, men of truth, hating covetousness; and place such over them, to be rulers of thousands, and rulers of hundreds, rulers of fifties, and rulers of tens. Exodus 18:21**

Key Verse: **You should also look for able men among all the people, men who fear God, are trustworthy, and hate dishonest gain; set such men over them as officers over thousands, hundreds, fifties, and tens. Exodus 18:21**

As You Read the Scripture

Exodus 18:1. We really don't know much about Jethro. His name in Hebrew means "excellence." Possibly that was his title because of his office as priest, and his real name was Reuel ("friend of God"?) as he is called in Exodus 2:18. But, maybe it was Hobab ("beloved") as Judges 4:11 says. But in Numbers 10:29, Hobab is Moses' brother-in-law! There is an interesting theory that the Hebrew name for God, "Yahweh," and many of their religious traditions came from the Midianites, who were distant cousins of the Israelites, and that Moses learned these things while staying with Jethro. The idea seems doubtful to me, but it is certainly true that God's people have never shrunk from learning from the cultures where they lived. Our chapter for today tells how Jethro the Midianite is able to serve as a very effective "process consultant" to Moses. Can you think of other times when foreigners played an important role in Israel's history? (What about Rahab and Ruth?)

Verse 7. Moses was evidently glad to see his father-in-law, for he kissed him in the traditional formal Oriental manner. They asked after each other's welfare (literally "peace") and went into Moses' tent. But, strange to our way of thinking, no mention is made of the reunion between Moses and his wife and sons.

Verse 8. There is some evidence here that the Israelites still thought of other gods as existing, though without the power of their deity. The notion that there is but one God in all the world, though implied in Deuteronomy 6:4, did not become completely common in Israel for a long time. Solomon built altars to foreign deities to please his wives, and the prophets still tried to persuade the people to leave the foreign idols alone.

Verse 13. Moses' custom of judging the people is still a tradition among the sheiks of the nomadic Arabs today. But this was a sizable nation, and the administrative responsibilities took all day. Not even a dictator can function without assistants.

Verse 15. The people came "to inquire of God." The distinction between church law and civil law that we know today was long in coming. To whom do you go with your troubles, your minister or your lawyer? Paul exhorts the early church to exhaust ecclesiastical remedies first, before resorting to the civil courts (1 Cor. 6:1-8). In the time of Moses, the Lord was sought, like an ancient oracle, on many matters, both large and small.

Verses 19-23. Jethro sets forth a very reasonable proposal, which Moses instantly agrees to. The problem, and its solution, is not unlike the decision made by the early Christians to appoint some of their number to take over the menial table duties from the apostles, so that they could go about their religious tasks. (See Acts 6:1-6; could this be the origin of the office of the deacon, meaning "one who serves"?) In Moses' case, the resulting arrangement is certainly more efficient. It is almost like a military arrangement, with officers over regiments, battalions, companies, and squadrons. But it may also mark the beginnings of democracy in ancient Israel; certainly many more people are being brought into decision-making positions in their government.

The Scripture and the Main Question

Organization

In the old days, clergy were a lot like lawyers. I once read in the ancient minutes of a rural congregation in Appalachia how two farmers appealed to the officials of their church for a ruling on where their fence line should run. The minutes stipulated that "the pastor of the church shall journey with them to the site, and upon hearing their arguments, shall decide where the fence should be; and for his labor and expense, the disputants shall pay him each one cask of good whiskey." They don't do things quite that way in my church today.

When the Israelites set out from Egypt they were certainly not a highly organized nation. No doubt they had ways of governing themselves, but these were probably largely patriarchal. Heads of households would rule on smaller matters, then clan chieftains, and eventually the elder statesmen of a tribe. Lack of leadership over the nation as a whole would have been one of the contributing factors to their increasing enslavement by the Egyptians. Without a Joseph there was no one to intercede for them with the pharaoh, and no one to give a sense of unity and cohesion to all the children of Israel. Good government, good management, is essential to the survival of any organization; as the organization grows, the old cousin-system ceases to function very effectively.

Those who argue for less government have their point. Thomas Paine wrote in *Common Sense:* "Government, even in its best state, is but a necessary evil; in its worst state, an intolerable one." And perhaps *Don Quixote* has it even better: "The good governor should have a broken leg and keep at home." But those who complain about government change their tune when they are in need of it. The children of Israel, in their cry to God (Exod. 2:23), were really asking for someone to come and take charge. If you pray for a Moses to lead you out of your Egypt, you had better be prepared for Moses to take charge. And take charge he did. How he was able to take that crowd of slaves and shape them into a powerful, well-governed, ethical nation is a mystery to me. But in this chapter, some of the answers to that mystery are made clear.

Advice and Consent

The words in the subhead are from the United States Constitution (Article II, Section 2, Paragraph 2), though I suspect they come from further back in British legal tradition. The paragraph has to do with the powers of the president to make treaties and appointments, subject to the advice and consent of the Senate. It is, of course, impossible to govern at all without the consent of the governed, either by their free choice or by forcing it on them. And any wise governor will keep a ready line of communication open with other officials and the citizenry. One of the marks of great leadership is the ability to take advice, and Moses here demonstrates it.

What is even more remarkable is that he's willing to take advice from his father-in-law. Because of the inevitable tension brought on naturally by the in-law relationship, such relatives are much maligned in our culture. But it does not have to be so and should not. I never knew my father-in-law, a wise and respected pediatrician who died before my wife and I met, but her mother was one of the principal figures of my formative years. A woman without much formal education, my mother-in-law taught the young adult Sunday school class in her church for so long that they were hardly young adults at all. I was privileged to learn many things from her, including theology, poetry, and common sense. Simon Peter apparently got along well with his mother-in-law too (Matt. 8:14), and one of the most loving relationships in the Bible existed between two in-laws (Ruth 1:14-18). Good advice is precious, and it should be accepted, even from those we might be inclined to resent.

Also evident in our story, though not explicitly stated, is Moses' ability to work with those under him. He apparently made good appointments (v. 25) and was willing to let them take responsibility for much of the decision making so necessary to good government. Bishop James Pike is credited with saying, "No one possesses authority who is not under authority." Thus Moses' obedience to God gave him the ability to elicit loyalty from those under him. The truly great leader has lines of communication open, both up and down.

The Elders of Israel

The word *elder* is used as a governmental term many times in the five books of Moses, including Exodus 18:18, and today most Christian denominations are governed by elders. In the episcopal churches, such as The United Methodist Church, the office of elder is fulfilled in the ordained ministry. The English word *priest* comes from the same root, and those who are ordained as ministers of the Word and sacraments are elders. Even some Baptist clergy are ordained by a "presbytery," with more than one congregation uniting to lay hands on one to be set apart to the preaching office. The point is that good organization in any church, or for that matter in any secular community, depends on the training and selection of able leaders, as well as the cooperation of the community as a whole. Perhaps the key text in the Bible for this concept is Ephesians 4:15-16:

Speaking the truth in love, we must grow up in every way into him who is the head, into Christ, from whom the whole body, joined and knit together by every ligament with which it is equipped, as each part is working properly, promotes the body's growth in building itself up in love.

Working together is difficult. Doing it all by yourself, as Moses attempted to do, however, is in the long run even harder. We have a task, both as a church and as individuals, to combine our gifts in such a way as to make our new Israel a genuine blessing.

Helping Adults Become Involved

Preparing to Teach

Apply the lesson of the lesson to your teaching of the lesson. In other words, try not to do this class all by yourself. Otherwise, you will be overworked, like Moses! Let me play Jethro to your Moses, and suggest that you appoint some folks from within your class to help you with the teaching. Here's one way you can do it: Call some of your class members and ask them to read the chapter carefully and be prepared to report on it when the class meets. You might give them an assignment card that would look like this:

> What principles of organization do you find in this chapter? Can you spot examples of them in the way our church is governed? In the secular governments—city, state, and nation? In the military? Are there ways that we can contribute more effectively to the life of our church by assisting our leaders? Could we have a more effective Sunday school class if we organized along such principles?

If it is not possible for you to make this assignment in advance, another way to handle it would be to take the first fifteen to twenty minutes of class time to give out the above card to everyone in the class and let each make a brief report. You, or someone you appoint, should take notes on the chalkboard or newsprint; at the end of the session your lesson will have almost taught itself. You might then spend the remaining minutes summarizing the principles you have gleaned from the material and making a list of ideas for your class's activities in the future.

This is the outline I suggest you follow:

> I.   A family reunion (18:1-9)
> II. A religious service (18:10-12)
> III. Moses' judging and Jethro's suggestion (18:13-23)
> IV. Moses implements the suggestion (18:24-27)

Introducing the Main Question

As was suggested above, the most effective way to introduce the question of cooperative leadership is to get your class members into leadership roles. If it is true that the best thing you can do for people is to ask them for help, then you will be paying a high compliment to your class members when you encourage them to take part.

Developing the Lesson

I. A family reunion (18:1-9)

Don't let the question of in-law relationships dominate the discussion; it could be a kind of red herring that gets them off the main subject. But it is an issue of real concern among most thoughtful Christians, so it would not be amiss to spend some time on it. Jethro seems to have been a very thoughtful person (his name means "excellence"). However, it has been suggested that this may have been his title as a priest among the Midianites. Maybe he was called "Your Excellency" or something like that. He was a man used to taking charge, and his visit to Moses is no exception. Do your in-laws try to take charge when they visit? If so, is this a source of friction? What can we learn from Moses' relationship with his wife's family that might help us in similar situations?

II. A religious service (18:10-12)

A good starting place is to worship together. There would be a lot less friction in families if we spent more time worshiping together. When I was growing up, and the in-laws came to visit, we always managed to go to church together. (Both of my grandfathers were preachers, so this wasn't too surprising.) And my wife's mother was a busy church person. The first time I went to visit them, prior to our marriage, the first thing we did was to go to their church for a family night supper. I clearly remember looking around at my future in-laws in the friendly setting of their church and thinking, "This is a family I want to be a part of." I can't think of a better way to get acquainted.

III. Moses' judging and Jethro's suggestion (18:13-23)

Moses, like all the judges who came after him, was a charismatic leader— that is, a gifted person who rose to the occasion. Such leaders are wonderful, but we will ruin them if we lean on them too heavily. We need to hold up their arms the way Aaron and Hur held up Moses' (Exod. 17:8-13). Are there ways in which your class can hold up your hands? Are there ways in which you and they can hold up the hands of other leaders in your congregation and community?

One word of caution: We need to be sure we are going into this with a sincere desire to help and with no thought of personal gain. Look at the important part of Jethro's advice in verse 21, concerning the character of the assistant judges.

IV. Moses implements the suggestion (18:24-27)

The important phrase here is "so Moses listened." We, too, need to listen, and if we hear any good counsel, we need, as Moses did, to put the plan to work at once.

Helping Class Members Act

This lesson lends itself well to labor outside the classroom. As you have sought to incorporate its principles into your teaching of the lesson, so you need to extend them beyond this session to other opportunities for service. There are surely many, both in your church and your community. For a closing session, you might have the class members list such opportunities, and each might choose one for personal implementation. You might ask each one to fill in the following blank: This week, I will volunteer to —————.

Planning for Next Sunday

Next Sunday may be the most important lesson in our whole series this quarter. Ask the class to read Exodus 19–20 carefully, and if possible, try their hand at stating the Ten Commandments in positive form.

God Desires Obedience

Background Scripture: Exodus 19:1–20:17

The Main Question

Do rules make you uncomfortable? They often bother me, even when I know they are probably good ones. A good example is the seatbelt law. I grumble to myself every time my car buzzes at me to remind me to fasten it. But, says a friend of mine, "That's just your car's way of telling you it loves you and wants you to be safe." Maybe so, but still I hate to be *told* when to be safe. I sometimes wish we had no rules.

But have you ever tried to play a game without rules? Once, years ago, some young friends and I decided to play a game of bridge with an extra rule: you could cheat if you could get away with it. There was no penalty for being caught cheating, you just had to take it back. The game wasn't much fun, and when it was over, the fellow who had been keeping the score won because he had cheated on that. We may argue over the rules and demand instant replay, but we know very well that if there are no rules, or if people disregard the rules, the game will be a failure.

So it is with life, and God knows it. God has given us some rules, not very complicated, but very essential, and when we all play the game of life by them it is very satisfying. Of course we make them complicated; yesterday's religious leaders and today's politicians have created a tangle of regulations. But through them all shines the deeper meaning of life: God's rules are fair, and we need to live by them. Our question this week is: Can we learn to love to do what we *have* to do? One way of asking the same question is to see if all those "Thou shalt nots" can be turned into "Thou shalts." Can we learn to view the law, not as a negative, but as a positive?

Selected Scripture

King James Version	New Revised Standard Version
Exodus 19:4-6a, 20:2-4, 7-17	*Exodus 19:4-6a, 20:2-4, 7-17*
4 Ye have seen what I did unto the Egyptians, and how I bare you on eagles' wings, and brought you unto myself.	4 You have seen what I did to the Egyptians, and how I bore you on eagles' wings and brought you to myself. 5 Now therefore, if you obey my voice and keep my covenant, you shall be my treasured possession out of all the peoples. Indeed, the whole earth is mine, 6 but you shall be for me a priestly kingdom and a holy nation.
5 Now therefore, if ye will obey my voice indeed, and keep my covenant, then ye shall be a peculiar treasure unto me above all people: for all the earth is mine:	
6 And ye shall be unto me a kingdom of priests, and an holy nation.	
20:2-4, 7-17	*20:2-4, 7-17*
2 I am the LORD thy God, which have brought thee out of the land of	2 I am the LORD your God, who brought you out of the land of

Egypt, out of the house of bondage.

3 Thou shalt have no other gods before me.

4 Thou shalt not make unto thee any graven image, or any likeness of any thing that is in heaven above, or that is in the earth beneath, or that is in the water under the earth.

....

7 Thou shalt not take the name of the LORD thy God in vain; for the LORD will not hold him guiltless and taketh his name in vain.

8 Remember the sabbath day, to keep it holy.

9 Six days shalt thou labour, and do all thy work:

10 But the seventh day is the sabbath of the LORD thy God: in it thou shalt not do any work, thou, nor thy son, nor thy daughter, thy manservant, nor thy maidservant, not thy cattle, nor thy stranger that is within thy gates:

11 For in six days the LORD made heaven and earth, the sea, and all that in them is, and rested the seventh day: wherefore the LORD blessed the sabbath day, and hallowed it.

12 Honour thy father and thy mother: that thy days may be long upon the land which the LORD thy God giveth thee.

13 Thou shalt not kill.

14 Thou shalt not commit adultery.

15 Thou shalt not steal.

16 Thou shalt not bear false witness against thy neighbour.

17 Thou shalt not covet thy neighbour's house, thou shalt not covet thy neighbour's wife, nor his manservant, nor his maidservant, nor his ox, nor his ass, nor any thing that is thy neighbour's.

Key Verse: **Now therefore, if ye will obey my voice indeed, and keep my covenant, then ye shall be a peculiar treasure unto me above all people: for all the earth is mine. Exodus 19:5**

Egypt, out of the house of slavery; 3 you shall have no other gods before me.

4 You shall not make for yourself an idol, whether in the form of anything that is in heaven above, or that is on the earth beneath, or that is in the water under the earth.

....

7 You shall not make wrongful use of the name of the LORD your God, for the LORD will not acquit anyone who misuses his name.

8 Remember the sabbath day, and keep it holy. 9 Six days you shall labor and do all your work. 10 But the seventh day is a sabbath to the LORD your God; you shall not do any work—you, your son or your daughter, your male or female slave, your livestock, or the alien resident in your towns. 11 For in six days the LORD made heaven and earth, the sea, and all that is in them, but rested the seventh day; therefore the LORD blessed the sabbath day and consecrated it.

12 Honor your father and your mother, so that your days may be long in the land that the LORD your God is giving you.

13 You shall not murder.

14 You shall not commit adultery.

15 You shall not steal.

16 You shall not bear false witness against your neighbor.

17 You shall not covet your neighbor's house; you shall not covet your neighbor's wife, or male or female slave, or ox, or donkey, or anything that belongs to your neighbor.

Key Verse: **Now therefore, if you obey my voice and keep my covenant, you shall be my treasured possession out of all the peoples. Indeed, the whole earth is mine. Exodus 19:5**

As You Read the Scripture

Exodus 19. God appears at Sinai (another theophany; see Lesson 2), and the people are prepared for the giving of the law.

Verse 1. It had taken them two months to cover the 150 miles between Egypt and Sinai.

Verse 2. It is understood that the mountain is Sinai, the same on which Moses met God at the burning bush. Moses has brought them to the place of his own religious experience to prepare them for theirs.

Verse 4. It is by the grace of God that they have been brought to this place.

Verse 5. The commandments are our half of the covenant to keep.

Verse 6. Compare this with 1 Peter 2:9.

Verse 7-15. Notice how Moses is fulfilling a priestly function, relaying messages back and forth between the Lord and the people.

Verse 12. The mountain is not to be touched. Those who live in the eastern United States will have a hard time understanding this, but if you have spent any time out west, you know that some of the Rockies rise up almost perpendicularly; you can stand next to a hill and reach out and touch it.

Verse 13. The holiness extends, like magnetism through iron filings, to the one who touches the mountain; no one should touch him.

Verse 16. These could have been natural phenomena, but the scene is like that of the burning bush, a miraculous sign of the presence of God.

Verses 21 and 24. There is danger that the people might break through the holy barrier, and also that God might break out! The image is one of the awesome presence of the holiness of God.

Chapter 20:1-17 The Ten Commandments is the name given in Exodus 34:28, but the literal translation is the "ten words." Probably in their original form they were quite brief. They are called "the covenant" in Exodus 25:16, which is literally "the testimony." They are also found in Deuteronomy 5:6-21, with slight variations. The Exodus version is considered to be the older of the two.

The commandments are not numbered in either Exodus or Deuteronomy, and so they have been numbered differently in different traditions:

	Jewish Tradition	Protestant Tradition	Catholic Tradition
1.	Verse 2	Verse 3	Verses 3-6
2.	Verses 3-6	Verses 4-6	Verse 7
3.	Verse 7	Verse 7	Verses 8-11
4.	Verses 8-11	Verses 8-11	Verse 12
5.	Verse 12	Verse 12	Verse 13
6.	Verse 13	Verse 13	Verse 14
7.	Verse 14	Verse 14	Verse 15
8.	Verse 15	Verse 15	Verse 16
9.	Verse 16	Verse 16	Verse 17a
10.	Verse 17	Verse 17	Verse 17b

The two tables of the law have also been divided in different ways. Our tradition usually divides them into 1-4 (religious duties) and 5-10 (ethical responsibility). In this way they can be grouped under the two great commandments given by Jesus (Matt. 22:37-39 and elsewhere).

FOURTH QUARTER

The Scripture and the Main Question

The Fear of God (19:1-25)

First there is the element of mystery, God shrouded in a dense cloud (v. 9). Then we have the solemn warning (v. 12) that the people must not so much as touch the holy mountain, under penalty of death. Not only that, but one must not even touch anyone who has touched the mountain, lest the penalty extend like magnetism, or like a warning not to grab hold of someone who has hold of a live wire (v. 13). Then there is the ceremonial washing and the abstinence from sexual activity (v. 15), as though the people must be "squeaky clean" in the presence of God. The scene culminates with thunder and lightning in the smoky cloud (v. 16) and a frightening blast on the ram's horn, followed by the violence of an earthquake (v. 18). Even the sight of God's appearing could be fatal (v. 21) and only the chosen, specially consecrated, representatives of the people (v. 22) dare to come close. Even they must stand back (v. 24) while Aaron and Moses intercede for them with the unapproachable mystery that is God.

This scene is surely in contrast with the almost casual reverence of much contemporary worship, whose trumpet gives a very "uncertain sound" (see 1 Cor. 14:8). There is something in this terrible vision that makes me think of how I felt as a child, going into a great cathedral, scrubbed and cleaned in my Sunday best, and struck with awe at the great and holy place. But that was small excitement compared to the ominous scene at this untouchable mountain. Here we have such a sense of God's utter holiness and apartness that we are filled with fear.

Our word *reverence* is simply not strong enough to describe the feeling that we are speaking about here. Another, lesser known, word is sometimes used to carry this idea: the word *numinous,* derived from a Latin root meaning "divine power and deity." It is not the same as ordinary "fear," which we would feel if a clear and present danger was nearby. You would feel fear if you believed that there was a man-eating tiger in the bushes nearby, but if you believed there were a holy ominous Presence nearby, it would cause you to be moved in a different way. We have a hard time describing this feeling because it is rarely experienced by enlightened moderns. Perhaps the primitive savage felt it in the thunderstorm. A friend of mine was in Managua, Nicaragua, some years ago when a violent earthquake shook that city. He was lying in his hotel bed when the quake started, and he sprung up to see what was going on. To his horror, he realized that the smooth tile floor on which he was standing was waving under his feet like the surface of a stream. He said, "The hair on the back of my neck stood on end, for I realized that the solidity of reality had become fluid. I was in for anything, I knew not what. My whole universe had been shaken to its foundations."

For Christians, accustomed to thinking of God in the close, personal way Jesus taught us, this vision of terror is a strange one. Could the loving God whom Jesus called Father really be like that? Sometimes it is necessary for parents to instill fear in their children to make them appreciate the terrible danger of a street filled with traffic or a bottle filled with poison. It is an act of caring love, though it may instill in the child all sorts of ominous feelings. But it may save a life. So do the laws of God come to us; they are frightening, yet they are a great comfort, for to know them and to respect them is to be able to live a joyful and productive life. Not to know them, or not to hold them in awe, leads ultimately to destruction.

The Ten Great Rules (20:1-17)

The word *Torah* means a great deal more than "Ten Commandments." Indeed, it refers to the whole Pentateuch, the five "books of Moses." In many places in the scriptures joy in God's rules is expressed. See, for instance Psalm 19, in which the natural order (vv. 1-6) is compared with the moral order (vv. 7-14). The law is

> More to be desired . . . than gold,
>> even much fine gold;
> sweeter also than honey,
>> and drippings of the honeycomb. (v. 10)

Or Psalm 119, in which the poet sings, for 176 verses, a remarkable acrostic song celebrating the happiness that the law brings.

> Oh, how I love your law!
>> It is my meditation all day long. (v. 97)

> Your word is a lamp to my feet
>> and a light to my path. (v. 105)

For those of us (and I think this is most of us) to whom rules are an irritant, it will help to think of them not so much as prohibitions against having any fun, but as guiding principles that God has given us to actually make life more fun. Jesus summed up the law (Matt. 22:37, 39) in a positive way: " 'You shall love the Lord your God with all your heart, and with all your soul, and with all your mind. . . . You shall love your neighbor as yourself.' "

Here is my attempt at putting the ten laws, most of which are stated in the negative, into positive form. Have a try at your own version.

1. Put God above everyone and everything else in your life.
2. See in everything beautiful evidence of the One who made all things.
3. Respect the name of God and keep your speech pure.
4. Keep a healthy rhythm to your life.
5. Honor your ancestors.
6. Respect and care for life.
7. Keep your promises.
8. Respect the property of others.
9. Tell the truth.
10. Be satisfied with what you have.

If we would adopt such an attitude toward life we would not only please God, but we would live joyfully in all our relationships.

Helping Adults Become Involved

Preparing to Teach

This is a tough lesson, both because it is so very important and because it is so very familiar. Coming at it in a fresh way will not be easy. Let me suggest this for a starter: There is an old litany, based on the commandments, that once was used regularly in churches as a service of preparation for Holy Communion, as an act of penitence and commitment. You can pray it by yourself in preparation for teaching this lesson, and you may decide to use it with your class. If so, read each of the commandments aloud, pausing after each for a time of silent meditation. After each meditation, close with the versicle: "Lord, have mercy upon me, and incline my heart to keep this law." Be sure to use the two great commandments of Jesus as well as the Ten Commandments. If you like, you can use them in the positive form in which I stated them in the preceding section.

If you decide to do it with your class, either at the beginning or the end of the class period, divide the versicle in half and say it like this:

> Leader: Lord, have mercy upon us.
> **People: And incline our hearts to keep this law.**

As an added preparation, in addition to a careful reading of the two chapters, you might want to improve on my "positive" stating of the ten rules.

Here's the outline I would follow:

> I. The untouchable mountain (19:1-25)
>   A. The invitation of God (19:1-8)
>   B. The people's preparation (19:9-15)
>   C. The theophany (19:16-25)
> II. The Ten Commandments (20:1-17)

Introducing the Main Question

Start with the idea that the rules are given to us for our own good. In that sense, they are intended to be good news, not bad. Begin by using the litany suggested above with the commandments stated in the positive, as you choose to say them.

An alternative procedure would be, if your class is large enough, to divide into ten groups (if you have fewer than ten people you can give some of them more than one commandment) and ask them to state the commandment in a positive way. (Note that you don't have to do this for numbers 4 and 5; they are already positive, but the group might like to work on stating the law in such a way that its underlying purpose is made clear. I suspect, for instance, that "Remember the sabbath day," really translates for many of your class members into "things you aren't supposed to do on Sunday.")

Yet one more exercise might be to try to state the Ten Commandments in as few words as possible. Here's my shot at it:

> 1. God first!
> 2. Pure worship!
> 3. Pure speech!
> 4. Rest regularly!
> 5. Honor parents!
> 6. Respect life!
> 7. Keep promises!
> 8. Respect property!
> 9. Respect truth!
> 10. Be satisfied!

How about that! I got them all in two words and all in the positive. But you could improve on it.

Developing the Lesson

I. The untouchable mountain (19:1-25)

In this section, talk with the class about the meaning of the expression "the fear of the Lord" (see Job 28:28; Ps. 111:10; Prov. 1:7; and many other places). There is a sense in which we are quite right to fear God, and another in which God is the one person in all the world whom we need not fear.

A. The invitation of God (19:1-8)

The covenant is not with Moses; that had happened at this same spot long before (Exod. 3). It is with the people, and they must now come into the presence of the Holy One.

B. The people's preparation (19:9-15)

In order to do so, they must get cleaned up a good bit. As in the later Temple, the people aren't allowed to go as close as the priests, but this is still a special occasion for them. For us Christians, the veil has been torn in two, and we are allowed access, through Christ, to the very presence of God (Heb. 10:19-23; see also 4:14-16).

C. The theophany (19:16-25)

A theophany is an appearance of God. Here in the "earthquake, wind and fire" we meet the God whom we both fear and love. The sound of the trumpet is like that of Gabriel (Matt. 24:31; 1 Cor. 15:52; 1 Thess. 4:16) summoning us to ultimate things.

II. The Ten Commandments (20:1-17)

If you have time, discuss all of the commandments, giving at least one sentence to set forth the reason behind the prohibition. For instance, I once heard a class of kindergarteners recite the Ten Commandments, following each with a sentence beginning "This means that. . . . " I waited with curiosity for number seven, wondering what a five-year-old would make of adultery. I was delighted when he announced, "This means God wants us to have happy families." I couldn't do better myself.

Helping Class Members Act

The class has the rules for the game, will they play according to the rules? Ask them to post the Ten Commandments somewhere they will see them every day.

Planning for Next Sunday

Have the class read Exodus 32–34 and keep their eyes open for golden calves.

God Forgives

Background Scripture: Exodus 32; 34:1-10

The Main Question

Sometimes there is not a thing you can do. I remember the story of a little girl who wandered into the living room to discover her mother's good scissors lying on the coffee table. She had some blunt scissors of her own, which she was allowed to use, but the shiny silver sharp scissors were too great a temptation for her. She picked them up, snapped them shut and open a few times, and looked about eagerly for something to cut. There on the back of the best chair was the antimacassar her great-aunt had crocheted. (If you don't know what an antimacassar is, ask your own great-aunt.) It was too inviting. With two snips, she cut it in half. At that moment her mother came into the room, took in the situation at a glance, snatched up the scissors, gave the child a smack, rushed into the bedroom, slammed the door, flung herself on the bed, and burst into tears.

Now we have here an impossible situation with no solutions. There is no way to get Auntie back from the grave to crochet another one of those things. The deed has been done. Suppose the little girl says, "I'm sorry; I'll never do it again." That won't undo the deed, and she most likely will do it again, or something like it. After the mother got over her tantrum and stopped crying, she heard the rapping of a tiny fist on her bedroom door, and a tearful little voice pleading, "Mommy, please take me back."

Do you think her mother took her back? Did God take back the shameful worshipers of the golden calf? Will God take you and me back? That is our question this week.

Selected Scripture

King James Version

Exodus 32:15-19, 30-34

15 And Moses turned, and went down from the mount, and the two tables of the testimony were in his hand: the tables were written on both their sides; on the one side and on the other were they written.

16 And the tables were the work of God, and the writing was the writing of God, graven upon the tables.

17 And when Joshua heard the noise of the people as they shouted, he said unto Moses, There is a noise of war in the camp.

18 And he said, It is not the voice of them that shout for mastery, nei-

New Revised Standard Version

Exodus 32:15-19, 30-34

15 Then Moses turned and went down from the mountain, carrying the two tablets of the covenant in his hands, tablets that were written on both sides, written on the front and on the back. 16 The tablets were the work of God, and the writing was the writing of God, engraved upon the tablets. 17 When Joshua heard the noise of the people as they shouted, he said to Moses, "There is a noise of war in the camp." 18 But he said,

"It is not the sound made by
     victors,
or the sound made by losers;

ther is it the voice of them that cry for being overcome: but the noise of them that sing do I hear.

19 And it came to pass, as soon as he came nigh unto the camp, that he saw the calf, and the dancing: and Moses' anger waxed hot, and he cast the tables out of his hands, and brake them beneath the mount.

....

30 And it came to pass on the morrow, that Moses said unto the people, Ye have sinned a great sin: and now I will go up unto the LORD; peradventure I shall make an atonement for your sin.

31 And Moses returned unto the LORD, and said, Oh, this people have sinned a great sin, and have made them gods of gold.

32 Yet now, if thou wilt forgive their sin—; and if not, blot me, I pray thee, out of thy book which thou hast written.

33 And the LORD said unto Moses, Whosoever hath sinned against me, him will I blot out of my book.

34 Therefore now go, lead the people unto the place of which I have spoken unto thee: behold, mine Angel shall go before thee: nevertheless in the day when I visit I will visit their sin upon them.

34:4-6

4 And he hewed two tables of stone like unto the first; and Moses rose up early in the morning, and went up unto mount Sinai, as the LORD had commanded him, and took in his hand the two tables of stone.

5 And the LORD descended in the cloud, and stood with him there, and proclaimed the name of the LORD.

6 And the LORD passed by before him, and proclaimed, The LORD, The LORD God, merciful and gracious, longsuffering, and abundant in goodness and truth.

it is the sound of revelers that I hear."

19 As soon as he came near the camp and saw the calf and the dancing, Moses' anger burned hot, and he threw the tablets from his hands and broke them at the foot of the mountain.

....

30 On the next day Moses said to the people, "You have sinned a great sin. But now I will go up to the LORD; perhaps I can make atonement for your sin." 31 So Moses returned to the LORD and said, "Alas, this people has sinned a great sin; they have made for themselves gods of gold. 32 But now, if you will only forgive their sin—but if not, blot me out of the book that you have written." 33 But the LORD said to Moses, "Whoever has sinned against me I will blot out of my book. 34 But now go, lead the people to the place about which I have spoken to you; see, my angel shall go in front of you. Nevertheless, when the day comes for punishment, I will punish them for their sin."

34:4-6

4 So Moses cut two tablets of stone like the former ones; and he rose early in the morning and went up on Mount Sinai, as the LORD had commanded him, and took in his hand the two tablets of stone. 5 The LORD descended in the cloud and stood with him there, and proclaimed the name, "The LORD." 6 The LORD passed before him, and proclaimed,

"The LORD, the LORD,
a God merciful and gracious,
slow to anger,
and abounding in steadfast love
and faithfulness.

FOURTH QUARTER

As You Read the Scripture

Exodus 32. In the interim since our last lesson (on Exod. 20), we have skipped over many details of the Law that grew out of the Ten Commandments. They involve civil and criminal laws (chaps. 21–22), rules for morality and religion (chaps. 22–23), a calendar of sabbaths and feasts (chap. 23), renewal of the covenant (chap. 24), and directions for the tabernacle and its worship services (chaps. 25–31). Now we encounter Aaron and the people, frustrated with Moses' long absence and ready to violate the very laws God is in the process of giving: the ban against the worship of other gods and the making of idols. The narrative serves as proof that the commandments were certainly needed.

Verse 2. It is natural for people to demand concrete assurance of their stability. Just as they will one day want a king during the uncertain days of the judges (1 Sam. 8:5), so also they want some certainty that they know who they are following. They have already begun to forget Moses.

Verse 3. Note the continued use of the plural "gods" (see v. 1). The Hebrew word for "god" has a plural form. It is most likely that the golden calf was made on a wooden frame and was gold-plated. (Certainly it would burn better; see v. 20.)

Verses 5-6. Aaron's complicity in the deed is clear, in spite of his protestation in verse 24. The celebration is remembered in the New Testament, in Stephen's defense (Acts 7:40-41) and by Paul in his criticism of the excesses of the early church at worship (1 Cor. 10:7). The Israelites weren't completely rejecting Yahweh; they had a hard time visualizing an invisible God, particularly now that Moses himself is out of their sight.

Verses 7-14. God informs Moses of what is going on, and Moses boldly argues with the Lord on behalf of the people. Moses' argument is successful (v. 14), and it seems that God's mind is changed (compare Jonah 3:10). What God demands is righteousness, and apparently God is willing to accept it in the repentance of either a whole nation, such as Nineveh, or one individual, such as Moses. Christians see in this a prefiguring of the atoning work of Jesus Christ.

Verses 15-35. These verses tell of the anger of Moses and the Lord. Although Moses is on the side of the people, and God has relented, there are still consequences the people must suffer.

Verse 32. Moses is willing to die for his people. Compare this to the willingness of Paul to suffer (Rom. 9:3). Ultimately, of course, it is just such willingness by Jesus that we Christians celebrate. Although Jesus was willing to die, he prayed, "Father, forgive them; for they do not know what they are doing" (Luke 23:34).

Exodus 34:1-10. Again we have skipped over much material, including the people's repentance, Moses' intercession on their behalf, and the wonderful theophany in which Moses, hiding in the cleft of the rock, is able to see only the afterglow of God's glory. In this passage, the tables of stone are reconsti-

tuted and the covenant is renewed, with the Lord revealed as a forgiving
God.

Verse 6. This is the height of the Old Testament's revelation of God's true
character (compare Num. 14:8; Ps. 86:15; Jon. 4:2).

The Scripture and the Main Question

There is a phrase that describes the attitude of some Christians toward God's
forgiveness: "cheap grace." How can grace be anything other than cheap? It
doesn't cost anything, does it? Grace, by definition, is a gift. How could it be
costly? The answer is that it is costly to the giver, and if we receive it flippantly,
lightly, or even arrogantly, we insult the giver. God's forgiveness hurts; it is
supremely expressed in the most hurtful form imaginable: a bloody cross.

So it is important for us to remember that God's forgiveness doesn't come
easily. It is, however, as sure as the sunrise to those who fear God's name
(Mal. 4:2). The story of the golden calf is about our rebellion and God's forgiveness, and it deserves our attention.

Our Need for Symbols

Christian symbols are fascinating. One of the earliest symbols used was the
fish, simply drawn in two arcs; it could be easily drawn with a toe in the sand and
could have been a kind of countersign among those who were under persecution and needed a means of identifying themselves to their fellows. Its use may
have begun when someone noticed that the Greek word for fish (IXTHUS)
contained the initials, in Greek of course, of a simple creed: Jesus Christ, God's
Son, Savior. It is still in use today; I just happened to glance down as I wrote this
and noticed that I am wearing a silver fish as a sign of church membership.

Another early symbol, and the most common, was the cross. We see it on
church steeples, on communion tables, hanging in chancels, worn around
people's necks, and printed on church letterheads. It has been used in over
a hundred different shapes. Indeed, crosses have been borrowed by many
secular agencies, such as the Red Cross. The cross is an international symbol
for hospitals and first-aid stations as well.

Why do we need symbols, or logos as they are called nowadays? The God
whom we worship is transcendent—that is, invisible—and greatly removed
from our world of things. So far is God above us or beyond us or before us
(we are struck with the language of space and time) that the idea of God
seems very unreal to us. In teaching our children, or even in "visualizing"
the eternal God for ourselves, we are comforted by things we can actually see
with our eyes. But it doesn't help us to be too literal. For this reason, when
the artists of the Renaissance began to be more and more proficient in using
proper perspective and anatomy in their sculpture and painting, the church
became more and more nervous about their use. The old mosaics with their
flat surfaces and stylized figures did not tempt us to worship them or to
think that God or Jesus really looked like that. We knew that they stood for
something else. But when the artists got better, their art became very disturbing to the church. Many of the reformers were so upset about it that
they nearly threw art out of the churches altogether, with the result that
colonial churches in early America were often very bare and plain. In some
denominations, they still are.

But there is a difference between a symbolic or artistic attempt to represent God, or God's presence, and a statue, like Aaron's golden calf, that we deem actually to *be* a god. There was a little carved African figure that sat in a corner in my parent's home. We called him Bud (I think after the god in Kipling's poem "Mandalay") and kept paper clips in his begging bowl. I thought he was sad and silly, and I never considered worshiping him. But some people did, and some still do. There seems to be, primitive perhaps, and therefore subtly embedded in our consciousness, a need to pin God down, to have a god we can touch and see, rather than a strange and distant deity like the invisible YHWH. So the Israelites cast a calf.

Does God's Mind Change?

And they got caught. But after expressing a great deal of anger, God listened to Moses' intercession (32:11-12, 31-32) with some clever bargaining ("You don't want to lose face do you?" [v. 12]) and God "changed his mind" (v. 14). And this is indicated in other places in the Bible (see Gen. 6:6; Amos 7:3, 6; Jon. 3:10; 1 Chron. 21:15). But how does this square with our image of the immutable, omnipotent God, in whom there is no "variation or shadow due to change" (James 1:17)? It helps me to think of what Leslie Weatherhead called "God's ultimate will vs. God's circumstantial will." Ultimately, God wants our redemption; in this, God never changes. But in confronting us, both in our failures and in our faulty repentance, God does appear to change, because of meeting us where we are. God always wants us to be moral and good, and to worship our Creator alone. But God understands us, even better than we understand ourselves, and the coming of Jesus Christ into our lives was proof of this. God is willing to go to any lengths to rescue us. It is we who change. And God, meeting us where we are, with unutterable love, appears to us to change, to enable us to become more like the unchangeable God.

Helping Adults Become Involved

Preparing to Teach

Again, be sure to read the material thoroughly, including the chapter we skipped, making sure you have facts in their context. Note that there has been a long aside (Exod. 21–31) containing a great deal about laws and regulations and religious activities, including the construction and use of the tabernacle. But the setting has not changed; we are still at Sinai. It was during all this dialogue between God and Moses that the people became bored and afraid, and slipped over into idolatry.

    I. The golden calf
        A. The people desert God and Moses
        B. Moses intercedes
        C. The anger of Moses
        D. The Levites
        E. Moses intercedes again
   II. The promise of God's presence
 III. The covenant renewed

Introducing the Main Question

I doubt your class is terribly tempted to make a golden calf. So your task as a teacher is to help them see the relevance of this lesson. What are our golden calves? They are anything that becomes more important to us than God, and in which we seek security. We have spoken about false gods (which we invent) and lesser gods (which are earthly things that we make into deities) in previous lessons, so we need not repeat the list now. Perhaps you still have a copy of the list your class made for lesson 3. If so, use it again; in any event, ask your class to suggest what the golden calves are in our society today. Some of the usual answers will be money, pleasure, fame, and power. But there are others, sometimes more hard to recognize: family, country, reputation, and so on.

You might also ask the class to think of persons in our day who are like Aaron—eager to give the people what they want, rather than what God wants. Not all of them are politicians. I know some clergy like that, some authors, some movie directors, some fad diet planners, and so on. Are we not all guilty of being Aaron sometimes? And do we not desperately need a Moses in our midst, to take a strong stand against such tendencies? If you know such a Moses, give your respect; if you don't, it may be up to you to be Moses to those around you.

Developing the Lesson

I. The golden calf

Start by helping the people know what their golden calves are. We may not make gold statues of them, but we may have things we worship.

A. The people desert God and Moses

This sort of apostasy is more common than not. In our day few claim to be atheists, not out loud at least, but there are many practicing atheists. Some people live as though there were no God, and our leaders play right along with them. In what sense do the people in your class desert God?

B. Moses intercedes

Moses' intercession for the Israelites set an example that was eventually supremely fulfilled in Jesus Christ, who entered the presence of God through the torn curtain and there made intercession for us. Moses is not Christ, but he is a type of Christ—that is, he has Christlike qualities. Moses was righteous (Heb. 11:23-28)—that is, he did these things by faith. We all need to be like this.

C. The anger of Moses

The breaking of the tablet on which Ten Commandments were written wasn't all a matter of Moses' temper. There is a tradition in the Talmud that Moses did it as if to say, "The people haven't seen the law yet; it is I who have broken it."

D. The Levites

This is an attempt to account for the origin of the Levitical priesthood.

E. Moses intercedes again

II. The promise of God's presence

You needn't cover this material, but at least quickly remind your class what happens in this chapter.

III. The covenant renewed

Here you need to bring in the discussion about the forgiving nature of God. A covenant is an agreement between two parties. Though we are forever breaking our half, God's half is being forever renewed.

Helping Class Members Act

Send the class members out to look for golden calves in their lives, and Aaronic preachers and politicians who are willing to cast them when the people want them. We too might break some tablets of stone in our anger.

Planning for Next Sunday

Have the class read the assignment and look for signs of the presence of God in their midst during the coming week.

LESSON 9   JULY 31

God Is with Us

Background Scripture: Exodus 25:1-9; 29:38-46; 40:16-38

The Main Question

Perhaps you have seen it: a painting by Norman Rockwell called *The Scoutmaster,* which depicts a thoughtful-looking man, standing outdoors under a starry sky. Behind him, illuminated by the light of a dying campfire, are some youngsters, curled up securely in their sleeping bags in their pup tent. The image is of a strong, caring person, standing guard through the night.

I chose this image for several reasons. For one, I have been both a Scout and a Scoutmaster, and I know something about how it feels. But my real reason for thinking of the Scoutmaster is the Bible itself. *Tabernacle* means "tent," and the image of passage from Exodus for this week is that of a God camped out with the Israelites in the wilderness. Indeed, when this idea is picked up in the New Testament (Rev. 21:3), the Greek can be literally translated, "See the tent of God is among mortals; God will pitch a tent with them, and be their God." Our main question can be summed up: What does it mean, on our life's journey, to be able to say, "Immanuel: God with us"?

Selected Scripture

King James Version

New Revised Standard Version

Exodus 25:1-8; 40:33c-38

1 And the LORD spake unto Moses, saying,

2 Speak unto the children of Israel, that they bring me an offering: of every man that giveth it willingly with his heart ye shall take my offering.

3 And this is the offering which ye shall take of them; gold, and silver, and brass,

4 And blue, and purple, and scarlet, and fine linen, and goats' hair,

5 And rams' skins dyed red, and badgers' skins, and shittim wood,

6 Oil for the light, spices for anointing oil, and for sweet incense,

7 Onyx stones, and stones to be set in the ephod, and in the breastplate.

8 And let them make me a sanctuary; that I may dwell among them.

29:42-46

42 This shall be a continual burnt offering throughout your generations at the door of the tabernacle of the congregation before the LORD: where I will meet you, to speak there unto thee.

43 And there I will meet with the children of Israel, and the tabernacle shall be sanctified by my glory.

44 And I will sanctify the tabernacle of the congregation, and the altar: I will sanctify also both Aaron and his sons, to minister to me in the priest's office. 5 And I will dwell among the children of Israel, and will be their God.

46 And they shall know that I am the LORD their God, that brought them forth out of the land of Egypt, that I may dwell among them: I am the LORD their God.

40:33c-38

33 So Moses finished the work.

34 Then a cloud covered the tent

Exodus 25:1-8; 40:33c-38

1 The LORD said to Moses: 2 Tell the Israelites to take for me an offering; from all whose hearts prompt them to give you shall receive the offering for me. 3 This is the offering that you shall receive from them: gold, silver, and bronze, 4 blue, purple, and crimson yarns and fine linen, goats' hair, 5 tanned rams' skins, fine leather, acacia wood, 6 oil for the lamps, spices for the anointing oil and for the fragrant incense, 7 onyx stones and gems to be set in the ephod and for the breastpiece. 8 And have them make me a sanctuary, so that I may dwell among them.

29:42-46

42 It shall be a regular burnt offering throughout your generations at the entrance of the tent of meeting before the LORD, where I will meet with you, to speak to you there. 43 I will meet with the Israelites there, and it shall be sanctified by my glory; 44 I will consecrate the tent of meeting and the altar; Aaron also and his sons I will consecrate, to serve me as priests. 45 I will dwell among the Israelites, and I will be their God. 46 And they shall know that I am the LORD their God, who brought them out of the land of Egypt that I might dwell among them; I am the LORD their God.

40:33c-38

33 So Moses finished the work.

34 Then the cloud covered the tent

of the congregation, and the glory of the LORD filled the tabernacle.

35 And Moses was not able to enter into the tent of the congregation, because the cloud abode thereon, and the glory of the LORD filled the tabernacle.

36 And when the cloud was taken up from over the tabernacle, the children of Israel went onward in all their journeys.

37 But if the cloud were not taken up, then they journeyed not until the day that it was taken up.

38 For the cloud of the LORD was upon the tabernacle by day, and fire was on it by night, in the sight of all the house of Israel, throughout all their journeys.

of meeting, and the glory of the LORD filled the tabernacle. 35 Moses was not able to enter the tent of meeting because the cloud settled upon it, and the glory of the LORD filled the tabernacle. 36 Whenever the cloud was taken up from the tabernacle, the Israelites would set out on each stage of their journey; 37 but if the cloud was not taken up, then they did not set out until the day that it was taken up. 38 For the cloud of the LORD was on the tabernacle by day, and fire was in the cloud by night before the eyes of all the house of Israel at each stage of their journey.

Key Verse: **And I will dwell among the children of Israel, and will be their God. Exodus 29:45**

Key Verse: **I will dwell among the Israelites, and I will be their God. Exodus 29:45**

As You Read the Scripture

This week we look at the material we skipped between the giving of the Law at Sinai and the people's apostasy with the golden calf. Make sure of the context by seeing where this week's passages fit into the outline.

Exodus 25:1-9. The offerings of the people.

Verse 2. Note that the offerings are voluntary (see 2 Cor. 9:7).

Verse 3. The metals listed are those the people carried with them. For a nomadic people, they were pretty well supplied!

Verse 4. The women wove the fabrics used (see 35:23, 25).

Verse 7. The *ephod* was a priestly garment, a kind of vest, supported by shoulder straps with engraved stones. On the front was a kind of pouch, called the breastpiece, hanging by gold chains and rings (see 28:6-12).

Exodus 25:10-27:21. The furniture of the tabernacle.

Exodus 28:1-43. The priesthood and its vestments.

Exodus 29:1-37. The consecration of the priests.

Exodus 29:38-46. The great altar and its offerings.

Verse 38. Two lambs a day would put a considerable dent in the herds of the people. In forty years, this would come to over 29,000 head! Then, of course, there were other sacrifices (see Num. 28). This important daily ritual was carried out, along with the meal and drink offerings, from the time of the Exodus to the destruction of Jerusalem in A.D. 70. Since that time, the Jews have not continued the practice of animal sacrifices.

Verse 40. A "measure" was an *ephah* (about a bushel), and a *hin* was about a gallon and a half.

Verses 42, 44. The "tent of meeting" sometimes refers to the tabernacle itself and sometimes to a kind of provisional meeting place set up outside the

the camp, as when God was angry with the people over the golden calf incident. (See 33:7-11.)

Exodus 30. Additional equipment for worship.

Exodus 31:1-11. Appointment of the craftsmen.

Exodus 31:12-18. The Sabbath law.

Exodus 31:1–34:45. The golden calf and God's forgiveness, which we studied last week.

Exodus 35–40. The ordinances carried out.

Exodus 40:16-38. Moses carried out God's instructions. We have come to the end of the book of the Exodus, and Moses faithfully does everything the Lord commanded. Now that the people are back in God's good graces, the Presence is once more felt in the midst of the people.

Verse 20. The "covenant" is literally the "testimony" and probably is the two tablets of stone containing the commandments. The "mercy seat" was more than a mere lid to the Ark (box), but was wrought with two cherubim, whose wings extended over it, between which the presence of God was thought to dwell (see 25:17-22).

Verse 35. This is the same cloud that we have been hearing about all during the story of the Exodus; it is like a sacrament, the outward sign of a spiritual truth, the presence of God's glory in the midst of the chosen people.

The Scripture and the Main Question

Where Is God?

When I was a boy, I lived next door to the church because my father was the pastor. One of the problems in living so close to the church is that it seems like part of your house, and you learn to take it pretty casually. (Maybe that's why Samuel had such a hard time hearing the voice of God in the Temple [1 Sam. 3:1-10].) I played all around holy things. Once, the custodian called me over to see some baby mice that had drowned in a toilet in the men's Bible class restroom; he thought that was something a small boy would like to see, and it was. But since then I have always had a hard time thinking of churches as sacred buildings.

But where *does* God live? I was told that God is everywhere, but that is not much different from saying that God is nowhere. Or is it? I remember growing up thinking that God was watching me all the time, but then I would get into some kind of trouble and hope that somehow God wouldn't find out about it. (I guess I meant my parents.)

When did you last have an experience or sense the presence of God? Was it in a church? Was it on a visit to the Grand Canyon? Was it when you looked through a telescope? Or a microscope? A professor of physical chemistry once said to me, "I don't see how you can look at a drop of ink under an electron microscope and not believe in God." A couple of times I have asked the members of my congregation to tell me about times when they have felt God to be near, and almost all of their experiences had the following in common: (1) they were in some sort of crisis, a war or an illness or some kind of desperate situation; and (2) other people were involved.

Is there any way we can cultivate what Brother Lawrence called *The Practice of the Presence of God,* so that we can know that we are cared for, not just in times of crisis, but all of the time, and even when we are alone?

FOURTH QUARTER

The Architecture of the Tabernacle

There were, of course, no graven images of God in the tent. But there were two cherubim (the plural of *cherub*). Cherubim were not fat babies as in some medieval pictures, from which we get the word *cherubic*. They were fearsome beasts (see Gen. 3:24; Ezek. 10; Ps. 99:1). And somehow, God was thought of as dwelling more or less between the wings of the two golden cherubim that were on the "mercy seat," the carved lid of the Ark where the Ten Commandments were kept (see Num. 7:89).

In our churches we usually have some central object to draw our attention. In some, where the proclamation of the Word has been seen as the most important part of worship, the pulpit is in the center. In others, coming out of a tradition in which the Eucharist is the high moment of worship, the communion table or altar first catches our eye. In many churches, these articles of furniture are together. Maybe God appears to us, in a sense, between the Word and the Sacrament, as between the wings of the cherubim in the Temple.

It is also notable that all of the furniture in the tabernacle was portable. There were rings on the corners of the tent (Exod. 25:12-14), through which acacia poles could be thrust, so that it could be readily moved. In our churches, for the most part, the furniture is pretty permanent, sometimes even screwed to the floor, so that no one can easily rearrange it. God moved with the people on their journey. To be more accurate, the people moved with God on their journey (Exod. 40:36).

Central to the act of worship among the Israelites was the great altar, where offerings were made to God of their flocks and produce. It seemed to them that God enjoyed smelling the fragrance of the cooking meat or grain (Exod. 29:41). It pleased God, in other words, for the people to remember every day that all their blessings came ultimately from God and were to be offered to God. This is true for us Christians as well (Rom. 12:1). Christ offered himself for us, and we are to offer ourselves to him.

The Offering

Then, as now, the people's commitment to God was expressed in the giving of gifts. In the desert, these gifts consisted of concrete things: metal, cloth, oil, wood. Later they would learn to bring their money, an extension of themselves, a symbol of their goods and services. And thus do we come with our offerings. An offering in a service of worship is not a collection. It is the people's giving of themselves.

If that is true, then God's self-giving also takes the form of an offering. God risks the created world by putting it in the hands of sinful human beings. God leaves the most important job in the world—the raising of children—to amateurs who have never done it before. And God risks the only begotten Son, the utter and complete gift, the self-emptying of the Eternal.

I asked at the beginning of this lesson, "Where is God?" I think now I am ready to give a partial answer to that question. God is wherever there is giving. God exists in relationship, in the eternal gift-giving that takes place between Father, Son, and Holy Spirit, and in the constant, ongoing giving between God and us, and between us and one another.

Helping Adults Become Involved

Preparing to Teach

There is a lot of material in this lesson, much of it strange to our ears. That strange house of worship with all its peculiar furniture dominates the scene. If you have time, you really ought to read the whole description of the tabernacle, so that the three brief passages we are assigned will fit into their proper space. In some of this material, I have made comparisons between the arrangement of the furnishings in the tabernacle and the way our own churches are equipped. You might want to walk through your own church building in your mind and see if any other similarities or differences suggest themselves.

Then, in keeping with a philosophy that we have tried to follow in these lessons, let's ask the questions: In what sense is God present in our classroom? In my preparation? In our study together? If I am right in suggesting that God is present in giving, then what gifts are being given in this study? Is there giving from me to you? From you to them? From them to us? From them to each other? From God to all of us? From us to God?

Here is this week's outline:

    I. The gifts of the people
   II. The great altar and its offerings
 III. Moses carries out God's instructions
       A. Assembly of the tabernacle
       B. God's glory in the tabernacle—the journey resumed

Introducing the Main Question

Divide the class into twos and ask them to take one minute to tell their partner what is their earliest memory of being in church as a child. Then ask them to tell their partner about a time when they experienced the presence of God or Jesus. When they have finished sharing, have them share with the whole group, calling out in a word or phrase something that would describe the church of their childhood. Then have them tell what the circumstances were when they felt God nearby. You may get responses like: "In a hospital room"; "At a youth conference"; "When I was in Vietnam." Close by asking them whether they feel God present here and now.

Developing the Lesson

I. The gifts of the people

It continues to surprise me how much stuff those Israelites had with them on their journey. I know they ripped off the Egyptians when they left, but how did they carry everything? Did they use pull-carts or travois? Did they load their cattle as beasts of burden? Somebody ought to make a list of every mention of bronze, gold, silver, yarns, leather, wood, linens, spices, oil, gems, jars, weapons, and the like and figure up the total weight. The people must have been pack-rats. Note that they gave a free-will offering of their goods, and that it was enough to do build and furnish the tabernacle.

II. The great altar and its offerings

Discuss briefly here the Israelites' sacrificial system, which is strange to modern ears, and show how it prefigures the sacrifice of Christ. You may get some help here from Hebrews 10:1-10.

When you mention the presence of God among the people at the tent, refer to God's camping out with us in Revelation 21:3-4. (Be sure to note that the words *dwelling* and *dwell* are the same as *tabernacle* or *tent*.) Perhaps if our church furniture went with us wherever we go, as did the tabernacle with the Israelites, we would experience the presence of God more readily on our journeys, at work, at school, at home and at play.

III. Moses carries out God's instructions

With this section, we come to the end of our journey through the book of the Exodus, which means "a journey outward." Perhaps it is appropriate to think also of the other way of looking at our spiritual quest, which we may call the "journey inward."

A. Assembly of the tabernacle

This brief description of the way things were set up reminds me in a strange way of watching the roustabouts put up a circus tent in a vacant field near the little town where I grew up. Circus people are the closest thing we have to nomads in our society today, and they are a vanishing breed.

Compare the things in the tent with the things in your church. Is this a valid way to list them?

The table of the show bread—our Lord's table
The lamps—our candles
The basin for washing—our baptismal font
The altar for burnt offerings—our table or altar
The Ark of the Covenant—our pulpit or lectern where the Bible, with
     its two Testaments or Covenants, is kept

B. God's glory in the tabernacle—the journey resumed.

Does God's glory rest in our church buildings? In church people, when they assemble? When they scatter for work and service? Does God go with us, or do we go with God?

Helping Class Members Act

Ask the class the questions in the preceding paragraph. Tell them good-bye, which means "God be with you."

Planning for Next Sunday

Say goodbye to Exodus, and hello (very briefly) to Leviticus. Have the class read Leviticus 25 and think about celebrations.

UNIT III: INSTRUCTIONS FOR LIFE

FOUR LESSONS   **AUGUST 7–28**

This unit takes key chapters from Leviticus, Numbers, and Deuteronomy to look at the instructions God gives to the newly emerging nation of Israel. The people are called upon to trust God completely, to remember that they are tenants on the earth, not its owners, and that, if they expect to prosper in this world, they must put their faith in God, and God alone. We will do well to put these principles to work in our own day.

Questions raised by these four lessons include: Who really owns the earth? What is our responsibility for it? Is the idea of private property outmoded? Does the ancient concept of the "jubilee" have anything to say to us in the here and now? Can we turn loose of the things that so dominate our lives? Where can we get the courage to tackle the difficult tasks that confront us? Is God on our side? Are we on God's side? How can we tell? We seem to be doing battle against giants; what will the outcome be? What is the point of it all, our chief end? Can we find, in relationships with God and others, fulfillment? And, in the last analysis, have we the moral courage to make the hard choice between the temptations of this world and the promises of the world unseen?

There is much in the Pentateuch (the first five books of the Bible) that we will have skipped over when we reach the end of these lessons, but we can safely say that we have skimmed the cream of them. There is hard, chewable, nourishing stuff in these scriptures, and the work we do will last us a lifetime.

LESSON 10   **AUGUST 7**

Celebrate God's Ownership

Background Scripture: Leviticus 25

The Main Question

We are all familiar with the basic cycles in our lives; simply to list a few key words will bring some of them to mind: weekend, Sunday dinner, midweek prayer meeting, spring break, summer vacation, Christmas holidays, and so on. Patterns become so fixed that they are hard to change.

But what about even more important patterns, the rhythm of our whole lives, or the pattern of history? It is good for both people and nations to take stock of themselves, to stop and regroup, to shake old and questionable habits, or renew those good ones that have been dropped along the way. And I can think of no more lovely idea than a Jubilee Year. The very word sounds like fun. (The Latin root is *jubilare,* to "shout for joy," and the Hebrew root is *yobhel,* "ram's horn," because such a horn was sounded to proclaim the season of liberty.)

Should we reinstitute such a celebration? How would it affect our lives? From what should we set ourselves free?

FOURTH QUARTER

Selected Scripture

King James Version	New Revised Standard Version

Leviticus 25:8-10, 23-28, 39-42

8 And thou shalt number seven sabbaths of years unto thee, seven times seven years; and the space of the seven sabbaths of years shall be unto thee forty and nine years.

9 Then shalt thou cause the trumpet of the jubile to sound on the tenth day of the seventh month, in the day of atonement shall ye make the trumpet sound throughout all your land.

10 And ye shall hallow the fiftieth year, and proclaim liberty throughout all the land unto all the inhabitants thereof: it shall be a jubile unto you; and ye shall return every man unto his possession, and ye shall return every man unto his family.

....

23 The land shall not be sold for ever: for the land is mine; for ye are strangers and sojourners with me.

24 And in all the land of your possession ye shall grant a redemption for the land.

25 If thy brother be waxen poor, and hath sold away some of his possession, and if any of his kin come to redeem it, then shall he redeem that which his brother sold.

26 And if the man have none to redeem it, and himself be able to redeem it;

27 Then let him count the years of the sale thereof, and restore the overplus unto the man to whom he sold it; that he may return unto his possession.

28 But if he be not able to restore it to him, then that which is sold shall remain in the hand of him that hath bought it until the year of jubile: and in the jubile it shall go out, and he shall return unto his possession.

Leviticus 25:8-10, 23-28, 39-42

8 You shall count off seven weeks of years, seven times seven years, so that the period of seven weeks of years gives forty-nine years. 9 Then you shall have the trumpet sounded loud; on the tenth day of the seventh month—on the day of atonement—you shall have the trumpet sounded throughout all your land. 10 And you shall hallow the fiftieth year and you shall proclaim liberty throughout the land to all its inhabitants. It shall be a jubilee for you: you shall return, every one of you, to your property, and every one of you to your family.

....

23 The land shall not be sold in perpetuity, for the land is mine; with me you are but aliens and tenants. 24 Throughout the land that you hold, you shall provide for the redemption of the land.

25 If anyone of your kin falls into difficulty and sells a piece of property, then the next of kin shall come and redeem what the relative has sold. 26 If the person has no one to redeem it, but then prospers and finds sufficient means to do so, 27 the years since its sale shall be computed and the difference shall be refunded to the person to whom it was sold, and the property shall be. returned.

39 And if thy brother that dwelleth by thee be waxen poor, and be sold unto thee; thou shalt not compel him to serve as a bondservant:

40 But as an hired servant, and as a sojourner, he shall be with thee, and shall serve thee unto the year of jubile:

41 And then shall he depart from thee, both he and his children with him, and shall return unto his own family, and unto the possession of his fathers shall he return.

42 For they are my servants, which I brought forth out of the land of Egypt: they shall not be sold as bondsmen.

39 If any who are dependent on you become so impoverished that they sell themselves to you, you shall not make them serve as slaves. 40 They shall remain with you as hired or bound laborers. They shall serve with you until the year of the jubilee. 41 Then they and their children with them shall be free from your authority; they shall go back to their own family, and return to their ancestral property. 42. For they are my servants, whom I brought out of the land of Egypt; they shall not be sold as slaves are sold.

Key Verse: **The land shall not be sold for ever; for the land is mine; for ye are strangers and sojourners with me. Leviticus 25:23**

Key Verse: **The land shall not be sold in perpetuity, for the land is mine; with me you are but aliens and tenants. Leviticus 25:23**

As You Read the Scripture

Leviticus 25. We have time this quarter for only one look at the book of Leviticus. The title of the book means "concerning the Levites," who were the descendants of Levi, Jacob's son. More specifically, they are the priestly tribe, Aaron and his descendants (see Exod. 32:25-29; Num. 3:1-13). The book is made up chiefly of ritual instructions for worship, atonement, purity, and ethical behavior.

Verses 1-7, 22-20. The sabbatical year.

Verse 2. The word *sabbath* means "rest."

Verse 4. A similar rule had already been described in Exodus 23:10-11, for the sake of poor people and animals, but here it is strengthened to explain how the land itself needs to rest. In addition to the need for fallow land to restore itself, the land belongs to God (v. 23) and has rights of its own.

Verse 5. The "unpruned vine" is literally in Hebrew, "Nazarite grapes," so that the grapes are left "unshorn" like one who has taken Nazaritic vows (see Num. 6:5).

Verses 8-19, 23-24. The year of jubilee, the fiftieth year (after seven times seven years) becomes a sabbath of sabbaths. We lack historical evidence that the Festival of Jubilees was ever actually put into practice. Is it then the description of an ideal existence, like the early Christian church's practice of having all things in common (Acts 2:44-45; 4:32-35), but that never became an actual way of life with the Hebrews? Such passages as Ruth 4 and 1 Kings 21 indicate that the law against the alienation of land was in force in those days. Certainly in later days such a law was needed (see Isa. 5:8; Mic. 2:2).

Verses 25-55. These verses list laws concerning loans and their redemption, the poor, servants, and slavery. All of these relate to the fundamental basis of the jubilee celebration, that all people and all things ultimately belong to the Lord, so that our use of them is always temporary (see vv. 23, 42, and 55).

Verses 29-34. Urban property was treated differently and could be owned permanently, whereas rural lands clearly ultimately belonged to God. The Levites, too, were a special case, for they did not have land of their own, only forty-eight cities in which they were allowed to live (see Lev. 35).

Verse 39. In those days, while Hebrews could never be slaves to each other, only indentured servants, permission was given for them to hold slaves from among the people of foreign nations. Even as late as the time of Christ slavery was an accepted custom, and it was not until the gospel began to make itself felt fully in relatively modern times that Christians have generally agreed that slavery of any kind is morally wrong. But these rules (such as v. 43) concerning the treatment of servants, and New Testament statements such as Paul's letter to Philemon, urging that the slave Onesimus be set free, and his declarations of equality in 1 Corinthians 12:13, Galatians 3:38 and Colossians 3:11, make it clear that long before our time God's love and mercy attacked this insidious practice.

The Scripture and the Main Question

"The Earth Is the Lord's"

The earth is the LORD's and all
    that is in it,
    the world, and those who live in it. (Ps. 24:1)

For every wild animal of the forest
    is mine,
    the cattle on a thousand hills. (Ps. 50:19)

If any doctrine in Holy Scripture is clear and unequivocable, it is surely the doctrine that the Lord, the Creator of the earth, is ultimately the Owner of all things. Even when we bring the offerings of "our" labors to God, it is not really an offering, for we own nothing. We ought continually to say with King David: "All things come from you, and of your own have we given you" (1 Chron. 29:14).

An attorney friend once told me that the first question he was asked by a teacher on the first day of law school was, "Why do you have to have a hunting license from the state to shoot a deer on your own property?" Who owns the deer? Does it belong to me if it is on my property? Does it belong to the state? The answer is that *nobody* owns the deer; it owns itself. To put it in terms of ecclesiastical law, God owns the deer. And God owns me. For that matter, God owns the state, too.

Stewardship is based on this principle. The word *steward* comes from a root meaning "styward," or pig keeper. In the ancient barter system, the keeper of the master's pigs was a responsible person, for the pigs were the household cash. So the styward eventually came to be the one who holds the purse strings of the master's property. To be a steward is to hold a regal office, to be entrusted with the goods of the Master of us all (see Jesus' story in Matt. 25:14-30).

The Right to Rest

The people, the rulers, even the land itself should take time off. There is a rabbinical saying that one of the reasons we should not plow on the sabbath, in addition to our own need for rest, is to honor the land's need to lie fallow. Don't even move a rock, for the rocks have a right to be left alone, at least for a while. The scriptures seem to teach that nature has an existence in its own right, apart from and having nothing to do with us. (See, for example, Ps. 104, in which the lions, the birds, and the sea creatures go about their business in their own season.) For that matter, God, too, needs to rest, and that is why we must all take time off (Exod. 20:11).

The Rhythm of Life

"Take time to smell the roses," says the adage; it is a description of a way of life. The American culture that I live in seems to have a "Type A" personality; we can't stop moving. When I was a child, we had what were called "blue laws." My parents wouldn't allow us to go to the movies on Sunday. We weren't even supposed to read the Sunday funnies until Monday after school. These blue laws were seen as old-fashioned prohibitions, irrelevant, immaterial, and unconstitutional, and eventually most of them got repealed. (Do you remember when the first convenience store opened in your town, so that there was a place to get an aspirin on Sunday?) And we all rejoiced when our freedom was established.

But we lost something in the process. To go at full speed seven days a week, to burn your candle at both ends, may give a lovely light, but you will burn up in a hurry. But candles were meant to burn up. Perhaps a better metaphor would be trees. If you let your trees alone to grow at a healthy rate, and harvest them properly, they are a renewable resource. There is no reason, theoretically, why the forests of the world shouldn't last forever, providing us with shade, oxygen, homes for wildlife, and, when appropriate, fuel and building materials. But we have seen fit to cut down thousand-year-old trees, which will not renew themselves in a hundred lifetimes, if then. We are destroying the rainforests of the world at the rate of a football field a second. It is as though some monster were stomping across the earth, with its giant feet wiping out our renewable resources with every step. They will soon be gone, and with them the ozone layer, and the seasons, and you and I.

All this is to say that the human race needs to capture a new sabbatical vision. We need to develop a healthy rhythm to our lives as individuals, as nations, and as a world. There need to be times when we rest, when the whole world, from the creatures of the North Sea to the mountain forests of Australia, can breathe and be renewed. It can, and must, begin with you and me. Our families need to set aside days to be together. Our churches need to come and rejoice in the Lord's house. We need, for the sake of our sanity, to turn loose, at least for a jubilee season, all the precious things and creatures we think we own, but that belong to the Lord of all the earth. We are like the juggler on the vaudeville circuit, who has a number of spinning plates, precariously balanced on the top of rods. Just as he manages to get them all going at once, one starts to wobble and he must rush to start it going, but then he has to run to another one. How long will this race go on?

Today's lesson calls us to an enjoyment of God's world that we can never know as long as we keep running. We must stop and smell the roses. We must "let go and let God" be in charge. We must take a sabbatical. If you have to go to the store on Sunday to get an antacid tablet, you'd better ask yourself, "Why is my stomach hurting in the first place?" Could it be that you have been trying to be in charge of a world that belongs to God alone?

Helping Adults Become Involved

Preparing to Teach

This week, instead of frantically looking for illustrations or laboriously poring over the text to make sure you have crossed every *t* and dotted every *i*, just read the Scripture and then sit down to pray and meditate and ask for the guidance of the Spirit. Is that a cop out? Well, probably it is if you try this method every Sunday. But just once, say every seven Sundays or every seven years or maybe every forty-nine Sundays, you should get some rest. When do preachers and Sunday school teachers get a sabbatical anyway?

Here's the outline:

I. The sabbatical year
II. The year of jubilee
III. The redemption of the land
IV. The redemption of houses
V. Loans to the poor
VI. Hebrew slavery

Introducing the Main Question

List the seasons of the church year on a chalkboard or newsprint and ask whether they make sense in terms of our need for spiritual sabbaticals.

Advent: a time of anticipation and adventure.
Christmas: a time of sharing and rejoicing.
Epiphany: a time of spreading the good news.
Lent: a time of soul searching and spiritual house cleaning.
Easter: a time of pure celebration; a jubilee.
Pentecost: a time of steady hard work and Spirit-filled duty.

Or you might have the class draw up a typical week in their lives. Ask this question: Does it follow a healthy rhythm?

As another possible approach, you might have someone read aloud Ecclesiastes 3:1-12 and discuss what it has to say about our life-styles.

However you go about it, set your folks to thinking about what it means to live as people who belong to God, in a world that belongs to God, living lives that are offered to God, and facing a future that is in God's hands.

Developing the Lesson

I. The sabbatical year

The land itself needs a rest. One wonders how the keepers of the old Levitical law of a sabbath for the land would react to our modern tendency to use chemicals to make the soil produce beyond its means. Certainly they would have approved, in principle at least, with modern methods of crop rotation, in which different plants, some of which return nutrients to the soil, are alternated with others. To use a field beyond its means is as foolish as eating up seed corn; in the long run, the farmer pays for it. But there is more here than mere practicality; there is also the lesson that the land belongs ultimately to the Lord (v. 23) and that we are all tenant farmers.

II. The year of jubilee

Not only the land, but all property is a trust from God. I have heard chanted at funerals a lugubrious old verse, each stanza of which ends with the line: "But all you can keep in your cold, dead hand is what you have given away." This is a questionable text for a funeral oration, but it describes reality. We are sojourners here. If for no other reason than our concern for future generations we must not think that things belong to us forever. I remember the joy with which my mother photographed everything in her house, and she sent copies to all her friends and relations, accompanied with a mimeographed list containing such information as "this belonged to your great-grandfather" and "we bought this at a rummage sale summer before last." Everybody indicated his or her first choice for an inheritance, and she delighted in seeing that most of us got what we wanted.

III. The redemption of the land

You needn't spend much time on this. Let it suffice to say that the same fundamental principle is being applied here: Our use of all things is temporary. God is ultimately the owner of all things.

IV. The redemption of houses

V. Loans to the poor

VI. Hebrew slavery

Thank God the institution of slavery has been essentially stamped out by our enlightened understanding of our basic humanity. See the discussion of this changing position in the comments in "As You Read the Scripture." Again the fundamental principle applies: Nothing and nobody belongs to us. Although the passage seems to be a defense of slavery, actually it is given to the Israelites as a limitation of the right of one person to own another. When carried to its logical result, as in the New Testament, this principle leads to the realization that no form of slavery should exist, including that created by unjust employers who make virtual slaves of their workers by exploiting their need for survival, or governments that take advantage of persons at the expense of their freedom.

Helping Class Members Act

A brief summation of the underlying theme of this chapter might be this: Go forth from this class and travel light. If you can help the class members to see that things are not the source of happiness, you have done them a good turn. They will be better stewards of the creation. The fact that we are only the caretakers of the world should make us more tolerant of others and more ready to share the world's goods with those who are in need. Your class needs a sabbatical, even from Bible study. Tell them to take the week off.

Planning for Next Sunday

Have the class read Numbers 13–14, after they have had a good rest.

Accept God's Guidance

Background Scripture: Numbers 13–14

The Main Question

Courage is a secondary virtue—that is, it makes a difference what you are courageous about. There are times when to act with courage is foolish. But there are times when it pays to stand up and take risks, even when most everybody disagrees with you. Of course, you will probably agree, that is true when *you* know what God wants, even if nobody else does.

But it is hard to know what God wants. The spies in this week's lesson were discouraging in their account of the promised land. But Caleb and Joshua brought in a minority report, saying, in effect, "Have courage! We can do it!" The people sided with the majority, and the result was an extension of their wilderness wanderings. Most of them never made it to the "land flowing with milk and honey."

Can we always know when to "strike while the iron is hot"? Sometimes, as in this case, popular opinion runs the other way. It would be a shame not to take advantage of an opportunity. If we do not, we may get left behind. Most of us, when we get into situations like this, go through a lot of agony. Should I or shouldn't I? Like the proverbial mule who starved to death equidistant from two bales of hay, we perish in our indecisiveness. Where shall we get the courage to risk? And how shall we know when the time to risk has come?

We know that we can never be certain about the future. On what basis, then, shall we make tough decisions that involve risk? Will God gamble with us?

Selected Scripture

King James Version

Numbers 13:25-28, 30-31

25 And they returned from searching of the land after forty days.

26 And they went and came to Moses, and to Aaron, and to all the congregation of the children of Israel, unto the wilderness of Paran, to Kadesh; and brought back word unto them, and unto all the congregation, and shewed them the fruit of the land.

27 And they told him, and said, We came unto the land whither thou sentest us, and surely it floweth with milk and honey; and this is the fruit of it.

New Revised Standard Version

Numbers 13:25-28, 30-31

25 At the end of forty days they returned from spying out the land. 26 And they came to Moses and Aaron and to all the congregation of the Israelites in the wilderness of Paran, at Kadesh; they brought back word to them and to all the congregation, and showed them the fruit of the land. 27 And they told him, "We came to the land to which you sent us; it flows with milk and honey, and this is its fruit. 28 Yet the people who live in the land are strong, and the towns are fortified and very large; and besides, we saw the descendants of Anak there."

28 Nevertheless the people be strong that dwell in the land, and the cities are walled, and very great: and moreover we saw the children of Anak there.

....

30 And Caleb stilled the people before Moses, and said, Let us go up at once, and possess it; for we are well able to overcome it.

31 But the men that went up with him said, We be not able to go up against the people; for they are stronger than we.

14:6-10a, 28-30

6 And Joshua the son of Nun, and Caleb the son of Jephunneh, which were of them that searched the land, rent their clothes:

7 And they spake unto all the company of the children of Israel, saying, The land, which we passed through to search it, is an exceeding good land.

8 If the LORD delight in us, then he will bring us into this land, and give it us; a land which floweth with milk and honey.

9 Only rebel not ye against the LORD, neither fear ye the people of the land; for they are bread for us: their defence is departed from them, and the LORD is with us: fear them not.

10 But all the congregation bade stone them with stones.

....

28 Say unto them, As truly as I live, saith the LORD, as ye have spoken in mine ears, so will I do to you:

29 Your carcasses shall fall in this wilderness; and all that were numbered of you, according to your whole number, from twenty years old and upward, which have murmured against me,

30 Doubtless ye shall not come into the land, concerning which I sware to make you dwell therein, save Caleb the son of Jephunneh, and Joshua the son of Nun.

....

30 But Caleb quieted the people before Moses, and said, "Let us go up at once and occupy it, for we are well able to overcome it." 31 Then the men who had gone up with him said, "We are not able to go up against this people, for they are stronger than we."

14:6-10a, 28-30

6 And Joshua son of Nun and Caleb son of Jephunneh, who were among those who had spied out the land, tore their clothes 7 and said to all the congregation of the Israelites, "The land that we went through as spies is an exceedingly good land. 8 If the LORD is pleased with us, he will bring us into this land and give it to us, a land that flows with milk and honey. 9 Only, do not rebel against the LORD; and do not fear the people of the land, for they are no more than bread for us; their protection is removed from them, and the LORD is with us; do not fear them." 10 But the whole congregation threatened to stone them.

....

28 Say to them, "As I live," says the LORD, "I will do to you the very things I heard you say: 29 your dead bodies shall fall in this very wilderness; and of all your number, included in the census, from twenty years old and upward, who have complained against me, not one of you shall come into the land in which I swore to settle you, except Caleb son of Jephunneh and Joshua son of Nun.

FOURTH QUARTER

Key Verses: **If the LORD delight in us, then he will bring us into this land, and give it us; a land which floweth with milk and honey. Only rebel not ye against the LORD, neither fear ye the people of the land; for they are bread for us: their defence is departed from them, and the LORD is with us: fear them not. Numbers 14:8-9**

Key Verses: **"If the LORD is pleased with us, he will bring us into this land and give it to us, a land that flows with milk and honey. Only, do not rebel against the LORD; and do not fear the people of the land, for they are no more than bread for us; their protection is removed from them, and the LORD is with us; do not fear them." Numbers 14:8-9**

As You Read the Scripture

The book of Numbers gets its title from the census that was taken of all the people of Israel. But the census, in fact, only takes up a couple of chapters; the others are filled with stories of the wilderness journey, many of which we would not have without this book. Such an account is our lesson this week in Numbers 13 and 14, the story of the spies and their report.

Numbers 13:1-16. The spies are chosen, two from each of the twelve tribes, representing a cross-section of the Hebrew people. Their names are of interest, but we have space to look at only the two who turned out to be heroes. *Caleb* means "dog" in Hebrew, which is interesting because *dog* became an insult applied to Gentiles. *Hoshea* means "salvation" or "deliverance" (it is the name as Hosea, the prophet), and in the form *Joshua*, to which Moses changed it, adding the root *YHWH* to the name, it is the same name as Jesus, meaning "The LORD is salvation." (In another form it is Isaiah, and with the name El [God] it is formed into Elisha, so it is very common among the later Hebrews. It is worth noting that the name Elijah means "El is YHWH" or "God is the LORD.")

Verses 21-22. They covered the whole length of the land, from the Negeb desert in the south to Hamath, in what is now Lebanon. This was a distance of some 180 miles, so it is no wonder that it took them forty days.

Verse 23. Two men carried the grapes, not because they were so heavy, but in order to hold the huge bunch clear of the ground. This symbol has become a favorite among contemporary Jews; the Israeli Ministry of Tourism uses it as a logo on their literature and on the sides of their tour buses. It is almost as though they were saying once more, "Come, spy out this land!"

Verse 30. Caleb is at first a minority of one, but later (14:6-9) Joshua joins him in encouraging the people.

Verse 33. The Nephilim are mentioned in only one other place in the Bible, Genesis 6;4, where they appear to be the result of a union between divine and human beings. That, of course, was before the flood. However, the people of Canaan did seem to be of rather large stature. (See Deut. 2:10 and the description of Goliath in 1 Sam. 17:4-7.)

Numbers 14. The people are fearful, and their lack of courage causes God to turn against them.

Verse 9. "A land flowing with milk and honey" is a metaphor for a rich and fertile land. It occurs nineteen times in the Bible, and is older than Joshua and Caleb (see Exod. 3:8 for its first use). The phrase is to be contrasted with the report in 13:32, "a land that devours its inhabitants"—in other words, not fertile enough to sustain them. It is believed that in the days of the early Christian church, new converts, on the occasion of their baptism, were dressed in white robes and given milk and honey to drink as a symbol of their entry into the promised land.

Verse 18. In his plea, Moses uses the gracious description of God found in Exodus 34:6-7. Even though God forgives us, we are not always delivered from the consequences of our sin (see Rom. 6:23).

The Scripture and the Main Question

Relativity

The size of something depends a lot on where you are standing when you look at it. I remember a very pompous pastor, of whom I stood in awe. He carried himself with vast dignity, looked at others down his nose, and spoke with an autocratic air. One day, when I was standing quite close to him in a crowd, I realized that I was a good two inches taller than he. I had always felt shorter! After that I was far more natural in his presence.

I was a member of a college fraternity, but we all ate in the college dining hall. Some of the brothers said, "There's a man in town who will let us rent half of his house. We can pool our money, buy tables, chairs, dishes, and kitchen equipment, hire a cook, and eat better and cheaper in our own space." Ignorant of the restaurant business, and not very anxious to risk my parents' money in a shaky venture, I argued against the plan. But I was outvoted, and we did it anyway. It turned out to be a marvelous experience; we had a lot of fun, and I turned from a skinny freshman into a plump sophomore. I simply did not have the vision or the courage to risk what turned out to be a happy undertaking.

Of course, conservatives like me are important to a group. We keep those with boundless enthusiasm from running off the end of the dock. But if everybody were like me, we would never do anything. There come times when healthy and holy risks must be taken. Even though the enemy looks like a giant, it may be shorter than we think, especially if God is on our side. But how do we know God is on our side? How does one decide whether a venture is worth undertaking?

Check It Out

One way is to explore the possibilities. Joshua and Caleb and company took a considerable risk on behalf of their fellow Israelites. In every age there are pioneer spirits who are willing to make the first venture into unknown territory. Now that the astronauts have been to the moon, I suppose the rest of us can go there eventually, or to even further planets. But those astronauts, brave as they were, were always connected to Ground Control by their computers. How much more intrepid were the Spanish conquistadors, who conquered the vast nations of the New World with one cannon and a few helmeted troops. They were undoubtedly ruthless and despicable, but you have to admire their courage! I have never been the sort of person who would make a good spy behind the enemy lines. Gilt-edged securities for me; I would rather live in an Egypt I know, with all its drawbacks, than venture into a Canaan I do not know. But I know enough to realize that this timidity on my part is partially sinful. When God says a thing is a good idea, I ought to have the courage to do it. Thank heavens for courageous folks who live on the cutting edge!

FOURTH QUARTER

Living by Grace

When I was about seven years old, my mother decided that I needed to learn to swim. There were a lot of lakes and creeks about, and she knew that it was dangerous for me not to know and that, if I didn't learn, I would be missing out on one of life's great pleasures. So she sent me to a class of other small boys, conducted by a lifeguard on the banks of Lake Susan, a cold mountain pond. It was a watershed experience, and I think worth describing. In those days, boys were expected to wear two-piece bathing suits. (The little town in which I grew up was that conservative.) So we all wore sleeveless undershirts. I took my father's fountain pen, dipped it in blue ink, and wrote LIFE GUARD on my shirt, so people wouldn't think I was appearing in public in my unmentionables.

I stood shivering in the icy waters of Lake Susan, with my feet on the gooshy bottom, and heard the lifeguard say, "All right, men, first we will do the dead man's float." I didn't like the sound of that at all. In spite of his insistence that the water would support me, I knew that my skinny frame would sink down out of sight into the goosh and my mother would never see me again. Somehow, I gained the courage to try, and sure enough, as I thrashed about, the water went up my nose, I strangled and choked, and the lifeguard had to pick me up by my now bright blue undershirt and set me shivering on the bank to dry. "I told you it wouldn't support me," I cried. "You didn't give it a chance," he said. "You tried to support yourself. Just relax and let the water support you."

Now, whether I was afraid of my mother or decided to trust the lifeguard or was just too stubborn not to quit, eventually I did relax and the water did support me! Today I am a pretty good swimmer; in fact, swimming is the one sport in which I excel. That first step was the hardest. I have never felt anything, before or since, so liberating. The water *will* support you. And so will life. To venture out in trust is to discover that God has wonderful plans for us, that life is worth living, and that there is joy in living in the promised land. From this side it may appear to be populated with giants, but that is not true. They can be overcome. One person plus God is a majority. When we go forth armed with the confidence of faith, we can and will live victoriously in the world. A faith in God, like that of Joshua and Caleb (14:9), reduces the size of the enemies that are arrayed against us, adds cubits to our own stature, and enables us to grow into the "measure of the stature of the fullness of Christ" (Eph. 4:13).

There *are* giants out there. Life is not easy. But when God goes with us, the giants can be overcome. "In the world you face persecution," said Jesus. "But take courage; I have conquered the world!" (John 16:33). The decision to act, to venture into the promised land, can be made with certainty when we remember that we are not venturing in our own strength, but in the strength of God. No astronaut has a better line of communication with ground control than we Christians do with the "ground of our being." When we are in touch with that strength and operate on that rather than our own, all things are possible.

Helping Adults Become Involved

Preparing to Teach

This is a difficult lesson. The story of the spies is a good story, but it is a fairly obvious one, and to develop a lesson in depth on it will not be easy. But, and again Scripture guides us in teaching the lesson, we are not going in our own strength. Trust God and venture into class feeling that you can overcome giants. Read the lesson carefully and think, from your own reading and experiences, of those who have overcome giants. Some that come to my mind are David and Goliath, the colonists during the American Revolution, Frodo in Tolkien's *The Lord of the Rings,* and Robinson Crusoe. And there is the greatest story, that of Jesus and his disciples, who, against all the powers of the day, turned the Roman Empire upside down (Acts 17:6). Perhaps your class will be able to come up with some others as you talk together. And think of yourself as doing battle with giants; the inertia of the average church school class is a formidable foe. You can do it, Joshua! Here's my outline:

      I. Spying out the land
          A. Appointing the spies
          B. The territory surveyed
          C. The spies report
     II. The intercession of Moses
          A. The people complain
          B. The Lord's anger
          C. Moses intercedes
          D. God forgives, but there are consequences

Introducing the Main Question

Start the lesson by talking about courage. It is, as I have said, a secondary virtue. There are courageous fools, who rush in where angels know better. You don't want to encourage your people to rashness. But courage is much needed. Every time a child stands up for a drug-free life, against the temptations of peers, it is a great victory. And there are times when we need to set out to joust with the windmills of our society, however foolish the world may think us. Most people have more courage than they realize. The purpose of this lesson is to arm us against dread, that we may do battle against the powers of darkness in our time. We don't have to think in terms of cosmic conflicts or heroic quests. It takes a lot of gumption just to keep the faith from breakfast to bedtime. The giants out there are not as tall as we think. This lesson will help us to grow a little taller, marching in the strength of God.

Developing the Lesson

I. Spying out the land

If you have a Bible map, spot for your class the Wilderness of Paran (Num. 12:16), which is the setting of this story and the starting point of the spying expedition. It is an area about fifty miles south of Beer Sheba, which is the southern end of the Holy Land (the phrase "from Dan to Beersheba" occurs many times in the Bible; see Judg. 20:1; 1 Sam. 3:20). If the spies went from there all the way to the entrance of Hamath, the northern border of Israel (near Dan), they covered considerable territory. They were on the borders of the land of promise, but had difficulty getting up the nerve to make the plunge.

A. Appointing the spies

This is a good example of the democratic process, making sure that all the tribes are represented. But sometimes if the group is too broadly represented, as in this case, they will have difficulty agreeing on a common report. It is often best to choose a small group who can grow to trust one another, learn to work together, and arrive at a common understanding of their task.

B. The territory surveyed

We are told (v. 25) that it took the spies forty days to cover the country. Bear in mind that the number forty in the Bible is often used to mean an indeterminate time of considerable duration. (Remember how it rained forty days and forty nights in the flood story; see also Jon. 3:4.)

C. The spies report

It is a good land, says the first report (v. 27), but by the time they get through disagreeing it isn't all that good (v. 32). In the midst of this report, the strong word of Caleb stands out: "We can do it!" It takes courage to be a minority of one (Joshua doesn't speak up until the next chapter); Caleb, whose name means "dog," may have been like a bulldog.

II. The intercession of Moses
A. The people complain

Here we go again! Once more they want to go back to Egypt. It's a good thing they didn't! Who knows what the history of the world would have been had they given up at this point? How quick these people are to want to choose another leader! The more I read this story, the more I admire the stubbornness, patience, and leadership abilities of Moses.

B. The Lord's anger

The Lord doesn't seem to have as much patience as Moses! But the Lord's standards are always higher than ours.

C. Moses intercedes

Again Moses is a type of Christ for his people, interceding on their behalf. His beautiful statement in verse 18 is a quote from the Lord's own words in Exodus 34:6-7. Note that they contain both God's mercy and judgment.

D. God forgives, but there are consequences

What seems to be the safe and secure thing turns out in the long run to be deadly. One who hesitates is lost. Because of their mistrust at this point, the Israelites have actually increased their pain.

Helping Class Members Act

Ask your class to name some of the giants they will have to fight in the coming week. Tell them to be of good courage (see Num. 13:20).

Planning for Next Sunday

We go next to Deuteronomy 6. Encourage them to read it, suggesting that this is one of the Bible's greatest chapters.

Love the Lord Your God

Background Scripture: Deuteronomy 6

The Main Question

In his book *Man's Search for Meaning,* Jewish psychiatrist Victor Frankl describes his dreadful experiences in a Nazi death-camp during World War II. Stripped of all dignity, separated from his family, cold and hungry and in terror of his life, the young man stood naked, waiting to go he knew not where. His captors threw him the clothing of another man who had perished in the gas chamber. As Frankl put on the ill-fitting pants and shirt, he felt in the pockets, and his fingers closed on a slip of paper. When he was out of the sight of his guards he stole a look at it. It contained two sentences in Hebrew: "Shema Yisroel" it began ("Hear, O Israel, the LORD our God, the LORD is one, and you shall love the LORD your God with all your heart, and with all your soul, and with all your might"). The remainder of his book tells how, in the months of fearful degradation, these words remained with him, and how, through the search for meaning in his life, he learned the secret of survival.

Most of us do not find our backs to the wall quite like that. But everyone has the same question to answer: What does my life mean? Frankl believed that the will to meaning (not the will to pleasure or power) is what keeps us going. But where do we find that meaning? When Jesus was asked, "What is the great commandment?" he answered by quoting these words from Deuteronomy, and adding Leviticus 19:18, "You shall love your neighbor as yourself." It is never inappropriate to ask the question again. Let us do so now.

Selected Scripture

King James Version	New Revised Standard Version
Deuteronomy 6:1-13	*Deuteronomy 6:1-13*
1 Now these are the commandments, the statutes, and the judgments, which the LORD your God commanded to teach you, that ye might do them in the land whither ye go to possess it:	1 Now this is the commandment—the statutes and the ordinances—that the LORD your God charged me to teach you to observe in the land that you are about to cross into and occupy, 2 so that you
2 That you mightest fear the LORD thy God, to keep all his statutes and his commandments, which I command thee, thou, and thy son, and thy son's son, all the days of thy life; and that thy days may be prolonged.	and your children and your children's children may fear the LORD your God all the days of your life, and keep all his decrees and his commandments that I am commanding you, so that your days may be long. 3 Hear therefore, O Israel,
3 Hear therefore, O Israel, and observe to do it; that it may be well with thee, and that ye may increase mightily, as the LORD God of thy fathers hath promised thee, in the	and observe them diligently, so that it may go well with you, and so that you may multiply greatly in a land flowing with milk and honey, as the

land that floweth with milk and honey.

4 Hear, O Israel: The LORD our God is one LORD:

5 And thou shalt love the LORD thy God with all thine heart, and with all thy soul, and with all thy might.

6 And these words, which I command thee this day, shall be in thine heart:

7 And thou shalt teach them diligently unto thy children, and shalt talk of them when thou sittest in thine house, and when thou walkest by the way, and when thou liest down, and when thou risest up.

8 And thou shalt bind them for a sign upon thine hand, and they shall be as frontlets between thine eyes.

9 And thou shalt write them upon the posts of thy house, and on thy gates.

10 And it shall be, when the LORD thy God shall have brought thee into the land which he sware unto thy fathers, to Abraham, to Isaac, and to Jacob, to give thee great and goodly cities, which thou buildest not,

11 And houses full of all good things, which thou filledst not, and wells digged, which thou diggedst not, vineyards and olive trees, which thou plantedst not; when thou shalt have eaten and be full;

12 Then beware lest thou forget the LORD, which brought thee forth out of the land of Egypt, from the house of bondage.

13 Thou shalt fear the LORD thy God, and serve him, and shalt swear by his name.

Key Verses: **Hear, O Israel: The LORD our God is one LORD: And thou shalt love the LORD thy God with all thine heart, and with all thy soul, and with all thy might. Deuteronomy 6:4-5**

LORD, the God of your ancestors, has promised you.

4 Hear, O Israel: The LORD is our God, the LORD alone. 5 You shall love the LORD your God with all your heart, and with all your soul, and with all your might. 6 Keep these words that I am commanding you today in your heart. 7 Recite them to your children and talk about them when you are at home and when you are away, when you lie down and when you rise. 8 Bind them as a sign on your hand, fix them as an emblem on your forehead, 9 and write them on the doorposts of your house and on your gates.

10 When the LORD your God has brought you into the land that he swore to your ancestors, to Abraham, to Isaac, and to Jacob, to give you—a land with fine, large cities that you did not build, 11 houses filled with all sorts of goods that you did not fill, hewn cisterns that you did not hew, vineyards and olive groves that you did not plant—and when you have eaten your fill, 12 take care that you do not forget the LORD, who brought you out of the land of Egypt, out of the house of slavery. 13 The LORD your God you shall fear; him you shall serve, and by his name alone you shall swear.

Key Verses: **Hear, O Israel: The LORD is our God, the LORD alone. You shall love the LORD your God with all your heart, and with all your soul, and with all your might. Deuteronomy 6:4-5**

As You Read the Scripture

Our last two lessons give us a chance to look at the fifth book in the Bible, Deuteronomy. Its name means "a second law" or "the law repeated." Indeed the Ten Commandments are repeated, with slight variations, in chapter 5. The book is written in a different style from that of Genesis–Numbers, and it is thought by many scholars to be related to the reform of Josiah (2 Kings 22–23), in which a lost book of the Law is discovered during repairs to the Temple (2 Kings 22:8). Deuteronomy may even have been that book. Certainly it is an important one. It is one of four Old Testament books most often quoted in the New Testament (the other three being Genesis, Isaiah, and Psalms); Jesus, according to Matthew, quotes from it three times in refuting the tempter (Matt. 4:1-11). But of all the passages in this book, made up mostly of Moses' speeches before his death, certainly the greatest is the key verse in today's lesson.

Deuteronomy 6:3. Here again is the phrase "a land flowing with milk and honey," which is the way a shepherd, not a farmer, would speak of paradise.

Verses 4-5. This is the key sentence in all the Hebrew Scriptures. It is known among the Hebrews by its opening word, the *shema*. It can be translated in several different ways, but in Hebrew it is quite terse, consisting of four Hebrew words: "YHWH, our God, YHWH, one."

It cannot be overemphasized how important this statement is in the ancient, polytheistic world, and the world that pulls at us from so many directions today. It has a certain similarity with the Muslim credo: "There is but one God, Allah, and Mohammed is his prophet."

Verse 7. The rudiments of religious education.

Verse 8. The pious Jew to this day takes these prescriptions literally and wears on the left forearm and on the forehead a small box, called a phylactery, on which is written verse 4. The *mezuza* is a small box, containing the passage as well, placed at the righthand doorpost of the house, and in some cases in each room. Beautiful as these reminders are, it is more important that these words be kept in our heart (v. 6).

Verses 10-15. The danger is that when the people cease to be nomads and become farmers, they will think they have won their bread by the sweat of their backs and will be tempted to forget that it was God who called them. That is why this central truth must be driven home so firmly.

Verses 16-19. The incident at Massah (Exod. 17:1-7) is brought up as an example of how shaky the people's faith is and how discouragement may at any moment lead them to think God is not going to deliver them. Their sin is not atheism but pessimism.

Verses 20-25. "Tell me the old, old story," the song goes. This brief section is a basic primer for the young Jew who wants to know what his or her heritage means. It is reminiscent of the question the youngest child asks at every Passover seder, "Why is this night different from all other nights?" It is a kind of creed of Hebrew tradition, and we would do well to teach it to our own children, along with the essential tenets of the faith given in the New Testament concerning Jesus Christ.

The Scripture and the Main Question

Foundation

We need to teach a course in remedial theology in most of our churches. Most of us are so caught up in the busyness of being religious, minding our morals, doing our duties, arguing over details, and generally working at the task of the church, that we lose sight of the foundation on which all our business is based. This fresh look at Israel's summons to its fundamental faith will be a good start at a basic theology on which all our action must depend, lest it be mere activity. We are fond of saying, "He's not really alive, he's just existing." The existentialists have taught us that phrase inside out, saying, "He's alive all right, breathing, but not really existing." Much of our daily activities are mere functions, having lost touch with their roots.

I am told that during World War II the British artillery produced a training film in which they photographed a crack team in the act of moving their piece into position, setting up, loading, aiming, firing, and moving on. The idea was that a new crew could watch the experts do it, with each soldier keeping his eye on his counterpart, and so learning what would be expected of him during an actual firing. To their astonishment, the makers of the training film noticed that one member of the crew did nothing but stand stock still throughout the entire operation. Upon investigation, they discovered that this soldier was a remnant from a previous war. His job was originally to hold the horses that drew the caisson, to keep them from bolting when the cannon fired. Like the fireman on a diesel locomotive, he had no useful function to perform.

How much of what we do from day to day has a genuine theological basis? What is the real purpose for our being here on this earth? Here we have the answer. The Shema was called "the Great Commandment" by Jesus (Matt. 22:36-40; Mark 12:29-34; Luke 10:27-28), and to it he added the law of neighborly love from Leviticus 19:18. Jesus' answer to the question What's the greatest commandment? was in keeping with the best Jewish thought on the subject, for the rabbis had long discussed which among the 613 laws in the Torah was primary. Both Jews and Christians consider it God's primary rule, in which all the law and the prophets are summed up.

A similar answer was given by the assembly of English divines at Westminster Abbey in 1648, with the drafting of what they called The Shorter Catechism. Question number one is as follows:

Q. What is the chief end of man?
A Man's chief end is to glorify God, and enjoy him forever.

Except for the non-inclusive nature of the language, that theological statement is true for us today. I would suggest phrasing it like this:

Q. What's the point of life?
A. The point of life is to praise and glorify God.

How would you word it? Secular philosophers would ask the question like this: Of all the good things in the world, what's the greatest? Is it life itself? Is it liberty? Is it the pursuit of happiness? None of the above, important as they are, Deuteronomy 6:4-5 tells us. It is love for God.

But what does it mean to love God with all your heart and soul and might? Love God with your whole being.

We are accustomed to dividing the person into three parts: body, mind, and spirit. Once, when I was serving a rural congregation, I tried to impress on the people the importance of using both the mind and the emotions in worship. I quoted the adage "One who sings prays twice." To me that means when you add the music to the words you have added the emotion to the intellect. One of the church members responded, "Yep, and one who taps his foot prays three times!" He's right. We are to praise God not only with our minds and hearts, but with our bodies. The whole being is to love God.

Relationship

But we still must ask what that means. Let me suggest, as a chapter in our remedial theology course, that we need to remember every day that God exists in relationship. God exists in relationships within the Godhead. The Father loves the Son, the Son loves the Spirit, and the Spirit loves the Father. And God exists in relationship to us ("God so loved the world . . "). And we exist, or ought to, in relationship with one another.

Things are not of ultimate significance. Not even people are of ultimate significance. But love, the *relationship* between people is. Of course you can have people without relationships, but you can't have relationships without people. People, apart from other people—that is, God and each other—don't really exist, we only live.

I would carry it a step further. It has been said that God put us in the world to love people and use things, and that the trouble with us is that we love things and use people. I would say that God put us in the world to love both people and things, and the trouble is that we use people and use things. As Martin Buber, the philosopher, put it, we need to be in an "I-Thou" relationship with God, the world, and each other, not an "I-It" relationship. What is most important is not possessions, not power, not even people, but *people in relationship.* That is why we can rejoice in the foundation on which we stand. Listen, everybody within the sound of my voice. God, the Lord, our God is One, and we are to love God with everything in our being. And that means we are to love each other.

Helping Adults Become Involved

Preparing to Teach

Once more the text dictates how you should teach. Remember as you prepare your lesson to love God above all things, and that means that you are to love the members of your class in the same way that you love and respect yourself. If you can keep that foundation under you as you teach, you will do well.

Don't be stuck with my words. Use your own. Decide for yourself what *you* mean by "Love God with your whole being." If you do so love God, how will that affect what you do as a teacher?

It will mean, of course, that you will carefully read God's Word and carefully prepare to teach God's people. In a sense nothing will be different. But in another sense, one which I cannot find the words to express, you and your class will be bound together with a true bond.

Here's the outline:

I. The Great Commandment
II. The importance of keeping it
III. The instruction of children

FOURTH QUARTER

Introducing the Main Question

I like deserted island questions. It's fun to ask a class, "If you were going to be on a deserted island and could take only, say, six things with you, in addition to food and drink, what would they be? My list would be:

> my glasses
> a dictionary
> paper and pencil
> the Bible
> Shakespeare plays
> my wife

Not necessarily in that order. What would your list be? What I value most in the world is relationships, and those six things would help me experience most of them. Could you use this method to help your class come to grips with the question What is most important to you?

Developing the Lesson

I. *The Great Commandment*

The first three verses are a kind of introduction; Moses is about to give Israel the charge that was given him by God in 5:31, and he wants their attention. "Listen!" he says, grabbing their attention just as God does with the opening word of the Shema.

After giving the basic law, Moses charges them to fill up their lives and those of their children with this law: on your heart, in your conversation, coming and going, walking and sleeping. Have the class read verses 4-9 aloud together, perhaps more than once.

II. *The importance of keeping it*

As long as the Israelites are nomads, they will be more or less obligated to remember that God is leading them through the desert, but now that they are about to become an agrarian people, they will forget that God gave them those things, too. Remind your class that most of us go around thinking that heat comes from thermostats and bread comes from the grocery store.

III. *The instruction of children*

It is absolutely necessary that the next generation know what we have been through. Probably half of the people who read what I am writing now will not remember Pearl Harbor, which was a watershed in my life. But what is really frightening is that I meet responsible adults all the time who don't remember the assassination of John F. Kennedy or the Vietnam war. How can I expect them to remember something Moses said over three thousand years ago? Our work is cut out for us. Someone has said that the Christian church is always only one generation away from extinction. The greatest mission field in the world is our children. We dare not neglect them.

Encourage your class members to learn the Shema, the Ten Commandments, and the Apostles' Creed by heart—and to teach them to their children.

Helping Class Members Act

I think this is the hardest lesson we have had this quarter, in terms of translating it into action, for what God is asking for here is not for us to act, but to remember. Suggest that the class memorize a verse or passage of Scripture that best sums up what they believe, and teach it to their children.

Planning for Next Sunday

Have them read Deuteronomy 28, the last look at the Pentateuch.

Choose to Obey

Background Scripture: Deuteronomy 28

The Main Question

Does it work? That's the main question in this chapter. But we must be careful how we ask it because we are forbidden from putting God to the test (see Deut. 6:16; Luke 4:12.) A well-meaning Christian friend tried to give me a lapel pin that had on it the words *Try Jesus.* I declined it, saying, "I'm forbidden to put God to the test." It seems to be asking of me, "Put Jesus to the test, and see if your life gets better."

And yet, we *are* invited to try God. Read the account in Malachi 3:10, in which God promises what will happen to you if you tithe. And isn't Jesus always reaching his hand out to us, like he did to Peter, inviting us to walk on life's trouble waters (Matt. 4:28-33)? Isn't accepting Christ a little like stepping into a dark abyss, a leap of faith in which we do not know the outcome?

So there is a sense in which God calls for our trust, inviting us in Deuteronomy 28 to choose between a blessing and a curse. How shall we respond to this invitation? The main drive of the chapter seems to set forth a clear tit for tat: Do this, and that will happen. Is life really that way? In what sense can we say: "If you keep God's commandments it will go well with you, if not, it will go badly"? This is one of the toughest questions in the world, but let's have a go at it.

Selected Scripture

King James Version	New Revised Standard Version
Deuteronomy 28:1-6, 15-19, 64-66	*Deuteronomy 28:1-6, 15-19, 64-66*
1 And it shall come to pass, if thou shalt hearken diligently unto the voice of the LORD thy God, to	1 If you will only obey the LORD your God, by diligently observing all his commandments that I am com-

observe and to do all his commandments which I command thee this day, that the LORD thy God will set thee on high above all nations of the earth:

2 And all these blessings shall come on thee, and overtake thee, if thou shalt hearken unto the voice of the LORD thy God.

3 Blessed shalt thou be in the city, and blessed shalt thou be in the field.

4 Blessed shall be the fruit of thy body, and the fruit of thy ground, and the fruit of thy cattle, the increase of thy kine, and the flocks of thy sheep.

5 Blessed shall be thy basket and thy store.

6 Blessed shalt thou be when thou comest in, and blessed shalt thou be when thou goest out.

....

15 But it shall come to pass, if thou wilt not hearken unto the voice of the LORD thy God, to observe to do all his commandments and his statutes which I command thee this day; that all these curses shall come upon thee, and overtake thee:

16 Cursed shalt thou be in the city, and cursed shalt thou be in the field.

17 Cursed shall be thy basket and thy store.

18 Cursed shall be the fruit of thy body, and the fruit of thy land, the increase of thy kine, and the flocks of thy sheep.

19 Cursed shalt thou be when thou comest in, and cursed shalt thou be when thou goest out.

....

64 And the LORD shall scatter thee among all people, from the one end of the earth even unto the other; and there thou shalt serve other gods, which neither thou nor thy fathers have known, even wood and stone.

65 And among these nations shalt thou find no ease, neither shall the

manding you today, the LORD your God will set you high above all the nations of the earth; 2 all these blessings shall come upon you and overtake you, if you obey the LORD your God:

3 Blessed shall you be in the city, and blessed shall you be in the field.

4 Blessed shall be the fruit of your womb, the fruit of your ground, and the fruit of your livestock, both the increase of your cattle and the issue of your flock.

5 Blessed shall be your basket and your kneading bowl.

6 Blessed shall you be when you come in, and blessed shall you be when you go out.

....

15 But if you will not obey the LORD your God by diligently observing all his commandments and decrees, which I am commanding you today, then all these curses shall come upon you and overtake you:

16 Cursed shall you be in the city, and cursed shall you be in the field.

17 Cursed shall be your basket and your kneading bowl.

18 Cursed shall be the fruit of your womb, the fruit of your ground, the increase of your cattle and the issue of your flock.

19 Cursed shall you be when you come in, and cursed shall you be when you go out.

....

64 The LORD will scatter you among all peoples, from one end of the earth to the other; and there you shall serve other gods, of wood and stone, which neither you nor your ancestors have known. 65 Among those nations you shall find no ease, no resting place for the sole of your foot. There the LORD will

sole of thy foot have rest: but the LORD shall give thee there a trembling heart, and failing of eyes, and sorrow of mind:

66 And thy life shall hang in doubt before thee; and thou shalt fear day and night, and shalt have none assurance of thy life.

give you a trembling heart, failing eyes, and a languishing spirit. 66 Your life shall hang in doubt before you; night and day you shall be in dread, with no assurance of your life.

Key Verse: **And all these blessings shall come on thee, and overtake thee, if thou shalt hearken unto the voice of the LORD thy God. Deuteronomy 28:2**

Key Verse: **All these blessings shall come upon you and overtake you, if you obey the LORD your God. Deuteronomy 28:2**

As You Read the Scripture

Deuteronomy 28. This chapter is neatly divided into two sections: blessings (vv. 1-14) and curses (vv. 15-58). Such a listing of good news and bad news is a familiar form of biblical teaching. (Compare Jesus' blessings and woes in the Sermon on the Plain in Luke 6:20-26, and the list of good things versus bad things mentioned in Lev. 26.) Each of the two sections is introduced by parallel descriptions of how these blessings and curses reach into all of life—city and country, family, flocks, food, everything (compare vv. 3-6 and 16-19). It appears that the writer prefers the punishment method of discipline to the reward method, because the section on bad news is about four times as long as the list of good things that will happen if the people are obedient.

Verse 5. For another use of the kneading bowl, see Exodus 12:34, and for examples of the basket as a container for bread, see Genesis 40:17, Leviticus 8:2, and Matthew 14:20.

Verse 7. "Seven ways" is like our expression "every which way but loose." The use of seven is a typical biblical superlative as used by Jesus in Matthew 18:21-22.

Verse 12. The promise of opening all the gifts of heaven to the obedient people is echoed in the similar passage in Malachi 3:10-12, which is another proof that the Lord is benevolent to those who are faithful. The opening of the windows of heaven means that there will be plenty of rain, which in that arid part of the world is essential to prosperity (see Lev. 26:4; Deut. 11:10).

Verse 13. Heads vs. tails (See the converse in Luke 14:7-11).

Verses 23-24. In contrast, those who disobey the Lord will *not* experience the opening of the windows of heaven. Instead, there will be a disastrous drought, in fact, a dust storm (see Lev. 26:19).

Verse 27. Disease will also be a result of disobedience (see Ps. 38). "The boils of Egypt" refers to the plague in Exodus 9. "Ulcers" is rendered in the King James Version as *emerods* (hemorrhoids). (For one of the most astonishing passages in all of the Bible, see the story of the "golden hemorrhoids" in 1 Sam. 5-6. The "tumors" are probably related to something like the bubonic plague.)

Verse 28. Wisely, Moses recognizes that mental, as well as physical, diseases are related to sinful behavior.

Verse 30. Even romance is subject to curse for the disobedient. The idea of "I planted but another harvested" is the common result of a life lived at the expense of others. All the calamities in verses 30-34 are those one can expect to happen when the nation is overtaken by a foreign power. One result of disobedience will be military defeat.

Verse 49. This may be a reference to the Babylonian captivity. Some scholars believe that the book of Deuteronomy may actually have been written at that time. It bears some similarities in style and content to some of the passages in the prophecy of Jeremiah.

The Scripture and the Main Question

Reward and Punishment

Psalm 37:25 is disturbing:

> I have been young, and now am old,
>   yet I have not seen the righteous forsaken
>   or their children begging bread.

It is disturbing because everyone can give a counterexample. Lots of times I have seen righteous people in financial trouble or with other problems. And there are many places in the Bible where this simple doctrine of reward and punishment is contradicted. When people asked Jesus (John 9:2) who had sinned to cause a certain man to be born blind, he answered, "Nobody. It wasn't due to sin." And on another occasion (Matt. 5:45), he told us that God makes the "sun rise on the evil and on the good, and sends rain on the righteous and on the unrighteous." A whole book (Job) was written to demonstrate that sometimes a righteous man undergoes terrible calamities..

Certainly there *is* a relationship between sin and suffering. Sometimes it is obvious—people have headaches, bloodshot eyes, and other symptoms that are directly related to sinful behavior. In Psalm 103:3, the parallelism makes the relationship clear as it praises the Lord, "who forgives all your iniquity, who heals all your diseases."

It appears at first that, in Deuteronomy 28, God is offering a simple bargain: Do this, and you will be blessed; don't do this, and you will be cursed. But is it that simple? In his commentary on Deuteronomy in *The Interpreter's Bible*, G. Ernest Wright says:

> The blessings are not conceived primarily to be God's rewards for moral goodness, nor are the curses primarily his punishment for moral turpitude. There is a deeper note here than a shallow religion of moralism. Israel as a nation, as a social, political, and economic organism, exists in covenant with her Lord. To deny or rebel against God is to break the covenant and violate that which has created, sustained, and composed nationality. Deuteronomy, in presenting the ideal or revealed order . . . gives the conditions upon which Israelite life can be sustained, and does not fail to make quite clear the results of rebellion. To disobey the divine Lord is to betray life itself as Israel understood it. Consequently, the choice is indeed one between life and death, for the blessing is life and the curse is death (cf. 30:15-20). It is important, then, that this deeper basis of ch. 28 be understood; otherwise it will be interpreted, as has too commonly been done, in a

superficial and moralistic manner. The primary concern here is not with rewards; it is rather with the conditions which must be met if life with all its hope and promise is to be found. (*The Interpreter's Bible,* vol. 2 [Nashville: Abingdon Press, 1953], pp. 493-94)

When we stated the Ten Commandments in positive form, we tried to see them, not merely as negative prohibitions, but as life-giving principles. It's the difference between saying, "Don't run in the street or I'll spank you" and "I love you, so take care of yourself."

Opposites

This chapter is certainly not divided equally. A great many more verses (54) are devoted to curses than to blessings (14). That ratio is about 80/20. Why so much more bad news than good news? Maybe it's like the old saying that it takes more muscles to frown than to smile. Certainly life is like that. You don't spend near as much time gathering eggs as you do shoveling out the hen-ouse. Look at the book of Psalms and compare the number of praise/rejoicing psalms to those that have to do with lamentations and cursings—about the same ratio there, too. Goodness is simple; evil is complicated.

But we do not live in a dualistic universe. It is not true that God is the god of good and heaven, and the devil is the god of evil and hell. The devil isn't the equal and opposite of God. The devil isn't even in charge of hell, but will be cast into it (Rev. 20:10). Evil is to good as cold is to hot or as darkness is to light. Only the light has an existence of its own; the darkness comes when the light is taken away. There is no such thing as a dark bulb that, when turned on, darkens a room. Deuteronomy 28 calls us to the light, as does the first letter of John (1:5-7):

God is light and in him there is no darkness at all. If we say that we have fellowship with him while we are walking in darkness, we lie and do not do what is true; but if we walk in the light as he himself is in the light, we have fellowship with one another, and the blood of Jesus his Son cleanses us from all sin.

Jesus, too, divided the world into light and darkness, sheep and goats: "Happy are you who are poor, hungry, weeping and reviled by the world," he said, "but woe to you that are rich, well fed, laughing and well thought of by the world" (see Luke 6:20-26). He had a way of turning things upside down, both to astonish us and to force us to see the truth. As sure as light overcomes darkness, if we are obedient, we will be blessed in the city and in the country, at the office and in the kitchen, when we come out and when we go in.

Helping Adults Become Involved

Preparing to Teach

Our question this week is a very difficult one. Thousand of volumes have been written on it, and the Bible itself seems divided on the question. So do not expect your class to easily come to a solution. But you would not be a teacher if you did not enjoy wrestling with tough problems. Teaching is the hardest work in the world—but worth it. So I encourage you to take the challenge of this lesson and go for a good class.

Apply the principle of the Scripture to the manner of your teaching. If you will obey the Lord your God by diligently observing all of God's commandments, the Lord will make you a good teacher, and all these blessings shall come upon you: Blessed will you be in your study and in your teaching; blessed will your discussions be; blessed will be your class members.

But if you will not obey the Lord your God by diligently observing all of God's commandments, the Lord will pull the pedagogical pavement out from under you, and these curses shall come upon you: Cursed will you be in your study and in your teaching; you will have sorry discussions; your class members will be miserable.

In other words, be enthusiastic, God filled, in your preparation and your teaching. Trust God to provide the inspiration and the skills, and depend on God to cause something to happen in your classroom. In the light of that, by all means begin with a prayer for enlightenment. You may use this one:

God of all truth: you are the Source of all knowledge and the inspiration of all who study. Give me the skill to interpret your Word for my class so that they may hear it and understand it and believe it and act upon it. I ask this in the name of Jesus Christ, the Master Teacher. Amen.

The outline is as follows:

I. The choice
II. The blessings
III. The curses

Introducing the Main Question

Begin with the illustration of the *Try Jesus* lapel pin or by reading Psalm 37 and the other biblical references to sin and suffering. But let me offer one other possibility: Ask your class to imagine that a charged 220 volt line of electricity can speak. It might say something like: "If you hook my leads up to a generator, I will provide power for you with which you can do all sorts of good things. But if you are so foolish as to grab my leads in your two hands, I will electrocute you." Is the electricity just waiting in the wire to zap somebody who makes the wrong move? No, it's just being what electricity is. In the same sense, God isn't some primitive Jove, sitting on a cloud with a quiverful of thunderbolts, just waiting until we do something wrong and zap us. No, God is (see Exod. 3:14). God cares for us and wants us to obey the commandments, because if we do, that is the way to life; but if we do not, that is the way to death. We have a choice to make between life and death (see Deut. 30:19), and God dearly wants us to make the right one.

Developing the Lesson

I. The choice

Begin this lesson with an overview of the whole chapter, so that your class will see how the blessings and banes are played off each other. Bring in

Luke's version of the Beatitudes as another example, and ask the class to consider their lives as a constant succession of such choices. As Christians, we daily choose between life and death.

II. The blessings

This is the shorter of the two lists. Your class might enjoy making a list on the chalkboard of all the blessings they can think of, and another list of all the things that frighten them. But don't spend too much time on this. Note how simple this chapter's list of blessings is: children, produce, livestock, food on the table, safety in your coming and going, and a place of importance in the world (v. 13). What more could you ask for?

III. The curses

The curses, on the other hand, are numerous and complicated: disease, drought, heat, blight, mildew, dust storms, death, insanity, blindness, sexual frustration, robbery, impotence, bad knees, poor crops, locusts, foreign domination, cannibalism, family hostility, failing eyesight, and dissatisfaction with life. (This is only a partial list; read the chapter.) The most ominous curse is the last one: "You shall offer yourselves for sale to your enemies as male and female slaves, but there will be no buyer" (Deut. 28:68).

It doesn't take much to satisfy us, but there are a million ways to make us miserable.

Helping Class Members Act

End the class session Deuteronomy 30:15-20, or perhaps Joshua 24:15. Help the class members to see that every moment of every day is a choice between good and evil (God and devil?), life and death. It is good to decide now, rather than later, in a moment of passion. Conclude with a prayer of commitment to the things of God.

Planning for Next Sunday

Next Sunday, we begin a new year of the *International Lesson Annual*. Be sure you have purchased your new *Annual* for 1994–1995. For our first unit of study, beginning next Sunday, we will begin a study entitled, "From the Conquest to the Kingdom"—a study of Joshua, Judges, I and II Samuel, and I Kings. Encourage your class to browse through the book of Joshua before next week's session.

Have a wonderful year of study during 1994–95!